WASHINGTON HIKING

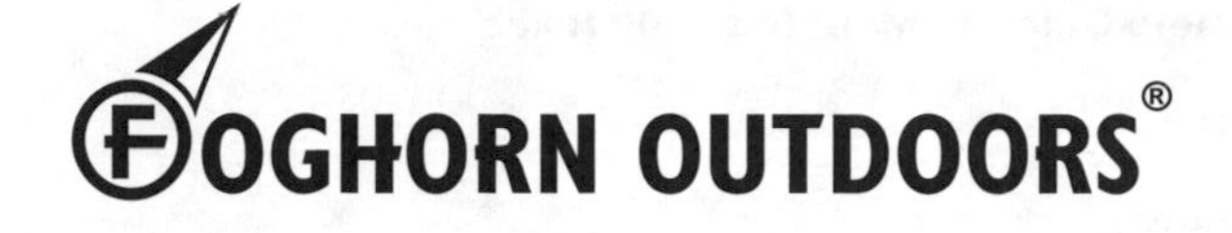

WASHINGTON HIKING

The Complete Guide to More Than 400 Hikes

First Edition

Scott Leonard

FOGHORN OUTDOORS WASHINGTON HIKING
The Complete Guide to More Than 400 Hikes

First Edition

Scott Leonard

Printing History
1st edition—March 2005
5 4 3 2 1

Avalon Travel Publishing
An Imprint of
Avalon Publishing Group, Inc.

ISBN: 1-56691-772-7
ISSN: 1553-9075

Series Manager: Ellie Behrstock
Editors: Grace Fujimoto, Elizabeth McCue
Acquisitions Editor: Rebecca K. Browning
Copy Editor: Karen Gaynor Bleske
Proofreader: Donna Leverenz
Graphics Coordinator: Deb Dutcher
Production Coordinator: Darren Alessi
Cover and Interior Designer: Darren Alessi
Map Editor: Kat Smith
Cartographers: Mike Morgenfeld, Kat Kalamaras
Indexer: Laura Welcome

Front cover photo: © Chris Duval

Printed in the United States of America by Worzalla.

About the Author

© SCOTT LEONARD

Scott Leonard has been hiking in Washington for nearly 10 years. A Pacific Northwest native, Scott started his outdoor adventures in the forests and high deserts of Oregon before coming to Washington during college and exploring the Olympic Mountains. After years of hiking in the state for recreation, Scott spent several years at the nonprofit EarthCorps, specializing in trail construction projects. So he has not only hiked many of Washington's trails, but has built several of them as well.

While writing *Foghorn Outdoors Washington Hiking,* Scott spent much of two summers on the trail, logging more than 1,000 miles. That much trail time is not without peril, as he escaped disaster on the Gray Wolf River by braving record rains in October 2003. Although bears have been frequent acquaintances, he fears no wildlife more than the tent-eating field mouse.

Scott's love lies first with the Olympic Mountains, but he enjoys exploring all of the Northwest's wilderness areas. He also has a strong passion for the outdoors, both in experiencing the environment and in protecting it. He is currently studying environmental law at Lewis & Clark University in Portland, Oregon.

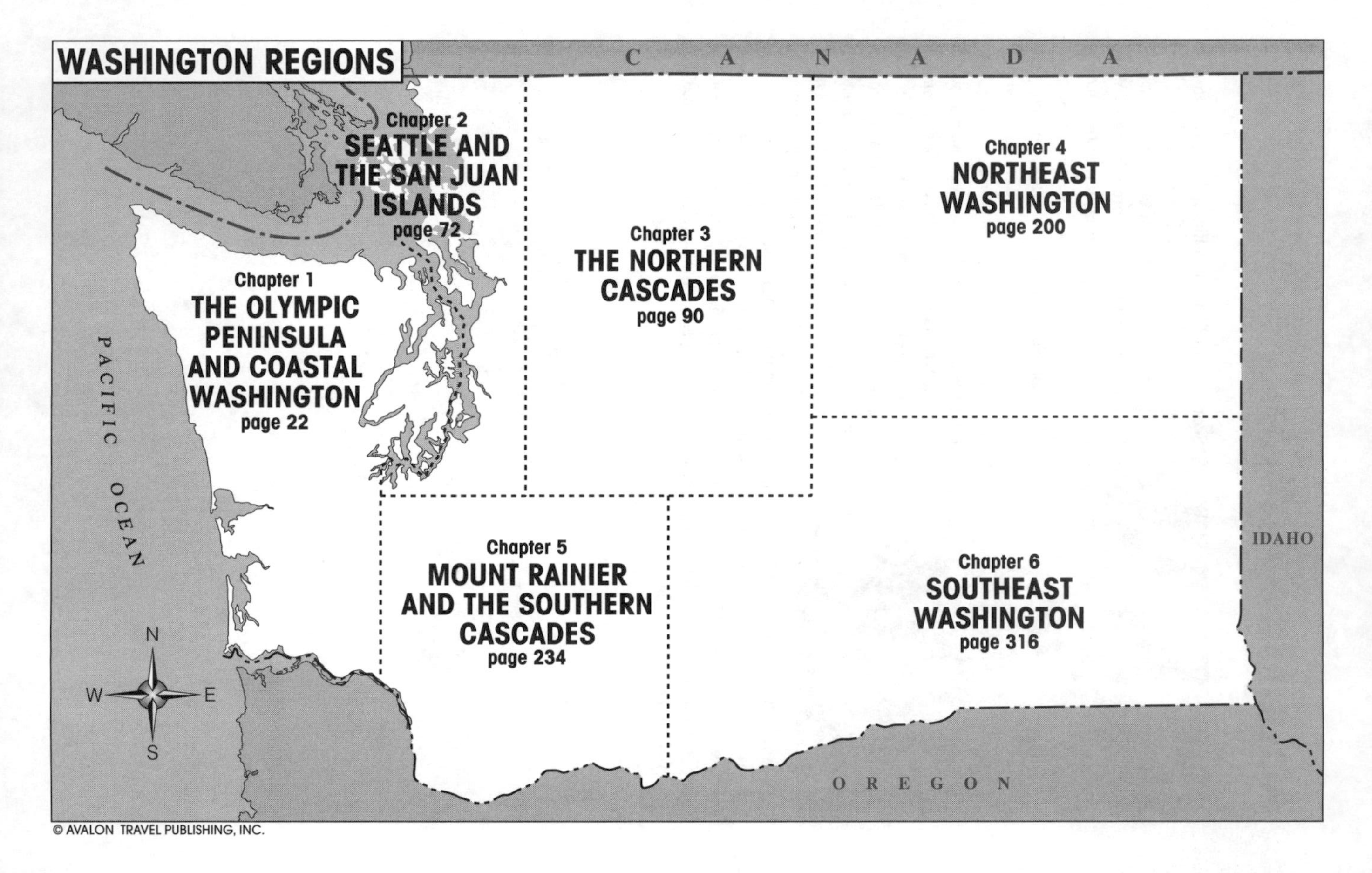

WASHINGTON REGIONS
C A N A D A
Chapter 2
SEATTLE AND THE SAN JUAN ISLANDS
page 72
Chapter 1
THE OLYMPIC PENINSULA AND COASTAL WASHINGTON
page 22
Chapter 3
THE NORTHERN CASCADES
page 90
Chapter 4
NORTHEAST WASHINGTON
page 200
Chapter 5
MOUNT RAINIER AND THE SOUTHERN CASCADES
page 234
Chapter 6
SOUTHEAST WASHINGTON
page 316
PACIFIC OCEAN
IDAHO
O R E G O N
N
W
E
S
© AVALON TRAVEL PUBLISHING, INC.

Contents

How to Use this Book x

About the Trail Profiles • About the Maps

Introduction 1

Hiking Tips 3

The 10 Essentials 3

Proper Clothing • Water Supply • Extra Food • Fire Starter • Map and Compass • First-Aid Kit • Sun Protection • Light Source • Multipurpose Knife • Emergency Kit

Bears, Cougars, and Rattlesnakes 6

Bears • Cougars • Rattlesnakes

Protecting the Outdoors 9

Planning Your Trip • Hiking and Camping • Taking Out Your Trash • Leaving What You Find • Lighting Campfires • Encountering Wildlife • Respecting Other Hikers

Hiking with Dogs 10

Permits 10

Northwest Forest Pass • National Parks Passes and Permits

Best Hikes 13

Top 10 Easy Hikes 13

Top 10 Weekend Backpacking Trips 13

Top 10 Lake Hikes 14

Top 10 Hikes to See Wildflowers 14

Top 10 Hikes to See Waterfalls 15

Top 10 Hikes with Kids 15

Top 10 Summits . . . 16
Top 10 Hikes for Berry Picking . . . 16

The Olympic Peninsula and Coastal Washington . . . 19

Including:
- Brothers Wilderness
- Buckhorn Wilderness
- Colonel Bob Wilderness
- Lake Crescent
- Lake Quinault
- Makah Indian Reservation
- Mount Skokomish Wilderness
- Olympic National Forest
- Olympic National Park
- Willapa Bay
- Wonder Mountain Wilderness

Seattle and the San Juan Islands . . . 69

Including:
- Chuckanut Mountain
- Cougar Mountain Regional Park
- Deception Pass State Park
- Moran State Park
- Orcas Island
- Puget Sound
- Snohomish County
- Tennant Lake County Park
- Whidbey Island

The Northern Cascades . . . 87

Including:
- Alpine Lakes Wilderness
- Boulder River Wilderness
- Cedar River Municipal Watershed
- Clearwater Wilderness
- Diablo Lake
- Glacier Peak Wilderness
- Henry M. Jackson Wilderness
- Lake Chelan National Recreation Area
- Lake Chelan Sawtooth Wilderness
- Lake Wenatchee
- Mount Baker Wilderness
- Mount Baker–Snoqualmie National Forest
- Mount Pilchuck State Park
- Mount Si Natural Resources Conservation Area
- Noisy-Diobsud Wilderness
- Norse Peak Wilderness
- North Cascades National Park
- Okanogan National Forest
- Pasayten Wilderness
- Ross Lake National Recreation Area
- Snoqualmie Pass
- Tiger Mountain State Park
- Twin Falls State Park
- Wallace Falls State Park
- Washington Pass
- Wenatchee National Forest

Northeast Washington . . . 197

Including:
- Colville National Forest
- Little Spokane River Natural Area
- Metaline Falls
- Okanogan National Forest
- Pasayten Wilderness
- Salmo-Priest Wilderness

Mount Rainier and the Southern Cascades 231

Including:

- Battle Ground State Park
- Beacon Rock State Park
- Castle Rock
- Chinook Pass
- Gifford Pinchot National Forest
- Glacier View Wilderness
- Goat Rocks Wilderness
- Indian Heaven Wilderness
- Mount Adams Wilderness
- The Mountain
- Mount Baker–Snoqualmie National Forest
- Mount Rainier National Park
- Mount St. Helens National Volcanic Monument
- Silver Lake State Park
- Stevens Canyon
- Tatoosh Wilderness
- Trapper Creek Wilderness
- Trout Lake
- Wenatchee National Forest
- White Pass
- William O. Douglas Wilderness

Southeast Washington 313

Including:

- Juniper Dunes Wilderness
- L. T. Murray Wildlife Refuge
- Moses Lake
- Palouse Falls
- South Columbia Basin Wildlife Area
- Umatilla National Forest
- Wenaha-Tucannon Wilderness

Resources 333

National Parks 334

National Forests 334

Parks, Recreation Areas, and Other Resources 336

Map Resources 337

Hiking Clubs and Groups 337

Index 339

How to Use this Book

Foghorn Outdoors Washington Hiking is divided into six chapters based on major regional areas in the state. Each chapter begins with a map of the area, which is further broken down into detail maps. These detail maps show the location of all the hikes in that chapter.

This guide can be navigated easily in two ways:

1. If you know the name of the specific trail you want to hike, or the name of the surrounding geographical area or nearby feature (town, national or state park, forest, mountain, lake, river, etc.), look it up in the index and turn to the corresponding page.

2. If you know the general area you want to visit, turn to the map at the beginning of the chapter that covers the area. Each chapter map is broken down into detail maps, which show by number all the hikes in that chapter. You can then determine which trails are in or near your destination by their corresponding numbers. Hikes are listed sequentially in each chapter so you can turn to the page with the corresponding map number for the hike you're interested in.

Our Commitment

We are committed to making *Foghorn Outdoors Washington Hiking* the most accurate and enjoyable hiking guide to the state. With this first edition you can rest assured that every hiking trail in this book has been carefully reviewed and accompanied by the most up-to-date information. Be aware that with the passing of time some of the fees listed herein may have changed, and trails may have closed unexpectedly. If you have a specific need or concern, it's best to call the location ahead of time.

If you would like to comment on the book, whether it's to suggest a hike we overlooked, or to let us know about any noteworthy experience–good or bad–that occurred while using *Foghorn Outdoors Washington Hiking* as your guide, we would appreciate hearing from you. Please address correspondence to:

Foghorn Outdoors Washington Hiking, first edition
Avalon Travel Publishing
1400 65th Street, Suite 250
Emeryville, CA 94608

email: atpfeedback@avalonpub.com
If you send us an email, please put "Washington Hiking" in the subject line.

About the Trail Profiles

Each hike in this book is listed in a consistent, easy-to-read format to help you choose the ideal hike. From a general overview of the setting to detailed driving directions, the profile will provide all the information you need. Here is an example:

Map number and hike number

Round-trip mileage (unless otherwise noted) and the approximate amount of time needed to complete the hike (actual times can vary widely, especially on longer hikes)

Map on which the trailhead can be found and page number on which the map can be found

Symbol indicating that the hike is listed among the author's top picks

The difficulty rating (boot—rated 1–5) is based on the steepness of the trail and how difficult it is to traverse; the quality rating (mountain—rated 1–10) is based largely on scenic beauty, but it also takes into account how crowded the trail is and whether noise of nearby civilization is audible

General location of the trail, named by its proximity to the nearest major town or landmark

1 Somewhere USA Hike

9.0 mi/5.0 hrs 4 8

At the mouth of the Somewhere River on Lake Someplace

Map 1.2, page 24

(F) Each hike in this book begins with a brief overview of its setting. The description typically covers what kind of terrain to expect, what might be seen, and any conditions that may make the hike difficult to navigate.

User Groups: This section notes the types of uses that are permitted on the trail, including hikers, mountain bikers, horseback riders, and dogs. Wheelchair access is also noted here.

Open Seasons: This section notes the times of year the trail is accessible.

Permits: This section notes whether a permit is required for hiking, or, if the hike spans more than one day, whether one is required for camping. Any fees are also noted here. The Hiking Tips section describes passes that are commonly required.

Maps: This section provides information on how to obtain detailed trail maps of the hike and its environs. Whenever applicable, names of U.S. Geologic Survey (USGS) topographic maps and national forest maps are also included; contact information for these and other map sources are noted in the Resources section at the back of this book.

Directions: This section provides mile-by-mile driving directions to the trailhead from the nearest major town.

Contact: This section provides an address and phone number for each hike. The contact is usually the agency maintaining the trail but may also be a trail club or other organization.

About the Maps

This book is divided into chapters based on regions; an overview map of these regions precedes the table of contents and is printed on the inside of the back cover. At the start of each chapter, you'll find a map of the entire region, enhanced by a grid that divides the region into smaller sections. These sections are then enlarged into individual detail maps. Trailheads are noted on the detail maps by number.

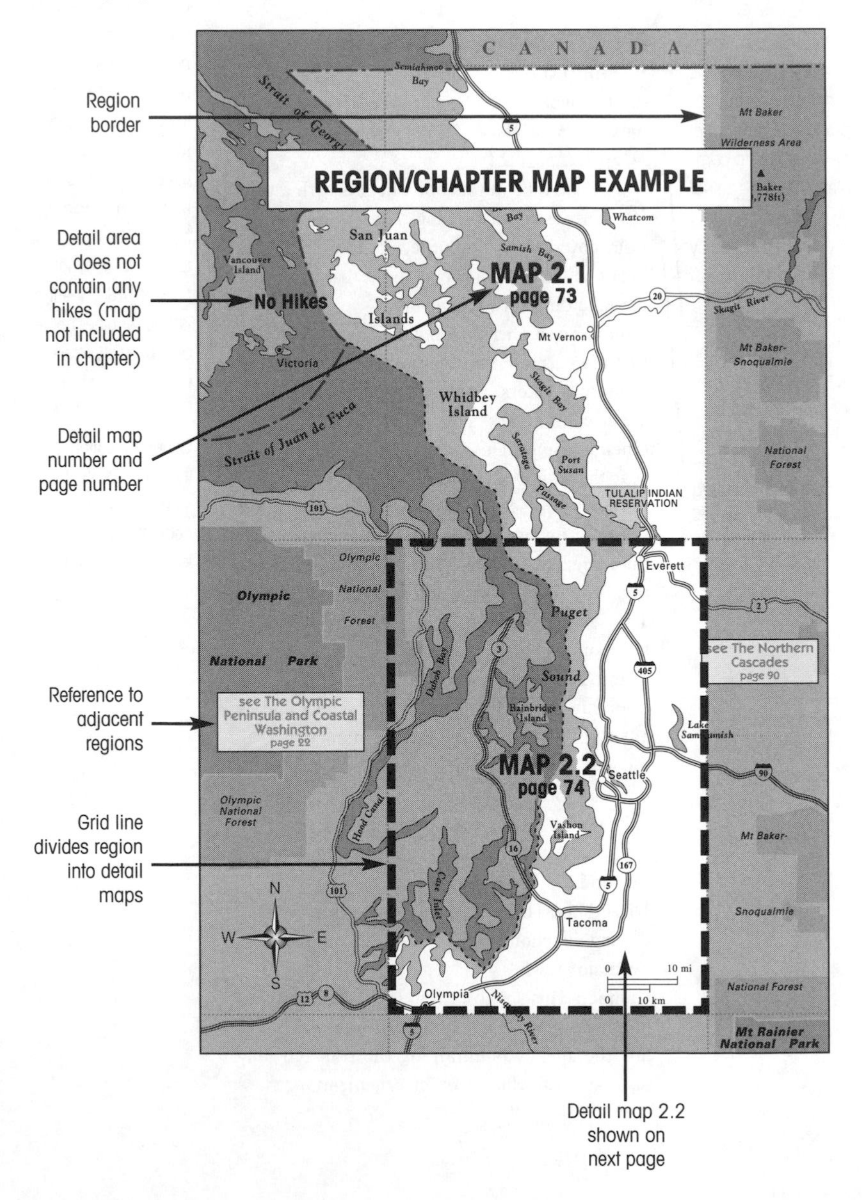

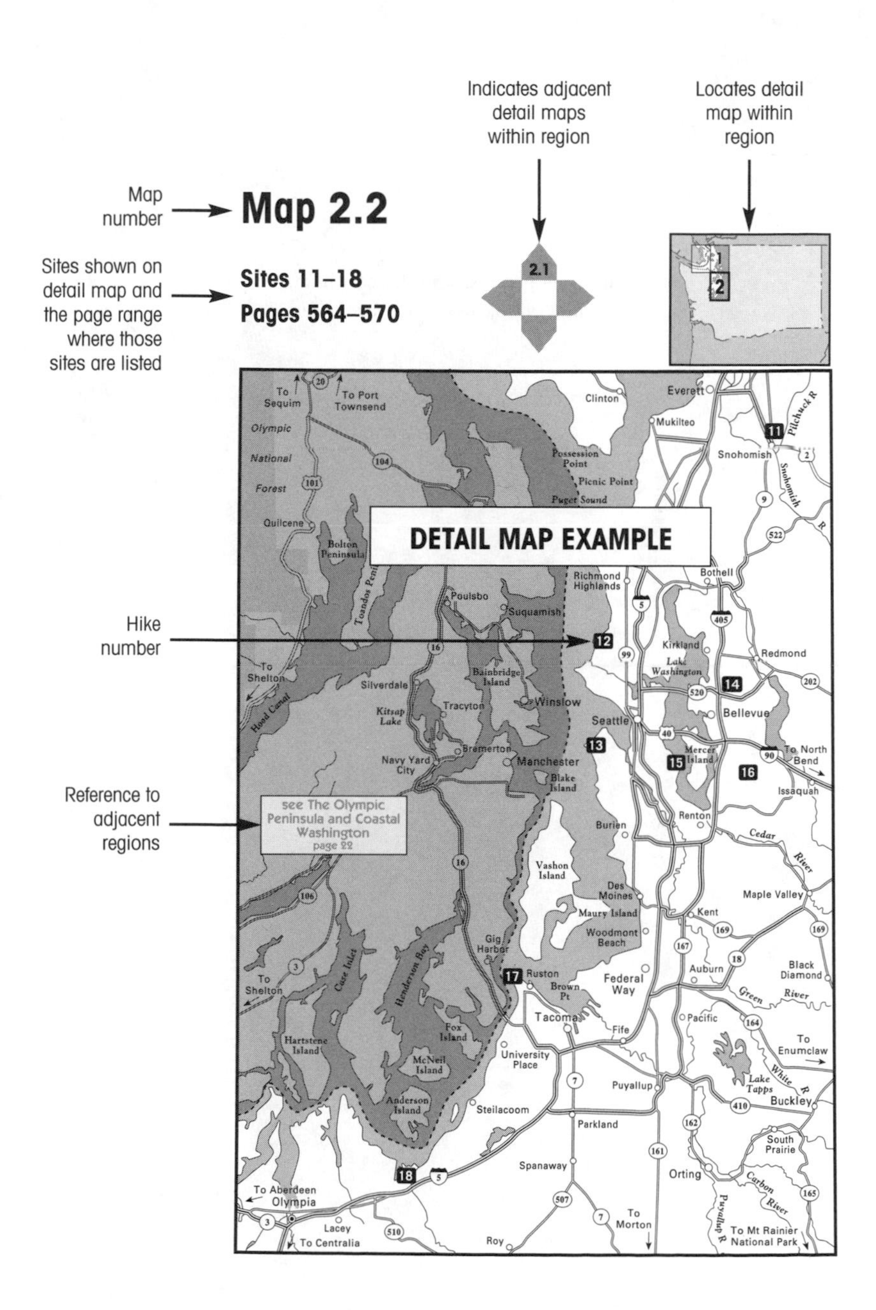

Indicates adjacent detail maps within region
Locates detail map within region
Map number
Map 2.2
Sites shown on detail map and the page range where those sites are listed
Sites 11–18
Pages 564–570
2.1
1
2
Hike number
Reference to adjacent regions
DETAIL MAP EXAMPLE
see The Olympic Peninsula and Coastal Washington page 22
To Sequim
To Port Townsend
Olympic National Forest
Quilcene
Bolton Peninsula
Toandos Peninsula
Clinton
Everett
Mukilteo
Pilchuck R
Snohomish
Snohomish R
Possession Point
Picnic Point
Puget Sound
Richmond Highlands
Bothell
Poulsbo
Suquamish
Kirkland
Lake Washington
Redmond
To Shelton
Hood Canal
Silverdale
Bainbridge Island
Winslow
Bellevue
Kitsap Lake
Tracyton
Seattle
Bremerton
Mercer Island
To North Bend
Navy Yard City
Manchester
Blake Island
Issaquah
Renton
Burien
Cedar River
Vashon Island
Des Moines
Maple Valley
Maury Island
Kent
Woodmont Beach
Gig Harbor
Auburn
Black Diamond
Ruston
Federal Way
Brown Pt
Green River
Case Inlet
Henderson Bay
Tacoma
Pacific
Fife
To Enumclaw
Hartstene Island
Fox Island
McNeil Island
University Place
Lake Tapps
White R
Puyallup
Buckley
Anderson Island
Steilacoom
Parkland
South Prairie
Spanaway
Orting
Carbon River
To Aberdeen
Olympia
To Morton
Puyallup R
To Mt Rainier National Park
Lacey
To Centralia
Roy

For my grandparents, who shared with me the
Pokey Little Puppy and a love for the outdoors

Introduction

Introduction

If you love the outdoors, Washington has everything you could ever ask for. In any given season, you'll find Washingtonians outdoors in our beloved wildernesses. First and foremost in our hearts is the mountains, where we hike, ski, snowshoe, rock climb, mountain bike, and camp year-round. The Olympics, slick with nearly 200 inches of annual rainfall, reign over the northwestern corner of the state. The Cascades divide Washington into its wet and dry halves and are never far from sight. The Cascades are also home to some of America's prettiest peaks, like Mount Rainier and Mount Baker, and countless alpine meadows and glaciers. One of the world's most restless mountains, Mount Saint Helens, is here as well. Not content with its new face from its major eruption in 1980, the mountain is in the process of rebuilding. Washington's mountains are places of peace and quiet, where the worries of city life quickly give way to the delights of wild natural beauty.

But Washington is more than just mountains. Any trail in the state is a grand trip, from the beaches and sea stacks of the coast to the expansive alpine meadows of the high country. With lush old-growth forests on its western side and dry deserts at its eastern end, Washington contains a wide range of plant life and terrain within its 71,303 square miles. We have rumbling rivers, gurgling streams, and breathtaking waterfalls left and right—many of which start as glaciers, something that Washington has more of than the rest of the United States combined (excluding Alaska). Washington is an incredibly diverse state, and as the ultimate trail authority, *Foghorn Outdoors Washington Hiking* will help you explore every inch of it.

More than 400 trails are included in this book, and during my time with Earthcorps, a local nonprofit, I even helped build some of them. Every trail is different, and you can find the perfect trek for any region or time frame. One weekend you may be looking for a quick hike close to Seattle (try the Alpine Lakes Wilderness), while on another weekend you may want to spend a few days exploring Washington's backcountry (like Glacier Peak Wilderness). And when your mother-in-law is in town, scenic Mount Rainier is the quintessential place to go (or you can just show her the mountain on a state license plate).

In the process of writing this book, I spent over three months camping under the stars. My trusty Subaru packed on over 12,000 miles while carrying me back and forth across the state. On the trail, deer became regular companions and elk crossed my path more frequently than a hunter could ever hope for. And my, oh my, the bears I've seen—though, admittedly, none was quite as terrorizing as the ravenous camp mouse. Still, my hairiest situation yet occurred in October 2003 as I was hiking solo in the Olympics. While traversing the Grand, Cameron, Dosewallips, and Gray Wolf drainages, I had the unfortunate opportunity to experience record rainfalls—more than nine inches in 24 hours. One mighty storm awakened me in the middle of the night as windy gusts dragged me and my tent across the meadow. As rivers rose, I jumped raging creeks, endured miles off trail, and scooted along fallen logs spanning the violent Gray Wolf. I've never been wetter or more worried, but I survived to relate an experience I'll never forget.

More than a year of my life was spent hiking and researching *Washington Hiking*. I hope that you enjoy using this guide as much as I enjoyed creating it. Open it up, find a trip, and have a blast!

Hiking Tips

The 10 Essentials

Going out for a quick afternoon on the trail? Better bring the 10 Essentials. Heading into the backcountry for a weeklong trek across the Pasayten Wilderness? Better bring the 10 Essentials. It doesn't matter what your intended trip, you never know what you're going to come across (or what's going to come across you), and it's better to prevent problems before they start. Pack the 10 Essentials every time, and you'll have a lot less to worry about.

Proper Clothing

Here in Washington, the weather can turn at the drop of a hat. In every season, rain seems never more than a few hours away. We didn't get a reputation for wet weather for nothing. During the summer, thunder showers or snow storms can give even experienced hikers a surprise. So it's best to bring extra clothing for those unexpected weather fronts.

Clothing that can ward off the cold is extremely important. Most accidents in the wilderness are the result of, or complicated by, hypothermia, which can set in quickly and with little warning. Once a person starts getting cold, the ability to think and further protect him- or herself heads downhill. Symptoms of hypothermia include fatigue, drowsiness, unwillingness to go on, a feeling of deep cold or numbness, poor coordination, and mumbling. To avoid this, bring clothes that are easily layered. During the summer, that can be as simple as a pair of wool pants or a warm fleece. During the winter, wool or synthetic fleeces are effective against the cold. A stocking cap is extremely helpful since a big chunk of body heat is lost through the head. Extra socks are helpful for keeping feet warm and comfortable. You can be vulnerable even in the summer–bitter July snowstorms are not unheard of.

Rain gear, such as jacket, pants, and a hat or hood, is equally important during all seasons, but especially during the fall and spring when it's practically impossible to head outdoors without it. Even if there is no rain in the forecast, be prepared for it. (Local weather reporters are forecasting for the cities, not the mountains.) And short but serious rainstorms in any season are the norm, not exception, in Washington.

When dressing for a hike, it's important to avoid cotton clothing, especially if rain is at all a possibility. Once cotton gets wet, it can draw off body heat, causing hypothermia to set in quickly. Wool and polypropylene are good alternatives. If you get wet wearing cotton, take it off if you have another layer that is not cotton.

Water Supply

Be sure to drink lots of water, even if it's not that hot out. Staying properly hydrated can prevent heat exhaustion. Symptoms of heat exhaustion include excessive sweating, gradual weakness, nausea, anxiety, and eventually loss of consciousness. Usually, the skin becomes pale and clammy or cold, the pulse slows, and blood pressure may drop. Heat exhaustion is often unexpected but very serious; someone experiencing heat exhaustion will have difficulty getting out of a wilderness setting and will need assistance–not always an easy task.

You may not be able to carry from the trailhead all the water you'll need for a long hike. Be prepared to get water from streams or rivers along the trail, and never drink untreated water in the wild. A stream may look crystal clear and be ice cold, but it can also be full of nasty parasites and viruses. If you catch a good case of *giardia* or *cryptosporidia,* you could be incapacitated for a good full week.

Treating water is easy. The old-fashioned method is simply to boil it. A full, rolling boil for one minute is adequate to purify water. These days, the marketplace is also full of high- and low-tech water filters. These systems are great because they keep the water cold and don't impart any taste. Plus, once you purchase a filter system, you don't need to ever buy again. Finally, there are iodine and chlorine systems that quickly and easily purify water. If you're comfortable drinking bleach and don't mind a strange taste, these will do the trick.

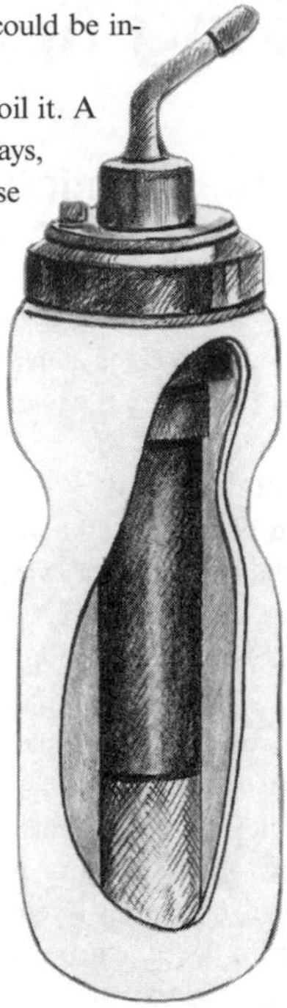

Water filters are a wise investment since all wilderness water should be considered contaminated. Make sure the filter can be easily cleaned or has a replaceable cartridge. The filter pores must be 0.4 microns or less to remove bacteria.

Extra Food

The lore of the backcountry is filled with tales of folks who head out for a quick day hike and end up spending a night (or more) in the wilderness. Planning on just an afternoon away from the kitchen, they don't bring enough food to last into the night or morning. Not only is an empty stomach a restless stomach, it can be dangerous, as well. A full stomach provides energy to help ward off hypothermia and keeps the mind clear for the task at hand: Not getting even more lost!

When packing food for an outing, include a little extra gorp or an extra energy bar. This will come in extremely handy on that night you're wandering back to the trailhead later than planned. A grizzled old veteran of the backcountry once passed on a helpful tip when it comes to packing extra food. Extra food is meant for an emergency; the last thing you want to do is eat it in a nonemergency because it looked good and then need it later. So, he packed something nutritious that he'd consider eating only in an emergency: canned dog food.

Fire Starter

Some people prefer matches while others choose to bring along a lighter. Either way, it's important to have something with which to start a fire. Don't think that you can start your fire by rubbing two sticks together. Even when it's dry, sticks don't like to start up easily. So be certain to purchase some quality waterproof matches (you can make your own with paraffin wax and wooden matches), or carry a couple of lighters. Regardless of your choice, keep them packed away in a safe and dry place (like a sandwich baggie). Besides a starter, bring along something to keep the fire going for a bit. Fire pellets are available at any outdoor store. Do-it-yourselfers will be glad to know that toilet paper is highly flammable, as are cotton balls dipped in Vaseline. Starting a fire when it's cold, dark, and wet can save your life.

Map and Compass

You need to carry a map and compass on your person *every* time you hit the trail. Whether you're going up Mount Si with the rest of Seattle or venturing into the vacant backcountry of the North Cascades National Park, you really need to carry a map and compass. No matter how familiar you think you are with a trail, you can get lost. Not only should you carry the two, but you also need to know how to use them.

A map is not always a map. You can't rely on the map that AAA gave you out on the trail. Instead, it's best to purchase a quality topographic map for use on the trail. A quality topographic map allows hikers to follow their steps more accurately and is infinitely more helpful for figuring out where you are when you're lost. Green Trails of Seattle makes high-quality topo maps for 90 percent of Washington trails. The USGS and National Geographic also make good topo maps.

Now that it's the 21st century, GPS devices are becoming more popular. These are great toys to play with while out on the trail. Some folks even swear by them. But a GPS device often won't work in a thick forest canopy. A good old-fashioned compass, on the other hand, is significantly cheaper and won't ever die on you when the batteries run out.

First-Aid Kit

A first-aid kit is an important essential to carry while out on the trail. With twigs, rocks, and bears lurking around every corner, hiking can be dangerous business. Injuries can range from small abrasions to serious breaks, and a simple but well-stocked first-aid kit can be a lifesaver. It's best to purchase a first-aid kit at outdoors stores. Kits come in different sizes, depending on your use, and include the fundamentals. Also, a number of organizations provide medical training for backcountry situations. Courses run from one-day seminars in simple first aid all the way to monthlong classes for wilderness EMT. Outdoor enthusiasts who go out on a regular basis should consider a course in Wilderness First Aid (WOOFA) or Wilderness First Response (WOOFER).

Band-aids come in every kit but are only helpful for small, nonserious cuts or abrasions. Here are a few things that are especially important and can come in handy in an emergency:

- Ibuprofen: It works very well to combat swelling. Twist an ankle or suffer a nasty bruise and reducing the swelling quickly becomes an important consideration.
- Athletic tape and gauze: These are helpful in treating twisted or strained joints. A firm wrap with athletic tape will make the three-mile hobble to the car less of an ordeal.
- Travel-size supplies of general medicines: Items like Alka-Seltzer or NyQuil are multipurpose and practical.

Finally: the only thing better than having a first-aid kit on the trail is not needing one!

Sun Protection

Most hikers don't think that fierce sunburns are a serious concern in notoriously gray Washington. But during the summer, the sun can be extremely brutal, especially at higher altitudes where a few thousand feet of atmosphere can be sorely missed. A full day in the blazing sun is hard on the eyes as well.

Don't let the sun spoil an otherwise great day in the outdoors. Sunscreen is worth its weight in gold out on the trail. Be sure to apply it regularly, and keep kids lathered up as well. It helps to bring a hat and lightweight clothing with long sleeves, both of which can make sunscreen almost unnecessary. Finally, many hikers swear by a good pair of sunglasses. Perhaps obvious during the summer, sunglasses are also a snowshoer's best friend. Snow blindness is a serious threat on beautiful sunny days during the winter.

All of these measures will make a trip more enjoyable as well as safer. Avoiding sunburn is also extremely helpful in warding off heat stroke, a serious condition in the backcountry.

Light Source

Countless times even veteran hikers intend to go out only for a "quick" day hike and ended up finishing in the dark. There were just too many things to see, too many lakes to swim in, and too many peaks to bag on that "short" hike. Often, getting back to the car or camp before it's dark requires the hard task of leaving a beautiful place while it's still light out. Or perhaps while out on an easy forest hike, you're on schedule to get back before dark, but the thick forest canopy brings on night an hour or two early. There are lots of ways to get stuck in the outdoors in the dark. And what good are a map and compass if you can't see them? Plan ahead and bring an adequate light source. The market is flooded these days with cheap (and not so cheap) headlamps. Headlamps are basically small flashlights that fit around your head. They're great because they're bright and they keep your hands free to beat back brush on the trail or hungry fellow campers around the dinner stove.

Multipurpose Knife

For outdoors enthusiasts, the multipurpose Swiss army knife is one of the greatest ideas since sliced bread. Handy utility knives come in all shapes and sizes and are made by about a hundred different companies. A high-quality utility knife will come in handy in a multitude of situations. The features available include: big knives and little knives, saws and scissors, corkscrews and screwdrivers, and about 30 other fun little tools. They are useful almost everywhere, except at the airport.

Emergency Kit

You'll probably have a hard time finding a pre-prepared emergency kit for sale at any store. Instead, this is something that you can quickly and inexpensively assemble yourself.

- Space blanket: Find these at any outdoor store or army surplus store. They're small, shiny blankets that insulate extremely well, are highly visible, and will make do in place of a tent when needed.
- Signal mirror: The small mirror that comes attached to some compasses works perfectly. A signal mirror is handy when you're lost. Catch the glare of the sun, and you can signal your position to search and rescue hikers or planes.
- Whistle: Again, if you get really lost, don't waste your breath screaming and hollering. You'll lose it quickly, and it doesn't carry far anyhow. Blow your whistle all day or night long, and you'll still be able to talk to the trees (or yourself).

Bears, Cougars, and Rattlesnakes

Hiking is all about being outdoors. Fresh air, colorful wildflowers, expansive mountain views, and a little peace and quiet are what folks are after as they embark on the trail. The great outdoors is also home to creatures big and small. About 99 percent of all wildlife is completely harmless to hikers. The only wildlife that pose a danger to us humans are bears, cougars, and rattlesnakes. Fortunately, 99 percent of all encounters with these big predators are nothing more than a memorable story. Coming across bears, cougars, and rattlesnakes may be frightening, but they don't need to be dangerous as long as you follow a few simple precautions.

Bears

The most common worry of novice hikers when they hit the trail is running into a bear. Bears are big, furry, and naturally a bit scary at first sight. But in reality, bears want little to do with people and much prefer to avoid us altogether. The chance of getting into a fist fight with a bear

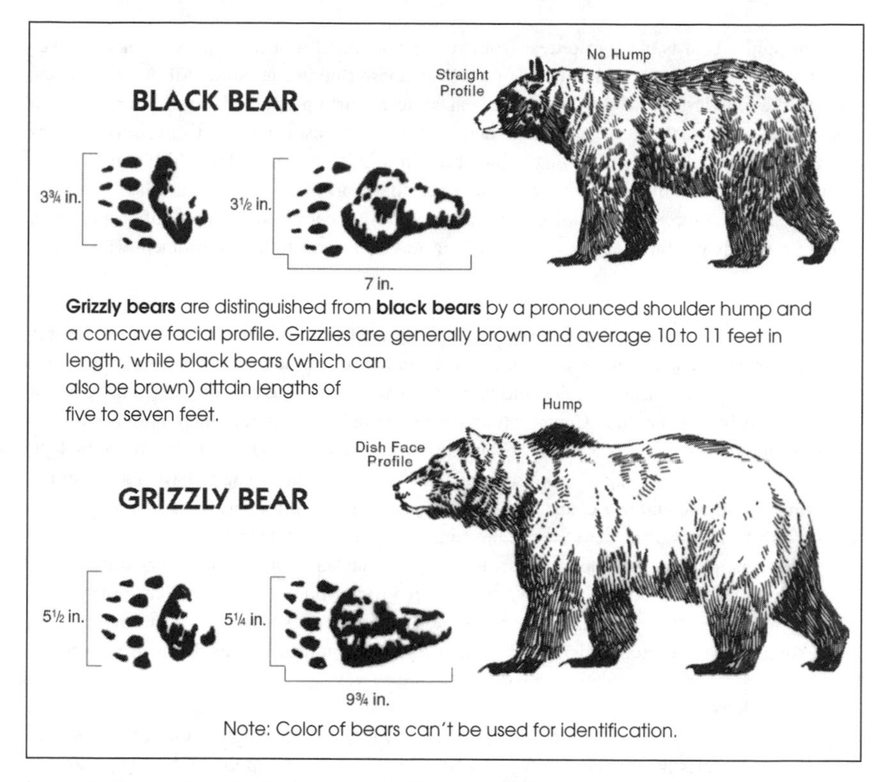

Grizzly bears are distinguished from **black bears** by a pronounced shoulder hump and a concave facial profile. Grizzlies are generally brown and average 10 to 11 feet in length, while black bears (which can also be brown) attain lengths of five to seven feet.

Note: Color of bears can't be used for identification.

is rare in Washington. In all of our state's history, there have only been three attacks and one fatality recorded. As long as you stay away from a bear's cubs and a bear's food, they will almost certainly leave you alone.

What kind of bears will you see out on the trail? Most likely it will be a black bear, but Washington is home to grizzly bears as well. Black bears, whose thick coats range from light tan to cinnamon to black in color and appearance, are by far the most numerous, with approximately 25,000 spread throughout our state. Grizzly bears are much rarer, numbering less than 50, and are primarily located along the Canadian border in the Pasayten Wilderness and Selkirk Mountains. Grizzlies have a distinctive hump on their shoulder.

The old image of Yogi the Bear stealing picnic baskets is not that far off. Bears love to get a hold of human food, so an effective way to avoid seeing a bear at all is proper food storage. When camping, be sure to use a bear hang. Collect all food, toiletries, and anything else with scent in a stuff sack and hang it in a tree. The sack should be at least 12 feet off the ground and eight feet from the tree trunk. This is the easiest way to avoid an unwanted bear encounter.

Should you come across a bear on the trail, stay calm. It's okay to be scared, but with a few precautions, you will be completely safe. First, know that your object is not to intimidate the bear but simply to let it know you are not easy prey. Make yourself look big by standing tall, waving your arms, or even holding open your jacket. Second, don't look it in the eye. Bears consider eye contact to be aggressive and an invitation to a confrontation. Third, speak loudly and firmly to the bear. Bears are nearsighted and can't make out objects from afar. But a human voice means humans, and a bear is likely to retreat from your presence. If a bear advances, it is very likely only trying to get a better look. Finally, if the bear doesn't budge, go around it in a wide circle. In case the unlikely should occur and the bear attacks, curl up in a ball, cover your neck, and take a cheap shot at the nose. Bears hate being hit in their sensitive noses. Conversely, if a grizzly is attacking you, play dead. Trying to hit a bear from this position is difficult: If you can cover your neck with one hand and swing with the other, that works. Protecting yourself is first priority. If the bear is especially aggressive, it's necessary to fight back. Don't let fear of bears prevent you from getting out there; it's rare to see a bear and even rarer to have a problem with one.

Cougars

With millions of acres of wilderness, Washington is home to cougars, bobcats, and lynx. Bobcats and lynx are small and highly withdrawn. If you encounter one of these recluses, you're in a small minority. Cougars are also very shy, and encounters with these big cats are rare; only 2,500 of these big cats live in our state. Cougar attacks are extremely uncommon; there have been few in recent years and only one fatality in Washington ever. You're more likely to be struck by lightning than attacked by a cougar. In most circumstances, you're just going to have a great story.

If you should encounter a cougar in the wild, you want to intimidate it as best as possible. First, don't run! A cougar views something running from it as dinner. Second, get big by waving your arms, jumping around, and spreading open a jacket. Cougars have very little interest in a tough fight. Third, don't bend down to pick up a rock; you only look smaller to the cougar. Fourth, stare the cougar down. In the wilderness, a menacing stare-down is intimidating. Finally, should a cougar attack, fight back with everything you have and as dirtily as possible.

Rattlesnakes

Fortunately, rattlesnakes are few and far between in much of Washington. Out of a dozen different snake species in our state, only the western rattlesnake, *Crotalus viridisis,* is poisonous. The rattler is found only east of the Cascades and more frequently in the southern half. Western rattlesnakes look much like the more common gopher snake. How can you tell if it's a rattlesnake or not? You'll know as soon as you hear its distinctive rattle.

The best way to avoid a rattler bite is to be aware of your surroundings. Walk only where you can see your next footstep; that is, don't go running through open grass or around rocky outcrops. While hiking in rattler country, wear boots that extend at least to the ankles and even a pair of long pants. Should you hear a hair-raising rattle, stay calm; rattlesnakes are rarely aggressive and would prefer to avoid a confrontation if given a chance.

If you should be one of the unfortunate few bitten by a rattlesnake in Washington, stay calm. You have several things in your favor. First, rattlesnake bites are not venomous 80 percent of the time. Second, despite their legend, rattlesnake bites are rarely deadly. Rattler bites are most serious in small persons and when the bite is on the face, neck, or on an artery. Third, treat the bite appropriately:

- Do not suck the venom by mouth; apply a Sawyer Extractor if available.
- Wrapping or constricting the area is not necessary. On a limb, you may tightly wrap the limb (without cutting off total blood supply) *above* the bite, from heart toward the bite.
- Do not cut the bite area.
- Do not take any medicine, not even aspirin or ibuprofen.
- Finally, calmly but immediately seek medical attention.

Remember that a snake bite sounds awfully scary, but they are rarely fatal.

Protecting the Outdoors

It's Friday afternoon, work has been a trial all week, and there's only one thing on your mind: getting outdoors and hitting the trail for the weekend. For many of us, nature is a getaway from the confines of urban living. The irony of it all, however, is that the more people head to the backcountry, the less wild it truly is. That means that it takes a collective effort from all trail users to keep the outdoors as pristine as it was 100 years ago. This effort is so important, in fact, that the organization Leave No Trace has created an ideology for low-impact use of our wilderness. (For more information on Leave No Trace Center for Outdoor Ethics and their values, check out their website at www.lnt.org.) Here are a few principles which we all can follow to ensure that the great outdoors continues to be great.

Planning Your Trip

A little careful planning and preparation not only makes your trip safer, but it also makes it easy to minimize resource damage. Make sure you know the regulations, such as group size limits or campfire regulations, before hitting the trail. Prepare for any special circumstances an area may have, such as the need for ice axes or water filters. Many places are used heavily during summer weekends. Schedule your trip for a weekday or an off-season, and you'll encounter far fewer fellow bipeds.

Hiking and Camping

One of the most important principles for hikers and campers here in Washington is to minimize one's impact on the land. Many of our greatest and most heavily used trails visit fragile environments, such as alpine meadows and lakeshores. These ecosystems are easily injured by walking or camping. Take care to travel only on the main trail, never cut a switchback, and avoid the social trails—small, unofficial trails that are made over years by hikers cutting trails—that spider web many a high meadow. When camping, pitch camp in already established sites, never on a meadow. Take care in selecting a site for a camp kitchen and when heading off for the bathroom. Being aware of your impact not only improves the experience for yourself but also for those who follow you.

Taking Out Your Trash

It goes without saying that trash does not belong in the great outdoors. That goes for all trash, regardless of whether it's biodegradable or not. From food packaging to the food itself, it has to go out the way it came in: on your back. Ditto for toilet paper. As far as human waste goes, dig a cat hole for your waste, and pack all toilet paper and hygiene products in bags to take with you. It may be nasty, but it's only fair for others.

Leaving What You Find

The old saying goes, "Take only photographs and leave only footprints." Well, if you're walking on durable surfaces like you should be, you won't even leave footprints. And it's best to leave the artifacts of nature where they belong: in nature. By doing so, you ensure that others can enjoy them as well. If you see something interesting, remember that it is only there because the hiker in front of you let it be for you to find. The same goes for attractive rocks, deer and elk antlers, and wildflowers. Avoid altering sites by digging trenches, building lean-tos, or harming trees.

Lighting Campfires

Thanks to Smokey the Bear, we all know the seriousness of forest fires. If you're going to have a fire, make sure it's out before going to sleep or leaving camp. But there are other important considerations for campfires. Here in Washington, many national forests and wildernesses have fire bans above an elevation of 3,500 feet. At these higher altitudes, trees grow slowly and depend greatly on decomposition of downed trees. Burning downed limbs and trees robs the ecosystems of much-needed nutrients, an impact that lasts centuries. Carry a camp stove any time you plan on cooking while backpacking.

Encountering Wildlife

No chasing the deer. No throwing rocks at the chipmunks. No bareback riding the elk. And no wrestling the bears. In all seriousness, the most important way we can respect wildlife is by not feeding them. Chipmunks may be cute, but feeding them only makes them fat and dependent on people for food. Keep a clean camp without food on the ground, and be sure to hang food anytime you're separated from it. A good bear hang is as much about keeping the bears out of the food as it is about keeping the mice and squirrels from eating it.

Respecting Other Hikers

If you are considerate of others on the trail, they are likely to return the favor. This includes such simple things as yielding right of way to those who are trudging uphill, keeping noise to a minimum, and observing any use regulations, such as no mountain bikes or no fires. If possible, try to set up camp off trail and out of sight. Together, everyone can equally enjoy the beauties of hiking in Washington.

Hiking with Dogs

While not everyone may have a dog, nearly everyone has an opinion about dogs on the trail. Hiking with canine friends can be a great experience, not only for us but for them, as well. What dog doesn't love being out on the trail, roaming the wild and in touch with his ancestral roots? That's great, but there are a few matters that must be considered before taking a dog out on the trail. First, be aware that national parks do not allow dogs on any trail at any time. However, dogs are allowed throughout national forests and any wildernesses contained within them. Second, dogs should be on trail at all times. Dogs can create an enormous amount of erosion when roaming off trail, and they're frequent switchback cutters. Third, dogs must be under control at all times. Leashes are not always mandatory because many dogs are obedient and do very well while unleashed. But if you're not going to use a leash, your dog should respond to commands well and not bother other hikers. Finally, be aware that dogs and wildlife don't mix well. Dogs love to chase chipmunks, rabbits, deer, and anything else that moves. But from the chipmunk's point of view, a big, slobbering beast chasing you is stressful and unequivocally bad. Not only that, but dogs can incite aggression in bears or cougars. An unleashed dog can quickly transform a peaceful bear into a raging assault of claws and teeth. Plus, bears and cougars find dogs to be especially tasty. Don't hesitate to bring your dog out on the trail as long as you take the dog's interests, as well as other hikers' interests, into consideration.

Permits

You've got your pack ready, done your food shopping, purchased the right maps, and even wrestled the kids into the car. But do you have the right permits? Here in Washington, there are several permits that you may need before you can hit the trail. Headed for a national forest? Read up on the Northwest Forest Pass. Driving down to Mount Rainier or the Olympics? You probably need a National Parks Pass. Backpacking in a national park? Don't forget your backcountry camping permit.

Northwest Forest Pass

The Northwest Forest Pass is the most widely used permit in our state. The pass is accepted at 680 day-use recreation sites in Washington and Oregon. Almost every trailhead in every national forest in Washington requires a NWFP for parking. Remarkably, a Northwest Forest Pass is all that is required in the North Cascades National Park. The Colville National Forest is the one agency that is not participating in the NWFP program; access to trailheads in the Colville is free. Senior citizens take note: in lieu of a NWFP, the federal Golden Eagle, Golden Access, and Golden Age passes are accepted.

The Northwest Forest Pass costs $30 and is valid for one year from date of purchase. It's interchangeable between vehicles in the same household. Day passes may also be purchased, at a cost of $5 per day. More than 240 vendors across the northwest offer the pass. These include all ranger stations, most outdoor stores, and many service stations in recreational areas. Passes can also be ordered online through Nature of the Northwest at www.naturenw.org. Proceeds from Northwest Forest Passes go toward improvements at recreational sites, including refurbishing trailheads, trail maintenance and construction, and environmental education. There is a lot of controversy over the pass, as critics contend that national forests are public lands and already paid for by federal taxes. They have a point, but the revenue serves to supplement ever-dwindling forest service budgets.

National Parks Passes and Permits

No question, the United States has the world's premier national park system. From Acadia National Park in Maine to Denali National Park in Alaska, the United States has taken care to preserve our most important ecosystems for future generations to enjoy. Here in Washington, we have North Cascades, Olympic, and Mount Rainier National Parks to savor. Each park has slightly different rules.

North Cascades National Park

This is the easiest and cheapest park to visit in Washington. All trailheads accessing the park require the Northwest Forest Pass for parking and day use. Overnight backpackers must register for a backcountry camping permit, called a Wilderness Permit in this park. These permits are free and are required for any overnight stay within the North Cascades National Park Service Complex (that includes Lake Chelan and Ross Lake National Recreation Areas). The national park limits the number of visitors at backcountry camps; thus, they require permits for any overnight stay. Permits are available from the Wilderness Information Center in Marblemount, North Cascades Visitor Center in Newhalem, Methow Valley Visitor Center in Winthrop, and Golden West Visitor Center in Stehekin. Just because they're free, don't think you can get away without a Wilderness Permit. Park rangers don't hesitate to hand out hefty fines.

Olympic National Park

Olympic National Park offers a mix of regulations. Some areas are accessible for free, but most require a fee. Passes are required at the following entrances: Hoh, Sol Duc, Elwha, Hurricane Ridge, and Skokomish. Passes are not required at the Quinault or other rivers. To access park entrances requiring passes, visitors have several options. A Single Visit Vehicle Permit costs $10 and is good for seven days. An Olympic National Park Annual Pass costs $30 and is good for one year. Also accepted are a variety of national passes. National parks passes include the National Parks Pass ($50), which is good at any national park in the United States for one year;

the Golden Access Pass, which is available to persons who are blind or permanently disabled and allows lifetime admittance to any national park for free; and the Golden Age Pass, which is available to persons 62 years or older and allows lifetime admittance to any national park for a one-time fee of $10.

Backpackers need to follow more rules. Whether you start at a national park trailhead or one located on national forest land, you need a backcountry camping permit, called a Wilderness Camping Permit, to camp within the national park. Here's how they work. You can pick one up at the Wilderness Information Center in Port Angeles or staffed ranger stations at Hoodsport, Staircase, Hurricane Ridge, Hoh, and Quinault. The cost is $5 per permit (good for parties up to 12 people), plus $2 per night per person. One person going out for three nights costs $11 (5+6). Three people going out for two nights costs $17 (5+4+4+4). Thankfully, there is no charge for youth 16 years of age and under.

Mount Rainier National Park

Mount Rainier requires fees for car access to some areas while other parts of the park are free. Driving through the park along State Route 410 (from Enumclaw to Yakima) and State Route 123 (south to State Route 12 and Packwood) are both free. Parking at all trailheads along these two routes are free. Access via Paradise-Longmire Road, Stevens Canyon Road, White River Road, Carbon River Road, and Mowich Lake Road all require one of three passes: A Single Visit Vehicle Permit ($10 and good for seven days), a Mount Rainier National Park Annual Pass ($30 and good for one year), or a variety of national parks passes (described under Olympics National Park), which are good for one year at all national parks in the United States.

Backpackers can rejoice, for a stay in the backcountry is free (maybe). A backcountry camping permit, called a Wilderness Camping Permit in this park, is required for all overnight stays within the park and is completely free. These permits are required because the park service has quotas on the number of visitors at backcountry camps. During the summer, a reservation is highly recommended for most backcountry camps, and the cost per reservation is $20, good for 1–12 people for up to 14 nights. If you're feeling confused, it's best to check out the Mount Rainier website or call the Wilderness Information Center listed for the hike you are considering for current availability.

Best Hikes

Top 10 Easy Hikes

Mount Townsend, The Olympic Peninsula and Coastal Washington, page 53. A popular trail to the summit of a large, meadowy butte in the Eastern Olympic Mountains.

Upper Big Quilcene, The Olympic Peninsula and Coastal Washington, page 54. Grand old-growth forest gives way to meadows and great views from Marmot Pass.

Deception Pass State Park, Seattle and the San Juan Islands, page 78. Miles of trail along the most beautiful stretch of coastline in the Puget Sound.

Nisqually Wildlife Refuge, Seattle and the San Juan Islands, page 84. A pair of trails winds through one of western Washington's largest bird refuges near Olympia.

Mount Pilchuck, The Northern Cascades, page 121. A popular summit hike ends at a lookout filled with historic information and views.

Glacier Basin, The Northern Cascades, page 125. A bike and hike along the Mountain Loop Highway finds glaciers and meadows.

Middle Fork Snoqualmie River, The Northern Cascades, page 169. Old-growth forest highlights this great river hike, less than an hour from Seattle.

Snow Lake, The Northern Cascades, page 176. A popular trail in the Alpine Lakes Wilderness through old-growth forest and meadows ending in a spectacular lake basin.

Esmerelda Basin, The Northern Cascades, page 192. The beauty-to-difficulty ratio is off the charts on this Alpine Lake favorite.

Tolmie Peak Lookout, Mount Rainier and the Southern Cascades, page 250. A pair of high-country lakes on the way to a great lookout next to Mount Rainier.

Top 10 Weekend Backpacking Trips

Ozette Triangle, The Olympic Peninsula and Coastal Washington, page 30. This is the most popular route along the coast and visits historic Wedding Rocks.

Lena Lakes, The Olympic Peninsula and Coastal Washington, page 58. A demanding hike through beautiful forests to an alpine playground.

Oval Lakes, The Northern Cascades, page 150. This is the most glorious part of the Sawtooth Range, east of Lake Chelan.

Phelps Creek (Spider Meadow), The Northern Cascades, page 154. An easy trip to a magnificent valley, topped by an easily accessible glacier to play on.

Cady Creek/Little Wenatchee Loop, The Northern Cascades, page 159. Follow PCT through wide open meadows while enjoying great views of Glacier Peak.

Necklace Valley, The Northern Cascades, page 161. A long valley of high lakes just 1.5 hours from Seattle.

The Enchantments, The Northern Cascades, page 191. Hands down, this is Washington's premier alpine trail, but miles of lakes, meadows, and peaks come at a breathtaking price.

Salmo Loop, Northeast Washington, page 224. Stuck in the most northeastern corner of Washington, this may be the wildest trip in the state.

Summerland/Panhandle Gap, Mount Rainier and the Southern Cascades, page 258. The best route to the high country of Mount Rainier, an admirable distinction.

Goat Ridge, Mount Rainier and the Southern Cascades, page 283. Miles of meadows, a great lake, and always good chances to see many goats.

Top 10 Lake Hikes

Seven Lakes Basin Loop, The Olympic Peninsula and Coastal Washington, page 39. The loop route is best, with countless great lakes and eye-popping views of the Olympics' biggest mountains.

Flapjack Lakes, The Olympic Peninsula and Coastal Washington, page 63. A pair of lakes beneath a ring of rocky peaks and easily accessible, to boot.

Galena Chain Lakes, The Northern Cascades, page 104. There are no fewer than five lakes along this easy loop trail on the northern slopes of Mount Baker.

Lake 22, The Northern Cascades, page 122. Just an hour from Seattle, the trail enjoys old-growth forest, a cascading stream, and a beautiful lake.

Eagle Lakes, The Northern Cascades, page 153. A dandy of the Sawtooth Range east of Lake Chelan; be ready for the occasional motorbike.

Blanca Lake, The Northern Cascades, page 157. Not far off Highway 2, this is the crown jewel in the Henry M. Jackson Wilderness.

Foss Lakes, The Northern Cascades, page 161. An easy 1.5-hour drive from Seattle, this valley of wonderful lakes is an off-season favorite.

Rachel Lake, The Northern Cascades, page 179. Just east of Snoqualmie Pass, the popularity of this trail doesn't steal from its scenic appeal.

The Enchantments, The Northern Cascades, page 191. Washington's greatest collection of high lakes, all framed by higher peaks.

Snow and Bench Lakes, Mount Rainier and the Southern Cascades, page 270. Short, flat, and beautiful, this is one of Mount Rainer's best trails.

Top 10 Hikes to See Wildflowers

Silver Lakes, The Olympic Peninsula and Coastal Washington, page 54. Above these lightly forested lakes lie meadowy slopes covered in aster and lupine.

Skyline Divide, The Northern Cascades, page 97. The wildflowers have competition from the rest of the scenery on this ridge north of Mount Baker.

Meadow Mountain, The Northern Cascades, page 119. The name says it all–a mountain aflame in wildflowers in July.

West Cady Ridge, The Northern Cascades, page 158. Nearly four miles of meadowy ridge running to PCT, east of Everett.

Dutch Miller Gap, The Northern Cascades, page 170. Great meadows at the head of the Middle Fork Snoqualmie River outside of North Bend.

Horseshoe Basin (Pasayten), Northeastern Washington, page 205. Literal square miles of meadows cover this remote section of the Pasayten Wilderness.

Spray Park, Mount Rainier and the Southern Cascades, page 251. Against lofty competition, perhaps Mount Rainier's best meadows.

Berkeley and Grand Parks, Mount Rainier and the Southern Cascades, page 252. After the flowers and cascading streams of Berkeley Park, prepare for the sheer size of Grand Park.

Skyline Loop, Mount Rainier and the Southern Cascades, page 268. Right out of Paradise Lodge at Mount Rainier, this is one for the whole family.

Yakima Rim, Southeast Washington, page 321. Early-season blooms in April and May make this trail the perfect choice to get out after the long winter.

Top 10 Hikes to See Waterfalls

Marymere Falls, The Olympic Peninsula and Coastal Washington, page 33. If the Olympic rain isn't enough, the mist from Marymere is sure to soak you through.

Sol Duc Falls/Lover's Lane, The Olympic Peninsula and Coastal Washington, page 38. Three parallel cascades pour into a narrow gorge among beautiful forests.

Whatcom Falls, Seattle and the San Juan Islands, page 75. One of the many reasons Bellingham is one of Washington's best communities.

Boulder River, The Northern Cascades, page 116. Several tall cascades fall into the river among old-growth forest.

Chewuch River, The Northern Cascades, page 136. The mighty Chewuch pouring over exposed rock makes a great contrast to the ruins of the surrounding burned forest.

Wallace Falls, The Northern Cascades, page 157. A great trail leads to the 265-foot fall in one of Washington's best state parks.

Twin Falls, The Northern Cascades, page 168. A giant drop of 150 feet caps a series of cascades on the North Fork Snoqualmie, 45 minutes from Seattle.

Denny Creek and Lake Melakwa, The Northern Cascades, page 175. Two big falls invite hikers to soak in the refreshment around their bases.

Comet Falls/Van Trump Park, Mount Rainier and the Southern Cascades, page 264. The 320-foot drop of Comet Falls is a welcome sight on the way to Van Trump Park at Mount Rainier.

Palouse Falls State Park, Southeast Washington, page 324. An enormous devil's punchbowl in the middle of the eastern Washington desert.

Top 10 Hikes with Kids

Ozette Triangle, The Olympic Peninsula and Coastal Washington, page 30. Kids who love tidal pools and the beach will love this loop.

Hurricane Hill, The Olympic Peninsula and Coastal Washington, page 41. A better view of the Olympic Mountains is hard to find than from this meadow ramble.

Staircase Rapids, The Olympic Peninsula and Coastal Washington, page 61. This follows the North Fork Skokomish River as its pours over numerous cascades.

Rainy Lake Nature Trail, The Northern Cascades, page 129. This easy and level nature trail ends up at one of the North Cascades' prettiest settings.

Iron Goat, The Northern Cascades, page 165. One of Washington's best rails-to-trails projects features lots of historic artifacts.

Talapus and Olallie Lakes, The Northern Cascades, page 173. A pair of forested lakes, perfect for first-time camping trips less than an hour from Seattle.

Cedar Flats, Mount Rainier and the Southern Cascades, page 245. This short, level loop trail ventures through a forest of enormous old-growth.

Ape Cave, Mount Rainier and the Southern Cascades, page 246. Two miles of lava cave just south of Mount St. Helens.

Paradise Nature Trails, Mount Rainier and the Southern Cascades, page 266. Numerous trails explore the open meadows at the base of Mount Rainier.

Grove of the Patriarchs, Mount Rainier and the Southern Cascades, page 272. This stand of 1,000-year-old old-growth forest sits on a small island in the Ohanapecosh River.

Top 10 Summits

Mount Constitution (Moran State Park), Seattle and the San Juan Islands, page 76. Although it's less than 3,000 feet in height, the panoramic view of Puget Sound and the San Juan Islands is terrific.

Church Mountain, The Northern Cascades, page 95. Old-growth forest gives way to acres of meadows and incredible views of Mount Baker.

Park Butte/Railroad Grade/Scott Paul Trail, The Northern Cascades, page 106. Miles of meadow wandering ends up at a lookout on the south slopes of Mount Baker.

Monogram Lake/Lookout Mountain, The Northern Cascades, page 110. Good luck counting the number of North Cascade peaks in sight from this old lookout.

Goat Flats, The Northern Cascades, page 120. A lake for swimming and acres of meadows prelude the steep climb to an old lookout.

lookout atop Oregon Butte

Granite Mountain, The Northern Cascades, page 173. The view from the lookout site ranges from Mount Rainier to Glacier Peak.

Mount David, The Northern Cascades, page 185. Survive the 5,000-plus feet of elevation gain and enjoy the view.

Columbia Mountain, Northeast Washington, page 218. Right on Highway 20 in North-Central Washington, this trail offers the best view of the Kettle Range.

Mount Fremont Lookout, Mount Rainier and the Southern Cascades, page 253. There is no better summit from which to gaze out upon Mount Rainier National Park.

Oregon Butte, Southeastern Washington, page 328. This trail visits a lookout atop the best viewpoint in all of the region.

Top 10 Hikes for Berry Picking

Six Ridge, The Olympic Peninsula and Coastal Washington, page 64. This long, remote ridge is open and exposed, perfect conditions for a bellyful of berries.

Lake Ann, The Northern Cascades, page 103. The trail drops into a valley chock full of juicy black huckleberries before climbing to beautiful Lake Ann.

Sauk Mountain, The Northern Cascades, page 108. Since the trail never leaves a meadow setting, expect to find berries the entire way.

Huckleberry Mountain, The Northern Cascades, page 117. Look for it off the Mountain Loop Highway; the name says it all.

Mount Dickerman, The Northern Cascades, page 124. Huge fields of huckleberries reward those who endure the strenuous climb.

Pratt Lake, The Northern Cascades, page 174. You'll find salmonberries, thimbleberries, and huckleberries galore along this trail in August.

Juniper Ridge, Mount Rainier and the Southern Cascades, page 294. As you ramble along miles of huckleberry bushes, peer east to Mount Adams and west to Mount St. Helens.

Dark Meadow, Mount Rainier and the Southern Cascades, page 297. Home to some of Washington's juiciest black huckleberries.

Indian Heaven, Mount Rainier and the Southern Cascades, page 301. Native Americans came here year after year for a reason, and that was to pick berries in a beautiful setting.

Race Track, Mount Rainier and the Southern Cascades, page 302. This trail explores the southern end of Indian Heaven Wilderness in search of its best berry fields.

Chapter 1

© SCOTT LEONARD

The Olympic Peninsula and Coastal Washington

The Olympic Peninsula and Coastal Washington

The Olympics are justifiably famous (or infamous) for the crazy amount of rain that visits the peninsula. The west-side river valleys get about 140 inches a year, and the region tops out at 200 inches a year near the crest. Yes, more than 200 inches, which amounts to more than 18 vertical feet of water. There may be other, drier regions of Washington, but the Olympic Peninsula is one of the United States' most unique places. Three distinct and highly beautiful environments grace this isolated and lightly inhabited peninsula.

On the west side is the Pacific Ocean and the Olympic Coast Wilderness, where picturesque sea stacks and tidal pools bless one of the West Coast's finest stretches of coastline. Protected by wilderness and wildlife designations, the Olympic Coast is one of the most scenic places on the peninsula. Bald eagles patrol the skies, while sea otters play in the surf. January storms roll in one after another, each giving way to welcome and frequent doses of sunshine. Luckily for hikers, trails run the length of the Olympic Coast, and Cape Flattery, Shi Shi Beach, and Ozette Triangle make good days hikes or overnighters. Longer trips can be made along the North, Central, or South Coast Trails. Regardless of the season, the coast is a special place to visit.

Farther inland are the area's famous rainforests, with trees growing to immense proportions and moss blanketing anything that will sit still for a minute (or so it seems). If you've never visited the Olympic rainforest, you're in for a treat. The home of one of the United States' few rainforests, the west side of the peninsula grows some of the earth's largest trees. Forests teeming with gargantuan specimens of western hemlock, Sitka spruce, and western red cedar cover the land. Towering some 200–300 feet overhead, these grand forests form giant canopies, beneath which grow dense understories of vine maple, elderberry, devil's club, and salmonberry. On rare spring or fall days when it's not raining, humidity hangs in the air, wetting everything it touches, even Gore-Tex. The Bogachiel, Hoh, and Quinault River Valleys are full of trails that explore this great area.

Finally, the Olympic Mountains, with their subalpine meadows and flowing glaciers, are one of Washington's wildest and most beautiful ranges. First, a little geology. The Olympics are profoundly unique in that they have a circular shape, known as a radial formation. The river drainages start in the center of the range and flow outward in all directions. The Olympics are very young, at least geologically speaking. The oldest rocks are only 55 million years old, with most rocks closer to 40 million years of age. The mountains got their start as deposits of lava and sedimentation under the Pacific Ocean. Gradually they were bent out of shape by the Juan de Fuca plate colliding offshore with the continental plate. The light sedimentary rocks, driven below the heavier continental plate, eventually broke through and sprang like a cork to the surface, creating the dome/circular shape. More recently (about 14,000 years ago), the Ice Age left its mark on the range. The Cordilleran ice sheet scraped past and around the mountains, creating the picturesque Hood Canal. Alpine glaciers spread down the valleys for miles from their starting points, producing distinctive U-shaped valleys. To say the least, the Olympics are a great place to geek out on geology.

They are also home to an abundance of wildlife. Several unique species call these forests home, including Roosevelt elk, Olympic salamanders, and Olympic marmots. The park offers some of our best chances to see black bears. Late summer in the high country is practically a bear mecca, when the sedate creatures gorge themselves into a stupor on ripe huckleberries. Wolf packs prowled these mountains before humans wiped them out in the early 20th century. While talks of reintroduction to the area have quieted down recently, wilderness lovers can only hope for such an action.

Of the Olympics' many rivers, the largest (or at least longest) of them is the Elwha River, flowing northward into the Straight of Juan de Fuca. The glacier-fed Elwha was once one of our region's most productive rivers, bearing populations of all five northwest salmon species. This came to an end when two dams were built on the river in the early 1900s, cutting off most of the spawning ground. Happily, these dams are slated for removal by the end of the decade. While full restoration may take 30 years or more, hope remains for future major runs on the river. Also on the north peninsula are trails out of Hurricane Ridge, an outstanding visitor center at 6,000 feet. After hiking, grab dinner and a beer in scenic Port Angeles.

The northeastern portion of the range is distinguishable by its relatively light rainfall, where the mountains receive as little as 20 inches of annual rainfall—an anomaly in this rainy region. Most fronts move off the Pacific in a southwest to northeast direction over the mountain range, and as wet air from the ocean crosses the range, the water is squeezed out over the western side. By the time air reaches the east side, much of the rain has fallen already, leaving the "rain shadow" dry. All of the retirees flocking to Sequim couldn't be happier. While this region is noticeably drier (tell that to someone hiking here in October), it has some extraordinary richness in landscape and forests.

Moving southward, the rest of the eastern side of the range is comprised of rivers dropping quickly from high mountain crests to the Hood Canal. This area receives its fair share of rain, certainly more than the rain shadow. Its major rivers include the Dosewallips, Duckabush, Hamma Hamma, and Skokomish Rivers.

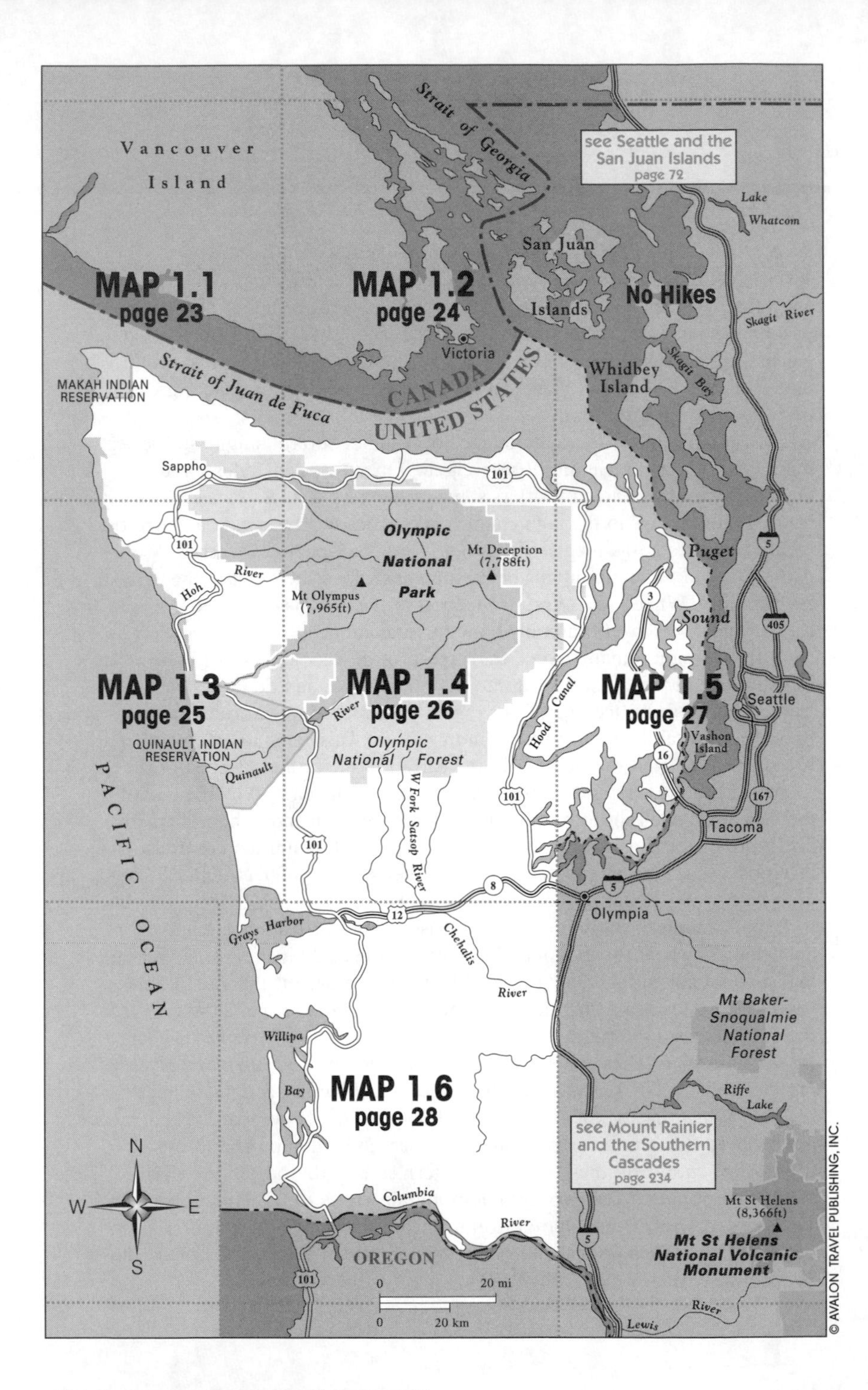
Strait of Georgia
Vancouver Island
see Seattle and the San Juan Islands page 72
Lake Whatcom
San Juan Islands
MAP 1.1 page 23
MAP 1.2 page 24
No Hikes
Skagit River
Victoria
Skagit Bay
Strait of Juan de Fuca
CANADA
UNITED STATES
Whidbey Island
MAKAH INDIAN RESERVATION
Sappho
101
Olympic National Park
Mt Deception (7,788ft)
Mt Olympus (7,965ft)
Hoh River
Puget Sound
3
5
405
MAP 1.3 page 25
MAP 1.4 page 26
MAP 1.5 page 27
Seattle
Hood Canal
Vashon Island
QUINAULT INDIAN RESERVATION
Quinault
River
Olympic National Forest
W Fork Satsop River
16
167
Tacoma
PACIFIC OCEAN
8
12
Olympia
Grays Harbor
Chehalis River
Mt Baker-Snoqualmie National Forest
Willipa Bay
MAP 1.6 page 28
Riffe Lake
see Mount Rainier and the Southern Cascades page 234
N
W
E
S
Columbia River
Mt St Helens (8,366ft)
Mt St Helens National Volcanic Monument
OREGON
0
20 mi
20 km
Lewis River
© AVALON TRAVEL PUBLISHING, INC.

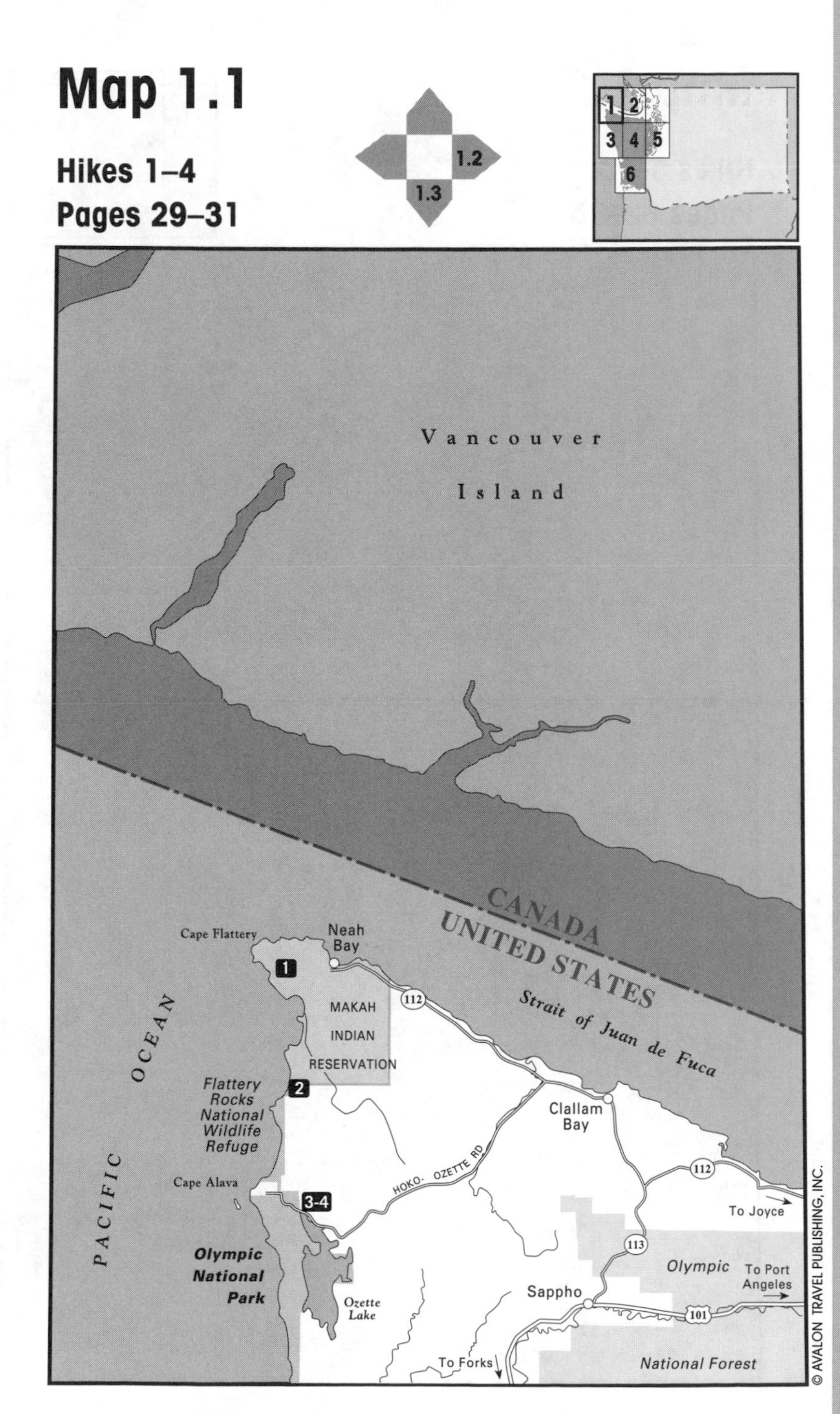
Map 1.1
Hikes 1–4
Pages 29–31
1.2
1.3
1
2
3
4
5
6
Vancouver Island
CANADA
UNITED STATES
Strait of Juan de Fuca
Cape Flattery
Neah Bay
MAKAH INDIAN RESERVATION
112
PACIFIC OCEAN
Flattery Rocks National Wildlife Refuge
Clallam Bay
Cape Alava
3-4
HOKO- OZETTE RD
To Joyce
113
Olympic National Park
Ozette Lake
Sappho
Olympic
To Port Angeles
101
To Forks
National Forest
© AVALON TRAVEL PUBLISHING, INC.

Map 1.2

Hikes 5–10
Pages 32–35

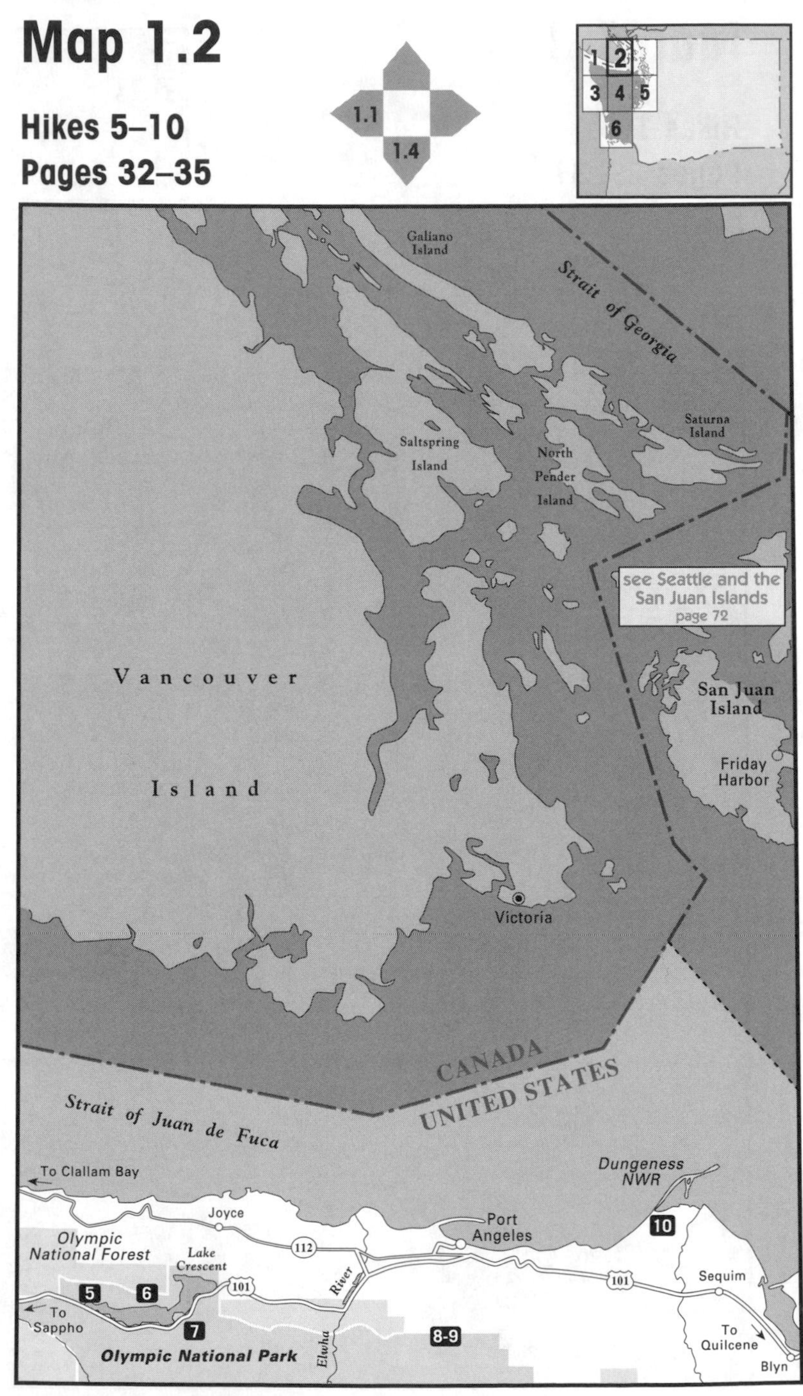

Map 1.3

Hikes 11–14
Pages 36–37

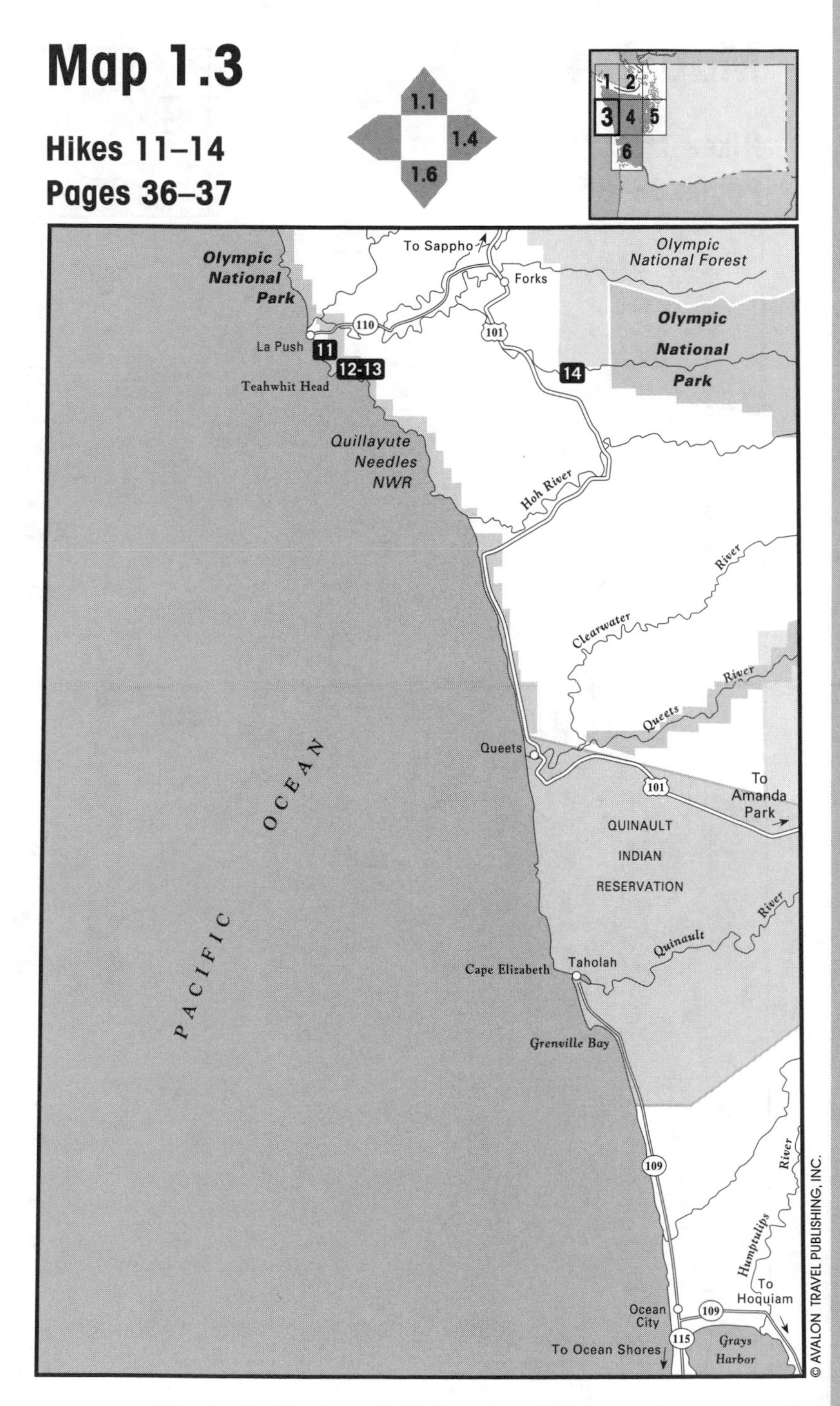

Map 1.4

Hikes 15–57
Pages 38–65

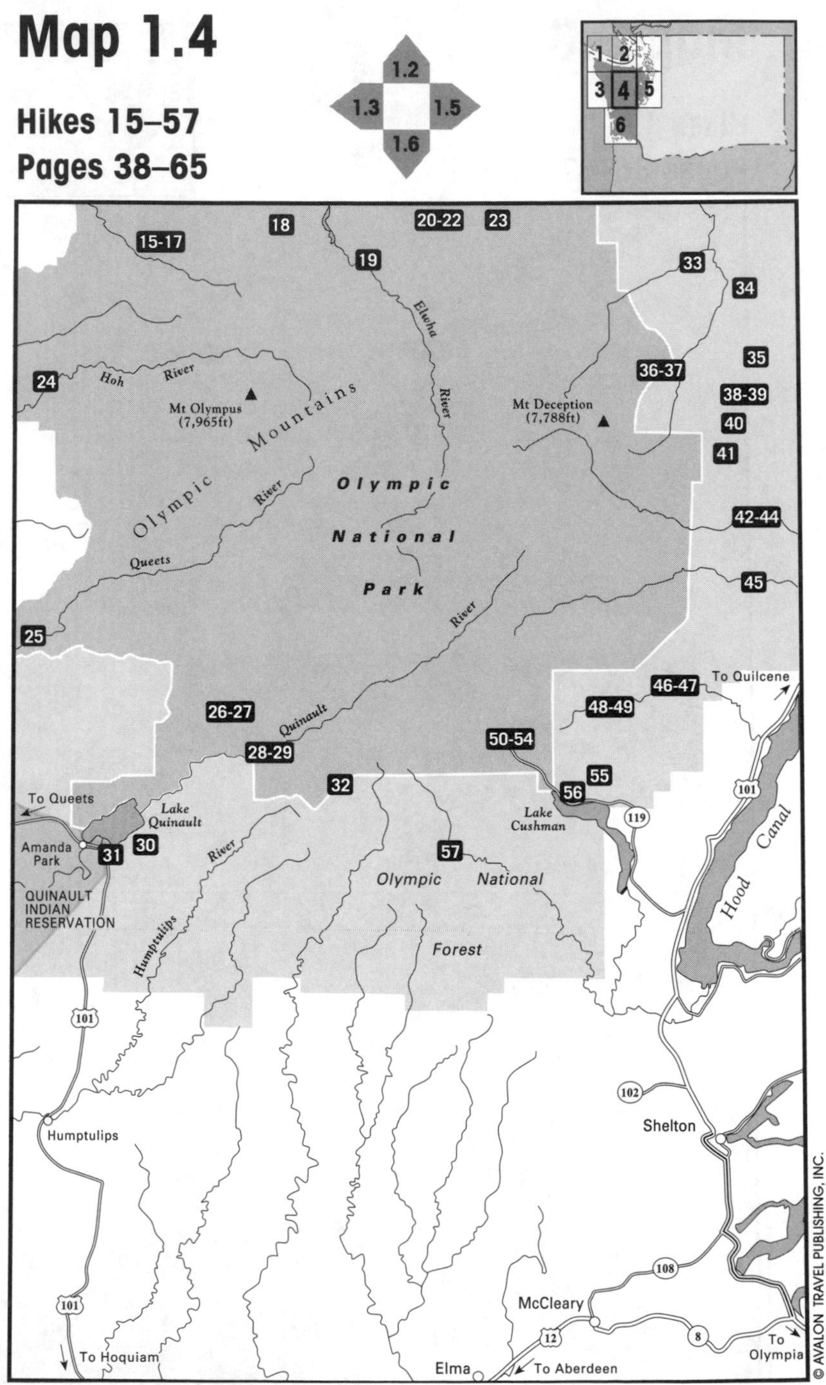

Map 1.5

Hike 58
Page 66

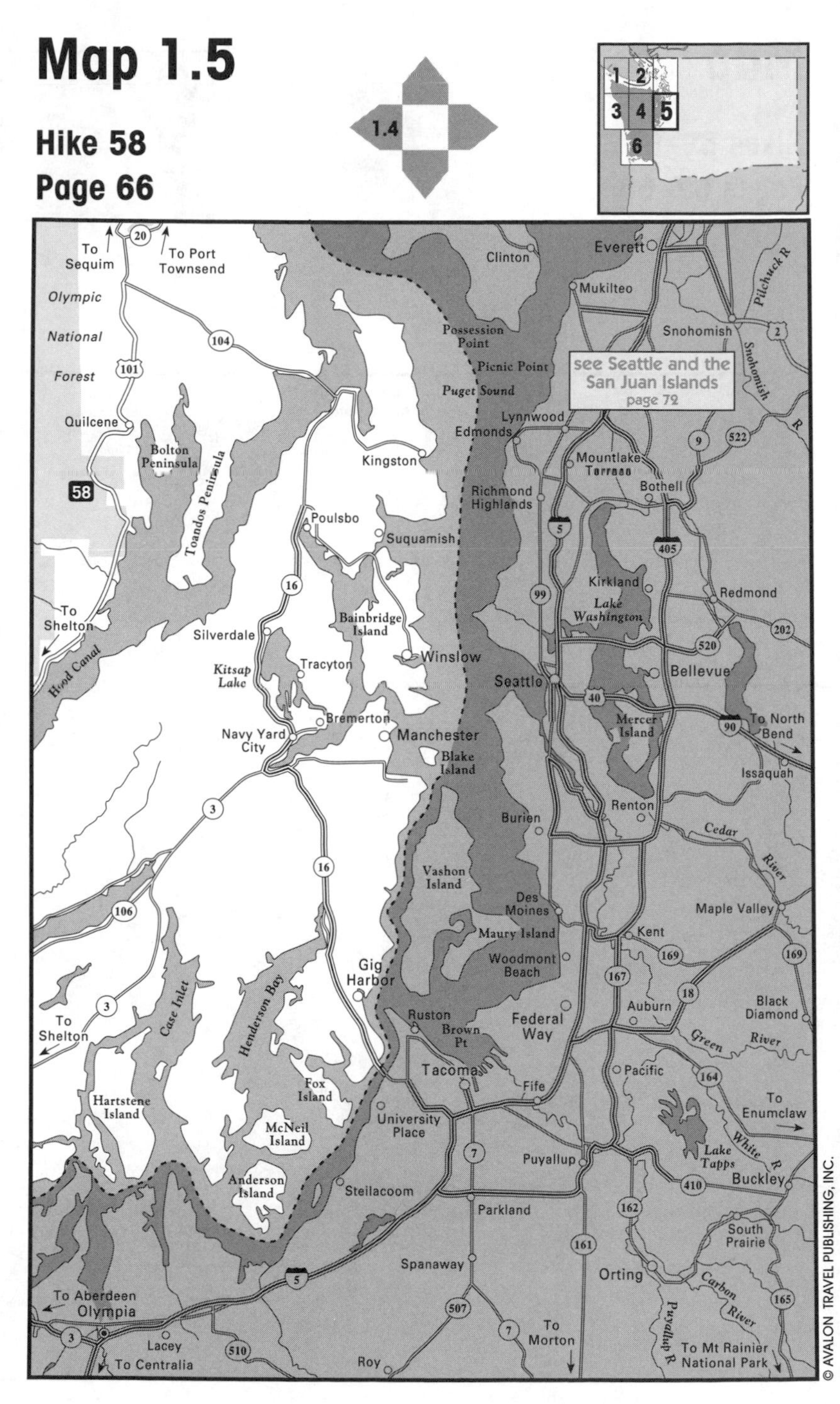

Map 1.6

Hikes 59–61
Pages 67–68

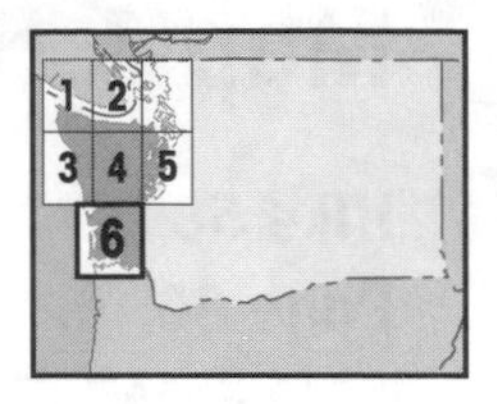

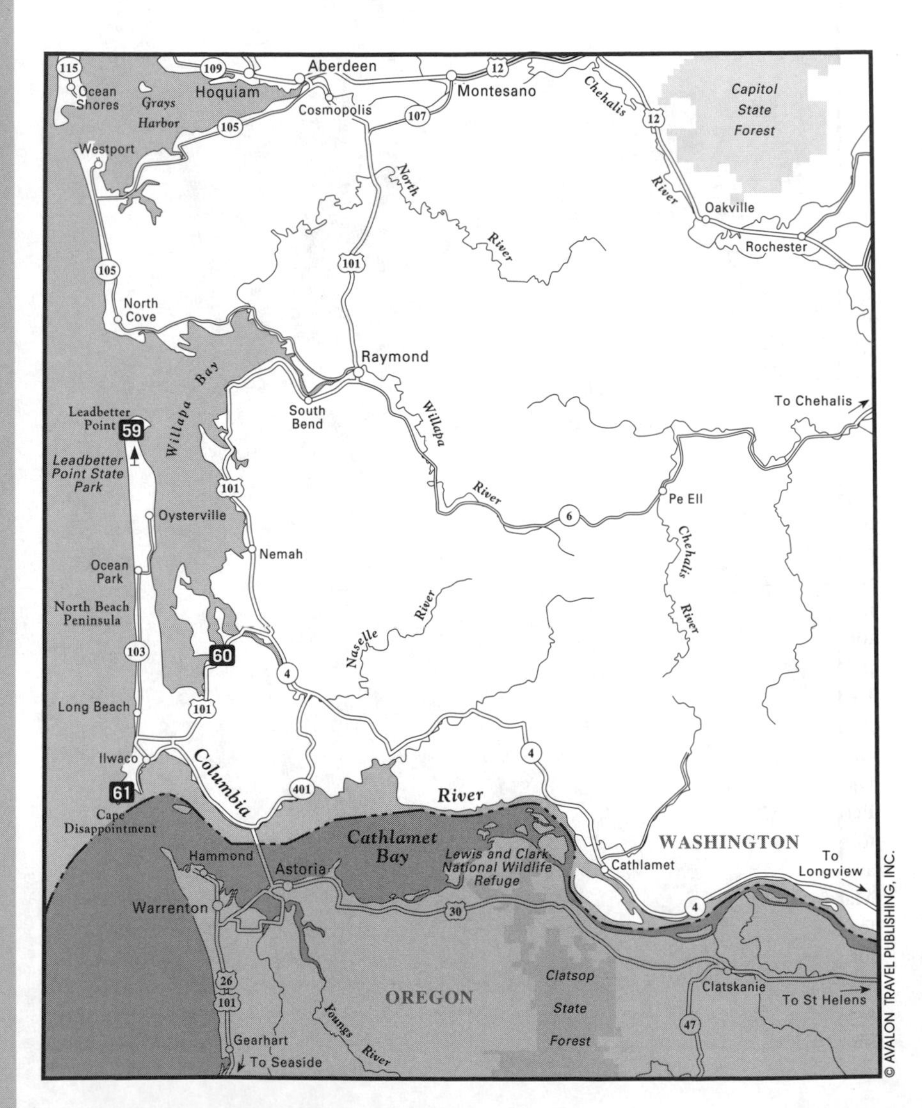

1 CAPE FLATTERY

1.5 mi/1.0 hr

northwest of Neah Bay on the Makah Indian Reservation

Map 1.1, page 23

A newly refurbished trail leads through great coastal forest to one of the Washington coast's most scenic places. The Makah Nation rebuilt Cape Flattery Trail several years back, taking a dangerous, muddy trail to near perfection. Four observation decks hover above sea cliffs overlooking the cape, providing views of ocean and wildlife. Birds and sea life flock to the area year-round. During the spring and fall, it's possible to sight gray whales.

Cape Flattery Trail works its way through a coastal forest of large old-growth cedars and firs. Many boardwalks and bridges along the way keep feet dry on this once infamously muddy trail. The trail pops out of the forest at the cape, above the Olympic Coast National Marine Sanctuary. The sanctuary designation provides protection for numerous animals. Scores of cormorants and tufted puffins make their way in and out of homes in the sea cliffs. Below in the water, sea lions swim from cove to cove on the prowl for a meal. From mid-March through mid-April, Cape Flattery is a prime location for spotting migrating gray whales; binoculars are a must. Cape Flattery may be a long way from the rest of Washington, but North America's most northwestern point is awesome.

User Groups: Hikers and leashed dogs. No horses or mountain bikes are allowed. No wheelchair access.

Open Seasons: This trail is accessible year-round.

Permits: A Makah Recreation Pass is required to park here. An annual pass costs $7 and is available at most businesses in Neah Bay.

Maps: For topographic maps, ask Green Trails for No. 98S, Cape Flattery, or ask the USGS for Cape Flattery.

Directions: From Port Angeles, drive 5 miles west on U.S. 101 to Highway 112. Turn right (north) onto Highway 112 and drive 63 miles to Neah Bay. At the west end of town, turn left on Cape Flattery Road and drive to Cape Loop Road. Turn right and drive to the signed trailhead at road's end.

Contact: Makah Tribe, P.O. Box 115, Neah Bay, WA 98357, 360/645-2201.

2 SHI SHI BEACH

4.0–9.6 mi/2.0 hrs–2 days

south of the Makah Indian Reservation in Olympic National Park

Map 1.1, page 23

Protected from development by wilderness designations, more than 75 miles of Olympic Coast remain in pristine condition, untamed by humans. This rich habitat sustains a biodiversity that offers unparalleled opportunities for seeing wildlife. And its most beautiful section lies here, from the wide, sandy shores of Shi Shi Beach to the rugged sea stacks at Point of the Arches.

The Makah Tribe recently began rebuilding Shi Shi Beach Trail from its reservation, providing a new and easier access to this beach. The trail travels 2 muddy miles through forest before breaking out onto Shi Shi Beach. Two miles of beach stretching southward offer great strolling, even when the weather fails to cooperate (which is often). The beach is a good point to turn around, for those looking for a shorter hike.

Shi Shi Beach ends where Point of the Arches begins. Here, a large grouping of enormous sea stacks spread out into the sea off a point. Tidal pools abound here, offering excellent chances for seeing starfish and urchins. Sea otters often play in the water while bald eagles soar overhead in perpetual wind.

The trip to Point of the Arches (4.8 miles) can easily be done in one day, but camping is a popular activity along Shi Shi. Permits, however, must be obtained from the park service. Good sites are found regularly along the shore. Water should be obtained at Petroleum Creek (3.3 miles), which must be forded to access Point of the Arches. It is an easy crossing made easier by low tides. Traveling south of Point of the Arches brings hikers to Cape Alava and the Ozette Triangle, not a recommended approach.

User Groups: Hikers only. No dogs, horses, or mountain bikes are allowed. No wheelchair access.

Open Seasons: This trail is accessible year-round.

Permits: A Makah Recreation Pass is required to park here. An annual pass costs $7 and is available at most businesses in Neah Bay. Overnight stays within the national park require backcountry camping permits, which are available at the Wilderness Information Center in Port Angeles.

Maps: For a map of Olympic National Park, contact the Outdoor Recreation Information Center at the downtown Seattle REI. For topographic maps, ask Green Trails for No. 98S, Cape Flattery, or ask the USGS for Makah Bay and Ozette.

Directions: From Port Angeles, drive 5 miles west on U.S. 101 to Highway 112. Turn right (north) onto Highway 112 and drive 63 miles to Neah Bay. At the west end of town, turn left on Cape Flattery Road and drive 3 miles to Hobuck Beach Road. Turn left, cross the Waatch River, and drive to Sooes River. Here, Hobuck Beach Road becomes Sooes Beach Road. Cross the Sooes River and drive to the clearly marked trailhead on the right. The parking area here is for day use only. Overnight visitors can pay local homeowners (who have signs advertising parking) to park on their private property (where their cars will be secure).

Contact: Makah Tribe, P.O. Box 115, Neah Bay, WA 98357, 360/645-2201; Olympic Wilderness Information Center, 600 East Park Avenue, Port Angeles, WA 98362-6798, 360/565-3130.

3 OZETTE TRIANGLE

9.0 mi/1–2 days

northwest of Forks in Olympic National Park

Map 1.1, page 23

No route in Washington claims a heritage quite like the Ozette Triangle. Three trails form this triangle, with the leg along the beach home to Wedding Rocks. Wedding Rocks bear petroglyphs carved by Native Americans hun-

© SCOTT LEONARD

Wedding Rocks, along Ozette Triangle

dreds of years ago. Their illustrations depict orcas, the sun and moon, and even a ship of western explorers. Even without Wedding Rocks, this beach would be highly popular. Large sea stacks set among larger islands, countless tidepools brimming with sea life, bald eagles aplenty, and even the possible sightings of gray whales make this a pleasurable trip.

Cape Alava and Sand Point Trails lead to the beach from Lake Ozette. Each trail is three miles long, flat, and forested by big trees. Boardwalk covers most of each trail and can be slippery; watch out! Starting on the northern route (Cape Alava) will drop you off at a coastline full of sea stacks and wildlife. The numerous campsites near Cape Alava require reservations (from the Port Angeles Wilderness Information Center) because of large summer crowds.

Head south from Cape Alava among countless tidal pools, brimming with life. Wedding Rocks are one mile south from Cape Alava, scattered around a jutting point; they are above the high tide line. The site is legendary for attracting cultists and other New Age folk, but you're more likely to run across sea otters floating offshore in beds of kelp. The beach extends south two miles before intersecting Sand Point Trail. Here, a large headland juts into the sea and provides an excellent vantage point from atop it. The Ozette Triangle is rightfully one of the peninsula's most valued trails.

User Groups: Hikers only. No dogs, horses, or mountain bikes are allowed. No wheelchair access.

Open Seasons: This trail is accessible year-round.

Permits: There is a $1 daily parking fee here, payable at the trailhead. Overnight stays within the national park require backcountry camping permits, which are available at the Wilderness Information Center in Port Angeles.

Maps: For a map of Olympic National Park, contact the Outdoor Recreation Information Center at the downtown Seattle REI. For topographic maps, ask Green Trails for No. 135S, Ozette, or ask the USGS for Ozette.

Directions: From Port Angeles, drive east 5 miles on U.S. 101 to Highway 112. Turn right (west) and drive 49 miles to Hoko/Ozette Lake Road. Turn left and drive 21 miles to the well-signed trailhead at Lake Ozette.

Contact: Olympic National Park, Wilderness Information Center, 3002 Mount Angeles Road, Port Angeles, WA 98362, 360/565-3100.

4 NORTH WILDERNESS BEACH

19.7 mi one-way/2–3 days 3 10

west of Forks in Olympic National Park

Map 1.1, page 23

This stretch of the Olympic coastline is one of the wildest and most scenic beaches anywhere in the United States. North Wilderness Beach features countless tidal pools packed with creatures crawling, swimming, or simply affixed to the rocks. Unremitting waves roll in through the fog to break apart on the sea stacks jutting into the Pacific Ocean. Sea otters, eagles, herons, cormorants, and ducks are all likely sightings.

Access to North Wilderness Beach Route is via Sandpoint Trail, three miles of virgin coastal forest. The travelway heads south along sandy beaches, but at times may test ankles with stretches of cobbles and boulders. Several times the trail is driven on land because of impassibility around a point. Circular signs (painted like bull's-eyes and visible from the shore) indicate these points. Also, it is important to carry a tide table, as 12 sections of trail require passage at low or medium tides. Green Trails maps indicate points that require passages during low tides.

The route encounters the tall cliffs of Yellow Bank (4.5 miles). A pair of memorials stand along the route; Norwegian Memorial (9.9 miles), marked by an obelisk, and Chilean Memorial (16.5 miles). The travelway crosses Cedar Creek (11.3 miles), a necessary ford, and rounds Cape Johnson (15 miles). Hole in the Wall appears south of Cape Johnson, a rock formation forming a natural arch, where hikers can capture a postcard moment. The route ends at the sea stacks of Rialto Beach.

Throughout the route, camping is plentiful, with numerous sites on the shore. Campfires are not permitted between Wedding Rocks, north of Sand Point, and Yellow Banks. Elsewhere, be sure to gather only driftwood from the beach.

User Groups: Hikers only. No dogs, horses, or mountain bikes are allowed. No wheelchair access.

Open Seasons: This trail is accessible year-round.

Permits: There is a $1 daily parking fee here, payable at the trailhead. Overnight stays within the national park require backcountry camping permits, which are available at the Wilderness Information Center in Port Angeles.

Maps: For a map of Olympic National Park, contact the Outdoor Recreation Information Center at the downtown Seattle REI. For topographic maps, ask Green Trails for No. 130S, Lake Ozette, or ask the USGS for Ozette, Allens Bay, and La Push.

Directions: From Port Angeles, drive east 5 miles on U.S. 101 to Highway 112. Turn right (west) and drive 49 miles to Hoko/Ozette Lake Road. Turn left and drive 21 miles to the well-signed trailhead at Lake Ozette.

Contact: Olympic National Park, Wilderness Information Center, 3002 Mount Angeles Road, Port Angeles, WA 98362, 360/565-3100.

5 PYRAMID MOUNTAIN

7.0 mi/3.5 hrs 3 6

north of Lake Crescent in Olympic National Park

Map 1.2, page 24

Pyramid Mountain Trail provides a good workout through old-growth forest culminating at a wonderful cabin lookout. From the top, peer out over the Strait of Juan de Fuca to Canada and over Lake Crescent to the Olympics. The lookout was built during World War II so the army could watch for incoming enemy aircraft. Fortunately none arrived but the lookout remained. The cabin on stilts perches atop the 3,100-foot peak, not high by Olympic standards, but good enough to work up a sweat and enjoy it.

Pyramid Mountain Trail starts off in a previously logged forest but soon enters old-growth forest. Mixed with the large conifers are numerous Pacific madrona, the Northwest's distinctive broadleaved evergreen. Madrona is known for its uniquely papery bark that comes off in ragged shreds to reveal fine, smooth wood. These handsome trees produce small, bell-shaped flowers in the spring. Madrona trees deserve close inspection and always garner admiration.

The trail climbs through forest, crossing June Creek, which often runs below ground at this spot. It's a good idea to bring your own water on this hike, especially on warm days. The trail eventually reaches the ridgeline, where devastating clear-cuts have revealed views of the strait. After several false summits, the trail finally reaches the lookout. Be a bit careful up here; the north side of the mountain features a precipitous drop. The views extend in every direction. Lake Crescent is a beautiful green jewel to the south, while the strait is wide and large to the north.

User Groups: Hikers only. No dogs, horses, or mountain bikes are allowed. No wheelchair access.

Open Seasons: This trail is accessible April–October.

Permits: Permits are not required. Parking and access are free.

Maps: For a map of Olympic National Park, contact the Outdoor Recreation Information Center at the downtown Seattle REI. For topographic maps, ask Green Trails for No. 101, Lake Crescent, or ask the USGS for Lake Crescent.

Directions: From Port Angeles, drive west 28 miles on U.S. 101 to North Shore Road. Turn right and drive about 3 miles to the well-signed trailhead on the left side of the road.

Contact: Olympic National Park, Wilderness Information Center, 3002 Mount Angeles Road, Port Angeles, WA 98362, 360/565-3100.

6 SPRUCE RAILROAD

8.0 mi/4.0 hrs

north shore of Lake Crescent in Olympic National Park

Map 1.2, page 24

Anyone who has ever navigated the twisty section of U.S. 101 as it passes Lake Crescent knows the beauty of the emerald lake. With lush green forests and high mountain ridges containing the waters, Lake Crescent often stands out in the memories of passing motorists. That is to say nothing of the memories it leaves in hikers who walk the shores of Lake Crescent on the Spruce Railroad Trail.

Four miles of trail edge the lake along a former railroad built by the U.S. Army. This rail route once carried high-quality spruce timber to Seattle and eastward for production of World War I airplanes. Metal eventually replaced wood in aircraft production and the army sold the route, allowing the railway to be successfully converted into a level, easy-to-walk trail. The highlight is Devil's Punchbowl, 1.1 miles from the east trailhead. Here, a small cove from the lake is encircled by cliffs of pillow basalt. The depth of this popular swimming hole is reportedly more than 300 feet. Spruce Railroad Trail continues another three miles below towering cliffs where Pacific madrona cling to the walls. Lush forest covers parts of the trail, but Lake Crescent rarely leaves your sight. A trailhead exists at the west end, also. This hike is extremely well suited for families and for the off-season. It's a local winter favorite.

User Groups: Hikers only. No dogs, horses, or mountain bikes are allowed. No wheelchair access.

Open Seasons: This trail is accessible year-round.

Permits: Permits are not required. Parking and access are free.

Maps: For a map of Olympic National Park, contact the Outdoor Recreation Information Center at the downtown Seattle REI. For topographic maps, ask Green Trails for No. 101, Lake Crescent, or ask the USGS for Lake Crescent.

Directions: From Port Angeles, drive west 28 miles on U.S. 101 to North Shore Road. Turn right and drive 5 miles to the well-signed trailhead.

Contact: Olympic National Park, Wilderness Information Center, 3002 Mount Angeles Road, Port Angeles, WA 98362, 360/565-3100.

7 MARYMERE FALLS

1.4 mi/1.0 hr

south of Lake Crescent in Olympic National Park

Map 1.2, page 24

Marymere Falls Trail offers hikers of all ages and abilities a great view of the Olympics' best waterfall. A short stroll through old forest and a climb up a large series of crib steps presents visitors with a vantage point well positioned for the showcase cascade. Falls Creek shoots over Marymere Falls and tumbles more than 100 feet. With adequate flow, the creek plummets so fiercely that surrounding trees and ferns sway. A delicate mist covers all who lean over the railing. Marymere is a beautiful spot and is popular in the summer with the many people passing by on U.S. 101. Ferns and mosses grow upon everything in the forest, a great example of what the Olympic forests are all about. The route starts at Storm King Ranger Station, follows the Barnes Creek Trail for .5 mile, then cuts off by crossing Barnes Creek and Falls Creek before ascending to the viewpoint.

User Groups: Hikers only. No dogs, horses, or mountain bikes are allowed. No wheelchair access.

Open Seasons: This trail is accessible year-round.

Permits: Permits are not required. Parking and access are free.

Maps: For a map of Olympic National Park, contact the Outdoor Recreation Information Center at the downtown Seattle REI. For topographic maps, ask Green Trails for No. 101, Lake Crescent, or ask the USGS for Lake Crescent.

Directions: From Port Angeles, drive west 20 miles on U.S. 101 to the well-signed Storm

King Ranger Station. Turn right and drive 200 yards to Lake Crescent Road. Turn right for the trailhead at Storm King Ranger Station.

Contact: Olympic National Park, Wilderness Information Center, 3002 Mount Angeles Road, Port Angeles, WA 98362, 360/565-3100.

8 HEATHER PARK/ MOUNT ANGELES

10.0 mi one-way/5.5 hrs

south of Port Angeles in Olympic National Park

Map 1.2, page 24

A popular route for Port Angeles visitors, Heather Park Trail delivers grand views into the Olympics from along windswept ridges. Meadows are the name of the game along the upper sections. An outstanding parkland basin is found at Heather Park, while several accessible peaks offer views stretching over the heart of the Olympic Range. The route can also be completed from Hurricane Ridge Visitor Center, a less strenuous but busier choice.

Heather Park Trail leaves Heart o' the Hills in pleasant but unspectacular second-growth forest and climbs steadily to timberline and Heather Park (4.1 miles). The wide open basin rests between the pinnacles of First Peak and Second Peak. Meadows of heather and lupine fill in the voids between scattered subalpine fir trees, and several campsites are to be had. This is a good turnaround.

Heather Park Trail continues, climbing below the base of Mount Angeles (6 miles), whose summit is accessible by an easy social trail. Beyond, the trail drops to a junction with Sunrise Trail (6.3 miles), a highly used route that leads west to Hurricane Ridge Visitor Center. It's 3.5 miles of ridgeline hiking through open forest and meadows. Sunrise Trail gains less elevation and has its own social trail to the top of Mount Angeles.

User Groups: Hikers and horses. No dogs or mountain bikes are allowed. No wheelchair access.

Open Seasons: This trail is accessible mid-June–October.

Permits: Permits are not required. Parking and access are free.

Maps: For a map of Olympic National Park, contact the Outdoor Recreation Information Center at the downtown Seattle REI. For topographic maps, ask Green Trails for No. 103, Port Angeles, and No. 135, Mount Angeles, or ask the USGS for Port Angeles and Mount Angeles.

Directions: From Port Angeles, drive north 2 miles on Race Street as it turns into Mount Angeles Road. Veer right at the well-signed fork and continue on Mount Angeles Road 5 miles to the trailhead immediately before the national park entrance booth. The trailhead is down a short access road.

Contact: Olympic National Park, Wilderness Information Center, 3002 Mount Angeles Road, Port Angeles, WA 98362, 360/565-3100.

9 KLAHHANE RIDGE

13.0 mi/6.5 hr

south of Port Angeles in Olympic National Park

Map 1.2, page 24

Klahhane Ridge Trail is much more than just Klahhane Ridge. For starters, the Klahhane Ridge Trail passes Lake Angeles, one of the peninsula's larger subalpine lakes, set beneath cliffs. Talk about picturesque. Second, the trail makes an outstanding loop when combined with Mount Angeles Trail. This 12.9-mile round-trip samples all of the best of the North Olympics. And the trail leads out along Klahhane Ridge, a place where open meadows and small trees give way to sweeping views of the interior Olympics. It may well be the best sampler of the Olympics around.

Klahhane Ridge Trail leaves Heart o' the Hills and climbs steadily through forest to Lake Angeles (3.7 miles). The lake is very popular with visitors to the North Peninsula, particularly on weekends. One would think the steep trip would weed folks out, but apparently not enough. A few camps are found around the lake. The trail continues up to Klahhane Ridge (5 miles), where distant vistas make their appearance, extending in every direction. The cities of Port Angeles and Victoria are visible to the north. Klahhane Ridge Trail ends at a junction with Mount Angeles Trail (6.5 miles), where turning north takes you through spectacular Heather Park and back to Heart o' the Hills.

User Groups: Hikers and horses. No dogs or mountain bikes are allowed. No wheelchair access.

Open Seasons: This trail is accessible mid-June–October.

Permits: Permits are not required. Parking and access are free.

Maps: For a map of Olympic National Park, contact the Outdoor Recreation Information Center at the downtown Seattle REI. For topographic maps, ask Green Trails for No. 103, Port Angeles, and No. 135, Mount Angeles, or ask the USGS for Port Angeles and Mount Angeles.

Directions: From Port Angeles, drive north 2 miles on Race Street as it turns into Mount Angeles Road. Veer right at the well-signed fork and continue on Mount Angeles Road 5 miles to the trailhead immediately before the national park entrance booth. The trailhead is down a short road on the right.

Contact: Olympic National Park, Wilderness Information Center, 3002 Mount Angeles Road, Port Angeles, WA 98362, 360/565-3100.

10 DUNGENESS SPIT

10.0 mi/5.0 hrs

north of Sequim on the northeast tip of the Olympic Peninsula

Map 1.2, page 24

Set within Dungeness National Wildlife Refuge, Dungeness Spit is undoubtedly one of the state's premier sites to watch wildlife. The refuge hosts a rich and diverse ecosystem that is home to birds, critters by land and sea, and numerous fish and shellfish. The trail is less of a trail and more of a walk on a great beach.

Dungeness Spit juts into the Strait of Juan de Fuca 5.5 miles, creating a quiet harbor and bay of tide flats. The spit is constantly growing, being added to from nearby bluffs eroding sandy sediments into the strait. At the end of the spit stands a historic lighthouse built in 1857 and still open to the public.

The refuge sees more than 250 species of birds each year, mainly shorebirds and waterfowl, some migratory and some permanent residents–definitely a bird-watcher's dream. More than 50 mammals of both land and sea live here, too. Harbor seals occasionally use the tip of the spit as a pup-raising site. In the bay, eelgrass beds provide a nursery for young salmon and steelhead adjusting to saltwater. This is a wonderful place to enjoy the wildlife.

User Groups: Hikers and horses (horses allowed except on summer weekends). No dogs or mountains bikes are allowed. The trail is wheelchair accessible (to several lookouts, not the spit).

Open Seasons: Most of this area is accessible year-round (some parts are closed seasonally to protect wildlife feeding and nesting).

Permits: The entrance fee is $3 per family daily. Admission is free with a federal duck stamp, a Golden Eagle Pass, a Golden Age Pass, or a Golden Access passport.

Maps: For a topographic map, ask the USGS for Dungeness.

Directions: From U.S. 101, go just west of Sequim and turn north on Kitchen-Dick Road. Continue for 3 miles to the Dungeness Recreation Area. Go through the recreation area to the refuge parking lot at the end of the road. The well-marked trailhead is located immediately before the parking area.

Contact: Dungeness National Wildlife Refuge, Washington Maritime NWR Complex, 33 South Barr Road, Port Angeles, WA 98362, 360/457-8451.

11 SECOND BEACH

2.4 mi/2.0 hrs

south of La Push on the central Olympic Coast

Map 1.3, page 25

Second Beach is a place to do some thinking. Sit and stare at the many sea stacks out among the waves. Watch waves crash through the large archway to the north. Spy eagles and gulls tangling high overhead. The months of March, April, and October may bring migrating whales past you not far offshore. When you tire of resting, walk along the sandy beach. It is in pristine condition, save for a little garbage that floats in from the ocean. Well over a mile long, Second Beach provides lots to see: driftwood, crabs, eagles, sea otters, and who knows what else. The trail down to the beach (.7 mile) is easy to negotiate, being flat and wide the whole way save for the last few hundred yards. A wide pile of driftwood stands between the trail and beach, requiring a bit of scrambling, but it's nothing much. Second Beach is well worth a couple of extra hours for anyone on the way to La Push.

User Groups: Hikers and leashed dogs. No horses or mountain bikes are allowed. No wheelchair access.

Open Seasons: This trail is accessible year-round.

Permits: Permits are not required. Parking and access are free.

Maps: For a map of Olympic National Park, contact the Outdoor Recreation Information Center at the downtown Seattle REI. For topographic maps, ask Green Trails for No. 163S, La Push, or ask the USGS for Toleak Point.

Directions: From Port Angeles, drive west 54 miles on U.S. 101 to La Push Road (Highway 110; just before the town of Forks). Turn right and drive 8 miles to a Y, where the road splits. Stay left, on La Push Road, and drive 4.5 miles to the signed trailhead on the left.

Contact: Olympic National Park, Wilderness Information Center, 3002 Mount Angeles Road, Port Angeles, WA 98362, 360/565-3100.

12 THIRD BEACH

2.6 mi/2.0–3.0 hrs

south of La Push on the central Olympic Coast

Map 1.3, page 25

Snaking its way through a nice lowland forest, Third Beach Trail accesses a long strip of extravagant Olympic coast. The beach is wide and sandy for nearly its entire length, well over a mile, and bends inward slightly to make a crescent. The resulting bay was named Strawberry Bay after the ubiquitous strawberry plant in the coastal forests. Tall, rocky cliffs mark the north end of the crescent and are impassable, no matter your skill level. As you look to the south, beyond Taylor Point, a number of sea stacks are visible in the distance. It's easy for hikers of all abilities to see such great things, as the trail down to the beach loses very little elevation and is wide and well maintained. As you hike through the forest, the increasing roar of the ocean signals your progress, as does the increasing size of massive cedar trees. Although some may say that Second Beach is more scenic, Third Beach is a great trip as well.

User Groups: Hikers and leashed dogs. No horses or mountain bikes are allowed. No wheelchair access.

Open Seasons: This trail is accessible year-round.

Permits: Permits are not required. Parking and access are free.

Maps: For a map of Olympic National Park, contact the Outdoor Recreation Information Center at the downtown Seattle REI. For topographic maps, ask Green Trails for No. 163S, La Push, or ask the USGS for Toleak Point.

Directions: From Port Angeles, drive west 54 miles on U.S. 101 to La Push Road (Highway 110; just before the town of Forks). Turn right and drive 8 miles to a Y, where the road splits. Stay left, on La Push Road, and drive 3 miles to the signed trailhead on the left.

Contact: Olympic National Park, Wilderness Information Center, 3002 Mount Angeles Road, Port Angeles, WA 98362, 360/565-3100.

13 CENTRAL WILDERNESS BEACH

16.7 mi one-way/2 days 

south of La Push on the central Olympic Coast

Map 1.3, page 25

As beautiful as the other long beach routes, Third Beach to Oil City provides a bit more of a hiking challenge. This is the South Coast Beach Travelway, and it requires that several overland bypasses and three creeks be crossed. Not that any of these obstacles is too much to overcome. The South Travelway has some great scenery, including Giants Graveyard, Alexander Island, and an extraordinary abundance of birds and sea life. Bald eagles and blue herons regularly sweep the shores in search of dinner, while sea otters play it cool, reclining in the water and eating shellfish off their stomachs.

Access the route via Third Beach, hiking south above Taylor's Point, impassable along the water. Many times hikers must avoid impassable coastline by hiking trails on land; it's important to carry a map to properly identify these sections. Five miles of great beach present views of Giants Graveyard (4.2 miles), Strawberry Point (6.5 miles), and Toleak Point (7.2 miles), appropriate images of the rugged coastline.

The middle section of Southern Travelway requires fords of Falls Creek (8.5 miles), Goodman Creek (9 miles), and Mosquito Creek (11.5 miles). If it's been wet recently, expect them to be difficult. The lower section of Southern Travelway uses beach, with Alexander Island offshore, and a long 3.5-mile overland route bypassing Hoh Head. This leaves you just north of the trailhead at Oil City (16.7 miles), near the mouth of the Hoh River. Campsites are spread throughout the trip, usually tucked away on shore but visible from the beach.

User Groups: Hikers only. No dogs, horses, or mountain bikes are allowed. No wheelchair access.

Open Seasons: This trail is accessible year-round.

Permits: Permits are not required. Parking and access are free.

Maps: For a map of Olympic National Park, contact the Outdoor Recreation Information Center at the downtown Seattle REI. For topographic maps, ask Green Trails for No. 163, La Push, or ask the USGS for Toleak Point and Hoh Head.

Directions: From Port Angeles, drive west 54 miles on U.S. 101 to La Push Road (Highway 110; just before the town of Forks). Turn right and drive 8 miles to a Y, where the road splits. Stay left, on La Push Road, and drive 3 miles to the signed trailhead on the left.

Contact: Olympic National Park, Wilderness Information Center, 3002 Mount Angeles Road, Port Angeles, WA 98362, 360/565-3100.

14 BOGACHIEL RIVER

41.6 mi/4 days 

southeast of Forks in Olympic National Park

Map 1.3, page 25

Let the masses drive the road up the Hoh River and visit the overpopulated Hoh River Valley. Follow the wiser hikers who access the Bogachiel River for the same gargantuan trees covered in moss, the same cascading streams filled with juvenile salmon, and the same forests teeming with wildlife—but with considerably more solitude.

An OK day hike, Bogachiel River Trail makes for an outstanding river valley trek. Beginning along an old logging road, the trail soon enters the national park and virgin rainforest (2 miles). Massive trees fill the forests, awash in green from the heavy rains off the Pacific Ocean. The mostly flat trail moves in and out of the forest, regularly nearing the river and passing camps. Maintenance on the trail often fails to keep up with the regular washouts from heavy winter rains, so be ready for some route-finding along the way.

After Flapjack Camp (10 miles), Bogachiel River Trail leaves the main branch of the river and slowly climbs with North Fork Bogachiel

River toward High Divide. This is the trail's best section, where at 15 Mile Shelter (14.5 miles) the river surges through a deep gorge. After Hyak Camp (17.6 miles) and 21 Mile Camp (20.8 miles), the trail overlooks the Bogachiel and vast meadows. Those who plan for it can connect this trail to Mink Lake or Deer Lake Trails (25.5 miles) for through-hikes via the Sol Duc Valley. This route is truly wild country, where elk and ancient trees far outnumber bipeds.

User Groups: Hikers and horses. No dogs or mountain bikes are allowed. No wheelchair access.

Open Seasons: This trail is usually accessible year-round (up to about 15 Mile Camp, where the winter snowpack becomes quite deep).

Permits: A federal Northwest Forest Pass is required to park here. Overnight stays within the national park require backcountry camping permits, which are available at the Wilderness Information Center in Port Angeles.

Maps: For a map of Olympic National Park, contact the Outdoor Recreation Information Center at the downtown Seattle REI. For topographic maps, ask Green Trails for No. 132, Spruce Mountain, No. 133, Mount Tom, and No. 134, Mount Olympus, or ask the USGS for Reade Hill, Indian Pass, Hunger Mountain, Slide Peak, and Bogachiel Peak.

Directions: From Forks, drive south 6 miles on U.S. 101 to Undie Road. Turn left (east) and drive 4 miles to the trailhead at road's end.

Contact: Olympic National Park, Wilderness Information Center, 3002 Mount Angeles Road, Port Angeles, WA 98362, 360/565-3100.

15 SOL DUC FALLS/ LOVER'S LANE

5.6 mi/3.0 hrs

south of Lake Crescent in Olympic National Park

Map 1.4, page 26

This is not an exclusive trail for sweethearts. Sure, a couple in love are apt to find this the perfect stroll. But those even more likely to find this a great trail are those who love an easy hike along a great trail through the forest. That group includes couples and kids, seasoned hikers, singles, groups, and anyone between. Add to the pleasure of Lover's Lane the excitement of Sol Duc Falls, one of the Olympics' premier photo ops, and you have a widely agreed-upon fun hike.

The trail departs from the Sol Duc Hot Springs Resort, where folks can relax weary muscles in a number of springs, and starts off into an old-growth forest. The Sol Duc River is never far away and calls out with its incessant rushing. The trail crosses three streams on easy-to-negotiate footbridges, each a nice interruption in the scenery.

Before three miles are underfoot, the trail arrives at Sol Duc Falls. Here, the river makes an abrupt turn and cascades from three notches into a narrow gorge. The forest is incredibly green in these parts and moss seems omnipresent. Regardless of your romantic pursuits, Lover's Lane is a trail for all.

User Groups: Hikers only. No dogs, horses, or mountain bikes are allowed. No wheelchair access.

Open Seasons: This trail is accessible year-round.

Permits: A federal National Parks Pass is required to park here.

Maps: For a map of Olympic National Park, contact the Outdoor Recreation Information Center at the downtown Seattle REI. For topographic maps, ask Green Trails for No. 133, Mount Tom, or ask the USGS for Bogachiel Peak.

Directions: From Port Angeles, drive west 30 miles on U.S. 101 to well-signed Sol Duc Hot Springs Road. Turn left (south) and drive 14 miles to the trailhead at road's end.

Contact: Olympic National Park, Wilderness Information Center, 3002 Mount Angeles Road, Port Angeles, WA 98362, 360/565-3100.

16 SEVEN LAKES BASIN LOOP

20.1 mi/2 days

south of Lake Crescent in Olympic National Park

Map 1.4, page 26

This is one of the peninsula's greatest hikes, a exceptional journey into one of the best lake basins in Washington. The destination is High Divide and the numerous lakes of the area. The divide is more than 5,000 feet in elevation, making this meadow territory. Views open wide to the south, revealing Mount Olympus at close range. Wildlife is plentiful in this part of the park, where regular sightings include black bear, ravens, Roosevelt elk, picas, and Olympic marmots. If you have a camera, please bring it. During July, wildflowers are prolific and difficult not to trample underfoot.

The trail makes a loop by heading up the Sol Duc River to High Divide, then coming back via Deer Lake and Canyon Creek. The trail up the Sol Duc River is a trip through pristine old-growth forests along a river making constant cascades and falls. After the Appleton Pass Trail cuts off at 4.8 miles, the Sol Duc Trail climbs vigorously up Bridge Creek to High Divide. Camps are frequent, but Sol Duc Park and Heart Lake are highly recommended.

From High Divide, Mount Olympus and the Bailey Range ring the Hoh Valley. Head north on the High Divide to the Seven Lakes Basin, a series of not seven but actually eight subalpine lakes. The lakes lie on a gentle slope facing the north, meaning snow can linger well into July. To curb overuse, campsites here must be reserved with the Wilderness Information Center. The trail leaves the basin and drops to Deer Lake. Here, one trail leads down to the trailhead via Canyon Creek, another long string of waterfalls.

User Groups: Hikers only. No dogs, horses, or mountain bikes are allowed. No wheelchair access.

Open Seasons: This trail is accessible July–October.

Permits: A National Parks Pass is required to park here. Overnight stays within the national park require backcountry camping permits, which are available at the Wilderness Information Center in Port Angeles.

Maps: For a map of Olympic National Park, contact the Outdoor Recreation Information Center at the downtown Seattle REI. For topographic maps, ask Green Trails for No. 133, Mount Tom, and No. 134, Mount Olympus, or ask the USGS for Bogachiel Peak and Mount Carrie.

Directions: From Port Angeles, drive west 30 miles on U.S. 101 to well-signed Sol Duc Hot Springs Road. Turn left (south) and drive 14 miles to the trailhead at road's end.

Contact: Olympic National Park, Wilderness Information Center, 3002 Mount Angeles Road, Port Angeles, WA 98362, 360/565-3100.

17 APPLETON PASS

14.8 mi/8.0 hrs

south of Lake Crescent in Olympic National Park

Map 1.4, page 26

Appleton Pass Trail provides a crossing from the Sol Duc to the Elwha drainages. It's also an alternate route up to Boulder Lake and a great entry to acres of open meadows and parkland. The Sol Duc Valley is full of waterfalls, and this route passes by several of them.

From the trailhead, the route uses Sol Duc River Trail for the first 4.8 miles. Along the way is Sol Duc Falls, a popular day hike. This section of trail passes through cool forests of old-growth timber. Appleton Pass Trail climbs steeply via a tiring number of switchbacks to the pass. Just before the pass, it reaches the timberline, and spacious meadows break out in abundance.

Small Oyster Lake is a short side trail from the pass and well recommended. Mount Appleton stands to the north, cloaked in wildflowers and heather during the early summer. For through-hikers, the trail continues beyond the pass down the South Fork of Boulder Creek. Just before the trail converges with North Fork

Trail, Boulder Creek makes a tremendous leap into a deep pool, followed by several smaller cascades, a wonderful sight.

User Groups: Hikers and horses. No dogs or mountain bikes are allowed. No wheelchair access.

Open Seasons: This trail is accessible July–October.

Permits: A National Parks Pass is required to park here. Overnight stays within the national park require backcountry camping permits, which are available at the Wilderness Information Center in Port Angeles.

Maps: For a map of Olympic National Park, contact the Outdoor Recreation Information Center at the downtown Seattle REI. For topographic maps, ask Green Trails for No. 133, Mount Tom, and No. 134, Mount Olympus, or ask the USGS for Bogachiel Peak and Mount Carrie.

Directions: From Port Angeles, drive west 30 miles on U.S. 101 to well-signed Sol Duc Hot Springs Road. Turn left (south) and drive 14 miles to the trailhead at road's end.

Contact: Olympic National Park, Wilderness Information Center, 3002 Mount Angeles Road, Port Angeles, WA 98362, 360/565-3100.

18 BOULDER LAKE

11.2 mi/6.0 hrs

southwest of Port Angeles in Olympic National Park

Map 1.4, page 26

Although Boulder Lake is a great destination, it's often forgotten for the soothing water of Olympic Hot Springs. The hot springs draw the majority of visitors (understandably), but they miss out on a great hike. The hike is a relatively easy one, climbing gradually through virgin forests. At the base of Boulder Peak, small Boulder Lake sits within open forests of subalpine fir and mountain hemlock. In spite of the lake's beauty, you're more likely to remember your soak in the Olympic Hot Springs on the way back down the trail.

The first 2.2 miles of the trail are old roadbed, terminating at Boulder Creek Camp. The hot springs are just across Boulder Creek. Consisting of several pools collecting hot mineral water, the springs feel primitive and natural. Save it for your muscles on the way down, when they'll be more thankful. The trail splits .5 mile beyond the camp; the left fork goes to Appleton Pass, the right fork travels another two miles to Boulder Lake. Campsites can be found around the lake within the open forest. View seekers can scramble Boulder Peak.

At the lake, the trail turns into Happy Lake Ridge Trail, an optional return of 10 miles to Hot Springs Road, two miles below the trailhead. Most of the hike is on the ridge, within open spreads of subalpine meadows. Happy Lake sits at the midpoint of the ridge, perfect for longer stays. It's nice, but we prefer the hot springs.

User Groups: Hikers and horses. No dogs or mountain bikes are allowed. No wheelchair access.

Open Seasons: This trail is accessible June–October.

Permits: A National Parks Pass is required to park here. Overnight stays within the national park require backcountry camping permits, which are available at the Wilderness Information Center in Port Angeles.

Maps: For a map of Olympic National Park, contact the Outdoor Recreation Information Center at the downtown Seattle REI. For topographic maps, ask Green Trails for No. 134, Mount Olympus, or ask the USGS for Mount Carrie.

Directions: From Port Angeles, drive west 8 miles on U.S. 101 to Elwha Hot Springs Road. Turn left (south) and drive 10 miles, into the national park, to the road's end at a barrier with a well-signed trailhead.

Contact: Olympic National Park, Wilderness Information Center, 3002 Mount Angeles Road, Port Angeles, WA 98362, 360/565-3100.

19 ELWHA RIVER

54.2 mi/3–5 days

southwest of Port Angeles in Olympic National Park

Map 1.4, page 26

The Elwha River serves as the main artery of the Olympic Mountains. For more than 25 miles, the trail closely follows a historic and well-traveled route deep into the heart of the range. The Elwha was used for ages by local tribes to delve into the mountains for hunting and ceremonial reasons. In the late 1800s, the Press Expedition (a contingent of newspapermen and explorers) followed it on their trek across the mountain range. It has been an often-visited trail by backpackers and hikers for decades and is thought of as the spirit of the Olympics. The glacially fed waters boom through magnificent forests, a setting for many a backcountry tale. Sounds like a great place, doesn't it?

Elwha Trail travels deep into the Olympics to Low Divide. There are many campsites and shelters, and they receive heavy use in the summer. Old-growth forest breaks to reveal the river in stands of alder and maple. The trail forks at Chicago Camp (25 miles). The north fork heads to Elwha Basin, while the south fork proceeds up to Low Divide and the North Fork Quinault. It's an amazing trek for those who complete it, and especially great when done with a friend.

Day hikers will also find much to see and do within several miles of the trailhead. Side trails (1.2 miles in) lead down to Goblin's Gate (1.7 miles), where the Elwha passes through a narrow gorge. From here, a small network of trails finds the sites of old homesteads and large meadows. These are great places to see deer, elk, and even black bears.

User Groups: Hikers and horses. No dogs or mountain bikes are allowed. No wheelchair access.

Open Seasons: The lower part of this trail is usually accessible year-round (upper part is accessible June–October).

Permits: A National Parks Pass is required to park here. Overnight stays within the national park require backcountry camping permits, which are available at the Wilderness Information Center in Port Angeles.

Maps: For a map of Olympic National Park, contact the Outdoor Recreation Information Center at the downtown Seattle REI. For topographic maps, ask Green Trails for No. 134, Mount Olympus, No. 135, Mount Angeles, No. 166, Mount Christie, and No. 167, Mount Steel, or ask the USGS for Hurricane Hill, Mount Angeles, McCartney Peak, Chimney Peak, and Mount Christie.

Directions: From Port Angeles, drive west 8 miles on U.S. 101 to Elwha Hot Springs Road. Turn left (south) and drive 4 miles to the cutoff for Whiskey Bend Road. Turn left and drive 5 miles to the trailhead at road's end.

Contact: Olympic National Park, Wilderness Information Center, 3002 Mount Angeles Road, Port Angeles, WA 98362, 360/565-3100.

20 HURRICANE HILL

3.2 mi/2.0 hrs

south of Port Angeles in Olympic National Park

Map 1.4, page 26

Visitors to Hurricane Ridge should and very often do hike this trail. Why? Because no trail in the Olympics offers such easy access to such exceptional views. The trail is completely within the high country, where windswept ridges are covered in lush, green meadows. The open trail offers nonstop views to the north and south, and the summit of Hurricane Hill is one giant panoramic vista. The hike is relatively easy and can be made by hikers of all abilities at their own pace.

Hurricane Hill Trail starts off on a cleared roadbed and gently climbs for its entire length. Wildflowers are in full gear during late June, while the last vestiges of the winter's snowpack hang on. Eventually the roadbed ends, but the trail remains wide and easy to hike. At the top of Hurricane Hill are wide knolls, perfect for a picnic or extended rest before heading back

to the car. It's likely you'll want to stick around for awhile, mostly for the views. Much of the Olympic interior is revealed, including the Bailey Range and most of the Elwha drainage. The views to the north include the Strait of Juan de Fuca, Vancouver Island, and to the east, the Cascades. If there is any one trail that will endear the Olympics to its visitors, this is surely it.

User Groups: Hikers only. No dogs, horses, or mountain bikes are allowed. No wheelchair access.

Open Seasons: This trail is accessible June–October.

Permits: A National Parks Pass is required to park here.

Maps: For a map of Olympic National Park, contact the Outdoor Recreation Information Center at the downtown Seattle REI. For topographic maps, ask Green Trails for No. 134, Mount Olympus, or ask the USGS for Hurricane Hill.

Directions: From Port Angeles, drive north 2 miles on Race Street as it turns into Mount Angeles Road. Veer right at the well-signed fork and continue on Mount Angeles Road 19 miles, past the lower and upper visitors centers, to the well-signed trailhead.

Contact: Olympic National Park, Wilderness Information Center, 3002 Mount Angeles Road, Port Angeles, WA 98362, 360/565-3100.

21 GRAND RIDGE

8.0 mi/4.0 hrs

south of Port Angeles in Olympic National Park

Map 1.4, page 26

The National Park Service was once crazy about cars. It hoped to build a road through the park connecting Obstruction Point to Deer Park. Fortunately, the park service realized it would be insane to destroy such a beautiful area and abandoned the idea after surveying the route. Survey markers from the Bureau of Public Roads still line the trail, the intended course. Barren, open, and windy, Grand Ridge offers views of the Gray Wolf River drainage and many northern Olympic peaks. It's a great trip for those visiting Obstruction Point and the Hurricane Ridge area.

The trail primarily follows the southern side of Grand Ridge. This area is extremely barren, where even krummholz (small, distorted trees that look more like bushes) struggle to establish a foothold. Thin soils and intense winds work together to keep this area devoid of trees and full of views. A couple of high points offer good scramble opportunities and panoramic views: Elk Mountain (1.5 miles) and Maiden Peak (4 miles). Be sure to bring water, as hot days are even hotter on this south-facing slope. And be aware that when the wind picks up, which is often, you can expect 50–60 mph gusts to knock you around. Usually the wind blows you into the mountain, a good thing, because the drop down the mountain is precipitous.

User Groups: Hikers only. No dogs, horses, or mountain bikes are allowed. No wheelchair access.

Open Seasons: This trail is usually accessible May–October.

Permits: A National Parks Pass is required to park at Hurricane Hill; parking at Deer Park is free.

Maps: For a map of Olympic National Park, contact the Outdoor Recreation Information Center at the downtown Seattle REI. For topographic maps, ask Green Trails for No. 135, Mount Angeles, or ask the USGS for Mount Angeles and Maiden Peak.

Directions: From Port Angeles, drive north 2 miles on Race Street as it turns into Mount Angeles Road. Veer right at the well-signed fork and continue on Mount Angeles Road 17 miles to Obstruction Point Road. Turn left and drive 7 miles to road's end and Obstruction Point Trailhead.

Contact: Olympic National Park, Wilderness Information Center, 3002 Mount Angeles Road, Port Angeles, WA 98362, 360/565-3100.

22 GRAND PASS

12.0 mi/1–2 days

south of Port Angeles in Olympic National Park

Map 1.4, page 26

This is one of the Olympics' most popular destinations and with good reason. Easily accessible and very beautiful, Grand and Moose Lakes are favorite campgrounds. Farther up Grand Valley are plentiful subalpine meadows and rough, rocky slopes leading to Grand Pass, where views reach for miles around. Throw in two routes to the valley from Obstruction Peak (each of which is terrific), and you have a popular and well-visited spot in the North Olympics.

Leaving Obstruction Point, you are faced with two possible routes. Grand Pass Trail traverses Lillian Ridge, well above 6,000 feet and awash in mountain views, before dropping to Grand Lake. Alternatively, Badger Valley Trail makes its way through meadows and Alaskan cedar groves before climbing to Grand Lake. The best option is to make this a small loop, along the ridge on the way in and up the valley on the way out.

Overnight guests to Grand and Moose Lakes are required to secure a permit and reservation from the Wilderness Information Center. While there are numerous sites, they often fill up in the summer. The lakes are bordered by beautiful forests and rocky valley hillsides. Beyond, Grand Pass Trail passes small Gladys Lake and climbs steeply to Grand Pass. The rocky and barren territory is a testament to the snowpacks that linger well into summer along these north-facing inclines. From Grand Pass, the Olympics are at hand and breathtaking.

User Groups: Hikers only. No dogs, horses, or mountain bikes are allowed. No wheelchair access.

Open Seasons: This trail is usually accessible June–October.

Permits: A National Parks Pass is required to park here. Overnight stays at Grand or Moose Lake require reservations and backcountry camping permits, which are available at the Wilderness Information Center in Port Angeles.

Maps: For a map of Olympic National Park, contact the Outdoor Recreation Information Center at the downtown Seattle REI. For topographic maps, ask Green Trails for No. 135, Mount Angeles, or ask the USGS for Mount Angeles, Maiden Peak, and Wellesley Peak.

Directions: From Port Angeles, drive north 2 miles on Race Street as it turns into Mount Angeles Road. Veer right at the well-signed fork and continue on Mount Angeles Road 17 miles to Obstruction Point Road. Turn left and drive 7 miles to road's end and Obstruction Point Trailhead.

Contact: Olympic National Park, Wilderness Information Center, 3002 Mount Angeles Road, Port Angeles, WA 98362, 360/565-3100.

23 CAMERON CREEK

32.0 mi/4 days

south of Sequim in Olympic National Park

Map 1.4, page 26

The best backcountry locations often require an extra bit of effort to reach. Perhaps it is that extra exertion that makes some places so special and memorable. Cameron Creek is one of those places. It requires more than a few miles of approach hiking before you even embark on the long trail itself. Don't fret, time-conscious hikers; the journey along the trail and the vast mountain meadows deep within Cameron Basin are reward enough.

Cameron Creek Trail begins at Three Forks, where the creek joins Grand Creek and Gray Wolf River. The best access is via Three Forks Trail, a steep drop from Deer Park. While it's possible to hike up from the Lower Gray Wolf, river crossings are necessary and difficult. Cameron Creek Trail heads up the valley 7 miles, passing through beautiful forests of Douglas fir. Lower Cameron Camp (4 miles from Three Forks) is the primary campground.

Cameron Trail becomes more rugged near its headwaters, sometimes blown out by the

creek. The upper basin is pure parkland, where wildflowers and waterfalls cover the landscape. Although it's a tough climb, Cameron Pass rewards with deep wilderness views. Mount Claywood and Sentinel Peak beckon from across Lost River Basin, one of the wildest places on the peninsula. The trail eventually drops to Dosewallips River. Campsites for the second night are scattered along the trail and throughout Cameron Basin.

User Groups: Hikers only. No dogs, horses, or mountain bikes are allowed. No wheelchair access.

Open Seasons: This trail is accessible June–early October.

Permits: Parking and access are free. Overnight stays within the national park require backcountry camping permits, which are available at the Wilderness Information Center in Port Angeles.

Maps: For a map of Olympic National Park, contact the Outdoor Recreation Information Center at the downtown Seattle REI. For topographic maps, ask Green Trails for No. 135, Mount Angeles, and No. 136, Tyler Peak, or ask the USGS for Tyler Peak, Maiden Peak, and Wellesley Peak.

Directions: From Port Angeles, drive east 5 miles on U.S. 101 to Deer Park Road. Turn right (south) and drive 17 miles to the well-signed trailhead.

Contact: Olympic National Park, Wilderness Information Center, 3002 Mount Angeles Road, Port Angeles, WA 98362, 360/565-3100.

24 HOH RIVER

34.0 mi/1–4 days

southeast of Forks in Olympic National Park

Map 1.4, page 26

The Hoh Valley is world famous for the enormous size of its forests. Known as cathedrals, the forest canopy stands 200 feet above, filtering sunlight onto numerous ferns and draping mosses. This trail is also popular because it is the route for those seeking the pinnacle of the Olympic Mountains, Mount Olympus. Never mind the herds of people (or elk), for trees with trunks that wouldn't fit in your living room are calling from above.

The entire trail is outstanding. The first 12 miles are flat and well laid out, avoiding many ups and downs. It's a constant biology lesson in growth limits, as behemoth trees compete to outgrow each other. Many places along the trail allow for full appreciation of a river's ecology. Eagles and ravens stand atop trees looking for salmon or steelhead within the river. American dippers patrol the waterline while herds of Roosevelt elk graze along the forest floor. There are several well-interspersed campgrounds throughout. At 9.5 miles is Hoh Lake Trail cutoff, a trip for another day.

After 12 miles, the trail begins to slowly climb. The river courses through a spectacular canyon more than 100 feet deep by the time a hiker reaches the 13-mile mark. Hoh Trail crosses the canyon on a well-built bridge and begins its true ascent. Through a series of switchbacks, the trail passes through the forest and into a deep ravine. Beyond lies Glacier Meadows, where Olympus stands tall above terminating glaciers, revealing fields of blooming wildflowers among piles of glacial moraine. There are numerous camps here, all on a first-come first-served basis for the many backpackers and mountain climbers. This is the climax of the Olympics, standing beneath mighty Olympus and above miles and miles of rainforest. Enjoy your hike out.

User Groups: Hikers and horses. No dogs or mountain bikes are allowed. No wheelchair access.

Open Seasons: This trail is usually accessible April–October.

Permits: A National Parks Pass is required to park here. Overnight stays within the national park require backcountry camping permits, which are available at the Hoh Ranger Station (at the end of Hoh River Road, 360/374-6925).

Maps: For a map of Olympic National Park, contact the Outdoor Recreation Information

Center at the downtown Seattle REI. For topographic maps, ask Green Trails for No. 133, Mount Tom, and No. 134, Mount Olympus, or ask the USGS for Owl Mountain, Mount Tom, Bogachiel Peak, Mount Carrie, and Mount Olympus.

Directions: From Port Angeles, drive south 14 miles on U.S. 101 to Upper Hoh River Road. Turn left (east) and drive 18 miles to the Hoh Ranger Station and trailhead.

Contact: Olympic National Park, Wilderness Information Center, 3002 Mount Angeles Road, Port Angeles, WA 98362, 360/565-3100.

25 QUEETS RIVER

30.8 mi/2–3 days

south of Forks in Olympic National Park

Map 1.4, page 26

Queets River Trail is all about two things: forests chock-full of enormous trees and total seclusion. Trees here grow to tremendous sizes, with Sitka spruce, western hemlock, western red cedar, and Douglas fir creating a community of giants. In fact, the Queets is home to the world's largest living Douglas fir, a monster with a trunk 14.5 feet in diameter and a broken top 221 feet above the ground. While as impressive as the Hoh, this valley receives just a fraction of the visitors. That's because of a necessary river ford just beyond the trailhead. The river can be forded only during times of low water (late summer or fall) and should be undertaken with care at any time; once you're past, though, traveling is easy.

The trail travels roughly 15 miles along the river. The forest often gives way to glades of big leaf maple and the cutting river. Bears outnumber people here. The world's largest Douglas fir is two miles in, just off Kloochman Rock Trail heading north. There are three established camps along the trail, easily providing sufficient camping for the few backpackers on this trail. The first is Spruce Bottom (6 miles). Sticking on the trail will eventually take you to the Pelton Creek Shelter (15 miles), where the trail ends. It is certainly possible to carry on farther to Queets Basin, but it's a bushwhack. It's enough to sit down, enjoy the permeating quiet of the wilderness, and smile.

User Groups: Hikers and horses. No dogs or mountain bikes are allowed. No wheelchair access.

Open Seasons: This trail is usually accessible May–October.

Permits: Parking is free. Overnight stays within the national park require backcountry camping permits, which are available at the Wilderness Information Center in Port Angeles.

Maps: For a map of Olympic National Park, contact the Outdoor Recreation Information Center at the downtown Seattle REI. For topographic maps, ask Green Trails for No. 165, Kloochman Rock, or ask the USGS for Stequaleho Creek, Kloochman Rock, and Bob Creek.

Directions: From Forks, drive south on U.S. 101 to Queets River Road. Turn left (east) and drive 14 miles to the trailhead at road's end.

Contact: Olympic National Park, Wilderness Information Center, 3002 Mount Angeles Road, Port Angeles, WA 98362, 360/565-3100.

26 SKYLINE RIDGE

45.0 mi/5–6 days

northeast of Quinault in Olympic National Park

Map 1.4, page 26

Sure to test even the toughest hikers, Skyline Ridge rewards with one of the most beautiful hikes on the peninsula. The trail never leaves the high country as it follows the ridge separating the large Quinault and Queets Valleys. The views up here are unbelievable, with Mount Olympus standing just one ridge away. Watch the sun set from this high place and the fog roll in from the Pacific Ocean, visible in the distance. And stay on your toes, as this is the perfect place to spot black bears as they drunkenly wolf down huckleberries. The Quinault is said to sport some of the highest black bear concentrations in the state,

so be ready for some excitement. Mile after mile, the Skyline consistently offers the best of the Olympics.

The route must be accessed by Three Lakes Trail (6.5 miles) or North Fork Quinault Trail (16 miles; see listing in this chapter). The best route is via North Fork Quinault, making a loop. Climbing out of Low Divide, Skyline Trail skirts several basins of meadows and rises to Beauty Pass (7.4 miles from Low Divide). A side trail heads to Lake Beauty and campsites with views of Olympus.

Beyond, the trail is difficult to follow and marked by rock cairns. Excellent map and route-finding skills are needed here. Skyline Trail heads for Three Prune Camp (18 miles), switching between the Quinault and Queets Valleys several times. Water can be difficult to find here until Three Prune. The trail begins its decent to Three Lakes, the last spot for camping, and Three Lakes Trail back to the trailhead. By the time you get back to the car, you'll already be planning next year's trip.

User Groups: Hikers only. No dogs, horses, or mountain bikes are allowed. No wheelchair access.

Open Seasons: This trail is usually accessible August–September (depending on the previous winter's snowpack).

Permits: Parking is free. Overnight stays within the national park require backcountry camping permits, which are available at Quinault Ranger Station.

Maps: For a map of Olympic National Park, contact the Outdoor Recreation Information Center at the downtown Seattle REI. For topographic maps, ask Green Trails for No. 166, Mount Christie, or ask the USGS for Bunch Lake, Kimta Peak, and Mount Christie.

Directions: From Forks, travel south on U.S. 101 to North Shore Road at Lake Quinault. Turn left (east) and drive 17 miles to North Fork Ranger Station at road's end.

Contact: Olympic National Park, Wilderness Information Center, 3002 Mount Angeles Road, Port Angeles, WA 98362, 360/565-3100.

27 NORTH FORK QUINAULT

31.4 mi/3–4 days 2 8

northeast of Quinault in Olympic National Park

Map 1.4, page 26

With headwaters at Low Divide, North Fork Trail provided the way for many a party of explorers. From this popular junction, used by the Press Expedition, Army Lieutenant Joseph P. O'Neil, and others, the river flows more than 30 miles to the Pacific through beautiful high country and forests of enormous size in the lowlands. Its link to Low Divide makes it a well-used route for folks coming or going to the Elwha River. It also makes a great counterpart to Skyline Trail, which skirts the North Fork's upper ridge. There's no end to things to see as the trail crosses numerous beautiful creeks and even the river itself. It passes through superb forests of trees swollen to large, rainforest dimensions, and hikers often encounter wildlife.

The trail follows the river all the way to its source at Low Divide. Campsites and shelters occur regularly throughout this section of trail, including Wolf Bar (2.5 miles), Halfway House (5.2 miles), Elip Creek, (6.5 miles), Trapper Shelter (8.5 miles), and 12 Mile (11.5 miles). Be prepared for several easy creek crossings. The ascent up the valley is modest, making these 12 miles pass quickly underfoot.

After a good day's hike, the trail crosses the North Fork at 16 Mile Camp (12.3 miles). This river crossing can be difficult if not impassable during times of high flow. If coming from the Elwha, beware. A U-turn here makes the return trip more than 40 miles. Beyond, the trail climbs to Low Divide, an open meadow surrounded by waterfalls. Low Divide Ranger Station lies just beyond the Skyline Trail junction.

User Groups: Hikers and horses. No dogs or mountain bikes are allowed. No wheelchair access.

Open Seasons: This trail is accessible June–October.

Permits: A federal Northwest Forest Pass is required to park here. Overnight stays within the national park require backcountry camping permits, which are available at Quinault Ranger Station.

Maps: For a map of Olympic National Park, contact the Outdoor Recreation Information Center at the downtown Seattle REI. For topographic maps, ask Green Trails for No. 166, Mount Christie, or ask the USGS for Bunch Lake, Kitma Peak, and Mount Christie.

Directions: From Forks, travel south on U.S. 101 to North Shore Road at Lake Quinault. Turn left (east) and drive 17 miles to North Fork Ranger Station at road's end.

Contact: Olympic National Park, Wilderness Information Center, 3002 Mount Angeles Road, Port Angeles, WA 98362, 360/565-3100.

28 ENCHANTED VALLEY

36.0 mi/4 days 3 10

east of Quinault in Olympic National Park

Map 1.4, page 26

Undoubtedly one of Washington's most beautiful places, Enchanted Valley leaves visitors reminiscing about their trip here for years to come. East Fork Quinault Trail travels through old-growth forests of giant trees to the steep cliffs and waterfalls of Enchanted Valley. The wide and wild valley offers miles of exploration and loads of views of the tall peaks enclosing the Quinault. The trail eventually finds the high-country playground of Anderson Pass, home to glaciers and acres of meadows.

East Fork Quinault Trail immediately crosses Graves Creek, where a bridge was recently blown out by heavy rains; call the Wilderness Information Center to see if a ford is required. The trail travels 13 level and easy miles among ancient trees growing in a lush and humid forest. Elk and deer roam the thick understory. The forest gives way to clearings as the trail nears Enchanted Valley. A ford of the river is required here, difficult at times of high water. Countless waterfalls cascade from the vertical cliffs on both sides of the valley. The valley is home to a ranger station and old chalet, now closed to visitors except in emergencies.

East Quinault Trail continues out of the Enchanted Valley and finally begins climbing to reach Anderson Pass and several glaciers. This high country is home to huckleberries and their biggest fans: black bears. Good places to pitch a tent are found at O'Neil Creek Camp (6.7 miles), Enchanted Valley Camp (13.1 miles), and Anderson Pass Camp (18 miles).

User Groups: Hikers and horses. No dogs or mountain bikes are allowed. No wheelchair access.

Open Seasons: This trail is accessible June–September.

Permits: Parking is free. Overnight stays within the national park require backcountry camping permits, which are available at Quinault Ranger Station on North Shore Road.

Maps: For a map of Olympic National Park, contact the Outdoor Recreation Information Center at the downtown Seattle REI. For topographic maps, ask Green Trails for No. 166, Mount Christie, and No. 167, Mount Steel, or ask the USGS for Mount Hoquiam, Mount Olson, Mount Steel, and Chimney Peak.

Directions: From Forks, drive south on U.S. 101 to South Shore Road. Turn left (east) and drive 18.5 miles to Graves Creek Ranger Station and the signed trailhead.

Contact: Olympic National Park, Wilderness Information Center, 3002 Mount Angeles Road, Port Angeles, WA 98362, 360/565-3100.

29 GRAVES CREEK

18.0 mi/2 days 3 8

northeast of Quinault in Olympic National Park

Map 1.4, page 26

Sometimes the itch to visit the Quinault area cannot be denied. The desire to see big trees, experience high-country meadows, and hear the boom of a roaring creek must be met. Fortunately, Graves Creek Trail scratches these itches without the considerable crowds of people found in the Enchanted Valley.

Graves Creek Trail begins soon after crossing Graves Creek on Quinault River Trail. It climbs gently above Graves Creek, which roars from within a box canyon for most of its descent. The trail makes a lot of ups and downs, but the overall trend is definitely up. At 3.2 miles the trail crosses Graves Creek, which can be difficult at times of high water (fall and spring). The forest breaks as meadows take over, a place where most hikers linger to fill up on huckleberries. The trail reaches Sundown Lake, set within a small glacial cirque complete with campsites. The trail eventually winds up at Six Ridge Pass and continues as Six Ridge Trail.

User Groups: Hikers only. No dogs, horses, or mountain bikes are allowed. No wheelchair access.

Open Seasons: This trail is accessible July–October.

Permits: No permits are needed for parking. Overnight stays within the national park require backcountry camping permits, which are available at Quinault Ranger Station on North Shore Road.

Maps: For a map of Olympic National Park, contact the Outdoor Recreation Information Center at the downtown Seattle REI. For topographic maps, ask Green Trails for No. 166, Mount Christie, or ask the USGS for Mount Hoquim.

Directions: From Forks, drive south on U.S. 101 to South Shore Road. Turn left (east) and drive 18.5 miles to Graves Creek Ranger Station and the signed trailhead.

Contact: Olympic National Park, Wilderness Information Center, 3002 Mount Angeles Road, Port Angeles, WA 98362, 360/565-3100.

30 COLONEL BOB MOUNTAIN

14.4 mi/8.0 hrs 4 9

east of Quinault in the Colonel Bob Wilderness of Olympic National Forest

Map 1.4, page 26

It's a hard climb from the bottoms of the Quinault Valley to the peaks of the southern ridge, the home of Colonel Bob Mountain. The overall elevation gain is greater than 4,000 feet, much of it covered twice. The trail climbs out of the rainforests of the lower valley to subalpine meadows, where ridges and views seem to extend for days on end. While crowds of folks bump into each other down in the Enchanted Valley, far fewer people are to be found up here. Trips to Colonel Bob during June and July are absolutely wonderful, when the wildflowers are in full bloom and snowfields linger on distant mountains.

Colonel Bob Trail is a true scaling of the peak, starting directly from the Quinault River. The trail heads up through a forest of Douglas fir and western red cedar. Mosses, lichens, and ferns grow on anything that can support them. The trail eventually reaches the camps of Mulkey Shelter (4 miles) and Moonshine Flats (6 miles).

The trail now climbs steeply to a ridge and dishearteningly drops down the other side. Take courage in knowing that while you must give back some elevation, open meadows await you. The trail navigates between the surrounding peaks before ascending Colonel Bob. The views are grand from on top, revealing much of the southern Olympics.

User Groups: Hikers and leashed dogs. No horses or mountain bikes are allowed. No wheelchair access.

Open Seasons: This trail is accessible mid-June–October.

Permits: A federal Northwest Forest Pass is required to park here.

Maps: For a map of Olympic National Forest, contact the Outdoor Recreation Information Center at the downtown Seattle REI. For topographic maps, ask Green Trails for No. 197, Quinault Lake, and No. 198, Griswold, or ask the USGS for Lake Quinault East and Colonel Bob.

Directions: From Forks, drive south on U.S. 101 to South Shore Road. Turn left (east) and drive 6 miles to the signed trailhead on the right side of the road.

Contact: Olympic National Forest, Quilcene

Ranger Station, 295142 U.S. 101 South, Quilcene, WA 98376, 360/765-2200.

31 LAKE QUINAULT LOOP

0.6–4.0 mi/0.5–2.0 hrs 1 9

on the shores of Lake Quinault in Olympic National Forest

Map 1.4, page 26

Lake Quinault Loop is one of three trails on the south side of the lake. Built within exceptional old-growth forests, the three trails offer two loops and a creek hike. The shortest of the three is Rain Forest Trail, a loop that finds its way into a stand of 500 year-old Douglas firs. Signs are placed along the path to enlighten hikers on the forest's ecology. The trail also passes a great stretch of Willaby Creek running through a gorge.

The second loop is a larger undertaking of 4 miles. It ventures farther into the forest, crossing a swamp on well-built puncheons and passing Cascade Falls on Falls Creek. It returns to the trailhead via Lake Quinault Shoreline Trail. The final hike is into Willaby Creek. A steady forest of immense proportions follows hikers to a granddaddy of cedars. The trail crosses the creek, which can be tricky, and eventually peters out. All three trails offer typically large Olympic forests full of moss and ferns. These are trails for the whole family to relish, regardless of age or hiking ability.

User Groups: Hikers and leashed dogs. No horses or mountain bikes are allowed. No wheelchair access.

Open Seasons: This area is accessible year-round.

Permits: A federal Northwest Forest Pass is required to park here.

Maps: For a map of Olympic National Forest, contact the Outdoor Recreation Information Center at the downtown Seattle REI. For topographic maps, ask Green Trails for No. 197, Quinault Lake, or ask the USGS for Lake Quinault East.

Directions: From Forks, drive south on U.S. 101 to South Shore Road. Turn left (east) and drive 1.5 miles to the signed trailhead on the right side of the road.

Contact: Olympic National Forest, Quilcene Ranger Station, 295142 U.S. 101 South, Quilcene, WA 98376, 360/765-2200.

32 WYNOOCHEE PASS

7.2 mi/4.0 hrs 2 8

east of Quinault in Olympic National Park

Map 1.4, page 26

This is not a long trail, and that's the beauty of it. Smart hikers know that Wynoochee Pass provides easy access to Sundown Lake and the incredible high country of the area. These spots add many additional miles and feet of elevation when accessed via two other converging trails. The few hikers who visit this trail each year find superb forests of mountain hemlock and silver fir along the route. It's nearly the perfect trail; not too long, incredibly scenic, and rarely used.

Wynoochee Pass Trail begins along an old logging road within the national forest before quickly entering the pristine confines of the national park. The trail is set high above the Wynoochee River, which is nearly at the end of its journey. The trail makes a few switchbacks up to the small meadow at Wynoochee Pass, elevation 3,600 feet and just over two miles from the trailhead. From here, hikers should follow a lightly used footpath for one mile to Sundown Lake and meadowy Sundown Pass. Since it's so far out of the way, it's understandable that so few people visit this part of the Olympics. But others' loss is your gain on Wynoochee Pass Trail. In the best sense of the term, it really is a getaway.

User Groups: Hikers only. No dogs, horses, or mountain bikes are allowed. No wheelchair access.

Open Seasons: This trail is accessible May–November.

Permits: A federal Northwest Forest Pass is required to park here.

Maps: For a map of Olympic National Park,

contact the Outdoor Recreation Information Center at the downtown Seattle REI. For topographic maps, ask Green Trails for No. 166, Mount Christie, or ask the USGS for Mount Hoquim.

Directions: From Aberdeen, drive west 9 miles to Wynoochee River Road (just before Montesano). Turn left (north) and drive 33 miles to Forest Service Road 2270 (at a four-way intersection). Go straight on Forest Service Road 2270 and drive 12 miles to Forest Service Road 2270-400. Turn right and drive 2 miles to the signed trailhead.

Contact: Olympic National Park, Wilderness Information Center, 3002 Mount Angeles Road, Port Angeles, WA 98362, 360/565-3100.

33 GRAY WOLF RIVER

30.2 mi/3–4 days

south of Sequim in Olympic National Park

Map 1.4, page 26

When the rain gives you pause about your planned trip to the west side of the peninsula, the little-visited Gray Wolf may be one of your better options. It's conveniently situated in the rain shadow of the Olympics, where much less rain falls than in other parts of the peninsula. So when it's raining on the west side, you're likely to luck out and stay dry in the rain shadow. The trail is quite long with the best parts, of course, far up the trail. The lower section of Gray Wolf is lowland river hiking. It's only above Three Forks, where Cameron and Grand Creeks join Gray Wolf, that the trail develops real personality.

Skip the lower half of the river and access Gray Wolf via Three Forks Trail (5.5 miles). From here, Gray Wolf Trail passes through beautiful forests of hemlock, cedar, and Douglas fir. A shelter is at Falls Camp (10.7 miles). From here, one can hike a way trail three miles up to Cedar Lake, a very large subalpine lake set within a large meadow. This little-visited spot alone is well worth a trip of several days.

Gray Wolf Trail continues by crossing the river several times and then beginning its real ascent. The basin at the head of the Gray Wolf is rather large and expansive. Several high tarns are set amid groves of mountain hemlocks and bare slides of shale. The basin is surrounded by high peaks, including the Needles as they extend from Mount Deception. The trail continues by steeply descending to Dosewallips River Trail.

User Groups: Hikers only. No dogs, horses, or mountain bikes are allowed. No wheelchair access.

Open Seasons: This trail is usually accessible May–October.

Permits: A federal Northwest Forest Pass is required to park here. Overnight stays require backcountry camping permits, which are available at the Quilcene Ranger Station.

Maps: For a map of Olympic National Park, contact the Outdoor Recreation Information Center at the downtown Seattle REI. For topographic maps, ask Green Trails for No. 135, Mount Angeles, and No. 136, Tyler Peak, or ask the USGS for Tyler Peak, Maiden Peak, and Wellesley Peak.

Directions: From Sequim, drive 3 miles east on U.S. 101 to Palo Alto Road. Turn right (south) and drive 7.5 miles to Forest Service Road 2880. Turn right and drive 1 mile to Forest Service Road 2870. Turn right and drive .5 mile to the signed trailhead.

Contact: Olympic National Forest, Quilcene Ranger Station, 295142 U.S. 101 South, Quilcene, WA 98376, 360/765-2200.

34 MOUNT ZION

3.6 mi/2.0 hrs

west of Quilcene in Olympic National Forest

Map 1.4, page 26

This is one of the Olympics' easier, more accessible peaks. It's not one of the tallest peaks, yet it offers its fair share of views from the northeast corner of the peninsula. A forested trail deposits hikers at a fairly flat, open summit. In comparison to the rest of the Olympics, it is in close proximity to Seattle, making it a great day hike for those with an itch for the Olympics.

The trail's best attraction is the many rhododendrons that grace the forest blanketing the route. They are in full bloom during June and are likely to be one the lasting memories of the hike. The trail gains just 1,300 feet on its ascent, pretty light fare for summit hikes. The forest eventually gives way near the summit to grand views of Olympic ranges and peaks. Mount Baker and the Cascades are visible beyond Puget Sound on clear days. On days that aren't so clear, fear not. Mount Zion is in the Olympic rain shadow, a corner of the mountain range that receives much less rain than the other parts of the peninsula. So when it's raining elsewhere, Mount Zion will be much drier. In sum, Mount Zion is a wonderful trail for easy hiking and basking in the sun.

User Groups: Hikers, leashed dogs, horses, mountain bikes, and motorcycles. No wheelchair access.

Open Seasons: This trail is accessible mid-May–November (accessible nearly year-round with snowshoes).

Permits: A federal Northwest Forest Pass is required to park here.

Maps: For a map of Olympic National Forest, contact the Outdoor Recreation Information Center at the downtown Seattle REI. For topographic maps, ask Green Trails for No. 136, Tyler Peak, or ask the USGS for Mount Zion.

Directions: From Quilcene, drive north 1.5 miles on U.S. 101 to Lords Lake Road. Follow Lords Lake Road to the lake and turn left onto Forest Service Road 28. Drive to Bon Jon Pass and turn right onto Forest Service Road 2810. The trailhead is 2 miles ahead on the left.

Contact: Olympic National Forest, Quilcene Ranger Station, 295142 U.S. 101 South, Quilcene, WA 98376, 360/765-2200.

35 TUBAL CAIN

17.4 mi/2 days

west of Quilcene in the Buckhorn Wilderness of Olympic National Forest

Map 1.4, page 26

Tubal Cain Trail is more than a secluded forest or place of expansive mountain views. Unlike most wilderness settings, the route features a good deal of evidence of mankind. Along the route are a pair of easy-to-find old mines. Here, copper, manganese, and other minerals were extracted from the flanks of Iron and Buckhorn Mountains. But another unexpected find is made along a side trail, deep within a high basin. Tull Canyon is the final resting place for an old Air Force B-17. The plane crashed here more than 50 years ago and has been left intact.

The trail immediately crosses Silver Creek to climb the valley within thick growth of rhododendrons, in full bloom in June. At 3.2 miles is the junction with Tull Canyon Trail. Tubal Cain Mine (and campground) lies on the east side of the creek a short .5 mile later. The shaft of the mine ventures into the mountain nearly 3,000 feet. Although the mine shaft is unsafe for exploration, there are many old relics left outside the mine. From Tubal Cain Mine, the trail becomes more scenic as it climbs to Buckhorn Lake (5.5 miles). This is a good turnaround for day hikers. Buckhorn and Iron Mountains stand imposingly across the valley at this point, guarding their treasures. The trail ends at Marmot Pass among meadows awash in wildflowers during July.

User Groups: Hikers, leashed dogs, and horses. No mountain bikes are allowed. No wheelchair access.

Open Seasons: This trail is accessible June–October.

Permits: A federal Northwest Forest Pass is required to park here.

Maps: For a map of Olympic National Forest, contact the Outdoor Recreation Information Center at the downtown Seattle REI. For topographic maps, ask Green Trails for No. 136,

Tyler Peak, or ask the USGS for Mount Townsend and Mount Deception.

Directions: From Sequim, drive 3 miles east on U.S. 101 to Palo Alto Road. Turn right (south) and drive 7.5 miles to Forest Service Road 28. Stay left and drive 1 mile to Forest Service Road 2860. Turn right and drive a long 14.5 miles to the signed trailhead.

Contact: Olympic National Forest, Quilcene Ranger Station, 295142 U.S. 101 South, Quilcene, WA 98376, 360/765-2200.

36 ROYAL BASIN

16.2 mi/2 days

south of Sequim in Olympic National Park

Map 1.4, page 26

Unrivaled in beauty, Royal Basin Trail travels miles of old-growth forest before finding acres of parkland meadows beneath towering peaks. This is one trail that guidebook authors prefer to keep mum about.

Royal Basin Trail begins along Dungeness River Trail one mile from the trailhead, where Royal Creek enters the river. Stay to the right on Royal Basin Trail. Easy to follow and well maintained, the trail serves hikers of all abilities as it courses through forest and avalanche tracks. Progress up the trail is easy to gauge as the forest changes from Douglas firs and western hemlocks to silver firs, yellow cedars, and finally subalpine firs. Campsites are found at the first meadow, a good alternative to the traditional campground a mile farther at Royal Lake.

The trail clambers over a terrace to reach Royal Lake. The large basin reveals Mount Deception, the Olympics' second-highest peak, and the always impressive Needles, a long, jagged ridge. Explore to your heart's content, but stay on established trails, please. Parkland and meadows abound here, with wildflowers that catch fire in early summer. At the top of the basin is Royal Glacier, which you can walk on, while a trip to the shoulder below Mount Deception is also possible, revealing the Elwha River drainage. Royal Basin is sure to capture your heart. So hike Royal Basin and then lie about where you've been to anyone who asks.

User Groups: Hikers only. No dogs, horses, or mountain bikes are allowed. No wheelchair access.

Open Seasons: This trail is usually accessible mid-June–October.

Permits: A federal Northwest Forest Pass is required to park here. Overnight stays require backcountry camping permits, which are available at the Quilcene Ranger Station.

Maps: For a map of Olympic National Park, contact the Outdoor Recreation Information Center at the downtown Seattle REI. For topographic maps, ask Green Trails for No. 136, Tyler Peak, or ask the USGS for Mount Deception.

Directions: From Sequim, drive 3 miles east on U.S. 101 to Palo Alto Road. Turn right (south) and drive 7.5 miles to Forest Service Road 28. Stay left and drive 1 mile to Forest Service Road 2860. Turn right and drive 11 miles to signed Dungeness Trailhead.

Contact: Olympic National Park, Wilderness Information Center, 3002 Mount Angeles Road, Port Angeles, WA 98362, 360/565-3100; Quilcene Ranger District, 295142 U.S. 101 South, P.O. Box 280, Quilcene, WA 98376, 360/765-2200.

37 UPPER DUNGENESS

12.4 mi/6.0 hrs

west of Quilcene in the Buckhorn Wilderness of Olympic National Forest

Map 1.4, page 26

The Upper Dungeness River is one of the most picturesque of the Olympics' many rivers, and this trail captures much of its scenic beauty. The trail follows the Dungeness as it passes through outstanding forests and eventually reaches a major junction, high within a mountain basin. Along the way is Heather Creek Trail, a nonmaintained route heading directly into the Olympics' wild interior. Add the fact that the Dungeness receives less rain than most of the peninsula, and you have a popular off-season hike.

The trail makes its way along the valley bottom for the first mile to a junction with Royal

Basin Trail. Cross Royal Creek to stay on Dungeness Trail. The forest here is superb, with large Douglas firs, red cedars, and western hemlocks towering over an open understory. The trail eventually crosses the Dungeness to the east side and comes to Camp Handy, at 3.2 miles. Great camps are found within this slightly wooded meadow.

From Camp Handy, Heather Creek Trail continues up the valley alongside the Dungeness for another four miles. This stretch is not maintained and is fairly undisturbed wilderness. Dungeness Trail leaves Camp Handy to begin climbing out of the valley and into parkland meadows. The trail ends at Boulder Camp, the junction with Constance Pass Trail and Big Quilcene Trail.

User Groups: Hikers, leashed dogs, and horses. No mountain bikes are allowed. No wheelchair access.

Open Seasons: This trail is accessible June–October.

Permits: A federal Northwest Forest Pass is required to park here.

Maps: For a map of Olympic National Forest, contact the Outdoor Recreation Information Center at the downtown Seattle REI. For topographic maps, ask Green Trails for No. 136, Tyler Peak, or ask the USGS for Mount Deception, Tyler Peak, and Mount Zion.

Directions: From Sequim, drive 3 miles east on U.S. 101 to Palo Alto Road. Turn right (south) and drive 7.5 miles to Forest Service Road 28. Stay left and drive 1 mile to Forest Service Road 2860. Turn right and drive 11 miles to signed Dungeness Trailhead.

Contact: Olympic National Forest, Quilcene Ranger Station, 295142 U.S. 101 South, Quilcene, WA 98376, 360/765-2200.

38 MOUNT TOWNSEND

7.8 mi/4.5 hrs

west of Quilcene in Buckhorn Wilderness of Olympic National Forest

Map 1.4, page 26

Upon reaching the top of Mount Townsend, hikers may be hard-pressed to decide if they're in the midst of mountains or perched above long stretches of Puget waterways. This lofty summit strategically puts you smack dab in the middle of the two settings. The grand, competing vistas are likely to vie for your attention for the length of your stay here. Be thankful. High mountain meadows scrubbed by forceful winds, complete with requisite berries, complement the experience. It's no wonder that Mount Townsend is one of the peninsula's more popular day hikes.

Mount Townsend Trail climbs steadily throughout its length. The couple of miles pass through forest punctuated by rhododendrons (catch them blooming in June). At 2.5 miles lies Camp Windy (not nearly as windy as Townsend's summit), and the trail soon reaches a junction with Silver Lakes Trail. Mount Townsend Trail harshly climbs through opening meadows, full of late summer's huckleberries. Snow and wind limit the growth of the subalpine trees, leaving vistas for hikers. The summit is long and flat with superb views. Nearly the full range of the Cascades lines the east, while Mount Deception and The Needles are highlights of the Olympic Range. The trail continues for another 1.4 miles down to Little Quilcene River Trail.

User Groups: Hikers, leashed dogs, and horses. No mountain bikes are allowed. No wheelchair access.

Open Seasons: This trail is accessible June–October.

Permits: A federal Northwest Forest Pass is required to park here.

Maps: For a map of Olympic National Forest, contact the Outdoor Recreation Information Center at the downtown Seattle REI. For topographic maps, ask Green Trails for No. 136, Tyler Peak, or ask the USGS for Mount Townsend.

Directions: From Quilcene, drive 1 mile south on U.S. 101 to Penny Creek Road. Turn right (west) and drive 1.5 miles to Big Quilcene Road. Stay to the left at this Y and drive 3 miles to the Forest Service boundary and paved Forest Service Road 27. Drive 9 miles to Forest

Service Road 2760. Drive 1 mile to the trailhead at road's end.

Contact: Olympic National Forest, Quilcene Ranger Station, 295142 U.S. 101 South, Quilcene, WA 98376, 360/765-2200.

39 SILVER LAKES

10.8 mi/6.0 hrs

west of Quilcene in the Buckhorn Wilderness of Olympic National Forest

Map 1.4, page 26

It takes a harsh rainstorm to ruin a trip to Silver Lakes. And that's a less-than-likely proposition since this trail is snugly tucked away in the peninsula's rain shadow. Silver Lakes nestle within a large basin rimmed with jagged peaks. Subalpine firs are amply spread around the lakes, mingling with meadows of heather. Alpine flowers add strokes of color unlikely to be forgotten for a long time after the trip. Throw in some good scrambles at the end to an extremely pleasant trail and you have yourself a thoroughly agreeable trip.

Silver Lakes Trail begins on Mount Townsend Trail, 2.9 miles from the trailhead (see listing in this chapter). The trail immediately drops into the forested valley, crosses Silver Creek, and makes a quick ascent to the larger Silver Lake. The smaller and less visited lake is just before the larger one, to the west off a visible side trail.

Parkland surrounds the lake, with large meadows of wildflowers mingling with small stands of subalpine fir. There are several campsites for overnight guests. The lake is favored by swimmers and fishermen alike. Be sure to scramble the slope rising to the south, between rocky peaks, for more wildflowers and the prime views.

User Groups: Hikers, leashed dogs, and horses. No mountain bikes are allowed. No wheelchair access.

Open Seasons: This trail is accessible July–October.

Permits: A federal Northwest Forest Pass is required to park here.

Maps: For a map of Olympic National Forest, contact the Outdoor Recreation Information Center at the downtown Seattle REI. For topographic maps, ask Green Trails for No. 136, Tyler Peak, or ask the USGS for Mount Townsend.

Directions: From Quilcene, drive 1 mile south on U.S. 101 to Penny Creek Road. Turn right (west) and drive 1.5 miles to Big Quilcene Road. Stay to the left at this Y and drive 3 miles to the Forest Service boundary and paved Forest Service Road 27. Drive 9 miles to Forest Service Road 2760. Drive 1 mile to the trailhead at road's end.

Contact: Olympic National Forest, Quilcene Ranger Station, 295142 U.S. 101 South, Quilcene, WA 98376, 360/765-2200.

40 UPPER BIG QUILCENE

10.6 mi/5.5 hrs

west of Quilcene in the Buckhorn Wilderness of Olympic National Forest

Map 1.4, page 26

Rarely can hikers get to such an outstanding viewpoint, with so much wild country spread before them, than with Upper Big Quilcene Trail. Passing through virgin timber and open, pristine meadows, the trail delivers hikers to Marmot Pass. This is an opportunity to view many of the Olympics' most impressive peaks, including Mount Mystery and Mount Deception. The trail is one of the best on the peninsula's east side and perfect for an outing with the dog.

The trail follows the river for several miles, where the forest consists of old-growth Douglas fir, western hemlock, and western red cedar. In June, rhododendrons light up the understory with fragrant blossoms. The trail then climbs gently but steadily out of the valley. Good camps are at Shelter Rock (2.6 mi) and Camp Mystery (4.6 mi), each next to water. The trail eventually broaches the confines of forest and finds itself at Marmot Pass, where one can finally see all that is to the north of the ridge. Grand views of near and far mountains are plentiful. The trail junctions here with

Tubal Cain Trail before dropping to Boulder Camp. Constance Pass and Upper Dungeness Trails meet at Boulder Camp.
User Groups: Hikers and leashed dogs. No horses or mountain bikes are allowed. No wheelchair access.
Open Seasons: This trail is accessible July–October.
Permits: A federal Northwest Forest Pass is required to park here.
Maps: For a map of Olympic National Forest, contact the Outdoor Recreation Information Center at the downtown Seattle REI. For topographic maps, ask Green Trails for No. 136, Tyler Peak, or ask the USGS for Mount Townsend and Mount Deception.
Directions: From Quilcene, drive 1 mile south on U.S. 101 to Penny Creek Road. Turn right (west) and drive 1.5 miles to Big Quilcene Road. Stay left at this Y and drive 3 miles to the Forest Service boundary and paved Forest Service Road 27. Drive 6 miles to Forest Service Road 2750. Stay to the left and drive 4.5 miles to the signed trailhead.
Contact: Olympic National Forest, Quilcene Ranger Station, 295142 U.S. 101 South, Quilcene, WA 98376, 360/765-2200.

41 TUNNEL CREEK
8.2 mi/4.5 hrs

west of Quilcene in the Buckhorn Wilderness of Olympic National Forest

Map 1.4, page 26

The trail up Tunnel Creek leads to a pair of subalpine lakes and a pass with far-reaching views. It's a popular day hike, whisking hikers from old-growth forests along the valley floor to open meadows and views up high. Never mind the steep final ascent to the lakes and 50-50 Pass, as you'll have plenty of time to rest while surveying the mountainous horizon.

The trail ventures easily through great forests of Douglas fir and western red cedar accompanied by numerous rhododendrons (blooming in June) for 2.7 miles. Here, the trail encounters Tunnel Creek Shelter, with a few campsites. Beyond this point, the route steeply climbs to the Twin Lakes (3.7 miles). The lakes are situated in a tiny basin and bounded by mountain hemlocks, an appealing setting. The trail climbs a bit more to 50-50 Pass, at elevation 5,050 feet. This is mostly just a rocky promontory, but the views are grand during clear weather. Nowhere is Mount Constance better seen, with pockets of snow often finding refuge among the many crags and faces. Views toward Puget Sound stand out as well. This is the ideal place to turn around; otherwise, a sharp descent awaits, into a valley other than where your car is parked.
User Groups: Hikers, leashed dogs, and horses. No mountain bikes are allowed. No wheelchair access.
Open Seasons: This trail is accessible mid-June–October.
Permits: A federal Northwest Forest Pass is required to park here.
Maps: For a map of Olympic National Forest, contact the Outdoor Recreation Information Center at the downtown Seattle REI. For topographic maps, ask Green Trails for No. 136, Tyler Peak, and No. 168, The Brothers, or ask the USGS for Mount Townsend.
Directions: From Quilcene, drive 1 mile south on U.S. 101 to Penny Creek Road. Turn right (west) and drive 1.5 miles to Big Quilcene Road. Stay left at this Y and drive 3 miles to the Forest Service boundary and Forest Service Road 2740. Stay to the left at this Y and drive 6.5 miles to the signed trailhead.
Contact: Olympic National Forest, Quilcene Ranger Station, 295142 U.S. 101 South, Quilcene, WA 98376, 360/765-2200.

42 WEST FORK DOSEWALLIPS
31.0 mi/3–4 days

south of Quilcene in Olympic National Park

Map 1.4, page 26

West Fork Dosewallips Trail is half of one of the premier routes for trekking across the Olympic Range. Making its way along the west

fork of its namesake, the trail reaches Anderson Pass and connects to the legendary Enchanted Valley. This route has had its troubles in recent years. Several years ago, a new suspension bridge was blown out after only a year. Rebuilt, the bridge was again damaged in 2003. Be sure to call the Wilderness Information Center for current access status.

West Fork Dosewallips Trail begins 1.4 miles up Dosewallips River Trail (actually 6.5 miles because the road is permanently out five miles below the trailhead) at a signed junction. After a short distance lies the troubled bridge crossing over a beautiful canyon. Beyond, the trail weaves through grand old-growth forest. Big Timber Camp is at 4.2 miles (from the Dosewallips Ranger Station) and Diamond Meadows at 6.6 miles.

The trail climbs to Honeymoon Meadows, wide open meadows of grass and flowers, and eventually to Anderson Pass (access to the Enchanted Valley). This low pass is a real playground, with a trail leading to Anderson Glacier and its craggy home, the highlight of the trip. A final camp is just below the pass.

User Groups: Hikers and horses. No dogs or mountain bikes are allowed. No wheelchair access.

Open Seasons: This trail is accessible June–October.

Permits: A federal Northwest Forest Pass is required to park here. Overnight stays within the national park require backcountry camping permits, which are available at the Quilcene Ranger Station.

Maps: For a map of Olympic National Park, contact the Outdoor Recreation Information Center at the downtown Seattle REI. For topographic maps, ask Green Trails for No. 168, The Brothers, and No. 167, Mount Steel, or ask the USGS for The Brothers and Mount Steel.

Directions: From Quilcene, drive south 11.5 miles on U.S. 101 to Dosewallips River Road. Turn right (west) and drive about 10 miles to the road's end at a washout. The trail is on the right side of the road and climbs above the washout before returning to the road, 5 miles from Dosewallips Ranger Station.

Contact: Olympic National Park, Wilderness Information Center, 3002 Mount Angeles Road, Port Angeles, WA 98362, 360/565-3100.

43 MAIN FORK DOSEWALLIPS RIVER

40.0 mi/4 days

south of Quilcene in Olympic National Park

Map 1.4, page 26

This exceptionally beautiful river valley has suddenly become much more remote. A few years back, the river wiped out the road to the trailhead, adding roughly five miles to the hike. This has weeded out a considerable number of visitors, and now this is a wilderness lover's dream come true. But don't worry about hiking an extra five miles, all of it on the old road. The hike is easily worth it.

After five miles along the old road, the abandoned car camp of Muscott Flats appears. The trail begins here at the ranger station. Dosewallips River Trail follows the river before splitting at 1.5 miles. Stay on the right fork to continue along the main Dosewallips Trail. Dosewallips Trail makes a long journey through typically grand forests of Douglas fir, hemlock, and cedar and passes three established camps on its way to Dose Meadows Camp, 12.5 miles from the end of the road.

The final 2.5 miles is the best part as it breaks out into spacious meadows. The trail begins a more steady ascent from here to Hayden Pass. Along the way is 1,000 Acre Meadow, a wildflower mecca off trail to the southeast for adventurous types. Those who make it to the pass will be rewarded. Countless peaks outline several valleys streaking away from this point. And, of course, Mount Olympus shines from the west.

User Groups: Hikers and horses. No dogs or mountain bikes are allowed. No wheelchair access.

Open Seasons: This trail is usually accessible mid-May–October.

Permits: A federal Northwest Forest Pass is required to park at the road washout. Overnight stays within the national park require backcountry camping permits, which are available at the Quilcene Ranger Station.
Maps: For a map of Olympic National Park, contact the Outdoor Recreation Information Center at the downtown Seattle REI. For topographic maps, ask Green Trails for No. 135, Mount Angeles, No. 136, Tyler Peak, and No. 168, The Brothers, or ask the USGS for The Brothers, Mount Deception, and Wellesley Peak.
Directions: From Quilcene, drive south 11.5 miles on U.S. 101 to Dosewallips River Road. Turn right (west) and drive about 10 miles to the road's end at a washout. The trail is on the right side of the road and climbs above the washout before returning to the road, 5 miles from Dosewallips Ranger Station.
Contact: Olympic National Park, Wilderness Information Center, 3002 Mount Angeles Road, Port Angeles, WA 98362, 360/565-3100.

44 LAKE CONSTANCE
10.0 mi/6.0 hrs

south of Quilcene in Olympic National Park

Map 1.4, page 26

You're likely to hear two things about Lake Constance. First, folks always mention the incredible beauty of the lake. Craggy Mount Constance towers above mountain hemlocks and subalpine firs that border the deep blue lake. But there's a catch, which you're also likely to hear about Lake Constance. The trail is unbelievably steep—3,300 feet in just two miles. That's steep enough to be the toughest climb in the Olympics and steep enough that you can forget about switchbacks. The trail heads straight up the ridge. Your arms will get as much of a workout as your legs as you grab onto roots and branches, pulling yourself up what barely qualifies as a trail. It's a very difficult climb and should not be undertaken by those not ready for a strenuous ascent.

Camping is available at the lake, but because of heavy use, a permit and reservation are required for overnight stays. There are lots of opportunities to explore around the lake, but staying on established trails is important to prevent further ecosystem damage. Also, don't forget that the road up the Dosewallips is out and requires about three miles of hiking on the old road to get to the trail. Get in shape and make it up to Lake Constance, for it is well worth the effort.
User Groups: Hikers only. No dogs, horses, or mountain bikes are allowed. No wheelchair access.
Open Seasons: This trail is usually accessible June–October.
Permits: A federal Northwest Forest Pass is required to park here. Overnight stays at Lake Constance require reservations and backcountry camping permits.
Maps: For a map of Olympic National Park, contact the Outdoor Recreation Information Center at the downtown Seattle REI. For topographic maps, ask Green Trails for No. 168, The Brothers, or ask the USGS for The Brothers.
Directions: From Quilcene, drive south 11.5 miles on U.S. 101 to Dosewallips River Road. Turn right (west) and drive about 10 miles to the road's end at a washout. The trail is on the right side of the road and climbs above the washout before returning to the road, 3 miles from Lake Constance Trail.
Contact: Olympic National Park, Wilderness Information Center, 3002 Mount Angeles Road, Port Angeles, WA 98362, 360/565-3100.

45 DUCKABUSH RIVER
43.6 mi/3–4 days

south of Quilcene in the Brothers Wilderness of Olympic National Forest and Olympic National Park

Map 1.4, page 26

The Duckabush ranks as one of the longest river valley trails on the peninsula. It starts just six miles from Hood Canal and makes a long

trek up to the river's headwaters. Much of the forest is big old-growth, and wildlife is regularly seen throughout the valley. Yet Duckabush Trail receives only moderate use, tapering off significantly farther up the lengthy valley. As wilderness lovers would say, "Other people's loss is our gain."

The main reasons few people venture far into the Duckabush are Little Hump and Big Hump. Elevation gains of 500 feet and 1,100 feet weed out many a noncommitted day hiker. Thank Big Hump, however, for preventing timber-cutting in the upper river valley. This obstacle kept much of the valley forested in old-growth, the main theme of the trail.

Good spots to throw down for the night are found at 5 Mile and 10 Mile Camps. The trail finally reaches the steep walls of Duckabush Basin after 20 miles. The trail makes a steep ascent to La Crosse Basin, a beautiful collection of high-country lakes, and O'Neil Pass. O'Neil Pass features scenery so spectacular that it's pretty much beyond compare to anything else in the Olympics. Magnificent mountains, valleys, and rivers sum it up best. It may be a lot of hard work to get very far on Duckabush Trail, but it will be well remembered.

User Groups: Hikers and horses. No dogs or mountain bikes are allowed. No wheelchair access.

Open Seasons: The lower part of this trail is accessible year-round (upper part is accessible July–October).

Permits: A federal Northwest Forest Pass is required to park here. Overnight stays require backcountry camping permits, which are available at Hoodsport Ranger Station.

Maps: For a map of Olympic National Park, contact the Outdoor Recreation Information Center at the downtown Seattle REI. For topographic maps, ask Green Trails for No. 167, Mount Steel, and No. 168, The Brothers, or ask the USGS for Mount Steel, The Brothers, and Mount Jupiter.

Directions: From Quilcene, drive 16 miles south on U.S. 101 to the Duckabush River Road (Forest Service Road 2510). Turn right (west) and drive 5.5 miles to Forest Service Road 2510-060. Turn right and drive .1 mile to a large parking lot and the signed trailhead.

Contact: Olympic National Park, Wilderness Information Center, 3002 Mount Angeles Road, Port Angeles, WA 98362, 360/565-3100; Olympic National Forest, Hoodsport Ranger District, 150 North Lake Cushman Road, Hoodsport, WA 98548, 360/877-5254.

46 LENA LAKES

6.0–12.0 mi/3.5 hrs–2 days 5 10

south of Quilcene in Olympic National Park

Map 1.4, page 26

Upper Lena Lake may possibly render hikers speechless with its beauty and open views. Meanwhile, the trail up to Lena Lake will certainly leave hikers breathless with its intense steep ascent and sections that require something more akin to scrambling than hiking. Lower Lena Lake is a much less strenuous excursion. Both lakes are great day hikes but also feature many campsites for overnight visits.

Lena Lake Trail climbs gently but steadily through three miles of shady forest to Lower Lena Lake. Dogs and mountain bikes are allowed up to this point, where numerous camps encircle the large lake. Upper Lena Lake Trail continues from the northeast corner of the lake and climbs strenuously for another three miles. This section features switchback after switchback as it ascends the steep valley. Be prepared for a rocky, narrow, and brushy trip.

The upper lake sits among some of the Olympics' best parkland meadows. Mount Bretherton stands to the south while Mount Lena fills the northern horizon. The National Park Service maintains numerous campsites around the eastern and southern shores of the lake. Footpaths create weblike patterns into the lakeside meadows. Be careful of treading

© SCOTT LEONARD

Upper Lena Lake, a strenuous but popular hike on Olympic westside

into revegetation plots, where the park is aiding regrowth of the very sensitive meadow ecosystem. Although Upper Lena Lake receives many visitors during the summer, it is worthy of all the attention it receives.

User Groups: Hikers only. No dogs, horses, or mountain bikes are allowed. No wheelchair access.

Open Seasons: This trail is accessible July–October.

Permits: A federal Northwest Forest Pass is required to park here. Overnight stays require backcountry camping permits, which are available at the park boundary.

Maps: For a map of Olympic National Park, contact the Outdoor Recreation Information Center at the downtown Seattle REI. For topographic maps, ask Green Trails for No. 168, The Brothers, or ask the USGS for Mount Washington and The Brothers.

Directions: From Quilcene, drive south 24 miles on U.S. 101 to Forest Service Road 25. Turn right and drive 8 miles to the Lena Lakes Trailhead.

Contact: Olympic National Park, Wilderness Information Center, 3002 Mount Angeles Road, Port Angeles, WA 98362, 360/565-3100.

47 THE BROTHERS

3.0 mi/2.0 hrs 3 5

south of Quilcene in the Brothers Wilderness of Olympic National Forest

Map 1.4, page 26

While The Brothers are the most easily recognized Olympic peaks from Seattle, visitors to the peninsula rarely hike this trail. That's because The Brothers Trail is primarily used by climbers to reach the base camp for a shot at the mountain's summit. The trail to the base camp is hikable for almost anyone, but since you won't see much, it's hardly worth it. To really appreciate The Brothers, you would have to go beyond the trail and ascend the mountain, which is not a job for amateurs. So unless you're ready for some real mountaineering, The Brothers Trail is best left as a through-way for climbers.

The trail begins near the northwest corner of Lena Lake, where Lena Creek empties into the lake. It is rocky and overcome with roots in places. It even requires some careful maneuvering over boulder fields. The trail enters the Valley of Silent Men, named for the climbers from Lena Lake passing through before the sun rises or the conversation heats up. The

trail passes back and forth over East Lena Creek several times and after three miles crosses one last time, skirts a small pond, and ends at The Brothers base camp. Most hikers should turn around here.

Beyond the base camp, climbing The Brothers is recommended only with the proper gear and training. It's a pretty serious ascent, not a scramble for novices. Hikers intending to go up to the summit should consult climbing guides containing this peak or with the ranger station in Quilcene.

User Groups: Hikers, leashed dogs, and horses. No mountain bikes are allowed. No wheelchair access.

Open Seasons: This trail is accessible June–October.

Permits: A federal Northwest Forest Pass is required to park here.

Maps: For a map of Olympic National Forest, contact the Outdoor Recreation Information Center at the downtown Seattle REI. For topographic maps, ask Green Trails for No. 168, The Brothers, or ask the USGS for Mount Washington and The Brothers.

Directions: From Quilcene, drive south 24 miles on U.S. 101 to Forest Service Road 25. Turn right and drive 8 miles to the Lena Lakes Trailhead.

Contact: Olympic National Forest, Hoodsport Ranger Station, 150 North Lake Cushman Road, Hoodsport, WA 98548, 360/877-5254.

48 PUTVIN

8.0 mi/4.0 hrs

south of Quilcene in Mount Skokomish Wilderness of Olympic National Forest and in Olympic National Park

Map 1.4, page 26

Putvin Trail includes much of what is great about the Olympics. There are forests full of trees big enough to make your neck sore. There are prime subalpine meadows, full of heather and huckleberries, enough to make your mouth water. And, of course, there are outstanding views, enough to make you rub your eyes. It's a steep trail, gaining 3,400 feet in just four miles. But as the pilgrims once said, there's redemption in suffering.

Putvin Trail starts off in the river bottom of the Hamma Hamma, climbing through an old logging tract. The trail eventually enters the Mount Skokomish Wilderness (1.5 miles) and a land of big trees. After briefly leveling out, Putvin resumes climbing, arriving at several small tarns. Keep going, as this is not Lake of the Angels. It is farther yet, set within a small glacier cirque called the Valley of Heaven. Heaven indeed. The lake is absolutely beautiful, surrounded by meadows and craggy peaks. Mount Skokomish and Mount Stone flank the valley's two ends. For outstanding views, hike the small footpath up to the long ridge separating the two peaks. From here, Putvin Trail's anonymity is hard to understand.

User Groups: Hikers and leashed dogs. No horses or mountain bikers are allowed. No wheelchair access.

Open Seasons: This trail is accessible mid-June–November.

Permits: A federal Northwest Forest Pass is required to park here. Overnight stays require backcountry camping permits, which are available at Hoodsport Ranger Station.

Maps: For a map of Olympic National Park and Olympic National Forest, contact the Outdoor Recreation Information Center at the downtown Seattle REI. For topographic maps, ask Green Trails for No. 167, Mount Steel, and No. 168, The Brothers, or ask the USGS for Mount Skokomish.

Directions: From Hoodsport, drive 14 miles north on U.S. 101 to Forest Service Road 25 (Hamma Hamma Recreation Area). Turn left (west) and drive 12 miles to the Putvin Historical Marker. The trail is on the right side of the road.

Contact: Olympic National Forest, Hoodsport Ranger Station, 150 North Lake Cushman Road, Hoodsport, WA 98548, 360/877-5254; Olympic National Park, Wilderness Information Center, 3002 Mount Angeles Road, Port Angeles, WA 98362, 360/565-3100.

49 MILDRED LAKES

9.8 mi/6.0 hrs

northwest of Hoodsport in Mount Skokomish Wilderness of Olympic National Forest

Map 1.4, page 26

Although Mildred Lakes is gaining in popularity, you're likely to experience fewer fellow hikers here than elsewhere in the Olympics. The Forest Service provides little maintenance on the trail to help keep this sensitive area in good condition, as an easy trail would likely lead to overuse. Nonetheless, Mildred Lakes are still out there and very much worth visiting.

The trail climbs through an old logging tract before entering virgin forest. The trail is relatively easy to follow through the pleasant forest of hemlock and fir. Before long, however, the trail becomes increasingly infested with rocks and roots. At about three miles, you must cross a ravine more than 20 feet deep. Now the trail becomes really rough. Head straight up the steep mountainside, pulling yourself up by rocks and roots. At 4.9 miles, crest the ridge to find the Mildred Lakes Basin.

The basin holds three lakes bordered by subalpine firs and meadows of heather. The Sawtooth Range runs along the north and western part of the basin, with Mount Cruiser and Mount Lincoln acting as bookends to the jagged ridge. There are a fair number of campsites up here, but Leave-No-Trace principles are to be emphasized, as heavy past use has been detrimental to the area.

User Groups: Hikers and leashed dogs. No horses or mountain bikes are allowed. No wheelchair access.

Open Seasons: This trail is accessible July–October.

Permits: A federal Northwest Forest Pass is required to park here.

Maps: For a map of Olympic National Forest, contact the Outdoor Recreation Information Center at the downtown Seattle REI. For topographic maps, ask Green Trails for No. 167, Mount Steel, or ask the USGS for Mount Skokomish.

Directions: From Hoodsport, drive north 14 miles on U.S. 101 to Forest Service Road 25 (Hamma Hamma Recreation Area). Turn left (west) and drive 14 miles to Mildred Lakes Trailhead at road's end.

Contact: Olympic National Forest, Hoodsport Ranger Station, 150 North Lake Cushman Road, Hoodsport, WA 98548, 360/877-5254.

50 STAIRCASE RAPIDS

2.0 mi/1.0 hr

northwest of Hoodsport in Olympic National Park

Map 1.4, page 26

Walks through the forest rarely get better than this. Set along the North Fork Skokomish River within an old-growth forest, Staircase Rapids Trail is perfect for families and older hikers. The flat, level trail encounters several sites where the river pours over bedrock or rumbles over rapids. And it all occurs within one of the eastern Olympics' most beautiful old-growth forests. The trail has a bit of history, as well, as it was part of the original route taken by the O'Neil Expedition in 1890. This is an excellent destination or just a side trip to a bigger excursion.

The trail starts at Staircase Ranger Station on the west side of the river. The exceptional old-growth forest is highlighted by Big Cedar (accessible by a side trail signed "Big Cedar"). Definitely check it out. Along the way to the rapids are Red Reef, an outcropping of red limestone that does its best to hold back the rushing river, and Dolly Varden Pool, where rocky cliffs loom over the river as it rumbles between large boulders. The climax of the walk is Staircase Rapids, a series of regularly spaced terraces over which the river spills. This is easily one of the Olympics' most scenic stretches of river and well worth a visit.

User Groups: Hikers only. No dogs, horses, or mountain bikes are allowed. No wheelchair access.

Open Seasons: This trail is accessible year-round.

Permits: A National Parks Pass is required to park here.
Maps: For a map of Olympic National Park, contact the Outdoor Recreation Information Center at the downtown Seattle REI. For topographic maps, ask Green Trails for No. 167, Mount Steel, or ask the USGS for Mount Skokomish.
Directions: From Hoodsport, drive west 9 miles on Lake Cushman Road (Highway 119) to Forest Service Road 24 (a T intersection). Turn left and drive 6.5 miles to Staircase Ranger Station for the trailhead and trailhead parking.
Contact: Olympic National Park, Wilderness Information Center, 3002 Mount Angeles Road, Port Angeles, WA 98362, 360/565-3100.

51 NORTH FORK SKOKOMISH

25.2 mi/2–3 days 1 8

northwest of Hoodsport in Olympic National Park

Map 1.4, page 26

The western rivers of the Olympic Mountains rightfully share reputations for forests of enormous proportions. While the North Fork Skokomish remains out of this limelight, it's no less impressive. The trail follows the North Fork Skokomish for 10 miles at relative ease, passing through a virgin forest full of massive trees. This route is historical, as well, having been blazed by Army Lieutenant Joseph P. O'Neil on the first east-west expedition of the Olympics in the winter of 1890.

The trail leaves Staircase Ranger Station along an old roadbed. It quickly encounters the Beaver Fire of 1985, where new firs are growing up among towering burned snags. At five miles, the trail crosses the Skokomish via a bridge where the slate-gray water passes through a beautiful box canyon bordered by colossal Douglas firs. The trail crosses several large streams, two of which lack a bridge and may be tricky in times of heavy runoff.

Camp Pleasant (6.4 miles) and Nine Stream Camp (9.3 miles) make for great places to spend the night and build a fire. After Nine Stream, the trail begins its ascent to First Divide through large mountain hemlocks and Douglas firs. After 3.5 miles of climbing, the trail reaches First Divide and several small tarns. Views into the upper Duckabush reward the long trek. Just beyond the pass, Home Sweet Home (13.5 miles) offers another great site for camping in a meadow setting.
User Groups: Hikers and horses. No dogs or mountain bikes are allowed. No wheelchair access.
Open Seasons: The lower part of this trail is accessible year-round. The upper part is accessible June–October.
Permits: A National Parks Pass is required to park here. Overnight stays in the national park require backcountry camping permits, which are available at Hoodsport Ranger Station or at the trailhead.
Maps: For a map of Olympic National Park, contact the Outdoor Recreation Information Center at the downtown Seattle REI. For topographic maps, ask Green Trails for No. 167, Mount Steel, or ask the USGS for Mount Skokomish, Mount Olson, and Mount Steel.
Directions: From Hoodsport, drive west 9 miles on Lake Cushman Road (Highway 119) to Forest Service Road 24 (a T intersection). Turn left and drive 6.5 miles to Staircase Ranger Station for the trailhead and trailhead parking.
Contact: Olympic National Park, Wilderness Information Center, 3002 Mount Angeles Road, Port Angeles, WA 98362, 360/565-3100; Olympic National Forest, Hoodsport Ranger Station, 150 North Lake Cushman Road, Hoodsport, WA 98548, 360/877-5254.

52 WAGONWHEEL LAKE

5.8 mi/3.5 hrs 5 6

northwest of Hoodsport in Olympic National Park

Map 1.4, page 26

When people mention Wagonwheel Lake, they mostly condemn it to being nothing more than a conditioning hike. Consider that neither an insult nor compliment; it's mostly just the truth.

After all, the trail makes a brutal ascent of 3,200 feet in less than three miles. For most hikers, a pace of 1,000 feet per mile is considered "difficult." Throw in the fact that there are few views to be had along the way or at the lake and you get only the diehards or the foolhardy on the trail.

Nearly the entire length of the trail is a steep climb through the forest. The lower part of the trail climbs via switchback through second-growth forest tamed by fire before eventually reaching some old-growth hemlock. After nearly three miles of huffing and puffing, hikers are delivered to Wagonwheel Lake, set within a small basin on the north side of Copper Mountain and bounded by a dense forest offering relatively no views. With all the hard work, why come here? Because a day in the woods is always a good day.

User Groups: Hikers only. No dogs, horses, or mountain bikes are allowed. No wheelchair access.

Open Seasons: This trail is accessible July–November.

Permits: A National Parks Pass is required to park here. Overnight stays in the national park require backcountry camping permits, which are available at Hoodsport Ranger Station.

Maps: For a map of Olympic National Park, contact the Outdoor Recreation Information Center at the downtown Seattle REI. For topographic maps, ask Green Trails for No. 167, Mount Steel, or ask the USGS for Mount Skokomish.

Directions: From Hoodsport, drive west 9 miles on Lake Cushman Road (Highway 119) to Forest Service Road 24 (a T intersection). Turn left and drive 6.5 miles to Staircase Ranger Station for the trailhead and trailhead parking.

Contact: Olympic National Park, Wilderness Information Center, 3002 Mount Angeles Road, Port Angeles, WA 98362, 360/565-3100; Olympic National Forest, Hoodsport Ranger Station, 150 North Lake Cushman Road, Hoodsport, WA 98548, 360/877-5254.

53 FLAPJACK LAKES

16.0 mi/2 days

northwest of Hoodsport in Olympic National Park

Map 1.4, page 26

Flapjack Lakes is one of the most scenic and popular destinations in Olympic National Park. So popular, in fact, the Park Service instituted a permit system limiting the number of overnight campers here. Don't let that deter you, however, as it's a must hike on any to-do list of Olympic trails. Plus, Flapjack Lakes are easily accessible, especially for families on a weekend excursion.

The route follows North Fork Skokomish Trail for 3.5 miles, where Flapjack Lake Trail takes off to the east. The trail steadily ascends through a forest of impressively large trees while following Donahue Creek. At seven miles, the trail splits, with the left fork heading to Black and White Lakes. Stay to the right and find old mountain hemlocks, subalpine firs, and yellow cedars surrounding the two lakes. Mount Cruiser and the jagged ridge leading to Mount Lincoln enclose the eastern view; a way trail leading up to the Gladys Divide is a great side trip.

If the thought of crowds at Flapjacks is unappealing, an attractive alternative is Black and White Lakes. From the fork, a mile of walking brings hikers to an open ridge below Mount Gladys. The lakes are small and have fewer campsites, but they are much more open and offer outstanding views of the entire North Fork Skokomish drainage. With several options for exploration, Flapjack Lakes are definitely a destination for Olympic enthusiasts to undertake.

User Groups: Hikers only. No dogs, horses, or mountain bikes are allowed. No wheelchair access.

Open Seasons: This trail is accessible mid-May–October.

Permits: A National Parks Pass is required to park at North Fork Skokomish Trailhead. Overnight stays in the national park require backcountry camping permits, which are available at Staircase Ranger Station.

Maps: For a map of Olympic National Park, contact the Outdoor Recreation Information Center at the downtown Seattle REI. For topographic maps, ask Green Trails for No. 167, Mount Steel, or ask the USGS for Mount Skokomish and Mount Olson.

Directions: From Hoodsport, drive west 9 miles on Lake Cushman Road (Highway 119) to Forest Service Road 24 (a T intersection). Turn left and drive 6.5 miles to Staircase Ranger Station for the trailhead and trailhead parking.

Contact: Olympic National Park, Wilderness Information Center, 3002 Mount Angeles Road, Port Angeles, WA 98362, 360/565-3100.

54 SIX RIDGE

32.8 mi/3–4 days

northwest of Hoodsport in Olympic National Park

Map 1.4, page 26

If you are considering hiking Six Ridge, you are to be commended. You have a thirst for adventure and are undeterred by difficult ascents. You appreciate grand mountain views, love mountain meadows full of blooming wildflowers, and enjoy wilderness best when it's solitary. Six Ridge Trail is all that and more.

To access Six Ridge, one must first travel North Fork Skokomish Trail 5.6 miles, a flat and easy walk. Skokomish Trail crosses the river here and Six Ridge turns south. After crossing Seven Stream, the trail climbs gradually through forest to achieve the eastern end of Six Ridge. From here are eight miles of ridge walking. The trail passes through exceptional subalpine meadows for much of the route, although fields of scree, talus, and even snow are common. There are several camps on the ridge, most notably McGravey Lakes at 8.5 miles up the ridge. The trail technically ends at Six Ridge Pass, where it becomes Graves Creek Trail but continues to Lake Sundown in 1.2 miles.

User Groups: Hikers only. No dogs, horses, or mountain bikes are allowed. No wheelchair access.

Open Seasons: This trail is accessible mid-July–October.

Permits: A National Parks Pass is required to park here. Overnight stays in the national park require backcountry camping permits, which are available at the Staircase Ranger Station.

Maps: For a map of Olympic National Park, contact the Outdoor Recreation Information Center at the downtown Seattle REI. For topographic maps, ask Green Trails for No. 166, Mount Christie, and No. 167, Mount Steel, or ask the USGS for Mount Skokomish, Mount Olson, and Mount Hoquim.

Directions: From Hoodsport, drive west 9 miles on Lake Cushman Road (Highway 119) to Forest Service Road 24 (a T intersection). Turn left and drive 6.5 miles to Staircase Ranger Station for the trailhead and trailhead parking.

Contact: Olympic National Park, Wilderness Information Center, 3002 Mount Angeles Road, Port Angeles, WA 98362, 360/565-3100.

55 MOUNT ELLINOR

6.2 mi/3.0 hrs

northwest of Hoodsport in Mount Skokomish Wilderness of Olympic National Forest

Map 1.4, page 26

Tucked away in the southeastern corner of the Olympic Peninsula, Mount Ellinor is rarely high on peoples' radar when they are looking for a hike. It gets less attention than other nearby spots, such as Mount Rose or Flapjack Lakes. But the trip is no less beautiful and actually features some the area's best views.

The trail has two trailheads, the lower one adding about 1.5 miles and 800 feet elevation gain to the trip. Since it's not much farther, the lower trailhead is the better choice, as it follows a well-forested ridge that should not be missed. The trail is a steady climb, rarely leveling out for more than a few yards. The forest breaks into avalanche chutes and meadows about .5 mile from the summit. At the top, views of Hood Canal, Lake Cushman, and neighboring Olympic peaks can be found. Neither well known nor frequently visited, Mount Ellinor makes for a perfect day getaway.

User Groups: Hikers and leashed dogs. No horses or mountain bikes are allowed. No wheelchair access.

Open Seasons: This trail is accessible mid-June–November (accessible year-round with ice ax).

Permits: A federal Northwest Forest Pass is required to park here.

Maps: For a map of Olympic National Forest, contact the Outdoor Recreation Information Center at the downtown Seattle REI. For topographic maps, ask Green Trails for No. 167, Mount Steel, and No. 168, The Brothers, or ask the USGS for Mount Washington and Mount Skokomish.

Directions: From Hoodsport, drive east 9 miles on Hoodsport Road (County Road 44) to Forest Service Road 24. Turn right and drive 1.5 miles to Forest Service Road 2419 (Big Creek Road). Turn left and drive 6 miles to Forest Service Road 2419-014. Turn left and drive 1 mile to the signed trailhead at road's end.

Contact: Olympic National Forest, Hoodsport Ranger Station, 150 North Lake Cushman Road, Hoodsport, WA 98548, 360/877-5254.

56 MOUNT ROSE

6.4 mi/3.5 hr

northwest of Hoodsport in Mount Skokomish Wilderness of Olympic National Forest

Map 1.4, page 26

Mount Rose is one of the more popular summits in the southeastern Olympic Mountains. Which means it must be awfully scenic, as it is certainly not an easy route. The trail is unique for a summit route in that it is a loop. Laid out like a lasso, the trail ascends straight to the summit and then makes a circle along the ridge to the trail again. Overall elevation gain is 3,500 feet in just about three miles.

The trail navigates a mile of second-growth timber before entering the wilderness. The rise to the junction (1.8 miles) is rather steep despite the many switchbacks. Head to the right for the more gradual route along the ridge. The trail has peek-a-boo views of neighboring peaks and drainages. The summit is forested save for a small chuck of basalt that reaches up roughly 30 feet. From the top are grand, panoramic views of Hood Canal and numerous Olympic peaks. Good luck, and enjoy the workout.

User Groups: Hikers and leashed dogs. No horses or mountain bikes are allowed. No wheelchair access.

Open Seasons: This trail is accessible July–October.

Permits: Permits are not required. Parking and access are free.

Maps: For a map of Olympic National Forest, contact the Outdoor Recreation Information Center at the downtown Seattle REI. For topographic maps, ask Green Trails for No. 167, Mount Steel, or ask the USGS for Lightning Peak and Mount Skokomish.

Directions: From Hoodsport, drive west 9 miles on Lake Cushman Road (Highway 119) to Forest Service Road 24 (a T intersection). Turn left and drive 3 miles to the signed trailhead on the right side of the road.

Contact: Olympic National Forest, Hoodsport Ranger Station, 150 North Lake Cushman Road, Hoodsport, WA 98548, 360/877-5254.

57 UPPER SOUTH FORK SKOKOMISH

15.0 mi/1–2 days

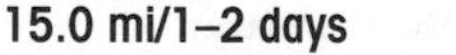

west of Hoodsport in the Wonder Mountain Wilderness and Olympic National Park

Map 1.4, page 26

Upper South Fork Skokomish Trail is a great route through a typically great Olympic river valley. Unfortunately, it is much shorter than it once was. This trail has just what one could want out of Olympic river hike: a forest composed of large trees, a river carving through occasional canyons, and meadows at the river's headwaters along a high mountain ridge. And throw in an absence of people on the trail, which is all right with the folks who know of this place.

The trail leaves the road and sets off into a forest of large cedars, firs, and hemlocks, all old-growth and of good size. Streams and creeks regularly cross the trail, but few give any trouble. The trail crosses the river twice via bridges and makes a detour into the Startup Creek valley. Soon after the route enters the national park, it becomes little more than a beaten footpath. It's not exceptionally difficult to follow as long as snow isn't lingering on the ground (after mid-June). The trail climbs gradually through the headwaters of the South Fork of the Skokomish, eventually reaching Sundown Pass and Lake Sundown, a remote place of meadows and open subalpine forests. Backpackers will find overnight spots at Camp Riley (5.4 miles) and Sundown Pass.

User Groups: Hikers and horses. No dogs or mountain bikes are allowed. No wheelchair access.

Open Seasons: This trail is accessible mid-June–October.

Permits: A federal Northwest Forest Pass is required to park here.

Maps: For a map of Olympic National Park and Olympic National Forest, contact the Outdoor Recreation Information Center at the downtown Seattle REI. For topographic maps, ask Green Trails for No. 166, Mount Christie, No. 167, Mount Steel, and No. 199, Mount Tebo, or ask the USGS for Lightning Peak, Mount Tebo, Mount Olson, and Mount Hoquim.

Directions: From Hoodsport, drive south 7 miles to Skokomish Valley Road. Turn right (west) and drive 5.5 miles to Forest Service Road 23. Turn right and drive 13 miles to Forest Service Road 2361. Turn right and drive 5.5 miles to the signed trailhead at road's end.

Contact: Olympic National Forest, Hoodsport Ranger Station, 150 North Lake Cushman Road, Hoodsport, WA 98548, 360/877-5254.

58 RAINBOW CANYON

1.0 mi/0.5 hr

south of Quilcene in the Buckhorn Wilderness of Olympic National Forest

Map 1.5, page 27

This is a great leg-stretcher for those making a long trek along U.S. 101. Just outside Rainbow Campground (which is right off the highway), a short .5-mile hike accesses a nice waterfall on the way to Rainbow Canyon on the Big Quilcene River. The trail's drop is not much to speak of, making it easily accessible to hikers of all abilities.

Forests of Douglas fir tower over an understory that includes vine maple, a tangle of brilliant colors in September. An overlook peers into Elbo Creek, where the waterfall cascades into a small pool. The trail continues down to the Big Quilcene River, where it makes a gentle turn within the canyon walls. Moss and ferns line the sides. When the kids are getting antsy in the back seat, Rainbow Canyon is just the thing to burn off a little energy. Total distance for the round-trip excursion is just one mile.

User Groups: Hikers and leashed dogs. No horses or mountain bikes are allowed. No wheelchair access.

Open Seasons: This trail is accessible year-round.

Permits: Permits are not required. Parking and access are free.

Maps: For a map of Olympic National Forest, contact the Outdoor Recreation Information Center at the downtown Seattle REI. For topographic maps, ask the USGS for Mount Walker.

Directions: From Quilcene, drive 5 miles south on U.S. 101 to Rainbow Campground. While the trail begins from within the campground, it is a group site and the gate will be locked. Park across Highway 101 and walk into the site. The trailhead is at the back of the campground.

Contact: Olympic National Forest, Quilcene Ranger Station, 295142 U.S. 101 South, Quilcene, WA 98376, 360/765-2200.

59 LEADBETTER POINT

2.6–8.3 mi/1.5–4.5 hrs

northern tip of Long Beach in southwestern Washington

Map 1.6, page 28

It may not appear as though there is much going on at Leadbetter Point, but in fact the tip of Long Beach is extremely rich in wildlife. Comprising sand dunes and miles of grasses waving in the strong breeze, the area can look barren and a bit forbidding. On closer inspection, however, you'll see that hundreds of thousands of seabirds and shorebirds make this place home for a part of each year. Leadbetter Point is a bird-watcher's dream, home to snowy plovers, grouse, bald eagles, great herons, and woodpeckers. Although it's a good visit anytime of the year, winter is the peak of bird season. Just be ready for soggy trail in places.

A small network of trails courses around the ever-changing peninsula. Taken altogether, they make an 8.3-mile loop that includes sand dunes, coastal forest, Willapa Bay, and a stretch along the beach. Shorter hikes include Blue Trail, a 2.6-mile round-trip out to the Pacific Ocean. All of the trails are fairly level, climbing only over sand dunes and grassy knolls. The park is managed by State Parks but is also a National Wildlife Refuge because of its importance as a migratory stop for birds. Dogs are not allowed on any trails.

User Groups: Hikers only. No dogs, horses, or mountain bikes are allowed. No wheelchair access.

Open Seasons: This trail is accessible year-round.

Permits: A $5 day-use fee is required to park here and is payable at the trailhead, or you can get an annual State Parks Pass for $30; contact Washington State Parks and Recreation, 360/902-8500.

Maps: For topographic maps, ask the USGS for Oysterville and North Cove.

Directions: From Long Beach, drive north 18 miles on Highway 103 (Pacific Way) to Leadbetter Point State Park. The route passes through Oysterville and is well signed. The trailhead is at the end of the road within the Leadbetter Point State Park.

Contact: Willapa National Wildlife Refuge, 3888 U.S. 101, Ilwaco, WA 98624-9707, 360/484-3482.

60 LONG ISLAND

1.0–5.0 mi/2.0–5.0 hrs

in Willapa Bay in Southwestern Washington

Map 1.6, page 28

Talk about secluded. As the name implies, this is an island, and it's one with no bridges. One reaches Long Island by boat or kayak, with no other options. If that's not a problem (it actually makes the trip all the more special), then Long Island is a real gem.

Roughly five miles of trail and even more old road crisscross the island, two miles wide by seven miles long. Hiking along the shore is a real wildlife getaway, with a plethora of seabirds and shorebirds stopping by on their yearly migrations. Bald eagles, grouse, great herons, and snowy plovers are just a few of the many winged inhabitants. Inland, deer, bear, and elk are some of the bigger mammals to be found.

The highlight of the island is the ancient cedar grove in the center of the island. After crossing the bay to the island by boat (the crossing is about 200 feet and can be done only at high tide), hike north on the old logging road about 2.5 miles to the signed "Trail of the Ancient Cedars." Turn left and in .5 mile you will be among a large grove of massive cedars. Spared from logging because of its hard-to-reach locale, the stand is certain to instill a sense of awe for a forest that once covered the entire island. There are a number of primitive campgrounds around the lake, although there is no water during the summer.

User Groups: Hikers only. No dogs, horses, or mountain bikes are allowed. No wheelchair access.

Open Seasons: This trail is accessible year-round.

Permits: Permits are not required. Parking and access are free.
Maps: For topographic maps, ask the USGS for Long Island.
Directions: From Long Beach, drive north 13 miles on U.S. 101 to the signed Refuge Headquarters and trailhead.
Contact: Willapa National Wildlife Refuge, 3888 U.S. 101, Ilwaco, WA 98624-9707, 360/484-3482.

61 CAPE DISAPPOINTMENT STATE PARK

0.5–9.0 mi /0.5–4.5 hrs 1 10

southwest of Ilwaco in southwest Washington

Map 1.6, page 28

A network of trails through Cape Disappointment State Park makes for a great combination of forest and coastal hiking. All of the trails are extremely easy and highly scenic, providing parents a prime locale to take the kids on the weekend. Formerly known as Fort Canby, the state park covers the grounds where Lewis and Clark spent a wet winter. On Cape Disappointment, Washington's most southwestern point, the park overlooks both the Columbia River and Pacific Ocean.

The main route through the park is Washington Coast Trail, a long trek that gets its southern start here. Patched together from several trails, this 4.5-mile segment bisects the park through old-growth forest to link a pair of old lighthouses. Folks spending a full day here will want to hike the length of it, the best way to see the park.

Families looking for a shorter trip should hike to Beard's Hollow. The trail travels just .5 mile through coastal forest and sand dunes before finding the secluded cove, a gateway to more than 20 miles of beach to the north. Another beauty is Cape Disappointment Lighthouse Trail, 1.4 miles to the West Coast's oldest working lighthouse. Be sure to check out the Lewis and Clark Interpretive Center, atop a pair of enormous gun emplacements from World Wars I and II. The center features a cornucopia of artifacts from the Corps of Discovery's journey 200 years ago.

User Groups: Hikers, leashed dogs, and mountain bikes. No horses are allowed. Parts of the trails are wheelchair accessible.
Open Seasons: This area is accessible year-round.
Permits: A $5 day-use fee is required to park here and is payable at the trailhead, or you can get an annual State Parks Pass for $30; contact Washington State Parks and Recreation, 360/902-8500.
Maps: For topographic maps, ask the USGS for Cape Disappointment.
Directions: From Long Beach, drive south 3.5 miles on Pacific Way to Ilwaco. Turn right on North Head Road and drive 2.5 miles to North Head Lighthouse Road. Turn right and drive .5 miles to the well-signed park entrance. The main trailhead is located at the Lewis and Clark Interpretive Center, inside the park entrance.
Contact: Cape Disappointment State Park, P.O. Box 488, Ilwaco WA, 98624, 360/642-3078.

Chapter 2

Seattle and the San Juan Islands

Seattle and the San Juan Islands

Who says you have to go far from Seattle to enjoy the great outdoors? The Puget Sound area is undoubtedly one of the United State's most scenic locales for a major urban area, which is great for Seattleites. The North Cascades may be just an hour or two drive from Seattle, but the secluded parks and beaches of this region are even closer. Stretching from the San Juan Islands in Puget Sound (accessible only by ferry, one of the prettiest boat rides you'll ever embark upon) down to Seattle and Olympia, a strong network of state and city parks have preserved a bit of the wilderness for people to enjoy quickly and easily. Thanks to easy trails and loads of wildlife, these places are excellent trips for young hikers in training.

A number of great parks line the Sound, many located on the San Juans. Moran State Park is the best, not simply among these, but among all of Washington's state parks. Situated on horseshoe-shaped Orcas Island, the park boasts Mount Constitution as its highlight. From the lofty height of 2,409 feet, Mount Constitution lays Puget Sound and the Strait of Juan de Fuca below you. This makes a great hike, but the peak is accessible on four wheels as well. In Anacortes, Washington Park is a little-explored gem. It's convenient to access for people passing through Anacortes on their way to other places–be one of the few to stop and explore the trails and shoreline of this city park. On Whidbey Island are Deception Pass, Fort Ebey, and South Whidbey State Parks. These are great destinations any time of the year, with miles of trail along the water. Lucky visitors may spot sea lions or orcas swimming and playing in the sound.

Back on the mainland are several great wildlife refuges. The Puget Sound region sees millions of birds pass through the area each spring and fall on their way to warmer climes. Refuges like Tennant Lake near Bellingham, Padilla Bay near Mount Vernon, and Nisqually Wildlife Refuge near Olympia offer exceptional opportunities for quiet walks and wildlife sightings. Ducks and geese might be lounging in the marshlands while goshawks and falcons patrol the air in search of dinner.

And let's not forget the wealth of forests and trails within the city limits, either; Seattle's city park system rivals any in the nation. Carkeek Park overlooks Puget Sound from high bluffs and is home to one of Seattle's few remaining salmon streams (fall runs of salmon can still be seen in Piper Creek). Seward Park covers Bailey Peninsula in Lake Washington and still boasts some old-growth timber. At Discovery Park on the Sound, hikers can enjoy sunsets from on the hill or explore the tidal pools of Puget Sound during low tides. There's a lot to do in Seattle's own backyard.

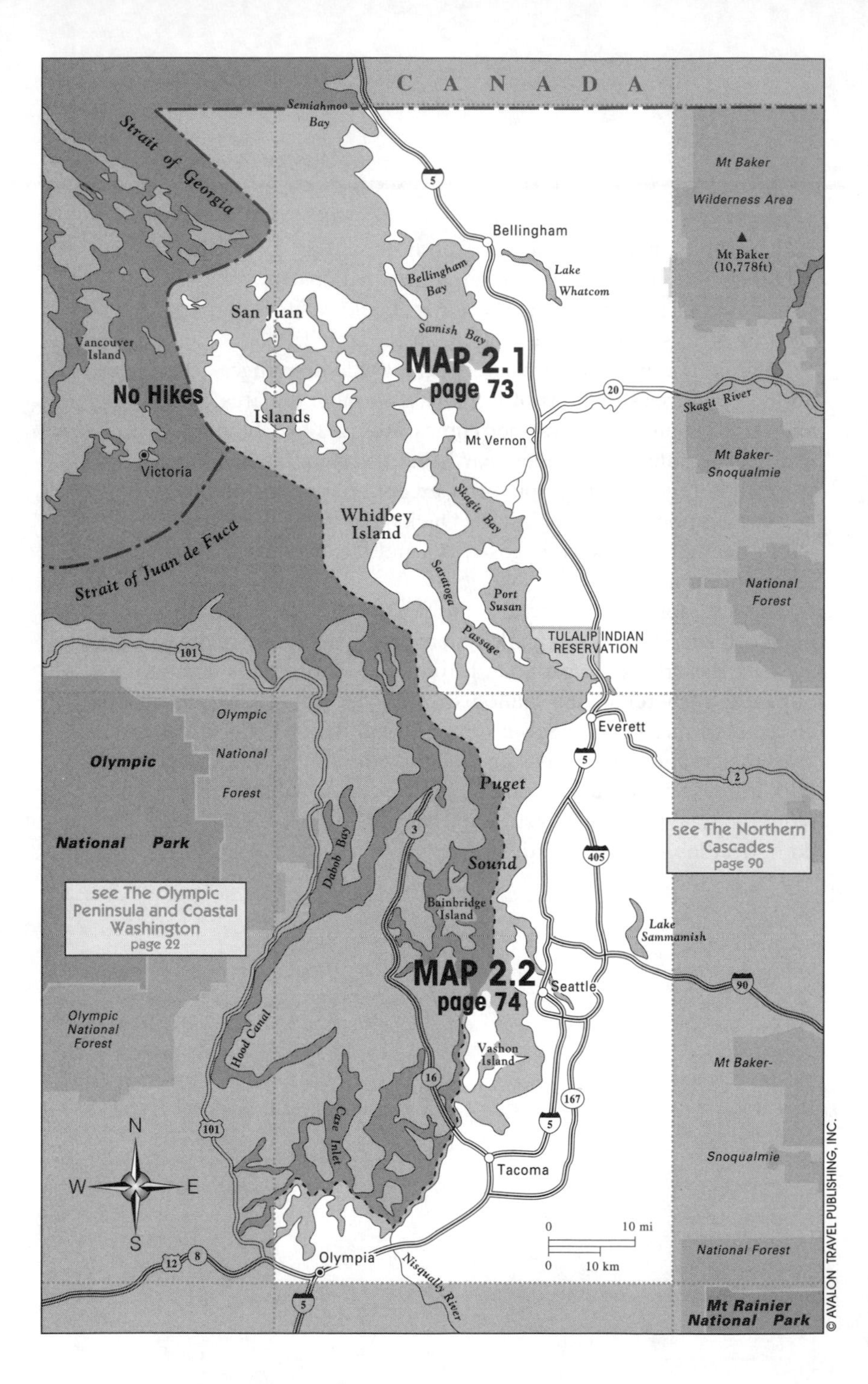
CANADA
Semiahmoo Bay
Strait of Georgia
Mt Baker
Wilderness Area
Mt Baker (10,778ft)
Bellingham
Lake Whatcom
Bellingham Bay
San Juan
Islands
Samish Bay
Vancouver Island
No Hikes
MAP 2.1
page 73
Skagit River
Mt Vernon
Victoria
Mt Baker-
Snoqualmie
Whidbey Island
Skagit Bay
Strait of Juan de Fuca
Saratoga Passage
Port Susan
National
Forest
TULALIP INDIAN RESERVATION
Olympic
National
Forest
Everett
Olympic
National Park
Puget
Sound
Dabob Bay
see The Northern Cascades
page 90
see The Olympic Peninsula and Coastal Washington
page 22
Bainbridge Island
Lake Sammamish
MAP 2.2
page 74
Seattle
Olympic National Forest
Hood Canal
Vashon Island
Mt Baker-
Snoqualmie
Case Inlet
Tacoma
N
W
E
S
0
10 mi
0
10 km
National Forest
Olympia
Nisqually River
Mt Rainier
National Park
© AVALON TRAVEL PUBLISHING, INC.

Map 2.1

Hikes 1–10
Pages 75–80

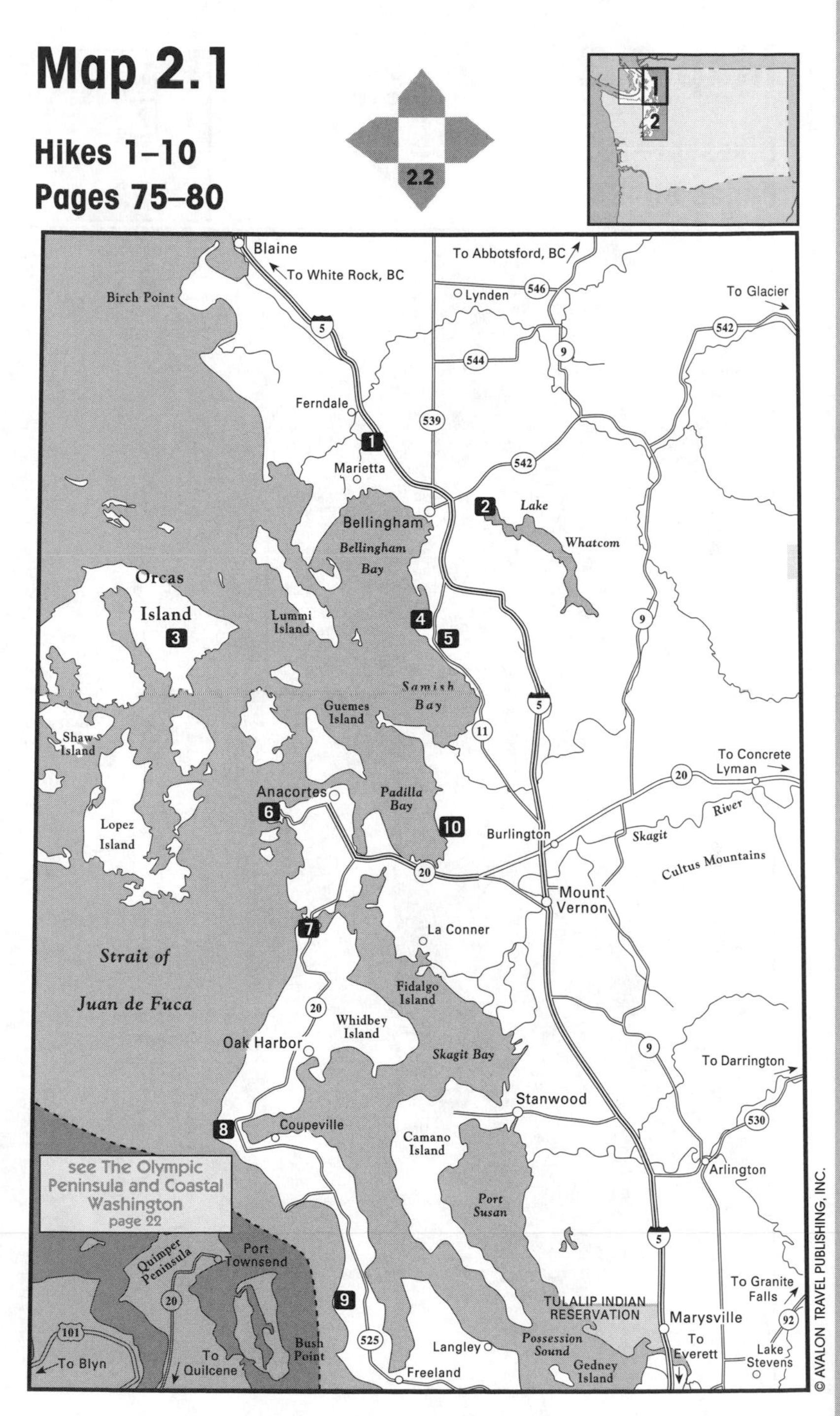

Map 2.2

Hikes 11–18
Pages 80–84

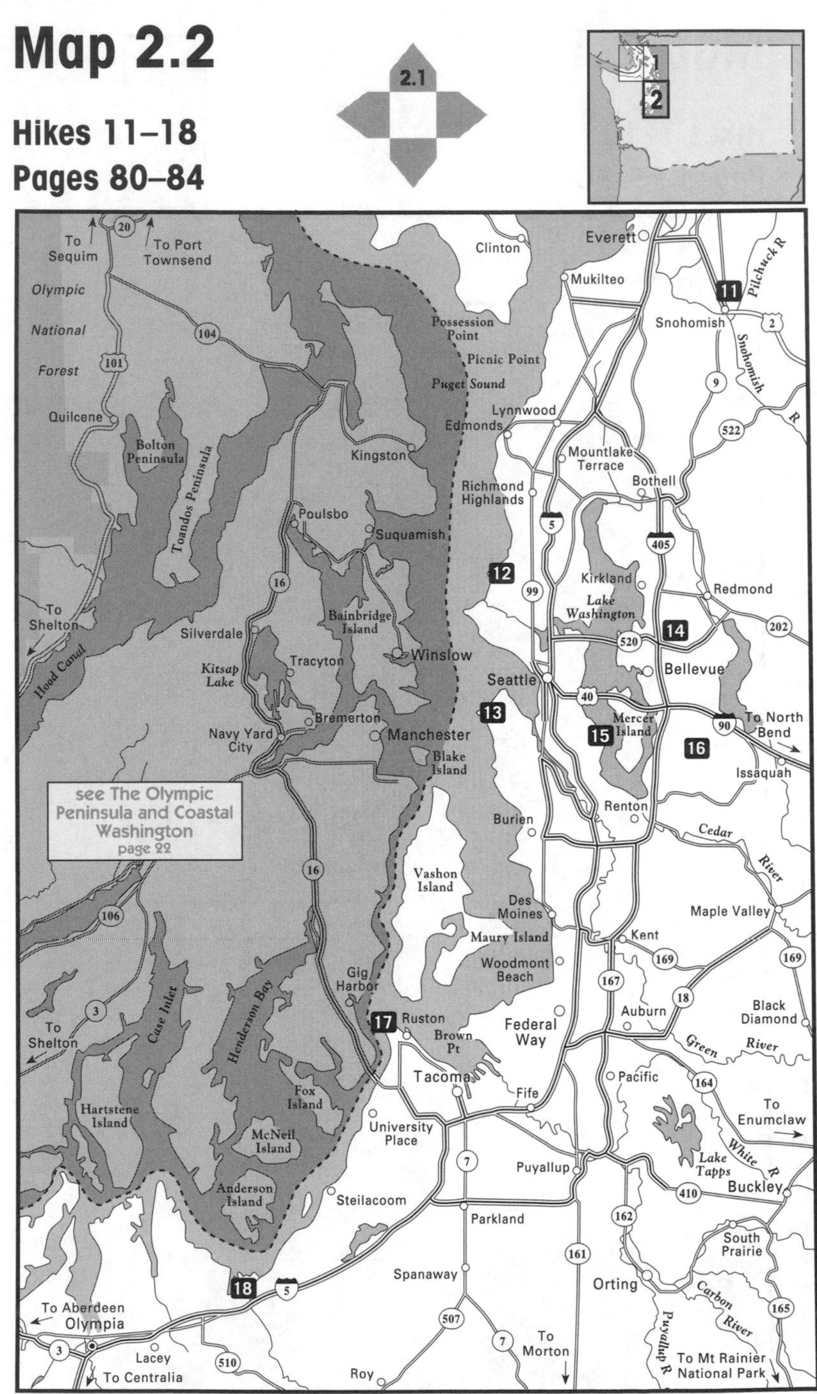

1 TENNANT LAKE

0.8–4.4 mi/1.0–2.5 hr

south of Ferndale in Tennant Lake County Park

Map 2.1, page 73

Pristine wetlands are hard to come by within the lower Nooksack River Valley, inundated by suburban sprawl and the spreading fields of agriculture, Fortunately, Tennant Lake Wildlife Area has preserved a chunk of these lands that are so important to wildlife. Spread over 624 acres, Tennant Lake Wildlife Area is an important spring and fall stopover for thousands of migratory birds, who make extensive use of the shallow lake and surrounding wetlands, fields, and forest. Three flat, easy trails meander through the park, a prime winter walk.

Tennant Lake Marsh Boardwalk is a 1.4-mile loop that explores most of the park. A well-built boardwalk helps to keep feet dry as the trail explores the marshes and wetlands. The route passes a 50-foot observation tower, which provides an awesome panoramic view of the area. A pair of binoculars comes in handy from the top. A longer hike can be made by following River Dike Trail (2.2 miles one-way). The trail follows the meandering Nooksack River through forest, wetlands, and neighboring farmlands. Finally, Hovander Park Trail (.4 mile one-way) visits the historic Hovander Homestead along wooded boardwalk.

User Groups: Hikers and mountain bikes. No dogs or horses are allowed. Two of the trails are wheelchair accessible.

Open Seasons: This area is accessible year-round.

Permits: Permits are not required. Parking and access are free.

Maps: Maps of the trail system are posted at trailheads. For a topographic map, ask the USGS for Ferndale.

Directions: From Seattle, drive north on I-5 to Ferndale (Exit 262). Turn left (west) on Main Street and drive .5 mile to Hovander Road. Turn left and drive to Nielsen Avenue. Turn right and follow signs to Tennant Lake Interpretive Center (end of Nielsen Avenue). The trailhead is at the interpretive center.

Contact: Tennant Lake Interpretive Center, 5236 Nielsen Road, Ferndale, WA 98248, 360/384-3064.

2 WHATCOM FALLS

0.5–2.0 mi/0.5–1.0 hr

in Bellingham

Map 2.1, page 73

Residents of Bellingham are lucky to have Whatcom Falls in their own backyard. In one of Washington's best municipal parks, several miles of trail explore Whatcom Creek and its large sets of falls. The park is ideal for rambling as the network of trails weaves along the creek and through the forest. Pipeline Trail is the main artery of the park, running for several miles along Whatcom Creek. This park was once the scene of a tragic accident. In the late 1990s, several people were killed when a natural-gas pipeline exploded, igniting a fire along half of the park. Burned trees and denuded slopes are a testament to this sad misfortune, but the area is quickly revegetating. A fish hatchery is in the center of the park and is open to the public. Access to the hatchery is via an old stone bridge constructed by the Depression-era Works Progress Administration. The scenic bridge overlooks Whatcom Falls, just one in a series of cascades. A short distance downstream are another set of falls, viewable from Pipeline Trail.

User Groups: Hikers, leashed dogs, and mountain bikes. No horses are allowed. Parts of the trails are wheelchair accessible.

Open Seasons: This area is accessible year-round.

Permits: Permits are not required. Parking and access are free.

Maps: Maps of the trail system are posted at trailheads. For a topographic map, ask the USGS for Bellingham South.

Directions: From downtown Bellingham, drive east on Lakeway Drive to Electric Avenue.

Turn right and drive .25 mile to Silver Beach Road. Turn left into the park entrance. The trailhead is on the west side of the parking lot.
Contact: Bellingham City Parks, 3424 Meridian Street, Bellingham, WA 98225, 360/676-6985.

3 MORAN STATE PARK
0.5–7.4 mi/0.5–4.0 hr

on Orcas Island in Moran State Park

Map 2.1, page 73

One of Washington's most beautiful and most popular state parks, Moran State Park rarely fails to impress. Situated on Orcas Island, the park is crowned by 2,409-foot Mount Constitution. It's the highest point in the San Juan Island chain, and the views from the summit are unbelievable. More than 30 miles of hiking trails lie within the park, exploring everything from forested lakes to the historic stone tower atop Mount Constitution. Whether you're visiting Orcas Island for a day or staying overnight at the campground, the trails of Moran State Park are well worth hiking.

The diversity of trails allows visitors to find a hike that is best for them. Many trails are short and flat. Among the best of the easy trails is Cascade Falls Trail, a quick .5-mile hike to the large waterfall on Cascade Creek. This is a real gusher during the springtime. Longer but just as flat is Mountain Lake Loop Trail, a 3.9-mile route around the park's largest body of water. Mountain Lake Trail starts at the large campground along the lake's shores.

The most popular destination for many visitors is the summit of Mount Constitution. Although one can drive to the top, Twin Lakes Trail is a survey of the park. Twin Lakes Trail skirts Mountain Lake before following a creek to Twin Lakes (1.5 miles), where loops circle both small lakes. The latter half of the trail switchbacks steeply to the summit (3.7 miles), where an old stone watchtower provides a panorama. The San Juans and Puget Sound are revealed in full glory, while Mount Baker rests behind the growing city of Bellingham.

User Groups: Hikers, leashed dogs, and mountain bikes (mountain bikes allowed September 15–May 15). No horses are allowed. No wheelchair access.
Open Seasons: This area is accessible year-round.
Permits: A $5 day-use fee is required to park here and is payable at the trailhead, or you can get an annual State Parks Pass for $30; contact Washington State Parks and Recreation, 360/902-8500.
Maps: Maps of the trail system are available at trailheads. For a topographic map, ask the USGS for Mount Constitution.
Directions: From the ferry terminal on Orcas Island, drive 13 miles on Horseshoe Highway (Orcas Road) to the park entrance. There are several trailheads within the park, all of them well signed.
Contact: Moran State Park, Star Route 22, Eastsound, WA, 98245, 360/376-2326.

4 LARRABEE STATE PARK
0.5–8.0 mi/1.0–4.0 hr

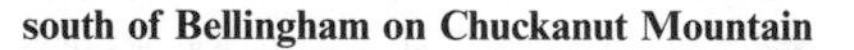

south of Bellingham on Chuckanut Mountain

Map 2.1, page 73

Spanning an area from the shores of Puget Sound to the crest of Chuckanut Mountain, Larrabee State Park is a treasure for hikers. Larrabee was Washington's first state park and even today is one of its largest. A diverse mix of trails varies from a beach ramble to a hike to several high, forested lakes. Trails to Clayton Beach and Teddy Bear Cove (each about .5 mile round-trip, accessible from Highline Road) drop to the sandy shores of Chuckanut Bay and Puget Sound. The beaches are strewn with boulders and driftwood. Best of all, this area lies within the rain shadow of the Olympic Peninsula, meaning it receives about half the rain of the Seattle area.

Longer trails lead up the western slopes of Chuckanut Mountain to Fragrance (2 miles) and Lost Lakes (4 miles). Surrounded by lush forests, these large lakes are favorite haunts for

both campers and anglers. Along the way to the lakes are numerous viewpoints of the San Juan Islands and Strait of Juan de Fuca.
User Groups: Hikers, leashed dogs, horses, and mountain bikes. No wheelchair access.
Open Seasons: This area is accessible year-round.
Permits: A $5 day-use fee is required to park here and is payable at the trailhead, or you can get an annual State Parks Pass for $30; contact Washington State Parks and Recreation, 360/902-8500.
Maps: For a topographic map, ask the USGS for Bellingham South.
Directions: From Seattle, drive north on I-5 to Chuckanut Drive (Exit 231). Turn left (west) and drive 14.5 miles to the park entrance. The trailhead is just inside the park entrance.
Contact: Larrabee State Park, 245 Chuckanut Drive, Bellingham, WA 98226, 360/676-2093.

5 PINE AND CEDAR LAKES

4.8 mi/3.0 hr 3 9

south of Bellingham on Chuckanut Mountain

Map 2.1, page 73

Famous as a colorful drive during the fall, Chuckanut Mountain also has some great trails. Here, on the eastern end of the long mountain ridge, are Pine and Cedar Lakes. These are a pair of mountain lakes well regarded for their views and fishing. A single trail leads to both of them, just a few hundred yards apart. Pine and Cedar Lakes Trail climbs steeply for the first 1.5 miles through a terrific forest of broad-leafed trees. It's hikable year-round, but October is a grand time to visit, when the forest is ignited by autumn color. The trail reaches a junction–Cedar Lake to the left and Pine Lake to the right. Both lakes are forested and have a subalpine feel to them, odd given that the altitude here is 1,600 feet. Several campsites are also found at each lake. A loop trail encircles Cedar Lake, which also has a side trail leading to a high viewpoint.
User Groups: Hikers, leashed dogs, horses, and mountain bikes. No wheelchair access.
Open Seasons: This area is accessible year-round.
Permits: Permits are not required. Parking and access are free.
Maps: For a topographic map, ask the USGS for Bellingham South.
Directions: From Bellingham, drive south on I-5 to North Lake Samish Exit. Turn right (west) onto North Lake Samish Drive and drive to Old Samish Road. Turn left and drive 2.5 miles to the signed trailhead on the left.
Contact: Whatcom County Parks and Recreation, 3373 Mount Baker Highway, Bellingham, WA 98226, 360/733-2900.

6 WASHINGTON PARK

2.6 mi/1.5 hr

in Anacortes on Puget Sound

Map 2.1, page 73

On the shores of Puget Sound and within the city limits of Anacortes, Washington Park gets far less attention than it deserves. Thousands of people pass right by the park on their way to the ferry to the San Juan Islands. But Washington Park is just as great, with more than 40,000 feet of shoreline and a 220-acre forest of cedar, fir, and madrona. Washington Park sits on a rocky point of Fidalgo Head, a large peninsula surrounded by saltwater and views. Although a road rounds the park, the best views are from Fidalgo Head Loop Trail, the main route through the park.

Fidalgo Head Loop Trail explores the perimeters of the park with frequent views of Puget Sound and the San Juan Islands. Numerous small side trails depart from this main artery, so it's a good idea to check out a trail map at the trailhead. Juniper Point and Burrows Trail are good, quick add-ons to Loop Trail. Elevation gains are modest, and the trail is easy enough for hikers of all abilities. Wildlife is plentiful, especially waterfowl. Brant, loons, murrelets, scoters, grebes, and hooded mergansers are frequently sighted, so a camera or binoculars are handy.

User Groups: Hikers, leashed dogs, and mountain bikes. No horses are allowed. No wheelchair access.
Open Seasons: This area is accessible year-round.
Permits: Permits are not required. Parking and access are free.
Maps: For a topographic map, ask the USGS for Anacortes North.
Directions: From Seattle, drive north on I-5 to Highway 20 (Exit 230). Head west on Highway 20 to Anacortes. Take Commercial Street to 12th Street. Turn left and drive 3 miles to Washington Park. The trailhead is located at the parking lot, just inside the park entrance.
Contact: Anacortes Parks and Recreation, P.O. Box 547, Anacortes, WA 98221, 360/293-1918.

7 DECEPTION PASS STATE PARK

1.0–12.0 mi/1.0–6.0 hr

on northern Whidbey Island in Deception Pass State Park

Map 2.1, page 73

A wide network of trails winds throughout this park, one of Washington State's most beautiful. More than 35 miles of trails lead through great forests to loads of seashore exploring. Tides rush water through the pass between Skagit Bay and Rosario Strait as though it were a river. Beaches edged by contorted pines and madronas offer chances to see orcas and sea otters in the water. Numerous upland trails offer great opportunities for runs and more extended hiking.

The park is split between Fidalgo Island and Whidbey Island. A large bridge spans the pass to connect the two islands. The best beach hiking is along Rosario Beach, on Fidalgo Island, where the Samish legend of the Maiden of Deception Pass is recounted. Signed reader boards provide maps for a number of trails around Rosario Beach and Bowman Bay. Be sure to pick up a map, which shows trails and distances, to see the route and distance of the hike you wish to take.

On Whidbey Island, trails of interest include one running from West Point, on Rosario Strait, along the pass channel to Haypus Point and Goose Rock. The many upland trails on this side of the island are often visited by mountain bikers. In all, there are nine islands within the state park, some of which can be reached only by canoe. More than 250 campsites are here for those wishing to spend the night, but they go quickly, as nearly three million people a year visit the park. Finally, it pays to be cautious when hiking here. The park staff spends a considerable amount of time performing first aid and rescue for folks, especially kids, who wander too close to cliff edges.
User Groups: Hikers, leashed dogs, and mountain bikes. No horses are allowed. Some trails are wheelchair accessible.
Open Seasons: This area is accessible year-round.
Permits: A $5 day-use fee is required to park here and is payable at the trailhead, or you can get an annual State Parks Pass for $30; contact Washington State Parks and Recreation, 360/902-8500.
Maps: Maps of the trail system are available at trailheads. For a topographic map, ask the USGS for Deception Pass.
Directions: From Mount Vernon, drive west 18 miles on Highway 20 toward Oak Harbor. Entrances to the park, before and after crossing Deception Pass by way of a high bridge, are along Highway 20 and well signed. Trail maps at each entrance show the exact locations of each trailhead.
Contact: Deception Pass State Park, Highway 20, Oak Harbor, WA 98277, 360/675-2417.

8 FORT EBEY

6.0 mi/3.0 hr

south of Oak Harbor on Whidbey Island

Map 2.1, page 73

Shake those wintertime blues and enjoy the drier climate of Whidbey Island. Situated in the rain shadow of the Olympic Mountains, America's longest island gets less than half the annual rainfall of Seattle. Fort Ebey is a great alternative to the crowds of people visiting the better-known Deception Pass State Park. A large trail network of more than 20 miles spreads out over the forested park, popular with mountain bikers. The highlight of Fort Ebey is Bluff Trail, six miles of wide, level trail extending along the high cliffs bordering the water. This is the most popular and scenic trail in the park, with outstanding views of the Olympic Mountains and Strait of Juan de Fuca. Lucky hikers may see a pod of orcas in the water below. Although rain is sparse here, wind isn't; remember an extra layer in all seasons. The park has several large cannon emplacements along the hillside overlooking the Strait of Juan de Fuca. Together with similar emplacements at Fort Worden and Fort Casey, these cannons formed a "Triangle of Fire," rendering the Puget Sound invulnerable to invasion during World War II. Fortunately, the invasion never arrived. There is a large car campground in the park, which is bordered by Kettles Park with even more trails to explore.

User Groups: Hikers, leashed dogs, and mountain bikes. No horses are allowed. No wheelchair access.

Open Seasons: This area is accessible year-round.

Permits: A $5 day-use fee is required to park here and is payable at the trailhead, or you can get an annual State Parks Pass for $30; contact Washington State Parks and Recreation, 360/902-8500.

Maps: Maps of the trail system are posted at trailheads. For a topographic map, ask the USGS for Port Townsend North.

Directions: From the ferry terminal in Clinton, on Whidbey Island, drive north 30 miles on Highway 525 to Libby Road. Turn left (west) and drive 1 mile to Valley Drive. Turn left and drive right into the park entrance. The trailhead is inside the park entrance and marked by a sign.

Contact: Fort Ebey State Park, 395 Fort Ebey Road, Coupeville, WA 98239, 360/678-4636.

9 SOUTH WHIDBEY STATE PARK

1.0–1.5 mi/1.0 hr 1 9

north of Clinton on Whidbey Island

Map 2.1, page 73

South Whidbey State Park remains far less known than its sister to the north, Deception Pass, but its scenery is just as great. On Admiralty Inlet, between Bush and Lagoon Points, the park offers great strolling along the peaceful beach or hiking within a stand of old-growth forest. From the day-use parking area, an unnamed path leads down to the water. The sandy beach stretches nearly a mile along Smugglers Cove. Wind-swept trees appear gnarly and stunted, growing out of the sides of the steep hillsides. Don't be surprised to spot sea otters playing and feeding offshore. A one-mile signed nature loop investigates the cliffs overlooking Admiralty Inlet, where lucky hikers can spot orcas in the water. For a quick and shady hike, Wilbert Trail winds 1.5 miles through an old, large forest of fir and cedar. All trails are family friendly. South Whidbey State Park is also home to a large car campground.

User Groups: Hikers and leashed dogs. No horses or mountain bikes are allowed. No wheelchair access.

Open Seasons: This area is accessible year-round.

Permits: A $5 day-use fee is required to park here and is payable at the trailhead, or you can get an annual State Parks Pass for $30; contact Washington State Parks and Recreation, 360/902-8500.

Maps: Maps of the trail system are posted at trailheads. For a topographic map, ask the USGS for Freeland.

Directions: From the ferry terminal in Clinton, drive north 10.5 miles on Highway 525 to Bush Point Road. Turn left and drive 5 miles (as the road becomes Smugglers Cove Road) to the park entrance on the left. The trailhead is inside the park entrance and marked by a sign.

Contact: South Whidbey State Park, 4128 Smugglers Cove Road, Freeland, WA 98249, 360/331-4559.

10 PADILLA BAY

0.8–4.6 mi/0.5–2.5 hr

west of Mount Vernon on Puget Sound

Map 2.1, page 73

On the shores of large Padilla Bay, this wildlife refuge provides excellent walks through important wildlife habitat. Although the area was disturbed for agricultural use more than 100 years ago, the area is flourishing as bird habitat today. Thousands of migrating marsh and shore birds stop through the reserve during the spring and fall. The area is also important habitat for many marine animals. Open year-round, Padilla Bay makes a great place to stretch the legs during winter.

A pair of trails explores the federally protected reserve. Upland Trail, a short .8-mile loop, leaves from the Breazeale Center to explore open meadows and sparse forest. Interpretive guides are available from the Breazeale Center, explaining different sightings along the way. The beginning of the trail reaches a viewing platform and is accessible to wheelchairs.

A longer hike can be made along Shore Trail, a 2.3-mile graveled path along a dike bordering Padilla Bay. The route explores the tidal slough and open mud flats of the bay, a good place to see wildlife. Views of the Olympics and even Mount Baker can be had while enjoying the salty marine air of Puget Sound. The path ends at Bayview State Park, home to a large campground.

User Groups: Hikers, leashed dogs, and mountain bikes (dogs and mountain bikes allowed on Shore Trail). No horses are allowed. Parts of the trails are wheelchair accessible.

Open Seasons: This area is accessible year-round.

Permits: Permits are not required. Parking and access are free.

Maps: Maps of the trail system are posted at trailheads. For a topographic map, ask the USGS for Anacortes South and LaConner.

Directions: From Seattle, drive north on I-5 to Highway 20 (Exit 230). Turn left (west) and drive 5 miles to Farm to Market Road. Turn right (north) and drive 2 miles to Josh Wilson Road. Turn left and drive 1.5 miles to Bayview-Edison Road. Turn right and drive .5 miles to Breazeale Interpretive Center, where the trailhead is located.

Contact: Padilla Bay National Estuarine Research Reserve, 10441 Bayview-Edison Road, Mount Vernon, WA 98273, 360/428-1558.

11 SNOHOMISH CENTENNIAL TRAIL

1.0–17.0 mi/1.0 hr–1 day

in Snohomish County

Map 2.2, page 74

One of Washington's many rails-to-trails projects, Snohomish Centennial Trail runs along 17 miles of old railroad line. The original segment of trail ran from Lake Stevens to Snohomish, but recent years have seen lengthy additions (an extra 10 miles between Lake Stevens and Arlington). Total length of the trail now runs 17 miles and is likely to continue growing. The trail rambles through the rural countryside of Snohomish County, through open fields into dense, shady forest. Views of the surrounding Cascade Mountains are nearly constant (except when in the woods, of course). This is a very popular mountain bike and equestrian trail. The 7 miles between Lake Stevens and Snohomish are paved. Hikers can take the trail for as long as they please; since the views are fairly consistent, they can turn around at any point.

User Groups: Hikers, leashed dogs, horses, and mountain bikes. The trail is wheelchair accessible (the trail is a mix of gravel and pavement).

Open Seasons: This area is accessible year-round.

Permits: Permits are not required. Parking and access are free.

Maps: For topographic maps, ask the USGS for Snohomish and Lake Stevens.

Directions: From Seattle, drive north on I-5 to Highway 2 (Exit 194). Drive east to the town

of Snohomish. The trailhead is at the intersection of Maple Street and Pine Avenue.
Contact: Snohomish County Parks and Recreation, 9623 32nd Street Southeast, Everett, WA 98205, 425/388-6600.

12 CARKEEK PARK
0.5–3.0 mi/0.5–2.0 hr

in Seattle on Puget Sound

Map 2.2, page 74

A flurry of recent work at Carkeek Park has turned it into one of Seattle's best in-city destinations for hiking. Trail work combined with revegetative plantings along several routes has shored up eroded areas and erased evidence of overuse and abuse. Stream restoration work has turned Piper Creek, which runs through the park, into one of Seattle's most promising salmon streams. Visit Carkeek in the spring or fall and you're likely to see salmon struggling up the short creek on their way to spawn. Wetland Trail is made of well-constructed boardwalk and explores Piper Creek for .5 mile. Other trails head up into the young forest covering the slopes of Carkeek Park. North Bluff Trail hits several great viewpoints overlooking Puget Sound and the wide beach below. Carkeek is a wonderful hideaway within the city limits.
User Groups: Hikers, leashed dogs, and mountain bikes. No horses are allowed. No wheelchair access.
Open Seasons: This area is accessible year-round.
Permits: Permits are not required. Parking and access are free.
Maps: Maps of the trail system are available at the trailhead kiosk.
Directions: From I-5 in Seattle, exit at Northgate Way (Exit 173). Head west on Northgate Way (it becomes 105th Street) to Greenwood Avenue. Turn right and drive to 110th Street. Turn left and drive about 1 mile as the street becomes Northwest Carkeek Park Road and curves down to the park entrance. The trailhead is located at the main parking lot within the park, at the end of the road.
Contact: Seattle City Parks and Recreation, 100 Dexter Avenue North, Seattle, WA 98109, 206/684-4075.

13 DISCOVERY PARK
2.8 mi/1.5 hr

in Seattle along Puget Sound

Map 2.2, page 74

Discovery Park is a perfect model of reclaiming an abandoned military base and releasing it to public use. Seattle City Parks took over the former Fort Lawton years ago and has turned it into one of the city's premier open spaces. The park sits on a high bluff overlooking Puget Sound. Watching the sun set over the Olympic Mountains from here makes for an evening to remember. Seven miles of trail explore the park, but the highlight is 2.8-mile Nature Loop Trail. The route enjoys a little bit of everything, passing old army barracks, weaving through old forest, and hitting a number of great viewpoints. Several steep side trails offer access to the sandy beach. The beach is well worth exploring during low tide, when tidal pools and their inhabitants (crabs, mussels, and tiny fish) are exposed. Although Discovery Park is in the midst of Washington's largest city, it's easy to feel as though you're miles away.
User Groups: Hikers, leashed dogs, and mountain bikes. No horses are allowed. No wheelchair access.
Open Seasons: This area is accessible year-round.
Permits: Permits are not required. Parking and access are free.
Maps: Maps of the trail system are posted at trailheads. For a topographic map, ask the USGS for Seattle North.
Directions: From Ballard (in Seattle), drive south on 15th Avenue Northwest to Emerson Street. Turn right and drive to West Gilman Street. Turn right and drive 2 miles to the park

entrance. The main trailhead at the visitors center is .2 mile inside the entrance on the left.
Contact: Seattle City Parks and Recreation, 100 Dexter Avenue North, Seattle, WA 98109, 206/684-4075.

14 BRIDLE TRAILS
1.0–4.8 mi/1.0–2.5 hr

in Bellevue

Map 2.2, page 74

In the heart of Bellevue, Bridle Trails State Park is like stepping into a vortex. As busy shoppers crowd into the nearby shopping mall, a small oasis of lush forest crisscrossed by miles of trails offers a peaceful getaway. Hikers be forewarned, however, as this is a popular and heavily used equestrian park. The occasional piles of horse apples are a small price for such an accessible forest getaway. Nearly 30 miles of trail form a large network within the 500 acres of park. Few specific routes exist, as the best strategy is to just start rambling through the woods. A popular choice is to hike the perimeter of the park, a 4.8-mile loop. All trails within the park are relatively flat, wide, and easy to negotiate, and some are as short as 1 mile. Bridle Trails offers great springtime hiking, when the Cascades are full of snow but trillium and other flowers are blooming within the park.
User Groups: Hikers, leashed dogs, and horses. No mountain bikes are allowed. No wheelchair access.
Open Seasons: This area is accessible year-round.
Permits: A $5 day-use fee is required to park here and is payable at the trailhead, or you can get an annual State Parks Pass for $30; contact Washington State Parks and Recreation, 360/902-8500.
Maps: Maps of the trail system are posted at trailheads. For a topographic map, ask the USGS for Bellevue North.
Directions: From I-405 in Bellevue, take Exit 17. Turn right onto 116th Avenue and drive to Northeast 53rd Street. The park entrance is on the left. The main trailhead is near the park entrance at the main parking area.
Contact: Washington State Parks and Recreation, P.O. Box 42650, Olympia, WA 98504-2669, 360/902-8844.

15 SEWARD PARK
1.8 mi/1.0 hr

in Seattle on Lake Washington

Map 2.2, page 74

One doesn't have to go far from Seattle to enjoy a stand of magnificent old-growth forest. In fact, one needn't even leave the city limits. On Bailey Peninsula, which juts into Lake Washington in South Seattle, Seward Park contains the largest stand of forest in the city. A wide, flat trail explores the forest and makes a loop along the waterfront. The forest has many large, towering Douglas firs and beautiful madronas with their peeling bark. A rich understory of salal, thimbleberry, and salmonberry creates a cool, peaceful interior. Although there is a network of small social trails, it's best to stick to the established path to avoid getting lost. The trail cuts through the park to the shore of Lake Washington. From here, hikers can walk the shore back to the parking area.
User Groups: Hikers, leashed dogs, and mountain bikes. No horses are allowed. The trails are wheelchair accessible.
Open Seasons: This area is accessible year-round.
Permits: Permits are not required. Parking and access are free.
Maps: Maps of the trail system are posted at trailheads. For a topographic map, ask the USGS for Seattle South.
Directions: From I-5 northbound, take Swift Avenue (exit 161) toward Albro Place. Turn right onto Swift Avenue and drive to Eddy Street. Turn left and drive to Beacon Avenue South. Turn left and drive to Orcas Street. Turn right and follow this street as it becomes Lake Washington Boulevard and hits the well-signed

Seward Park. The trailhead is at the main parking area at the end of the park entrance road.

Contact: Seattle City Parks and Recreation, 100 Dexter Avenue North, Seattle, WA 98109, 206/684-4075.

16 COUGAR MOUNTAIN

0.5–6.0 mi/0.5–3.0 hr

south of Bellevue in Cougar Mountain Regional Park

Map 2.2, page 74

The most western of the Issaquah Alps, Cougar Mountain is sanctuary in Seattle's backyard. Now encroached upon by development on all sides, the county park has become a near island of forest. Despite the close proximity of the city, Cougar Mountain and its large network of trails can feel like a step into the wilderness. A pair of trailheads offers access to roughly 30 miles of trail crisscrossing the 3,000 acres of Cougar Mountain. Red Town lies near the bottom on the south side while a second trailhead exists atop the mountain at Anti-Aircraft Peak. This area is great for wintertime hiking, when snow covers much of the Cascades. Pick up a map, available at trailheads, to choose which hike you want to do.

From Red Town, a number of hikes can be custom-made. Coal Creek Trail runs through an open forest of big-leaf maple and red alder, encountering numerous mining artifacts. This area was heavily mined for coal until as recently as the 1960s. Be sure to carry a map, for many trails venture off the main artery. Good side trips include Bagley Seam Trail, Wildside Trail, and Rainbow Town Trail.

From Anti-Aircraft Peak, Anti-Aircraft Trail delves into the open forest that covers the mountain. Deer make common company along the way, as do coyotes and mountain beavers. Again, bring a map when hiking here. The trails are unmarked and it's easy to get turned around. The trails provide several opportunities for easy or challenging loops.

User Groups: Hikers, leashed dogs, horses, and mountain bikes. No wheelchair access.

Open Seasons: This area is accessible year round.

Permits: Permits are not required. Parking and access are free.

Maps: Maps of the trail system are posted at trailheads. For a topographic map, ask the USGS for Bellevue South.

Directions: For Red Town, take Exit 13 off I-90 and turn south on Lakemount Boulevard. Drive 3 miles to the signed entrance on the left.

For Radar Park, which allows access to Anti-Aircraft Peak, take Exit 11 off I-90. Drive south on Southeast Newport Way to 164th Avenue. Turn right and drive to Cougar Mountain Drive. Turn right and drive 1 mile to the signed entrance.

Contact: Cougar Mountain Regional Wildland Park, King County Parks and Recreation, 201 South Jackson Street, Suite 700, Seattle, WA 98104, 206/296-8687.

17 POINT DEFIANCE

1.2–4.1 mi/2.0–4.0 hr

in Tacoma on Puget Sound

Map 2.2, page 74

The feather in Tacoma's cap, Point Defiance is a rare respite from the noise of the city. Secluded on a large point jutting into Commencement Bay, Point Defiance lays claim to miles of waterfront and some of the Puget Sound's best views. While its exact ranking is left open to debate, Point Defiance is unquestionably one of the largest urban parks in North America. Large conifer forests grace nearly 20 miles of trail, a welcome change of scenery from Tacoma's industrial core. Point Defiance is also home to the city's zoo and aquarium; the roar of an elephant shouldn't be a surprise. Tacoma locals dearly love Point Defiance.

There are several options for exploring Point Defiance. Short walks can be made along Waterfront Promenade, stretching from Owen Beach to a small assortment of restaurants. This short trail (.6 mile) is paved and accessible to wheelchairs. Other trails take on more

natural forms (dirt pathways) through the forest. Running along the cliffs that mark the edge of much of the park, Square Trail Outer Loop (4.1 miles) is by far the most scenic. It visits numerous overlooks of the sound, and scenes of the Tacoma Narrow Bridge are especially great. Triangle Trail Inner Loop (3.3 miles) makes a shorter trip with a couple of viewpoints of the sound, but it mostly stays within the forest. The most popular route is Spine Trail (2.1 miles), which runs straight through the park to a commanding viewpoint of Gig Harbor and the Narrows. Whatever your choice, enjoy the shady forest and rich ecosystem; even deer live within the park.

User Groups: Hikers, leashed dogs, and mountain bikes. No horses are allowed. The Waterfront Promenade is wheelchair accessible.

Open Seasons: This area is accessible year-round.

Permits: Permits are not required. Parking and access are free.

Maps: Maps of the trail system are posted at trailheads. For a topographic map, ask the USGS for Gig Harbor.

Directions: From I-5 in Tacoma, drive west on Highway 16 to Pearl Street exit. Turn right (north) and drive about 6 miles to the road's end at Point Defiance Park. Parking and trailheads are throughout the park.

Contact: Metro Parks Tacoma, 4702 South 19th Street, Tacoma, WA 98405, 253/305-1000.

18 NISQUALLY NATIONAL WILDLIFE REFUGE

1.0–5.0 mi/0.5–2.5 hr

north of Olympia on Puget Sound

Map 2.2, page 74

One of Western Washington's largest undisturbed estuaries, Nisqually National Wildlife Refuge is an unnoticed treasure along I-5. Here, where freshwater meets saltwater, a rich habitat exists for animals of all sorts but especially birds. Thousands of migratory birds pass through the refuge each spring and fall on their way to warming climates or feeding grounds. Mallards, widgeons, teal, Canada geese, red-tailed hawks, and great blue heron are regular sightings. Fortunately for those of us stuck on the ground, two loop trails explore this area.

© SCOTT LEONARD

Nisqually National Wildlife Refuge, along boardwalk

Much of the refuge is an expansive collection of marshes. The wide, slow-flowing Nisqually runs through the middle, but where the river ends and the sound begins is difficult to discern. Two loop trails run through the refuge. Both feature viewing platforms and blinds, where visitors can spy on wildlife without being noticed. It's a good idea to bring a pair of binoculars. A nice visitors center is open Wednesday–Sunday year-round.

Twin Barns Trail is a short one-mile loop with many interpretive signs explaining the history and ecology of the area. It's a great introduction to the refuge and the animals that live here. The trail is completely built of wooden boardwalk, making it accessible to all. A longer hike can be made by hiking Brown Farm Dike Trail, a five-mile loop around the perimeter of the refuge. This flat trail gets users close to the Nisqually River, Puget Sound, and McAllister Creek.

User Groups: Hikers only. No dogs, horses, or mountain bikes are allowed. The shorter of the two loops is wheelchair accessible.

Open Seasons: This area is accessible year-round.

Permits: A $3 day-use fee is required to park here and is payable at the trailhead.

Maps: Maps of the trail system are available at the visitor center. For a topographic map, ask the USGS for Nisqually.

Directions: From Seattle, drive south on I-5 to Nisqually (Exit 114). Turn right (west) onto Brown Farm Road and drive .3 mile to the well-signed trailhead.

Contact: Nisqually National Wildlife Refuge, 100 Brown Farm Road, Olympia, WA 98516, 360/753-9467.

Chapter 3

© SCOTT LEONARD

The Northern Cascades

The Northern Cascades

This region is home to a sizable chunk of Washington's greatest forests, mountains, and rivers. Hundreds of trails crisscross the enormous region, and nearly every one of them is great and exciting. It's truly hard to go wrong when setting out in the North Cascades. It's all a scenic playground, from ancient old-growth forests to alpine meadows, from wild and rushing rivers to enormous glaciers. (There are more glaciers here than in the rest of the lower 48 states combined!) The North Cascades are the playground of the Puget Sound region, with tons of trails less than two hours away.

Thanks to careful and diligent conservation, much of the North Cascades' natural beauty remains for us to enjoy. The region is home to one national park (North Cascades) and eight federally protected wildernesses (Alpine Lakes, Boulder River, Glacier Peak, Henry M. Jackson, Lake Chelan–Sawtooth, Mount Baker, Noisy-Diobsud, and Pasayten). Together, they make more than 2.5 million acres of protected land, possibly with more on the way. Another wilderness (the Big Sky, near Skykomish) has wide support from local communities and congresspeople and is very close to becoming official. (Unfortunately, a conservative congressman from California has repeatedly blocked this bill.)

The Alpine Lakes Wilderness offers the most easily accessed trails. Situated between Interstate 90 and Highway 2, many of these trailheads are less than a 90-minute drive from Seattle. Alpine Lakes is home to—you guessed it—hundreds of alpine lakes (technically subalpine). On the north side is the town of Leavenworth, up for debate as either cute or campy. Here, all buildings are required to incorporate Bavarian architecture, and it is certainly unlike any other town in the state (or outside of the Alps). It's interesting, to say the least. When you're itching to get outdoors for a quick hike, Alpine Lakes is a great place to start your search.

On the north side of Highway 2 are Henry M. Jackson and Glacier Peak Wildernesses. These two areas take up much of the North Cascades' central portion, about 670,000 acres. With glistening white glaciers covering its 10,541-foot summit, Glacier Peak is naturally the central focus of the area. Cady Ridge (both of them), Image Lake, and Buck Creek Pass are just a few of the excellent hikes in these wildernesses. These areas are also easily accessed by the Mountain Loop Highway. Cutting into the Cascades from Darrington, the route makes a large loop around the Boulder River Wilderness. This area is home to easy trails (Lake 22, Heather Lake, Goat Flats) and difficult trails alike (Mount Dickerson, Stujack Pass, Poodle Dog Pass).

Even with all these attractions, this isn't even half of what the North Cascades have to offer. The Mount Baker Wilderness, for one, contains alpine meadows that are absolutely amazing in July (when they're alive with wildflowers) and completely delicious in late August (when they're smothered in huckleberries). The insane beauty of Mount Baker and Mount Shuksan can almost go without saying. Head up Route 542 out of Bellingham for access to trails like Lake Ann, Hannegan Pass, and Chain Lakes.

Although North Cascades National Park and the Pasayten Wilderness are actually neighbors, they seem to be one entity. These two areas extend along a 70-mile stretch of the Canadian border, totaling 1,150,000 acres. Access is via Route 20, where glacier-capped mountains and old forests are regular sights from the road. Such a big area requires longer trips, and there are plenty to be found here. Day hikes to Driveway Butte and Desolation Peak are certainly possible, but such a short taste will definitely leave you wanting to spend at least four or five days on the trail. Copper Ridge, Whatcom Pass, Devil's Dome Loop, Boundary Trail, and Cathedral Basin are classics of the region. Folks on their way to the Pasayten will love the town of Winthrop, where the theme is Old West. A stop at Winthrop Brewing Company's local brewpub is a must, especially after your hike!

Finally, the east side of the Cascades is drier and often a great destination when the west side is rainy. (Like the Olympics, the Cascades act like a big squeegee, forcing moist air from the ocean to release most of its rain on the west side.) Many of the wilderness areas stretch across the Cascade Crest and have portions that benefit from this rain shadow effect. Highway 97 runs along the east side of the Cascades and provides access to many of these dry trails. The Lake Chelan–Sawtooth Wilderness is the heart and soul of the east side, with high, craggy peaks and mind-boggling views.

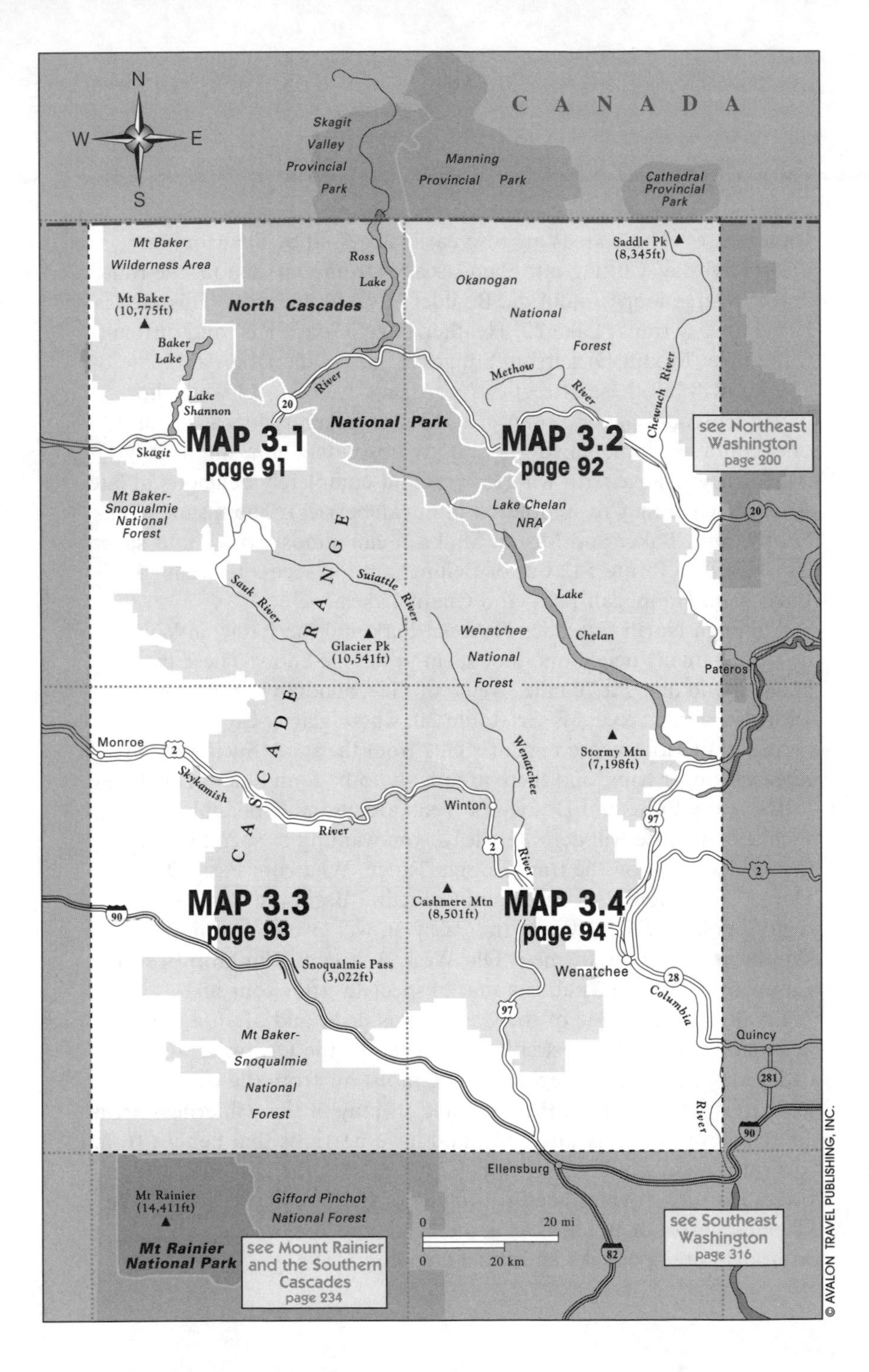

N
S
W
E
CANADA
Skagit Valley Provincial Park
Manning Provincial Park
Cathedral Provincial Park
Mt Baker Wilderness Area
Mt Baker (10,775ft)
Baker Lake
Lake Shannon
Ross Lake
North Cascades National Park
River
20
Skagit
Okanogan National Forest
Saddle Pk (8,345ft)
Methow River
Chewuch River
MAP 3.1
page 91
MAP 3.2
page 92
see Northeast Washington page 200
Mt Baker-Snoqualmie National Forest
CASCADE RANGE
Lake Chelan NRA
Lake Chelan
Sauk River
Suiattle River
Glacier Pk (10,541ft)
Wenatchee National Forest
Pateros
Monroe
2
Skykamish River
Stormy Mtn (7,198ft)
Wenatchee River
Winton
97
MAP 3.3
page 93
Cashmere Mtn (8,501ft)
MAP 3.4
page 94
90
Snoqualmie Pass (3,022ft)
Wenatchee
28
Columbia River
Quincy
281
Mt Baker-Snoqualmie National Forest
Ellensburg
Mt Rainier (14,411ft)
Mt Rainier National Park
Gifford Pinchot National Forest
see Mount Rainier and the Southern Cascades page 234
0
20 mi
20 km
82
see Southeast Washington page 316

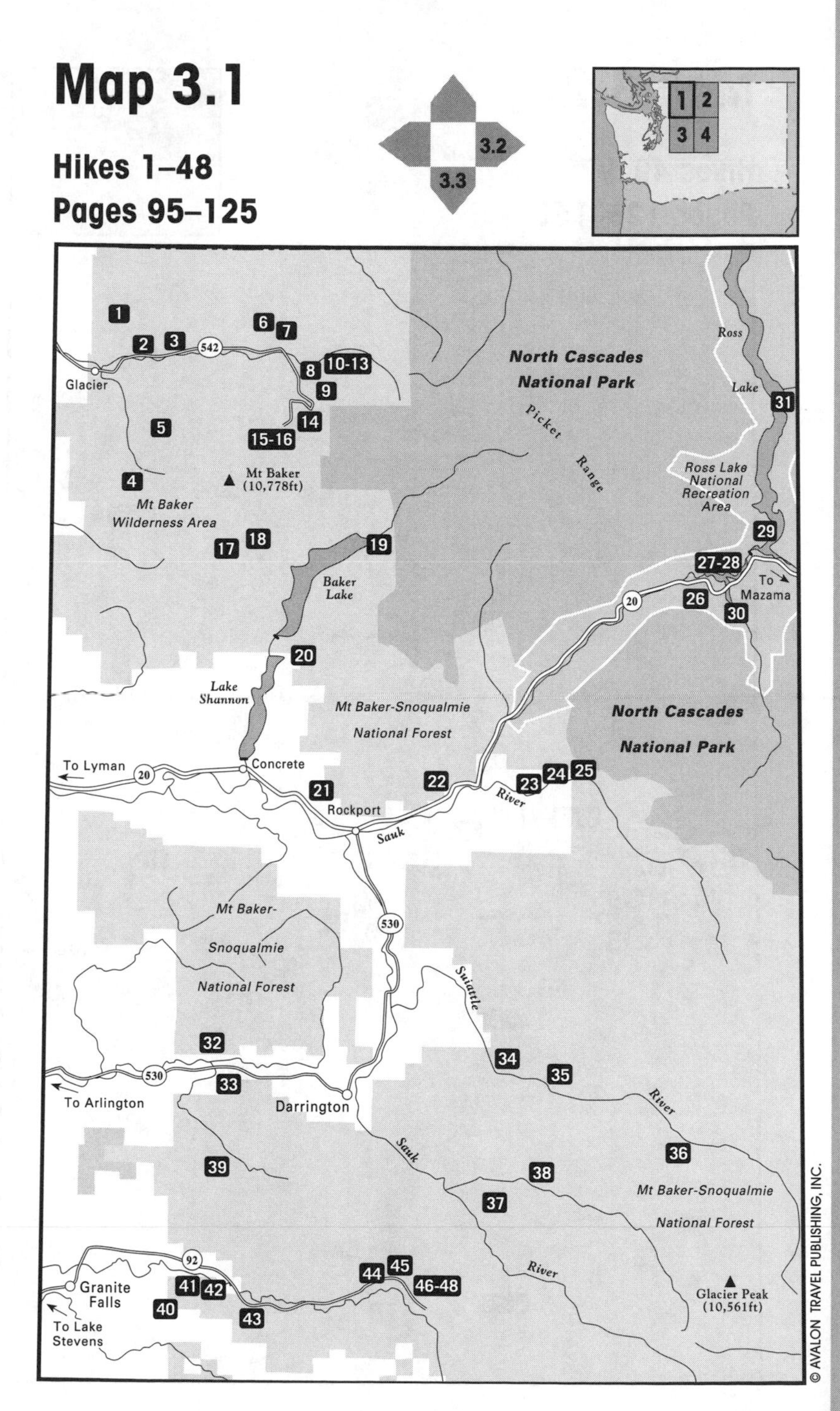
Map 3.1
Hikes 1–48
Pages 95–125
3.2
3.3
1
2
3
4
542
Glacier
5
6
7
8
9
10-13
14
15-16
Mt Baker
(10,778ft)
Mt Baker
Wilderness Area
17
18
19
Baker
Lake
20
Lake
Shannon
North Cascades
National Park
Picket
Range
Ross
Lake
31
Ross Lake
National
Recreation
Area
29
27-28
To
Mazama
26
30
20
North Cascades
National Park
Mt Baker-Snoqualmie
National Forest
To Lyman
20
Concrete
21
Rockport
22
23
24
25
River
Sauk
530
Mt Baker-
Snoqualmie
National Forest
Suiattle
32
530
To Arlington
33
Darrington
34
35
River
36
Sauk
39
38
37
Mt Baker-Snoqualmie
National Forest
92
Granite
Falls
To Lake
Stevens
40
41
42
43
44
45
46-48
River
Glacier Peak
(10,561ft)
© AVALON TRAVEL PUBLISHING, INC.

Map 3.2

Hikes 49–97
Pages 126–156

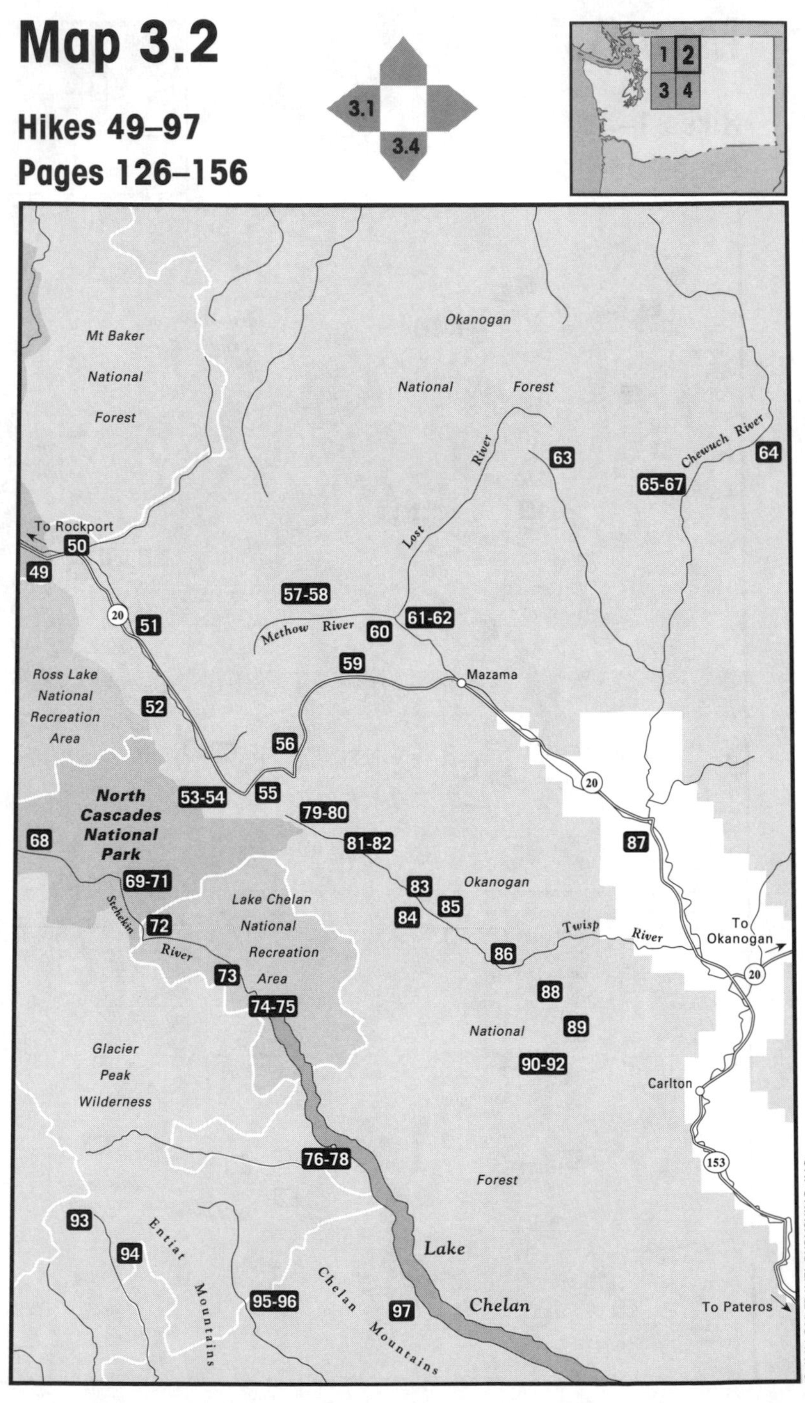

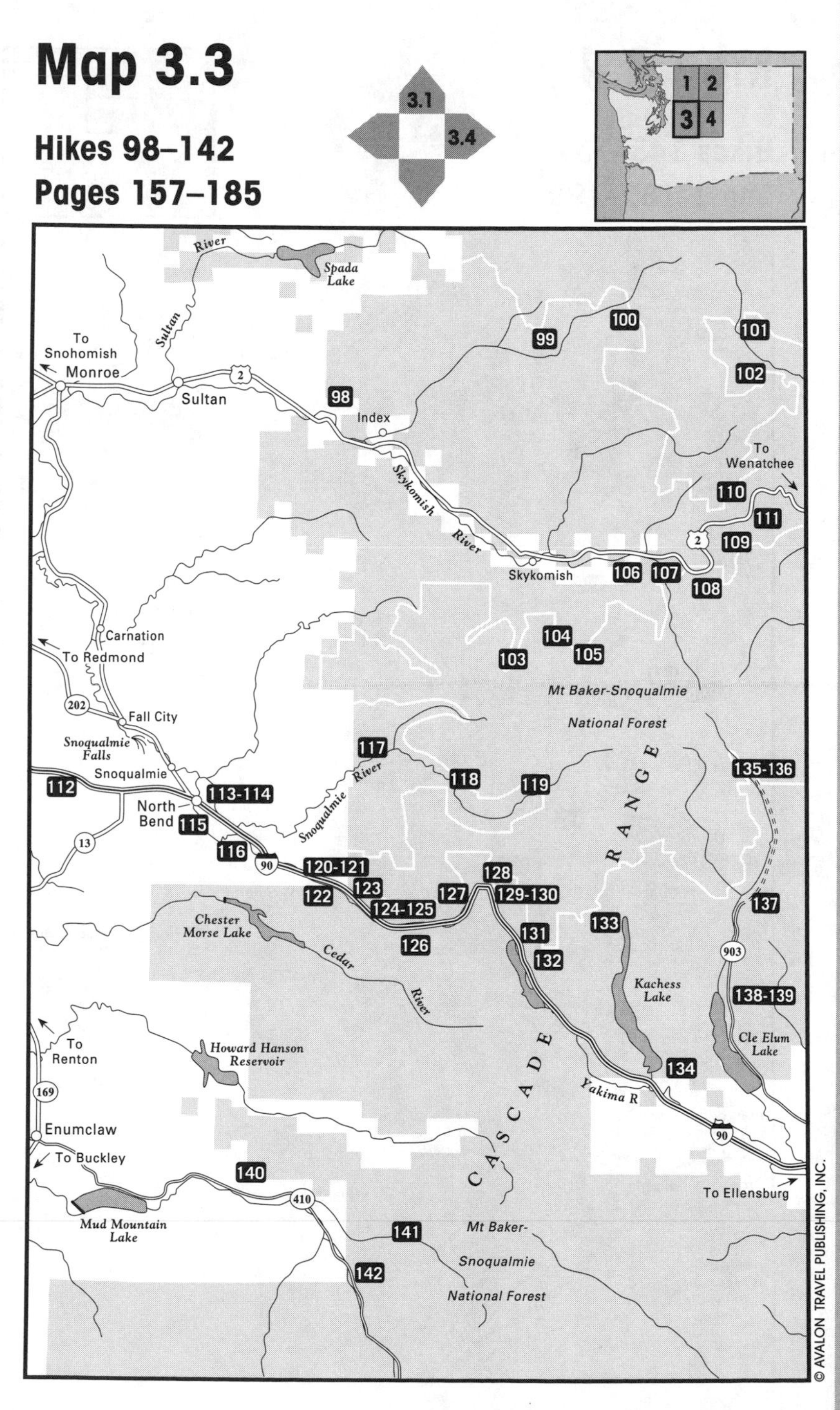

Map 3.3
Hikes 98–142
Pages 157–185
3.1
3.4
1 2
3 4
River
Spada Lake
Sultan
To Snohomish
Monroe
Sultan
2
98
99
100
101
102
Index
Skykomish River
To Wenatchee
110
111
109
2
Skykomish
106
107
108
Carnation
To Redmond
104
103
105
Mt Baker-Snoqualmie National Forest
202
Fall City
Snoqualmie Falls
Snoqualmie
117
Snoqualmie River
118
119
135-136
112
113-114
North Bend
115
13
116
90
120-121
122
123
124-125
127
128
129-130
137
Chester Morse Lake
126
131
133
132
903
Cedar River
Kachess Lake
138-139
Cle Elum Lake
To Renton
Howard Hanson Reservoir
134
169
Yakima R
Enumclaw
90
To Buckley
140
CASCADE RANGE
To Ellensburg
410
Mud Mountain Lake
141
Mt Baker-Snoqualmie National Forest
142
© AVALON TRAVEL PUBLISHING, INC.

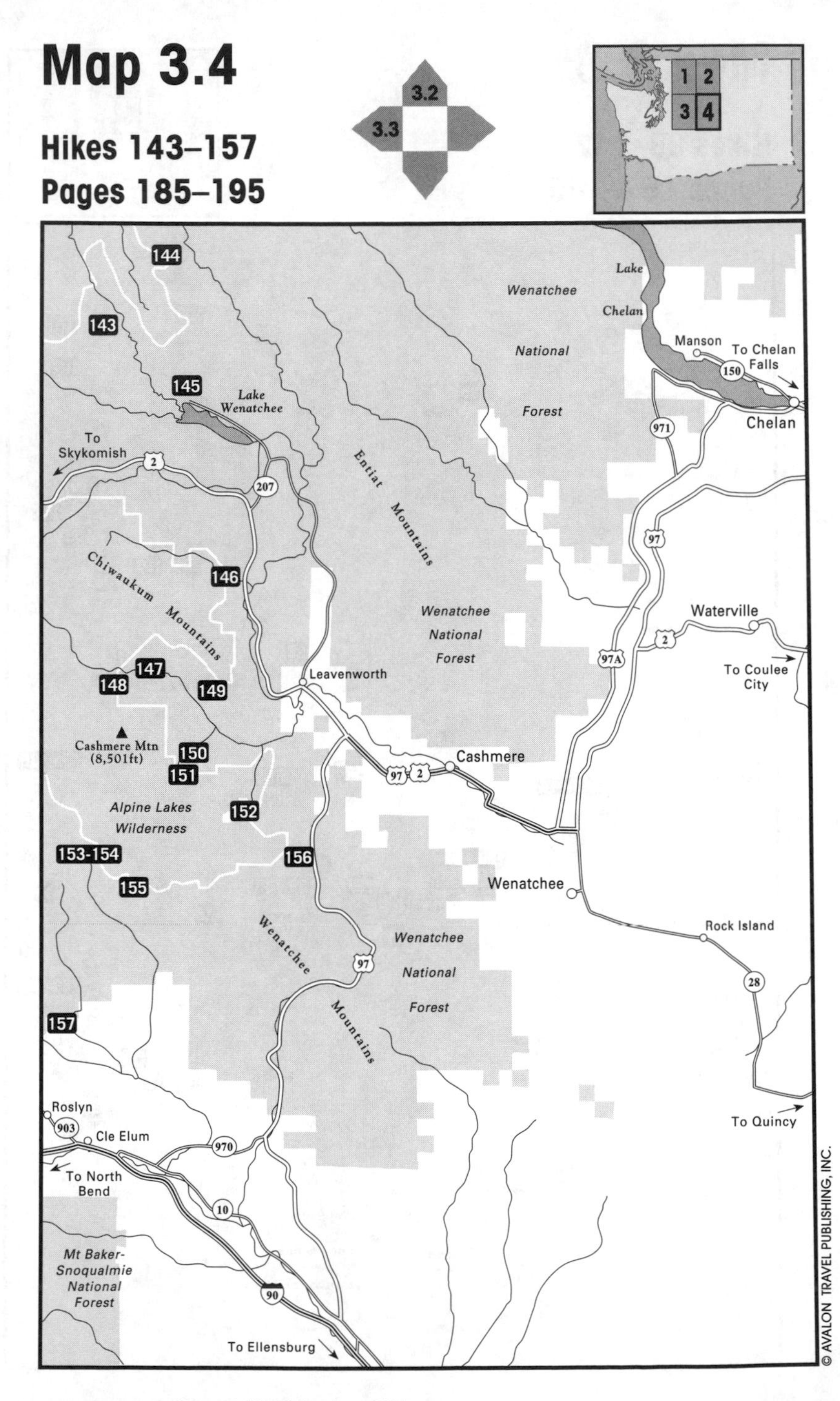
Map 3.4
Hikes 143–157
Pages 185–195
3.2
3.3
1
2
3
4
144
143
145
Lake Wenatchee
To Skykomish
2
207
Lake
Chelan
Wenatchee
National
Forest
Manson
To Chelan Falls
150
Chelan
971
Entiat Mountains
97
Chiwaukum Mountains
146
Wenatchee
National
Forest
Waterville
2
97A
To Coulee City
147
148
149
Leavenworth
Cashmere Mtn (8,501ft)
150
151
Cashmere
97
2
Alpine Lakes
Wilderness
152
153-154
156
155
Wenatchee
Rock Island
Wenatchee Mountains
Wenatchee
National
Forest
97
28
157
Roslyn
903
Cle Elum
970
To North Bend
To Quincy
10
Mt Baker-
Snoqualmie
National
Forest
90
To Ellensburg
© AVALON TRAVEL PUBLISHING, INC.

1 DAMFINO LAKES

1.4–19.6 mi/1.0–5.0 hr

east of Bellingham in Mount Baker–Snoqualmie National Forest

Map 3.1, page 91

Damfino Lakes are merely a starting point for hiking and exploration, as Damfino Lakes serve as a junction to several beautiful hikes. Canyon Ridge, regarded highly by the few who know of it, is accessible only via this trail. Excelsior Ridge, normally a long, steep climb, is achieved much more easily via Damfino Lakes Trail. Damfino Lakes Trail is more about what lies beyond the lakes than the lakes themselves.

Damfino Lakes Trail climbs gently through forest to the pair of lakes (.7 mile). From here, turn north and encounter the high meadow run of Canyon Ridge Trail (up to 9.8 miles one-way). Turn north at the lakes to head to Cowap Peak (elevation 5,658 feet), a summit for great views. A map and compass are highly recommended for these two trails.

Turn south at the lakes to climb gradually to the vast meadows of Excelsior Ridge (3 miles). This is a quicker and much easier shortcut to the ridge (one-third of the elevation gain and half the distance than from the traditional trailhead). So don't head for Damfino Lakes and stop there; the two small lakes are just the beginning.

User Groups: Canyon Ridge Trail is open to hikers, leashed dogs, horses, llamas, bicycles, and motorcycles. South of Damfino Lakes is open to hikers and leashed dogs. Boundary Way Trail is open to hikers, leashed dogs, and llamas. No wheelchair access.

Open Seasons: This area is usually accessible August–September.

Permits: A federal Northwest Forest Pass is required to park here.

Maps: For a map of Mount Baker–Snoqualmie National Forest, contact the Outdoor Recreation Information Center at the downtown Seattle REI. For topographic maps, ask Green Trails for No. 13, Mount Baker, or ask the USGS for Bearpaw Mountain.

Directions: From Bellingham, drive 36 miles east on Highway 542 (Mount Baker Highway) to Canyon Creek Road (Forest Service Road 31). Turn left (north) and drive 14.5 miles to the trailhead, on the right side at a sharp turn in the road.

Contact: Mount Baker–Snoqualmie National Forest, Glacier Public Service Center, Glacier, WA 98244, 360/599-2714.

2 CHURCH MOUNTAIN

8.4 mi/6.0 hr

east of Bellingham in Mount Baker–Snoqualmie National Forest

Map 3.1, page 91

One of the North Fork Nooksack River's finest hikes is fittingly one of its first. Church Mountain Trail rises through old-growth forest to an enormous basin and peak with views over the broad river valley to Mount Baker, Mount Shuksan, and much of Canada. It's not an easy height to achieve, as the 3,600-foot climb in just over four miles will attest. The trail offers enough wonder and inspiring views to more than make up for any weariness in the legs.

Church Mountain Trail starts off in a mean fashion, with a breath-stealing climb of switchbacks. These first two miles are mostly deep within virgin forest, with big trees providing welcome shade on warm, sunny days. The trail breaks out into the mountain's large glacial cirque, covered in subalpine meadows and streams. During July and early August, basin walls come afire with blooming wildflowers while heather and lupine thrive in the basin. This is a good turnaround for some, with Mount Baker directly across the basin, a real postcard view.

The final two miles are a steep ascent up basin walls, at times on tricky footing. This section is hot, dry, and exposed; plenty of water is a must. From atop Church Mountain, the views are panoramic and a topographic map is a necessity to identify the numerous mountains.

User Groups: Hikers and leashed dogs. No

horses or mountain bikes are allowed. No wheelchair access.

Open Seasons: This trail is usually accessible mid-July–early October.

Permits: A federal Northwest Forest Pass is required to park here.

Maps: For a map of Mount Baker–Snoqualmie National Forest, contact the Outdoor Recreation Information Center at the downtown Seattle REI. For topographic maps, ask Green Trails for No. 13, Mount Baker, or ask the USGS for Bearpaw Mountain.

Directions: From Bellingham, drive east 38 miles on Highway 542 (Mount Baker Highway) to Church Mountain Road (Forest Service Road 3040). Turn left (north) and drive 2.5 miles to the trailhead at road's end.

Contact: Mount Baker–Snoqualmie National Forest, Glacier Public Service Center, Glacier, WA 98244, 360/599-2714.

3 EXCELSIOR RIDGE

11.2 mi/8.0 hr

east of Bellingham in Mount Baker Wilderness of Mount Baker–Snoqualmie National Forest

Map 3.1, page 91

In a land where tough ascents and endless switchbacks are an accepted way of life on the trail, this hike makes others look tame. Excelsior Trail and Welcome Pass Trail climb from the valley floor to Excelsior Ridge, covered in meadows with views of mountains in every direction. Connecting them is High Divide Trail, 4.5 miles of ridgeline meadows. There's very little you won't see along this outstanding route.

To complete the whole loop, you must arrange a drop-off between the two trailheads. Better yet, drop off mountain bikes at the upper trailhead (Welcome Pass) and pick them up after hiking for an easy ride back to the car. For a one-way up-and-back trip, Welcome Pass is the best bet. Excelsior and Welcome Pass Trails both entail many switchbacks at an excruciating grade. The trails are mostly forested by old-growth, but they are nonetheless dry and hot.

The two trails are connected by High Divide Trail, which runs for 4.5 miles along the ridge. Views of Mount Baker and Mount Shuksan, just across the Nooksack River, are outstanding. The trail runs through seemingly endless meadows of wildflowers. Tomyhoi, Border Peaks, and a lot of Canada are visible from up here. Its south-facing orientation means that snow melts sooner here, making this one of the first trails to open in the valley.

User Groups: Hikers, leashed dogs, horses (horses allowed August 1–November 1), and llamas. No mountain bikes are allowed. No wheelchair access.

Open Seasons: This trail is usually accessible mid-June–early October.

Permits: A federal Northwest Forest Pass is required to park here.

Maps: For a map of Mount Baker–Snoqualmie National Forest, contact the Outdoor Recreation Information Center at the downtown Seattle REI. For topographic maps, ask Green Trails for No. 13, Mount Baker, and No. 14, Mount Shuksan, or ask the USGS for Bearpaw Mountain.

Directions: From Bellingham, drive east 41 miles on Highway 542 (Mount Baker Highway) to an unsigned trailhead on the left (north) side of the highway. This is Excelsior Pass Trailhead and is immediately past Nooksack Falls.

For Welcome Pass Trailhead, drive another 4.5 miles to Forest Service Road 3060. Turn left and drive 1 mile to the trailhead at road's end.

Contact: Mount Baker–Snoqualmie National Forest, Glacier Public Service Center, Glacier, WA 98244, 360/599-2714.

4 HELIOTROPE RIDGE

5.0 mi/3.0 hr

east of Bellingham in Mount Baker Wilderness of Mount Baker–Snoqualmie National Forest

Map 3.1, page 91

One of the best opportunities to see and hear a living glacier lies at the end of this popular trail. Heliotrope Ridge Trail ascends through beautiful forests to the terminus of the Coleman Glaciers. This is the most popular route for climbers who seek the summit of Mount Baker, which towers above the route. Huge glacial moraines shape the terrain above timberline, including the brightly layered Chromatic Moraine at the head of Glacier Creek. There's no shortage of hikers along the trail, but that should not detract from the great views and the ability to feel the mass of the slowly moving glaciers.

The trail leaves the trailhead and steadily ascends through beautiful forests of old-growth timber, crossing several ice-cold creeks. After two miles, the trail forks. The left fork crosses Heliotrope Creek and scrambles up to an overlook near an arm of the Coleman Glacier, where it terminates into a morass of mud and ice. Colorful Chromatic Moraine is just across the way.

The right fork at the junction climbs to a rocky terrain of wildflowers and whistling marmots. Mount Baker towers above a wide open area of scrambling opportunities. Climbers continue from here to the Coleman Glacier base camp. Be aware that the trickle of a stream you crossed in the morning may be a river by the afternoon. Plan carefully. Also, exploration on glaciers is not recommended without proper equipment and expertise—glacial crevasses prefer to swallow the foolish.

User Groups: Hikers and leashed dogs. No horses or mountain bikes are allowed. No wheelchair access.

Open Seasons: This trail is accessible August–early October.

Permits: A federal Northwest Forest Pass is required to park here.

Maps: For a map of Mount Baker–Snoqualmie National Forest, contact the Outdoor Recreation Information Center at the downtown Seattle REI. For topographic maps, ask Green Trails for No. 13, Mount Baker, or ask the USGS for Mount Baker and Goat Mountain.

Directions: From Bellingham, drive east 34 miles on Highway 542 (Mount Baker Highway) to Glacier Creek Road (Forest Service Road 39). Turn right (south) and drive 8.5 miles to the signed trailhead on the left.

Contact: Mount Baker–Snoqualmie National Forest, Glacier Public Service Center, Glacier, WA 98244, 360/599-2714.

5 SKYLINE DIVIDE

7.0 mi/4.0 hr

east of Bellingham in Mount Baker Wilderness of Mount Baker–Snoqualmie National Forest

Map 3.1, page 91

Catch a sunset from Skyline Divide, and you'll never stop talking about it. This long ridge extending from Mount Baker is covered in meadows. Views stretch from the North Cascades to Puget Sound and from Mount Baker to British Columbia. The Skyline Trail truly lives in the sky.

The road to the trailhead was washed out in 2003; call the ranger station in Glacier for an update on repairs. Skyline Trail climbs two miles through grand forest of Pacific silver fir and western hemlock. The grade is constant and not difficult. Before long, the trail reaches the divide, and Mount Baker seems close enough to touch. The North Cascades unfold to the east for miles, and there is no end to the peaks one can identify. The ridge is dry and hot, so bring plenty of water.

Skyline Trail carries on south for another 1.5 miles, going up and down with the ridge and heading ever closer to Baker. To the west are the San Juan Islands in the sound, and Vancouver, British Columbia, is also discernible. Sunsets from here dazzle and are well worth the night hike down. Very little camping is found on the ridge; consider a hike by moonlight another part of a remarkable experience.

User Groups: Hikers, leashed dogs, and horses. No mountain bikes are allowed. No wheelchair access.

Open Seasons: This trail is accessible July–early October.

Permits: A federal Northwest Forest Pass is required to park here.

Maps: For a map of Mount Baker–Snoqualmie National Forest, contact the Outdoor Recreation Information Center at the downtown Seattle REI. For topographic maps, ask Green Trails for No. 13, Mount Baker, or ask the USGS for Mount Baker and Bearpaw Mountain.

Directions: From Bellingham, drive east 34 miles on Highway 542 (Mount Baker Highway) to Glacier Creek Road (Forest Service Road 39). Turn right (south) and quickly turn left onto Forest Service Road 37. Drive 15 miles to the trailhead at road's end.

Contact: Mount Baker–Snoqualmie National Forest, Glacier Public Service Center, Glacier, WA 98244, 360/599-2714.

6 YELLOW ASTER BUTTE

7.2 mi/3.5 hr 3 8

east of Bellingham in Mount Baker Wilderness of Mount Baker–Snoqualmie National Forest

Map 3.1, page 91

This trail to the high country offers just about everything one could ask for in a trail. Wildflowers and huckleberries fill wide open meadows. A basin of subalpine lakes opens to reveal outstanding views of Baker and Shuksan, and a scramble yields Tomyhoi Peak. Best of all, the trail starts high, saving energy for high-country rambling. Bring your swimsuit, as the lakes are too enticing to turn down. It's hard to imagine what's missing in this great subalpine parkland.

The route begins on Tomyhoi Lake Trail, which switchbacks through avalanche chutes and thick brush to a signed junction (1.4 miles). Take a left and climb through open meadows with nonstop views to the lake basin. Indian paintbrush, monkey flowers, and penstemon are just a few of the flowers you'll find blooming in late July. Facing south toward the sun, this trail can be very hot; bring extra water or a filter.

The basin is full of numerous small lakes, perfect for a dip. The meadows are delicate and deteriorating because of heavy use; camp only in designated sites and follow strict Leave-No-Trace principles. For the hardy, a well-used path leads to the top of Yellow Aster Butte and big views of Mount Larrabee, Border Peaks, and Mount Baker. Yellow Aster Butte is a must-do for dedicated North Cascades hikers.

User Groups: Hikers and leashed dogs. No horses or mountain bikes are allowed. No wheelchair access.

Open Seasons: This trail is accessible July–early October.

© SCOTT LEONARD

American (R) and Canadian (L) Border Peaks, from Yellow Aster Butte

Permits: A federal Northwest Forest Pass is required to park here.
Maps: For a map of Mount Baker–Snoqualmie National Forest, contact the Outdoor Recreation Information Center at the downtown Seattle REI. For topographic maps, ask Green Trails for No. 14, Mount Shuksan, or ask the USGS for Mount Larrabee.
Directions: From Bellingham, drive east 46 miles on Highway 542 (Mount Baker Highway) to Twin Lakes Road (Forest Service Road 3065), just beyond the Department of Transportation facility. Turn left (north) and drive 5 miles to the signed trailhead (where the road makes several switchbacks on an exposed slope).
Contact: Mount Baker–Snoqualmie National Forest, Glacier Public Service Center, Glacier, WA 98244, 360/599-2714.

7 WINCHESTER MOUNTAIN

3.8 mi/2.5 hr

east of Bellingham in Mount Baker Wilderness of Mount Baker–Snoqualmie National Forest

Map 3.1, page 91

Winchester Mountain is home to a back-country favorite: an abandoned fire lookout. Built in 1935, the lookout is no longer used by the Forest Service but receives regular maintenance from a dedicated volunteer group. From up here, much of the North Cascades, in Washington and Canada, are revealed. Add to the spectacular views an enjoyable trail, flush with ripe huckleberries in September, and you have a great trail.

Winchester Mountain Trail is accessible at Twin Lakes (elevation 5,200 feet), an old base camp for miners and prospectors. The trail climbs steeply through meadows and patches of alpine trees. Be aware that the upper part of the trail is home to a hazardous snowfield that does not melt until late summer. Don't cross it without an ice ax. Otherwise it's best to drop below the snowfield and reconnect to the trail at the other side. The trail is a constant climb, but it's only 1,300 feet gain in about two miles. Bring water and a tolerance for other hikers.
User Groups: Hikers and leashed dogs. No horses or mountain bikes are allowed. No wheelchair access.
Open Seasons: This trail is usually accessible late July–early October. (September is the ideal month to hike the trail, with the best chances of avoiding the snow field.)
Permits: A federal Northwest Forest Pass is required to park here.
Maps: For a map of Mount Baker–Snoqualmie National Forest, contact the Outdoor Recreation Information Center at the downtown Seattle REI. For topographic maps, ask Green Trails for No. 14, Mount Shuksan, or ask the USGS for Mount Larrabee.
Directions: From Bellingham, drive east 46 miles on Highway 542 (Mount Baker Highway) to Twin Lakes Road (Forest Service Road 3065), just beyond the Department of Transportation facility. Turn left (north) and drive 7 miles to the signed trailhead at road's end. The last two miles are not recommended for passenger cars. A four-wheel-drive vehicle with high clearance is highly recommended.
Contact: Mount Baker–Snoqualmie National Forest, Glacier Public Service Center, Glacier, WA 98244, 360/599-2714.

8 GOAT MOUNTAIN

6.4 mi/4.5 hr

east of Bellingham in Mount Baker Wilderness of Mount Baker–Snoqualmie National Forest

Map 3.1, page 91

When June rolls around and the urge to explore the high country is strong, Goat Mountain is your sanctuary. The trail to this former lookout site lies on the south side of the mountain, making it one of the first to melt out in the summer. With views of Mount Shuksan and countless other peaks and ridges, this is a great first hike of the season. The climb is extremely strenuous, with more than 2,900 feet of elevation gain in just three miles, so it's a sure way to test your fitness for the coming summer of hiking.

Goat Mountain Trail is a steady climb up the side of the mountain. The first part passes through typically great forests of the Nooksack Valley. The trail enters Mount Baker Wilderness (2 miles) just as the forest gives way to open meadows. Huckleberries are as plentiful as the views of Shuksan and Baker. Be sure to bring water on this taxing ascent, as you won't find any on the way other than old patches of snow.

Below the summit sits an old lookout site, abandoned and torn down long ago. The views are excellent, and a long lunch break is well deserved after the hike. Those who are feeling adventurous and have the extra energy can continue scrambling up the ridge to the true summit, where the views only get better.

User Groups: Hikers, leashed dogs, and horses (horses allowed August 1–November 1). No mountain bikes are allowed. No wheelchair access.

Open Seasons: This trail is accessible late-June–October.

Permits: A federal Northwest Forest Pass is required to park here.

Maps: For a map of Mount Baker–Snoqualmie National Forest, contact the Outdoor Recreation Information Center at the downtown Seattle REI. For topographic maps, ask Green Trails for No. 14, Mount Shuksan, or ask the USGS for Mount Larrabee.

Directions: From Bellingham, drive east 46 miles on Highway 542 (Mount Baker Highway) to Hannegan Pass Road (Forest Service Road 32). Turn left and drive 2.5 miles to the trailhead on the left side. Parking is on the left immediately before the trailhead.

Contact: Mount Baker–Snoqualmie National Forest, Glacier Public Service Center, Glacier, WA 98244, 360/599-2714.

9 NOOKSACK CIRQUE

9.0 mi/5.0 hr

east of Bellingham in Mount Baker Wilderness of Mount Baker–Snoqualmie National Forest

Map 3.1, page 91

Unlike any other trail in this valley, Nooksack Cirque Trail is an easy river hike with little elevation gain. This is a welcome respite from the area's straight-up, straight-down trails. Miles of forest rambling delivers hikers to Nooksack Cirque, one of the most easily accessible and largest glacial cirques you'll ever lay eyes upon.

Nooksack Cirque Trail starts by fording Ruth Creek (cross downed logs for a drier experience) and follows an old logging road. It's second-growth forest until the road ends at the wilderness boundary (3 miles), where old-growth forest starts. The two forests are hugely different. Enormous western hemlocks and Pacific silver firs give the feeling that one has been suddenly transported to the Olympic rainforests. Look for colonnades, straight lines of three or four ancient trees growing from a decomposed log.

The final mile is not maintained and becomes brushier as one goes along. Several times the trail breaks out onto the riverbed and route-finding is necessary (but not difficult—head upstream!). At the end sits the large, open cirque beneath the Nooksack Glacier. The ice-scraped cliffs covered in waterfalls are impressive if you're willing to endure the bushwhack. There are two large campsites about .5 mile inside the wilderness boundary.

User Groups: Hikers and leashed dogs. No horses or mountain bikes are allowed. No wheelchair access.

Open Seasons: This trail is usually accessible year-round.

Permits: A federal Northwest Forest Pass is required to park here.

Maps: For a map of Mount Baker–Snoqualmie National Forest, contact the Outdoor Recreation Information Center at the downtown Seattle REI. For topographic maps, ask Green

Trails for No. 14, Mount Shuksan, or ask the USGS for Mount Larrabee, Mount Sefrit, and Mount Shuksan.

Directions: From Bellingham, drive east 46 miles on Highway 542 (Mount Baker Highway) to Forest Service Road 32, just before you cross the Nooksack River. Turn left and drive 2 miles to Forest Service Road 34. Turn right and drive 1.5 miles to the trailhead at road's end.

Contact: Mount Baker–Snoqualmie National Forest, Glacier Public Service Center, Glacier, WA 98244, 360/599-2714.

10 HANNEGAN PASS

10.0 mi/5.0 hr

east of Bellingham in Mount Baker Wilderness of Mount Baker–Snoqualmie National Forest

Map 3.1, page 91

More than a backcountry entrance to North Cascades National Park, Hannegan Trail is absolutely beautiful to boot. Passing beneath the looming Nooksack Ridge up to Hannegan Pass and down to Boundary Camp, the trail is one of the most scenic valley hikes anywhere. Leading to Copper Ridge, Chilliwack River, and Whatcom Pass, Hannegan Trail is a popular segment of longer treks. But the trail reaches Hannegan Peak, one of the best vistas in all of the North Cascades.

Hannegan Trail follows Ruth Creek back to its headwaters beneath Ruth Mountain. Much of the route is open avalanche chutes, revealing the enormous, vertical ridges on either side. Soon, the 7,100-foot Ruth Mountain appears with its enormous glacier and glacially polished walls. Beneath Ruth is Hannegan Camp (3.5 miles), a large and picturesque campground.

Hannegan Trail climbs to the meadows of Hannegan Pass (4 miles) and down to Boundary Camp (5 miles). At the pass is Hannegan Peak Trail, a steep pitch through meadows to the 6,186-foot peak. The views are grand, including Ruth, Mount Shuksan, Mount Baker, the Picketts, and countless other Cascade peaks. Just about every footstep along this hike is unbelievably beautiful. To hike this trail and not visit Hannegan Peak is a missed opportunity.

User Groups: Hikers, leashed dogs, and horses. No mountain bikes are allowed. No wheelchair access.

Open Seasons: This trail is usually accessible July–early October.

Permits: A federal Northwest Forest Pass is required to park here. Overnight stays within the national park (Boundary Camp or beyond) require backcountry camping permits, which are available at Glacier Public Service Center. No permit is required for staying at Hannegan Camp.

Maps: For a map of Mount Baker–Snoqualmie National Forest, contact the Outdoor Recreation Information Center at the downtown Seattle REI. For topographic maps, ask Green Trails for No. 14, Mount Shuksan, or ask the USGS for Mount Sefrit.

Directions: From Bellingham, drive east 46 miles on Highway 542 (Mount Baker Highway) to Hannegan Pass Road (Forest Service Road 32). Turn left and drive 5 miles to the signed trailhead at road's end.

Contact: Mount Baker–Snoqualmie National Forest, Glacier Public Service Center, Glacier, WA 98244, 360/599-2714.

11 COPPER RIDGE LOOP

34.5 mi/4–5 days

east of Bellingham in North Cascades National Park

Map 3.1, page 91

Strike up a conversation with a North Cascades hiking veteran and you'll invariably be asked, "Have you done Copper Ridge yet?" This backcountry trek maintains cultlike popularity, thanks to being one of the most scenic and beloved routes in the state. Views and meadows abound along this high-country route. Several lakes highlight the ridge run, which also leads to an old lookout. The wild ridge is isolated in the upper national park and makes an excellent loop with Chilliwack Trail.

Copper Ridge is accessible via Hannegan

Pass (see previous listing). At Boundary Camp (5 miles) the trail splits–up to Copper Ridge and down to Chilliwack River (see listing in this chapter). Your direction will depend upon available camp reservations (the National Park Service requires permits to camp within the park). Much of the trail enjoys open meadows. Great views, but it's hot and dry, too; prepare to pack water.

Copper Ridge Trail leaves Boundary Camp and climbs around Hells Gorge to the ridge. Silesia Camp and Egg Lake Camp (8.2 miles) offer great camps and a refreshing dip in Egg Lake. An old lookout offers the route's highest point at 6,260 feet (10.7 miles). Below the long arm of Copper Mountain lies Copper Lake Camp (11.9 miles). The trail continues four additional miles on the ridge before dropping to Chilliwack River (19.4 miles). Become a North Cascades veteran and make plans for Copper Ridge.

User Groups: Hikers and horses. No dogs or mountain bikes are allowed. No wheelchair access.

Open Seasons: This trail is usually accessible August–September.

Permits: A federal Northwest Forest Pass is required to park here. Overnight stays within the national park require backcountry camping permits, which are are available at Glacier Public Service Center.

Maps: For a map of North Cascades National Park, contact the Outdoor Recreation Information Center at the downtown Seattle REI. For a topographic map, ask Green Trails for No. 14, Mount Shuksan, and No. 15, Mount Challenger, or ask the USGS for Mount Sefrit and Copper Mountain.

Directions: From Bellingham, drive east 46 miles on Highway 542 (Mount Baker Highway) to Hannegan Pass Road (Forest Service Road 32). Turn left and drive 5 miles to the signed trailhead at road's end.

Contact: North Cascades National Park, Wilderness Information Center, 7280 Ranger Station Road, Marblemount, WA 98267, 360/873-4500; Mount Baker–Snoqualmie National Forest, Glacier Public Service Center, Glacier, WA 98244, 360/599-2714.

12 WHATCOM PASS

34.0 mi/4 days

east of Bellingham in North Cascades National Park

Map 3.1, page 91

The legend of Whatcom Pass frequently and quickly makes its way around hiking circles. It's not a legend of Sasquatch or a miner's ghost, but instead true accounts of the beauty found at Whatcom Pass. Nestled at the base of the Picket Range, Whatcom Pass enjoys the North Cascades' most impressive range. Some old-timers even proclaim Whatcom Pass the king of all backcountry destinations. That sounds about right.

The route follows the beautiful Hannegan Pass and Chilliwack River Trails (see listings in this chapter) to Brush Creek (12.3 miles). By this point, the scenery should have knocked your boots off. Brush Creek Trail splits from the Chilliwack and climbs five miles to the subalpine splendor of Whatcom Pass. Graybeal Camp sits at 12.3 miles, but pass it up for a camp near the pass. Take care in this delicate ecosystem by staying on established trails and avoiding campfires. Appreciate the view of Mount Challenger and its enormous glacier. Make great side trips by scrambling north to Tapto Lakes or south along the Whatcom Arm.

User Groups: Hikers only. No dogs, horses, or mountain bikes are allowed. No wheelchair access.

Open Seasons: This trail is accessible August–September.

Permits: A federal Northwest Forest Pass is required to park here. Overnight stays within the national park require reservations and backcountry camping permits, which are available at Glacier Public Service Center.

Maps: For a map of North Cascades National Park, contact the Outdoor Recreation Information Center at the downtown Seattle REI.

For topographic maps, ask Green Trails for No. 14, Mount Shuksan, and No. 15, Mount Challenger, or ask the USGS for Mount Sefrit, Copper Mountain, Mount Redoubt, Mount Challenger, and Mount Blum.

Directions: From Bellingham, drive east 46 miles on Highway 542 (Mount Baker Highway) to Hannegan Pass Road (Forest Service Road 32). Turn left and drive 5 miles to the signed trailhead at road's end.

Contact: North Cascades National Park, Wilderness Information Center, 7280 Ranger Station Road, Marblemount, WA 98267, 360/873-4500; Mount Baker–Snoqualmie National Forest, Glacier Public Service Center, Glacier, WA 98244, 360/599-2714.

13 CHILLIWACK RIVER

40.0 mi/4 days

east of Bellingham in North Cascades National Park

Map 3.1, page 91

As the miles pass underfoot on Chilliwack River Trail, the solitude of the wilderness grows ever more lonely. Most often hiked to reach Copper Ridge or Whatcom Pass, Chilliwack River Trail is grand by itself, too. Miles of large old-growth forest tower over the trail, pleasantly following the rambling river. This is real wilderness, where bears and elk are regular hiking partners. Regardless of one's destination, Chilliwack River Trail is an enjoyable journey.

Chilliwack Trail is accessible via Boundary Camp on Hannegan Pass Trail (5 miles). Chilliwack Trail drops through ever-thickening forest to Copper Creek Camp (8.5 miles) and U.S. Cabin Camp (11.1 miles). The trail crosses the river at one of the state's unique river crossings: A cable car whisks hikers above the river to the opposite shore.

Brush Creek Trail (12.9 miles) ventures south up to Whatcom Pass (12.9 miles) while Copper Ridge Trail climbs to the west (16.5 miles). Beyond this point, the trail rambles through beautiful lowland river forests, where green dominates the scenery. Bear Creek Camp (18.3 miles) and Little Chilliwack Camp (20.7 miles) offer campsites before entering Canada (24 miles one-way). Few ever make it so deep into this wild place.

User Groups: Hikers and horses. No dogs or mountain bikes are allowed. No wheelchair access.

Open Seasons: This trail is accessible from Hannegan Pass July–September and from Canada nearly year-round.

Permits: A federal Northwest Forest Pass is required to park at the Hannegan Pass trailhead. Overnight stays within the national park require backcountry camping permits.

Maps: For a map of North Cascades National Park, contact the Outdoor Recreation Information Center at the downtown Seattle REI. For topographic maps, ask Green Trails for No. 14, Mount Shuksan, and No. 15, Mount Challenger, or ask the USGS for Mount Sefrit and Copper Mountain.

Directions: From Bellingham, drive east 46 miles on Highway 542 (Mount Baker Highway) to Hannegan Pass Road (Forest Service Road 32). Turn left and drive 5 miles to the signed trailhead at road's end.

Contact: North Cascades National Park, Wilderness Information Center, 7280 Ranger Station Road, Marblemount, WA 98267, 360/873-4500.

14 LAKE ANN

8.6 mi/6.0 hr

east of Bellingham in Mount Baker Wilderness of Mount Baker–Snoqualmie National Forest

Map 3.1, page 91

When you finally crest the meadowy pass and spot Lake Ann lying beneath Mount Shuksan, you will know that you have arrived someplace special. Rocky alpine meadows surround this high-country lake, while the towering cliffs and glaciers of Mount Shuksan stand above. The journey is through four miles of old-growth forest and berry-filled meadows. This is one of the best hikes in an area full of beautiful country.

Lake Ann Trail quickly drops through forest

Mount Baker, from along Lake Ann Trail, a great hike

into Swift Creek Basin (1.5 miles). Despite an average of 700 inches of snow each winter, mountain hemlocks swell massively. In the basin, acres of meadows brim with huckleberries, making this a sweet hike in August. The trail crosses Swift Creek (look downstream to Mount Baker) and climbs two miles through more meadows to a pass above Lake Ann.

Surrounded by alpine meadows and mountain views, Lake Ann presents a nice place to rest awhile. Take a dip in the cool water while watching marmots play in the meadows. On Mount Shuksan, the Curtis Glaciers can be heard breaking and settling in the summer heat. There is plenty of camping space, but it can go quickly. This trail is a perfect midweek or late-season trip.

User Groups: Hikers and leashed dogs. No horses or mountain bikes are allowed. No wheelchair access.

Open Seasons: This area is usually accessible July–early October.

Permits: A federal Northwest Forest Pass is required to park here.

Maps: For a map of Mount Baker–Snoqualmie National Forest, contact the Outdoor Recreation Information Center at the downtown Seattle REI. For topographic maps, ask Green Trails for No. 14, Mount Shuksan, or ask the USGS for Shuksan Arm.

Directions: From Bellingham, drive east 56 miles on Highway 542 (Mount Baker Highway) to the signed trailhead on the left, past Heather Meadows Visitor Center.

Contact: Mount Baker–Snoqualmie National Forest, Glacier Public Service Center, Glacier, WA 98244, 360/599-2714.

15 GALENA CHAIN LAKES

6.5 mi/4.0 hr 3 8

east of Bellingham in Mount Baker Wilderness of Mount Baker–Snoqualmie National Forest

Map 3.1, page 91

Galena Chain Lakes have been a backcountry destination for hikers and backpackers for generations. Nestled among towering mountains, these four lakes are picturesque examples of the subalpine. Chain Lakes are immersed in meadows and huckleberries and offer lots of great camping. They can be fished for dinner as well. This trail is great for families and is accessible for both day hikers visiting Heather Meadows as well as overnight backpackers.

The route is best done as a loop, starting at Artist Point. Chain Lakes Trail heads toward Ptarmigan Ridge before turning right at a signed junction (1 mile). Before you know it, you've reached Mazama Lake (2 miles). There are four choice camps here, set on the small ridge between the lake and Mount Baker. The trail makes its way to large Iceberg Lake, which sits below the vertical walls of Table Mountain. Reportedly, the fish are biggest here. A side trail leads to four camps along Hayes Lake, which requires a bit of up and down.

To exit the basin, the trail climbs to a saddle between Table and Mazama Dome, the best vista of the trail, and drops two steep miles to the visitors center. Wild Goose Trail returns hikers to Artist Point, but drivers passing through here are always happy to pick up a few riders for the two-mile drive. This is a popular trail in season.

User Groups: Hikers and leashed dogs. No horses or mountain bikes are allowed. No wheelchair access.

Open Seasons: This trail is usually accessible July–September.

Permits: A federal Northwest Forest Pass is required to park here.

Maps: For a map of Mount Baker–Snoqualmie National Forest, contact the Outdoor Recreation Information Center at the downtown Seattle REI. For topographic maps, ask Green Trails for No. 14, Mount Shuksan, or ask the USGS for Shuksan Arm.

Directions: From Bellingham, drive east 58 miles on Highway 542 (Mount Baker Highway) to Artist's Point at the end of the highway. The trailhead is on the northwest side of the parking lot.

Contact: Mount Baker–Snoqualmie National Forest, Glacier Public Service Center, Glacier, WA 98244, 360/599-2714.

16 PTARMIGAN RIDGE

8.0 mi/4.0 hr

east of Bellingham in Mount Baker Wilderness of Mount Baker–Snoqualmie National Forest

Map 3.1, page 91

Just as one might expect from an arm of Mount Baker, Ptarmigan Ridge Trail revels in an excess of natural beauty. Wildflowers paint miles of meadows while even more miles of views extend in all directions. Mount Shuksan looms from the east, and Mount Baker towers directly above. Marmots and picas are local residents, living it up with location, location, location. It's not possible to ask too much of Ptarmigan Ridge on a sunny, summer day.

Before leaving, be aware of several safety issues. Snowfields linger along the route well into summer, sometimes all year long. They are steep and should be crossed only by experienced hikers. Along this precipitous ridge, a misstep can have grave consequences. Mount Baker's weather changes rapidly, so be ready to use map and compass should a storm blow in and create a whiteout. That said, Ptarmigan Ridge Trail presents an exciting trip for those prepared for it.

The route uses Chain Lakes Trail before cutting left at a signed junction (1 mile). Ptarmigan Ridge Trail follows the cusp of the ridge as it ascends to Coleman Pinnacle (4.5 miles). Along the way are miles of wildflower meadows and fields of rock. Summer days are blistering hot in the sun, so extra water is a must. A scramble to the top of Coleman Pinnacle rewards with close views of Rainbow Glacier and Mount Baker. Climbers use this route to approach Mount Baker from Camp Kiser.

User Groups: Hikers and leashed dogs. No horses or mountain bikes are allowed. No wheelchair access.

Open Seasons: This trail is accessible August–September.

Permits: A federal Northwest Forest Pass is required to park here.

Maps: For a map of Mount Baker–Snoqualmie National Forest, contact the Outdoor Recreation Information Center at the downtown Seattle REI. For topographic maps, ask Green Trails for No. 14, Mount Shuksan (No. 13, Mount Baker, is helpful in identifying ridges and peaks on the mountain), or ask the USGS for Shuksan Arm.

Directions: From Bellingham, drive east 58 miles on Highway 542 (Mount Baker Highway)

to Artist's Point at the end of the highway. The trailhead is on the northwest side of the parking lot.

Contact: Mount Baker–Snoqualmie National Forest, Glacier Public Service Center, Glacier, WA 98244, 360/599-2714.

17 BELL PASS/CATHEDRAL PASS/MAZAMA PARK

17.0 mi/1–2 days

3 9

east of Bellingham in Mount Baker Wilderness of Mount Baker–Snoqualmie National Forest

Map 3.1, page 91

On the southwestern slopes of Washington's youngest volcano, Bell Pass Trail offers a more reclusive entry into the wonders of the Mount Baker high country. The trail presents a longer route into a parkland of expansive meadows, crackling glaciers, and wide vistas. That means fewer people travel along it than on the Park Butte and Scott Paul Trails, an enticing consideration.

Bell Pass Trail begins along Elbow Lake Trail, cutting switchbacks through the forest on its way to a junction (3.5 miles); Bell Pass Trail heads to the right. Elk sightings are an ordinary occurrence here. The trail departs the forest to find itself at Bell Pass (5.5 miles), where views of the Twin Sister Range are great. The trail levels out while it traverses above Ridley Creek. The meadows of Mazama Park (8.5 miles) are exceptional anytime in summer, but especially so in July during full bloom. Campsites are here. The trail continues up through Cathedral Pass to meet Park Butte Trail. A great lookout sits atop Park Butte, well worth the extra effort.

User Groups: Hikers, leashed dogs, and horses. No mountain bikes are allowed. No wheelchair access.

Open Seasons: This area is accessible July–October.

Permits: A federal Northwest Forest Pass is required to park here.

Maps: For a map of Mount Baker–Snoqualmie National Forest, contact the Outdoor Recreation Information Center at the downtown Seattle REI. For topographic maps, ask Green Trails for No. 45, Hamilton, or ask the USGS for Twin Sisters Mountain and Mount Baker.

Directions: From Sedro-Woolley, drive east 16 miles on Highway 20 to Mile Marker 82. Turn left (north) on Baker Lake Highway (Forest Service Road 11) and drive 12 miles to Forest Service Road 12. Turn left and drive 14 miles to a signed spur road on the left. Turn left on this road and drive .25 mile to Elbow Lake Trailhead.

Contact: Mount Baker–Snoqualmie National Forest, Mount Baker Ranger District Office, 810 Highway 20, Sedro-Woolley, WA 98284, 360/856-5700.

18 PARK BUTTE/RAILROAD GRADE/SCOTT PAUL TRAIL

7.0–8.0 mi/4.0 hr

3 10

east of Bellingham in Mount Baker Wilderness of Mount Baker–Snoqualmie National Forest

Map 3.1, page 91

This is arguably the finest terrain in all of the North Cascades. Three trails lead to high subalpine meadows set at the foot of Mount Baker, where glaciers crumble off the mountain and the sky opens up around you. Spend days roaming the high country here, spotting wildflowers and wildlife. The three trails form a network offering wide exploration, so it's best to have a map when picking your route through this area. Campsites spread throughout the area for magical overnight stays. This place attracts lots of visitors, so come for the scenery, not the solitude.

Park Butte Trail (7 miles round-trip, up and back) climbs through forest to open meadows and Park Butte lookout. The trail crosses Sulphur and Rocky Creeks (clear in the morning but milky white with glacial flour by afternoon). Marmots whistle from meadows while picas peep from atop boulders. The trail splits in Morovitz Meadow (2 miles); the left fork climbs a ridge to the lookout, with views of the mountain and Twin Sisters.

Scott Paul Trail (8 miles round-trip loop) leaves the Park Butte Trail in Morovitz Meadow to climb up Metcalf Moraine and meet the interesting terminus of Easton Glacier. The moraine exposes barren rock and mud, detailing an infant landscape before mountain meadows encroach. The trail continues east through meadows to climb a high crest with views of Mount Shuksan and the North Cascades before dropping through forest to the trailhead. Railroad Grade (6 miles round-trip, up and back) is a side trail shooting up to the mountain out of Morovitz Meadow. The trail is on a moraine created by the Easton Glacier and brings you close to the living glacier.

User Groups: Hikers, leashed dogs, and horses. No mountain bikes are allowed. No wheelchair access.

Open Seasons: This area is accessible July–October.

Permits: A federal Northwest Forest Pass is required to park here.

Maps: For a map of Mount Baker–Snoqualmie National Forest, contact the Outdoor Recreation Information Center at the downtown Seattle REI. For topographic maps, ask Green Trails for No. 45, Hamilton, or ask the USGS for Baker Pass.

Directions: From Sedro-Woolley, drive east 16 miles on Highway 20 to Mile Marker 82. Turn left (north) on Baker Lake Highway (Forest Service Road 11) and drive 12 miles to Forest Service Road 12. Turn left and drive 3.5 miles to Forest Service Road 13. Turn right and drive 5.5 miles to the trailhead at road's end.

Contact: Mount Baker–Snoqualmie National Forest, Mount Baker Ranger District Office, 810 Highway 20, Sedro-Woolley, WA 98284, 360/856-5700.

19 BAKER LAKE AND BAKER RIVER

3.6–28.6 mi/2.0 hr–2 days

east of Sedro-Woolley in Mount Baker–Snoqualmie National Forest

Map 3.1, page 91

For year-round forest wandering, Mount Baker presents hikers these two trails. Baker Lake Trail meanders 14.3 miles along the eastern shore of the large, dogleg-shaped lake. Baker River Trail continues from the north part of the lake and ventures eight miles up the river into North Cascades Park. Exceptional old-growth forests line the lengths of both trails, and water is always at hand. These are great trails for both day hikes and more extended adventures.

Short hikes along Baker Lake Trail are best begun from the south end. The trail contours along the eastern shores of the lake through stands of large trees. Anderson Point, a good turnaround, juts into the lake with campsites (1.8 miles); there are also three other campgrounds. The grade is level and easy, perfect for families with small children.

At the north end of the lake is Baker River Trail. Baker River Trail passes through terrific stands of virgin timber and even a beaver pond as it follows the river. In contrast to wildlife, people are relatively scarce here. The maintained trail ends when it crosses Sulphide Creek, impassable during times of high water. If you ford the river, a social trail continues beside the milky river five miles before truly petering out. For the adventurous, solitude and an enjoyable time are highly likely.

User Groups: Hikers, leashed dogs, and horses. No mountain bikes are allowed. No wheelchair access.

Open Seasons: This trail is accessible year-round.

Permits: A federal Northwest Forest Pass is required to park here.

Maps: For a map of Mount Baker–Snoqualmie National Forest, contact the Outdoor Recreation Information Center at the downtown Seattle REI. For topographic maps, ask Green

Trails for No. 46, Lake Shannon, or ask the USGS for Welker Peak, Bacon Peak, and Mount Shuksan.

Directions: From Sedro-Woolley, drive east 16 miles on Highway 20 to Mile Marker 82. Turn left (north) on Baker Lake Highway (Forest Service Road 11). For Baker Lake Trailhead, drive 14 miles to Baker Dam Road. Turn right and drive across Upper Baker Dam to Forest Service Road 1107. Turn left and drive 1 mile to the trailhead on the left side. For Baker River Trailhead, drive 25.5 miles on Forest Service Road 11 to the trailhead at road's end.

Contact: Mount Baker–Snoqualmie National Forest, Mount Baker Ranger District Office, 810 Highway 20, Sedro-Woolley, WA 98284, 360/856-5700.

20 ANDERSON AND WATSON LAKES

2.5 mi/2.0 hr

east of Bellingham in Noisy-Diobsud Wilderness of Mount Baker–Snoqualmie National Forest

Map 3.1, page 91

High in the Noisy-Diobsud Wilderness is a trail with several options. Watson Lakes Trail passes by Anderson Butte, a former lookout site full of views, on its way to two sets of picturesque subalpine lakes. Accessible by hikers of all abilities, these lakes serve grand views of distant peaks and offer superb fishing for those with dinner in mind. Throw in old-growth forest and subalpine meadows, and this is a day hike or overnight trip that has it all.

Watson Lakes Trail leaves the lofty trailhead (elevation 4,200 feet) and proceeds through virgin timber and meadows to Anderson Butte junction (.9 mile). A .5-mile climb achieves the summit, a great place to see Mount Baker and North Cascade peaks. Include this side trip in a hike to the lakes.

Watson Lakes Trail soon arrives at another junction (1.5 miles). To the right are Anderson Lakes (2 miles), three small subalpine lakes surrounded by meadows and trees. The left fork in the trail leads over a shoulder and down to Watson Lakes (2.5 miles), a larger pair of lakes with more mountain views. Both lakes are ringed by big trees and meadows. Camping at both lakes is in designated sites only. Also, both lake basins are notoriously buggy. Access to both sets of lakes is easy and hikers of all abilities will enjoy visiting them.

User Groups: Hikers and leashed dogs. No horses or mountain bikes are allowed. No wheelchair access.

Open Seasons: This area is accessible mid-June–October.

Permits: A federal Northwest Forest Pass is required to park here.

Maps: For a map of Mount Baker–Snoqualmie National Forest, contact the Outdoor Recreation Information Center at the downtown Seattle REI. For topographic maps, ask Green Trails for No. 46, Lake Shannon, or ask the USGS for Bacon Peak.

Directions: From Sedro-Woolley, drive east 16 miles on Highway 20 to Mile Marker 82. Turn left (north) on Baker Lake Highway (Forest Service Road 11). Drive 14 miles to Baker Dam Road. Turn right and drive across Upper Baker Dam to Forest Service Road 1107. Turn left and drive 10 miles to Forest Service Road 022. Turn left and drive to the trailhead at road's end.

Contact: Mount Baker–Snoqualmie National Forest, Mount Baker Ranger District Office, 810 Highway 20, Sedro-Woolley, WA 98284, 360/856-5700.

21 SAUK MOUNTAIN

4.2 mi/4.0 hr

west of Marblemount in Mount Baker–Snoqualmie National Forest

Map 3.1, page 91

This is a great short day hike that offers outstanding vistas the entire way. Sauk Mountain Trail starts and ends in meadows smothered with alpine flowers. Most would say that it's difficult to find anything better than that. Of course, the terrific nature of the trail attracts loads of folks, but solitude is always difficult to find so close to Highway 20.

The trail is well laid out, with many switchbacks cutting the 1,300 feet of elevation gain to a much easier grade. This is exclusive meadow country, and in midsummer, flower enthusiasts will find themselves in heaven. Expect to find paintbrush, phlox, tiger lilies, aster, columbine, and lupine on display. Sauk Mountain Trail splits (1.5 miles), with the left fork heading to the summit and the right fork leading down to Sauk Lake, which is set between the rocky slopes of Sauk and Bald Mountains. The summit is a former fire lookout site with panoramic views. Gaze from the San Juans to the rugged North Cascades, from Mount Baker and Mount Shuksan all the way south to Mount Rainier. This trail gets a lot of use, so please stick to the path and don't cut switchbacks.

User Groups: Hikers and leashed dogs. No horses or mountain bikes are allowed. No wheelchair access.

Open Seasons: This trail is accessible mid-June–October.

Permits: A federal Northwest Forest Pass is required to park here.

Maps: For a map of Mount Baker–Snoqualmie National Forest, contact the Outdoor Recreation Information Center at the downtown Seattle REI. For topographic maps, ask Green Trails for No. 46, Lake Shannon, or ask the USGS for Sauk Mountain.

Directions: From Sedro-Woolley, drive east on Highway 20 for 32 miles. At Mile Marker 96, turn left on Sauk Mountain Road (Forest Service Road 1030). Follow Forest Service Road 1030 for 7 miles to the junction of Forest Service Road 1036. Turn right on Road 1036 and follow to the road's end, where the trailhead is located.

Contact: Mount Baker–Snoqualmie National Forest, Mount Baker Ranger District Office, 810 Highway 20, Sedro-Woolley, WA 98284, 360/856-5700.

22 THORNTON LAKES

9.5 mi/5.0 hr

west of Newhalem in North Cascades National Park

Map 3.1, page 91

The three Thornton Lakes are high in an outstretched arm of Mount Triumph along the western side of North Cascades National Park. The trail does not offer much until near the very end, where Mount Triumph and Thornton Lakes come into view along a ridge crest. Here, Mount Triumph towers over the lakes while Eldorado Peak stands to the south. The best views are not at the lake but rather atop Trappers Peak to the north.

Thornton Lakes Trail was never actually built by a trail crew but instead was fashioned over time simply by boots. The first half of the trail follows an old logging road, brushy with alders, before finding the makeshift trail. It climbs steeply through second-growth forest before breaking out into open meadows.

The trail reaches a ridge (4.5 miles) above Lower Thornton Lake, where hikers have three options. For access to the lower lake, the biggest of the three, drop down the ridge along the obvious trail. The upper lakes, often covered with snow and ice well into summer, are reached by traversing the west slopes of the lower lake along small footpaths. And finally, view seekers should follow the ridge crest to the north to scramble Trappers Peak. From up here, the close Pickett Range comes into full view along with much of the surrounding North Cascades. There are not many sites for camping here, so the trip is definitely recommended as a day hike.

User Groups: Hikers only. No dogs, horses, or mountain bikes are allowed. No wheelchair access.

Open Seasons: This trail is accessible July–October.

Permits: A federal Northwest Forest Pass is required to park here.

Maps: For a map of North Cascades National Park, contact the Outdoor Recreation Information Center at the downtown Seattle REI.

For topographic maps, ask Green Trails for No. 47, Marblemount, or ask the USGS for Mount Triumph.

Directions: Drive east on Highway 20 from Marblemount. Look for the Thornton Lakes Trail sign near Mile Marker 117. Turn north on the gravel road and drive 5 miles to the road's end, where the trailhead is located.

Contact: North Cascades National Park, Wilderness Information Center, 7280 Ranger Station Road, Marblemount, WA 98267, 360/873-4500.

23 MONOGRAM LAKE/ LOOKOUT MOUNTAIN

9.4 mi/5.0 hr 5 10

east of Marblemount in Mount Baker–Snoqualmie National Forest and North Cascades National Park

Map 3.1, page 91

At the western edge of North Cascades National Park are two exceptional destinations accessible from one trail. Monogram Lake sits in a small cirque on a high alpine ridge, framed by meadows and high mountain views. On the other hand, the lookout atop creatively named Lookout Mountain offers scores of extraordinary vistas of North Cascade peaks. The catch is well over 4,000 feet of elevation gain from the trailhead to either point. Don't worry about reaching only one. It will still be a memorable trip, and there's something left for next weekend.

Both routes begin on Lookout Mountain Trail, a treacherously steep series of switchbacks through shady old-growth forest. The trail splits (2.8 miles), with Lookout Mountain to the left and Monogram Lake to the right. Lookout Mountain Trail continues climbing harshly but now through open meadows teeming with blooming wildflowers in July and early August. At the summit (4.7 miles, 5,719 feet) rests a functional lookout at the edge of a mighty drop-off. As expected, the views are spectacular from this height.

Monogram Lake Trail soon enters wildflower meadows and traverses open slopes to the lake (4.9 miles). This is national park territory, a place where dogs are strictly not allowed. A multitude of exploring exists around the lake, perfect for those with an itch for scrambling. Backpackers can stay at Monogram Lake Camp, but don't forget reservations with the Park Service.

User Groups: Monogram Lake Trail is open to hikers. Lookout Mountain Trail is open to hikers and leashed dogs. No horses or mountain bikes are allowed. No wheelchair access.

Open Seasons: This trail is accessible mid-July–October.

Permits: A federal Northwest Forest Pass is required to park here.

Maps: For a map of Mount Baker–Snoqualmie National Forest and North Cascades National Park, contact the Outdoor Recreation Information Center at the downtown Seattle REI. For topographic maps, ask Green Trails for No. 47, Marblemount, or ask the USGS for Big Devil Peak.

Directions: From Sedro-Woolley, drive east on Highway 20 for 39 miles to the community of Marblemount. On the east end of town, turn right on the Cascade River Road, which immediately crosses the Skagit River. Drive 6.5 miles on Cascade River Road to the signed trailhead on the north side of the road, just inside the national forest boundary.

Contact: North Cascades National Park, Wilderness Information Center, 7280 Ranger Station Road, Marblemount, WA 98267, 360/873-4500.

24 HIDDEN LAKE PEAKS

9.0 mi/5.0 hr 4 9

east of Marblemount in Mount Baker–Snoqualmie National Forest and North Cascades National Park

Map 3.1, page 91

An aura surrounds trails that are open for short periods each year. Thanks to heavy winter snowfall, some routes are accessible just a few fleeting months each summer. Thus trips to these destinations are rare and special. That's the case with Hidden Lake, often locked away from hikers by snow until late summer. But if you bide your time, you won't be disappointed. Hidden Lake and its accompanying lookout are high in the sky but surrounded by even higher Cascade peaks.

Hidden Lake Peaks Trail is classic North Cascades: lots of elevation gain. As usual, the 3,500 feet of climbing is well worth it. The trail climbs through a forest of Pacific silver fir before giving way to the meadows and views of Sibley Creek Basin. Sunbathing marmots on the granite boulders are as common as lingering patches of snow.

Hidden Lake Peaks Trail climbs to a saddle from which Hidden Lake is finally revealed. Hikers can either drop to the lake or climb to Hidden Lake Lookout for views. If snow lingers along either route, it's best to simply enjoy the great views from the saddle.

User Groups: Hikers and leashed dogs (up to the park boundary at the saddle). No horses or mountain bikes are allowed. No wheelchair access.

Open Seasons: This trail is accessible August–October.

Permits: A federal Northwest Forest Pass is required to park here.

Maps: For a map of Mount Baker–Snoqualmie National Forest and North Cascades National Park, contact the Outdoor Recreation Information Center at the downtown Seattle REI. For topographic maps, ask Green Trails for No. 48, Diablo Dam, and No. 80, Cascade Pass, or ask the USGS for Eldorado Peak and Sonny Boy Lake.

Directions: From Sedro-Woolley, drive east on Highway 20 for 39 miles to the community of Marblemount. On the east end of town, turn right on Cascade River Road, which immediately crosses the Skagit River. At about 10 miles, turn left onto Sibley Creek Road (Forest Service Road 1540, also signed "Hidden Lake Trail") and drive to the end, about 5 miles.

Contact: North Cascades National Park, Wilderness Information Center, 7280 Ranger Station Road, Marblemount, WA 98267, 360/873-4500.

25 CASCADE PASS

7.4 mi/3.5 hr

east of Marblemount in North Cascades National Park

Map 3.1, page 91

From the parking lot at the trailhead, there is little doubt that Cascade Pass Trail is one magnificent hike. With the mighty Johannesburg Mountain to the south, Cascade Pass Trail carries hikers to the Cascade Crest at the foot of several tall, massive peaks. Wildflowers and glacial views are the norm along the entire route, an entrance to the Stehekin Valley and much of North Cascades National Park.

Cascade Pass Trail climbs steadily but gently throughout its length. A grand forest of mountain hemlock and Pacific silver fir offers welcome shade before breaking into expansive meadows. At Cascade Pass (3.7 miles), acres of wildflowers compete for attention with the neighboring glacier-capped ridges and peaks. This is a dry trail, so bring plenty of water. Also, this area sees plenty of traffic, so stay on designated trails and make this a day hike only.

Cascade Pass is a fine turnaround, but options for further exploration do exist. Sahale Arm Trail heads north from the pass, gaining big elevation and bigger views. A less difficult path heads in the opposite direction to scale Mix-up Peak and find a small tarn. Trekkers will be glad to know that Cascade Pass Trail continues east and drops to the Stehekin River. This route to Lake Chelan has been used for thousands of years by Native American traders.

User Groups: Hikers only. No dogs, horses, or mountain bikes are allowed. No wheelchair access.

Open Seasons: This trail is accessible July–October.

Permits: A federal Northwest Forest Pass is required to park here.

Maps: For a map of North Cascades National Park, contact the Outdoor Recreation Information Center at the downtown Seattle REI. For topographic maps, ask Green Trails for

No. 80, Cascade Pass, or ask the USGS for Cascade Pass.

Directions: From the town of Marblemount on Highway 20, drive 23 miles on Cascade River Road to the trailhead at road's end.

Contact: North Cascades National Park, Wilderness Information Center, 7280 Ranger Station Road, Marblemount, WA 98267, 360/873-4500.

26 PYRAMID LAKE

4.2 mi/2.0 hr

south of Diablo in Ross Lake National Recreation Area

Map 3.1, page 91

Pyramid Lake Trail provides easy access to a deep lake set far below the towering summit of Pyramid Peak. The trail follows the gentle Pyramid Creek through a forest of large and small trees, where a recent burn killed some trees but spared others. The trail is a popular one since it's one of the easier hikes within the park. It's a great destination for folks passing through the park along the highway and looking for a short hike to stretch the legs.

Pyramid Lake Trail gains 1,500 feet in two miles. Closely spaced lodgepole pine and Douglas fir compete to revegetate the forest after a slope-clearing fire. Farther on, larger trees begin appearing, particularly some western red cedars. The trail crosses the creek at the one-mile mark, which may result in some wet feet during times of heavy flow. The trail climbs at a steady rate to the lake, bound by vertical cliffs on two sides. Pyramid Peak stands tall to the southwest, seemingly barren and without a tree to speak of. The lake lies within a National Research Area because of the high levels of biodiversity here. Camping is strictly prohibited, and exploration around the lake should be confined to clearly established trails. Please keep dogs on leashes at all times!

User Groups: Hikers and leashed dogs. No horses or mountain bikes are allowed. No wheelchair access.

Open Seasons: This trail is accessible May–October.

Permits: A federal Northwest Forest Pass is required to park here.

Maps: For a map of North Cascades National Park, contact the Outdoor Recreation Information Center at the downtown Seattle REI. For topographic maps, ask Green Trails for No. 48, Diablo Dam, or ask the USGS for Diablo Dam and Ross Dam.

Directions: From Newhalem, drive east on Highway 20 to the trailhead on the north side of the road, just beyond Mile Marker 126.

Contact: North Cascades National Park, Wilderness Information Center, 7280 Ranger Station Road, Marblemount, WA 98267, 360/873-4500.

27 SOURDOUGH MOUNTAIN

11.5 mi/6.0 hr

5 9

north of Diablo in Ross Lake National Recreation Area and North Cascades National Park

Map 3.1, page 91

Sourdough Mountain Trail is all about two very simple things: unrivaled views of the North Cascades and steepness. Views extend in every direction, up, down, east and west, and north and south. Countless peaks are within sight, including Colonial and Snowfield Peaks and the celebrated Picket Range, often called simply "the Pickets." This vista comes with a dear cost, however, as the trail is one of the steepest you'll come across. From trailhead to summit is a grueling 5,100-foot ascent in just 5.7 miles. It's a real hoofer, but those who complete it will not soon forget it.

Sourdough Mountain Trail gets to work immediately, climbing 3,000 feet in the first three miles. Great forests of Douglas fir and western hemlock provide shade along the exhausting climb. The trail eventually reaches grand subalpine meadows and the sky-high summit. Sourdough Lookout sits atop the 5,985-foot summit. The panoramic views are top-notch and difficult to duplicate within the park. A pair of camps are on either side of the lookout for those wishing to recover tired legs with a night's rest.

User Groups: Hikers only. No dogs, horses,

or mountain bikes are allowed. No wheelchair access.

Open Seasons: This trail is accessible July–October.

Permits: A federal Northwest Forest Pass is required to park here.

Maps: For a map of North Cascades National Park, contact the Outdoor Recreation Information Center at the downtown Seattle REI. For topographic maps, ask Green Trails for No. 48, Diablo Dam, and No. 16, Ross Lake, or ask the USGS for Diablo Dam and Ross Dam.

Directions: From Marblemount, drive east on Highway 20. Turn left at the town of Diablo, near Mile Marker 126. Sourdough Mountain Trailhead is behind the domed swimming pool near the back of the town.

Contact: North Cascades National Park, Wilderness Information Center, 7280 Ranger Station Road, Marblemount, WA 98267, 360/873-4500.

28 DIABLO LAKE

7.6 mi/4.0 hr

near Diablo in Ross Lake National Recreation Area

Map 3.1, page 91

By itself, Diablo Lake Trail is an excellent way to pass an afternoon, with views of emerald Diablo Lake and pristine old-growth forests. There are a multitude of activities, however, that can be enjoyed in conjunction with the trail to make the day that much more memorable. For instance, during the summer, hike the trail to Ross Dam and then take a Seattle City Light ferry on the lake back down to the trailhead. Tours of the dams are also available, allowing folks to see why their lights turn on at the flip of a switch. Several campgrounds and picnic sites are also nearby for those using their cars as a base.

Diablo Lake Trail actually never nears the lakeshore, and instead takes a higher route that provides more views. Numerous peaks and ridges of the North Cascades are visible along the trail, especially from the viewpoint halfway down the trail. The trail is a great place to bird-watch, as scores of species make the forests here their home. While there is some elevation gain along the route, few hikers will have any difficulty with it. That makes it great for families (but keep an eye on little ones near the viewpoints). The trail eventually connects to Ross Dam, the end of one lake but the beginning of another.

User Groups: Hikers and leashed dogs. No horses or mountain bikes are allowed. No wheelchair access.

Open Seasons: This trail is accessible when Highway 20 is open. Highway 20 closure depends on seasonal snow, and it is usually closed November–April.

Permits: A federal Northwest Forest Pass is required to park here.

Maps: For a map of North Cascades National Park, contact the Outdoor Recreation Information Center at the downtown Seattle REI. For topographic maps, ask Green Trails for No. 48, Diablo Dam, or ask the USGS for Diablo Dam and Ross Dam.

Directions: From Marblemount, drive east on Highway 20. Turn left at Diablo Dam. The parking area is before crossing the dam, which is closed to car traffic. The trailhead is a .5-mile walk down the old road.

Contact: North Cascades National Park, Wilderness Information Center, 7280 Ranger Station Road, Marblemount, WA 98267, 360/873-4500.

29 BEAVER LOOP

32.5 mi/4 days

west of Ross Lake in North Cascades National Park

Map 3.1, page 91

Not so long ago, glaciers a mile thick slid down the Big Beaver and Little Beaver Valleys, carving them into wide U-shaped troughs. If you need proof, the Beaver Loop through the two valleys will surely provide it. This well-known backpacking route gains little elevation but enjoys some of Washington's largest stands of old-growth forest. Beaver Pass offers grand views of enormous valleys framed by even larger peaks.

The route follows Little Beaver Creek before crossing into Big Beaver Creek Valley. It's necessary to arrange a water taxi with Ross Lake Resort to deposit yourself at the mouth of Little Beaver Creek. Little Beaver Trail threads up the valley through 11 miles of remarkable forest. Camps are situated at the boat landing, at Perry Creek at 4.6 miles, and Stillwell Camp at 11.2 miles.

At Stillwell Camp, Big Beaver Trail cuts off and climbs to the pass. This requires a ford of Little Beaver Creek, difficult if not impossible in early summer when the snows are in full melt, so be prepared. At Big Beaver Pass (13.7 miles and home to Beaver Pass Camp), exploration will yield amazing views into the Luna Valley and its basin, while the Picketts tower over the valley. Big Beaver Trail drops into the wide, U-shaped valley and travels 13.5 miles to Ross Lake through stands of western red cedar more than 1,000 years old. The cedars alone are worth the 26.5 miles. Luna Camp is 2.7 miles from Beaver Pass, 39 Mile Camp is seven miles from the pass, and Pumpkin Mountain Camp is at Ross Lake. To get back to the car, hike the Ross Lake Trail six miles or make arrangements with the water taxi for a pickup at Big Beaver.

User Groups: Hikers only. No dogs, horses, or mountain bikes are allowed. No wheelchair access.

Open Seasons: This trail is accessible July–September.

Permits: A federal Northwest Forest Pass is required to park here. Overnight stays within the national park require reservations and backcountry camping permits, which are available at the Wilderness Information Center.

Maps: For a map of North Cascades National Park, contact the Outdoor Recreation Information Center at the downtown Seattle REI. For topographic maps, ask Green Trails for No. 15, Mount Challenger, and No. 16, Ross Lake, or ask the USGS for Pumpkin Mountain, Mount Prophet, Mount Redoubt, Mount Spickard, and Hozomeen Mountain.

Directions: From Marblemount, drive east 20 miles on Highway 20 to signed Diablo Dam. Turn left and cross the dam and turn immediately right for the parking area for Ross Lake Resort. Here, a ferry carries passengers to the Ross Lake Water Taxi for transportation to the trailheads.

Contact: North Cascades National Park, Wilderness Information Center, 7280 Ranger Station Road, Marblemount, WA 98267, 360/873-4500; Ross Lake Resort Water Taxi, 206/386-4437.

30 THUNDER CREEK

38.8 mi/4 days

south of Diablo Lake in North Cascades National Park

Map 3.1, page 91

This is one of the North Cascades' classic routes, leading deep into the park and out to Lake Chelan. The trail is also great for short day hikes up the creek, as there is plenty to see and do within the first several miles. Immense, icy peaks line the valley ridges while massive cedars and firs fill the forest along the trail. Thunder Creek is deservedly considered one of the park's classic hikes.

Thunder Creek Trail sets off within a large forest of western red cedar and Douglas fir. Hikers looking for a short day hike will enjoy Thunder Creek Nature Loop (.5 mile up Thunder Creek Trail), a one-mile loop that ventures off into old-growth forest. Thunder Creek Trail stays relatively flat for 7.5 miles to McAllister Camp, a good turnaround for long day hikes. Here, a bridge spans the creek as it rushes through a small canyon of granite, a wonderful place for lunch.

Farther along Thunder Creek Trail, the wilderness grows deeper, with views of rugged, glacial peaks to the west. Enormous glaciers cover these mountains and provide the creek with much of its rock flour. The trail continues through the forested valley to Park Creek Pass, a one-way total of 19.4 miles. Stehekin lies eight miles beyond. Numerous campsites are situated throughout the valley. Thunder

Creek makes a wonderful segment of a long trek through the North Cascades.

User Groups: Hikers, leashed dogs (dogs allowed on the first 6.5 miles but not within the national park), and horses. No mountain bikes are allowed. No wheelchair access.

Open Seasons: This trail is accessible April–November.

Permits: A federal Northwest Forest Pass is required to park here. Overnight stays within the national park require backcountry camping permits, which are available at the Wilderness Information Center.

Maps: For a map of North Cascades National Park, contact the Outdoor Recreation Information Center at the downtown Seattle REI. For topographic maps, ask Green Trails for No. 48, Diablo Dam, No. 49, Mount Logan, and No. 81, McGregor Mountain, or ask the USGS for Ross Dam, Forbidden Peak, and Mount Logan.

Directions: From Newhalem, drive east on Highway 20 to Mile Marker 130 and Colonial Creek Campground. Turn right and park in the lot above the boat ramp. The signed trailhead is located at the end of the parking lot.

Contact: North Cascades National Park, Wilderness Information Center, 7280 Ranger Station Road, Marblemount, WA 98267, 360/873-4500.

31 DESOLATION PEAK

13.6 mi/8.0 hr

east of Ross Lake in North Cascades National Park

Map 3.1, page 91

Jack Kerouac made Desolation Peak world-famous when he included the mountain in his book *Desolation Angels.* The book is based on his time with the Forest Service, when he was stationed at the still-functional lookout atop the lofty peak. Kerouac has helped to keep the peak a well-visited locale despite its truly desolate location.

Ross Lake Resort offers boat transportation to Desolation Landing near Lightning Creek. After disembarking from the boat, hike Desolation Peak Trail north along Ross Lake for two miles before making a very steep ascent to Desolation Peak. Although there is some shade along the way, much of the hillside was burned in a fire 75 years ago and gets a lot of sun. The views improve as the elevation increases, creating the opportunity for regular breaks. Bringing extra water is a must, as snow is the only source this high. From the open slopes of Desolation Peak, numerous peaks and ridges are visible. Ross Lake appears particularly agreeable after such a long hike. Overnight hikers will enjoy Desolation Camp, just below tree line.

User Groups: Hikers only. No dogs, horses, or mountain bikes are allowed. No wheelchair access.

Open Seasons: This trail is accessible mid-June–September.

Permits: A federal Northwest Forest Pass is required to park here. Overnight stays within the national park require reservations and backcountry camping permits, which are available at the Wilderness Information Center.

Maps: For a map of North Cascades National Park, contact the Outdoor Recreation Information Center at the downtown Seattle REI. For topographic maps, ask Green Trails for No. 16, Ross Lake, or ask the USGS for Hozomeen Mountain.

Directions: From Marblemount, drive east 20 miles on Highway 20 to signed Diablo Dam. Turn left and cross the dam and turn immediately right for the parking area for Ross Lake Resort. Here, a ferry carries passengers to the Ross Lake Water Taxi for transportation to the trailheads.

Contact: North Cascades National Park, Wilderness Information Center, 7280 Ranger Station Road, Marblemount, WA 98267, 360/873-4500; Ross Lake Resort Water Taxi, 206/386-4437.

32 MOUNT HIGGINS

9.0 mi/5.0 hr

west of Darrington in Mount Baker–Snoqualmie National Forest

Map 3.1, page 91

Mount Higgins is best known by Mountain Loop Highway drivers as the first big mountain they

pass under. Highly visible from the road is the long band of rock capping the ridge and leading into the tilted slats of Mount Higgins. The hike up is every bit as rewarding and as strenuous as it would seem from the car.

Mount Higgins Trail endures 3,300 feet of harsh elevation gain on the way. That's a lot of climbing, and only boggy and buggy Myrtle Lake offers a little respite along the way. Weary hikers who turn back early will still have a good time, but they miss the climax that makes all the hard work worth it. After passing a clear-cut, the trail enters virgin national forest. The grade eventually levels out, and the Myrtle Lake Trail soon breaks to the left, at 3.3 miles. Myrtle Lake is a short .5 mile away. Mount Higgins Trail continues climbing to an abandoned lookout post, just below the summits of Mount Higgins. These peaks are best left to true rock climbers. The view from the old lookout encompasses miles of mountains, including the Olympics across Puget Sound.

User Groups: Hikers and leashed dogs. No horses or mountain bikes are allowed. No wheelchair access.

Open Seasons: This trail is accessible July–October.

Permits: A federal Northwest Forest Pass is required to park here.

Maps: For a map of Mount Baker–Snoqualmie National Forest, contact the Outdoor Recreation Information Center at the downtown Seattle REI. For topographic maps, ask Green Trails for No. 77, Oso, or ask the USGS for Oso.

Directions: From Arlington, drive east 16 miles on the Mountain Loop Highway (Highway 530) to C-Post Road (just before Mile Marker 38). Turn right (north) onto C-Post Road. Continue on the road for 2.8 miles after crossing over the North Fork Stillaguamish River. The road dead-ends at the signed trailhead, and the trail is on the right side (east) of the road. Some parking is available along the road.

Contact: Mount Baker–Snoqualmie National Forest, Darrington Ranger Station, 1405 Emmens Street, Darrington, WA 98241, 360/436-1155.

33 BOULDER RIVER

8.6 mi/4.5 hr 2 8

within the Boulder River Wilderness southwest of the town of Darrington

Map 3.1, page 91

When the snow still lingers in the alpine regions during the springtime, Boulder River Trail offers an excellent chance to stretch the legs and get ready for summer. The trail wanders four miles into the river valley to a picturesque setting of camps. Along the way are several outstanding waterfalls dropping into the river, which makes much of its way through narrow gorges. With little elevation gain, the trail is a favorite for hikers of all ages and abilities.

Boulder River Trail follows an old logging road to the wilderness boundary, where great old-growth forest begins (1 mile). The first of Boulder's two high waterfalls soon comes into view. While this is a nice turnaround spot for the less serious, it's advisable to trek the next three miles.

Boulder River Trail continues through exceptional old-growth forests, often high above the noisy river. Early-season hikers will en-

© SCOTT LEONARD

Boulder River Trail, a good year-round hike

counter numerous trilliums and other understory flowers in full bloom. The trail empties out onto the river's banks (4.3 miles), where Three Fingers Peak can be seen up the valley. Expect to linger here a while. Boulder River is a great overnight trip as well, with several campsites clustered around the end of the trail.

User Groups: Hikers and leashed dogs. No horses or mountain bikes are allowed. No wheelchair access.

Open Seasons: This trail is accessible year-round.

Permits: A federal Northwest Forest Pass is required to park here.

Maps: For a map of Mount Baker–Snoqualmie National Forest, contact the Outdoor Recreation Information Center at the downtown Seattle REI. For topographic maps, ask Green Trails for No. 77, Oso, and No. 109, Granite Falls, or ask the USGS for Granite Falls.

Directions: From Arlington, drive east on Mountain Loop Highway (Highway 530) to French Creek Road. Turn right and drive 4 miles to the trailhead at road's end.

Contact: Mount Baker–Snoqualmie National Forest, Darrington Ranger Station, 1405 Emmens Street, Darrington, WA 98241, 360/436-1155.

34 HUCKLEBERRY MOUNTAIN

14.0 mi/9.0 hr

east of Darrington in Glacier Peak Wilderness of Mount Baker–Snoqualmie National Forest

Map 3.1, page 91

Huckleberry Mountain is a hike for the serious North Cascade hiker. Few trails in the state are as strenuous as Huckleberry Mountain—5,000 feet of vertical ascent in seven miles is evidence of that. But don't be scared off too easily. If you are looking for a rough, challenging hike, there is no better trail than this. The route climbs steeply through layers of forest zones before emerging among mountaintop meadows and expansive views.

Huckleberry Mountain Trail heads in one direction, which is up. Take relief in the cascading streams running nearby and the shade provided by the old-growth forest. The trail finally levels out after five miles, where it finds the crest of large, wide Huckleberry Mountain. The trail now heads north along the ridge before ending at the site of an old lookout. The expansive views soothe weary legs.

There are camps along the trail for those wishing to make a night of it. Be sure to carry extra water; once the snow is gone, so is your water. An early start is recommended for day hikers and backpackers alike. A group of lakes several miles north are accessible only by cross-country travel.

Note: Suiattle River Road was severely washed out in 2003, and a timeline for repair was not set at time of publication. Call ahead to see if the trail is accessible.

User Groups: Hikers, leashed dogs, and horses. No mountain bikes are allowed. No wheelchair access.

Open Seasons: This trail is accessible July–October.

Permits: A federal Northwest Forest Pass is required to park here.

Maps: For a map of Mount Baker–Snoqualmie National Forest, contact the Outdoor Recreation Information Center at the downtown Seattle REI. For topographic maps, ask Green Trails for No. 79, Snowking Mountain, or ask the USGS for Huckleberry Mountain.

Directions: From Darrington, drive north 7 miles on Highway 530 toward Rockport to Suiattle River Road (Forest Service Road 26). Turn right and drive 15 miles to the trailhead on the left.

Contact: Mount Baker–Snoqualmie National Forest, Darrington Ranger Station, 1405 Emmens Street, Darrington, WA 98241, 360/436-1155.

35 GREEN MOUNTAIN

8.0 mi/5.0 hr

west of Darrington in Glacier Peak Wilderness of Mount Baker–Snoqualmie National Forest

Map 3.1, page 91

Green Mountain has it all. Enjoy lush old-growth forest before breaking out into wide

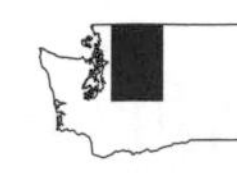

open meadows that give the mountain its name. Wildflowers cover the slopes in bright colors during July, while August brings a feast of huckleberries. Several small tarns tucked into a small basin present the perfect place for a rest and meal before the final ascent to the climax of the route. At the top of Green Mountain, at a lofty 6,500 feet, stands an old lookout soaking up panoramic views of the Cascades. There's not much one can ask of a trail that Green Mountain doesn't deliver.

Green Mountain trail starts high, at 3,500 feet, making it easier to stomach than most trails in the area. The forest breaks after one mile to revel in unbroken views. Several small tarns (2.5 miles) offer a rest stop (or turnaround) before the final climb to the summit. Built in 1933, the historic lookout perseveres atop Green Mountain. Glacier Peak rises spectacularly to the east while countless ridges and peaks fill the horizon. If we had just one day to spend hiking in the Mountain Loop Highway region, this would be it.

Note: Suiattle River Road was severely washed out in 2003, and a timeline for repair was not set at time of publication. Call ahead to see if the trail is accessible.

User Groups: Hikers, leashed dogs, and horses. No mountain bikes are allowed. No wheelchair access.

Open Seasons: This trail is accessible July–October.

Permits: A federal Northwest Forest Pass is required to park here.

Maps: For a map of Mount Baker–Snoqualmie National Forest, contact the Outdoor Recreation Information Center at the downtown Seattle REI. For topographic maps, ask Green Trails for No. 80, Cascade Pass, or ask the USGS for Downey Mountain.

Directions: From Darrington, drive north 7 miles on Highway 530 toward Rockport to Suiattle River Road (Forest Service Road 26). Turn right and drive 20.5 miles to Forest Service Road 2680. Turn left (north) and drive 6 miles to the trailhead at road's end.

Contact: Mount Baker–Snoqualmie National Forest, Darrington Ranger Station, 1405 Emmens Street, Darrington, WA 98241, 360/436-1155.

36 IMAGE LAKE

33.0 mi/3–4 days

in Glacier Peak Wilderness of Mount Baker–Snoqualmie National Forest

Map 3.1, page 91

When you finally reach Image Lake, you'll likely recognize the spectacular scene from numerous book covers and friends' pictures. Understandably, it's one of Washington's best-known scenes. Within a small high-country cirque, Image Lake reflects perfectly the majestic Glacier Peak, just seven miles distant.

The route follows Suiattle River Trail before breaking away and climbing to the upper ridge. The river valley is one of Washington's finest, filled with a lush forest of ancient timber. At 10.8 miles, veer left on Miners Ridge Trail and climb 5.5 miles to the subalpine splendor of Miners Ridge and Image Lake.

The trip can be done in three days, if you're quick, but it's best to take at least four days. It's possible to stay at a different camp each night. First- and last-night campsites can be found at Canyon Creek Camp (6.5 miles) and before Miners Ridge Trail junction (9.5 miles). Numerous campsites are at Image Lake and on Miners Ridge, but they manage to go quickly on summer weekends. One mile beyond Image Lake is Lady Camp with equally great views. Activities other than gazing at Glacier Peak include rambling along Miners Ridge, covered in wildflowers during July. Near the western end sits a lookout still maintained by the Forest Service.

Note: Suiattle River Road was severely washed out in 2003, and a timeline for repair was not set at time of publication. Call ahead to see if the trail is accessible.

User Groups: Hikers and leashed dogs. No horses or mountain bikes are allowed. No wheelchair access.

Open Seasons: This trail is accessible July–September.

Permits: A federal Northwest Forest Pass is required to park here.
Maps: For a map of Mount Baker–Snoqualmie National Forest, contact the Outdoor Recreation Information Center at the downtown Seattle REI. For topographic maps, ask Green Trails for No. 112, Glacier Peak, or ask the USGS for Lime Mountain and Gamma Peak.
Directions: From Darrington, drive north 7 miles on Highway 530 toward Rockport to Suiattle River Road (Forest Service Road 26). Drive 24 miles on Suiattle River Road to the trailhead at road's end.
Contact: Mount Baker–Snoqualmie National Forest, Darrington Ranger Station, 1405 Emmens Street, Darrington, WA 98241, 360/436-1155.

37 MOUNT PUGH (STUJACK PASS)

7.0 mi/5.0 hr

in Mount Baker–Snoqualmie National Forest

Map 3.1, page 91

In true North Cascades form, Mount Pugh Trail makes a challenging climb (nearly 4,000 feet) to expansive views that encompass a multitude of peaks. Stujack Pass is a small saddle on the ridge below mighty Pugh Mountain. The terrain is inspiring, where patches of small, weather-beaten trees grow in gardens of rock and heather. If this isn't enough, there is a footpath that leads to the summit of Mount Pugh. The question won't be if you want to summit Mount Pugh. The question will be if you have the energy to summit.

Mount Pugh Trail is in good shape to the pass, but beyond it is not much more than a rocky path. The trail moves through old-growth forest and encounters small Lake Meten (1.5 miles). Get used to switchbacks, for they are the story of the day. The forest eventually breaks and the route provides loads of views as it scales the rocky slope. Stujack Pass is a welcome sight. It's a great reward when you hit the pass and so much is finally revealed to the east. Hearty hikers can climb another 1,500 feet (in just 1.5 miles) to the summit via a tricky foot path along the ridge. From the summit, views from Rainier to Baker embrace too much of the Cascades to absorb in just one afternoon.
User Groups: Hikers and leashed dogs. No horses or mountain bikes are allowed. No wheelchair access.
Open Seasons: This trail is accessible August–October.
Permits: A federal Northwest Forest Pass is required to park here.
Maps: For a map of Mount Baker–Snoqualmie National Forest, contact the Outdoor Recreation Information Center at the downtown Seattle REI. For topographic maps, ask Green Trails for No. 111, Sloan Peak, or ask the USGS for Pugh Mountain and White Chuck Mountain.
Directions: From Darrington, drive east 14 miles on Mountain Loop Highway to Forest Service Road 2095. Turn left and drive 1.5 miles to the trailhead on the right.
Contact: Mount Baker–Snoqualmie National Forest, Darrington Ranger Station, 1405 Emmens Street, Darrington, WA 98241, 360/436-1155.

38 MEADOW MOUNTAIN

21.0 mi/2–3 days

in Glacier Peak Wilderness of Mount Baker–Snoqualmie National Forest

Map 3.1, page 91

A long approach to Meadow Mountain has made it much wilder than many of its counterparts. Closure of the access road added 5.5 miles to the hike, weeding out the day-hiker crowd. That's good news for those seeking an easy but satisfying weekend trip to sublime meadows and mountain views. Huckleberries, wildflowers, and marmots are all over, indulging hikers in paradise. The trail gets only better the farther one travels, tracing an open ridge to Fire Mountain.

The first 5.5 miles are along Forest Service Road 2710, whose closure is a mixed blessing. It's never much fun to hike a road, but say goodbye to the crowds. Meadow Mountain Trail climbs steeply and quickly to a pass, where the trail forks (7.5 miles). The left route drops slightly to Meadow Lake (8.2 miles), encircled by rocky cliffs and meadows. The main trail follows the ridge east, passing through subalpine parkland. Big Glacier Peak stands almost alarmingly close. Emerald and Diamond Lakes (10.5 miles) lie to the north of the trail, requiring some easy cross-country travel. Few spots are as peaceful Meadow Mountain. Campsites are scattered along the route but good, established sites are found at each of the lakes.

User Groups: Hikers, leashed dogs, and horses. No mountain bikes are allowed. No wheelchair access.

Open Seasons: This trail is accessible July–October.

Permits: A federal Northwest Forest Pass is required to park here.

Maps: For a map of Mount Baker–Snoqualmie National Forest, contact the Outdoor Recreation Information Center at the downtown Seattle REI. For topographic maps, ask Green Trails for No. 111, Sloan Peak, and No. 112, Glacier Peak, or ask the USGS for Pugh Mountain and Glacier Peak.

Directions: From Darrington, drive east 9 miles on Mountain Loop Highway to White Chuck Road (Forest Service Road 23). Turn left (east) and drive 6 miles to Forest Service Road 27 (signed "Meadow Mountain Trail"). Turn left (north) and drive 2.4 miles to Forest Service Road 2710, which is gated, and the new trailhead.

Contact: Mount Baker–Snoqualmie National Forest, Darrington Ranger Station, 1405 Emmens Street, Darrington, WA 98241, 360/436-1155.

39 GOAT FLATS

10.0 mi/5.0 hr

in the Boulder River Wilderness, within Mount Baker–Snoqualmie National Forest

Map 3.1, page 91

It's hard to believe that such great hiking is so close to the Seattle area. Proximity to the city brings out the crowds, but the high-country beauty of Goat Flats deserves to be experienced by all. Three Fingers Trail travels five miles to the paradise of Goat Flats. Ancient forests surrender to views of old, craggy mountains. This is undoubtedly the best stretch of trail in Boulder River Wilderness.

Three Fingers Trail climbs through old-growth forest before encountering Saddle Lake (2.5 miles), modest in size but inviting nonetheless. Overnight guests need to make camp at least 200 feet from the lake. Three Fingers Trail continues its ascent through alpine meadows and increasingly rewarding views. Goat Flats sit in a particularly wide saddle along the ridge (5.5 miles), offering a grand perspective on the Cascades. Enjoy the meadows overflowing with flowers in midsummer and the huckleberries in the late summer. The trail continues one mile to Tin Can Gap and another mile to an old lookout atop Three Fingers. Tin Can Gap is too strenuous of an effort to be worthwhile and the lookout is usually reserved for climbers. Bring your lunch, stick to Goat Flats, and you'll be talking about it for months.

User Groups: Hikers and leashed dogs. No horses or mountain bikes are allowed. No wheelchair access.

Open Seasons: This trail is accessible July–October.

Permits: A federal Northwest Forest Pass is required to park here.

Maps: For a map of Mount Baker–Snoqualmie National Forest, contact the Outdoor Recreation Information Center at the downtown Seattle REI. For topographic maps, ask Green Trails for No. 109, Granite Falls, and No. 110, Silverton, or ask the USGS for Granite Falls and Silverton.

Directions: From Granite Falls, drive 7 miles east to Tupso Pass Road (Forest Service Road 41). Turn right and drive this long, gravel road to its end, 18 miles later. Watch for road markers, as many small roads branch off the main road, Forest Service Road 41.

Contact: Mount Baker–Snoqualmie National Forest, Verlot Public Service Center, 33515 Mountain Loop Highway, Granite Falls, WA 98252, 360/691-7791.

40 MOUNT PILCHUCK

6.0 mi/3.5 hr

east of Verlot in Mount Baker–Snoqualmie National Forest and Mount Pilchuck State Park

Map 3.1, page 91

An outstanding hike, the greatest attraction along Mount Pilchuck Trail is undoubtedly the restored fire lookout at the summit. Built in 1920, the lookout was restored by the Everett Chapter of the Mountaineers to a condition equaling the outstanding views from within. The lookout peers out to the entire Puget Sound Basin, with Seattle's buildings distant specks, up to Mount Baker and over many North Cascade peaks to Glacier Peak. The lookout contains a full history of the site as well as a great map of visible peaks. This is all on top of a hike through a beautiful old-growth forest and parkland meadows among the granite slabs of the mountain.

Mount Pilchuck Trail begins within a forest teeming with giant mountain hemlocks. The trail climbs steadily the entire way but never at an excruciating grade. The trail turns north and works its way around Little Pilchuck to enter the north basin. Hemlocks and Alaskan yellow cedar find ground amid enormous slabs of granite. Snow lingers late into summer along this north-facing basin, although it rarely poses a problem. The ascent to the summit is the steepest part of the trail but well worth it. On a sunny day, there is no grander view of the Puget Sound Basin. Check the weather, as Pilchuck has a nasty legend for fast-arriving fog, a definite view spoiler.

User Groups: Hikers and leashed dogs. No horses or mountain bikes are allowed. No wheelchair access.

Open Seasons: This trail is accessible June–November.

Permits: A federal Northwest Forest Pass is required to park here.

Maps: For a map of Mount Baker–Snoqualmie National Forest, contact the Outdoor Recreation Information Center at the downtown Seattle REI. For topographic maps, ask Green Trails for No. 109, Granite Falls, or ask the USGS for Granite Falls.

Directions: From Granite Falls, drive east 12 miles on Mountain Loop Highway (Highway 530) to Pilchuck Road (Forest Service Road 42). Turn right and drive 7 miles to the trailhead at road's end.

Contact: Mount Baker–Snoqualmie National Forest, Verlot Public Service Center, 33515 Mountain Loop Highway, Granite Falls, WA 98252, 360/691-7791.

41 HEATHER LAKE

3.8 mi/3.0 hr

east of Granite Falls in Mount Baker–Snoqualmie National Forest

Map 3.1, page 91

Below the north face of Mount Pilchuck, Heather Lake is one of the Mountain Loop Highway's most beautiful day hikes. A stretch among giant timber brings Heather Lake, inviting hikers to stick around for a while with a loop around the lake. In the latter part of summer, tasty huckleberries stain your hands while lofty peaks strain your neck. For proximity to the Seattle area and overall grandeur, there are few better destinations.

Heather Lake Trail climbs steadily but at an easy grade. While the path may have been overcome by roots or rocks at times, it is wide enough to easily accommodate the crowds that hike it. The first mile winds through long-ago-logged land, with enormous cedar stumps testament to the old forests. Notice several 80-foot western hemlocks growing atop cedar stumps, with roots snaking to the ground. Soon, the trail enters virgin forest set upon steep slopes, and one can begin to see the challenges the old lumberjacks faced. The trail drops into Heather Lake Basin, with views of Mount Pilchuck's steep walls and a trail with numerous structures to take you around the lake. Time your hike right (in August) and feast on berries.

User Groups: Hikers and leashed dogs. No

horses or mountain bikes are allowed. No wheelchair access.

Open Seasons: This trail is accessible mid-May–November.

Permits: A federal Northwest Forest Pass is required to park here.

Maps: For a map of Mount Baker–Snoqualmie National Forest, contact the Outdoor Recreation Information Center at the downtown Seattle REI. For topographic maps, ask Green Trails for No. 109, Granite Falls, or ask the USGS for Verlot.

Directions: From Granite Falls, drive east 12 miles on the Mountain Loop Highway (Highway 530) to Pilchuck Road (Forest Service Road 42). Turn right and drive 1.5 miles to the signed trailhead.

Contact: Mount Baker–Snoqualmie National Forest, Verlot Public Service Center, 33515 Mountain Loop Highway, Granite Falls, WA 98252, 360/691-7791.

42 LAKE 22

5.4 mi/4.0 hr

east of Granite Falls in Mount Baker–Snoqualmie National Forest

Map 3.1, page 91

The designation of Lake 22 Research Natural Area preserved the landscape around this trail, making it the jewel of the southern Mountain Loop Highway. Climbing entirely through old-growth forest, the journey is as beautiful as the destination, which is a tall order in Lake 22's case. Along the trail, cascading waterfalls work to draw your attention from enormous Douglas firs and western red cedars. At the lake, steep walls leading to a rugged ridge of granite compete for attention with bushes of huckleberries.

Lake 22 Trail climbs steadily along 22 Creek, rumbling with several large cascades. The tread is well maintained, and the number of log structures is impressive. Just in time, the grade flattens and Lake 22 stands before you, guarded by the towering north face of Mount Pilchuck. The lake is stocked, so a fishing pole is put to good use here. This is a great day hike from Seattle and is very popular. But no size of crowd should keep hikers from experiencing Lake 22.

User Groups: Hikers only. No dogs, horses, or mountain bikes are allowed. No wheelchair access.

Open Seasons: This trail is accessible mid-May–November.

Permits: A federal Northwest Forest Pass is required to park here.

Maps: For a map of Mount Baker–Snoqualmie National Forest, contact the Outdoor Recreation Information Center at the downtown Seattle REI. For topographic maps, ask Green Trails for No. 109, Granite Falls, or ask the USGS for Verlot.

Directions: From Granite Falls, drive east 13 miles on the Mountain Loop Highway (Highway 530) to the signed trailhead on the right.

Contact: Mount Baker–Snoqualmie National Forest, Verlot Public Service Center, 33515 Mountain Loop Highway, Granite Falls, WA 98252, 360/691-7791.

43 ASHLAND LAKES/ BALD MOUNTAIN

4.0–9.8 mi/2.0–10.0 hr

south of Verlot on Washington Department of Natural Resources land

Map 3.1, page 91

This is one of the Seattle area's lesser-known hikes. On Washington Department of Natural Resources land, which is usually less than scenic, the Ashland Lakes and Bald Mountain area actually retains its old-growth forests and meadows. Perhaps the nickname Department of Nothing Left is not entirely appropriate after all. A small network of trails visits several sets of lakes and rides the crest of a long ridge. Much of it is easily accessible to hikers of all ages. For just an hour out of Seattle, it doesn't get much better than this.

Hikers can access Bald Mountain from the west or east end. Bald Mountain Trail runs along the crest of Bald Mountain, more like a ridge than a mountain. On the eastern side are Cutthroat Lakes (9.8 miles), a large grouping of tarns and small lakes set in subalpine meadows. On the western end of the trail are Ashland Lakes (4 miles). This pair of lakes, along with Beaver Plant Lake, are immersed in grand old-growth forest. DNR constructed nice, large campsites at each of the lakes. A little farther down the trail from these lakes are Twin Falls, where Wilson Creek makes an enormous cascade off a cliff into a small lake.

User Groups: Hikers and leashed dogs. No horses or mountain bikes are allowed. No wheelchair access.

Open Seasons: This trail is accessible May–November.

Permits: A federal Northwest Forest Pass is required to park here.

Maps: For a map of this area, contact the Outdoor Recreation Information Center at the downtown Seattle REI. For topographic maps, ask Green Trails for No. 110, Silverton, and No. 142, Index, or ask the USGS for Silverton and Index.

Directions: For Ashland Lakes, drive 4.5 miles east of Verlot to Forest Serice Road 4020. Turn right (south) and drive 2.3 miles to Forest Service Road 4021. Turn right and drive 1.5 miles to Forest Service Road 4021-016. Turn left onto Forest Service Road 4021-016 and drive to the Ashland trailhead at road's end.

For Cutthroat Lakes, drive east 7 miles from Verlot to Forest Service Road 4030. Turn right (south) and drive 1 mile to Forest Service Road 4032. Turn right and drive 8 miles to the trailhead at road's end.

Contact: Mount Baker–Snoqualmie National Forest, Verlot Public Service Center, 33515 Mountain Loop Highway, Granite Falls, WA 98252, 360/691-7791.

44 MOUNT FORGOTTEN MEADOWS

8.0 mi/5.0 hr

east of Granite Falls in Mount Baker–Snoqualmie National Forest

Map 3.1, page 91

When Perry Creek Trail breaks out of the forest onto the open ridge and Mount Forgotten stares down on you, the previous four miles of steep ascent become worth every step. Great mountain views are finally at hand. But the best is yet to come. Continuing to the meadows of Mount Forgotten delivers expansive and panoramic views of numerous North Cascades peaks.

At first, Perry Creek Trail climbs slowly through several open avalanche fields. As the trail enters the forest, Perry Creek Falls greets hikers as it rushes through a small gorge. From here, the trail gets mean. The route switchbacks up through old-growth forest of Alaskan yellow cedars and Pacific silver firs, whose shade and understory of huckleberries compensate for the climb.

Soon, the trail breaks out onto the ridge, with Mount Baker visible from afar and Mount Forgotten finally apparent. Just before the ridge, follow a small footpath to the right. Mount Forgotten Meadows await a few hundred yards away, with spectacular views of Glacier Peak and other surrounding mountains. There are few better picnic spots in the Mountain Loop Highway area.

User Groups: Hikers and leashed dogs. No horses or mountain bikes are allowed. No wheelchair access.

Open Seasons: This trail is accessible June–October.

Permits: A federal Northwest Forest Pass is required to park here.

Maps: For a map of Mount Baker–Snoqualmie National Forest, contact the Outdoor Recreation Information Center at the downtown Seattle REI. For topographic maps, ask Green Trails for No. 111, Sloan Peak, or ask the USGS for Bedal.

Directions: From Granite Falls, drive east 26 miles on Mountain Loop Highway (Highway 530) to Perry Creek Road (Forest Service Road 4063). Turn left and drive 1.5 miles (stay left at the fork) to the trailhead at road's end.

Contact: Mount Baker–Snoqualmie National Forest, Verlot Public Service Center, 33515 Mountain Loop Highway, Granite Falls, WA 98252, 360/691-7791.

45 MOUNT DICKERMAN

8.6 mi/5.0 hr

east of Granite Falls in Mount Baker–Snoqualmie National Forest

Map 3.1, page 91

Mount Dickerman persists as a Mountain Loop Highway favorite in spite of its punishing nature. After all, prolific berry bushes and expansive mountain views have the tendency to cancel out killer ascents. During the burly hike up countless switchbacks, keep your mind focused on the August berries that will surely revive your step. And during the final rise, keep your attention on the opening and expanding scenes, culminated by a near orgy of views at the summit.

Mount Dickerman Trail starts off as serious as a heart attack, making a full-on assault on the hillside. The valley floor disappears while you zigzag up through a cool forest with a few creeks for splashdowns. The trail levels off a bit to enter open meadows chock-full of huckleberry bushes. The trail keeps on climbing to make the final ascent to the summit. Glacier Peak is an imposing neighbor while all of the Monte Cristo peaks make their own appearance. It can be a busy trail in the summer, but as always with North Cascade summits, it's well worth it.

User Groups: Hikers and leashed dogs. No horses or mountain bikes are allowed. No wheelchair access.

Open Seasons: This trail is accessible July–October.

Permits: A federal Northwest Forest Pass is required to park here.

Maps: For a map of Mount Baker–Snoqualmie National Forest, contact the Outdoor Recreation Information Center at the downtown Seattle REI. For topographic maps, ask Green Trails for No. 111, Sloan Peak, or ask the USGS for Bedal.

Directions: From Granite Falls, drive east on the Mountain Loop Highway (Highway 530) for 28 miles. The signed trailhead is on the left (north) side of the highway.

Contact: Mount Baker–Snoqualmie National Forest, Verlot Public Service Center, 33515 Mountain Loop Highway, Granite Falls, WA 98252, 360/691-7791.

46 GOTHIC BASIN

9.0 mi/5.0 hr

east of Granite Falls in Henry M. Jackson Wilderness of Mount Baker–Snoqualmie National Forest

Map 3.1, page 91

While little remains of the once-bustling mining town of Monte Cristo, the miners' trails live on. The trail up to Gothic Basin, one of many mines in the area, reveals the job's greatest perk: unbelievable views of mountains and valleys. Indeed, Gothic Basin Trail is a testament to the hardiness of the old miners. In a successful effort to get to the worksite quickly, it makes a very steep ascent to the basin, a barren moonscape save for large Foggy Lake.

Hike or bike Monte Cristo Road 1.1 miles to Gothic Basin Trail, just before the road crosses the Sauk River. It's a quick and dirty climb to the basin using steep switchbacks, but several impressive waterfalls alleviate the tough ascent. Snow lingers late within several creek gorges, making the route strongly not recommended when significant snowpack remains on the hillside. The trail eventually reaches the Gothic Basin (4.6 miles), an expansive bowl of heather meadows. Del Campo and Gothic Peaks tower above Foggy Lake on either side. For the rockhounds out there, this is a great place to explore. Numerous types of rocks are found up here, including conglomerates, granite, limestone, and sandstone. It's amazing to think that this place used to be, for miners, just another day at the office.

User Groups: Hikers, leashed dogs, and mountain bikes (mountain bikes on Monte Cristo Road). No horses are allowed. No wheelchair access.

Open Seasons: This trail is accessible late July–October.

Permits: A federal Northwest Forest Pass is required to park here.
Maps: For a map of Mount Baker–Snoqualmie National Forest, contact the Outdoor Recreation Information Center at the downtown Seattle REI. For topographic maps, ask Green Trails for No. 111, Sloan Peak, and No. 143, Monte Cristo, or ask the USGS for Monte Cristo.
Directions: From Granite Falls, drive east 30 miles on the Mountain Loop Highway (Highway 530) to the trailhead at Barlow Pass.
Contact: Mount Baker–Snoqualmie National Forest, Verlot Public Service Center, 33515 Mountain Loop Highway, Granite Falls, WA 98252, 360/691-7791.

47 POODLE DOG PASS/ TWIN LAKES

17.4 mi/1–2 days

east of Granite Falls in Henry M. Jackson Wilderness of Mount Baker–Snoqualmie National Forest

Map 3.1, page 91

Poodle Dog Pass is one of the Mountain Loop Highway's premier hikes, set about as deep as one can get within the Cascades. This is high country, where meadows of heather cover the hillsides and mountain peaks dominate the skyline. The closure of Monte Cristo Road has made this a much longer trek, subsequently helping the path ditch most of its crowds. Rugged peaks and mountains are the theme to this hike, some of the best of the Monte Cristo region.

Accessing Poodle Dog Pass requires an easy four-mile hike or bike down Monte Cristo Road. While the road is closed to vehicles, it's not closed to mountain bikes, a popular way of cutting eight miles off the round-trip. From Monte Cristo, Poodle Dog Pass Trail steadily climbs out of the forest and into meadows, climbing over 1,600 feet in just 1.7 miles. From Poodle Dog Pass (1.7 miles), a side trail leads to large Silver Lake, set beneath the cliffs of Silvertip Peak. Beyond the pass, Twin Lakes Trail continues through superb terrain of meadows and rock fields, shooting right between Twin Peaks before dropping to Twin Lakes. The long ridge of Columbia Peak stands more than 2,400 feet above the lakes, creating a large, ringed basin. Established campsites are found at each of the three lakes, and camping should be restricted to these sites only.
User Groups: Hikers, leashed dogs, and mountain bikes (mountain bikes on Monte Cristo Road). No horses are allowed. No wheelchair access.
Open Seasons: This trail is accessible July–October.
Permits: A federal Northwest Forest Pass is required to park here.
Maps: For a map of Mount Baker–Snoqualmie National Forest, contact the Outdoor Recreation Information Center at the downtown Seattle REI. For topographic maps, ask Green Trails for No. 111, Sloan Peak, and No. 143, Monte Cristo, or ask the USGS for Monte Cristo.
Directions: From Granite Falls, drive east 30 miles on the Mountain Loop Highway (Highway 530) to Monte Cristo Trail at Barlow Pass.
Contact: Mount Baker–Snoqualmie National Forest, Verlot Public Service Center, 33515 Mountain Loop Highway, Granite Falls, WA 98252, 360/691-7791.

48 GLACIER BASIN

12.2 mi/8.0 hr

east of Granite Falls in Henry M. Jackson Wilderness of Mount Baker–Snoqualmie National Forest

Map 3.1, page 91

Glacier Basin has the ability to make a person feel about as big as an ant. With massive mountains towering several thousand feet above the basin on every side, any understanding of "perspective" slips off into the thin mountain air. The imposing cliffs and peaks of Cadet and Monte Cristo seem to redefine scale. Glacier Basin is the perfect locale to reset the human ego.

Glacier Basin Trail departs from the old town of Monte Cristo, an easy four-mile walk down the closed-to-vehicles Monte Cristo Road. A popular means for arriving here is via mountain bike, riding along the road and then hiking the trail. The trail sets off at a decent pace before sharply quickening in its ascent. Rising up the valley, the trail passes a dramatic waterfall on Glacier Creek before taking a turn up over Mystery Hill (6 miles), the place for overnight camps.

By now the forest has faded away and meadows fill in between talus slopes. Picas and marmots are heard frequently, just before they scuttle off beneath the rocks. The trail gradually levels out and enters the basin, which is filled with meadows and interlocked braids of creeks. This is beautiful alpine territory, not so long ago buried beneath massive glaciers.

User Groups: Hikers, leashed dogs, and mountain bikes (mountain bikes on Monte Cristo Road). No horses are allowed. No wheelchair access.

Open Seasons: This trail is accessible July–October.

Permits: A federal Northwest Forest Pass is required to park here.

Maps: For a map of Mount Baker–Snoqualmie National Forest, contact the Outdoor Recreation Information Center at the downtown Seattle REI. For topographic maps, ask Green Trails for No. 111, Sloan Peak, and No. 143, Monte Cristo, or ask the USGS for Monte Cristo and Blanca Lake.

Directions: From Granite Falls, drive east 30 miles on the Mountain Loop Highway (Highway 530) to the trailhead at Barlow Pass.

Contact: Mount Baker–Snoqualmie National Forest, Verlot Public Service Center, 33515 Mountain Loop Highway, Granite Falls, WA 98252, 360/691-7791.

49 FOURTH OF JULY PASS

12.2 mi/5.0 hr 2 8

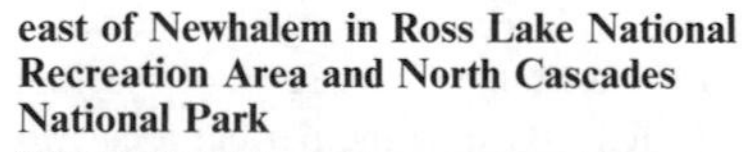

east of Newhalem in Ross Lake National Recreation Area and North Cascades National Park

Map 3.2, page 92

This is one of the few passes in the North Cascades that does not inspire a cold sweat in hikers. Unlike many of its kin, this is not a steep, near-vertical trail leading to the pass. On the contrary, the route along Panther Creek is extremely beautiful and easy to hike. Numerous cascades and waterfalls are the result of the creek's course over ever-present boulders. The total elevation gain of 1,800 feet is spread out over six miles, so Fourth of July Pass can be achieved by the whole family. Wide views of glacially capped mountains await at the top. And for those with the means for transportation, the trail continues to Thunder Creek for a great through-hike.

The best route up to the pass is definitely via Panther Creek. Panther Creek Trail stays near the gushing creek as it passes through a luxuriant forest of large western red cedars. At 3.1 miles is Panther Camp, with several sites. The trail begins to climb up the hillside when the creek makes a hard turn to the southeast to venture deep into the wilderness. Glaciers carved the pass long ago to avoid Ruby Mountain, leaving it wide and flat. Panther Potholes offer a cool respite on hot days. The best views are from Fourth of July Camp. From here are expansive views of the Neve Glacier sliding down off Snowfield Peak and Colonial Peak. The trail continues 2.5 miles to Thunder Creek Trail (2.1 miles from the trailhead).

User Groups: Hikers only. No dogs, horses, or mountain bikes are allowed. No wheelchair access.

Open Seasons: This trail is accessible July–October.

Permits: A federal Northwest Forest Pass is required to park here.

Maps: For a map of North Cascades National Park, contact the Outdoor Recreation Information Center at the downtown Seattle REI. For topographic maps, ask Green Trails for No. 48, Diablo Dam, and No. 49, Mount Logan, or ask the USGS for Crater Mountain and Ross Dam.

Directions: From Marblemount, drive east on Highway 20 to East Bank Trailhead, 8 miles beyond Colonial Creek Campground. Park at

East Bank Trailhead, cross the highway, and walk .3 mile east to the trailhead on the south side of the highway.

Contact: North Cascades National Park, Wilderness Information Center, 7280 Ranger Station Road, Marblemount, WA 98267, 360/873-4500.

50 DEVIL'S DOME LOOP

41.7 mi/4–5 days

east of Ross Lake in North Cascades National Park and Pasayten Wilderness

Map 3.2, page 92

The North Cascades National Park is well known for its large selection of extended backpacking trips. Devil's Dome Loop is one of its best, even trekking across part of the Pasayten Wilderness. Set along the high ridges east of Ross Lake, the loop encircles mammoth Jack Mountain while enjoying miles of far-flung vistas, acres of old-growth forests, and privacy in the deep wilderness. The route is a tough one and should be undertaken only by those ready for four or more days in the backcountry.

Heading counterclockwise, Jackita Ridge Trail climbs steeply from Canyon Creek onto the barren, rocky slopes of Crater Mountain. From here, 11 miles of trail traverses Jackita Ridge before encountering Devil's Ridge Trail at Devil's Pass. Devil's Ridge Trail heads east for another five miles of high-country hiking. From this point, the trail drops to Ross Lake. The East Bank Trail follows the shore 15 miles before returning to Canyon Creek Trailhead. While a four-day trip is possible, five or six days is much better.

Water is an important consideration, as the ridge is extremely dry once the snowpack has melted. Along the way are many established camps. Most notable are (from Canyon Creek Trailhead): Devil's Park (7 miles), Devil's Pass Shelter (16 miles), Skyline Camp (18 miles), Devil's Dome (20 miles), and Bear Skull (22 miles). The East Bank Trail has many camps spread along its shores. The Devil's Dome Loop is highly respected for its ability to challenge even veteran hikers.

User Groups: Hikers only. No dogs, horses, or mountain bikes are allowed. No wheelchair access.

Open Seasons: This area is accessible mid-July–October.

Permits: A federal Northwest Forest Pass is required to park here. Overnights stays within the national park require backcountry camping permits, which are available at the Wilderness Information Center.

Maps: For a map of North Cascades National Park, contact the Outdoor Recreation Information Center at the downtown Seattle REI. For topographic maps, ask Green Trails for No. 16, Ross Lake, No. 17, Jack Mountain, No. 48, Diablo Dam, and No. 49, Mount Logan, or ask the USGS for Crater Mountain, Azurite Peak, Shull Mountain, Jack Mountain, and Pumpkin Mountain.

Directions: From Marblemount, drive east on Highway 20 to the Canyon Creek Trailhead, near Mile Marker 142.

Contact: North Cascades National Park, Wilderness Information Center, 7280 Ranger Station Road, Marblemount, WA 98267, 360/873-4500.

51 EAST CREEK

16.0 mi/2 days

west of Winthrop in North Cascades Scenic Highway and Okanogan National Forest

Map 3.2, page 92

Despite an easily accessible trailhead on Highway 20, few people bother to visit East Creek. Perhaps the trail is overshadowed by the reputations of bigger, better-known trails. Other folks' loss is your gain should you undertake East Creek. Eight miles of trail travel through terrific old-growth forest and open meadow to Mebee Pass, where views are finally afforded. From the pass, scramble to surrounding peaks, peer into the long Methow River valley, bask in the sun, and most of all, enjoy the solitude.

East Creek Trail crosses Granite Creek via footbridge before making a quick ascent along East Creek. A ford of East Creek is

required (2.5 miles), a difficult endeavor when the winter's snows are still melting. Late July is best, as runoff has lowered but wildflowers are still in bloom. The trail continues up the valley, crossing numerous creeks. The last 1.5 miles is a steep climb up the side of the valley, breaking out of the forest into meadows. At the pass stands an old fire lookout, built in 1933 and recently renovated. Camps are situated at several places along the trail, but the best are just below Mebee Pass in the meadows.

User Groups: Hikers, leashed dogs, and horses. No mountain bikes are allowed. No wheelchair access.

Open Seasons: This trail is accessible July–October.

Permits: A federal Northwest Forest Pass is required to park here.

Maps: For a map of Okanogan National Forest, contact the Outdoor Recreation Information Center at the downtown Seattle REI. For topographic maps, ask Green Trails for No. 49, Mount Logan, or ask the USGS for Azurita Peak.

Directions: From Marblemount, drive east on Highway 20 to the East Creek Trailhead, near Mile Marker 146.

Contact: Okanogan National Forest, Methow Valley Ranger District, 24 West Chewuch Road, Winthrop, WA 98862, 509/996-4003.

52 EASY PASS/FISHER CREEK

7.0 mi/5.0 hr 5 9

east of Newhalem in Okanogan National Forest and North Cascades National Park

Map 3.2, page 92

Easy Pass is easily one of the biggest misnomers within the North Cascades, as there is nothing easy about it. After all, a rugged, rocky climb of 2,800 feet is rarely easy. It certainly isn't here. The scenery, however, is easy on the eyes. The colossal Mount Logan, cloaked in ice, stares from across the valley while Fisher Peak stands at the head of the basin. Wildflowers and wildlife roam freely below in the wild and undisturbed valley. The trail continues by dropping into the basin and wandering out Fisher Creek Valley to Thunder Creek, an exceptional trek.

Easy Pass Trail immediately crosses boulder-strewn Granite Creek and starts a long, arduous climb to the pass. After two miles, the trail breaks out of forest and enters an avalanche chute between the steep walls of Ragged Ridge. The name Easy Pass stems from the fact that this was the easiest (and only) place for a trail over Ragged Ridge. The trail finally reaches the pass after 3.5 miles. Here, subalpine larches claim whatever soil they can for a home, turning a brilliant gold in the fall. There is no camping at the pass.

For overnight trips, Easy Pass Trail continues down to Fisher Creek (within the national park). This is black-bear country, and the animals are frequently spotted roaming the hillsides munching on huckleberries. Fisher Camp is at the lower part of the flower-filled basin and makes a great overnight resting spot. The trail proceeds down through the forested valley to Thunder Creek, 11 miles from Easy Pass.

User Groups: Hikers and leashed dogs (dogs to Easy Pass only). No horses or mountain bikes are allowed. No wheelchair access.

Open Seasons: This trail is accessible mid-July–mid-October.

Permits: A federal Northwest Forest Pass is required to park here. Overnights stays within the national park require backcountry camping permits.

Maps: For a map of Okanogan National Forest and North Cascades National Park, contact the Outdoor Recreation Information Center at the downtown Seattle REI. For topographic maps, ask Green Trails for No. 49, Mount Logan, or ask the USGS for Mount Arriva and Mount Logan.

Directions: From Winthrop, drive about 40 miles west on Highway 20 (or 46 miles east from Marblemount) to Easy Pass Trailhead. The trailhead is on the south side of the highway.

Contact: North Cascades National Park, Wilderness Information Center, 7280 Ranger Station Road, Marblemount, WA 98267, 360/873-4500.

53 RAINY LAKE NATURE TRAIL

1.8 mi/1.0 hr 1 9

west of Winthrop in Okanogan National Forest

Map 3.2, page 92

The achievement of motoring up a pass is usually a call for celebration and a little leg stretching. Rainy Lake Nature Trail provides the perfect excuse to pull over and work out the cramps. Only a mile to the lake, with no elevation change, Rainy Lake Trail is easily accomplished by folks of all ages and abilities. The paved path has educational signs pointing out plant species or ecological processes. Some of the trees on the trail are downright imposing. At the end lies Rainy Lake, sitting within a glacial cirque. The Lyall Glacier sits above with its meltwater cascading into the lake. This is a great stop!

User Groups: Hikers and leashed dogs. No horses or mountain bikes are allowed. The trail is wheelchair accessible.

Open Seasons: This trail is accessible mid-June–October.

Permits: A federal Northwest Forest Pass is required to park here.

Maps: For a map of Okanogan National Forest, contact the Outdoor Recreation Information Center at the downtown Seattle REI. For topographic maps, ask Green Trails for No. 50, Washington Pass, or ask the USGS for Washington Pass.

Directions: From Newhalem, drive Highway 20 to Mile Marker 157. Turn right into the south trailhead. The north trailhead is only for Cutthroat Pass and the Pacific Crest Trail.

Contact: Okanogan National Forest, Methow Valley Ranger District, 24 West Chewuch Road, Winthrop, WA 98862, 509/996-4003.

54 LAKE ANN/MAPLE PASS

3.8–7.6 mi/2.0–4.5 hr 3 8

west of Winthrop in Okanogan National Forest

Map 3.2, page 92

With good reason, Lake Ann is one of Highway 20's most-often-recommended day hikes. Just two miles of hiking delivers a beautiful lake surrounded by towering ridges. It's a great place for bird-watching, offers the chance to do a little fishing, and makes for a nice picnic. Plus, it can be added as a side trip to Maple Pass.

Lake Ann Trail heads up through a great old-growth forest filled with Pacific silver fir and mountain hemlock. The path is well maintained and the grade climbs gently. Marmots are likely to greet you with a shrill whistle while you pass through the meadows. The trail divides (1.5 miles), with the Maple Pass Trail heading to the right. Stay to the left and soon you'll be at Lake Ann. (If you don't go back to do Maple Pass, your trip will be 3.8 miles round-trip.) Unfortunately there is no camping at Lake Ann because of previous overuse and abuse. The lake basin is a result of glacial carving nearly a million years ago. As the glacier retreated, the rocks and dirt it deposited formed a natural dam, creating Lake Ann. Meadows abound here, even on a small island in the south part of the lake. And there is always a chance of seeing a black bear here. So keep that picnic nearby at all times.

In local hiking circles, Maple Pass is considered one of the best day hikes in the region. And rightfully so, as this trail takes hikers above two shimmering blue lakes to a level with glaciers. It takes you through mountain meadows teeming with marmots and visited by mountain goats and black bears. Most impressively, it takes you on even terms with so many major peaks that you need six topo maps to name them all. This really is a trail to remember and visit again and again.

The loop is best started counterclockwise. This makes the ascent a little easier to handle. In the other direction, a sign forewarns,

"Trail beyond steeper but more scenic." Maple Pass Trail follows Lake Ann trail for 1.5 miles before climbing the basin wall to Heather Pass. Lake Ann glitters below and mountain heather lights up the meadows in August. Black Peak, 8,970 feet, emerges and rarely leaves your sight. The trail moves up the western ridge through high meadows. Alpine larches grace any fertile spot possible, and the northern peaks stand out. Maple Pass is a good climb, and from it an understanding of several major creek drainages can be had. On clear days, even Glacier Peak is visible. The trail, now even with the Lyall Glacier, continues down, moving between views of Rainy Lake and Lake Ann. A steep drop through a wonderful forest brings you to the car again. The experience will likely keep you coming back to Maple Pass.

User Groups: Hikers and leashed dogs (dogs allowed on the loop but may not complete it, as Maple Pass is in the national park). No horses or mountain bikes are allowed. No wheelchair access.

Open Seasons: This trail is usually accessible mid-July–early October.

Permits: A federal Northwest Forest Pass is required to park here.

Maps: For a map of Okanogan National Forest, contact the Outdoor Recreation Information Center at the downtown Seattle REI. For topographic maps for the Lake Ann Trail, ask Green Trails for No. 50, Washington Pass, or ask the USGS for Washington Pass. For topographic maps for Maple Pass, ask Green Trails for No. 49, Mount Logan, and No. 50, Washington Pass, or ask the USGS for Washington Pass and Mount Arriva.

Directions: From Newhalem, drive Highway 20 to Mile Marker 157. Turn right into the south trailhead. The north trailhead is only for Cutthroat Pass and the Pacific Crest Trail.

Contact: Okanogan National Forest, Methow Valley Ranger District, 24 West Chewuch Road, Winthrop, WA 98862, 509/996-4003.

55 BLUE LAKE

4.4 mi/2.5 hr

west of Winthrop in Okanogan National Forest

Map 3.2, page 92

Blue Lake is a natural masterpiece. To begin, Blue Lake Trail climbs through shady old-growth forests. The destination is a short two miles, a lake sparkling deep turquoise, making Blue Lake a most appropriate name. Enormous craggy peaks and ridges skirted in rock and talus stand to three sides. The 7,800-foot Early Winters Spires rise to the northeast trying to steal the show. And the high mountain subalpine forests bring it all to life.

Blue Lake is a truly fantastic hike, considering its easy accessibility and attractiveness in all seasons. The first mile of trail climbs gradually through virgin forest. Before long, it breaks into meadows, and Cutthroat Peak is visible across the valley. The trail was built well and receives good maintenance, as it seems much shorter than its stated distance. The path finds the lake before you know it. Mountain hemlock, alpine larch, and subalpine fir find home in the smallest crevasses and complete the scene. The alpine larch make a late-season hike here highly appealing. During autumn, the larch seem to catch on fire, their needles turning orange and then yellow before falling off. There is no camping allowed at Blue Lake, so please keep it to a day hike.

User Groups: Hikers and leashed dogs. No horses or mountain bikes are allowed. No wheelchair access.

Open Seasons: This trail is accessible mid-June–mid-October.

Permits: A federal Northwest Forest Pass is required to park here.

Maps: For a map of Okanogan National Forest, contact the Outdoor Recreation Information Center at the downtown Seattle REI. For topographic maps, ask Green Trails for No. 50, Washington Pass, or ask the USGS for Washington Pass.

Directions: From Winthrop, drive west on Highway 20 to Bluc Lakc Trailhcad. Thc signcd trailhead is on the left, about .5 mile west of Washington Pass.

Contact: Okanogan National Forest, Methow Valley Ranger District, 24 West Chewuch Road, Winthrop, WA 98862, 509/996-4003.

56 CUTTHROAT PASS

11.0 mi/6.0 hr

near Washington Pass in Okanogan National Forest

Map 3.2, page 92

Cutthroat Pass is perfect for all kinds of hikers, from beginners to the experienced, which has made it a popular destination over the years. The pass isn't a difficult journey, making it a great trip for first-timers in the North Cascades. Cutthroat Lake offers a good turnaround point for those uninterested in climbing to the pass and simply wanting a great, short day hike. Conversely, the views from the pass will inspire even the most trail hardened of hikers, who may think they have seen it all.

Cutthroat Pass Trail leisurely climbs through the valley's forest to a junction (1.7 miles). Here, Cutthroat Lake Trail breaks to the left. The lake is a short .25 mile down the trail, lined by boulders, forests, and steep basin walls. Those wanting an easy overnighter will find campsites here. Make sure it's an established site, though, and at least 200 feet from the lakeshore.

Continuing on Cutthroat Pass Trail takes hikers abruptly up to the pass. Expect a lot of wildflowers in the expansive meadows during the month of July. The views are exceptional, distant, and rewarding. Visitors often return home with stories of seeing or encountering mountains goats, who regularly frequent the area. Camps are situated around the pass, although water is nonexistent once the snowpack is gone. The pass sees its fair share of traffic because the Pacific Crest Trail runs right through it.

User Groups: Hikers, leashed dogs, and horses. No mountain bikes are allowed. No wheelchair access.

Open Seasons: This trail is acccssiblc July–September.

Permits: A federal Northwest Forest Pass is required to park here.

Maps: For a map of Okanogan National Forest, contact the Outdoor Recreation Information Center at the downtown Seattle REI. For topographic maps, ask Green Trails for No. 50, Washington Pass, or ask the USGS for Washington Pass.

Directions: From Winthrop, drive west 26 miles on Highway 20 to Forest Service Road 400. Turn right (north) and drive 1 mile to the trailhead at road's end.

Contact: Okanogan National Forest, Methow Valley Ranger District, 24 West Chewuch Road, Winthrop, WA 98862, 509/996-4003.

57 WEST FORK METHOW RIVER

16.0 mi/2–6 days

northwest of Mazama in Okanogan National Forest

Map 3.2, page 92

The West Fork of the Methow River serves as an access point to one of the Pacific Crest Trail's most scenic sections. The trail follows the river eight miles up the valley to the PCT. The trail along the river is well known by anglers, who come here to catch and release cutthroat and other trout. Campsites appear regularly along the way, usually directly on the river. The trail eventually leaves the riverside to reach the PCT.

From here, hikers have several options. They can join the PCT as it heads north through Brush Creek and along a high ridge to Hart's Pass (20.7 miles). Expect lots of meadows, views, and probably mountain goats. Or one can travel south on the PCT. The famous trail continues south through the river valley, up to meadowy ridges and on to Rainy Pass Trailhead via three major passes (26.4 miles). And the East Creek Trail ventures out of the Methow Valley to Mebee Pass, an old fire lookout, and eventually to East Creek Trailhead (17.9 miles). These three options require two cars, however, which

is sometimes a difficult undertaking. If you have only one car, there's no shame in hiking out the same way you came in.

User Groups: Hikers, leashed dogs, horses, and mountain bikes. No wheelchair access.

Open Seasons: This trail is accessible July–mid-October.

Permits: A federal Northwest Forest Pass is required to park here.

Maps: For a map of Okanogan National Forest, contact the Outdoor Recreation Information Center at the downtown Seattle REI. For topographic maps, ask Green Trails for No. 49, Mount Logan, and No. 50, Washington Pass, or ask the USGS for Robinson Mountain and Slate Peak.

Directions: From Winthrop, drive west 17 miles on Highway 20 to Mazama. Turn right (north) onto Mazama Road and drive .2 mile to Hart's Pass Road (County Road 9140/Forest Service Road 5400). Turn left and drive to Rattlesnake Trailhead, .3 mile beyond River Bend Campground.

Contact: Okanogan National Forest, Methow Valley Ranger District, 24 West Chewuch Road, Winthrop, WA 98862, 509/996-4003.

58 BUCKSKIN RIDGE

22.2 mi/2 days

northwest of Mazama in Pasayten Wilderness of Okanogan National Forest

Map 3.2, page 92

Thanks to Slate Pass, a trailhead conveniently situated at 6,200 feet of elevation, access to Buckskin Ridge is a piece of cake. Well, maybe a little more difficult than cake, but still, very little of the North Cascades is as accessible. Buckskin Ridge Trail runs the long, jagged ridge at a steady elevation. Major peaks of the Pasayten Wilderness are close enough to touch at times (or even climb). Buckskin Trail passes a pair of lakes before dropping to the Pasayten River, which offers a pair of excellent river hike loop options.

From Hart's Pass, hike the road up to Slate Pass (1.4 miles) and where Buckskin Ridge Trail begins. The trail enjoys open meadows for much of its length. The trail winds around the east side of the ridge to good camping at Silver Lake (6 miles) and on to Silver Pass (8 miles). The trail now runs the west side of the ridge, with all new peaks to admire. This segment has several steep and challenging sections, so be prepared for a slow time. Buckskin Lake (11.1 miles) marks the northern end of the ridge and also makes for a good campsite. The obvious return route is back along the ridge. But those seeking a loop can continue on Buckskin Trail to the Pasayten River. Here, trails up the West and Middle Forks return to Slate Peak. Each is about 35 miles in total length.

User Groups: Hikers, leashed dogs, and horses (horses permitted but highly not recommended). No mountain bikes are allowed. No wheelchair access.

Open Seasons: This trail is accessible July–October.

Permits: A federal Northwest Forest Pass is required to park here.

Maps: For a map of Okanogan National Forest, contact the Outdoor Recreation Information Center at the downtown Seattle REI. For topographic maps, ask Green Trails for No. 18, Pasayten Peak, and No. 50, Washington Pass, or ask the USGS for Slate Peak, Pasayten Peak, and Frosty Creek.

Directions: From Winthrop, drive west 17 miles on Highway 20 to Mazama. Turn right (north) onto Mazama Road and drive .2 mile to Hart's Pass Road (County Road 9140/Forest Service Road 5400). Turn left and drive 18.5 miles to Hart's Pass. Turn right on Forest Service Road 5400-600 and drive 5 miles to Slate Pass at road's end. Hart's Pass Road is prone to frequent washouts; call the ranger station for current status.

Contact: Okanogan National Forest, Methow Valley Ranger District, 24 West Chewuch Road, Winthrop, WA 98862, 509/996-4003.

59 DRIVEWAY BUTTE

8.0 mi/5.0 hr

north of Highway 20 in Okanogan National Forest

Map 3.2, page 92

This is a steep ascent to a former lookout site atop Driveway Butte. If the Forest Service once used a peak to scan for fires, you can be certain that it has an expansive view. Indeed it does, looking out over many surrounding valleys, ridges, and peaks, all the way into the Pasayten Wilderness. Driveway Butte Trail gains about 3,000 feet, which is no easy feat. Complicating the task is a trail that can be rocky and rough at times. For those prepared for a strenuous hike, however, the vista is a wonderful reward.

Driveway Butte Trail leaves Early Winters Creek very near Highway 20. The first two miles are brutal, climbing steeply up Indian Creek through forest. At a small pass, the trail heads around the headwaters of McGee Creek. Subalpine meadows finally appear before the top of the Butte, with grand views of Silver Star Mountain and many other Cascade peaks. Once the snow is gone, very little water is to be found along the trail, so carrying extra water is important, especially on hot summer days. The panoramic views will be well appreciated by those who accomplish the summit.

User Groups: Hikers, leashed dogs, and horses. No mountain bikes are allowed. No wheelchair access.

Open Seasons: This trail is accessible mid-May–October.

Permits: A federal Northwest Forest Pass is required to park here.

Maps: For a map of Okanogan National Forest, contact the Outdoor Recreation Information Center at the downtown Seattle REI. For topographic maps, ask Green Trails for No. 50, Washington Pass, or ask the USGS for Silverstar Mountain and Robinson Mountain.

Directions: From Winthrop, drive west on Highway 20 for 18.5 miles to Klipchuck Campground. Near the self-service fee station is a gated service road. The trail begins about 100 yards down this road.

Contact: Okanogan National Forest, Methow Valley Ranger Station, 24 West Chewuch Road, Winthrop, WA 98862, 509/996-4003.

60 WEST FORK PASAYTEN

31.0 mi/3–4 days

3 10

northwest of Mazama in Pasayten Wilderness of Okanogan National Forest

Map 3.2, page 92

The West Fork of the Pasayten is easily accessible via Slate Peak, a trailhead conveniently situated at an elevation of 6,800 feet. Start high and drop into the large, wide valley of the Pasayten's West Fork. The trail sticks to the river valley, passing through ancient forests of pine and fir with frequent views to the towering peaks lining the valley ridges. This trail experiences some of the Pasayten's wildest regions, where sightings of bear and other wildlife are frequent. Best of all, the trail makes two excellent loops when combined with trails that run along the top of the valley's ridges.

West Fork Pasayten Trail drops from the high vantage of Slate Peak into the river valley below. Snow lingers a little late on the north side of Slate Peak and you must ford the river (4 miles). That means late July or early August are prime times to hit this trail. Campsites are littered along the route, frequently right on the river. At 8.5 miles is a junction for Holman Creek and up to Pacific Crest Trail, the first of the two great loop possibilities. Hike up to Holman Pass and head south on PCT back to Slate Peak for a total of 21 miles. Many call this the best of PCT. Anywhere.

The main trail continues another seven miles to a major junction. Head south on the Buckskin Ridge Trail, a 16.6-mile trip back to Slate Peak. This section of trail can be obscure and difficult to find at times, but experienced routefinders will love it.

User Groups: Hikers, leashed dogs, and horses. No mountain bikes are allowed. No wheelchair access.

Open Seasons: This trail is accessible mid-July–mid-October.

Permits: A federal Northwest Forest Pass is required to park here. A free wilderness permit is also required to hike here and is available at the trailhead.

Maps: For a map of Okanogan National Forest, contact the Outdoor Recreation Information Center at the downtown Seattle REI. For topographic maps, ask Green Trails for No. 18, Pasayten Peak, and No. 50, Washington Pass, or ask the USGS for Slate Peak, Pasayten Peak, and Frosty Creek.

Directions: From Winthrop, drive west 17 miles on Highway 20 to Mazama. Turn right (north) onto Mazama Road and drive .2 mile to Hart's Pass Road (County Road 9140/Forest Service Road 5400). Turn left and drive 18.5 miles to Hart's Pass. Turn right on Forest Service Road 5400-600 and drive 5 miles to Slate Pass at road's end. Hart's Pass Road is prone to frequent washouts; call the ranger station for current status.

Contact: Okanogan National Forest, Methow Valley Ranger District, 24 West Chewuch Road, Winthrop, WA 98862, 509/996-4003.

61 ROBINSON PASS

55.0 mi/5–10 days

north of Mazama in Pasayten Wilderness of Okanogan National Forest

Map 3.2, page 92

By no means must you hike this trail 27.5 miles in only to come out the same 27.5 miles. Instead, Robinson Creek Trail can be drastically shortened or dramatically lengthened. Heading over Robinson Pass into the Middle Fork Pasayten River valley, the trail ventures into the most secluded section of the already remote wilderness. Numerous trails intersect the trail along the Pasayten River, making hikes easily customizable. Even a straight trip up and back isn't all that bad.

Robinson Creek Trail follows the creek to Robinson Pass (8.8 miles). Campsites are scattered along the creek and are usually forested; the better ones are near the pass. The trail now drops elevation for the next 19 miles down through the Pasayten River Valley. The wide, U-shaped valley is regularly broken up by enormous avalanche chutes, revealing the tall, rounded peaks lining the valley. Campsites are abundant in this valley and are often along the river.

Trails frequently break off to head over the ridge or up another major creek drainage. Trails lead up the West Fork of Pasayten (20.5 miles), Rock Creek (21.6 miles), and Frosty Creek (22.8 miles), each more desolate than the one before it. High-country treks can be made up to Freds Lake and Doris Lake (15.7 miles) or Tatoosh Buttes (20.7 miles). The Pasayten Wilderness is a place where grizzly bears and gray wolves still roam the countryside, and Robinson Creek Trail is the gateway to all of it.

User Groups: Hikers, leashed dogs, and horses. No mountain bikes are allowed. No wheelchair access.

Open Seasons: This trail is accessible mid-June–mid-October.

Permits: A federal Northwest Forest Pass is required to park here. A free wilderness permit is also required to hike here and is available at the trailhead.

Maps: For a map of Okanogan National Forest, contact the Outdoor Recreation Information Center at the downtown Seattle REI. For topographic maps, ask Green Trails for No. 18, Pasayten Peak, and No. 50, Washington Pass, or ask the USGS for Robinson Mountain, Slate Peak, Pasayten Peak, and Mount Lago.

Directions: From Winthrop, drive west 17 miles on Highway 20 to Mazama. Turn right (north) onto Mazama Road and drive .2 mile to Hart's Pass Road (County Road 9140/Forest Service Road 5400). Turn left and drive 9.5 miles to Robinson Creek Trailhead. Hart's Pass Road is prone to frequent washouts; call the ranger station for current status.

Contact: Okanogan National Forest, Methow Valley Ranger District, 24 West Chewuch Road, Winthrop, WA 98862, 509/996-4003.

62 LOST RIVER

8.5 mi/5.0 hr

northwest of Mazama in Pasayten Wilderness of Okanogan National Forest

Map 3.2, page 92

While the Pasayten Wilderness is best known for its long treks into the backcountry, it does have its share of great day hikes. This easy stroll through the woods leads to the convergence of two large gorges, the Lost River and Eureka Creek. Along the way, the Lost River makes for noisy company, cascading over boulders and small rapids. With very little elevation gain along the route, the trail is perfect for hikers of all abilities and families. As an additional bonus, the low-lying trail opens earlier than other high routes, making the Lost River a good springtime outing.

Monument Creek Trail follows Lost River through forests of pine and fir, regularly breaking out for views of the valley ridges. Four miles in, the trail comes to Eureka Creek. Spilling out of a deep gorge, the creek passes over impressive falls before joining the Lost River. Cross a bridge over Eureka to streamside campsites, a very pleasant place to have lunch or spend the night. The narrow Lost River Gorge is viewable from the end of the trail, although it gets even more rugged and remote up the valley–so much so that trail construction isn't possible up the gorge. Folks who are ready for serious cross-country navigation can leave the two streams' confluence and hike up to Pistol Pass and on to Monument Creek (15.4 miles), a strenuous, even hellish, up and down.

User Groups: Hikers, leashed dogs, and horses. No mountain bikes are allowed. No wheelchair access.

Open Seasons: This trail is accessible April–October.

Permits: A federal Northwest Forest Pass is required to park here.

Maps: For a map of Okanogan National Forest, contact the Outdoor Recreation Information Center at the downtown Seattle REI. For topographic maps, ask Green Trails for No. 50, Washington Pass, and No. 51, Mazama, or ask the USGS for Robinson Mountain and McLeod Mountain.

Directions: From Winthrop, drive west 17 miles on Highway 20 to Mazama. Turn right (north) onto Mazama Road and drive .2 mile to Hart's Pass Road (County Road 9140/Forest Service Road 5400). Turn left and drive 9.5 miles to Monument Creek Trailhead. Hart's Pass Road is prone to frequent washouts; call the ranger station for current status.

Contact: Okanogan National Forest, Methow Valley Ranger District, 24 West Chewuch Road, Winthrop, WA 98862, 509/996-4003.

63 BURCH MOUNTAIN

9.8 mi/5.5 hr

north of Winthrop in Okanogan National Forest

Map 3.2, page 92

From atop Burch Mountain, feel awash in a sea of rocky peaks, with waves of mountain ridges extending in every direction. The vastness of the Pasayten Wilderness is easily felt from this high point of 7,782 feet. Catch the trail during the early summer and the journey is as grand as the summit, with open forests providing cool shade and wildflowers taking over open meadows. Venture here later in the season and you're sure to experience hot, dry weather. If you come in August, bring plenty of water.

The route starts on Billy Goat Pass Trail, which gains a hefty 1,800 feet of elevation in three miles. At the pass, double back to the south on Burch Mountain Trail. This path scales the side of Eightmile Ridge at a less harsh pitch. Meadows and vistas are the norm along the way. After 1.5 miles, the trail has reached the base of Burch Mountain and a side trail scrambles to the summit. Big Craggy Peak lives up to its name across Eightmile Creek, while numerous other peaks and ridges shine in the not-so-far distance. Bring a map, for many of the peaks deserve to be identified.

User Groups: Hikers, leashed dogs, and horses.

No mountain bikes are allowed. No wheelchair access.

Open Seasons: This trail is accessible July–September.

Permits: A federal Northwest Forest Pass is required to park here.

Maps: For a map of Okanogan National Forest, contact the Outdoor Recreation Information Center at the downtown Seattle REI. For topographic maps, ask Green Trails for No. 19, Billy Goat Mountain, or ask the USGS for Billy Goat Mountain and Sweetgrass Butte.

Directions: From Winthrop, drive north on Chewuch River Road (across Highway 20 from the visitors center) 10 miles to Forest Service Road 5140. Turn left and drive 11 miles to the trailhead at road's end.

Contact: Okanogan National Forest, Methow Valley Ranger District, 24 West Chewuch Road, Winthrop, WA 98862, 509/996-4003.

64 CHEWUCH RIVER

36.0 mi/4 days

north of Winthrop in Pasayten Wilderness of Okanogan National Forest

Map 3.2, page 92

This long, river valley trail makes connections to several trails branching off into the Pasayten Wilderness before arriving at some of the area's most beautiful country. But it also makes for a good day hike, with Chewuch Falls a short three miles up the trail. Those looking for an extended trip will enjoy Remmel Lake at the head of the Chewuch. Trips up Tungsten Creek, Topaz Mountain, and Coleman Peak are also begun from the Chewuch River.

Chewuch River Trail is popular with those riding horses or driving stock, meaning that it can be wide and dusty. Overall, the hike gains little elevation as it passes through forests of lodgepole pine, some of it recently burned in 2003. Campsites are scattered along the length of the trail, and water is never far away. Keep plodding and the trail eventually rises into Remmel Basin to find Remmel Lake (18 miles), surrounded by meadows and larches. The high, flat terrain makes the surrounding 8,000-plus-feet peaks seem like rolling hills. At the lake, make camp at established campsites more than 200 feet from the lakeshore.

User Groups: Hikers, leashed dogs, and horses. No mountain bikes are allowed. No wheelchair access.

Open Seasons: This trail is accessible July–September.

Permits: A federal Northwest Forest Pass is required to park here. A free wilderness permit is also required to hike here and is available at the trailhead.

Maps: For a map of Okanogan National Forest, contact the Outdoor Recreation Information Center at the downtown Seattle REI. For topographic maps, ask Green Trails for No. 20, Coleman Peak, or ask the USGS for Coleman Peak, Bauerman Ridge, and Remmel Mountain.

Directions: From Winthrop, drive north on Chewuch River Road (across Highway 20 from the visitors center) 30 miles to Thirtymile Trailhead at road's end.

Contact: Okanogan National Forest, Methow Valley Ranger District, 24 West Chewuch Road, Winthrop, WA 98862, 509/996-4003.

65 COLEMAN RIDGE

31.7 mi/3–4 days

north of Winthrop in Pasayten Wilderness of Okanogan National Forest

Map 3.2, page 92

While Coleman Ridge Trail runs more than 20 miles along the high alpine ridge, the best part of the trip is contained in the upper part of ridge, near Four Point Lake. Here, scattered among glacially scraped boulders, are meadows full of early summer wildflowers and far-reaching vistas. Four Point Lake makes for a wonderful camp, where captivating stars illuminate the night sky.

The route follows the Chewuch River before making a lazy loop up to Coleman and back down. Hike the Chewuch River, passing Chewuch Falls along the way, until you reach Fire Creek Trail (6 miles), heading off to the left. You must ford the Chewuch, a difficult crossing when the snowpack runoff is high. The trail climbs up Fire Creek, eventually becoming Coleman Ridge Trail (10.7 miles), and finds a high mountain pass complete with views. Campsites are scattered along the route, with nice spots on the creek and a couple atop the ridge.

Coleman Ridge Trail heads north on the ridge and passes below Remmel Mountain, a worthy peak for an easy side trip. Four Point Lake is off a short side trail (16.5 miles). Be sure to use the established sites at the lake. The route then drops down Four Point Creek to the Chewuch River, 12.9 miles from the trailhead. Good times for a trip here are July, when wildflowers are blooming, and late September, when larches seem to have caught fire.

User Groups: Hikers, leashed dogs, and horses. No mountain bikes are allowed. No wheelchair access.

Open Seasons: This trail is accessible July–September.

Permits: A federal Northwest Forest Pass is required to park here. A free wilderness permit is also required to hike here and is available at the trailhead.

Maps: For a map of Okanogan National Forest, contact the Outdoor Recreation Information Center at the downtown Seattle REI. For topographic maps, ask Green Trails for No. 20, Coleman Peak, or ask the USGS for Coleman Peak, Mount Barney, and Bauerman Ridge.

Directions: From Winthrop, drive north on Chewuch River Road (across Highway 20 from the visitors center) 30 miles to Thirtymile Trailhead at road's end.

Contact: Okanogan National Forest, Methow Valley Ranger District, 24 West Chewuch Road, Winthrop, WA 98862, 509/996-4003.

66 CATHEDRAL BASIN

39.0 mi/5–6 days 4 10

north of Winthrop in Pasayten Wilderness of Okanogan National Forest

Map 3.2, page 92

For folks seeking to experience the best of what the Pasayten Wilderness has to offer, this is the trail. More than 20 miles from the nearest car lies resplendent Cathedral Basin. Lakes are set inside basins, illuminated by wildflowers in the summer, larches in the fall, and multitudes of stars every night. The Cathedral Pass journey is one of the prizes of the Pasayten.

The best access is via Andrews Creek, an excellent, although long, valley hike. It's 12.5 miles along the forested creek to Andrews Pass. Some of the route was very recently burned in 2003.

© SCOTT LEONARD

Cathedral Basin—Hard to get to but one of Washington's most beautiful places.

Throughout the valley are tremendous views of surrounding peaks and ridges. Camps are scattered regularly along the trail here. It's another three miles from the pass to a junction with Boundary Trail. Head east to encounter Lower Cathedral Lake (18.6 miles) and Upper Cathedral (20.5 miles). Campsites are scarce around the lakes, so be ready to set up camp near the Boundary Trail junction or other available sites.

Above the lakes, Cathedral Peak and Amphitheater Mountain form worthy sentinels, standing on either side of the pass. Marmots rumble across the tundralike meadows while bears forage for berries. Scrambles are possible up many of the neighboring peaks, where the views extend across the wilderness to the Cascades and Canada.

User Groups: Hikers, leashed dogs, and horses. No mountain bikes are allowed. No wheelchair access.

Open Seasons: This trail is accessible July–September.

Permits: A federal Northwest Forest Pass is required to park here. A free wilderness permit is also required to hike here and is available at the trailhead.

Maps: For a map of Okanogan National Forest, contact the Outdoor Recreation Information Center at the downtown Seattle REI. For topographic maps, ask Green Trails for No. 20, Coleman Peak, or ask the USGS for Coleman Peak, Mount Barney, and Remmel Mountain.

Directions: From Winthrop, drive north on Chewuch River Road (across Highway 20 from the visitors center) 24 miles to signed Andrew's Creek Trailhead.

Contact: Okanogan National Forest, Methow Valley Ranger District, 24 West Chewuch Road, Winthrop, WA 98862, 509/996-4003.

67 PEEPSIGHT

28.0 mi/3–4 days

north of Winthrop in Pasayten Wilderness of Okanogan National Forest

Map 3.2, page 92

Off Andrews Creek and normally a route to other places, the trail to Peepsight Mountain and Peepsight Lake is a worthy journey in itself. The eight-mile trail leaves Andrews Creek to scale the side of Peepsight Mountain. This is high country, full of meadows and views. A trip to Peepsight Mountain, elevation 8,146 feet, is a window on the Pasayten, laying much of the vast wilderness at your tired feet. And Peepsight Lake lies on the other side of the pass, but it usually opens later in the season because of snow melting slowly on the pass. The trail winds back down to Andrews Creek to form a loop.

The route follows Andrews Creek Trail to Peepsight Trail (8.5 miles). A ford of Andrews Creek is necessary, not an easy task in the early summer. Peepsight Trail climbs to a junction (12.6 miles); to the west lies Peepsight Lake, a welcome sight when fall larches are burning with color. Peepsight Mountain is an easy scramble from this trail. The right fork in the trail skirts Peepsight Mountain and makes for Crazy Man Pass and Rock Lake before dropping back to Andrews Pass, 12.5 miles from the trailhead. Campsites are found at many places along the route; when possible, stick to established sites.

User Groups: Hikers, leashed dogs, and horses. No mountain bikes are allowed. No wheelchair access.

Open Seasons: This trail is accessible August–September.

Permits: A federal Northwest Forest Pass is required to park here. A free wilderness permit is also required to hike here and is available at the trailhead.

Maps: For a map of Okanogan National Forest, contact the Outdoor Recreation Information Center at the downtown Seattle REI. For topographic maps, ask Green Trails for No. 20, Coleman Peak, or ask the USGS for Coleman Peak and Remmel Mountain.

Directions: From Winthrop, drive north on Chewuch River Road (across Highway 20 from the visitors center) 24 miles to signed Andrew's Creek Trailhead.

Contact: Okanogan National Forest, Methow Valley Ranger District, 24 West Chewuch Road, Winthrop, WA 98862, 509/996-4003.

68 HORSESHOE BASIN (STEHEKIN)

7.8–16.4 mi/2 days

north of Stehekin in North Cascades National Park

Map 3.2, page 92

Fortunately, one of the North Cascades' most beautiful basins is a convenient trip for folks on both the west side and east side of the Cascades. Hikers living on the rainy side of the state can reach Horseshoe Basin via Cascade Pass in 8.2 up-down-and-up-again miles. Eastsiders can take a shorter route via Stehekin, which involves a beautiful ferry ride on Lake Chelan. On either route, the enormous cliffs and waterfalls ringing Horseshoe Basin make for an awesome trip.

Folks seeking access to Horseshoe Basin from the west need to hike to Cascade Pass (3.7 miles; see listing in this chapter) and drop to the Stehekin River and Horseshoe Basin Trail junction (6.7 miles). From Chelan, ride the ferry to Stehekin and catch the shuttle to Cottonwood Campground, at the end of Stehekin Valley. From here, Horseshoe Basin junction is a quick hike (2.4 miles).

Horseshoe Basin Trail wanders up Basin Creek 1.5 miles to the head of the basin. Covered in meadows, the basin offers impressive views of the enormous mountains and glaciers towering 4,000 feet above. Campers, please stick to established campsites, scattered throughout the basin. This area is dotted by numerous mines, operated decades ago, and their remains are worth checking out. Horseshoe Basin is a North Cascades classic.

User Groups: Hikers only. No dogs, horses, or mountain bikes are allowed. No wheelchair access.

Open Seasons: This trail is accessible July–mid-October

Permits: A federal Northwest Forest Pass is required to park at Cascade Pass, for hikers entering from the west. Overnight stays within the national park require reservations and backcountry camping permits, which are available at the Wilderness Information Center in Marblemount or the visitors center in Stehekin.

Maps: For a map of North Cascades National Park, contact the Outdoor Recreation Information Center at the downtown Seattle REI. For topographic maps, ask Green Trails for No. 80, Cascade Pass, or ask the USGS for McGregor Mountain, Goode Mountain, and Mount Logan.

Directions: For the eastern entrance, from Wenatchee, drive north 33 miles on U.S. 97 to Chelan. Lady of the Lake Ferry Terminal is on U.S. 97 Alternate just before entering downtown. Catch the passenger ferry to Stehekin and ride the shuttle to Cottonwood Camp Trailhead.

For the western entrance, from the town of Marblemount on Highway 20, drive 23 miles on Cascade River Road to the Cascade Pass Trailhead at road's end.

Contact: North Cascades National Park, Golden West Visitor Center, Stehekin, WA, 360/856-5700, ext. 340; Lady of the Lake Ferry Service, 1418 West Woodin Avenue, Chelan, WA 98816, 509/682-4584.

69 NORTH FORK BRIDGE CREEK

19.4 mi/3 days

north of Stehekin in North Cascades National Park

Map 3.2, page 92

A high, rugged ridge dotted by glaciers surrounds the large basin at the head of North Fork Bridge Creek. The high peaks of Goode Mountain, Storm King, and Mount Logan stand impressively over the open, rocky expanse of North Fork Meadows. The splendor of it all is easily accessible via a gentle trail along valley floors and a trio of great camps, easy stuff for beginner backpackers.

North Fork Bridge Creek Trail is accessible through Stehekin, which requires a ride on the

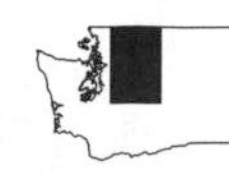

Lake Chelan passenger ferry. Catch the shuttle from Stehekin to Bridge Creek Trailhead. The first three miles are along Bridge Creek Trail. Shortly after crossing the creek, via bridge, North Fork Trail takes off to the left (north). At 5.2 miles is Walker Park Camp, for hikers and horses, while at 6.2 miles are Grizzly Creek Camps, one each for horses and hikers. Camping beyond is now forbidden because of excessive abuse in the meadows.

North Fork Bridge Creek Trail alternates between old forests and avalanche chutes. The views from the openings get successively better. From Grizzly Camps, it's a quick hike to North Fork Meadows (8.5 miles). The bulky valley walls shoot skyward to enormous peaks. Glaciers struggle to cling to the steep slopes. Enjoy.

User Groups: Hikers and horses. No dogs or mountain bikes are allowed. No wheelchair access.

Open Seasons: This trail is accessible July–mid-October

Permits: Overnight stays within the national park require reservations and backcountry camping permits, which are available at the visitors center in Stehekin.

Maps: For a map of North Cascades National Park, contact the Outdoor Recreation Information Center at the downtown Seattle REI. For topographic maps, ask Green Trails for No. 49, Mount Logan, and No. 81, McGregor Mountain, or ask the USGS for McGregor Mountain, Goode Mountain, and Mount Logan.

Directions: From Wenatchee, drive north 33 miles on U.S. 97 to Chelan. Lady of the Lake Ferry Terminal is on U.S. 97 Alternate just before entering downtown. Catch the passenger ferry to Stehekin and ride the shuttle to Bridge Creek Trailhead.

Contact: North Cascades National Park, Golden West Visitor Center, Stehekin, WA, 360/856-5700, ext. 340; Lady of the Lake Ferry Service, 1418 West Woodin Avenue, Chelan, WA 98816, 509/682-4584.

70 GOODE RIDGE

10.0 mi/6.0 hr

north of Stehekin in North Cascades National Park

Map 3.2, page 92

Doing things the old-fashioned way, Goode Ridge Trail starts low in the valley before climbing to a high valley ridge. Make no mistake; Goode Ridge Trail is a steep one, gaining 4,400 feet of elevation in just five miles. Its challenging but not overwhelming ascent is perfect for those who are craving some mean vistas but who aren't crazy enough to challenge McGregor Mountain to a fight.

Goode Ridge Trail is in the northern part of the Stehekin Valley. For that, one must hop the passenger ferry from Chelan and then a shuttle from Stehekin. All that is not possible for one day, so plan on camping in the valley somewhere at least one night. The trail makes a steady climb away from the river, passing through forests for the first half before breaking out into open meadows. Expect hot, dry weather during the summer and bring extra water. The trail eventually reaches the southern end of Goode Ridge. The views of the surrounding peaks, lakes, and valleys are impressive. McGregor, Goode, Storm King, and Glacier Peak are the most memorable from a long list of visible peaks.

User Groups: Hikers only. No dogs, horses, or mountain bikes are allowed. No wheelchair access.

Open Seasons: This trail is accessible July–September.

Permits: Overnight stays within the national park require reservations and backcountry camping permits, which are available at the visitors center in Stehekin.

Maps: For a map of North Cascades National Park, contact the Outdoor Recreation Information Center at the downtown Seattle REI. For topographic maps, ask Green Trails for No. 81, McGregor Mountain, or ask the USGS for Goode Mountain.

Directions: From Wenatchee, drive north 33

miles on U.S. 97 to Chelan. Lady of the Lake Ferry Terminal is on U.S. 97 Alternate just before entering downtown. Catch the passenger ferry to Stehekin and ride the shuttle to Goode Ridge Trailhead.

Contact: North Cascades National Park, Golden West Visitor Center, Stehekin, WA, 360/856-5700, ext. 340; Lady of the Lake Ferry Service, 1418 West Woodin Avenue, Chelan, WA 98816, 509/682-4584.

71 RAINBOW LAKE

23.8 mi/3 days

north of Stehekin in North Cascades National Park and Lake Chelan National Recreation Area

Map 3.2, page 92

Since there are no car-carrying ferries to Stehekin, there are no cars in the small town. A shuttle bus is your only option for access to the valley's nine trailheads. But the lack of a car makes through-hikes extremely easy. Rainbow Lake Trail is a perfect example. Have the shuttle drop you off upriver and hike your way back to Stehekin. This route is a grand one, via four creek valleys and a stop at a high alpine lake.

The route is best done from north to south, since the north trailhead is 1,000 feet higher. Disembark from the Stehekin shuttle at Bridge Creek Trailhead and hike the famed Pacific Crest Trail to South Fork Bridge Creek junction (6.8 miles). Good first-night camps are found at Sixmile Camp (6 miles) and South Fork Camp (6.8 miles). South Fork Bridge Creek Trail climbs to Bowan Pass (13.1 miles), passing Dans Camp (9.8 miles). The pass lies directly below the rocky and sheer face of Bowan Mountain.

Rainbow Lake rests just on the other side of the pass, set within open meadows dotted by larches, colorful in the early fall. An established camp is found here at 14 miles, near Rainbow Lake, and two more are at 15.4 miles and 16 miles, down in the North Fork Rainbow Creek Valley. Follow the trail through forests of pine and fir, out the valley, and down Rainbow Creek Trail to Stehekin. Enjoy a meal and a beer in Stehekin and then ride Lady of the Lake to Chelan and your unmissed auto.

User Groups: Hikers and horses. No dogs or mountain bikes are allowed. No wheelchair access.

Open Seasons: This trail is accessible July–September.

Permits: Overnight stays within the national park require reservations and backcountry camping permits, which are available at the visitors center in Stehekin.

Maps: For a map of North Cascades National Park, contact the Outdoor Recreation Information Center at the downtown Seattle REI. For topographic maps, ask Green Trails for No. 81, McGregor Mountain, and No. 82, Stehekin, or ask the USGS for McGregor Mountain, McAlester Mountain, and Stehekin.

Directions: From Wenatchee, drive north 33 miles on U.S. 97 to Chelan. Lady of the Lake Ferry Terminal is on U.S. 97 Alternate just before entering downtown. Catch the passenger ferry to Stehekin and ride the shuttle to to Bridge Creek Trailhead.

Contact: North Cascades National Park, Golden West Visitor Center, Stehekin, WA, 360/856-5700, ext. 340; Lady of the Lake Ferry Service, 1418 West Woodin Avenue, Chelan, WA 98816, 509/682-4584.

72 McGREGOR MOUNTAIN

15.4 mi/2–3 days

5 9

north of Stehekin in Lake Chelan National Recreation Area

Map 3.2, page 92

It's difficult to verify, but it's my opinion that McGregor Mountain is the steepest trail in the state. And with all the steep trails in the North Cascades, Olympics, and Mount Rainier, that's a fine distinction. From trailhead to summit, McGregor Mountain Trail climbs 6,300 feet. Few care to continue counting past 50 the number of switchbacks to the top of an 8,122-foot

peak. Keep in mind that pain on the trail always pays off at top.

High Bridge Trailhead is in the Stehekin River Valley, meaning you'll need to catch the passenger ferry from Chelan to Stehekin and subsequently ride the shuttle bus to High Bridge Camp. Start on Pacific Crest Trail before turning right (east) onto McGregor Mountain Trail (1.3 miles). The ascent starts immediately and doesn't end until Heaton Camp at 7,000 feet. Much of the trail lies in open, rocky meadows. The trail is dry, so bring enough water for hiking and for meals at camp. Heaton Camp offers exceptional views. A short scramble reaches the ridge below McGregor's summit, revealing far-flung views to the east. Finally, before you hit the trail, ask yourself, "Are you sure you want to do this when there's a nice bakery in Stehekin instead?"

User Groups: Hikers only. No dogs, horses, or mountain bikes are allowed. No wheelchair access.

Open Seasons: This trail is accessible July–September.

Permits: Permits are not required. Parking and access are free.

Maps: For a map of North Cascades National Park, contact the Outdoor Recreation Information Center at the downtown Seattle REI. For topographic maps, ask Green Trails for No. 81, McGregor Mountain, or ask the USGS for McGregor Mountain.

Directions: From Wenatchee, drive north 33 miles on U.S. 97 to Chelan. Lady of the Lake Ferry Terminal is on U.S. 97 Alternate just before entering downtown. Catch the passenger ferry to Stehekin and ride the shuttle to High Bridge Trailhead.

Contact: North Cascades National Park, Golden West Visitor Center, Stehekin, WA, 360/856-5700, ext. 340; Lady of the Lake Ferry Service, 1418 West Woodin Avenue, Chelan, WA 98816, 509/682-4584.

73 COMPANY/DEVORE CREEKS LOOP

27.5 mi/3 days 4 9

west of Stehekin in Glacier Peak Wilderness of Wenatchee National Forest

Map 3.2, page 92

This is another excellent through-hike within Stehekin Valley. The route heads up long, wide Company Creek Valley and circles around a sharp ridge of craggy peaks before dropping through Fourth of July Basin on the way to Stehekin. The crowds are rather thin along the trail, having been drawn to other, better known trails farther up the valley. That's good news for those who venture here, a wild place full of things to see.

The route begins on Company Creek Trail with a long but scenic climb to Hilgard Pass (11.3 miles). Avalanche chutes expose Tupshin and Devore Peaks for long distances. You must ford Company Creek five miles in, difficult during times of heavy runoff. Well-established campsites are found at 3.5 miles, 10 miles, and 11.5 miles. At 6,600 feet, Hilgard Pass offers some scenic views.

The route now drops 1,900 feet before gaining 1,800 back on the way to Tenmile Pass (15.8 miles). If it sounds like a lot of work, it is. But enormous Fourth of July Basin awaits on the other side. This is premier high country, with sweeping views of the Devore Creek drainage. Bears and coyotes are frequent visitors, but they rarely approach close enough for mug shots. Excellent second-night camps are found at Tenmile Pass and within Fourth of July Basin. The trail drops to Bird Creek Camp (20 miles) and Weaver Point Camp (25 miles) before arriving at Devore Creek Trailhead.

User Groups: Hikers, leashed dogs, and horses. No mountain bikes are allowed. No wheelchair access.

Open Seasons: This trail is accessible July–September.

Permits: Permits are not required. Parking and access are free.

Maps: For a map of Wenatchee National For-

est, contact the Outdoor Recreation Information Center at the downtown Seattle REI. For topographic maps, ask Green Trails for No. 81, McGregor Mountain, No. 82, Stehekin, No. 113, Holden, and No. 114, Lucerne, or ask the USGS for Stehekin, Mount Lyall, and Holden.
Directions: From Wenatchee, drive north 33 miles on U.S. 97 to Chelan. Lady of the Lake Ferry Terminal is on U.S. 97 Alternate just before entering downtown. Catch the passenger ferry to Stehekin and ride the shuttle to Company Creek Trailhead.
Contact: North Cascades National Park, Golden West Visitor Center, Stehekin, WA, 360/856-5700, ext. 340; Lady of the Lake Ferry Service, 1418 West Woodin Avenue, Chelan, WA 98816, 509/682-4584.

74 STEHEKIN TRAILS

0.5–9.0 mi/0.5–5.0 hr

around Stehekin north of Lake Chelan

Map 3.2, page 92

Accessible only by passenger ferry or plane, Stehekin is as remote as it gets. The small village consists of resorts and cabins, several small restaurants and bakeries, and no fewer than 12 campgrounds. Scattered around town and valley are 18 different trails, many of which are full-scale adventures (covered elsewhere in this chapter). Some are perfect day hikes for families, including Agnes Gorge, Bullion Loop (a section of PCT), and Rainbow Loop Trail.

Agnes Gorge Trail, on the north side of Agnes Creek (different trail), travels 2.5 easy miles up the creek as it runs through a tight chasm. At the end, the trail finds the creek as it passes over a small waterfall. Rainbow Loop Trail goes 5 miles along the eastern ridge above Stehekin. The trail gains little elevation and gets in a couple of views of Lake Chelan. Pacific Crest Trail also runs through the upper valley. Using the shuttle, make a 6.5-mile through-hike from Bullion Camp past Coon Lake up to Bridge Creek Camp. The Stehekin Valley is beautiful, and now you can say you've hiked PCT.

User Groups: Hikers, leashed dogs, and horses. No mountain bikes are allowed. No wheelchair access.
Open Seasons: This area is accessible March–November.
Permits: Permits are not required. Parking and access are free.
Maps: For a map of North Cascades National Park, contact the Outdoor Recreation Information Center at the downtown Seattle REI. For topographic maps, ask Green Trails for No. 82, Stehekin, and No. 81, McGregor Mountain, or ask the USGS for Stehekin.
Directions: From Wenatchee, drive north 33 miles on U.S. 97 to Chelan. Lady of the Lake Ferry Terminal is on U.S. 97 Alternate just before entering downtown. Catch the passenger ferry to Stehekin and ride the shuttle to the various trailheads.
Contact: North Cascades National Park, Golden West Visitor Center, Stehekin, WA, 360/856-5700, ext. 340; Lady of the Lake Ferry Service, 1418 West Woodin Avenue, Chelan, WA 98816, 509/682-4584.

75 CHELAN LAKESHORE

16.9 mi one-way/2–4 days 2 9

south of Stehekin in Lake Chelan–Sawtooth Wilderness of Okanogan National Forest

Map 3.2, page 92

April and May are great times to hike Lake Chelan Lakeshore Trail, before the summer's heat makes it unbearable. Besides, summers should be reserved for the alpine. Lakeshore Trail travels 17 miles along the eastern bank to the hamlet of Stehekin, soaking up much of the lake's scenery.

Park in the town of Chelan and ride the passenger ferry to the landing of Prince Creek, on the eastern shore. After your hike, catch lunch in Stehekin and a returning ferry to Chelan. The trail follows the lakeshore, often climbing a few hundred yards above the waterline. Open forests of enormous ponderosa pine and Douglas fir line the hillside, and snowy peaks appear across the lake.

A number of established camps lie along the trail, including Prince Creek, Cascade Creek (5.5 miles), Meadow Creek (7.6 miles), Moore Point (10.6 miles), Flick Creek (13.5 miles) and Purple Point, in Stehekin. The trail can be done in two days, but three or four days is best, allowing for great side trips. Spend a day hiking up Fish Creek to Boulder Lake or Prince Creek to the Sawtooth Range. It may be only a lakeshore trail, but those who hike it know there is much more to it than that.

User Groups: Hikers only. No dogs, horses, or mountain bikes are allowed. No wheelchair access.

Open Seasons: This trail is accessible year-round.

Permits: Permits are not required. Parking and access are free.

Maps: For a map of Okanogan National Forest, contact the Outdoor Recreation Information Center at the downtown Seattle REI. For topographic maps, ask Green Trails for No. 82, Stehekin, No. 114, Lucerne, and No. 115, Prince Creek, or ask the USGS for Prince Creek, Lucerne, and Stehekin.

Directions: From Wenatchee, drive north 33 miles on U.S. 97 to Chelan. Lady of the Lake Ferry Terminal is on U.S. 97 Alternate just before entering downtown. Catch the passenger ferry to Stehekin and ride the shuttle to Prince Creek Landing.

Contact: North Cascades National Park, Golden West Visitor Center, Stehekin, WA, 360/856-5700, ext. 340; Lady of the Lake Ferry Service, 1418 West Woodin Avenue, Chelan, WA 98816, 509/682-4584.

76 LYMAN LAKES

18.2 mi/3–4 days

west of Lake Chelan in Glacier Peak Wilderness of Wenatchee National Forest

Map 3.2, page 92

For years, this has been one of the state's most frequented glaciers. Dropping off into the upper lake, Lyman Glacier displays the workings of the Ice Age, albeit on a smaller scale. The hike is a great trip up Railroad Creek Valley to large Lyman Lake, an outstanding place to spend the night. Further adventures and wide open meadows await up the trail in this high-country parkland. The lakes are often visited as a stop along a larger loop, but they make for a great trip in themselves.

The trailhead is accessible via passenger ferry from Chelan. Disembark at Lucerne and catch a ride on a privately operated bus to the village of Holden. Railroad Creek Trail ascends the forested valley to Hart Lake (3.5 miles) and Lyman Lake (8.1 miles). Camps are scattered along the way and at Lyman Lake. Lyman Spur Trail (8.1) climbs to Spider Gap, a steep but scenic ascent.

Deep within Glacier Peak Wilderness, wildlife is found everywhere. Mountain goats roam the high ridges while deer and bear roam the valleys. Be sure to hang bear sacks when camping. The trail continues south another mile to the upper lake and meadow bliss. Lyman Glacier is safe for careful exploration. For those on an extended stay, a trip up to Cloudy Pass (12.1 miles) and Suiattle Pass (13.1 miles) delivers grand views of the Cascades.

User Groups: Hikers, leashed dogs, and horses. No mountain bikes are allowed. No wheelchair access.

Open Seasons: This trail is accessible July–October.

Permits: Permits are not required. Parking and access are free.

Maps: For a map of Wenatchee National Forest, contact the Outdoor Recreation Information Center at the downtown Seattle REI. For topographic maps, ask Green Trails for No. 113, Holden, or ask the USGS for Holden.

Directions: From Wenatchee, drive north 33 miles on U.S. 97 to Chelan. Lady of the Lake Ferry Terminal is on U.S. 97 Alternate just before entering downtown. Catch the passenger ferry to Lucerne, the drop-off for Holden. Take the bus to the town of Holden. The trailhead is located at Holden Campground.

Contact: North Cascades National Park, Golden West Visitor Center, Stehekin, WA, 360/856-5700, ext. 340; Lady of the Lake Ferry Service, 1418 West Woodin Avenue, Chelan, WA 98816, 509/682-4584.

77 DOMKE LAKE

7.0 mi/4.0 hr–2-plus days

west of Lake Chelan in Wenatchee National Forest

Map 3.2, page 92

This large lake sits within a small valley above and away from Lake Chelan. More than a mile long, the lake is a favorite stop for hikers, anglers, and families looking to do some camping. While the lake is accessible only by passenger ferry, it still receives a fair amount of traffic. While Domke Lake isn't as large as Lake Chelan, its water is warmer and thus more inviting for extended swims.

Domke Lake is just 3.5 miles from Lucerne, the boat drop-off point. The trail ascends just 1,000 feet to the forested lake. Camps are at the northeast and southeast corners while yet another camp is reached by boat on the western shore. Make the lake a base camp to explore the area on Domke Mountain Trail. Its junction is just below the lake on the main trail. Three miles of trail gain nearly 3,000 feet to a grand viewpoint of the lakes and imposing mountains.

User Groups: Hikers, leashed dogs, horses, and mountain bikes. No wheelchair access.

Open Seasons: This trail is accessible June–October.

Permits: Permits are not required. Parking and access are free.

Maps: For a map of Wenatchee National Forest, contact the Outdoor Recreation Information Center at the downtown Seattle REI. For topographic maps, ask Green Trails for No. 114, Lucerne, or ask the USGS for Lucerne.

Directions: From Wenatchee, drive north 33 miles on U.S. 97 to Chelan. Lady of the Lake Ferry Terminal is on U.S. 97 Alternate just before entering downtown. Catch the passenger ferry to Lucerne. The trailhead is located at the ferry stop.

Contact: North Cascades National Park, Golden West Visitor Center, Stehekin, WA, 360/856-5700, ext. 340; Lady of the Lake Ferry Service, 1418 West Woodin Avenue, Chelan, WA 98816, 509/682-4584.

78 EMERALD PARK

14.2 mi/1–3 days

within Glacier Peak Wilderness west of Lake Chelan

Map 3.2, page 92

Set below the high summits of the Chelan Mountains, Emerald Park is a lush escape from the surrounding dry climate. Green meadows sit within a deep, rocky basin, where Emerald Peak and Pinnacle Peak tower 3,000 feet above Emerald Park. The trail can be accomplished as a full day of hiking, but two or three days is best. The basin deserves exploration and a trip up to Millham Pass is well recommended. The area is remote and belongs mostly to coyotes and the stars.

A passenger ferry is the only option to the trailhead at Lucerne, three-quarters of the way up Lake Chelan on the western shore. The route spends 1.6 miles on Domke Lake Trail before heading off on Emerald Park Trail. A short .5 mile later the trail splits again; head to the left, saving Railroad Creek for another day. Five miles of trail slowly makes its way up the valley, gaining 3,000 feet. The trail is often far above the creek, making water scarce. At Emerald Park, the forest gives way to green, open meadows and astounding views of the basin. Emerald Park Camp is 7.1 miles from Lucerne.

User Groups: Hikers, leashed dogs, and horses. No mountain bikes are allowed. No wheelchair access.

Open Seasons: This trail is accessible May–October.

Permits: Permits are not required. Parking and access are free.

Maps: For a map of Wenatchee National Forest, contact the Outdoor Recreation Information Center at the downtown Seattle REI. For topographic maps, ask Green Trails for No.

114, Lucerne, or ask the USGS for Holden, Pinnacle Mountain, and Lucerne.
Directions: From Wenatchee, drive north 33 miles on U.S. 97 to Chelan. Lady of the Lake Ferry Terminal is on U.S. 97 Alternate just before entering downtown. Catch the passenger ferry to Lucerne. The trailhead is located at the ferry stop.
Contact: North Cascades National Park, Golden West Visitor Center, Stehekin, WA, 360/856-5700, ext. 340; Lady of the Lake Ferry Service, 1418 West Woodin Avenue, Chelan, WA 98816, 509/682-4584.

79 TWISP PASS

4.2 mi/3.0 hr

northwest of Twisp in Lake Chelan–Sawtooth Wilderness of Okanogan National Forest

Map 3.2, page 92

The upper Sawtooth Mountain Range is full of natural beauty; wildflowers envelop mountain meadows in color in the early summer while subalpine larches burn up the hillsides during the fall. The trail to Twisp Pass encounters both, as well as impressive views of crowded mountain peaks in all directions. It's one of the best day hikes in the Twisp Valley, but it also serves hikers looking for longer trips. The trail is a major route into the North Cascades National Park, on the western side of the pass. An additional 4.3 miles delivers hikers to Bridge Creek and a junction of four major trails. Day hikers will be content with the pass and Dagger Lake, just inside the park.

The trail is a steep one, gaining 2,400 feet on the way to the pass. The first two miles are well forested and come to a trail junction. The right fork heads up to Copper Pass, an equally impressive gap within the mighty Sawtooths. A great loop can be made via Copper Pass and Bridge Creek for 20.5 miles. Stay to the left for Twisp Pass, climbing steeply through rocky meadows to Twisp Pass. Water is scarce after the junction, so bring plenty. Lincoln Butte and Twisp Mountain stand tall on either side of the pass, while Dagger Lake sparkles from below. A quick mile's descent into the park arrives at an established camp at Dagger Lake. A backcountry permit from the national park is required for overnight stays here.
User Groups: Hikers, leashed dogs (up to Twisp Pass, but not beyond), and horses. No mountain bikes are allowed. No wheelchair access.
Open Seasons: This trail is accessible July–September.
Permits: A federal Northwest Forest Pass is required to park here.
Maps: For a map of Okanogan National Forest, contact the Outdoor Recreation Information Center at the downtown Seattle REI. For topographic maps, ask Green Trails for No. 82, Stehekin, or ask the USGS for Gilbert.
Directions: From Twisp, drive east 26 miles on Twisp River Road (Forest Service Road 44 becomes Forest Service Road 4440) to the trailhead at road's end.
Contact: Okanogan National Forest, Methow Valley Ranger Station, 24 West Chewuch Road, Winthrop, WA 98862, 509/996-4003.

80 NORTH CREEK

9.2 mi/4.5 hr

northwest of Twisp in Lake Chelan–Sawtooth Wilderness of Okanogan National Forest

Map 3.2, page 92

North Creek presents one of the Twisp Valley's more gentle and accessible lake hikes. The trail climbs just 2,200 feet over 4.6 miles, a relative cakewalk compared to the routes for some other lakes in the valley. The valley nearly encircles Gilbert Mountain, offering a chance to view the rugged peak from nearly every side. To add color to the scenery, wildflowers light up the open meadows around the lake during July.

After passing through an old timber harvest, the trail climbs through a forest of Douglas fir and ponderosa pine. The trail occasionally passes through avalanche chutes where snow can stick around into July some years. When it does, passage is difficult. Despite the arid conditions of Eastern Cascades, this valley received a fair amount of carving by Ice Age glaciers, leaving it flat and wide. The trail follows the creek for the most part, following the natural loop of the valley, eventually turning south before encountering the lake. Gilbert Mountain looms high above from the south, more than 2,000 feet overhead. Exploration above the lake is best avoided; vertical shafts and loose rock remain from previous mining activity, as well as fragile meadows that don't endure hiking boots well.

User Groups: Hikers, leashed dogs, and horses. No mountain bikes are allowed. No wheelchair access.

Open Seasons: This trail is accessible June–October.

Permits: A federal Northwest Forest Pass is required to park here.

Maps: For a map of Okanogan National Forest, contact the Outdoor Recreation Information Center at the downtown Seattle REI. For topographic maps, ask Green Trails for No. 82, Stehekin, or ask the USGS for Gilbert.

Directions: From Twisp, drive east 26 miles on Twisp River Road (Forest Service Road 44 becomes Forest Service Road 4440) to the trailhead at road's end.

Contact: Okanogan National Forest, Methow Valley Ranger Station, 24 West Chewuch Road, Winthrop, WA 98862, 509/996-4003.

81 LOUIS LAKE

11.4 mi/6.0 hr

northwest of Twisp in Lake Chelan–Sawtooth Wilderness of Okanogan National Forest

Map 3.2, page 92

Louis Lake is one of the best deals in the Twisp Valley. Less grueling than other routes in the valley, Louis Lake Trail visits the most scenic lakes in the Sawtooth Range. Grand examples of Englemann spruce, Douglas fir, and whitebark pine battle with mountain views for your attention. It's an epic bout, although the great ridges dominating the skyline win out. To top it all off, Louis Lake sits within a narrow, rugged valley surrounded by some of the range's most jagged ridges. Visitors from afar are well advised to give Louis Lake serious consideration as a recipient for their effort.

The route begins along South Creek Trail before Louis Lake Trail cuts to the south (2.1 miles). The trail heads straight toward the ridge before the valley turns 90 degrees, revealing a narrow slot. The forest breaks into meadows often, revealing South Creek Butte and Crescent Mountain. Louis Lake (5.3 miles) is a pictorial setting, surrounded by meadows of heather and harboring a small, tree-covered island. Steep valley walls lead to a sharp ridge around the basin, highlighted by a tall peak of 81,42 feet. Despite its popularity during the summer, Louis Lake is an outstanding Twisp Valley destination.

User Groups: Hikers, leashed dogs, and horses. No mountain bikes are allowed. No wheelchair access.

Open Seasons: This trail is accessible mid-June–October.

Permits: A federal Northwest Forest Pass is required to park here.

Maps: For a map of Okanogan National Forest, contact the Outdoor Recreation Information Center at the downtown Seattle REI. For topographic maps, ask Green Trails for No. 82, Stehekin, or ask the USGS for Gilbert.

Directions: From Twisp, drive east 22 miles on Twisp River Road (Forest Service Road 44 becomes Forest Service Road 4440) to South Creek Trailhead on the right.

Contact: Okanogan National Forest, Methow Valley Ranger Station, 24 West Chewuch Road, Winthrop, WA 98862, 509/996-4003.

82 SCATTER CREEK

8.6 mi/6.0 hr

5 8

northwest of Twisp in Lake Chelan–Sawtooth Wilderness of Okanogan National Forest

Map 3.2, page 92

The prime time to visit Scatter Lake is fall, when wildly colorful larches mark the perimeter of this deep blue pool. To add to the array of colors, afternoon sunlight brings out the deep red of high Abernathy Peak. Scatter Lake offers lots of color to make up for the

punishing hike. In fact, punishing may be a light word for 3,800 feet of elevation gain contained within four short miles. But that's the way of the Twisp Valley. The scenery around Scatter Lake easily makes up for it.

The route begins along Twisp River Trail but quickly turns onto Scatter Creek Trail (.2 mile). The trail begins a short series of switchbacks before abandoning them altogether for the alternative of a straight ascent up the valley. Scatter Creek is always at hand offering a cool refreshment. Scatter Creek Trail crosses the creek before climbing the final mile to the lake. Wildflowers are prolific in the open meadows during July. Abernathy Peak, 8,321 feet, looks down from the talus-strewn ridge around the lake basin.

User Groups: Hikers, leashed dogs, and horses. No mountain bikes are allowed. No wheelchair access.

Open Seasons: This trail is accessible June–October.

Permits: A federal Northwest Forest Pass is required to park here.

Maps: For a map of Okanogan National Forest, contact the Outdoor Recreation Information Center at the downtown Seattle REI. For topographic maps, ask Green Trails for No. 82, Stehekin, or ask the USGS for Gilbert and Midnight Mountain.

Directions: From Twisp, drive east 22 miles on Twisp River Road (Forest Service Road 44 becomes Forest Service Road 4440) to South Creek Trailhead on the right.

Contact: Okanogan National Forest, Methow Valley Ranger Station, 24 West Chewuch Road, Winthrop, WA 98862, 509/996-4003.

83 SLATE CREEK

10.2 mi/6.0 hr

northwest of Twisp in Lake Chelan–Sawtooth Wilderness of Okanogan National Forest

Map 3.2, page 92

Slate Lake is the most brutal of the Twisp Valley lake hikes. Other appropriate synonyms include terrorizing, demanding, and exceptionally beautiful. Such words go along with 3,800-foot elevation gains laid out over just three miles. The lake is set back within a recess along the Abernathy Ridge, nearly becoming a part of the Wolf Creek drainage. Instead, the lake drains into Little Slate Creek and down to Twisp River. The terrain is fairly open, as the forest struggles to thicken for lack of much precipitation. This makes for good views and excellent scrambling.

Slate Creek Trail gets all the work out of the way in the first three miles. In this stretch, the trail climbs straight up to a knob on the west side of the creek. This ascent is dry and extremely demanding on hot summer days. From this point, however, the views are outstanding. The rugged Sawtooth Range stretches out across from the entire length of the Twisp River. Midnight and 3 A.M. Mountains are directly across Little Slate Creek. From here, the trail follows at a nearly even grade along the ridge enclosing Slate Lake. Those with energy left can take advantage of the great scrambling opportunities around the lake. Despite the treacherous ascent up, Slate Lake is the best lake in the valley for those with an adventurous spirit.

User Groups: Hikers, leashed dogs, and horses. No mountain bikes are allowed. No wheelchair access.

Open Seasons: This trail is accessible June–October.

Permits: A federal Northwest Forest Pass is required to park here.

Maps: For a map of Okanogan National Forest, contact the Outdoor Recreation Information Center at the downtown Seattle REI. For topographic maps, ask Green Trails for No. 83, Buttermilk Butte, or ask the USGS for Midnight Mountain.

Directions: From Twisp, drive east 18 miles on Twisp River Road (Forest Service Road 44 becomes Forest Service Road 4440) to Slate Creek Trailhead on the right.

Contact: Okanogan National Forest, Methow Valley Ranger Station, 24 West Chewuch Road, Winthrop, WA 98862, 509/996-4003.

84 WILLIAMS CREEK

13.6 mi/8.0 hr

northwest of Twisp in Lake Chelan–Sawtooth Wilderness of Okanogan National Forest

Map 3.2, page 92

Williams Creek Trail starts low and ends high. Make no mistake about that. If you're into difficult 3,700-foot elevation gains, then perhaps this is the perfect trail for you. The most distinctive facet of the route is its passage through an old forest burn. Although the fire occurred decades ago, the forest remains open. Significant regenerative growth has taken place, staging an interesting example of forest dynamics.

Williams Lake is set within a great bowl, where Williams Butte and War Creek Ridge rim the basin. Meadows are prolific around the lake, with July flowers as bright as the sky. The trail to the lake follows the creek the entire way, staying to the north side. The trail is popular with equestrians, as there is a horse camp just before the lake. While the lake is stocked, fishing reviews are mixed. If you're going to hike almost seven miles, though, you might as well bring your pole and try to catch some lunch.

User Groups: Hikers, leashed dogs, and horses. No mountain bikes are allowed. No wheelchair access.

Open Seasons: This trail is accessible June–October.

Permits: A federal Northwest Forest Pass is required to park here.

Maps: For a map of Okanogan National Forest, contact the Outdoor Recreation Information Center at the downtown Seattle REI. For topographic maps, ask Green Trails for No. 82, Stehekin, and No. 83, Buttermilk Butte, or ask the USGS for Gilbert, Midnight Mountain, and Sun Mountain.

Directions: From Twisp, drive east 19 miles on Twisp River Road (Forest Service Road 44) to Mystery Campground. Turn left on Forest Service Road 4430, cross the river, and stay left for .5 mile to Williams Creek Trailhead on the right.

Contact: Okanogan National Forest, Methow Valley Ranger Station, 24 West Chewuch Road, Winthrop, WA 98862, 509/996-4003.

85 NORTH WAR CREEK

19.0 mi/2 days

west of Twisp in Lake Chelan–Sawtooth Wilderness of Okanogan National Forest

Map 3.2, page 92

North War Creek Trail is the most northern and scenic route to Chelan Summit Trail. The trail makes a long gradual ascent to War Creek Pass, where the high-country Lake Juanita awaits. A side trail leads to the summit of Boulder Butte, where the views of much of the North Cascades are superb. Most hikers on this trail are completing the longer Chelan Summit Loop and wish to exit via the Twisp River. Nonetheless, War Creek is a great excursion for those wanting to see what the Sawtooth Ridge has to offer.

North War Creek Trail parallels the stream for nearly its entire length. The grade is gentle until the end, where the last mile rises to the pass. Forests of old-growth pine and spruce blanket the valley, adding shade on hot days, although parts of the forest are scarred from a 1994 fire. The trail crests at War Creek Pass in a subalpine setting, where meadows cover the crest and views extend in many directions. Lake Juanita is below with a hiker and horse camp. The trail up to Boulder Butte is highly recommended and not to be missed by any who have ventured this far. From War Creek Pass, trails lead down Purple Creek to Stehekin, up Boulder Creek, and down the crest of the Sawtooth Mountains.

User Groups: Hikers, leashed dogs, and horses. No mountain bikes are allowed. No wheelchair access.

Open Seasons: This trail is accessible July–October.

Permits: A federal Northwest Forest Pass is required to park here.

Maps: For a map of Okanogan National Forest, contact the Outdoor Recreation Information

Center at the downtown Seattle REI. For topographic maps, ask Green Trails for No. 82, Stehekin, and No. 83, Buttermilk Butte, or ask the USGS for Sun Mountain and Oval Peak.
Directions: From Twisp, drive east 15 miles on Twisp River Road (Forest Service Road 44) to Forest Service Road 4430. Turn left on Forest Service Road 4430, cross the river, and stay right for 1 mile to Forest Service Road 100. Turn left and drive 1.5 miles to the trailhead at road's end.
Contact: Okanogan National Forest, Methow Valley Ranger Station, 24 West Chewuch Road, Winthrop, WA 98862, 509/996-4003.

86 OVAL LAKES

15.0–22.6 mi/2–3 days

west of Twisp in Lake Chelan–Sawtooth Wilderness of Okanogan National Forest

Map 3.2, page 92

The Sawtooth Range east of Lake Chelan is full of great adventures and destinations. Situated along the high mountainous crest, Oval Lakes are one of the range's most beautiful locales. These three lakes lie within small, rocky basins at the head of Oval Creek. Subalpine larches eke out a living here, at nearly 7,000 feet. The lakes have great camping and offer great exploration, with loads of views from Oval Pass.

The route begins on Eagle Creek Trail but soon cuts off on Oval Creek Trail (1.9 miles). The old forest provides welcome shade for a while but begins to break into meadows and views. West Oval Lake is achieved via a short side trail (at 7.2 miles) but is not open to camping. Check it out, get a taste of what's ahead, and continue to Middle Oval Lake (8.9 miles) or East Oval Lake (9.4 miles). The fishing's good but the camping's even better. One look at the rocky ridges ringing the lakes, and you'll know why this is called the Sawtooths.

Between West Oval and Middle Oval Lakes, be sure to hike a quick .25 mile to Oval Pass and views of Tuckaway Basin. Adventurous hikers with a map can initially follow Eagle Creek Trail to Eagle Pass and around Tuckaway Lake to Oval Pass, a lasso-shaped loop of 22.6 miles
User Groups: Hikers, leashed dogs, and horses. No mountain bikes are allowed. No wheelchair access.
Open Seasons: This trail is accessible July–October.
Permits: A federal Northwest Forest Pass is required to park here.
Maps: For a map of Okanogan National Forest, contact the Outdoor Recreation Information Center at the downtown Seattle REI. For topographic maps, ask Green Trails for No. 83, Buttermilk Butte, or ask the USGS for Sun Mountain and Oval Peak.
Directions: From Twisp, drive east 15 miles on Twisp River Road (Forest Service Road 44) to Forest Service Road 4430. Turn left on Forest Service Road 4430, cross the river, and stay to the left for 1 mile to Forest Service Road 080. Turn right and drive 1.5 miles to the trailhead at road's end.
Contact: Okanogan National Forest, Methow Valley Ranger Station, 24 West Chewuch Road, Winthrop, WA 98862, 509/996-4003.

87 WOLF CREEK

19.8 mi/2 days

west of Winthrop in Lake Chelan–Sawtooth Wilderness of Okanogan National Forest

Map 3.2, page 92

Gardner Meadows caps one of the region's most beautiful valley treks. Wolf Creek Trail ventures 10 miles into Wolf Creek valley, ending where Abernathy Ridge and Gardner Mountain loom high above the open parkland. Although the trail is popular with equestrians and hunters during fall, an abundance of wildlife awaits to be seen. Lupine and glacier lilies paint the meadows in color during early summer while deer and coyotes roam the open expanse. And there's no end to exploring off the main trail, as several nonmaintained trails lead into side valleys.

Wolf Creek Trail ascends gently over 10

miles to Gardner Meadows. The trail never strays far from the creek, which is locally known for booming bull trout populations. Most of the route passes through forests of huge Douglas fir and ponderosa pines. Side trails include one up the North Fork Wolf Creek at 2.7 miles, the South Fork Wolf Creek at 6.5 miles, and another up Hubbard Creek at 7.2 miles, none of which is maintained. Less maintenance, however, usually means more adventure.

Gardner Meadows is set upon wide open rolling hills. Patches of trees litter the terrain, which runs up to steep, scree-covered slopes. Scrambles farther up to Abernathy Lake or to the top of Abernathy Ridge are well advised for those looking for off-trail travel. Rumors continue to persist regarding gray wolves within the appropriately named valley. Reported sightings have not been confirmed and are more likely coyotes, which are abundant here. Sightings of gray wolves in the North Cascades have been confirmed only north of Highway 20.

User Groups: Hikers, leashed dogs, and horses. No mountain bikes are allowed. No wheelchair access.

Open Seasons: This trail is accessible June–October.

Permits: A federal Northwest Forest Pass is required to park here.

Maps: For a map of Okanogan National Forest, contact the Outdoor Recreation Information Center at the downtown Seattle REI. For topographic maps, ask Green Trails for No. 83, Buttermilk Butte, or ask the USGS for Thompson Ridge, Gilbert, and Midnight Mountain.

Directions: From Winthrop, drive east on Highway 20 to Twin Lakes Road (County Road 9120). Turn right (west) and drive 1.5 miles to Wolf Creek Road (County Road 1145). Turn right and drive 5 miles to the trailhead at road's end.

Contact: Okanogan National Forest, Methow Valley Ranger Station, 24 West Chewuch Road, Winthrop, WA 98862, 509/996-4003.

88 EAST FORK BUTTERMILK CREEK

15.0 mi/1–2 days 2 5

west of Twisp in Lake Chelan–Sawtooth Wilderness of Okanogan National Forest

Map 3.2, page 92

East Fork Buttermilk Creek is much like the West Fork. It's a hike through a forest that really isn't worth the time it takes to hike it. It's always nice to get out and enjoy nature, but there are many other trails within the area that are far more deserving of your time. That said, there are still some good things about this trail. Those good things are mainly limited to large forests near the creek and some great views at Hoodoo Pass. Unless you've hiked many other trails in the area and are looking for a new experience, East Fork Buttermilk Creek just isn't all that special.

The trail is laid out on an old mining road for the first four miles. Forests of Englemann spruce and lodgepole pine cover the valley and occasionally provide glimpses of surrounding ridges. The trail is not steep until it reaches the headwaters of the creek in Hoodoo Basin. Here, it abruptly ascends to Hoodoo Pass (7.5 miles). Views to the north and south are well worth a long stop here. The trail drops to Chelan Summit Trail (8.8 miles). Backpackers should plan on camping at Hoodoo Pass or at the junction of Chelan Summit Trail.

User Groups: Hikers, leashed dogs, and horses. No mountain bikes are allowed. No wheelchair access.

Open Seasons: This trail is accessible mid-June–October.

Permits: A federal Northwest Forest Pass is required to park here.

Maps: For a map of Okanogan National Forest, contact the Outdoor Recreation Information Center at the downtown Seattle REI. For topographic maps, ask Green Trails for No. 83, Buttermilk Butte, and No. 115, Prince Creek, or ask the USGS for Hoodoo Peak and Martin Peak.

Directions: From Twisp, drive east 11 miles on

Twisp River Road to Forest Service Road 43. Turn left and drive 6 miles to Forest Service Road 400. Turn right and drive 3.5 miles to the trailhead on the left.
Contact: Okanogan National Forest, Methow Valley Ranger Station, 24 West Chewuch Road, Winthrop, WA 98862, 509/996-4003.

89 LIBBY CREEK

10.4 mi/6.0 hr

southwest of Twisp in Lake Chelan–Sawtooth Wilderness of Okanogan National Forest

Map 3.2, page 92

Libby Lake sits within its own amphitheater. Large, towering walls of granite ringing the high lake give way to large slopes of boulders and talus. But the lake is not easy to reach. Several elevation drops along the way are relentlessly followed by difficult climbs. But Libby Lake is well regarded and always enjoyable.

Libby Creek Trail begins on an old logging road and climbs steadily before becoming a real trail. The path eventually drops to cross the North Fork of Libby Creek, a great time to dip one's head in the cold water and cool off. The trail remains within the wide, forested valley bottom, crossing another pair of small creeks, sometimes dry. Tall Hoodoo Peak is to the north. The trail makes a final charge upward just before the lake. Remnants of a very old cabin can be seen to the side of the trail, beaten up by heavy winter snowfalls. There are several campsites below the lake, a quiet and inviting overnight stay. The lake itself is ringed by broken talus and subalpine larches, subsisting in this harsh, almost barren, mountain hideaway.
User Groups: Hikers, leashed dogs, and horses. No mountain bikes are allowed. No wheelchair access.
Open Seasons: This trail is accessible July–September.
Permits: A federal Northwest Forest Pass is required to park here.
Maps: For a map of Okanogan National Forest, contact the Outdoor Recreation Information Center at the downtown Seattle REI. For topographic maps, ask Green Trails for No. 83, Buttermilk Butte, and No. 115, Prince Creek, or ask the USGS for Hoodoo Peak.
Directions: From Twisp, drive east 3 miles on Highway 20 to Highway 153. Turn right onto Okanogan County Road 1045 and drive to Forest Service Road 43. Turn left and drive 5.5 miles to Forest Service Road 4340. Turn left and drive 1.5 miles to Forest Service Road 4340-700. Turn right and drive 1.5 miles to Forest Service Road 4340-750. Turn left and drive to the signed trailhead.
Contact: Okanogan National Forest, Methow Valley Ranger Station, 24 West Chewuch Road, Winthrop, WA 98862, 509/996-4003.

90 MARTIN LAKES

14.2 mi/2 days

southwest of Twisp in Lake Chelan–Sawtooth Wilderness of Okanogan National Forest

Map 3.2, page 92

Martin Lakes are a great first experience of the Sawtooths, a place of high lakes and higher peaks. Surrounded on three sides by woods and on another by the larch-dotted base of Martin Peak, the lakes offer a lot of peace, quiet, and most likely, solitude. Dinner's never more than a few casts away, either, as the lakes sport a good deal of healthy trout. It's enough to make hungry hikers curse forgotten poles.

The trail is in good condition and makes a steady, modest incline. The route begins on Eagle Lakes Trail but splits onto Martin Creek Trail (2.3 miles). The trail regularly opens to provide views of the opposing ridge and beyond, preventing feelings of forest claustrophobia. The two Martin Lakes are down a short and signed side trail at 6.3 miles. Several good campsites are found at the lower lake. High peaks and ridges surround the large basin. Clark's nutcrackers swoop about the whitebark pines, and hawks give the numerous chipmunks chase.
User Groups: Hikers, leashed dogs, horses, mountain bikes, and motorcycles (motorcycles most of the way). No wheelchair access.

Open Seasons: This trail is accessible July–mid-October.
Permits: A federal Northwest Forest Pass is required to park here.
Maps: For a map of Okanogan National Forest, contact the Outdoor Recreation Information Center at the downtown Seattle REI. For topographic maps, ask Green Trails for No. 115, Prince Creek, or ask the USGS for Martin Peak.
Directions: From Pateros, drive north on Highway 153. Turn left onto Gold Creek Loop Road, south of the town of Carlton. Turn left (west) onto Forest Service Road 4340. Drive about 6 miles to Forest Service Road 4340-300. Turn left and drive for about 5 miles to the trailhead at road's end.
Contact: Okanogan National Forest, Methow Valley Ranger Station, 24 West Chewuch Road, Winthrop, WA 98862, 509/996-4003.

91 CRATER LAKE

7.4 mi/4.0 hr

southwest of Twisp in Lake Chelan–Sawtooth Wilderness of Okanogan National Forest

Map 3.2, page 92

Crater Lake is not the result of a large meteor hitting the Sawtooths. Nor was it created by a long-ago volcanic eruption. So erase the image of a crater from your mind, and replace it with tall, jagged ridges, craggy peaks, colorful larches, and blue mountain water. Voilà, you have a picture of the real Crater Lake. It's a good day hike and shows what the Sawtooths have to offer.

The route begins on Eagle Lake Trail, cutting to the right just after crossing Crater Creek (.5 mile). It moves quickly up the valley at a moderate grade. Crossing the creek again, it climbs more steeply. Before long, you'll be swearing the trail feels like more than the posted three miles from the junction. After a large granite outcrop, which reveals most of Eastern Washington, the trail levels off and hits the lake. There are several spots for camping at the outlet of the lake. This is a favorite spot for high-country anglers.

User Groups: Hikers, leashed dogs, horses, and mountain bikes. No wheelchair access.
Open Seasons: This trail is accessible July–mid-October.
Permits: A federal Northwest Forest Pass is required to park here.
Maps: For a map of Okanogan National Forest, contact the Outdoor Recreation Information Center at the downtown Seattle REI. For topographic maps, ask Green Trails for No. 115, Prince Creek, or ask the USGS for Martin Peak.
Directions: From Pateros, drive north on Highway 153. Turn left onto Gold Creek Loop Road, south of the town of Carlton. Turn left (west) onto Forest Service Road 4340. Drive about 6 miles to Forest Service Road 4340-300. Turn left and drive for about 5 miles to the trailhead at road's end.
Contact: Okanogan National Forest, Methow Valley Ranger Station, 24 West Chewuch Road, Winthrop, WA 98862, 509/996-4003.

92 EAGLE LAKES

12.3 mi/1–2 days

southwest of Twisp in Lake Chelan–Sawtooth Wilderness of Okanogan National Forest

Map 3.2, page 92

Take a trip to Eagle Lakes and you are likely to run into folks who have been coming here for 35 years or more. They enthusiastically call it home, and it's easy to understand why. Set below the towering granite walls of Mount Bigelow, Upper Eagle Lake enjoys a grand forest of subalpine larch and fir. A beautiful trail to the lakes and pretty decent fishing make this a popular choice in the South Sawtooth Range.

Eagle Lakes Trail climbs for much of its length but never too steeply. After Martin Lakes junction (2.5 miles), the forest begins to open up along Eagle Lakes Trail, providing a welcome view and appreciation of how far one has come. The trail passes granite outcroppings and very large Douglas firs and ponderosa pines. The junction for Upper Eagle Lake arrives first (5.8 miles) and climbs a short .5 mile to the lake.

Campsites ring the eastern shore, opposite the rocky slopes of the western shore. Upper Lake is definitely the better choice. Lower Eagle Lake Trail drops to the left (6.1 miles) to the more forested and larger lake, home to a horse camp.
User Groups: Hikers, leashed dogs, horses, mountain bikes, and motorcycles. No wheelchair access.
Open Seasons: This trail is accessible July–mid-October.
Permits: A federal Northwest Forest Pass is required to park here.
Maps: For a map of Okanogan National Forest, contact the Outdoor Recreation Information Center at the downtown Seattle REI. For topographic maps, ask Green Trails for No. 115, Prince Creek, or ask the USGS for Martin Peak.
Directions: From Pateros, drive north on Highway 153. Turn left onto Gold Creek Loop Road, south of the town of Carlton. Turn left (west) onto Forest Service Road 4340. Drive about 6 miles to Forest Service Road 4340-300. Turn left and drive for about 5 miles to the trailhead at road's end.
Contact: Okanogan National Forest, Methow Valley Ranger Station, 24 West Chewuch Road, Winthrop, WA 98862, 509/996-4003.

93 BUCK CREEK PASS

20.5 mi/2 days

north of Trinity in Glacier Peak Wilderness of Wenatchee National Forest

Map 3.2, page 92

Great by itself, Buck Creek Pass is also the means to grander ends. The pass is between three high peaks, each of them offering exceptional views of surrounding peaks and mountain ranges. The views are first-rate, but the wildflower meadows are what draw crowds of folks up the trail each year. In fact, Flower Dome could not be better named, for a blanket of flowers covers its entirety during July. Glacier Peak is a regular fixture, its mighty glaciers well revealed.

Buck Creek Trail leaves the town of Trinity along the road but quickly enters Glacier Peak Wilderness. The trail splits (2 miles), so stick to the left, cross the Chiwawa River via bridge, and head up Buck Creek Valley through large forests of Douglas fir, Englemann spruce, and hemlock.

Buck Creek Pass is achieved after a tiring 10 miles. Numerous campsites line the trail and are widespread at the pass. Once camp is set up, the exploration can begin. Absolutely necessary is a one-mile trip up Flower Dome, awash in wildflower color. Another trail climbs to the top of Liberty Cap. For the hearty, a difficult trail heads toward High Pass and barren Triad Lake. Much of the area is delicate and receives heavy traffic, so be sure to take care where you step.
User Groups: Hikers, leashed dogs, and horses. No mountain bikes are allowed. No wheelchair access.
Open Seasons: This trail is accessible July–September.
Permits: A federal Northwest Forest Pass is required to park here.
Maps: For a map of Wenatchee National Forest, contact the Outdoor Recreation Information Center at the downtown Seattle REI. For topographic maps, ask Green Trails for No. 113, Holden, or ask the USGS for Trinity, Clark Mountain, and Suiattle Pass.
Directions: From Leavenworth, drive west on Highway 2 to Highway 207, at Coles Corner. Veer Left to Fish Lake and drive 1 mile to Chiwawa Valley Road (Forest Service Road 62). Turn left and drive to Trinity. The trailhead is at road's end, just beyond Phelps Creek Campground.
Contact: Wenatchee National Forest, Lake Wenatchee Ranger District, 22976 Highway 207, Leavenworth, WA 98826, 509/763-3103.

94 PHELPS CREEK (SPIDER MEADOW)

17.0 mi/2 days

north of Lake Wenatchee in Glacier Peak Wilderness of Wenatchee National Forest

Map 3.2, page 92

Officially, the route is named Phelps Creek Trail. But within Washington hiking circles, it is better known as Spider Meadow, after the enormous meadows within the elongated valley. At the head of the valley slides Spider Glacier, Washington's easiest glacier to explore. Nearly a mile long but not more than 150 feet across, Spider Glacier ends at scenic Spider Gap, with views of the North Cascades. Few trails this scenic are this easy.

Phelps Creek Trail follows an old logging road but soon enters Glacier Peak Wilderness (1 mile). The forest grows older and larger, and edible mushrooms are regularly spotted. Chicken-of-the-woods and bear's head tooth fungus are easily identifiable by beginners, but be sure to leave trailside specimens alone for others to enjoy. The trail breaks into Spider Meadow (4 miles). The obvious U shape to the valley is the work of the valley's previous tenant, a glacier. Camping must be at established campsites, of which there are about 30 throughout the lower valley.

After climbing out of the meadow (5 miles), the trail climbs to Spider Glacier, to the east. This glacier is completely nontechnical and can be traversed easily by all. At the top is Spider Gap, with views to the north of the larger Lyman Glacier and various North Cascade peaks. There are an additional 10 campsites within this upper basin. Expect a lot of people here on summer weekends.

User Groups: Hikers, leashed dogs, and horses (horses allowed up to Spider Meadow only). No mountain bikes are allowed. No wheelchair access.

Open Seasons: This trail is accessible mid-June–September.

Permits: A federal Northwest Forest Pass is required to park here.

Maps: For a map of Wenatchee National Forest, contact the Outdoor Recreation Information Center at the downtown Seattle REI. For topographic maps, ask Green Trails for No. 113, Holden, or ask the USGS for Trinity, Holden, and Suiattle Pass.

Directions: From Leavenworth, drive west on Highway 2 to Highway 207, at Coles Corner. Turn left and drive to Fish Lake and drive 1 mile to Chiwawa Valley Road (Forest Service Road 62). Turn left and drive toward Trinity. Just before Trinity, turn right on Forest Service Road 6211 and drive to the trailhead at road's end.

Contact: Wenatchee National Forest, Lake Wenatchee Ranger District, 22976 Highway 207, Leavenworth, WA 98826, 509/763-3103.

95 ENTIAT MEADOWS

29.6 mi/3–4 days

northwest of Entiat in Glacier Peak Wilderness of Wenatchee National Forest

Map 3.2, page 92

After 15 miles, a trail needs to offer something special. I'm talking large peaks or glaciers, wide open meadows with wildflowers, or lots of wildlife. Actually, that's what Entiat River Trail delivers, making its easy but long route well worth the trip.

Entiat River Trail quietly follows the Entiat River to its headwaters, making little substantial change in elevation. The first 10 miles are forested by large Englemann spruce, silver fir, and Douglas fir. Soon, the valley opens into meadows, and Tin Pan Mountain welcomes you to true backcountry. The trail turns west with the valley and Seven Fingered Jack beckons from the end of the valley, encouraging hikers to keep moving. There are good camps throughout this section of the trail for resting tired feet. Many hours from the car, Entiat River Trail arrives at its terminus among meadows and enormous piles of glacier moraine.

Entiat Glacier covers the backside of Maude Mountain, breaking and crackling during warm summer days. Mountain goats regularly patrol the steep valley walls in pursuit of dinner. Their bright white coats are easy to spot. There are many deer in the valley and always a good chance of seeing a bear or cat. This spot is far from any civilization, a very welcome bargain indeed.

User Groups: Hikers, leashed dogs, and horses. No mountain bikes are allowed. No wheelchair access.

Open Seasons: This trail is accessible June–October.
Permits: A federal Northwest Forest Pass is required to park here.
Maps: For a map of Wenatchee National Forest, contact the Outdoor Recreation Information Center at the downtown Seattle REI. For topographic maps, ask Green Trails for No. 113, Holden, and No. 114, Lucerne, or ask the USGS for Holden and Saska Peak.
Directions: From Wenatchee, drive north along U.S. 97 Alternate to Entiat. Turn left on Entiat River Road and drive 38 miles to the road's end, where the trailhead is located.
Contact: Wenatchee National Forest, Entiat Ranger Station, 2108 Entiat Way, P.O. Box 476, Entiat, WA 98822, 509/784-1511.

96 ICE LAKES

25.6 mi/2–3 days

northwest of Entiat in Glacier Peak Wilderness of Wenatchee National Forest

Map 3.2, page 92

Ice Lakes are true high country. Other than subalpine larches and big mountains, there is little else here. No worries, because Ice Lakes is phenomenally beautiful. Think of the Enchantments, but without the crowds or discouraging permit process. The upper Entiat Mountains rise above Ice Valley and surround the lakes. Hike up here in late September and the larches will add radiant yellows and oranges to the landscape. Best of all, this trail is not exceptionally well known.

The journey to Ice Lakes is no piece of cake. First, hike eight miles up Entiat River Trail. Cross the Entiat (troublesome in the spring) and wind up Ice Creek Valley through a forest filled with large Englemann spruce. First-night spots can be found on either side of the Entiat River crossing (8 miles), where Pomas Creek runs into Ice Creek (8.8 miles), and at Ice Camp (12.7 miles).

At Ice Camp, the trail turns downright nasty, scaling the valley wall (a 1,300-foot climb in one mile). This section often requires 90 minutes or more, so don't be discouraged. At the top is Lower Ice Lake, and a short mile farther is Upper Ice Lake. There is lots of camping to be had at the lakes, particularly the lower one. Plan for time to kick back and relax here, as it's time well spent. There are lots of scrambles to be had from here, including an ascent of 9,082-foot Mount Maude.

User Groups: Hikers, leashed dogs, and horses (horses up to Ice Camp; they won't be able to make it farther). No mountain bikes are allowed. No wheelchair access.
Open Seasons: This trail is usually accessible mid-July–October.
Permits: A federal Northwest Forest Pass is required to park here.
Maps: For a map of Wenatchee National Forest, contact the Outdoor Recreation Information Center at the downtown Seattle REI. For topographic maps, ask Green Trails for No. 113, Holden, and No. 114, Lucerne, or ask the USGS for Holden, Saska Peak, and Pinnacle Mountain.
Directions: From Wenatchee, drive north along U.S. 97 Alternate to Entiat. Turn left on Entiat River Road and drive 38 miles to the road's end, where the well-signed trailhead is located.
Contact: Wenatchee National Forest, Entiat Ranger Station, 2108 Entiat Way, P.O. Box 476, Entiat, WA 98822, 509/784-1511.

97 PYRAMID MOUNTAIN

18.4 mi/1–2 days 2 9

west of Lake Chelan in Wenatchee National Forest

Map 3.2, page 92

Pyramid Mountain is for hikers looking to seemingly stand atop the state. From the lofty elevation of 8,243 feet, Pyramid Mountain provides a panorama rarely matched in the region. From the high ridge and even higher peak, one can see much of Lake Chelan, surrounding mountain ranges, and much of the Cascades. To attain such a high vantage is relatively easy thanks to a trailhead at 6,500 feet. Vistas this grand don't come this cheaply very often.

Pyramid Mountain Trail spends the length of its time along the Chelan Mountains ridgeline among sparse meadows and subalpine trees. Passing Crow Hill, the trail hits a junction (2.7 miles); stay right to skirt below Graham Mountain. Endure a pair of elevation losses before climbing Pyramid Mountain, where an old fire lookout once stood. Camping can be done in accordance with Leave-No-Trace principles, but fires are never a good idea in this dry climate. Carrying extra water is important here, where the summer sun is scorching.

User Groups: Hikers, leashed dogs, horses, and mountain bikes. No wheelchair access.

Open Seasons: This trail is accessible mid-July–September.

Permits: A federal Northwest Forest Pass is required to park here.

Maps: For a map of Wenatchee National Forest, contact the Outdoor Recreation Information Center at the downtown Seattle REI. For topographic maps, ask Green Trails for No. 114, Lucerne, or ask the USGS for Pyramid Mountain and Saksa Peak.

Directions: From Entiat, drive east on Entiat River Road to Forest Service Road 5900, just beyond Lake Creek Campground. Turn right and drive 8.5 miles to Forest Service Road 113 at Shady Pass. Turn left and drive 2 miles to the trailhead at road's end. This is a rough road and a high-clearance vehicle is recommended.

Contact: Wenatchee National Forest, Entiat Ranger Station, 2108 Entiat Way, P.O. Box 476, Entiat, WA 98822, 509/784-1511.

98 WALLACE FALLS

5.6 mi/3.0 hr

north of Gold Bar in Wallace Falls State Park

Map 3.3, page 93

There are few better trails within such easy reach of Seattle. Wallace Falls are some of the Cascades' best known waterfalls, with more than nine drops of at least 50 feet. The tallest cascade, with a drop of 265 feet, is visible from Highway 2. Why see something from the highway when you can check it out up close?

There are two options for reaching the falls, thanks to the hard work of volunteers. A direct route to the falls is achieved in 2.8 miles while a longer, gentler loop adds a mile. Either way, Wallace Falls is certainly made for the whole family and for all hikers. The trail leaves the trailhead before splitting into Woody Trail and Railroad Grade (the longer of the two). Traveling through forests of alder and fir, the trails meet near the bridge over the North Wallace River. Another mile up the trail reveals the numerous falls. It's wonderful during the spring, when snowmelt turns Wallace River into a torrent and adds spectacular drama to the falls. Also during the spring, many forest plants and flowers are in bloom, adding much color to the setting. The trail gets its fair share of visitors during the summer, but it's understandable why.

User Groups: Hikers and leashed dogs. No horses or mountain bikes are allowed. No wheelchair access.

Open Seasons: This trail is accessible year-round.

Permits: A $5 day-use fee is required to park here and is payable at the trailhead, or you can get an annual State Parks Pass for $30; contact Washington State Parks and Recreation, 360/902-8500.

Maps: For topographic maps, ask Green Trails for No. 142, Index, or ask the USGS for Gold Bar and Wallace Lake.

Directions: From Everett, drive east on U.S. 2 to the town of Gold Bar. Turn left (north) on 1st Street and follow the signs to the park entrance. The well-signed trailhead is near the main parking area in the park.

Contact: Wallace Falls State Park, P.O. Box 230, Gold Bar, WA 98251, 360/793-0420.

99 BLANCA LAKE

7.0 mi/4.0 hr

northeast of Index in Henry M. Jackson Wilderness of Mount Baker–Snoqualmie National Forest

Map 3.3, page 93

Below a trio of towering peaks, Blanca Lake makes a scenic trip. With the large Columbia Glacier feeding the lake a steady

stream of silt-filled runoff, the lake turns an intense turquoise and makes for fine photographs. The beauty of the lake and its surroundings are not without grinding effort. The trail makes a steep ascent to a pass at Virgin Lake before steeply dropping to the lake. From amid parkland meadows, however, views of Glacier Peak help to ease the leg-numbing switching.

Blanca Lake Trail dances the switchback shuffle, ascending 2,700 feet in just three miles. Forests of red cedar, Douglas fir, and western hemlock shade the way. Near the crest (2.7 miles), enjoy views of the inner peaks and ridges of the Cascades. Pass Virgin Lake and drop to Blanca Lake. Columbia Peak, Monte Cristo Peak, and Kyes Peak ring the large basin. Trails for exploration wander around the lake, but Columbia Glacier should be treated as off-limits. A number of good campsites ring the lake, but they see a lot of use, especially on summer weekends. Blanca Lake is well worth writing home about.

User Groups: Hikers and leashed dogs. No horses or mountain bikes are allowed. No wheelchair access.

Open Seasons: This trail is accessible July–October.

Permits: A federal Northwest Forest Pass is required to park here.

Maps: For a map of Mount Baker–Snoqualmie National Forest, contact the Outdoor Recreation Information Center at the downtown Seattle REI. For topographic maps, ask Green Trails for No. 143, Monte Cristo, or ask the USGS for Blanca Lake.

Directions: From Everett, drive east on U.S. 2 to Index. At the Index turnoff, turn left (north) onto the North Fork Skykomish River Road (Forest Road 63). Drive 18.1 miles to the trailhead.

Contact: Mount Baker–Snoqualmie National Forest, Skykomish Ranger Station, 74920 Northeast Stevens Pass Highway, Skykomish, WA 98288, 360/677-2414.

100 WEST CADY RIDGE

7.0–17.0 mi/1–2 days

north of Skykomish in Henry M. Jackson Wilderness of Mount Baker–Snoqualmie National Forest

Map 3.3, page 93

West Cady Ridge is blessed with miles of wide open big-sky meadows. The views are supreme from nearly every inch of the trail, which rides the crest of the ridge straight to PCT. Meadows of heather and wildflower aplenty cover the ridge, making July the time to hit this trail. Splendor this grand rarely comes at so easy a price. And topping it all off is the panoramic vista from atop Benchmark Mountain.

West Cady Ridge Trail reaches meadows in a quick but steep hike through great Cascade old-growth forest. The trees shrink before your eyes as you steadily climb higher. The trail finds the crest (3.5 miles, a good turnaround point for a shorter hike) and follows it to PCT (8.5 miles). There are some ups and downs, but at all times the trail is easy to follow. Huckleberries line the route, an encouragement to take things slowly. A side trail (at 7 miles) shoots up Benchmark Mountain to the summit. Backpackers are encouraged to explore this trail. At 5,816 feet, the summit reveals much of the Cascades. Hiking north on PCT brings hikers to Pass Creek Trail, which can be used to make a loop out of West Cady Ridge.

User Groups: Hikers, leashed dogs, and horses. No mountain bikes are allowed. No wheelchair access.

Open Seasons: This trail is accessible July–October.

Permits: A federal Northwest Forest Pass is required to park here.

Maps: For a map of Mount Baker–Snoqualmie National Forest, contact the Outdoor Recreation Information Center at the downtown Seattle REI. For topographic maps, ask Green Trails for No. 143, Monte Cristo, and No. 144, Benchmark Mountain, or ask the USGS for Blanca Lake and Benchmark Mountain.

Directions: From Everett, drive east on U.S.

2 to Index. At the Index turnoff, turn left (north) onto North Fork Skykomish River Road (Forest Service Road 63). Drive 20 miles to the trailhead on the right.
Contact: Mount Baker–Snoqualmie National Forest, Skykomish Ranger Station, 74920 Northeast Stevens Pass Highway, Skykomish, WA 98288, 360/677-2414.

101 CADY CREEK/ LITTLE WENATCHEE LOOP

19.0 mi/2–3 days

north of Lake Wenatchee in Henry M. Jackson Wilderness of Wenatchee National Forest

Map 3.3, page 93

This is an excellent trip along Pacific Crest Trail. Using Cady Creek and Little Wenatchee River Trails, the route offers access to a pair of superb high country destinations. Meadows of wildflowers and sweeping vistas are the name of the game here, one of PCT's most beautiful stretches. While the loop can be made in two days, three is far better. A more relaxed pace allows for side trips and more time in this exceptional place.

The route begins along Cady Creek, a gradual climb through old-growth forests to Cady Pass (5.2 miles). Cady Creek must be forded, but the cool water is refreshing on hot summer days. Hike north on PCT through terrific meadows to Lake Sally Ann (10 miles) below Skykomish Peak. Lake Sally Ann has several great campsites.

PCT continues north to Meander Meadow (12.3 miles), a large, flat basin overflowing with wildflowers. Several great camps are near the outlet of the meadow. Kodak Peak stands over the basin, offering panoramic views from the summit. Much of Glacier Peak and Henry M. Jackson Wildernesses are within sight. The route returns to the trailhead via Little Wenatchee River Trail, which is full of great forests and waterfalls. Much of PCT is along north-facing slopes, where snow lingers late into summer, a consideration. All in all, this is an outstanding three-day weekend.

User Groups: Hikers, leashed dogs, and horses. No mountain bikes are allowed. No wheelchair access.
Open Seasons: This trail is accessible mid-July–October.
Permits: A federal Northwest Forest Pass is required to park here.
Maps: For a map of Wenatchee National Forest, contact the Outdoor Recreation Information Center at the downtown Seattle REI. For topographic maps, ask Green Trails for No. 144, Benchmark Mountain, or ask the USGS for Poe Mountain and Benchmark Mountain.
Directions: From Leavenworth, drive west on U.S. 2 to Highway 207, at Coles Corner. Turn left and drive to Little Wenatchee Road (Forest Service Road 65). Veer left and drive to the signed trailhead at road's end.
Contact: Wenatchee National Forest, Lake Wenatchee Ranger Station, 22976 Highway 207, Leavenworth, WA 98826, 509/763-3103.

102 FORTUNE PONDS

17.0 mi/1–2 days

north of Skykomish in Henry M. Jackson Wilderness of Mount Baker–Snoqualmie National Forest

Map 3.3, page 93

Don't be fooled by the name of the hike. Tradition dictates that the hike be called Fortune Ponds, even though they are but a small feature of this wonderful route. The bigger features are Pear and Peach Lakes, two large high-country lakes enclosed by parkland meadows and outstanding views. And for those seeking even more adventure, a climb to the top of Fortune Mountain is easy and well recommended.

Meadow Creek Trail immediately climbs a steep valley wall through a burned-out forest. The trail levels out and gradually climbs along Meadow Creek. The creek must be crossed twice, a wet ordeal during the early summer. By the time the forest thins and eventually breaks, you reach Fortune Ponds. Benchmark Mountain stands to the north, framed nicely behind the lakes. The trail continues another

mile to Pear Lake and an intersection with Pacific Crest Trail. Peach Lake is to the south and over a small ridge. Subalpine fir and mountain hemlocks line the lakes, where established camps can be found. This is the high country, where huckleberries madly grow before bears can madly eat them. A side trail leads up Fortune Mountain, which at 5,903 feet presents much of the surrounding wilderness.

User Groups: Hikers, leashed dogs, and horses. No mountain bikes are allowed. No wheelchair access.

Open Seasons: This trail is accessible July–October.

Permits: A federal Northwest Forest Pass is required to park here.

Maps: For a map of Wenatchee National Forest, contact the Outdoor Recreation Information Center at the downtown Seattle REI. For topographic maps, ask Green Trails for No. 144, Benchmark Mountain, or ask the USGS for Captain Point and Benchmark Mountain.

Directions: From Everett, drive east on U.S. 2 until .5 mile east of the town of Skykomish. Turn left (north) onto the Beckler River Road (Forest Service Road 65) and drive for 6 miles to the junction with Rapid River Road (Forest Service Road 6530). Turn right and continue for 4.5 miles to trailhead.

Contact: Mount Baker–Snoqualmie National Forest, Skykomish Ranger Station, 74920 Northeast Stevens Pass Highway, Skykomish, WA 98288, 360/677-2414.

103 SNOQUALMIE AND DOROTHY LAKES

4.0–15.0 mi/2.5 hr–2 days 2 8

south of Skykomish in Alpine Lakes Wilderness of Mount Baker–Snoqualmie National Forest

Map 3.3, page 93

This great route offers two ways to experience it. Snoqualmie and Dorothy Lake Trails make a long, east-west journey through the Alpine Lakes Wilderness, progressing from the Taylor River in the Snoqualmie drainage over to the Miller River in the Skykomish drainage. Along the way are a number of great waterfalls and no fewer than five large lakes. There's lots to explore here with a chance for hikers of all abilities to experience it.

Snoqualmie, Dear, Bear, and Dorothy Lakes lie within 2.5 miles of each other. These big lakes feature grand forests reaching to the shores, with big peaks visible over the basin's gentle ridges. Quick and easy access is gained from Miller River Trailhead, just two miles from enormous Lake Dorothy. This access point is preferred by families and those seeking the lakes but not a long trek. From the west trailhead, the route makes a longer (15 miles round-trip), more scenic trek to the lakes. Also, a steep side trail (6.3 miles) shoots up to isolated Nordrum Lake. Campsites are located at each of the lakes.

User Groups: Hikers, leashed dogs, horses, and mountain bikes (horses and mountain bikes allowed on the first six miles of Taylor River Road). No wheelchair access.

Open Seasons: This trail is accessible mid-May–November.

Permits: A federal Northwest Forest Pass is required to park here.

Maps: For a map of Mount Baker–Snoqualmie National Forest, contact the Outdoor Recreation Information Center at the downtown Seattle REI. For topographic maps, ask Green Trails for No. 175, Skykomish, or ask the USGS for Snoqualmie Lake and Big Snow Mountain.

Directions: Taylor River Trailhead: From Seattle, drive east on I-90 to Exit 34. Turn left onto 468th Avenue North. At .6 mile, turn right onto Middle Fork Road (Forest Service Road 56). Stay on Forest Service Road 56 for 12.5 miles to the Taylor River Trailhead. Forest Service Road 56 splits just after it crosses the Taylor River; stay to the left. The trailhead is .5 mile farther at a gate.

East Miller River Trailhead: From Everett, drive east on U.S. 2 to Money Creek Campground, 2.8 miles before the town of Skykomish. Turn south onto the Old Cascade Highway.

The road is just west of the highway tunnel. Drive the Old Cascade Highway for 1 mile, then turn right (south) onto the Miller River Road (Forest Service Road 6410). Continue on Forest Service Road 6410 for 9.5 miles to the road's end at the trailhead.

Contact: Mount Baker–Snoqualmie National Forest, North Bend Ranger Station, 42404 Southeast North Bend Way, North Bend, WA 98045, 425/888-1421.

104 FOSS LAKES

13.6 mi/2 days

east of Skykomish in Alpine Lakes Wilderness of Mount Baker–Snoqualmie National Forest

Map 3.3, page 93

This classic Alpine Lakes Wilderness trail takes in no fewer than five lakes, offering a day hike or overnighter that never gets boring. The upper lakes are set among a rugged landscape once dominated by glaciers. Even today, it sees a lot of winter snow. But be forewarned: Within two hours of Seattle and with easy accessibility up to even the farthest lake, this trail sees a lot of use, even bordering on abuse. If you're willing to forgo solitude, then Foss Lakes is a must visit.

The trail begins very easily, with little elevation gain along the first 1.5 miles to Trout Lake. Along the way, the trail passes one of the biggest Douglas firs you'll ever see. Only the largest of families will be able to wrap their arms around this one. Surrounded by forest, Trout Lake whets the appetite for the alpine lakes to come. This is a good turnaround for less serious hikers.

From Trout Lake, West Fork Foss Trail climbs steeply to Lake Malachite, cruising in and out of forest alongside a beautiful cascading stream that offers needed refreshment on hot days. This is the trail's big climb, gaining 1,800 feet in two miles. From Lake Malachite, another three lakes (Copper, Little Heart, and Big Heart) lie within three miles' distance. The lakes seem to get better as you progress, with the blues of the lakes getting deeper and the rocky ridges getting steeper and higher. From Big Heart Lake, trails lead to Lake Angeline and the many ridges and lakes beyond. There is camping at each of the lakes, although it goes quickly during the summer season. These are true alpine lakes, sure to stick in your hiking memory.

User Groups: Hikers and leashed dogs. No horses or mountain bikes are allowed. No wheelchair access.

Open Seasons: This trail is usually accessible June–October.

Permits: A federal Northwest Forest Pass is required to park here.

Maps: For a map of Mount Baker–Snoqualmie National Forest, contact the Outdoor Recreation Information Center at the downtown Seattle REI. For topographic maps, ask Green Trails for No. 175, Skykomish, or ask the USGS for Big Snow Mountain and Skykomish.

Directions: From Everett, drive east on U.S. 2 to 1.7 miles east of the town of Skykomish. Turn right (south) onto Foss River Road (Forest Service Road 68). Stay on this main road, avoiding any turnoffs, to the trailhead at road's end.

Contact: Mount Baker–Snoqualmie National Forest, Skykomish Ranger Station, 74920 Northeast Stevens Pass Highway, Skykomish, WA 98288, 360/677-2414.

105 NECKLACE VALLEY

16.0 mi/1–2 days

west of Stevens Pass in Alpine Lakes Wilderness of Mount Baker–Snoqualmie National Forest

Map 3.3, page 93

It's a long, hard hike into Necklace Valley. After five miles of river valley, the trail climbs 2,500 feet in a little more than two miles. Not exactly the stuff for beginners. For those who endure the challenge of reaching the Necklace Valley, however, ample compensation awaits. The Necklace Valley hosts a string of handsome lakes dotting a narrow, high valley. On nearly all sides are rocky slopes and ridges, where patches of snow linger late into summer. The upper valley is wide and very open, leaving lots of room to explore.

Necklace Valley Trail quickly enters the wilderness (1.5 miles) and enjoys four miles of old-growth forest along the East Fork Foss River. From here, the trail shoots up through the forest quickly and mercilessly into Necklace Valley (7 miles). A map is a necessity up here, as there are a number of lakes and lots of room to get lost. The best plan of action is to just start wandering, as there is no such thing as a bad section of the Necklace Valley. The lower lakes are forested and provide good shelter, while the upper lakes are open with meadows. All of the lakes here have established campsites. The scenery only gets better as the trail follows the valley up past La Bohn Lakes to La Bohn Gap. From here, Mount Hinman and Bears Breast Mountain stand tall to the south and north.

User Groups: Hikers and leashed dogs. No horses or mountain bikes are allowed. No wheelchair access.

Open Seasons: This trail is accessible July–October.

Permits: A federal Northwest Forest Pass is required to park here.

Maps: For a map of Mount Baker–Snoqualmie National Forest, contact the Outdoor Recreation Information Center at the downtown Seattle REI. For topographic maps, ask Green Trails for No. 175, Skykomish, and No. 176, Stevens Pass, or ask the USGS for Skykomish, Big Snow Mountain, and Mount Daniel.

Directions: From Everett, drive east on U.S. 2 to 1.7 miles east of the town of Skykomish. Turn right (south) onto Foss River Road (Forest Service Road 68) and drive 4.1 miles to the trailhead.

Contact: Mount Baker–Snoqualmie National Forest, Skykomish Ranger Station, 74920 Northeast Stevens Pass Highway, Skykomish, WA 98288, 360/677-2414.

106 TONGA RIDGE

9.2 mi/5.0 hr

west of Stevens Pass in Alpine Lakes Wilderness of Mount Baker–Snoqualmie National Forest

Map 3.3, page 93

This is a great opportunity for the whole family to experience the high country. Starting out at a lofty 4,300 feet elevation, the trail rides out Tonga Ridge for more than four miles, offering Mount Sawyer and Fisher Lake for excellent side trips. The route stays below 5,000 feet the entire length, making for very little climbing yet excellent mountain views. The trail is popular with hikers because of its extensive meadows overflowing with huckleberries. Never mind the late August crowds; stay focused on the terrific views of nearby peaks.

Tonga Ridge Trail travels 4.6 miles along Tonga Ridge, connecting at each end to a part of Forest Service Road 6830-310. The first and closest trailhead is recommended, save for those looking for a shorter hike to Fisher Lake. Subalpine meadows dominate the route, as do great views of Mounts Hinman and Daniel. During August, hikers quickly take note of the plentiful huckleberry bushes. A side trail leads to the summit of Mount Sawyer for a 360-degree view of the surrounding peaks and much of the Cascades. A side trail also leads to Fisher Lake. The rough trail heads up and over a small crest to the large and impressive lake, set beneath towering cliffs.

User Groups: Hikers and leashed dogs. No horses or mountain bikes are allowed. No wheelchair access.

Open Seasons: This trail is accessible July–October.

Permits: A federal Northwest Forest Pass is required to park here.

Maps: For a map of Mount Baker–Snoqualmie National Forest, contact the Outdoor Recreation Information Center at the downtown Seattle REI. For topographic maps, ask Green Trails for No. 175, Skykomish, and No. 176,

Stevens Pass, or ask the USGS for Skykomish and Scenic.
Directions: From Everett, drive east on U.S. 2 to 1.7 miles east of the town of Skykomish. Turn right (south) onto Foss River Road (Forest Service Road 68). Drive on Forest Service Road 68 for 3.5 miles to Forest Service Road 6830. Turn left onto Forest Service Road 6830 and drive for 6 miles to Forest Service Road 6830-310. Turn right onto Forest Service Road 6830-310 and drive 1 mile to the end of the road.
Contact: Mount Baker–Snoqualmie National Forest, Skykomish Ranger Station, 74920 Northeast Stevens Pass Highway, Skykomish, WA 98288, 360/677-2414.

107 DECEPTION CREEK

20.6 mi/2 days

west of Stevens Pass in Alpine Lakes Wilderness of Mount Baker–Snoqualmie National Forest

Map 3.3, page 93

Some trips into the wilderness need not culminate at a vista or high alpine lake. Sometimes, simple travel within giant forests and along a cool, murmuring creek is the end in itself. That is certainly the case with Deception Creek, a great stroll through shady cool Cascade forest with access to high-country lakes. But the real point of Deception Creek is simply an excursion into wilderness.

Deception Creek Trail parallels the stream for six miles. It crosses the swirling creek below a nice waterfall (.5 mile). The route features a bit of up and down as it slowly climbs up the valley. This is Cascadia at its best, with the forest full of large Douglas firs, western red cedars, and western hemlocks. Moss grows on most everything while the forest floor becomes a carpet of ferns at times.

Deception Creek Trail eventually leaves the valley floor to ascend the valley wall. A connector trail (7.3 miles) leads up to Deception Lakes, a good option as a destination. Deception Pass (10.3 miles) is a junction for Pacific Crest Trail and Marmot and Hyas Lakes. Campsites are scattered liberally along the trail.
User Groups: Hikers and leashed dogs. No horses or mountain bikes are allowed. No wheelchair access.
Open Seasons: This trail is accessible April–November.
Permits: A federal Northwest Forest Pass is required to park here.
Maps: For a map of Mount Baker–Snoqualmie National Forest, contact the Outdoor Recreation Information Center at the downtown Seattle REI. For topographic maps, ask Green Trails for No. 176, Stevens Pass, or ask the USGS for Scenic and Mount Daniel.
Directions: From Everett, drive east on U.S. 2 to Forest Service Road 6088, immediately beyond Deception Falls picnic area. Turn right and drive .3 mile to the trailhead at road's end.
Contact: Mount Baker–Snoqualmie National Forest, Skykomish Ranger Station, 74920 Northeast Stevens Pass Highway, Skykomish, WA 98288, 360/677-2414.

108 SURPRISE LAKE

8.0 mi/4.0 hr

near Stevens Pass in Alpine Lakes Wilderness of Mount Baker–Snoqualmie National Forest

Map 3.3, page 93

By the time one has hiked a mile up Surprise Creek, the surprise should be over. Within the first half hour, it is readily evident that this is a beautiful hike. It gets only better as it progresses. But perhaps a surprise does exist, because the view from Pieper Pass seems almost too good to be true. This is a great part of the Alpine Lakes Wilderness, with many lakes and lots of stunning scenery.

Surprise Creek Trail quickly says good-bye to civilization and enters old-growth forest. Surprise Creek makes a number of small falls and cascades. The grade is gentle until the trail makes a quick rise to a narrow gap between two ridges. Reach the notch and Surprise Lake (4 miles); Glacier Lake is a bit farther up the

long, narrow basin (5 miles). Forest and meadow fringe the lakes, and the tall cliffs of Surprise Mountain drop to Glacier Lake. Numerous campsites are found around each lake.

For additional exploration, hike PCT up to 6,000-foot Pieper Pass to view the large glaciers on Mount Hinman and Mount Daniel. Spark Plug and Thunder Mountains are good scrambles as well. There is a lot of high country to explore around here, and likely more than a few extra surprises.

User Groups: Hikers and leashed dogs. No horses or mountain bikes are allowed. No wheelchair access.

Open Seasons: This trail is accessible July–October.

Permits: A federal Northwest Forest Pass is required to park here.

Maps: For a map of Mount Baker–Snoqualmie National Forest, contact the Outdoor Recreation Information Center at the downtown Seattle REI. For topographic maps, ask Green Trails for No. 176, Stevens Pass, or ask the USGS for Scenic.

Directions: From Everett, drive east on U.S. 2 to Mile Marker 58. Turn right (south) onto an unmarked road to the service center for Burlington-Northern Railroad. Cross the railroad tracks and turn onto the spur road on the far right. Continue for .2 mile to the trailhead.

Contact: Mount Baker–Snoqualmie National Forest, Skykomish Ranger Station, 74920 Northeast Stevens Pass Highway, Skykomish, WA 98288, 360/677-2414.

109 CHAIN LAKES

22.0 mi/2 days 3 9

near Stevens Pass in Alpine Lakes Wilderness of Wenatchee National Forest

Map 3.3, page 93

Chain Lakes are tucked way, way back in the Alpine Lakes Wilderness. Eleven miles from the nearest trailhead, there are few people back in these parts. Great old-growth forest lines much of the route before it breaks into subalpine meadows and views, with several spectacular lakes. Chain Lakes are an excellent destination for a long weekend. They definitely deserve three days for exploration rather than two cramped days spent mostly hiking.

Chain Lakes are accessible by either Stevens Pass or Icicle Creek out of Leavenworth. These are two different approaches to the shared segment of Chain Lakes Trail. From near Stevens Pass, PCT climbs above Josephine Lake and Lake Susan Jane before dropping into the Icicle Creek drainage and Chain Lakes Trail (5 miles). Traveling from Icicle Creek (6.5 miles) takes you through a more typical east-side forest, drier with more pines.

The two routes converge at Chain Lakes Trail, which climbs quickly to the lakes. Chain Lakes lie within a narrow basin, filled with parkland and meadows along the upper lakes, where jagged crags line the rim of the basin. There are several established campsites near the lower two lakes. The trail heads over the jagged ridge through a gap and drops to Doelle Lakes, two more great high lakes with camping.

User Groups: Hikers, leashed dogs, and horses (horses allowed day use of Chain Lakes). No mountain bikes are allowed. No wheelchair access.

Open Seasons: This trail is accessible July–October.

Permits: A federal Northwest Forest Pass is required to park here.

Maps: For a map of Mount Baker–Snoqualmie National Forest, contact the Outdoor Recreation Information Center at the downtown Seattle REI. For topographic maps, ask Green Trails for No. 176, Stevens Pass, and No. 177, Chiwaukum Mountains, or ask the USGS for Stevens Pass.

Directions: From Everett, drive east on U.S. 2 to Forest Service Road 6960 (about 4 miles east of Stevens Pass). Turn right and drive 4 miles to the parking lot at the road's gated end. Turn right (south) onto an unmarked road to the service center for Burlington-Northern Railroad. Cross the railroad tracks and turn onto the spur road on the far right. Continue for .2 mile to the trailhead.

Contact: Mount Baker–Snoqualmie National Forest, Skykomish Ranger Station, 74920 Northeast Stevens Pass Highway, Skykomish, WA 98288, 360/677-2414.

110 NASON RIDGE

6.0–22.1 mi/3.5 hr–2 days

east of Stevens Pass in Wenatchee National Forest

Map 3.3, page 93

This subalpine ridge provides hikers with a lot of trail and several excellent destinations. Running the length of Nason Ridge, Nason Ridge Trail passes three lakes and an alpine lookout, summits several peaks more than 6,000 feet elevation, and features five different access points. It is not, however, an easy ascent to any part of Nason Ridge. Every trailhead has at least 2,000 feet of climbing to the ridge. The splendor of Nason Ridge is well worth it.

The main attractions along the ridge are Rock Mountain and Lake (9.2 miles round-trip), Merritt Lake (6 miles round-trip), and Alpine Lookout. Rock Mountain (6,852 feet) stands on the western end of Nason Ridge. Rock Lake sits below, in a small cirque and surrounded by subalpine forest. Farther east are Crescent and Merritt Lakes. Merritt is accessible by its own trail right off Highway 2. The lakes on the ridge have established campsites that should be used at all times. Alpine Lookout is a staffed Forest Service fire watchtower, about five miles from Butcher Creek Trailhead. Spread out on the ridge between these points are 20 miles of trail threading through high meadow, the perfect place for mountain goats. The two ends of the trail also have trailheads, on Butcher Creek and Snowy Creek. These are accessible from Highway 2 and Lake Wenatchee. There is much to do and see on Nason Ridge, and it gets better later in the season.

User Groups: Hikers, leashed dogs, and mountain bikes. No horses are allowed. No wheelchair access.

Open Seasons: This trail is open mid-July–October.

Permits: A federal Northwest Forest Pass is required to park here.

Maps: For a map of Wenatchee National Forest, contact the Outdoor Recreation Information Center at the downtown Seattle REI. For topographic maps, ask Green Trails for No. 145, Lake Wenatchee, or ask the USGS for Labyrinth Mountain, Mount Howard, and Lake Wenatchee.

Directions: From Leavenworth, drive west on U.S. 2 to Forest Service Road 6910 for Alpine Lookout, Forest Service Road 657 for Merritt Lake or Rock Mountain Trailhead (on U.S. 2).

Contact: Wenatchee National Forest, Lake Wenatchee Ranger Station, 22976 Highway 207, Leavenworth, WA 98826, 509/763-3103.

111 IRON GOAT

12.0 mi one-way/6.0 hr

west of Stevens Pass along Highway 2

Map 3.3, page 93

Iron Goat Trail is the result of a lot of volunteer labor. Volunteers for Outdoor Washington have led the effort to remake an old railway into one of Washington's best rails-to-trails projects. The route follows the old path of the Great Northern Railway, the first rail service to cross Stevens Pass back in the late 1800s. Volunteers have done an excellent job of cleaning up debris, refurbishing the trail, and adding many interesting interpretive signs along the way. The route is great for families and hikers of all abilities–you can turn around at any point for a satisfying hike. Along the way are many old artifacts from the railway. Several tunnels lead off into the hillside, appearing as deep, dark caverns. As a railway, the route was plagued by trouble from the uncooperative Cascades. Snowslides and avalanches were frequent problems, as were fires. The trail is accessible at its two ends, each of which is on the west side of Stevens Pass. This is an excellent trip not only for families and young children, but for anyone crossing the pass and needing a break.

User Groups: Hikers and leashed dogs. No horses or mountain bikes are allowed. Part of the trail is wheelchair accessible (near Martin Creek).
Open Seasons: This trail is usually accessible April–November.
Permits: A federal Northwest Forest Pass is required to park at the trailheads.
Maps: Maps of this trail are best obtained at the trailheads. Current Green Trails and USGS maps do not show the Iron Goat.
Directions: From Everett, drive east on U.S. 2 beyond the town of Skykomish. At Mile Marker 55 (6 miles east of the town of Skykomish), turn left (north) onto the Old Cascade Highway (Forest Service Road 67). Drive 2.3 miles to Forest Service Road 6710 and turn left onto Forest Service Road 6710. Drive 1.4 miles to the Martin Creek Trailhead.

To get to Wellington Trailhead, drive to Mile Marker 64.3, just west of Stevens Pass, and turn left (north) onto the Old Cascade Highway. Drive 2.8 miles to Road 050. Turn right onto Road 050. Turn right and drive to the trailhead.
Contact: Mount Baker–Snoqualmie National Forest, Skykomish Ranger Station, 74920 Northeast Stevens Pass Highway, Skykomish, WA 98288, 360/677-2414.

112 TIGER MOUNTAIN

1.0–5.2 mi/1.0–5.0 hr

within Tiger Mountain State Forest

Map 3.3, page 93

Tiger Mountain State Forest is a shining example of what a great place Seattle is to live. More than 80 miles of trail lie within 13,000 acres of this wooded park less than a half hour from the city. That makes it the state's busiest trailhead, with cars often parked along the entrance all the way to the freeway. But don't be dismayed by the parking, as the many miles of wandering trails offer many chances for casual forest strolling or intensive hiking. The park's easy accessibility makes it extremely popular among hikers of all abilities and especially for families.

There are many trails to explore here. The best strategy is to peruse the signboard at the trailhead and pick one that suits your mood. Your own map will also be handy in navigating the vast network of trails. The most popular is West Tiger 3, which leads to the western summit. With an elevation gain of more than 2,000 feet in just 2.6 miles, it satisfies even serious hikers. It offers grand views of the Seattle and Puget Sound region, the adjacent Issaquah Alps, and even Mount Rainier. Other favorites with less climbing include Poo Poo Point Trail and Seattle View Trail. Easier, more level hikes include Around the Lake Trail, leading to Tradition Lake, and Bus Road Trail. Children will love Swamp Monster Trail, a level interpretive trail with signboards telling the story of a lovable raccoon.
User Groups: Hikers, leashed dogs, horses, and mountain bikers. No wheelchair access.
Open Seasons: This area is usually accessible year-round.
Permits: Permits are not required. Parking and access are free.
Maps: For topographic maps, ask Green Trails for No. 204S, Tiger Mountain, or ask the USGS for Fall City and Hobart.
Directions: From Seattle, drive east on I-90 to Exit 20, High Point Road. Take a right, and then another quick right, following the sign for Tradition Lake Trailhead. The gate is open seven days a week dawn–8 P.M.
Contact: Washington Department of Natural Resources, P.O. Box 47001, Olympia, WA 98504-7001, 360/902-1375.

113 MOUNT SI

8.0 mi/4.0 hr

north of North Bend in Mount Si Natural Resources Conservation Area

Map 3.3, page 93

Mount Si is like the Disneyland of Seattle hiking: more crowds than you can shake a stick at. Busloads of folks from the metropolitan area descend upon this mountain, the closest high peak to Seattle. It's literally the most heavily used trail in the state. Experienced and novice hikers alike come here for the views of the Cascades, Seattle, and Puget Sound Basin. The trail is steep and at times rocky, often used by folks as a late-spring training hike for the upcoming summer. It's certainly not an ideal trail for those seeking wilderness exploration, but it scratches the itch for wooded hikes and commanding views.

Mount Si Trail is a continuous climb through the forest. Views into the Snoqualmie River Valley are few until the top. A good stop is at Snag Flats (2 miles), where giant Douglas fir offer a great rest. This is the only level section of the trail, where extensive puncheon and turnpike has been installed by EarthCorps crews. A few interpretive signs discuss a fire that hit the area almost a century ago.

From Snag Flats is yet more incline, eventually turning into serious switchbacks. The summit, best left for those with rock-climbing experience, is marked by a haystack. The views from up here are wide, from Puget Sound to deep into the Cascades. Mount Rainier is often visible to the south. It's a great hike if you don't mind hiking with half of Seattle.

User Groups: Hikers and leashed dogs. No horses or mountain bikes are allowed. No wheelchair access.

Open Seasons: This trail is usually accessible May–November.

Permits: Permits are not required. Parking and access are free.

Maps: For topographic maps, ask Green Trails for No. 206S, Mount Si, or ask the USGS for Mount Si.

Directions: From Seattle, drive east on I-90 to Exit 32. Turn left on 468th Avenue and drive to North Bend Way. Turn left and drive to Mount Si Road. Turn right and drive 4 miles to the trailhead on the left.

Contact: Washington Department of Natural Resources, P.O. Box 47001, Olympia, WA 98504-7001, 360/902-1375.

114 LITTLE SI

5.0 mi/2.5 hr

north of North Bend in Mount Si Natural Resources Conservation Area

Map 3.3, page 93

Appropriately named, Little Si is Mount Si in a nutshell. A shorter hike, less of an incline, and fewer people all make this a nice early- or late-season hike when other, more intriguing trails are out of reach because of snow. The trail offers a pretty good workout nonetheless, making an ascent most of its length. There are a number of side trails, so it's best to have a map and good memory of which direction you came. The views from the top extend across the Snoqualmie Valley to Rattlesnake Mountain and up to Mount Si and Mount Washington.

Little Si Trail immediately climbs an outcropping of exposed rock. The main trail goes straight ahead while spur trails stray to the sides. These side trails can be good extracurricular journeys, and some great new ones have been built by EarthCorps crews. Most side trails lead to exposed rock heavily used by local climbers. Mostly second-growth forest covers the trail, although some granddaddy trees can be seen in places. The summit of the Little Si is exposed to reveal the surrounding countryside, quickly becoming "North Bend: The Strip Mall." A fun and manageable hike for the whole family.

User Groups: Hikers and leashed dogs. No horses or mountain bikes are allowed. No wheelchair access.

Open Seasons: This area is usually accessible March–December.

Permits: Permits are not required. Parking and access are free.

Maps: For topographic maps, ask Green Trails for No. 206S, Mount Si, or ask the USGS for North Bend.

Directions: From Seattle, drive east on I-90 to Exit 32. Turn left on 468th Avenue and drive to North Bend Way. Turn left and drive to Mount Si Road. Turn right and drive 1 mile to the trailhead on the left.

Contact: Washington Department of Natural Resources, P.O. Box 47001, Olympia, WA 98504-7001, 360/902-1375.

115 RATTLESNAKE MOUNTAIN

3.0–11.3 mi/1.5 hr

within the Cedar River Municipal Watershed and on Washington Department of Natural Resources Land

Map 3.3, page 93

Unbeknownst to most hikers, Rattlesnake Mountain Trail is actually an 11.3-mile trail that spans nearly the entire east-to-west length of the mountain. Most folks hike only the northern part of the trail to Rattlesnake Ledge, an immense outcropping of rock that offers great views of the surrounding area. The trail is new, built by Washington Trails Association and EarthCorps crews in conjunction with Mountains to Sound Greenway Trust and the City of Seattle. The new trail is a vast improvement over the old, which was essentially a straight-up assault on the hill. Now a consistent, manageable, and wide grade whisks hundreds of hikers to the ledge each day.

The route to Rattlesnake Ledge starts in the Cedar River watershed. The trail passes through second-growth forest rich in undergrowth flowers and ferns before arriving at the ledge (1.5 miles). The ledge literally drops straight down, so take care with dogs and children. Views extends across the Snoqualmie Valley to Mount Si and eastward into the watershed, the source of Seattle's drinking water.

The trail actually continues over the mountain. The view into the watershed grows bigger, and on clear days Mount Rainier looms surreally large to the south. The trail is a makeshift collection of trails and old logging roads, although a more continuous replacement is being built. The trail ends at Snoqualmie Point 11.3 miles later, making for a long and enjoyable hike with a car shuttle.

User Groups: Hikers and leashed dogs. No horses or mountain bikes are allowed. No wheelchair access.

Open Seasons: This trail is usually accessible year-round.

Permits: Permits are not required. Parking and access are free.

Maps: For topographic maps, ask Green Trails for No. 205S, Rattlesnake Mountain, or ask the USGS for North Bend.

Directions: From Seattle, drive east on I-90 to Exit 32. Turn right on 468th Avenue (becomes Southeast Edgewick Road) and drive 5 miles to the signed trailhead at Rattlesnake Lake.

Contact: Cedar River Watershed Education Center, 425/831-6780.

116 TWIN FALLS

2.6 mi/1.5 hr

east of North Bend in Twin Falls State Park

Map 3.3, page 93

Twin Falls Trail makes an excellent winter hike, when high-country trails are covered with the excessive white of winter's work and the rivers are flowing with Washington's most ordinary commodity, rain. Twin Falls are much more than just a pair; rather, the South Fork of the Snoqualmie River makes a series of cascades that concludes with an impressive plummet of more than 150 feet. The trail is easy going for hikers of all abilities. The journey is nothing to shake your head at, either, as it passes through old-growth forest and one particular granddaddy of a tree.

A well-maintained trail ambles alongside the Snoqualmie River to the falls. Several enormous cedars line the trail, spared the long, cutting arm of the timber industry. A number of boardwalks and bridges are strategically placed to keep feet dry in even the wettest of weather. At the falls (1.3 miles), a platform offers misty views of the falls. Above, a bridge spans the river in the midst of the cascades. The optimum time to visit is the winter and spring, when more than 75,000 gallons of water flow over the falls each minute. During dry summers, this torrent vanishes to just 200 gallons. The trail continues to connect to John Wayne

Pioneer Trail, which provides access to a trailhead at Exit 38.

User Groups: Hikers and leashed dogs. No horses or mountain bikes are allowed. No wheelchair access.

Open Seasons: This trail is accessible year-round.

Permits: A $5 day-use fee is required to park here and is payable at the trailhead, or you can get an annual State Parks Pass for $30; contact Washington State Parks and Recreation, 360/902-8500.

Maps: For topographic maps, ask Green Trails for No. 206, Bandera, or ask the USGS for Chester Morse Lake.

Directions: From Seattle, drive east on I-90 to Exit 34. Turn right off the freeway on 468th Avenue Southeast and drive south .5 mile to Southeast 159th Street. Drive .5 mile to the trailhead at road's end.

Contact: Washington State Parks and Recreation, P.O. Box 42650, Olympia, WA 98504-2669, 360/902-8844.

117 MIDDLE FORK SNOQUALMIE RIVER

1.0–10.0 mi/0.5–5.0 hr

northeast of North Bend in Mount Baker–Snoqualmie National Forest

Map 3.3, page 93

The Middle Fork of the Snoqualmie River is a fantastic trail close to the Seattle area and accessible year-round. Much of the trail passes through old-growth forests that survived the saw or ax. Along the upper reaches of trail are the privately operated Goldmeyer Hot Springs, one of the best in Washington. The trail has been undergoing an intense amount of reconstruction by the Forest Service in the past few years, opening up many more miles of trail along the river.

Middle Fork Trail works its way through the river valley for roughly 12 miles along the south shore. It is accessible at two trailheads, one near the Taylor River and another near Dingford Creek. Customize your hike by turning around when the mood strikes—even a stroll of just 1 mile out and back will feel satisfying. Near the Taylor River, at Middle Fork Trailhead, Middle Fork Trail crosses the river on a new, extraordinary wooden bridge and meanders up the river valley, swooping near and away from the river. Above Dingford Trailhead, the trail encounters routes up to Snow, Gem, and Wildcat Lakes. Goldmeyer Hot Springs are roughly five miles from the trailhead and require reservations. The Middle Fork rarely gets snow, making it an excellent escape during the winter.

User Groups: Hikers, leashed dogs, horses, and mountain bikes. No wheelchair access.

Open Seasons: This trail is accessible year-round.

Permits: A federal Northwest Forest Pass is required to park at the trailheads.

Maps: For a map of Mount Baker–Snoqualmie National Forest, contact the Outdoor Recreation Information Center at the downtown Seattle REI. For topographic maps, ask Green Trails for No. 174, Mount Si, No. 175, Skykomish, and No. 207, Snoqualmie Pass, or ask the USGS for Lake Phillipa and Snoqualmie Lake.

Directions: From Seattle, drive east on I-90 to Exit 34. Turn left onto 468th Avenue North and drive .6 mile to Middle Fork Road. Turn right and drive 3 miles to Forest Service Road 56. Turn left and drive 11 miles to Middle Fork Snoqualmie Trailhead.

To reach the upper trailhead at Dingford, continue on Forest Service Road 56 for 6 miles.

Contact: Mount Baker–Snoqualmie National Forest, North Bend Ranger Station, 42404 Southeast North Bend Way, North Bend, WA 98045, 425/888-1421.

118 DINGFORD CREEK

11.0 mi/6.0 hr

northeast of North Bend in Alpine Lake Wilderness of Mount Baker–Snoqualmie National Forest

Map 3.3, page 93

Hester and Myrtle Lakes are just two of many

wonderful high-country lakes off Dingford Creek Trail. Hester and Myrtle are the largest and best known, attracting a majority of Dingford Trail's visitors. The hikes to the lakes are exceptional and offer miles of further exploration in the high-country meadows. Old-growth forest of hemlock, cedar, and fir make the journey along rumbling Dingford Creek an excellent day hike.

Dingford Creek Trail makes a quick ascent through second-growth forest before leveling out and strolling through ancient forests. At three miles the trail splits; head right for Hester Lake (5.5 miles). Hester Lake is large and encircled by forests of subalpine fir and mountain hemlock. Anglers love the lake for its stocked trout. From here, adventurous folks can reach Little Hester Lake and explore Mount Price.

Dingford Creek Trail continues following the stream up to Myrtle Lake (5.5 miles), fringed with forest and talus shores. Folks with off-trail experience can get to three small lakes to the west or climb up to Big Snow Lake, which sits directly under Big Snow Mountain. The trail grows faint from Myrtle Lake but does head up to Little Myrtle Lake and two other, smaller lakes. Regardless of destination, any route up Dingford Creek Trail is outstanding.

User Groups: Hikers and leashed dogs. No horses or mountain bikes are allowed. No wheelchair access.

Open Seasons: This trail is accessible July–early November.

Permits: A federal Northwest Forest Pass is required to park here.

Maps: For a map of Mount Baker–Snoqualmie National Forest, contact the Outdoor Recreation Information Center at the downtown Seattle REI. For topographic maps, ask Green Trails for No. 175, Skykomish, or ask the USGS for Snoqualmie Lake and Big Snow Mountain.

Directions: From Seattle, drive east on I-90 to Exit 34. Turn left onto 468th Avenue North and drive .5 mile to Middle Fork Road. Turn right and drive 3 miles (via the left fork in the road). Turn left on Forest Service Road 56 and drive 14 miles to Dingford Trailhead. Park in the wide turnout on the right; the trailhead is on the left.

Contact: Mount Baker–Snoqualmie National Forest, North Bend Ranger Station, 42404 Southeast North Bend Way, North Bend, WA 98045, 425/888-1421.

119 DUTCH MILLER GAP

15.0 mi/8.0 hr 3 9

northeast of North Bend in Alpine Lake Wilderness of Mount Baker–Snoqualmie National Forest

Map 3.3, page 93

A trip to Dutch Miller Gap is a trip to the headwaters of the mighty Middle Fork Snoqualmie River. Here, deep within the river's valley, wilderness reigns supreme in the old-growth forests and meadows. Tall, rocky peaks dominate the wild landscape. As a bonus, there are several options for exploration in the high country, including Williams Lake and beautiful La Bohn Gap and La Bohn Lakes.

Middle Fork Snoqualmie Trail gradually climbs four miles up the valley alongside the river. The river makes a number of cascades and creates lots of pools for dipping. A short but noticeable rise, where the trail climbs a glacial step, delivers hikers into subalpine meadows with frequent rock slides. Camp Pedro is at six miles and has several great campsites.

After Camp Pedro, the trail splits, with the right fork climbing to Dutch Miller Gap through meadows and talus. The surrounding peaks tower over hikers at the pass. Expect lots of ripe huckleberries in August. The other fork leads up to Williams Lake, set within meadows in a glacial cirque. Footpaths lead up to La Bohn Gap, which features views as great as those of Dutch Miller, and down to the Necklace Valley. With so many excellent places up here, hikers can't go wrong.

User Groups: Hikers, leashed dogs, and horses. No mountain bikes are allowed. No wheelchair access.

Open Seasons: This trail is accessible July–October.

Permits: A federal Northwest Forest Pass is required to park here.

Maps: For a map of Mount Baker–Snoqualmie National Forest, contact the Outdoor Recreation Information Center at the downtown Seattle REI. For topographic maps, ask Green Trails for No. 175, Skykomish, and No. 176, Stevens Pass, or ask the USGS for Big Snow Mountain and Mount Daniel.

Directions: From Seattle, drive east on I-90 to Exit 34. Turn left onto 468th Avenue North and drive .5 mile to Middle Fork Road. Turn right and drive 3 miles (via the left fork in the road). Turn left on Forest Service Road 56 and drive 20 miles to the trailhead at road's end. Forest Service Road 56 is often very rough and may require a high-clearance vehicle.

Contact: Mount Baker–Snoqualmie National Forest, North Bend Ranger Station, 42404 Southeast North Bend Way, North Bend, WA 98045, 425/888-1421.

120 MOUNT DEFIANCE/ MASON LAKES

16.6 mi/8.0 hr

east of North Bend in Alpine Lakes Wilderness of Mount Baker–Snoqualmie National Forest

Map 3.3, page 93

New Ira Spring Trail couples great high lakes with a high peak chock-full of views. Recently rebuilt, the trail to Mount Defiance and Mason Lakes commemorates one of Washington's strongest wilderness advocates, trail guide guru Ira Spring. Fields of heather and huckleberries are prolific along this route, as are the blackflies and mosquitoes in early summer. This trail encounters numerous lakes stocked with trout and is complemented with a scramble atop Mount Defiance.

Ira Spring Trail travels two miles on an old road before the newly built trail begins with spectacular results. Lazy switchbacks climb through open meadows before it tops a crest and descends to a wide, forested basin and Mason Lake. The main trail continues east to Rainbow Lake, filled to the brim with what else, rainbow trout. A side trail leads to Island Lake, the prime swimming hole (deep, cool, and sunny). All of the lakes have several campsites, although they go quickly.

Just beyond Mason Lake lies the Mount Defiance Trail junction. Turn left and climb through huckleberry meadows to the great views atop the summit. Cascade peaks line the horizons to the north, east, and south, while Puget Sound Basin and the Olympics stand out to the west. It's a great viewpoint.

User Groups: Hikers and leashed dogs. No horses or mountain bikes are allowed. No wheelchair access.

Open Seasons: This trail is accessible July–October.

Permits: A federal Northwest Forest Pass is required to park here. A free wilderness permit is also required to hike here and is available at the trailhead.

Maps: For a map of Mount Baker–Snoqualmie National Forest, contact the Outdoor Recreation Information Center at the downtown Seattle REI. For topographic maps, ask Green Trails for No. 206, Bandera, or ask the USGS for Bandera.

Directions: From Seattle, drive east on I-90 to Exit 45. Turn left (north, over the freeway) to Forest Service Road 9030. Turn left and drive left .5 mile to Forest Service Road 9031. Veer left on Forest Service Road 9031 and drive 4 miles to the trailhead at road's end.

Contact: Mount Baker–Snoqualmie National Forest, North Bend Ranger Station, 42404 Southeast North Bend Way, North Bend, WA 98045, 425/888-1421.

121 BANDERA MOUNTAIN

7.0 mi/4.0 hr

east of North Bend in Alpine Lakes Wilderness of Mount Baker–Snoqualmie National Forest

Map 3.3, page 93

Bandera has a reputation for two things: a steep, difficult ascent and breathtaking panoramic

views. The second feature far outweighs the first. A new trail built by the Forest Service makes access to Bandera Trail much easier and should encourage even more folks to visit this great place. That's good for everyone, since Bandera is less than an hour from Seattle. The trail is awash in mountain views in every direction, offering one of Washington's best sunsets.

The route to Bandera follows Mason Lakes Trail for 2.5 miles before splitting off to the right at a signed junction. By this point, hikers are out of woods and immersed in wide open mountain meadows, kept in check by heavy snowpacks and regular (every 100 years or so) fires. The views are grand along the way and only get better as the trail reaches the summit of Bandera. Mount Rainier is enormous to the south, behind McClellan Butte. Miles and miles of forest and mountain ridges give way to Glacier Peak to the east and Mount Baker to the north. Total elevation gain is about 3,000 feet, a rough day's work, but the memories of the great views will outlast any soreness.

User Groups: Hikers and leashed dogs. No horses or mountain bikes are allowed. No wheelchair access.

Open Seasons: This trail is accessible June–mid-November.

Permits: A federal Northwest Forest Pass is required to park here. A free wilderness permit is also required to hike here and is available at the trailhead.

Maps: For a map of Mount Baker–Snoqualmie National Forest, contact the Outdoor Recreation Information Center at the downtown Seattle REI. For topographic maps, ask Green Trails for No. 206, Bandera, or ask the USGS for Bandera.

Directions: From Seattle, drive east on I-90 to Exit 45. Turn left (north, over the freeway) to Forest Service Road 9030. Turn left and drive left .5 mile to Forest Service Road 9031. Veer left on Forest Service Road 9031 and drive 4 miles to the trailhead at road's end.

Contact: Mount Baker–Snoqualmie National Forest, North Bend Ranger Station, 42404 Southeast North Bend Way, North Bend, WA 98045, 425/888-1421.

122 McCLELLAN BUTTE

9.2 mi/5.0 hr

east of North Bend in Mount Baker–Snoqualmie National Forest

Map 3.3, page 93

A tough, steep, rocky path leads to the top of McClellan Butte. Few hikers will have kind words for a trail that asks so much. That is, until hikers reach the top with miles of forests and peaks revealed at their feet. Adversity is often just an exercise in building character (thanks, Dad). McClellan Butte may be a difficult climb, but it's an excellent alternative to other trails that are busier and just as difficult (Mount Si, for instance).

McClellan Butte Trail climbs through forest for nearly its entire length. After .6 mile it intersects the Iron Horse Trail; follow it west .4 mile, then turn south on McClellan Butte Trail. A great number of steep switchbacks scale the hillside, crossing several avalanche chutes that can remain filled with snow until July. Be aware that when filled with snow, they are dangerous because of avalanches. Overuse has exposed many frustrating rocks and roots.

The trail eventually finds the southern edge of the butte at the border of the Cedar River watershed. The trail ends below the true summit, a rocky point with vertical walls, best left for rock climbers. Nevertheless, there are great views just below the summit, with Mount Rainier in the distance and Chester Morse Lake directly below. Think of all the character you just built after that treacherous climb. Cheers!

User Groups: Hikers and leashed dogs. No horses or mountain bikes are allowed. No wheelchair access.

Open Seasons: This trail is accessible July–October.

Permits: A federal Northwest Forest Pass is required to park here.

Maps: For a map of Mount Baker–Snoqualmie National Forest, contact the Outdoor Recreation

Information Center at the downtown Seattle REI. For topographic maps, ask Green Trails for No. 206, Bandera, or ask the USGS for Bandera.
Directions: From Seattle, drive east on I-90 to Exit 42. Turn right (south) and then turn left onto Forest Service Road 55. Drive .3 mile to a signed gravel road. Turn right and drive .2 mile to the trailhead at road's end.
Contact: Mount Baker-Snoqualmie National Forest, North Bend Ranger Station, 42404 Southeast North Bend Way, North Bend, WA 98045, 425/888-1421.

123 TALAPUS AND OLALLIE LAKES

4.0–6.0 mi/2.0–3.0 hr

east of North Bend in Alpine Lakes Wilderness of Mount Baker–Snoqualmie National Forest

Map 3.3, page 93

Although they're not showy or flashy, this pair of forested lakes can be the perfect respite from the city. Talapus and Olallie Lakes are greatly accessible, situated within an hour's drive of Seattle. The easy trail gains less than 1,000 feet, perfect for hikers young and old. The result during the summer is swarms of families to match the swarms of bugs. Regardless, the lakes make great overnight destinations with many nice campsites. And forests of virgin Douglas fir and western hemlock surround the lakes to offer shade for those not inclined to jump in the water.

Talapus Lake Trail begins on an old cat track but soon becomes a true trail. The trail dances a laid-back switchback shuffle through a cool, shady forest. Alpine Lakes Wilderness is entered just before a marshy area, below Talapus Lake. Many paths diverge from here, leading to good camping spots around Talapus. This trail is very busy, so the camping spots go early during the summer.

For Olallie Lake, continue .5 mile along the main trail to a junction; veer left for .5 mile to the forested shores of Olallie. Again, there are many camps along the lake for the many visitors. Keep in mind that both lakes harbor a lot of mosquitoes. Olallie visitors should follow Pratt Lake Trail above the lake for a picturesque view of Mount Rainier.
User Groups: Hikers and leashed dogs. No horses or mountain bikes are allowed. No wheelchair access.
Open Seasons: This trail is accessible June–October.
Permits: A federal Northwest Forest Pass is required to park here. A free wilderness permit is also required to hike here and is available at the trailhead.
Maps: For a map of Mount Baker–Snoqualmie National Forest, contact the Outdoor Recreation Information Center at the downtown Seattle REI. For topographic maps, ask Green Trails for No. 206, Bandera, or ask the USGS for Bandera.
Directions: From Seattle, drive east on I-90 to Exit 45. From the off-ramp, turn north (left) onto Forest Service Road 9031 for about .5 mile. Turn right onto Forest Service Road 9030 and drive 2 miles to road's end, where the trailhead is located.
Contact: Mount Baker–Snoqualmie National Forest, North Bend Ranger Station, 42404 Southeast North Bend Way, North Bend, WA 98045, 425/888-1421.

124 GRANITE MOUNTAIN

8.6 mi/5.0 hr 4 9

east of North Bend in Alpine Lakes Wilderness of Mount Baker–Snoqualmie National Forest

Map 3.3, page 93

Let's not mince words; Granite Mountain Trail is a hell of a climb to one of the best summit views in the region. The trail ascends nearly 4,000 feet in just over four miles but rewards with broad meadows of huckleberries and copious views of surrounding peaks. The summit is home to the last functioning fire lookout operated by the Forest Service in the area. If the Forest Service is here, you know it has views.

Granite Mountain Trail begins 1.3 miles up Pratt Lake Trail. As the hum of the freeway

fades away, Granite Mountain Trail takes off to the right. The ascent is certainly steep, making numerous switchbacks up through the forest. Be thankful for the shade, as there is unlikely to be any water on the route. The trail eventually emerges into open meadows with Mount Rainier off in the distance.

This south-facing slope melts out early in the year, but the trail soon levels out and jumps to the north slope of the hill. Here, snow lingers late and avalanche danger persists even into June. Head-turning views will likely slow your ascent and help to keep your heart rate reasonable. All of the Snoqualmie-area peaks are on parade as are Mount Baker and Glacier Peak on clear days.

User Groups: Hikers, leashed dogs, llamas, and goats. No horses or mountain bikes are allowed. No wheelchair access.

Open Seasons: This trail is accessible July–October.

Permits: A federal Northwest Forest Pass is required to park here.

Maps: For a map of Mount Baker–Snoqualmie National Forest, contact the Outdoor Recreation Information Center at the downtown Seattle REI. For topographic maps, ask Green Trails for No. 207, Snoqualmie Pass, or ask the USGS for Snoqualmie Pass.

Directions: From Seattle, drive east on I-90 to Exit 47. Turn left (north) from the off-ramp and turn left at the T in the road. Drive .5 mile to the signed trailhead.

Contact: Mount Baker–Snoqualmie National Forest, North Bend Ranger Station, 42404 Southeast North Bend Way, North Bend, WA 98045, 425/888-1421.

125 PRATT LAKE

11.4 mi/6.0 hr

east of North Bend in Alpine Lakes Wilderness of Mount Baker–Snoqualmie National Forest

Map 3.3, page 93

Pratt Lake is one of the nicest but least-visited destinations in Alpine Lakes Wilderness. The journey to the lake is just as great as the destination. Great forests, views of Mount Rainier, berries for everyone, and lots of lakeshore to explore are yours for the enjoying. What's more is that there are often few people along this route. That's amazing, since it is easily one of the best loops anywhere near I-90 and Seattle.

Pratt Lake Trail begins in the shade of forest, much needed during summer days. The trail climbs gently, crossing several small creeks on its way to Olallie Lake. It passes signed junctions for Granite Mountain and Talapus Lake. As the trail contours above Olallie Lake, the forest breaks for an amazing view of Mount Rainier.

The trail splits along a ridge; the left fork leads to Mount Defiance, so head right, down to Pratt Lake through fields of granite boulders. The chirping you hear is picas saying hello. Mount Roosevelt stands out across from the basin, above Pratt Lake. Numerous campsites are at the north end of the lake, where it drains into the Pratt River. Remnants of abandoned Pratt River Trail are on the western shore, ripe for exploration. At night, with the moon and stars at play in the sky, this place seems very far away from everything, yet it is less than an hour from Seattle.

User Groups: Hikers, leashed dogs, and llamas. No horses or mountain bikes are allowed. No wheelchair access.

Open Seasons: This trail is accessible mid-June–October.

Permits: A federal Northwest Forest Pass is required to park here. A free wilderness permit is also required to hike here and is available at the trailhead.

Maps: For a map of Mount Baker–Snoqualmie National Forest, contact the Outdoor Recreation Information Center at the downtown Seattle REI. For topographic maps, ask Green Trails for No. 206, Bandera, and No. 207, Snoqualmie Pass, or ask the USGS for Bandera and Snoqualmie Pass.

Directions: From Seattle, drive east on I-90 to Exit 47. Turn left (north) from the off-ramp and turn left at the T in the road. Drive .5 mile to the signed trailhead.

Contact: Mount Baker–Snoqualmie National Forest, North Bend Ranger Station, 42404 Southeast North Bend Way, North Bend, WA 98045, 425/888-1421.

126 ANNETTE LAKE

7.0 mi/4.0 hr

in the Mount Baker–Snoqualmie National Forest, south of Snoqualmie Pass

Map 3.3, page 93

Nothing is especially unique about Annette Lake. Then again, Annette is another beautiful alpine lake, set between large peaks, with waterfalls and beautiful forest. Add it all up, and it's definitely a great place to spend the day. The trail up to Annette Lake is fairly easy to hike, and that's never a bad thing.

Annette Lake Trail proceeds through dense forest on its way to the lake. In the beginning, the trail follows an old service road and soon crosses an old railway line (now Iron Horse Trail). Switchbacks rise steeply on the side of Silver Peak, high above Humpback Creek. Avalanche chutes open the canopy in places, providing some views of Humpback Mountain. The trail continues smoothly for the last mile, arriving at Annette Lake.

Annette Lake sits directly between Silver Peak and Abiel Peak. Steep cliffs drop into the woods and lingering snowfields that surround the lake. It's not your typically deep blue alpine lake, but it does make for some decent fishing. There is some camping around the lake for those seeking an overnighter.

User Groups: Hikers and leashed dogs. No horses or mountain bikes are allowed. No wheelchair access.

Open Seasons: This trail is accessible June–mid-November.

Permits: A federal Northwest Forest Pass is required to park here. A free wilderness permit is also required to hike here and is available at the trailhead.

Maps: For a map of Mount Baker–Snoqualmie National Forest, contact the Outdoor Recreation Information Center at the downtown Seattle REI. For topographic maps, ask Green Trails for No. 207, Snoqualmie Pass, or ask the USGS for Snoqualmie Lake and Lost Pass.

Directions: From Seattle, drive east on I-90 to Exit 47. Turn right (south) and then left on Forest Service Road 55. Drive .5 mile to the signed trailhead at road's end.

Contact: Mount Baker–Snoqualmie National Forest, North Bend Ranger Station, 42404 Southeast North Bend Way, North Bend, WA 98045, 425/888-1421.

127 DENNY CREEK AND LAKE MELAKWA

9.0 mi/4.5 hr

east of North Bend in Alpine Lakes Wilderness of Mount Baker–Snoqualmie National Forest

Map 3.3, page 93

This may well be the most beautiful hike in the I-90 corridor. Two series of incredible waterfalls parallel the trail. After crossing Hemlock Pass, Lake Melakwa sits within a beautiful, large basin, rimmed by jagged peaks giving way to forests of subalpine trees. This is a perfect introduction to all that the Alpine Lakes Wilderness has to offer; accordingly, it attracts flocks of people during the summer. Don't be dismayed, as there is plenty to see for all.

Denny Creek Trail begins along Denny Creek as cars and trucks pass overhead on I-90. The highway overpass preserves important corridors, allowing wildlife to move uninhibited through the forests. The trail encounters Keekwulee Falls at 1.5 miles; at two miles are Snowshoe Falls. These cascades form large pools on slabs of granite with lots of nooks and crannies.

The trail switchbacks up through avalanche chutes and fields of huckleberries to Hemlock Pass; Lake Melakwa lies another .3 mile beyond. There are many campsites at the lake, on both the eastern and western shores. Be sure to stay on footpaths, as the meadows here have taken a beating. Sharp-toothed Chair Peak is the tallest peak of the jagged rim around

the basin. More great lakes lie beyond Lake Melakwa for the adventurous. The trail drops with Melakwa Creek to Lower Tuscohatchie Lake, a favorite backcountry swimming hole.
User Groups: Hikers and leashed dogs. No horses or mountain bikes are allowed. No wheelchair access.
Open Seasons: This trail is accessible July–October.
Permits: A federal Northwest Forest Pass is required to park here. A free wilderness permit is also required to hike here and is available at the trailhead.
Maps: For a map of Mount Baker–Snoqualmie National Forest, contact the Outdoor Recreation Information Center at the downtown Seattle REI. For topographic maps, ask Green Trails for No. 207, Snoqualmie Pass, or ask the USGS for Snoqualmie Pass.
Directions: From Seattle, drive east on I-90 to Exit 47. Turn left (north) from the off-ramp and turn right at the T in the road. Drive .4 mile to Forest Service Road 58. Turn left and drive about 4 miles to the signed trailhead.
Contact: Mount Baker–Snoqualmie National Forest, North Bend Ranger Station, 42404 Southeast North Bend Way, North Bend, WA 98045, 425/888-1421.

128 SNOW LAKE

6.0 mi/3.0 hr

north of Snoqualmie Pass in Alpine Lakes Wilderness of Mount Baker–Snoqualmie National Forest

Map 3.3, page 93

Everything about this place seems supersized. Snow Lake is remarkably large, especially for an alpine lake. The basin itself is enormous, easily absorbing the large crowds that trek to the area. Big meadows satisfy appetites with large numbers of prime huckleberries. And of course the surrounding peaks and ridges are large, looming over the lake and making for some striking vistas. It's all large and all exceptionally grand.

Snow Lake Trail gently works its way toward tiny Source Lake. This section is mostly open, providing great views of the jagged valley ridges. Switchbacks climb steeply to a ridge looking down on Snow Lake. The trail is occasionally rocky, mostly because of the high use. The ridge is a turnaround point for many, as the trail then drops about 500 feet in .5 mile to Snow Lake. Unless you're on a strict time schedule (you shouldn't be), it's worth the effort to continue.

Snow Lake is cloaked in typical Alpine Lakes Wilderness beauty. The cliffs of Chair Peak tower over meadows and groves of mountain hemlock surrounding the lake. Camping at Snow Lake is discouraged because of the heavy use of the trail; alpine meadows have delicate makeups. If you're not satisfied with stopping here, then you're in for a treat. A climb over a steep ridge ends up at Gem and Wildcat Lakes.
User Groups: Hikers and leashed dogs. No horses or mountain bikes are allowed. No wheelchair access.
Open Seasons: This trail is accessible June–October.
Permits: A federal Northwest Forest Pass is required to park here. A free wilderness permit is also required to hike here and is available at the trailhead.
Maps: For a map of Mount Baker–Snoqualmie National Forest, contact the Outdoor Recreation Information Center at the downtown Seattle REI. For topographic maps, ask Green Trails for No. 207, Snoqualmie Pass, or ask the USGS for Bandera and Snoqualmie Pass.
Directions: From Seattle, drive east on I-90 to Exit 52 (West Summit). Turn left (under the freeway) and left again on Alpental Road. Drive .2 mile and turn right on Forest Service Road 9040. Drive 1.5 miles to a large gravel parking lot on the left. The trailhead is on the right.
Contact: Mount Baker–Snoqualmie National Forest, North Bend Ranger Station, 42404 Southeast North Bend Way, North Bend, WA 98045, 425/888-1421.

129 COMMONWEALTH BASIN/RED PASS

10.0 mi/5.0 hr 3 9

near Snoqualmie Pass in Alpine Lakes Wilderness of Mount Baker–Snoqualmie National Forest

Map 3.3, page 93

This is one of the better trails out of the Snoqualmie Pass area. The trailhead literally starts at Snoqualmie Pass and climbs 5 miles to a spectacular viewpoint atop Red Pass. Along the way are old-growth forests of enormous mountain hemlocks that give way to wide open meadows and fields of blueberry bushes. The trail needn't be hiked its entire length to be fully enjoyed. That makes this trail a great family hike, in case little ones get tuckered out early.

The first half of the route follows Pacific Crest Trail. Along this stretch, the trail gently and gradually climbs through shady forest to reach a junction (2.5 miles). Stick to the left on Commonwealth Basin Trail as the basin opens into parkland, meadows mixed with pockets of forest. You must make a crossing of Commonwealth Creek (4 miles), but it is unlikely to be much trouble by mid-July. The last mile is a descent climb of about 1,200 feet. Halfway up is Red Pond and a nice campsite. Finally, after more switchbacks, Red Pass is achieved. Views extend in nearly all directions, taking in countless peaks of the Alpine Lakes Wilderness.

User Groups: Hikers and leashed dogs. No horses or mountain bikes are allowed. No wheelchair access.

Open Seasons: This trail is accessible July–October.

Permits: A federal Northwest Forest Pass is required to park here.

Maps: For a map of Mount Baker–Snoqualmie National Forest, contact the Outdoor Recreation Information Center at the downtown Seattle REI. For topographic maps, ask Green Trails for No. 207, Snoqualmie Pass, or ask the USGS for Snoqualmie Pass.

Directions: From Seattle, drive east on I-90 to Exit 52. Turn north at the exit ramp and take the first right into the PCT-North parking area. The lot to the left is intended for stock; hikers can continue straight to the main parking lot. The trail starts at the east end of the parking lot.

Contact: Mount Baker–Snoqualmie National Forest, North Bend Ranger Station, 42404 Southeast North Bend Way, North Bend, WA 98045, 425/888-1421.

130 KENDALL KATWALK

11.0 mi/6.0 hr 3 10

north of Snoqualmie Pass in Alpine Lakes Wilderness of Mount Baker–Snoqualmie National Forest

Map 3.3, page 93

Without a doubt, Kendall Katwalk is one of the most unforgettable and exciting stretches of Pacific Crest Trail. Heading north from Snoqualmie Pass, PCT encounters a long granite wall on the side of Kendall Peak, with a slope of roughly 75 degrees. That's pretty close to vertical. With a little ingenuity and even more dynamite, trail engineers blasted a 100-yard stretch of trail into the slope. Named Kendall Katwalk, it's now famous across the country.

PCT leaves Snoqualmie Pass and wastes little time before beginning the ascent to the high country. Shady and well graded, the trail passes underfoot quickly. Stay right at Commonwealth Basin junction (2.5 miles) and continue climbing with PCT. The forest soon breaks, and numerous neighboring peaks and ridges come into view. In August, ripe huckleberries fuel the climb to Katwalk (5.5 miles). This is a crowded segment of PCT, but take the time to walk Katwalk a couple of times anyway. Although the trail is plenty wide, watch your step; Silver Creek Valley is a good 1,200-foot drop. Campers will need to hike an extra two miles to Gravel and Ridge Lakes.

User Groups: Hikers, leashed dogs, and horses. No mountain bikes are allowed. No wheelchair access.

Open Seasons: This trail is accessible mid-June–September.

Permits: A federal Northwest Forest Pass is required to park here.
Maps: For a map of Mount Baker–Snoqualmie National Forest, contact the Outdoor Recreation Information Center at the downtown Seattle REI. For topographic maps, ask Green Trails for No. 207, Snoqualmie Pass, or ask the USGS for Snoqualmie Pass.
Directions: From Seattle, drive east on I-90 to Exit 52. Turn north at the exit ramp and take the first right into the PCT-North parking area. The lot to the left is intended for stock; hikers can continue straight to the main parking lot. The trail starts at the east end of the parking lot.
Contact: Mount Baker–Snoqualmie National Forest, North Bend Ranger Station, 42404 Southeast North Bend Way, North Bend, WA 98045, 425/888-1421.

131 GOLD CREEK VALLEY

8.0 mi/4.0 hr

north of Snoqualmie Pass in Alpine Lakes Wilderness of Mount Baker–Snoqualmie National Forest

Map 3.3, page 93

Gold Creek Trail is an easy venture through old-growth forest on the east side of the crest. The trail gains just 400 feet of elevation in four miles of maintained trail, making it accessible by hikers of all abilities. Meadows and avalanche chutes are numerous, providing ample views of the surrounding peaks and ridges. Although it is along the Cascade Crest, the trail sits low in the valley. It is often one of the first trails in the area to be snow free. That makes it a great selection in June. Hikers looking for a challenge can continue on nonmaintained trails to Alaska or Joe Lakes, each situated high on the valley's ridges.

Gold Creek Trail travels for a mile before crossing into Alpine Lakes Wilderness. An old-growth forest of fir and hemlock provides needed shade as Gold Creek gushes with the winter's snowmelt. The trail crosses several streams along the way, including Gold Creek, and may be difficult or even impassable when stream flow is high. The route eventually crosses Silver Creek, where maintenance of the trail ends. From here, audacious hikers can bushwhack it to steep footpaths up to Alaska and Joe Lakes. These high lakes in small cirques are set within subalpine parkland. A specific destination is not required on Gold Creek Trail, as the entire length of the trail is excellent hiking.

User Groups: Hikers and leashed dogs. No horses or mountain bikes are allowed. No wheelchair access.
Open Seasons: This trail is accessible mid-May–November.
Permits: A federal Northwest Forest Pass is required to park here.
Maps: For a map of Mount Baker–Snoqualmie National Forest, contact the Outdoor Recreation Information Center at the downtown Seattle REI. For topographic maps, ask Green Trails for No. 207, Snoqualmie Pass, or ask the USGS for Chikamin Peak.
Directions: From Seattle, drive east on I-90 to Exit 54. Turn left and drive .2 mile to Forest Service Road 4832. Turn right and drive 1 mile to Forest Service Road 144. Turn left and drive 2 miles to the signed trailhead.
Contact: Mount Baker–Snoqualmie National Forest, North Bend Ranger Station, 42404 Southeast North Bend Way, North Bend, WA 98045, 425/888-1421.

132 MARGARET AND LILLIAN LAKES

9.2–10.6 mi/5.0–6.0 hr

northeast of Snoqualmie Pass in Alpine Lakes Wilderness of Wenatchee National Forest

Map 3.3, page 93

Margaret and Lillian Lakes are just two in a series of high-country lakes within the south end of Rampart Ridge. These subalpine lakes enjoy knockout views of the inner Cascade Crest. You'd never guess from the jumble of cars at the trailhead that this trail is a steep one or that it endures a stretch of road hiking for the first two miles. Never mind, for this is a great hike just 90 minutes from Seattle.

The signed trailhead is just uphill from the parking lot on Forest Service Road 4934. Passing through the gates, hike the old road for nearly two miles before finding true trail. Subalpine fir and mountain hemlock provide welcome shade on this hot, dry trail. Extra water will be appreciated during the summer heat. The trail soon splits at a saddle (3.5 miles), with the right fork dropping to Margaret Lake (4.6 miles). Rocky meadows surround the cool lake below Mount Margaret.

For a slightly longer hike, stay left at the junction, continuing to follow Rampart Ridge Trail down to Twin Lakes (4.5 miles) and on to Lake Lillian (5.3 miles). Both lakes revel in wildflower blooms in July, and views across Gold Creek to Kendall Peak are awesome. Campers need to stay away from lakeshores and find established sites. Adhere to the trails at all times, for these are fragile environs.

User Groups: Hikers and leashed dogs. No horses or mountain bikes are allowed. No wheelchair access.

Open Seasons: This trail is accessible mid-June–mid-October.

Permits: A federal Northwest Forest Pass is required to park here.

Maps: For a map of Wenatchee National Forest, contact the Outdoor Recreation Information Center at the downtown Seattle REI. For topographic maps, ask Green Trails for No. 207, Snoqualmie Pass, or ask the USGS for Chikamin Peak and Stampede Pass.

Directions: From Seattle, drive east on I-90 to Exit 54 (Hyak). Turn left and drive .3 mile to Forest Service Road 4832. Turn right and drive 5 miles to Forest Service Road 4934. Turn left and drive .5 mile to the parking area. The signed trailhead is a short walk up Forest Service Road 4934 behind a gated road.

Contact: Wenatchee National Forest, Cle Elum Ranger Station, 803 West 2nd Street, Cle Elum, WA 98922, 509/852-1100.

133 RACHEL LAKE

7.6 mi/4.0 hr

northeast of Snoqualmie Pass in Alpine Lakes Wilderness of Wentachee National Forest

Map 3.3, page 93

Rachel Lake is one of the most popular destinations along the I-90 corridor. Crowds are a given on just about any day of the week, a testament to the accessibility and beauty of the lakes basin. Rachel Lake Trail is perfect for folks looking for an undemanding but beautiful hike a little more than an hour from Seattle. The enjoyable hike leads to a basin of lakes neighbored by craggy peaks.

The first three miles of Rachel Lake Trail are relatively flat and pass quickly. This section passes through forest and occasional avalanche chutes, where colorful fireweed dominates the openings. The last mile gets interesting and much tougher, climbing steeply through a classic box canyon. The views begin to appear as you enter the high country. Rachel Lake is the largest of three lakes and many small tarns beneath Rampart Ridge, each tempting with their cool water.

Rampart Ridge and the lakes have seen a lot of use, with denuded areas abounding. This is unfortunate, as beautiful alpine meadows used to be prolific here. Alta Mountain stands tall to the north and offers a good scramble to the top. There is a lot of country to explore from Rachel Lake, and much of it already has been. Yet Rachel Lake is a beautiful destination and will always be a solidly popular day hike.

User Groups: Hikers and leashed dogs. No horses or mountain bikes are allowed. No wheelchair access.

Open Seasons: This trail is accessible June–October.

Permits: A federal Northwest Forest Pass is required to park here. A free wilderness permit is also required to hike here and is available at the trailhead.

Maps: For a map of Wenatchee National

Forest, contact the Outdoor Recreation Information Center at the downtown Seattle REI. For topographic maps, ask Green Trails for No. 207, Snoqualmie Pass, or ask the USGS for Snoqualmie Pass.
Directions: From Seattle, drive east on I-90 to Exit 62. Turn left on Kachess Lake Road and drive 5.5 miles to Forest Service Road 4930. Turn right and drive 3.5 miles to the trailhead at road's end.
Contact: Wenatchee National Forest, Cle Elum Ranger District, 803 West 2nd Street, Cle Elum, WA 98922, 509/852-1100.

134 KACHESS RIDGE

13.1 mi one-way/7.0 hr

north of Easton in Wenatchee National Forest

Map 3.3, page 93

High above two large reservoirs, Kachess Ridge Trail traverses more than 13 miles along a high, meadowy ridge. Along the way are several worthy side trips to high vistas or alpine lakes. The trail works well as a through-hike, but if two cars are out of the question, no worries. Four other access points make getting to a particular spot quite easy.

For a through-hike, it's best to travel north to south, conveniently losing 2,500 feet of net elevation along the way. The route follows the crest of No Name Ridge. At 2.3 miles is a junction for Red Mountain Trail, a seldom-used trail passing Little Joe Lake (nice) on the way to an alternate trailhead (not recommended). At 3.8 miles is the junction dropping to inviting Thorp Lake and another trailhead. A short .25 mile later a side trail heads steeply to the summit of Thorp Mountain, the high point of the trip, in both altitude and experience. At 5,854 feet, see much of the surrounding Cascades, most spectacularly Mount Rainier.

The trail follows the ridge three miles through meadows and continuous views, passing Know Creek Trail (another trailhead) and French Cabin Creek Trail (a fourth trailhead). The trail now begins its drop into Silver Creek Basin and down to the trailhead. Kachess Beacon Trail, 1.9 miles from the southern trailhead, leads up to a nice viewpoint at 4,615 feet.
User Groups: Hikers, leashed dogs, horses, and mountain bikes. No wheelchair access.
Open Seasons: This trail is accessible mid-June–October.
Permits: A federal Northwest Forest Pass is required to park here.
Maps: For a map of Wenatchee National Forest, contact the Outdoor Recreation Information Center at the downtown Seattle REI. For topographic maps, ask Green Trails for No. 208, Kachess Lake, or ask the USGS for Kachess Lake.
Directions: From Seattle, drive east on I-90 to Exit 70 (Easton). Drive north over the freeway and turn left on West Sparks Road. Drive one mile to Forest Service Road 4818. Turn right and drive one mile to Forest Service Road 203. Turn right and drive 2 miles to the signed trailhead at road's end.
Contact: Wenatchee National Forest, Cle Elum Ranger District, 803 West 2nd Street, Cle Elum, WA 98922, 509/852-1100.

135 DECEPTION PASS LOOP

14.7 mi/1–3 days

north of Cle Elum in Alpine Lakes Wilderness of Wentachee National Forest

Map 3.3, page 93

The climax of the trip is not at Deception Pass but instead beneath the amazing Cathedral Rock and the parkland surrounding its base. Cathedral Rock looms high above Pacific Crest Trail, with towering rock cliffs that somehow sing and make cathedral the only word fit to describe the peak. Throw in great views of the Wenatchee Mountains and Mount Stuart, and you have the makings for a great weekend of hiking.

The hike works either clockwise or counterclockwise, but the latter makes for less strenuous climbing and is described here. Start at Tucquala Lake and head north through Cle Elum Valley to the pass, which is wooded and offers few views. Here, Marmot Lake and Lake Clarice are four miles to the north along a down-and-up trail, each with campsites.

From Deception Pass, the route follows PCT south past impressive mountain hemlocks before arriving at the base of Cathedral Rock. A pair of stream crossings may be difficult in times of heavy runoff. At Cathedral Rock, the trail climbs to beautiful parkland meadows of huckleberries, heather, and small trees. Peggy's Pond lies a short .5 mile around the base of Cathedral Rock and is worth visiting. The route drops steeply to the trailhead via Cathedral Rock Trail, passing Squaw Lake along the way.

User Groups: Hikers, leashed dogs, and horses (horses will be unable to cross a blown-out ford on a stream along the PCT). No mountain bikes are allowed. No wheelchair access.

Open Seasons: This trail is accessible June–October.

Permits: A federal Northwest Forest Pass is required to park here.

Maps: For a map of Wenatchee National Forest, contact the Outdoor Recreation Information Center at the downtown Seattle REI. For topographic maps, ask Green Trails for No. 176, Stevens Pass, or ask the USGS for Mount Daniel and The Cradle.

Directions: From Seattle, drive east on I-90 to Exit 80 (Roslyn). Turn left on Bullfrog Cutoff Road and drive to Highway 903. Turn left and drive to Salmon La Sac and Forest Service Road 4330. Continue straight on Forest Service Road 4330 to Tucquala Meadows Trailhead at road's end.

Contact: Wenatchee National Forest, Cle Elum Ranger District, 803 West 2nd Street, Cle Elum, WA 98922, 509/852-1100.

136 TUCK AND ROBIN LAKES

12.8 mi/1–2 days 3 9

north of Cle Elum in Alpine Lakes Wilderness of Wentachee National Forest

Map 3.3, page 93

These two picturesque lakes are classics among folks who regularly hike this area. Set high on the west side of the Wenatchee Ridge, Robin Lake reveals typical but never-tiring beauty of mountain hemlocks, heather, and huckleberries. This is a great destination, but with a little more effort, Tuck Lake delivers an outstanding high-mountain landscape uncommon in the Northwest. At an elevation of 6,100 feet, vegetation becomes scarce, large bare slabs of Granite Mountain beg for exploration, and a feeling of high alpine is always in the air.

The trail begins on Deception Pass Trail. The first three miles are flat and easy as the trail moves up the upper reaches of the Cle Elum River Valley. From here, the trail climbs well up through lazy switchbacks and at 4.5 miles is the cutoff for Tuck and Robin Lakes. Turning right, the trail ascends steeply, 1,100 feet in two miles, on sometimes rocky and difficult trail. After two miles, you've arrived at Robin Lake in subalpine forest. Bare slabs of granite mix with patches of mountain hemlocks and heather. Tuck Lake is about 1.5 miles farther on a way path that can provide some difficulty, as it climbs another 900 feet. At Tuck, the landscape is barren, with large slabs of granite exposed for lack of any decent soil at such an altitude. Blue sky and massive peaks fill the horizon.

While camping is available at both lakes, don't count on getting a spot if you show up late. This is a popular trail, and disappearing vegetation is a concern with established campsites going early. During the summer and early fall, it is best as a day hike.

User Groups: Hikers and leashed dogs. No horses or mountain bikes are allowed. No wheelchair access.

Open Seasons: This trail is accessible late June–early October.

Permits: A federal Northwest Forest Pass is required to park here.

Maps: For a map of Wenatchee National Forest, contact the Outdoor Recreation Information Center at the downtown Seattle REI. For topographic maps, ask Green Trails for No.

176, Stevens Pass, or ask the USGS for Mount Daniel and The Cradle.

Directions: From Seattle, drive east on I-90 to Exit 80 (Roslyn). Turn left on Bullfrog Cutoff Road and drive to Highway 903. Turn left and drive to Salmon La Sac and Forest Service Road 4330. Continue straight on Forest Service Road 4330 to Tucquala Meadows Trailhead at road's end.

Contact: Wenatchee National Forest, Cle Elum Ranger District, 803 West 2nd Street, Cle Elum, WA 98922, 509/852-1100.

137 PADDY-GO-EASY PASS

6.0 mi/3.5 hr 3 8

north of Roslyn in Alpine Lakes Wilderness of Wenatchee National Forest

Map 3.3, page 93

Trailblazers must be sarcastic folk, especially when it comes to naming their new trails. Experienced hikers know as a general rule of thumb that when the word "easy" is used in a trail name, that trail is usually anything but easy. Regardless of the effort, hikers are often pleased with the outstanding views of many nearby peaks and ridges. The route travels outstanding high-country terrain, full of meadows covered in wildflowers. To top off the trip is Sprite Lake, an all-star lake set before The Cradle.

French Creek Trail makes a steady and steep ascent to the pass. Forest lines most of the way up before thinning to great meadows. This is a very colorful place in early July, when wildflowers are in full bloom. The trail gains roughly 2,700 feet in three miles. The pass is superb, with views of numerous peaks. Mounts Daniel, Stuart, and Rainier are particularly memorable. The pass lies at the crest of the Wenatchee Mountains, a beautiful ridge in its own right.

For further exploration, Sprite Lake lies a short distance over the pass within a small glacial cirque, with rocky slopes and scrubby subalpine trees. Across the valley below stands The Cradle, a tall, rocky, and barren peak. No, Paddy, it's not an easy hike, but it certainly is spectacular.

User Groups: Hikers, leashed dogs, and horses. No mountain bikes are allowed. No wheelchair access.

Open Seasons: This trail is accessible July–mid-October.

Permits: A federal Northwest Forest Pass is required to park here.

Maps: For a map of Wenatchee National Forest, contact the Outdoor Recreation Information Center at the downtown Seattle REI. For topographic maps, ask Green Trails for No. 176, Stevens Pass, or ask the USGS for The Cradle.

Directions: From Seattle, drive east on I-90 to Exit 80 (Roslyn). Turn left on Bullfrog Cutoff Road and drive to Highway 903. Turn left and drive to Salmon La Sac and Forest Service Road 4330. Continue straight on Forest Service Road 4330 to Paddy-Go-Easy Pass, 1 mile before road's end.

Contact: Wenatchee National Forest, Cle Elum Ranger Station, 803 West 2nd Street, Cle Elum, WA 98922, 509/852-1100.

138 WAPTUS RIVER VALLEY

29.6 mi/4 days 2 9

north of Salmon La Sac in Alpine Lakes Wilderness of Wenatchee National Forest

Map 3.3, page 93

Waptus River Valley is not an end in itself. The trail leads to a number of high-country destinations, including Spade Lake and Dutch Miller Gap, two highlights of the Alpine Lakes Wilderness. It's a bit like those old books in which you can choose your own adventure. Take a number of trips up the river, each with different destinations and results. Of course, Waptus River and Waptus Lake are not to be overlooked. The route up the valley is beautiful, while Waptus Lake is the Alpine Lakes' largest lake, with excellent camping.

Waptus River Trail follows the river closely within surrounding forests. Waptus Lake (8.5 miles) has campsites and views of massive Summit Chief and Bears Breast Mountains. The main trail skirts the lake and continues to the head of the valley, where it makes for Dutch Miller Gap. Near the top of the tough ascent to the pass lies Lake Ivanhoe, a high lake set within shores of granite. Dutch Miller Gap leads down into the Middle Fork Snoqualmie.

One of the most popular side trips is Spade Lake. From Waptus Lake, Spade Lake Trail climbs steeply to Spade Lake. The views are good until the lake, where they become excellent. Other adventures along Waptus River Trail include trails up gentle Trail Creek, Waptus Pass over to Escondido Creek, and Pacific Crest Trail, which crosses the valley just above Waptus Lake.

User Groups: Hikers, leashed dogs, and horses. No mountain bikes are allowed. No wheelchair access.

Open Seasons: This trail is accessible July–October.

Permits: A federal Northwest Forest Pass is required to park here.

Maps: For a map of Wenatchee National Forest, contact the Outdoor Recreation Information Center at the downtown Seattle REI. For topographic maps, ask Green Trails for No. 176, Stevens Pass, and No. 208, Kachess Lake, or ask the USGS for Mount Daniel and Polallie Ridge.

Directions: From Seattle, drive east on I-90 to Exit 80 (Roslyn). Turn left on Bullfrog Cutoff Road and drive to Highway 903. Turn left and drive to Salmon La Sac Campground. Waptus Trailhead is on the right, just after you cross Cle Elum River.

Contact: Wenatchee National Forest, Cle Elum Ranger Station, 803 West 2nd Street, Cle Elum, WA 98922, 509/852-1100.

139 JOLLY MOUNTAIN

12.4 mi/8.0 hr

north of Cle Elum in Wenatchee National Forest

Map 3.3, page 93

At 6,443 feet elevation, Jolly Mountain is well capable of delivering excellent views of surrounding ridges and mountains. On clear days, which are easier to come by here on the east side of the Cascades, the tall peak delivers. The route climbs up along Salmon La Sac Creek to a ridge, before making the final ascent to Jolly Mountain. The way is extremely steep, gaining more than 4,000 feet in just six miles of trail. This trail is definitely for the well conditioned, except for those traveling by mountain bike or motorcycle, which are allowed on the trail.

Jolly Mountain Trail makes a steady and steep climb up the creek valley, crossing it at 2.6 miles (difficult ford when the snows are still melting, until mid-July). The views are plentiful, as are the wildflowers blooming in early summer. The trail makes a final steep rise to the summit of Jolly Mountain. The peak provides wide views in all directions, and the vast size of Mount Stuart is readily apparent. The trail is very dry, so be sure to carry lots of water.

User Groups: Hikers, leashed dogs, horses, mountain bikes, and motorcycles. No wheelchair access.

Open Seasons: This trail is accessible June–November.

Permits: A federal Northwest Forest Pass is required to park here.

Maps: For a map of Wenatchee National Forest, contact the Outdoor Recreation Information Center at the downtown Seattle REI. For topographic maps, ask Green Trail for No. 208, Kachess Lake, or ask the USGS for Davis Peak.

Directions: From Seattle, drive east on I-90 to Exit 80 (Roslyn). Turn left on Bullfrog Cutoff Road and drive to Highway 903. Turn left and drive to Salmon La Sac. Jolly Mountain Trailhead is on the right, just beyond Cayuse Horse Camp.

Contact: Wenatchee National Forest, Cle Elum Ranger Station, 803 West 2nd Street, Cle Elum, WA 98922, 509/852-1100.

140 SUMMIT LAKE/ BEARHEAD MOUNTAIN

5.0–6.0 mi/3.0 hr

south of Enumclaw in Clearwater Wilderness of Mount Baker–Snoqualmie National Forest

Map 3.3, page 93

One trailhead provides access to these two destinations, one a high, subalpine lake and the other an even higher mountain summit. Most folks pick one and take it easy, rather than cram both hikes into one long, strenuous day. A trip to Summit Lake, an ideal midsummer swimming hole, is 2.5 miles one-way and a 1,000-foot elevation gain. A trip to the panoramic viewpoint of Bearhead Mountain is three miles one-way, climbing 1,700 feet.

The routes follow Summit Lake Trail into Clearwater Wilderness, climbing to Twin Lake (.8 mile). The trail splits here; Summit Lake Trail turns left while Carbon Trail heads right to Bearhead Mountain. The climb to Bearhead traverses the base of the mountain before turning to climb straight up the shoulder on Bearhead Mountain Trail (2.2 miles). From 6,089 feet, the views are stupendous. Mountains to the north, mountains to the east, and mountains to the south.

A slight majority of hikers turn toward Summit Lake and its meadowy shores. Wildflowers arrive in July while huckleberries wait until late August. Mount Rainier is easily seen from the shore, an incredible dream. Those with an itch for views will enjoy knowing that an easy scramble leaves from the lake to a peak rising west of the lake with great views.

User Groups: Hikers, leashed dogs, and horses. No mountain bikes are allowed. No wheelchair access.

Open Seasons: This trail is accessible mid-June–September.

Permits: A federal Northwest Forest Pass is required to park here.

Maps: For a map of Mount Baker–Snoqualmie National Forest, contact the Outdoor Recreation Information Center at the downtown Seattle REI. For topographic maps, ask Green Trails for No. 237, Enumclaw, or ask the USGS for Bearhead Mountain.

Directions: From Enumclaw, drive west 5 miles to Highway 165 (on the west side of Buckley). Turn left (south) and drive 10.5 miles to Carbon River Highway. Turn left and drive 7.7 miles to Cayada Creek Road (Forest Service Road 7810). Turn left and drive 7 miles to the trailhead at road's end.

Contact: Mount Baker–Snoqualmie National Forest, Enumclaw Ranger Station, 450 Roosevelt Avenue East, Enumclaw, WA 98022, 360/825-6585.

141 GREENWATER RIVER

15.2 mi/1–2 days

south of Enumclaw in Norse Peak Wilderness of Mount Baker–Snoqualmie National Forest

Map 3.3, page 93

In one of the few virgin river valleys left in the southern Mount Baker–Snoqualmie National Forest, Greenwater River Trail explores it all. Coursing more than 10 miles to Corral Pass, its highlights are several lakes gracing the route. Being rather flat and certainly easy, this is a great full day hike or overnight trip for young or beginner backpackers, especially early or late in the year, when snow still blankets the high country.

Greenwater River Trail never ventures far from the beautiful, lively river. Endure a quick spell of old logging before immersing yourself in an ancient forest of Douglas fir, western hemlock, and western red cedar. A pair of small lakes (Meeker and Upper Greenwater) appear at two and 2.4 miles. These lakes are good turnarounds for a short day hike. Continuing up, the trail passes a pair of signed junctions to Echo Lake (6.9 miles). A number of campgrounds are found at the south end of the lake (7.4 miles). Don't forget the fly rod, because the trout in this lake make a sizable dinner.

User Groups: Hikers, leashed dogs, and horses. No mountain bikes are allowed. No wheelchair access.

Open Seasons: This trail is accessible April–November.

Permits: A federal Northwest Forest Pass is required to park here.

Maps: For a map of Mount Baker–Snoqualmie National Forest, contact the Outdoor Recreation Information Center at the downtown Seattle REI. For topographic maps, ask Green Trails for No. 239, Lester, or ask the USGS for Lester SW.

Directions: From Enumclaw, drive east on Highway 410 20.5 miles to Greenwater Road (Forest Service Road 70). Turn left (north) and drive 10 miles to Forest Service Road 7033. Turn right and drive .5 mile to the signed trailhead on the right.

Contact: Mount Baker–Snoqualmie National Forest, Enumclaw Ranger Station, 450 Roosevelt Avenue East, Enumclaw, WA 98022, 360/825-6585.

142 NOBLE KNOB

7.4 mi/4.0 hr

south of Enumclaw in Norse Peak Wilderness of Mount Baker–Snoqualmie National Forest

Map 3.3, page 93

Tally it all up: $10 national park fee? No. Pure meadow bliss, complete with wildflowers in July? Yes. Long, taxing climb? No. Miles and miles of brilliant views? Yes. If you're not sold already, keep reading. The trail to Noble Knob is one of ease and excitement, a glorious ramble through the high country to a magnificent viewpoint. Noble Knob Trail starts high, at 5,700 feet elevation, an altitude that changes little throughout the hike. Skirting the base of Mutton Mountain and the slopes of Dalles Ridge, the trail arrives at the base of Noble Knob, a small rounded peak. A short side trail leads to the summit, the former site of a fire lookout. Mountain views appear from every direction (Olympics to the northwest), but of course Mount Rainier steals the show. Expect to see a lot of company on Noble Knob Trail, especially on summer weekends.

User Groups: Hikers, leashed dogs, horses, and mountain bikes. No wheelchair access.

Open Seasons: This trail is accessible June–September.

Permits: A federal Northwest Forest Pass is required to park here.

Maps: For a map of Mount Baker–Snoqualmie National Forest, contact the Outdoor Recreation Information Center at the downtown Seattle REI. For topographic maps, ask Green Trails for No. 239, Lester, or ask the USGS for Suntop and Lester SW.

Directions: From Enumclaw, drive east 32 miles on Highway 410 to Corral Pass Road (Forest Service Road 7174). Turn left (east) and drive 6.7 miles to the trailhead just before Corral Pass Campground.

Contact: Mount Baker–Snoqualmie National Forest, Enumclaw Ranger Station, 450 Roosevelt Avenue East, Enumclaw, WA 98022, 360/825-6585.

143 MOUNT DAVID

14.0 mi/8.0 hr

north of Lake Wenatchee in Glacier Peak Wilderness of Wenatchee National Forest

Map 3.4, page 94

This is about as high as one can get in the Glacier Peak Wilderness, other than Glacier Peak itself. It certainly feels that way. Tucked up north of Lake Wenatchee, Mount David towers over surrounding peaks for miles and miles. That leaves unmatched panoramic views for those who summit the challenging peak. Neighboring ridges and peaks fall away from beneath, melting into scores of other ridges as far as the eye can see. Challenging is an understatement for this trail. Make no mistake, this is a long, taxing ascent to the top. Alpine ridges and never-ending views make all the hard work worthwhile.

The route begins on Panther Creek Trail but Mount David Trail takes off to the right (west) after one mile. Here, the climbing begins. It's a

steady assault on the mountain, but thanks to the excellent layout of the trail, it's never too much. The total elevation gain is 5,100 feet, or what is known as a "full day." No water is to be found along the trail, so be sure to bring several liters per person. From the ridge, the views open up as the trail contours on or just below the sharp ridge. The mountain falls away precipitously at your feet, down to the valley bottom far below. The trail seems to become steeper nearer the end, but that is likely because of complaints from weary legs. A small scramble conquers the summit. There's no end to the visible peaks, certainly too many to list here. At 7,431 feet tall, Mount David feels like the top of the world.

User Groups: Hikers and leashed dogs. No horses or mountain bikes are allowed. No wheelchair access.

Open Seasons: This trail is accessible August–October.

Permits: A federal Northwest Forest Pass is required to park here.

Maps: For a map of Wenatchee National Forest, contact the Outdoor Recreation Information Center at the downtown Seattle REI. For topographic maps, ask Green Trails for No. 145, Wenatchee Lake, or ask the USGS for Wenatchee Lake.

Directions: From Leavenworth, drive west on U.S. 2 to Highway 207 (at Coles Corner). Turn right and drive to White River Road, north of Lake Wenatchee (Forest Service Road 6400). Turn right and drive to the trailhead at road's end.

Contact: Wenatchee National Forest, Lake Wenatchee Ranger Station, 22976 Highway 207, Leavenworth, WA 98826, 509/763-3103.

144 LITTLE GIANT PASS

10.0 mi/7.0 hr

north of Lake Wenatchee in Glacier Peak Wilderness of Wenatchee National Forest

Map 3.4, page 94

From Little Giant Pass, the views are nearly indescribable. From the pass, enjoy expansive views stretching miles to dozens of mountains and ridges. Don't forget to look down, as well, for the perspective of not one but two immense, glacially carved valleys at your feet. This is one knee-knocking, lung-busting, hell-raiser of a hike—3,800 vertical feet in a brisk five miles. In addition to views are vast wildflower meadows within beautiful basins.

Little Giant Trail begins with a ford of Chiwawa River, a wet ordeal in the summer and fall but an impassable obstacle any other time. The trail wastes no time and immediately begins a long series of switchbacks out of the valley. Old-growth forest covers the trail and keeps hikers cool with shade. The trail crosses Little Giant Creek (other than remnant snowpack, the route's only water source) and begins entering exposed meadows. The climbing isn't done until you reach the pass. The wide, U-shaped valleys of the Chiwawa and Napeequa Rivers reveal their glacial origins. Snowcapped peaks and ridges line the horizon in every direction. Remember extra water or a water filter on this trip; you'll definitely need it.

User Groups: Hikers, leashed dogs, and horses (horses not recommended). No mountain bikes are allowed. No wheelchair access.

Open Seasons: This trail is accessible June–October.

Permits: A federal Northwest Forest Pass is required to park here.

Maps: For a map of Wenatchee National Forest, contact the Outdoor Recreation Information Center at the downtown Seattle REI. For topographic maps, ask Green Trails for No. 113, Holden, or ask the USGS for Trinity and Clark Mountain.

Directions: From Leavenworth, drive west on U.S. 2 to Highway 207, at Coles Corner. Turn left, drive to Fish Lake, and drive 1 mile to Chiwawa Valley Road (Forest Service Road 62). Turn left and drive toward Trinity to Little Giant Trailhead on the left, 1.5 miles beyond Nineteenmile Campground.

Contact: Wenatchee National Forest, Lake Wenatchee Ranger Station, 22976 Highway 207, Leavenworth, WA 98826, 509/763-3103.

145 DIRTY FACE

9.0 mi/5.0 hr

north of Lake Wenatchee in Wenatchee National Forest

Map 3.4, page 94

We won't throw around terms such as cruel or nasty, but Dirty Face is not a stroll in the park. This trail is a straight-up assault on the mountain. Fair enough, for hikers are armed with endless switchbacks and Nalgenes of water to help achieve the top. A successful hiker is rewarded with views of Lake Wenatchee and numerous peaks of the Glacier Peak Wilderness. The site formerly hosted a Forest Service lookout to take advantage of the wide vista. Don't be discouraged if the hike sounds difficult. It is challenging, but it is beautiful as well.

Dirty Face Trail changes little over its length, composed entirely of switchbacks–reports vary between 70 and 90. After about 25 or so, the simple act of counting becomes easier said than done. The trail runs into an abandoned logging road (1.5 miles), which must be followed to its end, where the trail begins again. Ponderosa pine provides poor shade along the trail before patches of subalpine trees offer even less. The trail reaches a ridge, then switchbacks up even more to the former lookout site. The views are grand to the east and west, encompassing much of the Glacier Peak Wilderness. Lake Wenatchee glimmers in the sunshine below.

User Groups: Hikers, leashed dogs, horses, and mountain bikes. No wheelchair access.

Open Seasons: This trail is accessible mid-June–October.

Permits: A federal Northwest Forest Pass is required to park here.

Maps: For a map of Wenatchee National Forest, contact the Outdoor Recreation Information Center at the downtown Seattle REI. For topographic maps, ask Green Trails for No. 145, Wenatchee Lake, or ask the USGS for Wenatchee Lake.

Directions: From Leavenworth, drive west on U.S. 2 to Highway 207 (at Coles Corner). Turn right and drive to the trailhead at Lake Wenatchee Ranger Station.

Contact: Wenatchee National Forest, Lake Wenatchee Ranger Station, 22976 Highway 207, Leavenworth, WA 98826, 509/763-3103.

146 CHIWAUKUM CREEK

24.4 mi/2–3 days

near Leavenworth in Alpine Lakes Wilderness of Wenatchee National Forest

Map 3.4, page 94

Little-known Chiwaukum Creek is a trail corridor with all sorts of options. Several decades ago the road to the trailhead closed, adding a couple of miles to the hike in. Apparently an old road is grounds for dismissal of a trail, perhaps because there are so many other great hikes in the area. Fewer people sounds good. The options exist because the trail heads up the valley before splitting into North and South Forks. Each of these trails then splits again. It quickly becomes a full summer of weekends trying to hike it all. The crown jewel of the valley is Larch Lake, attained via 12 miles on North Fork Trail.

Chiwaukum Trail heads up the valley for six miles before splitting, staying close to the cool water of the creek among great forests of pine and fir. The beautiful and rarely traveled South Fork heads left, eventually splitting to reach Icicle Ridge Trail at Ladies Pass or Index Creek. The route via Ladies Pass travels between Lake Brigham and Lake Flora, outstanding high-country lakes. Also on the South Fork is a trail up Palmer Creek, to the Badlands and Icicle Ridge again.

North Fork Trail crosses Glacier Creek (8 miles) before climbing to reach the forested shores of Chiwaukum Lake (10 miles). Rocky mountain ridges surround the cool, blue water of the lake, as do numerous campsites. The trail continues to Larch Lake (12.2 miles), an area of meadows and jagged ridges. Larches and subalpine firs cover the landscape.

User Groups: Hikers, leashed dogs, and horses (horses allowed only to Glacier Creek).

No mountain bikes are allowed. No wheelchair access.

Open Seasons: This trail is accessible late July–October.

Permits: A federal Northwest Forest Pass is required to park here.

Maps: For a map of Wenatchee National Forest, contact the Outdoor Recreation Information Center at the downtown Seattle REI. For topographic maps, ask Green Trails for No. 177, Chiwaukum Mountains, or ask the USGS for Winton, Big Jim Mountain, and Chiwaukum Mountain.

Directions: From Stevens Pass, drive 25 miles east on U.S. 2 to Mile Marker 89. Turn right onto Chiwaukum Creek Road (Forest Service Road 7908) just beyond the marker. Drive to a junction and stay to the right. Drive to the road's end and the trailhead.

Contact: Wenatchee National Forest, Leavenworth Ranger Station, 600 Sherbourne, Leavenworth, WA 98826, 509/548-6977.

147 CHATTER CREEK/ LAKE EDNA

11.5 mi/8.0 hr

near Leavenworth in Alpine Lakes Wilderness of Wenatchee National Forest

Map 3.4, page 94

Some folks hike the Alpine Lakes for a relaxing time away from home. Others come here looking for a relentless workout that offers killer views. Chatter Creek Trail up to Lake Edna is definitely for the latter type of hiker. It gains nearly 4,000 feet in just over five miles. That is undoubtedly considered a workout. As steep as the trail may be, however, it pays off with a terrific lake set in parkland and panoramic views of the Cascades. Lake Edna is situated along Icicle Ridge Trail, making Chatter Creek a quick but grueling access to the high ridge trail.

Chatter Creek Trail quickly begins climbing, where old forests provide welcome shade on hot days. The trail crosses the creek (tricky before June) and continues its relentless ascent to the ridgeline (5 miles). At least it spends its last half among wide open meadows. The views begin to really emerge at this point.

Chatter Creek Trail contours a basin before making a final climb to the lake at 6,735 feet. The lake lies within a northside basin, so snow may linger well into August. The shores are fairly barren of trees; only scrubs and meadow endure this high up. The best vistas are found atop Cape Horn, a steep scramble to the west. At over 7,000 feet, much of the Cascades is exposed. Those planning to camp at the lake or along the ridge must use established campsites and refrain from camping on the fragile meadows.

User Groups: Hikers, leashed dogs, and horses. No mountain bikes are allowed. No wheelchair access.

Open Seasons: This trail is accessible July–October.

Permits: A federal Northwest Forest Pass is required to park here.

Maps: For a map of Wenatchee National Forest, contact the Outdoor Recreation Information Center at the downtown Seattle REI. For topographic maps, ask Green Trails for No. 177, Chiwaukum Mountains, or ask the USGS for Jack Ridge and Chiwaukum Mountain.

Directions: From Leavenworth, drive south on Icicle Creek Road (Forest Service Road 7600) 16 miles to Chatter Creek Campground and Trailhead, on the right.

Contact: Wenatchee National Forest, Leavenworth Ranger Station, 600 Sherbourne, Leavenworth, WA 98826, 509/548-6977.

148 JACK CREEK

23.2 mi/1–3 days

near Leavenworth in Alpine Lakes Wilderness of Wenatchee National Forest

Map 3.4, page 94

A lot awaits off Jack Creek Trail. Several trails lead off from Jack Creek, connecting to other major drainages of Icicle Creek and thereby creating spectacular loops for backpacking. Alone, the trail travels more than 11 miles to

Stuart Pass and exceptional subalpine parkland. Most of the route is forested, the trail surrounded by old-growth forests of Douglas fir, Englemann spruce, and pines. The full length of the trail is rarely traveled, making Jack Creek a preferred backcountry route.

Jack Creek Trail follows the stream closely for most of its length. The trail to Trout Lake cuts off just over a mile in. This is a great loop when connected to Eightmile Lake (see listing in this chapter). A couple of miles later another trail leads to Trout Lake, much more steeply. Meadow Creek heads off to the west, providing a pair of loops; one climbs to Blackjack Ridge and Cradle Lake, an excellent high-country route, while the other crosses Meadow Creek Pass and drops into French Creek. Any of these routes are well chosen.

Jack Creek Trail slowly but surely gains in elevation to Stuart Pass (11.6 miles, 6,400 feet). Mount Stuart looms large to the east, and the Esmerelda Peaks are in view. The trail is a great valley hike, with plenty of camping along the way. It's an excellent trail to simply see where you end up.

User Groups: Hikers, leashed dogs, and horses. No mountain bikes are allowed. No wheelchair access.

Open Seasons: This trail is accessible mid-June–November.

Permits: A federal Northwest Forest Pass is required to park here.

Maps: For a map of Wenatchee National Forest, contact the Outdoor Recreation Information Center at the downtown Seattle REI. For topographic maps, ask Green Trails for No. 177, Chiwaukum Mountains, and No. 210, Liberty, or ask the USGS for Jack Ridge and Mount Stuart.

Directions: From Leavenworth, drive south on Icicle Creek Road (Forest Service Road 7600) 16 miles to Trout/Jack Creek Trailhead on the left, just beyond Rock Island Campground.

Contact: Wenatchee National Forest, Leavenworth Ranger Station, 600 Sherbourne, Leavenworth, WA 98826, 509/548-6977.

149 ICICLE RIDGE

10.0–25.0 mi/3.5 hr–4 days 4 9

near Leavenworth in Alpine Lakes Wilderness of Wenatchee National Forest

Map 3.4, page 94

This long ridge trail is a favorite among Leavenworth locals. Extending for 25 miles and more, the trail takes in a wide variety of high country. Alpine meadows full of early summer flowers dominate nearly the entire route, while a number of high lakes occupy the western end. The route has a number of access points, both from Icicle Creek Road and the backcountry. Views are as prolific as the wildflowers, extending over much of the Alpine Lakes Wilderness and south to Mount Stuart and Mount Daniel. This high country is outstanding and thankfully preserved by the Alpine Lakes Wilderness.

At the eastern trailhead, Icicle Ridge Trail seemingly starts right in the town of Leavenworth. Little time is wasted in reaching the ridge, as the trail climbs quickly and steeply and then runs the crest. A steep trail from Icicle Creek Road via Fourth of July Creek reaches the ridge in this section. It's extremely dry in the summer, and the snow melts here before the rest of the trail, providing early access.

Icicle Ridge Trail drops off the ridge to cross Cabin Creek and reach large Lake Augusta, at 6,854 feet. Set beneath Big Jim Mountain, this is a great place for camping. The stars at night are surreal. The trail meanders along the north side of the ridge for a while, making junctions with Palmer Creek Trail and Index Creek Trail. Another ascent delivers Lakes Edna and craggy Cape Horn. Chatter Creek Trail accesses the ridge here in a 10-mile trip. The trail stays at or above 7,000 feet for several miles before dropping to Mary and Margaret Lakes. Hikers have access to Frosty or Whitehorse Creek Trails, both backcountry exits.

User Groups: Hikers, leashed dogs, and horses. No mountain bikes are allowed. No wheelchair access.

Open Seasons: This trail is accessible July–October (the eastern end opens in late May).
Permits: A federal Northwest Forest Pass is required to park here.
Maps: For a map of Wenatchee National Forest, contact the Outdoor Recreation Information Center at the downtown Seattle REI. For topographic maps, ask Green Trails for No. 177, Chiwaukum Mountains, and No. 178, Leavenworth, or ask the USGS for Big Jim Mountain, Cashmere Mountain, and Leavenworth.
Directions: From Leavenworth, drive south on Icicle Creek Road (Forest Service Road 7600) 16 miles to Chatter Creek Campground and Trailhead, on the right.
Contact: Wenatchee National Forest, Leavenworth Ranger Station, 600 Sherbourne, Leavenworth, WA 98826, 509/548-6977.

150 EIGHTMILE AND TROUT LAKE LOOP

18.0 mi/–2 days

near Leavenworth in Alpine Lakes Wilderness of Wenatchee National Forest

Map 3.4, page 94

This is an outstanding loop through tall, rocky ridges and mountains in the Alpine Lakes Wilderness. Windy Pass connects Trout Lake to Eightmile Lake via miles of excellent high-country hiking, achieving lakes and views that will not soon be forgotten. Windy Pass stands at 7,300 feet, revealing much of the surrounding wilderness. Cashmere Mountain stands to the east, Mount Stuart to the south, and countless other peaks and ridges line the horizon. Trout and Eightmile Lakes are excellent destinations by themselves for day hikes or overnighters.

The loop requires a car drop or hitchhike from a friendly passerby. Starting from Eightmile Creek, the trail climbs moderately to Little Eightmile Lake and Eightmile Lake (3.3 miles), each dwarfed by the surrounding mountains. Camping along this route requires hikers to obtain a permit at the Leavenworth Ranger Station. The trail next reaches open parkland meadows and Lake Caroline (6.8 miles).

The prime moment of the hike comes at Windy Pass (7,200 feet), one of the best panoramic views on any trail in the region. Flowers and larches add color to the scene, each at their own times of the year. The trail descends three miles from Windy Pass to Trout Lake (12.3 miles), surrounded by trees and even more high ridges and peaks. From Trout Lake, the trail drops to Icicle Creek (18 miles).
User Groups: Hikers, leashed dogs, and horses (horses day use only). No mountain bikes are allowed. No wheelchair access.
Open Seasons: This trail is accessible July–early November.
Permits: A federal Northwest Forest Pass is required to park here. Overnight stays require backcountry camping permits ($3 per person per day), which are available at Leavenworth Ranger Station.
Maps: For a map of Wenatchee National Forest, contact the Outdoor Recreation Information Center at the downtown Seattle REI. For topographic maps, ask Green Trails for No. 177, Chiwaukum Mountains, or ask the USGS for Cashmere Mountain and Jack Ridge.
Directions: From Leavenworth, drive south on Icicle Creek Road (Forest Service Road 7600) 10 miles to Forest Service Road 7601 (Bridge Creek Campground). Turn left and drive 3 miles to the signed trailhead on the right.
Contact: Wenatchee National Forest, Leavenworth Ranger Station, 600 Sherbourne, Leavenworth, WA 98826, 509/548-6977.

151 COLCHUCK AND STUART LAKES

9.0 mi/6.0 hr

near Leavenworth in Alpine Lakes Wilderness of Wenatchee National Forest

Map 3.4, page 94

These are two favorite destinations for many Alpine Lakes hikers. Each lake is a beautiful turquoise and is surrounded by great subalpine forests. Massive, rocky mountains enclose the lakes, and typically awesome mountain views are encountered along the trails. The lakes are great to hike no matter what your timeframe for the trip, as they are challenging day hikes as well as excellent overnighters. The trails can be fairly busy during the summer with day hikers, but an overnight permitting system keeps campers to a reasonable number. Colchuck and Stuart Lakes are wonderful and wild mountain lakes.

The route to the two lakes follows cool and refreshing Mountaineer Creek before splitting (2.5 miles). The left fork climbs to Colchuck Lake, a steep grade of switchbacks. A cool waterfall eases the pain. Colchuck Lake sits within patches of forest, directly beneath the enormous walls of Dragontail and Colchuck Peaks. Their rocky cliffs drop straight to the water.

From the junction, Stuart Lake Trail makes an easy and gentle climb through meadows to Stuart Lake. The way is full of views of the surrounding ridges and peaks, with Mount Stuart towering 4,000 feet above the lake. Impressive stuff, indeed. At both lakes, camping is grand. Regardless of which lake you choose, it's difficult to go wrong once you've stepped foot onto this trail.

User Groups: Hikers only. No dogs, horses, or mountain bikes are allowed. No wheelchair access.

Open Seasons: This area is accessible July–October.

Permits: A federal Northwest Forest Pass is required to park here. Overnight stays require backcountry camping permits ($3 per person per day), which are available at Leavenworth Ranger Station.

Maps: For a map of Wenatchee National Forest, contact the Outdoor Recreation Information Center at the downtown Seattle REI. For topographic maps, ask Green Trails for No. 177, Chiwaukum Mountains, and No. 209, Mount Stuart, or ask the USGS for Cashmere and Enchantment Lakes.

Directions: From Leavenworth, drive south on Icicle Creek Road (Forest Service Road 7600) 5 miles to Snow Creek Trailhead on the left.

Contact: Wenatchee National Forest, Leavenworth Ranger Station, 600 Sherbourne, Leavenworth, WA 98826, 509/548-6977.

152 THE ENCHANTMENTS

16.8 mi/2–4 days 5 10

south of Leavenworth in Alpine Lakes Wilderness of Wenatchee National Forest

Map 3.4, page 94

Ahh, the Enchantments. Just the thought of this spectacular playground of high country makes the heart warm. Nowhere is quite like the Enchantments; this is the Shangri-la of Washington hiking. This series of high basins is filled with lakes of unsurpassed quality, with acres of subalpine parkland. Larches are everywhere, making late September a time not to miss. These high ridges have the craggiest rock you've seen. No trail description can ever do justice to the true beauty of the Enchantments.

The Enchantments are best reached via Snow Lakes. An excellent loop can be made by hiking down Aasgard Pass to Colchuck Lake. This requires a car-drop, however. So this description will stick to the Snow Lakes access. Because of large crowds of people visiting the area, folks planning on staying overnight, which is recommended, must obtain a permit from the Leavenworth Ranger Station.

Snow Lakes Trail crosses Icicle Creek and immediately climbs to Snow Lakes (6.5 miles). Fortunately, much of the route is in old-growth forest. Snow Lakes are a common first-night camp for those unable to make it all the way to the Lower Enchantments. Between Snow Lakes and the first basin, the trail makes a very steep, rugged climb. The trees gradually give way, and hikers finally find themselves within the Enchantments (8 miles).

The Enchantments are a series of basins filled with lakes. A good map is necessary, as a network of trails laces the area. Marmots frolic in the meadows and sun themselves on the boulders while wind rustles the needles of subalpine firs and larches. The basins are rimmed by a number of ridges jutting into the sky with their sharp, craggy peaks. The main

trail passes lake after lake on its way farther up and deeper into the basin. Glaciers overhang many of the upper lakes and are often heard cracking and breaking. The trail reaches Aasgard Pass (10.7 miles) before dropping steeply to Colchuck Lake, far below. Backpackers looking to spend a night or two in the Enchantments have numerous campsite options. Dozens of sights are located at nearly every lake. Just remember to pitch it on a hard, durable, and established spot.

User Groups: Hikers only. No dogs, horses, or mountain bikes are allowed. No wheelchair access.

Open Seasons: This trail is accessible mid-July–October.

Permits: A federal Northwest Forest Pass is required to park here. Overnight stays within the Enchantments require backcountry camping permits, which are awarded by lottery at the Leavenworth Ranger Station.

Maps: For a map of Wenatchee National Forest, contact the Outdoor Recreation Information Center at the downtown Seattle REI. For topographic maps, ask Green Trails for No. 209S, The Enchantments, or ask the USGS for Cashmere, Enchantment Lakes, and Blewett.

Directions: From Leavenworth, drive south on Icicle Creek Road (Forest Service Road 7600) 5 miles to Snow Creek Trailhead on the left.

Contact: Wenatchee National Forest, Leavenworth Ranger Station, 600 Sherbourne, Leavenworth, WA 98826, 509/548-6977.

153 ESMERELDA BASIN

4.5 mi/3.0 hr

2 9

northwest of Cle Elum in Wenatchee National Forest

Map 3.4, page 94

The lazy trail to Esmerelda Basin is perfectly suited for those seeking subalpine meadows and rocky peaks without the difficulty of a major climb. Esmerelda Basin is filled with meadows of wildflowers set among rock. Total elevation gain is 1,700 feet, making it easy to understand the popularity of the trail. From the basin, several attractive options await. Fortune Creek Pass offers distant views of mountains. Alternatively, the trail meanders on the ridgeline to find small Lake Ann, set on the barren slopes of Ingalls Peak, an outstanding destination.

Esmerelda Basin Trail begins at a lofty elevation of 4,300 feet, providing an easy journey to a grand landscape. The route pleases immediately and consistently, passing back and forth between subalpine forests and open meadows. The rocky Esmerelda Peaks line the route to the south. Esmerelda Basin is about two miles from the trailhead. At this junction, head left to climb to Fortune Creek Pass, where the views become sublime. Turn right at the junction for another adventure, a trail riding the crest toward Fortune Peak and Lake Ann. These are highly recommended as extended day hikes.

User Groups: Hikers, leashed dogs, and horses. No mountain bikes are allowed. No wheelchair access.

Open Seasons: This trail is accessible July–October.

Permits: A federal Northwest Forest Pass is required to park here.

Maps: For a map of Wenatchee National Forest, contact the Outdoor Recreation Information Center at the downtown Seattle REI. For topographic maps, ask Green Trails for No. 209, Mount Stuart, or ask the USGS for Mount Stuart.

Directions: From Seattle, drive east on I-90 to Exit 86. Turn left on Highway 970 and drive 7 miles to Teanaway River Road. Turn left and drive 13 miles to Forest Service Road 9737. Drive 10 miles to the trailhead at road's end.

Contact: Wenatchee National Forest, Cle Elum Ranger Station, 803 West 2nd Street, Cle Elum, WA 98922, 509/852-1100.

154 LONGS PASS AND LAKE INGALLS

6.0–10.8 mi/3.5–6.0 hr

3 9

northwest of Cle Elum in Wenatchee National Forest

Map 3.4, page 94

Longs Pass and Lake Ingalls are two of the

Cle Elum area's best destinations. Larches are ablaze in the fall while amazing views of Mount Stuart linger year-round. The high elevation trailhead makes it easy to achieve the best of the eastern Cascades. Open subalpine forests provide constant views of surrounding peaks, valleys, and forests on a steady climb to Longs Pass and Lake Ingalls. From Longs Pass, the view of Mount Stuart is unbeatable, with the massive mountain staring directly at hikers from across Ingalls Creek. Lake Ingalls is bound by glacially scraped granite and patches of meadows. Day hikes as good as this are hard to come by so easily.

The route starts high, at 4,400 feet, on Esmerelda Basin Trail. At the first junction (.4 mile), veer right for Ingalls Way Trail. Two miles of switchbacks end at another junction; left for Lake Ingalls, right for Longs Pass. Both trails are moderately steep and exposed, so bring plenty of water. Open meadows are scattered with larches brightening the slopes in the fall. Longs Pass (3 miles) has the Cascades' best view of Stuart, set among superb meadows with larches to boot. Ingalls Lake (5.4 miles) rests directly beneath its own craggy mountain, Ingalls Peak. While they get quite dry and scorching hot in the dead of summer, both of these trails are wonderful early summer and fall trips.

User Groups: Hikers, leashed dogs, and horses. No mountain bikes are allowed. No wheelchair access.

Open Seasons: This trail is accessible July–October.

Permits: A federal Northwest Forest Pass is required to park here.

Maps: For a map of Wenatchee National Forest, contact the Outdoor Recreation Information Center at the downtown Seattle REI. For topographic maps, ask Green Trails for No. 209, Mount Stuart, or ask the USGS for Mount Stuart.

Directions: From Seattle, drive east on I-90 to Exit 86. Turn left on Highway 970 and drive 7 miles to Teanaway River Road. Turn left and drive 13 miles to Forest Service Road 9737. Drive 10 miles to the trailhead at road's end.

Contact: Wenatchee National Forest, Cle Elum Ranger Station, 803 West 2nd Street, Cle Elum, WA 98922, 509/852-1100.

155 BEVERLY TURNPIKE

6.4 mi/3.5 hr

northeast of Cle Elum in Wenatchee National Forest

Map 3.4, page 94

Connecting the Teanaway River to Ingalls Creek, Beverly and Turnpike Trails meet in the most beautiful of circumstances. At 5,800 feet, Beverly-Turnpike Pass is endowed with excellent views of mountain ridges and peaks, particularly the nearby and impressive Mount Stuart. Like most high-country routes, this trail passes through miles of subalpine meadows and revels in swaths of wildflowers. The route drops to the Ingalls Creek Trail, making for a good loop if a car-drop can be arranged.

Beverly Turnpike Trail climbs steadily from Teanaway River Valley up along Beverly Creek. It's not very impressive at first, as it travels an old road and passes through a clear-cut. As the trail progresses, however, unspoiled forests and meadows enter the scene. Rocky ridges line the way, their slopes covered in meadows. A trail cuts off to the right to Fourth Creek, also an access to Ingalls Creek. Stay left and follow the main trail to the pass. The best views are achieved here, where Mount Stuart appears to the north. A steep side trip up to Iron Peak, just before the pass, is well recommended for panoramic views. The route then follows Turnpike Creek through old-growth forest to Ingalls Creek and a necessary ford to reach that trail.

User Groups: Hikers, leashed dogs, and horses. No mountain bikes are allowed. No wheelchair access.

Open Seasons: This trail is accessible July–October.

Permits: A federal Northwest Forest Pass is required to park here.

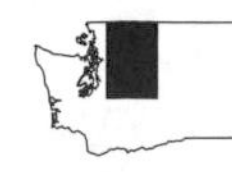

The Enchantments, Washington's best and most revered destination

Maps: For a map of Wenatchee National Forest, contact the Outdoor Recreation Information Center at the downtown Seattle REI. For topographic maps, ask Green Trails for No. 209, Mount Stuart, or ask the USGS for Red Top Mountain, Enchantment Lakes, and Mount Stuart.

Directions: From Seattle, drive east on I-90 to Exit 86. Turn left on Highway 970 and drive 7 miles to Teanaway River Road. Turn left and drive 13 miles to Forest Service Road 9737. Drive 3 miles to Forest Service Road 112. Turn right and drive 1.5 miles to the trailhead at road's end.

Contact: Wenatchee National Forest, Cle Elum Ranger Station, 803 West 2nd Street, Cle Elum, WA 98922, 509/852-1100.

156 INGALLS CREEK

32.0 mi/3–4 days

southeast of Leavenworth in Alpine Lakes Wilderness of Wenatchee National Forest

Map 3.4, page 94

The longest river hike in the Alpine Lakes Wilderness, this valley route leads to unbelievably beautiful country. Set below massive Mount Stuart and numerous other craggy peaks and mountains, Ingalls Creek makes an impressive trek through eastside forest to superb subalpine meadows. An early summer hike reveals untold treasures in melting snowfields and natural bouquets of wildflowers. Few treks left in the Alpine Lakes area can boast of such remoteness and wildness. That makes this a very special place to those who visit it.

Ingalls Creek Trail rarely strays far from the banks of Ingalls Creek. The route is mostly old-growth ponderosa pines and Douglas firs. Campsites are numerous along the trail, which keeps an easy grade for most of its path.

At Porcupine Creek (10 miles), the trail begins climbing, emerging from the forest into excellent subalpine parkland. Surrounding ridges and peaks break out into view. The Wenatchee Mountains, while quite big, pale in comparison to Mount Stuart directly to the north. Ingalls Lake is a favorite site, set among larches on granite slabs. While camping is not allowed at the lake, plentiful campsites are to be found nearby. The trail ends by climbing to Stuart Pass at 6,400 feet.

User Groups: Hikers, leashed dogs, and horses. No mountain bikes are allowed. No wheelchair access.

Open Seasons: This trail is accessible June–November.

Permits: A federal Northwest Forest Pass is required to park here.
Maps: For a map of Wenatchee National Forest, contact the Outdoor Recreation Information Center at the downtown Seattle REI. For topographic maps, ask Green Trails for No. 209, Mount Stuart, and No. 210, Liberty, or ask the USGS for Mount Stuart, Enchantment Lakes, and Blewett.
Directions: From Seattle, drive east on I-90 to Highway 970 (Exit 86). Drive north to U.S. 97. Drive north to Ingalls Creek Road, 12 miles north of Blewett Pass. Turn left and drive 1 mile to the trailhead at road's end.
Contact: Wenatchee National Forest, Leavenworth Ranger Station, 600 Sherbourne, Leavenworth, WA 98826, 509/548-6977.

157 YELLOW HILL AND ELBOW PEAK

6.0–10.0 mi/4.0–6.0 hr 3 9

northeast of Cle Elum in Wenatchee National Forest

Map 3.4, page 94

Yellow Hill and Elbow Peak are all about views. Situated in the Teanaway drainage, these two mountaintops offer wide vistas of the surrounding Cascades. The route itself is not anything special, being mainly composed of roads and dirt tracks fit for bikes. Nothing keeps hikers from enjoying these trails other than the steep climbs, but that's what trails offering breathtaking views are all about.

Yellow Hill Trail follows a logging road high above the Teanaway Valleys. Second-growth forests offer shade on this dry trail as it switchbacks up a ridge. The trees gradually thin out along the path, giving hikers great views of neighboring ridges and peaks. The trail makes it to Yellow Hill at three miles and 5,527 feet elevation. Mount Stuart appears surprisingly close while Mount Rainier stands to the south. Elbow Peak is another two miles of hiking along a high ridge, definitely a pleasant way to spend a few hours. The views are not much different from those at Yellow Hill, but people are much more scarce. From their lofty perches, both peaks provide a proper outlook on the numerous ridges and valleys of the Teanaway Valleys.

User Groups: Hikers, leashed dogs, horses, mountain bikes, and motorcycles. No wheelchair access.
Open Seasons: This trail is accessible mid-June–October.
Permits: A federal Northwest Forest Pass is required to park here.
Maps: For a map of Wenatchee National Forest, contact the Outdoor Recreation Information Center at the downtown Seattle REI. For topographic maps, ask Green Trails for No. 208, Kachess Lake, and No. 209, Mount Stuart, or ask the USGS for Cle Elum Lake, Teanaway Butte, and Davis Peak.
Directions: From Seattle, drive east on I-90 to Exit 86. Turn left on Highway 970 and drive 7 miles to Teanaway River Road. Turn left and drive 7 miles to West Fork Teanaway Road. Turn left and drive 1 mile to Middle Fork Teanaway Road. Turn right and drive 6 miles to the signed trailhead on the right.
Contact: Wenatchee National Forest, Cle Elum Ranger Station, 803 West 2nd Street, Cle Elum, WA 98922, 509/852-1100.

Chapter 4

© SCOTT LEONARD

Northeast Washington

Northeast Washington

It's easy to find folks who are experts on hiking in the Alpine Lakes or Glacier Peak Wildernesses. The same goes for finding authoritative voices on North Cascades National Park or even the desolate Pasayten Wilderness. But hikers with an intricate knowledge of northeastern Washington are few and far between. Sure, westsiders have plenty to keep them occupied with the Cascades and Olympic Mountains. But never visiting or exploring Colville National Forest is a missed opportunity.

Locals from places like Republic, Colville, or Metaline Falls don't mind this lack of attention because that means they have nearly two million acres of national forest practically to themselves. The likelihood of running into a crowd out here is pretty much zilch. In fact, except for hunting season, you're unlikely to see other folks in the backcountry.

The wild Kettle and Selkirk Ranges are two major subregions of northeast Washington, and they are crisscrossed by great trails. Hit the trail in the Kettle Range and don't be surprised by elk, deer, or even moose. When hiking in the Selkirks, be on the lookout for caribou, gray wolves, or even grizzlies. Transecting northeast Washington, Highway 20 from Anacortes to Newport is easily the state's most scenic highway. Expect to come across places like Republic, Kettle Falls, Colville, and Metaline Falls. Never heard of them? Most folks haven't.

The Kettle Mountains are located east of the Cascades proper but west of the mighty Columbia River rise. The range runs south to north, and most peaks top 7,000 feet of elevation. Many of the trails networking the mountains start low and work their way up to the main travelway, the Kettle Crest Trail, which runs along the length of the ridge. The Columbia Mountain Trail offers a great and quick experience of the Kettles. With a trailhead at Sherman Pass right on Highway 20, the trail climbs quickly to the peak of Columbia Mountain, giving up views for miles. The southwest side of the range was burned severely in 1988, but the Edds Mountain and Barnaby Butte Trails are still great trails despite the charred forest lining their routes.

Great trails are found in the low country, as well. Outside of Republic (another great small town, complete with a co-op grocery) are Fish and Swan Lakes. In addition to great fishing and a good car campground, trails loop each lake. On the east side of the Kettle Range is Hoodoo Canyon, a short hike through a narrow gorge, complemented by a lake and good campground.

Farther east (much farther east) lie the Selkirk Mountains. Many of the peaks in the Selkirks, like Grassy Top, Thunder Mountain, and Shedroof Mountain, fall in the 6,000- to 7,000-foot range. The most popular adventures in this area occur at Sullivan Lake, a large, glacially cut lake bordered by old forests. A pair of great campgrounds makes this a regular summer destination for families and boaters.

Tucked away into Washington's borders with Canada and Idaho, the Salmo-Priest Wilderness protects 40,000 acres of the Colville National Forest. The wilderness is shaped like a horseshoe and protects the high ridges framing Sullivan Creek. Several great trails explore the peaks and meadows of the Salmo-Priest. Crowell Ridge, Grassy Top, and Shedroof Divide are all fine trails.

In short, if you don't know the Selkirks or the Kettles, you should. It's well worth the trip from west of the Cascades to see how the other half plays.

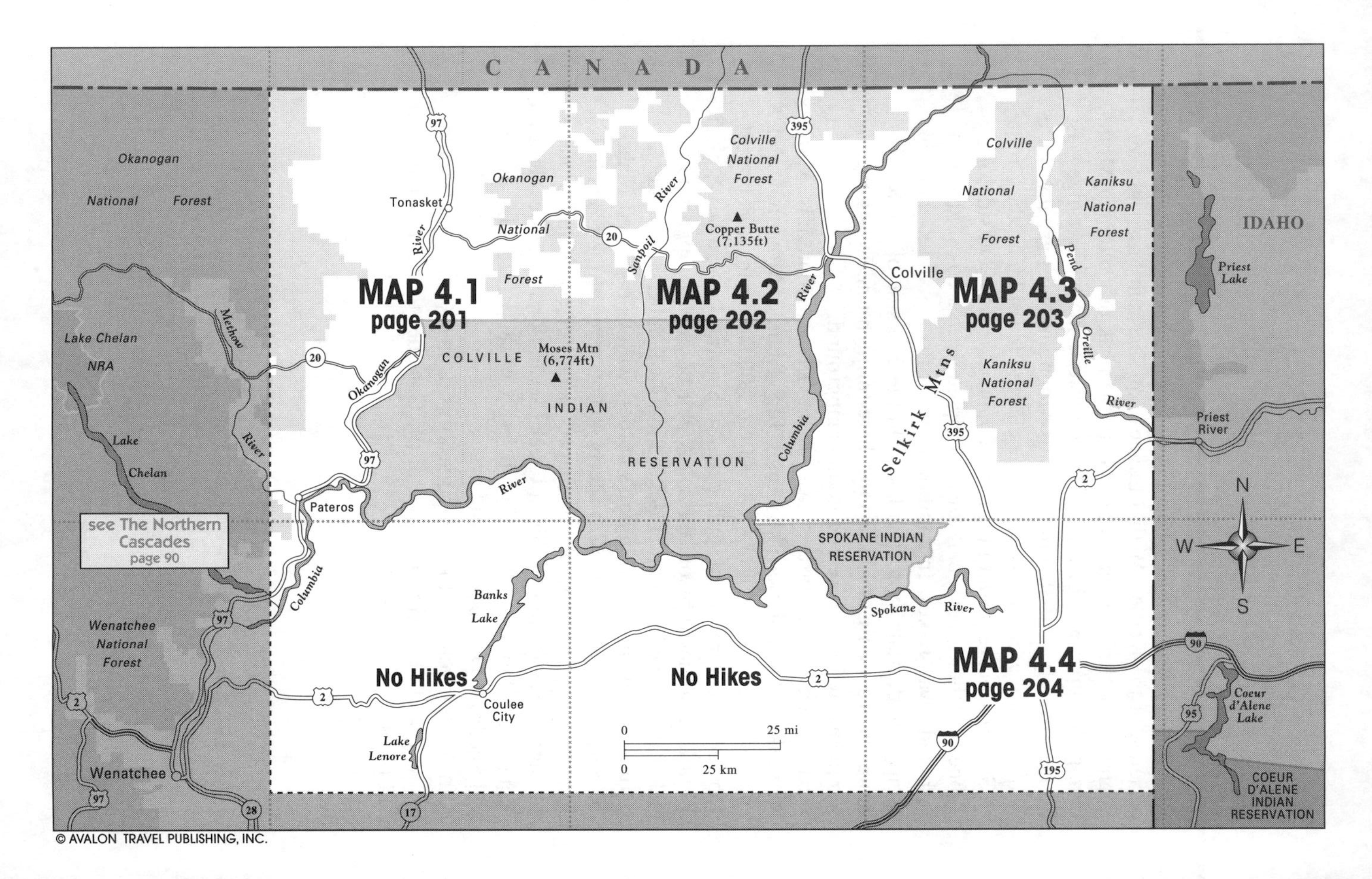

CANADA
Okanogan National Forest
Lake Chelan NRA
Methow River
Lake Chelan
see The Northern Cascades page 90
Wenatchee National Forest
Wenatchee
Tonasket
River
Okanogan National Forest
MAP 4.1
page 201
Okanogan
Pateros
Columbia
COLVILLE INDIAN RESERVATION
Moses Mtn (6,774ft)
River
Banks Lake
No Hikes
Coulee City
Lake Lenore
Sanpoil River
Colville National Forest
Copper Butte (7,135ft)
MAP 4.2
page 202
River
Columbia
No Hikes
25 mi
25 km
0
0
Colville
Colville National Forest
MAP 4.3
page 203
Kaniksu National Forest
Selkirk Mtns
Kaniksu National Forest
Pend Oreille River
SPOKANE INDIAN RESERVATION
Spokane River
MAP 4.4
page 204
IDAHO
Priest Lake
Priest River
N
W
E
S
Coeur d'Alene Lake
COEUR D'ALENE INDIAN RESERVATION

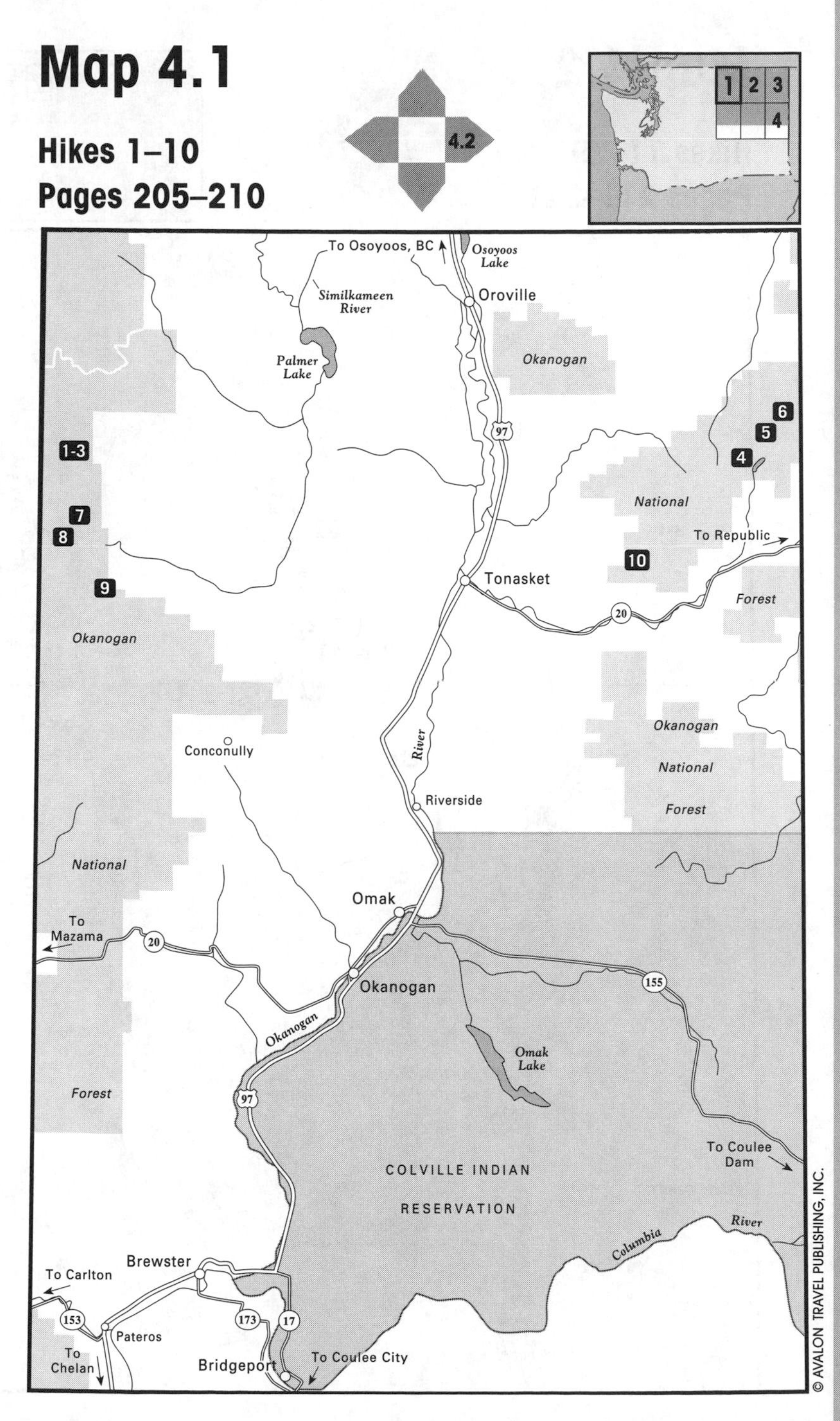
Map 4.1
Hikes 1–10
Pages 205–210
4.2
1
2
3
4
To Osoyoos, BC
Osoyoos Lake
Oroville
Similkameen River
Palmer Lake
Okanogan
97
1-3
7
8
9
6
5
4
National
To Republic
10
Tonasket
20
Forest
Okanogan
Conconully
River
Okanogan
National
Forest
Riverside
National
Omak
To Mazama
20
Okanogan
155
Okanogan
Omak Lake
97
Forest
To Coulee Dam
COLVILLE INDIAN
RESERVATION
River
Columbia
Brewster
To Carlton
153
Pateros
173
17
To Chelan
Bridgeport
To Coulee City
© AVALON TRAVEL PUBLISHING, INC.

Map 4.2

Hikes 11–29
Pages 211–221

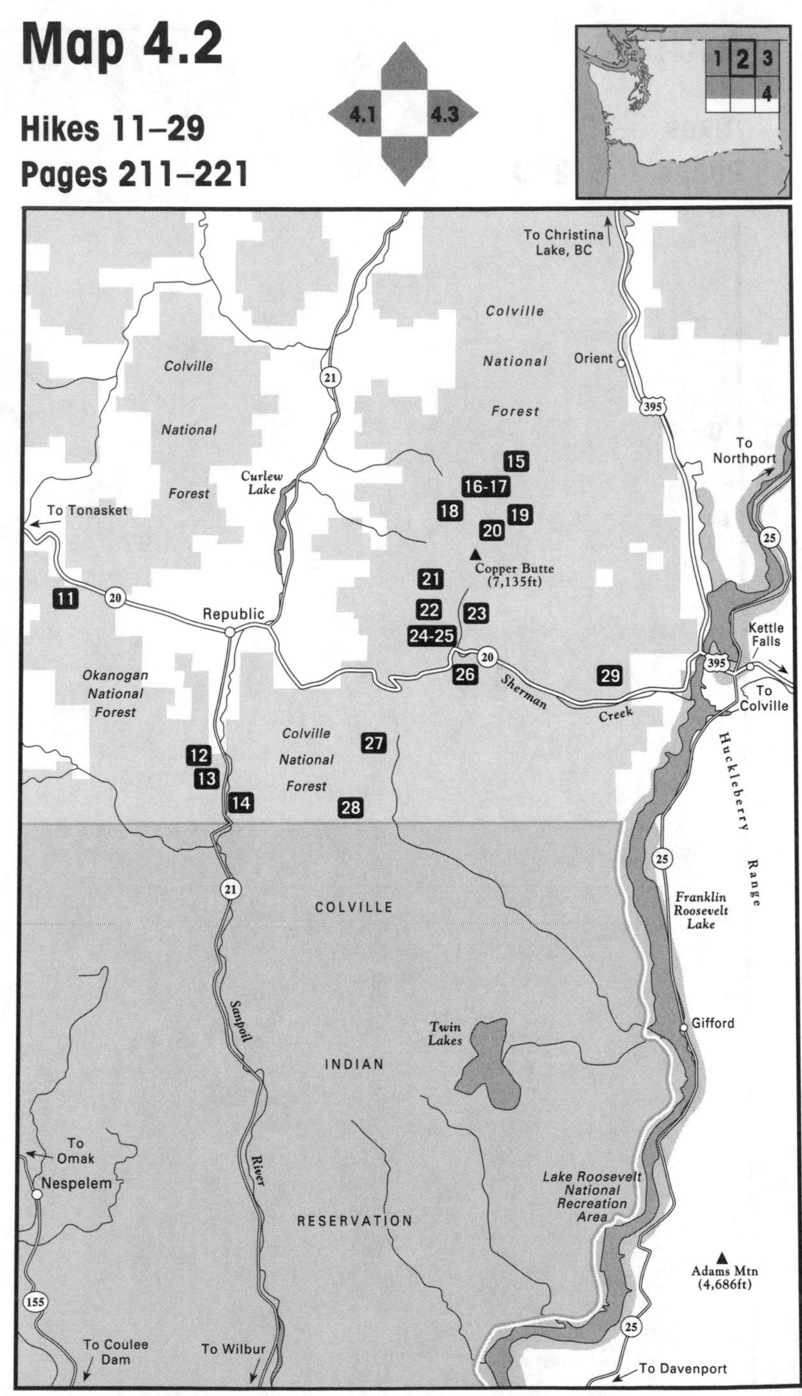

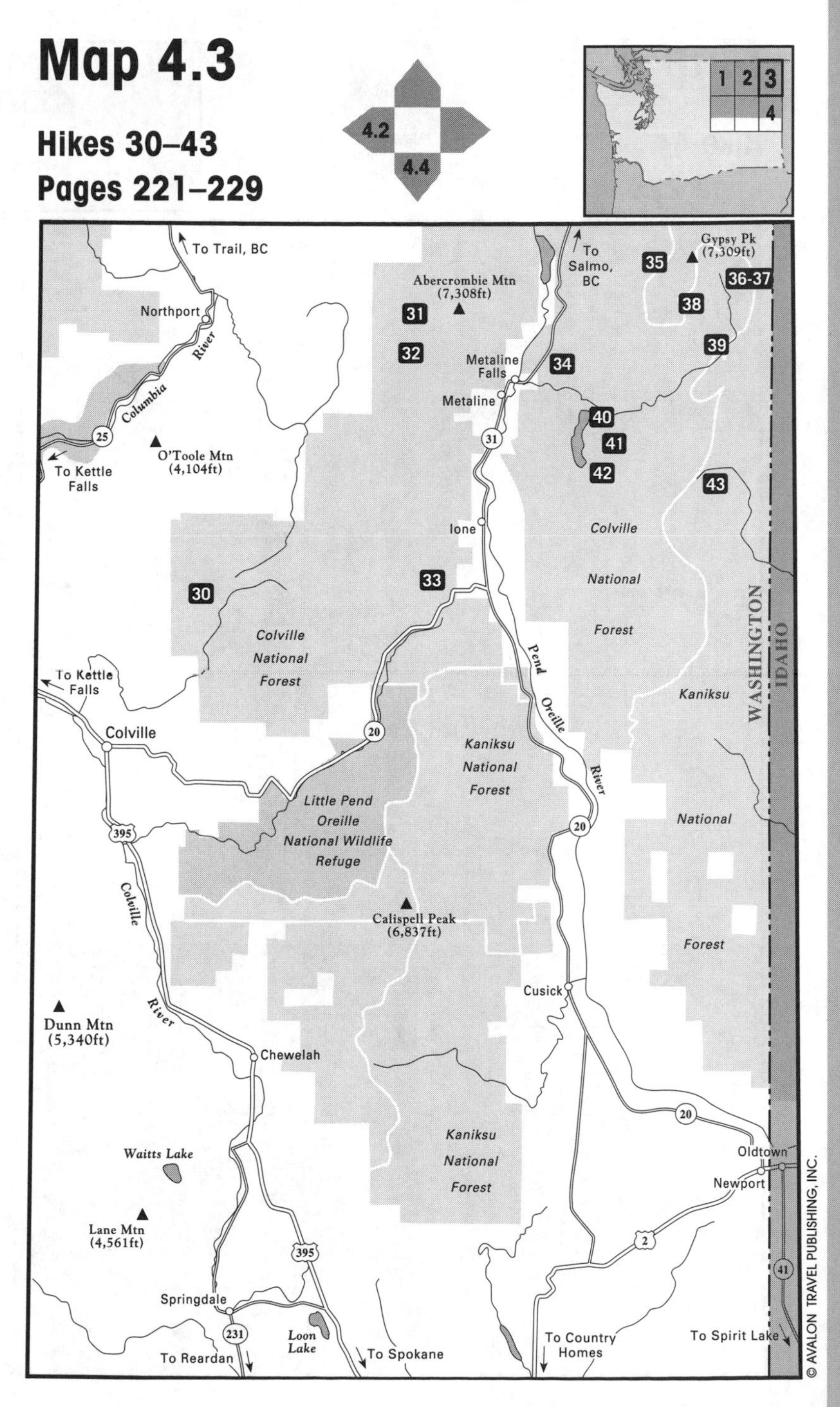
Map 4.3
Hikes 30–43
Pages 221–229
4.2
4.4
1
2
3
4
To Trail, BC
To Salmo, BC
Gypsy Pk (7,309ft)
35
36-37
Abercrombie Mtn (7,308ft)
31
38
Northport
32
39
Metaline Falls
34
Metaline
40
Columbia River
25
O'Toole Mtn (4,104ft)
31
41
To Kettle Falls
42
43
Ione
Colville National Forest
33
30
Colville National Forest
Pend Oreille River
WASHINGTON
IDAHO
To Kettle Falls
Kaniksu
Colville
20
Kaniksu National Forest
Little Pend Oreille National Wildlife Refuge
National
395
20
Colville River
Calispell Peak (6,837ft)
Forest
Cusick
Dunn Mtn (5,340ft)
Chewelah
20
Kaniksu National Forest
Waitts Lake
Oldtown
Newport
Lane Mtn (4,561ft)
2
395
41
Springdale
231
Loon Lake
To Reardan
To Spokane
To Country Homes
To Spirit Lake
© AVALON TRAVEL PUBLISHING, INC.

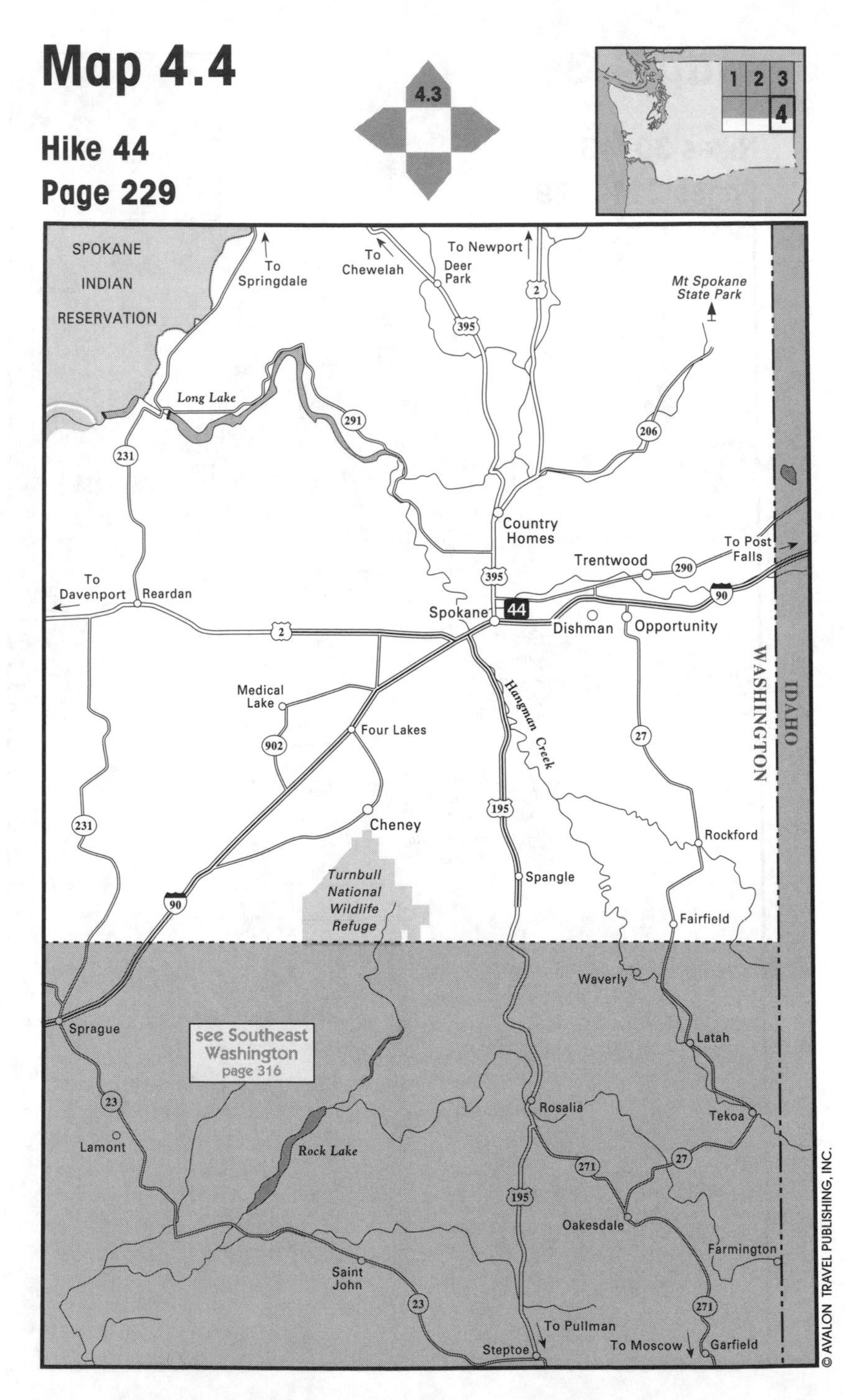

Map 4.4
Hike 44
Page 229
4.3
1
2
3
4
SPOKANE
INDIAN
RESERVATION
To Springdale
To Chewelah
Deer Park
To Newport
Mt Spokane State Park
Long Lake
291
395
2
206
231
Country Homes
Trentwood
290
To Post Falls
To Davenport
Reardan
Spokane
44
Dishman
Opportunity
90
2
Medical Lake
Four Lakes
902
Hangman Creek
27
WASHINGTON
IDAHO
231
Cheney
195
Rockford
Turnbull National Wildlife Refuge
Spangle
Fairfield
90
Waverly
Sprague
see Southeast Washington page 316
Latah
23
Rosalia
Tekoa
Lamont
Rock Lake
27
271
195
Oakesdale
Farmington
Saint John
23
271
To Pullman
Steptoe
To Moscow
Garfield
© AVALON TRAVEL PUBLISHING, INC.

1 BOUNDARY TRAIL

98.0 mi/9–10 days

near the Canadian border in Pasayten Wilderness of Okanogan National Forest

Map 4.1, page 201

One of Washington's granddaddy trails, Boundary Trail runs across the entirety of America's largest wilderness, the Pasayten. The route follows the Canadian border, hence the name. It is an extremely high route, much of it occurring at 6,000 feet or more. The area is completely wild and one of the few places in the lower 48 where grizzly bears and gray wolves still roam. The route needn't be hiked end to end; there are many great trips accessing just a part of the trail. At least eight major trails provide access for small loops.

The Boundary Trail begins at Castle Pass on Pacific Crest Trail. Start at Hart's Pass and hike north 18 miles to Castle Pass and "Ol' 533," the trail's number. From here, it heads east 73 miles to Iron Gate Trailhead, in the middle of nowhere. Along the way it climbs dozens of high passes and ridges, crosses the Pasayten River, and basks in endless views of mountains. The summer is a prime time to visit, when wildflowers are in bloom, as is the fall, when larches do their thing. Established camps are littered along the route, and off-trail camping is OK as long as it's low impact. Also, if you hike this route without the maps, you likely won't come back. Good luck.

User Groups: Hikers, leashed dogs, and horses. No mountain bikes are allowed. No wheelchair access.

Open Seasons: This trail is accessible July–September.

Permits: A federal Northwest Forest Pass is required to park here. A free wilderness permit is also required to hike here and is available at the trailhead.

Maps: For a map of Okanogan National Forest, contact the Outdoor Recreation Information Center at the downtown Seattle REI. For topographic maps, ask Green Trails for No. 17, Jack Mountain, No. 18, Pasayten Peak, No. 19, Billy Goat Mountain, No. 20, Coleman Peak, and No. 21, Horseshoe Basin, or ask the USGS for Horseshoe Basin, Bauerman Ridge, Remmel Mountain, and Ashnola Pass.

Directions: Harts Pass: From Winthrop, drive west 17 miles on Highway 20 to Mazama. Turn right (north) onto Mazama Road and drive .2 mile to Hart's Pass Road (County Road 9140/Forest Service Road 5400). Turn left and drive to Rattlesnake Trailhead, .3 mile beyond River Bend Campground.

Iron Gate: From Tonasket, drive north on Tonasket–Oroville Westside Road to Loomis-Oroville Road. Turn left and drive through Enterprise and Loomis to Sinlahekin Valley Road (County Road 9425). Turn right and drive 2 miles to Touts Coulee Road (Forest Service Road 39). Turn left and drive 14 miles to Iron Gate Road. Turn right and drive 5 miles to the trailhead at road's end.

Contact: Okanogan National Forest, Methow Valley Ranger District, 24 West Chewuch Road, Winthrop, WA 98862, 509/996-4003.

2 HORSESHOE BASIN (PASAYTEN)

13.0 mi/2–4 days

north of Winthrop in Pasayten Wilderness of Okanogan National Forest

Map 4.1, page 201

This is not the well-known Horseshoe Basin trail at the head of the Stehekin River. Instead, this is a much more remote and hence lesser-known Horseshoe Basin deep within the Pasayten Wilderness. The terrain, high rolling hills covered in tundralike meadows, is unlike that anywhere else in Washington. Many of the peaks top out over 8,000 feet, an impressive height. One of the best trails the Pasayten has to offer, Horseshoe Basin is appropriate for backpackers with moderate experience.

Starting at Iron Gate Trailhead, follow Boundary Trail as it climbs through scenic forest and meadow to Sunny Pass (5.2 miles). Boundary

Trail turns north and finds expansive Horseshoe Pass and Basin (6.7 miles). Incredible camps are found at Sunny Pass, Horseshoe Pass, Louden Lake, and Smith Lake. The ecosystem is delicate at this elevation and necessitates strict Leave-No-Trace camping.

The basin is ripe for exploration. Each of the many peaks is an easy walk, little more than 1,000 feet above the high pass. Armstrong Mountain lines the Canadian border while Arnold Peak and Horseshoe Mountain are worthy American peaks. Any side trip is highly recommended. Although the snowpack is gone by Memorial Day, be prepared for adverse weather, even a snowstorm, well into summer.

User Groups: Hikers, leashed dogs, and horses. No mountain bikes are allowed. No wheelchair access.

Open Seasons: This trail is accessible mid-May–October.

Permits: A federal Northwest Forest Pass is required to park here. A free wilderness permit is also required to hike here and is available at the trailhead.

Maps: For a map of Okanogan National Forest, contact the Outdoor Recreation Information Center at the downtown Seattle REI. For topographic maps, ask Green Trails for No. 21, Horseshoe Basin, or ask the USGS for Horseshoe Basin.

Directions: From Tonasket, drive north on Tonasket–Oroville Westside Road to Loomis-Oroville Road. Turn left and drive through Enterprise and Loomis to Sinlahekin Valley Road (County Road 9425). Turn right and drive 2 miles to Touts Coulee Road (Forest Service Road 39). Turn left and drive 14 miles to Iron Gate Road. Turn right and drive 5 miles to the trailhead at road's end.

Contact: Okanogan National Forest, Methow Valley Ranger District, 24 West Chewuch Road, Winthrop, WA 98862, 509/996-4003.

3 WINDY PEAK

12.8 mi/6.5 hr

north of Winthrop in Pasayten Wilderness of Okanogan National Forest

Map 4.1, page 201

The tallest point in the area, Windy Peak makes an attractive summit on clear days. There are no fewer than four different routes to the peak, but this wilderness trail up Windy Creek is the shortest and best. Passing through old-growth forests, it climbs to the vast open meadows along the flanks of Windy Peak. Wildflowers, views, and indeed a little wind is about all you'll find at 8,334 feet. This is one of Washington's most expansive views.

From Iron Gate Trailhead, begin on Boundary Trail but turn left on Clutch Creek Trail (.7 mile). Climbing the ridge through forests of fir and pine, the route turns right on Windy Peak Trail (4.4 miles). The trail climbs straight up, but it's a meadow walk from here on to the top. At the summit (6.4 miles), much of the Pasayten is laid bare at your feet, spread out in front of the Cascades Mountains. Don't forget extra water and food on this dry, strenuous trip.

User Groups: Hikers, leashed dogs, and horses. No mountain bikes are allowed. No wheelchair access.

Open Seasons: This trail is accessible July–October.

Permits: A federal Northwest Forest Pass is required to park here. A free wilderness permit is also required to hike here and is available at the trailhead.

Maps: For a map of Okanogan National Forest, contact the Outdoor Recreation Information Center at the downtown Seattle REI. For topographic maps, ask Green Trails for No. 21, Horseshoe Basin, or ask the USGS for Horseshoe Basin.

Directions: From Tonasket, drive north on Tonasket–Oroville Westside Road to Loomis-Oroville Road. Turn left and drive through Enterprise and Loomis to Sinlahekin Valley Road (County Road 9425). Turn right and drive 2

miles to Touts Coulee Road (Forest Service Road 39). Turn left and drive 20 miles to the trailhead at Long Swamp Campground.
Contact: Okanogan National Forest, Methow Valley Ranger District, 24 West Chewuch Road, Winthrop, WA 98862, 509/996-4003.

4 SOUTH SIDE BONAPARTE
11.2 mi/6.0 hrs 3 9

northwest of Tonasket in Okanogan National Forest

Map 4.1, page 201

Mount Bonaparte registers as one of eastern Washington's tallest summits, standing tall at 7,257 feet. Being that the peak is in the north-central part of the state, you're assured of spectacular views of distant mountains in every direction. South Side Trail is the shortest and easiest way to reach the summit out of four possible options. While much of the route is forested, the upper parts of the trail are fairly open, cloaked in meadows and steep slopes. The summit of Mount Bonaparte is rounded like a large dome, meaning trees obscure most views until one climbs the 90-year-old fire lookout stationed atop the mountain. That the lookout still stands is a testament to its hardy construction in 1914. The snow-capped North Cascades are readily visible to the west while the Kettle River Range stands to the east. Rarely seen mountains of Canada stand to the north.
User Groups: Hikers, leashed dogs, and horses. No mountain bikes are allowed. No wheelchair access.
Open Seasons: This trail is accessible May–November.
Permits: Permits are not required. Parking and access are free.
Maps: For a map of Okanogan National Forest, contact the Outdoor Recreation Information Center at the downtown Seattle REI. For a topographic map, ask the USGS for Mount Bonaparte.
Directions: From Tonasket, drive east 20 miles on Highway 20 to County Road 4953. Turn left (north) and drive 9 miles to Forest Service Road 33. Turn left and drive 7 miles to Forest Service Road 33-100. Turn left and drive 3.5 miles to the trailhead.
Contact: Okanogan National Forest, Tonasket Ranger Station, 1 West Winesap, Tonasket, WA 98855, 509/486-2186.

5 STRAWBERRY MOUNTAIN
3.0 mi/1.5 hrs 2 9

northwest of Tonasket in Okanogan National Forest

Map 4.1, page 201

While the summit of big brother Mount Bonaparte towers over little brother Strawberry Mountain, the latter boasts the easier and more enjoyable hike. Strawberry Trail climbs from a great campground on Lost Lake up through some magnificent old-growth forest. Enormous ponderosa pines, Douglas firs, and western larches highlight the trip to Strawberry Mountain's summit. These trees have survived through the centuries thanks to strong natural defenses against fire (thick bark, wide spacing). The trail climbs the north side of the mountain steadily but gently all the way to the top. Although the summit is more than 2,500 feet below the peak of Mount Bonaparte, the forest breaks open to reveal great views of Lost and Bonaparte Lakes below. Strawberry Trail is a definite must-hike trail for anyone camping at Lost Lake or in the general area. And proving that life is truly sweet, you can expect to find strawberries (small ones) along the route.
User Groups: Hikers, leashed dogs, and horses. No mountain bikes are allowed. No wheelchair access.
Open Seasons: This trail is accessible May–November.
Permits: Permits are not required. Parking and access are free.
Maps: For a map of Okanogan National Forest, contact the Outdoor Recreation Information Center at the downtown Seattle REI. For a topographic map, ask the USGS for Mount Bonaparte.
Directions: From Tonasket, drive east 20 miles

on Highway 20 to Bonaparte Lake Road (County Road 4953). Turn left (north) and drive 9 miles to Forest Service Road 33. Turn left and drive 5.5 miles to Lost Lake Campground. The trailhead is 50 yards down the small side road (Forest Service Road 33-050) immediately before the campground (but park in the campground's day-use area).
Contact: Okanogan National Forest, Tonasket Ranger Station, 1 West Winesap, Tonasket, WA 98855, 509/486-2186.

6 BIG TREE BOTANICAL LOOP

0.7 mi/0.5 hrs 1 9

northwest of Tonasket in Okanogan National Forest

Map 4.1, page 201

Big trees indeed. This easy-to-navigate trail shows that the east side of the Cascades can grow enormous evergreens much like the west side does. The short loop trail, with a wide, flat, and graveled path for wheelchair access, walks through an old-growth forest of ponderosa pine, Douglas fir, Englemann spruce, and western larch. Many of the trees are upward of 300 years old. Although the forest underwent selective logging about 40 years ago (to remove trees doomed to die by bark beetles), the forest is a great example of eastern climax forests. The trees are widely spaced with a sparse undergrowth of grasses and small shrubs. These understory plants are meant to burn regularly, at low intensities. The fire burns quickly with little chance to ignite the large trees. At the end of the loop is the highlight of the hike, where two gigantic western larches grow in a small depression. These two granddaddy tamaracks are more than 900 years old, on par with some of the biggest trees in the Olympics. Here's to another 900 years!
User Groups: Hikers and leashed dogs. No horses or mountain bikes are allowed. This trail is wheelchair accessible.
Open Seasons: This trail is accessible year-round.
Permits: Permits are not required. Parking and access are free.
Maps: For a map of Okanogan National Forest, contact the Outdoor Recreation Information Center at the downtown Seattle REI. For a topographic map, ask the USGS for Mount Bonaparte.
Directions: From Tonasket, drive east on Highway 20 to Bonaparte Lake Road (County Road 4953). Turn left (north) and drive 9 miles to Forest Service Road 33. Turn left and drive 3.5 miles to the well-signed trailhead and parking area on the right side of the road.
Contact: Okanogan National Forest, Tonasket Ranger Station, 1 West Winesap, Tonasket, WA 98855, 509/486-2186.

7 TIFFANY MOUNTAIN

8.2 mi/4.5 hr

east of Winthrop in Okanogan National Forest

Map 4.1, page 201

The roadless area surrounding Tiffany Mountain is distinct from the rest of the North Cascades. High, rolling hills dominate the horizons, while wetlands and meadows populate many of the valleys. Open forests of fir and pine create beautiful parkland on the slopes of mountains, while their summits are covered in wildflowers, grasses, and mosses. It's a more subtle beauty than the jagged peaks of the North Cascades. If you're here in July, expect a lot of green for such an easterly locale.

Tiffany Mountain is reachable via four routes, making a loop trip easy and promising. Pick or choose, but Tiffany Lake Trail is the best choice. This route passes timbered Tiffany Lake (an excellent base camp) before climbing to Whistler Pass. The four trails converge here and may be confusing, so bring a map and compass. A scramble to the top of Tiffany Mountain yields vistas extending for miles. Peer into the vast Pasayten Wilderness, then turn and survey much of the Cascade Range. A walk along flowered Freezeout Ridge is an easier but equally great side trip. The area is protected as a botanical reserve, so if camping here, stick to established camps and observe strict Leave-No-Trace principles.

User Groups: Hikers, leashed dogs, horses, and mountain bikes. No wheelchair access.

Open Seasons: This trail is accessible mid-June–September.

Permits: A federal Northwest Forest Pass is required to park here.

Maps: For a map of Okanogan National Forest, contact the Outdoor Recreation Information Center at the downtown Seattle REI. For topographic maps, ask Green Trails for No. 53, Tiffany Mountain, or ask the USGS for Tiffany Mountain.

Directions: From the town of Conconully, drive Okanogan County Road 2017 around the reservoir for three miles. Turn right onto Forest Service Road 37 and continue for 21 miles. After crossing Bernhardt Creek, turn right onto Forest Service Road 39 and drive 8 miles north to Tiffany Springs Campground and the trailhead.

Contact: Okanogan National Forest, Methow Valley Ranger District, 24 West Chewuch Road, Winthrop, WA 98862, 509/996-4003.

8 BERNHARDT MINE

5.0 mi/3.0 hr

northeast of Winthrop in Okanogan National Forest

Map 4.1, page 201

Mention the word "mine" to a hiker, and you're likely to get a nasty scowl in return. After all, who wants to toil along a trail just to check out a big hole? Well, Bernhardt Mine Trail is really much more than a field trip to an old mine. The trail passes several old, barely standing cabins along the way, testaments to the hardy living of the old settlers. And there's the mine itself, a tame model of extraction compared to modern practices, when bulldozers rip up entire hillsides and chemical solutions strip streams into lifelessness. Enjoy the mine, but keep hiking to Clark Peak, where you'll forget all about industry thanks to sweeping meadows of wildflowers that reveal distant mountain ranges.

The route to the mine is steep but only two miles. Pass through soggy wetlands and climb almost straight up to the miner's cabin and an accompanying mine. Hike a little higher to intersect North Summit Trail. This trail runs north to Tiffany Mountain and makes possible an 11-mile loop (hike Freezeout Ridge Trail to Forest Service Road 39 and walk the road two miles to your car). If you're looking for something shorter, just scramble to the top of Clark Peak. Expansive views and grassy meadows will be your reward.

User Groups: Hikers, leashed dogs, horses, and mountain bikes. No wheelchair access.

Open Seasons: This trail is accessible July–mid-October.

Permits: A federal Northwest Forest Pass is required to park here.

Maps: For a map of Okanogan National Forest, contact the Outdoor Recreation Information Center at the downtown Seattle REI. For topographic maps, ask Green Trails for No. 53, Tiffany Mountain, or ask the USGS for Tiffany Mountain.

Directions: From the town of Conconully, drive Okanogan County Road 2017 around the reservoir three miles. Turn right onto Forest Service Road 37 and continue for 21 miles. After crossing Bernhardt Creek, turn right onto Forest Service Road 39 and drive 1 mile north to the trailhead on the right.

Contact: Okanogan National Forest, Methow Valley Ranger District, 24 West Chewuch Road, Winthrop, WA 98862, 509/996-4003.

9 GRANITE MOUNTAIN

11.0 mi/6.0 hr

northeast of Winthrop in Okanogan National Forest

Map 4.1, page 201

In the early 1990s, more than 700 local residents sent letters to the U.S. Forest Service, objecting to plans to build more than 30 miles of road through the Granite Mountain Roadless

Area. The roads were to help log thousands of acres of forest, spoiling one of the Okanogan's best forests. Fortunately for hikers today, their efforts were successful. Granite Mountain Trail climbs steeply to Granite's 7,366-foot summit, surveying the protected forests as well as many distant peaks and ranges. If you're not into a full hike, you can still obtain views from Little Granite Mountain, a six-mile round-trip.

Granite Mountain Trail climbs steeply through forests of lodgepole pine and fir to a small ridge. A side trail leads north to the top of Little Granite (2 miles). The main trail continues toward much larger Granite Mountain through a gap between ridges. A stiff scramble almost straight up leads to the summit and the requisite views. Although it passes near Little Granite Creek, the trail is usually very dry once the snowpack has disappeared, so extra water is a must.

User Groups: Hikers, leashed dogs, horses, and mountain bikes. No wheelchair access.

Open Seasons: This trail is accessible July–mid-October.

Permits: A federal Northwest Forest Pass is required to park here.

Maps: For a map of Okanogan National Forest, contact the Outdoor Recreation Information Center at the downtown Seattle REI. For topographic maps, ask Green Trails for No. 53, Tiffany Mountain, and No. 85, Loup Loup, or ask the USGS for West Conconully and Loup Loup Summit.

Directions: From Conconully, drive southwest 2 miles on Okanogan County Road 2017. The road branches to Forest Service Road 42 and Forest Service Road 37; turn right onto Road 37. Drive 1 mile and turn left onto Forest Service Road 37-100. Drive 4 miles and turn right onto Forest Service Road 37-120. The trailhead is .5 mile ahead, on the right.

Contact: Okanogan National Forest, Methow Valley Ranger District, 24 West Chewuch Road, Winthrop, WA 98862, 509/996-4003.

10 FOURTH OF JULY RIDGE

9.0 mi/5.0 hrs 3 8

northwest of Tonasket in Okanogan National Forest

Map 4.1, page 201

Fourth of July Ridge is less about big views than it is a trip back into time. Along the trail are several old cabins built more than 100 years ago by some of the region's first settlers. In the 19th century, folks slowly moved into the upper Okanogan for the deceptively rich natural resources of the area. Although the forests and prairies appear dry during much of the summer, this area is really an ideal place to raise cattle. Geologically, the land of the Okanogan is very old and composed of metamorphic rocks, a type of rock that is often home to vast mineral deposits. That attracted miners to these parts. The cabins along the ridge have long ago been abandoned, yet old artifacts can still found among their remains. After passing the cabins (1.5 miles), Fourth of July Trail slowly traverses Mount Bonaparte by climbing the southeast slope. At 3.5 miles is Lightning Spring, usually dry by June, and at 4.5 miles the trail intersects Southside Trail, access to Mount Bonaparte's summit (see listing for South Side Bonaparte in this chapter).

User Groups: Hikers, leashed dogs, and horses. No mountain bikes are allowed. No wheelchair access.

Open Seasons: This trail is accessible May–November.

Permits: Permits are not required. Parking and access are free.

Maps: For a map of Okanogan National Forest, contact the Outdoor Recreation Information Center at the downtown Seattle REI. For topographic maps, ask the USGS for Havillah and Mount Bonaparte

Directions: From Tonasket, drive north 15 miles on County Road 9467 (Tonasket-Havillah Road) to Forest Service Road 3230. Turn right and drive 4 miles to the signed trailhead.

Contact: Okanogan National Forest, Tonasket Ranger Station, 1 West Winesap, Tonasket, WA 98855, 509/486-2186.

11 FIR MOUNTAIN

4.0 mi/2.5 hrs

east of Tonasket in Okanogan National Forest

Map 4.2, page 202

Although the route up Fir Mountain is nothing to write home about, much of your sweat is paid off with a great summit view. Fir Mountain Trail shows no qualms about its intention of climbing straight up the hillside to the summit, a long craggy mass of exposed rock. The trail is mostly forested until it reaches the summit, meaning you'll have to wait until you're well invested in the hike to achieve any views. This is a good place to see deer or elk browsing in the forest, or to hear the whoomp-whoomp-whoomp of grouse. The summit has good vistas of the Kettle River Range and the white-capped North Cascades to the east. Expect the trail to be hot and dry with no water to be found along the way. The trailhead is across Highway 20 from Sweat Creek Campground, a nice place to call home for the night.

User Groups: Hikers and leashed dogs. No horses or mountain bikes are allowed. No wheelchair access.

Open Seasons: This trail is accessible May–October.

Permits: Permits are not required. Parking and access are free.

Maps: For a map of Okanogan National Forest, contact the Outdoor Recreation Information Center at the downtown Seattle REI. For a topographic map, ask the USGS for Wauconda Summit.

Directions: From Republic, drive west 9 miles on Highway 20 to Forest Service Road 31. Turn left (south) and drive 1.5 miles to the signed trailhead.

Contact: Okanogan National Forest, Tonasket Ranger Station, 1 West Winesap, Tonasket, WA 98855, 509/486-2186.

12 SWAN AND LONG LAKE LOOPS

1.3–1.8 mi/1.0 hr

south of Republic in Colville National Forest

Map 4.2, page 202

These are a pair of outstanding lakeshore loops leaving from a pair of great campgrounds. The two trails encircle Swan Lake (1.8 miles) and Long Lake (1.3 miles), passing through old-growth ponderosa pine forest with steady views of the lakes. Swan Lake is large and open atop a high plateau. Long

Long Lake, a short and easy lake loop near a car campground

Lake lies in a narrow valley between two rocky cliffs. The trails are flat and easy, perfect for hikers of all ages and abilities. Moose and elk are often heard calling out from around the lake during late evening, while loons, geese, and ducks fill the woods with sound during the morning. The two campgrounds are great for casual campers, as they feature full car-camping amenities. Anglers in pursuit of the well-stocked trout in the lakes will most appreciate the trails since they pass countless secluded fishing holes.

User Groups: Hikers, leashed dogs, and mountain bikes. No horses are allowed. No wheelchair access.

Open Seasons: This trail is accessible March–November.

Permits: Permits are not required. Parking and access are free.

Maps: For a map of Colville National Forest, contact the Outdoor Recreation Information Center at the downtown Seattle REI. For a topographic map, ask the USGS for Swan Lake.

Directions: From Republic, drive south 7.5 miles on Highway 21 to Scatter Creek Road. Turn right (west) and drive 7 miles to Swan Lake Campground. The trailhead is in the day-use area.

Contact: Colville National Forest, Republic Ranger Station, 180 North Jefferson, Republic, WA 99166, 509/775-7400.

13 TENMILE

5.0 mi/2.5 hrs

south of Republic in Colville National Forest

Map 4.2, page 202

Unlike many of the summit hikes in the area, Tenmile Trail hikes through a small, rugged canyon up into nice parkland forests of fir and pine. The route leaves San Poil Campground (conveniently situated alongside Highway 21) and climbs through the lightly forested canyon. Ponderosa pines line the steep walls while cottonwoods inhabit the wet canyon bottom. This is a great place to see deer, hear elk, and maybe even stumble across a moose. Don't forget about bears or the possibility of a rattlesnake. Tenmile Trail climbs 1.5 miles in the canyon before reaching the plateau above, a good turnaround point. The last mile works its way up through a draw to Tenmile Road, a good access point for those staying at Swan or Long Lake Campgrounds.

User Groups: Hikers and leashed dogs. No horses or mountain bikes are allowed. No wheelchair access.

Open Seasons: This trail is accessible June–October.

Permits: Permits are not required. Parking and access are free.

Maps: For a map of Colville National Forest, contact the Outdoor Recreation Information Center at the downtown Seattle REI. For topographic maps, ask the USGS for Bear Mountain and Swan Lake.

Directions: From Republic, drive 10 miles south on Highway 21 to San Poil Campground. Turn right (west) into the campground. The trailhead is near the day-use parking area.

For the upper trailhead, turn right onto Scatter Creek Road (7.5 miles from Republic) and drive 4 miles to Tenmile Road. Turn left and drive 2.5 miles to the signed trailhead.

Contact: Colville National Forest, Republic Ranger Station, 180 North Jefferson, Republic, WA 99166, 509/775-7400.

14 13 MILE

16.5 mi one-way/8.0 hrs

southeast of Republic in Colville National Forest

Map 4.2, page 202

A trail with options is 13 Mile, making for a great trek through the southern reach of the Kettle River Range. The route has three trailheads, making the entire stretch of trail (more than 16 miles) easily accessible. The views are unbeatable from the high ridge, whether they be looking out to other Kettle peaks or out over San Poil Valley.

All three trailheads offer something different and worthwhile. From 13 Mile Campground, the trail climbs quickly to views of the beautiful San Poil River canyon. Hawks and eagles looking for dinner are commonly seen high above the valley. The trail intersects Forest Service Road 2054 and the middle trailhead at about four miles. Thirteen Mile Trail continues east to grassy meadows along the south slopes of 13 Mile Mountain before dropping into a creek valley. Deer and elk are frequently encountered on this lightly used section of the route. The high point (in elevation) is achieved when the trail reaches the saddle between Fire and 17 Mile Mountains, just 2.5 miles from the east trailhead. The great thing about 13 Mile Trail is that with three trailheads, it's like three trails in one and each is equally fun. Water sources are undependable (especially in late summer) along this high route, so be sure to carry an adequate supply. A few camps are dispersed throughout, but best bets are to find a flat spot 50 yards from the trail and to call it home for the night.

User Groups: Hikers, leashed dogs, horses, and mountain bikes. No wheelchair access.

Open Seasons: This trail is accessible June–October.

Permits: Permits are not required. Parking and access are free.

Maps: For a map of Colville National Forest, contact the Outdoor Recreation Information Center at the downtown Seattle REI. For topographic maps, ask the USGS for Thirteenmile Creek, Bear Mountain, and Edds Mountain.

Directions: West access: From Republic, drive 13 miles south on Highway 21 to 13 Mile Campground on the left (east) side of the road. The 13 Mile Trailhead is within the campground.

East access: From Republic, drive east 7 miles to Hall Creek Road (County Road 99, which turns into Forest Service Road 2054). Turn right (south) and drive 5.5 miles to Forest Service Road 600. Turn left onto Forest Service Road 600 and drive 5 miles to the signed trailhead on the right (west) side of the road.

Middle Access: From Republic, drive east 7 miles to Hall Creek Road (County Road 99). Turn right (south) and drive 1.5 miles to County Road 233. Turn right and drive 1.5 miles to Forest Service Road 2053. Veer left and drive 1 mile to Forest Service Road 2054. Turn right and drive 5.5 miles to Cougar Trailhead.

Contact: Colville National Forest, Republic Ranger Station, 180 North Jefferson, Republic, WA 99166, 509/775-7400.

15 TAYLOR RIDGE

8.0 mi/4.0 hrs 2 8

northwest of Kettle Falls in Colville National Forest

Map 4.2, page 202

Taylor Ridge Trail has just about everything you could ask for from a trail. The route traverses the high ridge, frequently leaving the timber to take in good views of the surrounding peaks and valleys. Water is frequently available along the route and there are several good campsites, making overnight ventures a good bet. The trail is also split in half by a Forest Service road, making upper sections of the ridge easily accessible. From the bisecting road, the two segments are each about four miles in length. Head east on Taylor Ridge Trail to follow the ridge for a short while before dropping sharply to Boulder Creek. The trail to the west gently climbs higher, passing through meadows and vistas as the ridge works its way toward the Kettle Crest. Find camps near the road and up higher on the trail. Water can be found from several streams and springs along the route.

User Groups: Hikers, leashed dogs, horses, mountain bikes, and motorcycles. No wheelchair access.

Open Seasons: This trail is accessible May–October.

Permits: Permits are not required. Parking and access are free.

Maps: For a map of Colville National Forest, contact the Outdoor Recreation Information Center at the downtown Seattle REI. For topographic

maps, ask the USGS for Mount Leona and Bulldog Mountain.

Directions: From Kettle Falls, drive north 22 miles to Boulder–Deer Creek Road (Forest Service Road 6100). Turn left (west) and drive 8 miles to Forest Service Road 6113. Turn left (south) and drive 7 miles to the signed trailhead.

Contact: Colville National Forest, Kettle Falls Ranger Station, 255 West 11th Avenue, Kettle Falls, WA 99141, 509/738-7700.

16 PROFANITY

6.0 mi/3.5 hrs

northeast of Republic in Colville National Forest

Map 4.2, page 202

Rarely used by anyone other than hunters, Profanity Peak Trail offers a firsthand glimpse at the impact of forest fires on dry, east-side forests. The Leona Fire roared through this area in 2001, destroying much of the forest. Already, the area has begun to regenerate. Ground covers revealed by the now-gone canopy are doing extremely well in the sunlight. Seedlings have already taken root in many places and are working on creating a forest of their own. It's a welcome sight to see nature taking care of itself, especially after the doomsday coverage forest fires often receive.

The first half of Profanity Trail climbs through parts of the fire on its way up to Kettle Crest Trail. At this point, the views are grand to the east and west. Those with a cursing streak can exercise it by heading south on Kettle Crest Trail and scaling the summit of Profanity Peak. Grand vistas await those who do.

User Groups: Hikers, leashed dogs, horses, and mountain bikes. No wheelchair access.

Open Seasons: This trail is accessible May–October.

Permits: Permits are not required. Parking and access are free.

Maps: For a map of Colville National Forest, contact the Outdoor Recreation Information Center at the downtown Seattle REI. For a topographic map, ask the USGS for Mount Leona.

Directions: From Republic, drive east 2.5 miles on Highway 20 to Highway 21. Turn left (north) and drive 13 miles to Aeneas Creek Road (County Road 566). Turn right and drive 8 miles (the road becomes Forest Service Road 2160) to the trailhead at road's end.

Contact: Colville National Forest, Republic Ranger Station, 180 North Jefferson, Republic, WA 99166, 509/775-7400.

17 STICK PIN

2.6 mi/2.0 hrs

northwest of Kettle Falls in Colville National Forest

Map 4.2, page 202

Stick Pin, one of the many trails offering access to Kettle Crest Trail, is unique in that water is readily available nearly the length of the trail. Thanks go out to the trail engineer who laid out Stick Pin, as it follows the South Fork of Boulder Creek up to its headwaters in the Kettle River Range. The cool water is refreshing on hot summer days. Most of Stick Pin Trail is covered by thick forests of Douglas fir, western larch, and lodgepole pine. Deer and elk are plentiful in this area, as are easy-to-startle grouse. The trail threads between Ryan Hill and Stickpin Hill to make a steep climb up to Kettle Crest Trail and the requisite meadow views.

User Groups: Hikers, leashed dogs, horses, and mountain bikes. No wheelchair access.

Open Seasons: This trail is accessible May–October.

Permits: Permits are not required. Parking and access are free.

Maps: For a map of Colville National Forest, contact the Outdoor Recreation Information Center at the downtown Seattle REI. For a topographic map, ask the USGS for Mount Leona.

Directions: From Kettle Falls, drive west approximately 22 miles on Highway 20 to Albian Hill Road. Turn right (north) and drive 12.1 miles to Forest Service Road 2030-921, a small side road. Follow this road .5 mile to its end and the signed trailhead. A primitive camp is at the trailhead.

Contact: Colville National Forest, Kettle Falls Ranger Station, 255 West 11th Avenue, Kettle Falls, WA 99141, 509/738-7700.

18 LEONA

3.2 mi/1.5 hrs

northeast of Republic in Colville National Forest

Map 4.2, page 202

It may be hard to distinguish between the many trails leading up to Kettle Crest Trail, but Leona is one of the best. Much of the trail features glorious views of Curlew Valley and out to the North Cascades. And when you reach Kettle Crest Trail, you can gaze out over the Columbia River Valley and up and down the Kettle River Range. Leona Trail climbs steadily, but the grade is easily managed, especially since this is such a short trail. At the halfway point is Leona Spring, a rare source of water at this elevation. At the crest, hike north along signed Leona Loop Trail, which combines with Kettle Crest Trail to a make a six-mile loop (total). Cutting off from the loop is a trail to the summit of Leona, a well-recommended vista.

User Groups: Hikers, leashed dogs, horses, and mountain bikes. No wheelchair access.

Open Seasons: This trail is accessible May–October.

Permits: Permits are not required. Parking and access are free.

Maps: For a map of Colville National Forest, contact the Outdoor Recreation Information Center at the downtown Seattle REI. For a topographic map, ask the USGS for Mount Leona.

Directions: From Republic, drive east 2.5 miles on Highway 20 to Highway 21. Turn left (north) and drive 11.5 miles to St. Peter's Creek Road (County Road 584). Turn right (east) and drive 7 miles (it will turn into Forest Service Road 2157) to a roadblock and road's end. The trailhead is to the right of the roadblock.

Contact: Colville National Forest, Republic Ranger Station, 180 North Jefferson, Republic, WA 99166, 509/775-7400.

19 US MOUNTAIN

5.2 mi/3.0 hrs

northeast of Kettle Falls in Colville National Forest

Map 4.2, page 202

One of the few trails in this region not connecting to Kettle Crest Trail, US Mountain Trail instead undertakes a summit of the 6,200-foot peak. As can be expected, the summit opens to reveal meadows and spectacular views. Most notable is that from this vantage it is possible to see much of the Kettle River Range. US Mountain is set off to the east side of the divide, thus making the northern half of the mountains well discernable. US Mountain Trail makes a steady ascent on the mountain but is not terribly steep. The forest can be pretty thick in places, but parts of the trail are covered in swaths of meadows (and flowers during the early summer). Although the trail continues down into the South Fork Boulder Creek Valley, hikers are well advised to turn back after reaching the top of US Mountain. This is a hot and dry trail, so extra water is an important consideration.

User Groups: Hikers, leashed dogs, horses, mountain bikes, and motorcycles. No wheelchair access.

Open Seasons: This trail is accessible May–October.

Permits: Permits are not required. Parking and access are free.

Maps: For a map of Colville National Forest, contact the Outdoor Recreation Information Center at the downtown Seattle REI. For a topographic map, ask the USGS for Copper Butte.

Directions: From Kettle Falls, drive west approximately 22 miles on Highway 20 to Albian Hill Road. Turn right (north) and drive 7.3 miles to a difficult-to-find trailhead on the right (east) side of the road.

Contact: Colville National Forest, Kettle Falls Ranger Station, 255 West 11th Avenue, Kettle Falls, WA 99141, 509/738-7700.

20 OLD STAGE ROAD

3.2–10.6 mi/1.5–6.0 hrs

northeast of Republic in Colville National Forest

Map 4.2, page 202

As far as unique histories go, Old Stage Road Trail takes the cake. This is the last remaining section of the first Washington State Highway. Well, highway is hardly the proper word. How about calling it a bumpy, dusty, rocky route over the mountains? Today it's not so bad, thanks to lots of volunteer work from Inland Empire Chapter of Backcountry Horsemen of Washington. The trail is popular with folk on horseback but is perfectly suited for families on foot.

In 1892, the Washington Legislature commissioned a road to be built from Marblemount, west of the Cascades, to Marcus on the Columbia River. The old road came up from the west to the Kettle River Range and crossed it via this route. It lasted only about six years before a better route over Sherman Pass was recognized and built. Much of the hike is forested as the trail gently climbs to Kettle Crest Trail. The trail stretches up to the crest (1.6 miles), a good turnaround point for shorter excursions, before dropping down through forest. Hikers today will find a trail much more suited for boots than wagon wheels, but it is amazing to see what folks once went through just to get across the state.

User Groups: Hikers, leashed dogs, horses, and mountain bikes. No wheelchair access.

Open Seasons: This trail is accessible mid-May–October.

Permits: Permits are not required. Parking and access are free.

Maps: For a map of Colville National Forest, contact the Outdoor Recreation Information Center at the downtown Seattle REI. For a topographic map, ask the USGS for Copper Butte.

Directions: From Kettle Falls, drive 25 miles west on Highway 20 to Albian Hill Road (Forest Service Road 2030). Turn right (north) and drive 7.1 miles to Forest Service Road 2030-380. The signed trailhead lies a few hundred yards up Forest Service Road 2030-380.

Contact: Colville National Forest, Republic Ranger Station, 180 North Jefferson, Republic, WA 99166, 509/775-7400.

21 MARCUS

7.0 mi/3.5 hrs

northeast of Republic in Colville National Forest

Map 4.2, page 202

To say the least, Marcus Trail provides an easy and extremely beautiful access to Kettle Crest Trail. What should really be known about the trail is that leads to the foot of Copper Butte, the tallest point in the Kettle River Range. Parts of Copper Butte were burned by a 1996 fire. Marcus makes a steady ascent to Kettle Crest Trail. After two miles of old, open forest, the trail breaks out into open meadows, aflame in wildflower color during the early summer. The trail traverses a south-facing slope, making it accessible a little earlier than others in the area, but hot and dry, without water. Once you reach Kettle Crest Trail, don't miss the highlight of the trip, a summit of Copper Butte. At 7,135 feet, the peak soaks up the views of numerous distant mountain ranges within two countries and two states, with Glacier Peak to the west.

User Groups: Hikers, leashed dogs, horses, and mountain bikes. No wheelchair access.

Open Seasons: This trail is accessible May–October.

Permits: Permits are not required. Parking and access are free.

Maps: For a map of Colville National Forest, contact the Outdoor Recreation Information Center at the downtown Seattle REI. For topographic maps, ask the USGS for Cooke Mountain and Copper Butte.

Directions: From Republic, drive east on Highway 20 about 3 miles to Highway 21. Turn left (north) and drive 2.5 miles to County Road 284. Turn right and drive 2.5 miles until it turns into Forest Service Road 2152. Continue on Forest Service Road 2152 for 2.7 miles to Forest Service Road 2040. Turn left and drive 5.2 miles to Forest Service Road 250. Turn right and drive 1.5 miles to the signed trailhead. A primitive campsite is at the trailhead.

Contact: Colville National Forest, Republic Ranger Station, 180 North Jefferson, Republic, WA 99166, 509/775-7400.

22 SHERMAN

2.6 mi/1.5 hrs

east of Republic along SR20 in Colville National Forest

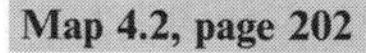

Map 4.2, page 202

Sherman Trail provides quick but difficult access to the northern section of Kettle Crest Trail. By itself, the trail is rather miserable. But Kettle Crest Trail is prime country for exploration, and it lends itself well to making longer trips possible. Sherman gains nearly 1,600 feet of elevation in a short 1.3 miles. Much of the route is within a thick, young forest. Although the views are eaten up by the surrounding thicket of trees, at least they provide shade on this normally hot and dry route. Not until you reach the end of the trail, along the crest of the range, does the forest break and the views come out. For hikers looking to continue along Kettle Crest Trail, Jungle Hill lies to the south (2 total miles) and Wapaloosie to the north (3.5 total miles).

User Groups: Hikers, leashed dogs, horses, and mountain bikes. No wheelchair access.

Open Seasons: This trail is accessible June–October.

Permits: Permits are not required. Parking and access are free.

Maps: For a map of Colville National Forest, contact the Outdoor Recreation Information Center at the downtown Seattle REI. For topographic maps, ask the USGS for Cooke Mountain and Copper Butte.

Directions: From Republic, drive east approximately 12 miles to Forest Service Road 2040. Turn left (north) and drive 2.5 miles to Forest Service Road 065. Turn right (east) and drive 2 miles to the signed trailhead.

Contact: Colville National Forest, Republic Ranger Station, 180 North Jefferson, Republic, WA 99166, 509/775-7400.

23 WAPALOOSIE

5.5 mi/3.0 hrs

northwest of Kettle Falls in Colville National Forest

Map 4.2, page 202

More than a worthy candidate for a tongue-twister contest, Wapaloosie is an excellent scenic route to North Kettle Crest Trail. The summit of Wapaloosie itself is a grand adventure, challenging for some hikers and just right for others. Wapaloosie Trail takes advantage of numerous switchbacks to make a slow but steady ascent on the mountain. The trail gains roughly 2,000 feet of elevation in a short 2.75 miles, not an effort to snicker at. After 1.5 miles, the trail breaks out into open slopes covered in grasses and wildflowers. Deer and elk are likely to be seen in the early mornings or late evenings. Hawks are regularly soaring above, keeping an eye on all below. Wapaloosie Trail reaches Kettle Crest Trail just below Wapaloosie Mountain. A short side trail leads to the summit, offering panoramic views of the surrounding countryside. This is a great way to get in some views and exercise at the same time.

User Groups: Hikers, leashed dogs, horses, and mountain bikes. No wheelchair access.

Open Seasons: This trail is accessible June–October.

Permits: Permits are not required. Parking and access are free.

Maps: For a map of Colville National Forest, contact the Outdoor Recreation Information Center at the downtown Seattle REI. For a topographic map, ask the USGS for Copper Butte.

Directions: From Kettle Falls, drive west approximately 22 miles on Highway 20 to Albian Hill Road. Turn right (north) and drive 3.2 miles to the signed trailhead.

Contact: Colville National Forest, Kettle Falls Ranger Station, 255 West 11th Avenue, Kettle Falls, WA 99141, 509/738-7700.

24 COLUMBIA MOUNTAIN

7.1 mi/3.5 hrs

east of Republic along SR20 in Colville National Forest

Map 4.2, page 202

Columbia Mountain offers the most easily accessible and most encompassing viewpoint within the Kettle River Range. Directly off Highway 20, Columbia Mountain Trail cuts off from Kettle Crest Trail to create a loop encircling the 6,700-foot butte. Within the loop is a side trail leading to an abandoned lookout and the summit of Columbia Mountain. This is one of the best vantages in the Kettle River Range, with long views of the divide to the north and south. The devastation of the 1988 White Mountain fire is readily apparent, with much of the southern mountain range nothing but miles of dead snags.

The route follows Kettle Crest Trail two miles through forest and eventually open meadows. On clear days, the North Cascades are well visible to the west. At Columbia Spring, a seasonal source of water, Columbia Mountain Trail cuts right and backtracks up the slopes. The trail diverges after .5 mile to create a loop around the mountain, much like a lasso. On the north side of the loop you'll find the trail up to the peak. Mountains appear across the distant horizons, with snow-capped peaks in Canada and Idaho joining in. Outside of the North Cascades, nowhere else along Highway 20 will you find a better hike.

© SCOTT LEONARD

View from Columbia Mountain (in Kettle Range), looking north

User Groups: Hikers, leashed dogs, horses, and mountain bikes. No wheelchair access.

Open Seasons: This trail is accessible June–October.

Permits: Permits are not required. Parking and access are free.

Maps: For a map of Colville National Forest, contact the Outdoor Recreation Information Center at the downtown Seattle REI. For a topographic map, ask the USGS for Sherman Peak.

Directions: From Republic, drive 17 miles east on Highway 20 to Sherman Pass. On the east side of the pass, turn left (north) into the signed trailhead.

Contact: Colville National Forest, Republic Ranger Station, 180 North Jefferson, Republic, WA 99166, 509/775-7400.

25 KETTLE CREST NORTH

30.3 mi one-way/3 days

northeast of Republic in Colville National Forest

Map 4.2, page 202

This is a long, rugged, and popular route through the high country of the Kettle River Range. Stretching 30 miles from Sherman Pass all the way to Deer Creek Summit, North Kettle Crest Trail starts high and stays that way. The trail climbs or skirts the base of numerous mountains and buttes, including Columbia (2 miles from Sherman Pass), Wapaloosie (7 miles), Copper (13 miles), Ryan Hill (20 miles), Profanity (22 miles), and Sentinel (28 miles). Each peak along the way can be scrambled to the top to reveal expansive views in all directions. Much of the route is swathed in open meadows of grass and wildflowers. June is usually a great month to get some color on the trail.

Although parts of Kettle Crest North Trail are relatively well traveled, much of the trail has few visitors most of the year (hunting season in the fall brings increased use). That means animals are aplenty in these parts, with deer, elk, and moose spotted along the trail regularly. Signs of bear and cougar are frequently seen along the trail; these big predators scratch trees to mark their territory, leaving behind stripped bark and exposed trunk. Campsites are scattered throughout the length of the trail. Water is a less dependable commodity. There are some springs and streams along the route, but by late summer they are not reliable; rationing of water is smart planning. The best bet is to set up a through-hike with a car at each end. Many access trails lead to the Kettle Crest, so many options exist for a customized hike. For a decent backpacking experience, there's no better trail in this area.

User Groups: Hikers, leashed dogs, horses, and mountain bikes. No wheelchair access.

Open Seasons: This trail is accessible June–October.

Permits: Permits are not required. Parking and access are free.

Maps: For a map of Colville National Forest, contact the Outdoor Recreation Information Center at the downtown Seattle REI. For topographic maps, ask the USGS for Sherman Peak, Copper Butte, and Mount Leona.

Directions: South access: From Republic, drive 17 miles east on Highway 20 to Sherman Pass. On the east side of the pass, turn left (north) into the signed trailhead.

North access: From Republic, drive north approximately 20 miles to the town of Curlew. Turn east on County Road 602 and drive 12 miles to Deer Creek Summit Trailhead.

Contact: Colville National Forest, Republic Ranger Station, 180 North Jefferson, Republic, WA 99166, 509/775-7400.

26 KETTLE CREST SOUTH

13.3 mi one-way/8.0 hrs 3 10

east of Republic along Highway 20 in Colville National Forest

Map 4.2, page 202

The southern leg of Kettle Crest Trail is highly memorable for two reasons. Most of this high route is along the crest of the Kettle River Range and thus offers expansive views of the surrounding country, from the North Cascade Mountains in the west to the Columbia River Valley to the east. Even more remarkable is the charred forest that covers much of the route. In 1988, eight lightning strikes created six fires. Because of extremely dry conditions, the fires merged to create the White Mountain Complex. The fire eventually burned more than 20,000 acres of forest, leaving behind miles of dead trees, known as snags. The fire burned along much of Kettle Crest Trail but did leave pockets of older forest. Where the fire burned, it burned hot and left little. As nature tends to do, the area is quickly recovering. Small pines and lush ground cover are filling in the area, well on the way to creating a forest of their own.

Kettle Crest South Trail truly follows the crest of this large range for much of its length. From Sherman Pass, it climbs around Sherman Peak and Snow Peak, each of which is tall and reached via side trails. Bald Mountain, Barnaby Buttes, and White Mountain are other peaks easily bagged along the way. It's best done as a through-hike, with a second car positioned at White Mountain Trailhead. Water can be obtained via several springs and streams scattered along the route. Campsites are strewn frequently along the route.

User Groups: Hikers, leashed dogs, horses, and mountain bikes. No wheelchair access.

Open Seasons: This trail is accessible June–October.

Permits: Permits are not required. Parking and access are free.

Maps: For a map of Colville National Forest, contact the Outdoor Recreation Information Center at the downtown Seattle REI.

For a topographic map, ask the USGS for Sherman Peak.

Directions: North access: From Republic, drive 17 miles east on Highway 20 to Sherman Pass. On the east side of the pass, turn left (north) into the signed trailhead.

South access: From Republic, drive 20 miles east on Highway 20 to Forest Service Road 2020 (about three miles beyond Sherman Pass). Turn right (south) and drive 5 miles to Forest Service Road 2014. Turn right and drive 4 miles to Forest Service Road 2020-250. Turn right and drive 3.5 miles to White Mountain Trailhead.

Contact: Colville National Forest, Kettle Falls Ranger Station, 255 West 11th Avenue, Kettle Falls, WA 99141, 509/738-7700.

27 EDDS MOUNTAIN

8.4 mi/4.0 hrs

southeast of Republic in Colville National Forest

Map 4.2, page 202

Edds Mountain Trail offers the most scenic route to South Kettle Crest Trail. The route passes below Edds Mountain and Bald Mountain, a pair of 6,800-foot peaks, each of which is an easy scramble to broad views. The North Cascades line the western horizon over Sanpoil Valley, while the Kettle River Range fills the east. Parts of the route are in forest, other parts are in open meadows. June is a great time to see wildflowers covering these south-facing slopes. The trail offers a great firsthand look at the White Mountain Complex fire of 1988, passing through several sections of charred forest that is once again teeming with plant life. Although the trail gains just 1,000 feet over four miles, parts of the path are steep and rocky. Extra water is a must on this hot and dry trail.

User Groups: Hikers, leashed dogs, horses, and mountain bikes. No wheelchair access.

Open Seasons: This trail is accessible June–October.

Permits: Permits are not required. Parking and access are free.

Maps: For a map of Colville National Forest, contact the Outdoor Recreation Information Center at the downtown Seattle REI. For a topographic map, ask the USGS for Edds Mountain.

Directions: From Republic, drive east 7 miles on Highway 20 to Hall Creek Road (County Road 99, which turns into Forest Service Road 2054). Turn right (south) and drive 4 miles to Forest Service Road 300. Turn left and drive 1.5 miles to road's end and the trailhead.

Contact: Colville National Forest, Republic Ranger Station, 180 North Jefferson, Republic, WA 99166, 509/775-7400.

28 BARNABY BUTTE

14.0 mi/8.0 hrs

southeast of Republic in Colville National Forest

Map 4.2, page 202

Barnaby Butte Trail offers a lot more than just a summit of the two rounded peaks. For starters, it offers a good workout. The trail climbs more than 3,000 feet over the course of seven miles, a decent day's work for anyone. Barnaby Butte Trail passes through a wide variety of ecosystems, most notably recently burned areas of forests. These patches were engulfed by the White Mountain Fire of 1988 and are now home to stands of small young pines. Animals are never far from this seldom-used route. These open areas make for great wildlife habitat, providing open space for deer to graze and countless snags from which hawks conduct their hunt. And, of course, the trail makes a grand summit of Barnaby Buttes, the site of a former lookout. The view of the southern Kettle River Range is great, and the bird's-eye view of the fire's impact is incredible. It's important to carry extra water and sunscreen on this trail because of its long and exposed (hot) nature. Water will likely not be available along the way.

User Groups: Hikers, leashed dogs, horses, and mountain bikes. No wheelchair access.

Open Seasons: This trail is accessible June–October.

Permits: Permits are not required. Parking and access are free.
Maps: For a map of Colville National Forest, contact the Outdoor Recreation Information Center at the downtown Seattle REI. For a topographic map, ask the USGS for Sherman Peak.
Directions: From Republic, drive east 7 miles on Highway 20 to Hall Creek Road (County Road 99, which turns into Forest Service Road 2054). Turn right (south) and drive 5.5 miles to Forest Service Road 600. Turn left onto Forest Service Road 600 and drive 7 miles to the signed trailhead on the left (east) side of the road. The first two miles of trail is old Road 680.
Contact: Colville National Forest, Republic Ranger Station, 180 North Jefferson, Republic, WA 99166, 509/775-7400.

29 HOODOO CANYON

4.5 mi/2.5 hrs

west of Kettle Falls in Colville National Forest

Map 4.2, page 202

Hoodoo Canyon provides one of the best day hikes in northeastern Washington. Departing from a great campground on a well-stocked fishing lake, Hoodoo Canyon Trail climbs the wall of a narrow canyon to a viewpoint. The way is steep and rough at times, but always well worth the effort. And it can all be done in a morning or afternoon hike, with enough time to make s'mores at Trout Lake under the stars.

Hoodoo Canyon Trail departs Trout Lake Campground and quickly switchbacks up the canyon wall. It then traverses the length of the canyon with Trout and Emerald Lakes reflecting from far below. The forest mingles with open slopes along the way, making the hike especially scenic. The trail can be rocky and narrow at points; be careful. The trail climbs to a bluff overlooking the glacially carved canyon. To the north are the eastern peaks of the Kettle River Range. The trail continues two miles down to Deadman Creek and a northern trailhead. The much better option is to return to Trout Lake and catch yourself some dinner.
User Groups: Hikers and leashed dogs. No horses or mountain bikes are allowed. No wheelchair access.
Open Seasons: This trail is accessible April–November.
Permits: Permits are not required. Parking and access are free.
Maps: For a map of Colville National Forest, contact the Outdoor Recreation Information Center at the downtown Seattle REI. For topographic maps, ask the USGS for Bangs Mountain, Boyds, and Jackknife Mountain.
Directions: From Kettle Falls, drive west 8 miles on Highway 20 to Trout Lake Road (Forest Service Road 020). Turn right (north) and drive 5 miles to Trout Lake Campground. The trailhead is within the campground.
Contact: Colville National Forest, Kettle Falls Ranger Station, 255 West 11th Avenue, Kettle Falls, WA 99141, 509/738-7700.

30 GILLETTE RIDGE

12.5 mi/6.0 hrs

north of Colville in Colville National Forest

Map 4.3, page 203

Gillette Ridge provides something of a rarity in the state: an easy-to-access and easy-to-complete ridge run. Starting at 4,700 feet, Gillette Ridge Trail traverses the crest of the ridge and tops out on the north section at 5,775 feet. Although there are a few saddles in which to lose hard-earned elevation, don't fret and instead munch on some huckleberries. The trail makes a good tour of the ridge, with plenty of views along the way. Various mountains appear from near and far on the horizons, but far more scenic is the valley below. It's hard to miss the distinctive U shape of the valley, sculpted roughly 12,000 years ago by glaciers. Even more impressive is that the glaciers that ground out Deep Creek Valley also smoothed out the ridge you're on. Back in 10,000 B.C., you'd be under hundreds of feet of ice. That's a refreshing thought on hot summer days, which is most of them up here. Water isn't to be found along the route, so bring plenty to drink with the huckleberries you'll harvest.

User Groups: Hikers, leashed dogs, horses, and mountain bikes. No wheelchair access.

Open Seasons: This trail is accessible mid-May–October.

Permits: Permits are not required. Parking and access are free.

Maps: For a map of Colville National Forest, contact the Outdoor Recreation Information Center at the downtown Seattle REI. For topographic maps, ask the USGS for Aladdin and Gillette Mountain.

Directions: From Colville, drive north approximately 14.5 miles on Alladin Road (County Road 9435) to Forest Service Road 500. Turn left (west) and drive 6 miles to the trailhead on the left side of the road.

Contact: Colville National Forest, Colville Ranger Station, 755 South Main, Colville, WA 99114, 509/684-7000.

31 ABERCROMBIE MOUNTAIN

6.5 mi/3.5 hrs

north of Colville in Colville National Forest

Map 4.3, page 203

From the high vantage point afforded by Abercrombie Mountain, one can seemingly peer into forever. At 7,308 feet, the peak is one of the tallest in eastern Washington. On clear days, visitors can literally look out over hundreds of square miles, well into Canada and Idaho. Just five miles from the Canadian border, the peak towers above the surrounding country. Trails scale Abercrombie from the east and west, but the road to the west trailhead is more accessible. Abercrombie Trail cuts steep switchbacks up the hillside, passing through a variety of environments, from forests of lodgepole pine to clear-cuts to forests long ago ravaged by fire. The remains of an old fire lookout lie strewn about the summit, remnants of a once-awesome place to wake up and go to work. Bring plenty of water, as this is hot and dry country with no refreshment along the way.

User Groups: Hikers, leashed dogs, and horses. No mountain bikes are allowed. No wheelchair access.

Open Seasons: This trail is accessible June–October.

Permits: Permits are not required. Parking and access are free.

Maps: For a map of Colville National Forest, contact the Outdoor Recreation Information Center at the downtown Seattle REI. For topographic maps, ask the USGS for Leadpoint and Abercrombie Mountain.

Directions: From Colville, drive north 25 miles on Alladin Road (County Road 9435) to Deep Creek Road (County Road 9445). Turn right and drive 7 miles to County Road 4720. Turn right and drive 2 miles to Forest Service Road 070. Drive 3.5 miles to road's end and the signed trailhead.

Contact: Colville National Forest, Colville Ranger Station, 755 South Main, Colville, WA 99114, 509/684-7000.

32 SHERLOCK PEAK

2.5 mi/2.0 hrs

north of Colville in Colville National Forest

Map 4.3, page 203

Abercrombie's little brother to the south, Sherlock Peak, is on par when it comes to bragging rights. While not as tall as Abercrombie Mountain, Sherlock Peak delivers a better journey to the final destination. The route starts high, resulting in a less strenuous hike. A seasonal cold-water spring is found along the route, providing a refresher early in the summer. And best of all, much of the route is in open forest and meadows. That may make the hike hotter, but it makes it more scenic, too. Just munch on some of the huckleberries found along the trail to make up for any sunburn. From the top of Sherlock, gaze east to the Selkirk Range running into Idaho and Canada or west to the Columbia River Valley.

User Groups: Hikers, leashed dogs, and horses. No mountain bikes are allowed. No wheelchair access.

Open Seasons: This trail is accessible June–October.

Permits: Permits are not required. Parking and access are free.

Maps: For a map of Colville National Forest, contact the Outdoor Recreation Information Center at the downtown Seattle REI. For topographic maps, ask the USGS for Leadpoint and Deep Lake.

Directions: From Colville, drive north 25 miles on Alladin Road (County Road 9435) to Deep Creek Road (County Road 9445). Turn right and drive 7 miles to County Road 4720. Turn right and drive 2 miles to Forest Service Road 070. Turn right and drive .5 mile to Forest Service Road 075, a rough dirt road. Drive 4 miles to road's end and the trailhead.

Contact: Colville National Forest, Colville Ranger Station, 755 South Main, Colville, WA 99114, 509/684-7000.

33 TIGER/COYOTE ROCK LOOPS

1.8–4.8 mi/1.0–2.5 hrs 1 8

west of Ione in Colville National Forest

Map 4.3, page 203

This pair of nice and easy loops makes for an excellent break from a long drive across Highway 20. With little elevation gain, Tiger and Coyote Rock Loops can be tackled by hikers of all abilities, particularly little ones. The two loops are situated in a small basin filled with wildlife. Beavers swim in Frater Lake while deer, elk, and moose often feed in the open meadows. Tiger Loop is the smaller of the two (1.8 miles) and takes only an hour to complete. It follows the shore of Frater Lake before journeying over to the waving grasses of Tiger Meadows. The trail junctions with Coyote Loop; turn left to return to the trailhead. Coyote Loop is just under five miles long, a more moderate distance for a full morning or afternoon. The trail passes through stands of Douglas fir and lodgepole pine to reach several viewpoints of the surrounding valley, at Coyote Rock and Shelter Rock. Be sure to bring water with you, as it won't be found along the way.

User Groups: Hikers, leashed dogs, mountain bikes, and motorcycles. No horses are allowed. No wheelchair access.

Open Seasons: This area is accessible April–November.

Permits: Permits are not required. Parking and access are free.

Maps: For a map of Colville National Forest, contact the Outdoor Recreation Information Center at the downtown Seattle REI. For a topographic map, ask the USGS for Ione.

Directions: From Ione, drive south on Highway 31 to the junction with Highway 20. Turn right (west) and drive approximately 15 miles to the well-signed trailhead on the right (north) side of the highway.

Contact: Colville National Forest, Colville Ranger Station, 755 South Main, Colville, WA 99114, 509/684-7000.

34 HALLIDAY/NORTH FORK

19.0 mi/2 days 4 5

east of Metaline Falls in the Salmo-Priest Wilderness of Colville National Forest

Map 4.3, page 203

This pair of trails combines to make a well-used route up to Crowell Ridge, in the northern arm of the Salmo-Priest Wilderness. Unfortunately, this promising route into the high country is actually a bit of a disappointment. For such a long trip, little water is to be found along the way. Much of the route is in the deep forest, revealing little of the surrounding mountains or valleys. And there's a big drop in the middle, resulting in a dreaded loss of hard-earned elevation. However, the trail offers an excellent opportunity to come across a large sampling of wildlife. Most folks have seen deer or grouse when out hiking. But how about moose or caribou? Or the symbol of wilderness, grizzly bears? You're likely to find them here.

The first trail is Halliday, which starts from Slate Creek and soon passes a marsh and ponds, a likely place to find moose feeding. Halliday then climbs the shoulder of Crowell Mountain before dropping sharply to North Fork Sullivan Trail. This trail doesn't get near the refreshing creek, which is rather annoying on hot days. Desperate hikers will have to bushwhack through underbrush for a cooldown. North Fork Trail climbs steeply in its last two miles to reach Crowell Ridge and spectacular payoff views. Inconveniently, the only campsite is a few miles below Crowell Ridge, a long and tiring day. With so much working against it, one might question why this backcountry route gets any use. Hunters love it.

User Groups: Hikers, leashed dogs, and horses. No mountain bikes are allowed. No wheelchair access.

Open Seasons: This trail is accessible May–October.

Permits: Permits are not required. Parking and access are free.

Maps: For a map of Colville National Forest, contact the Outdoor Recreation Information Center at the downtown Seattle REI. For topographic maps, ask the USGS for Boundary Dam and Gypsy Peak.

Directions: From Metaline Falls, drive north 6.5 miles on Highway 31 to Forest Service Road 180. Turn right and the trailhead is 200 yards down a dirt road, on the left of the large clearing.

Contact: Colville National Forest, Sullivan Lake Ranger Station, 12641 Sullivan Lake Road, Metaline Falls, WA 99153, 509/446-7500.

35 SLATE CREEK

8.6 mi/4.5 hrs

east of Metaline Falls in Colville National Forest

Map 4.3, page 203

Slate Creek is one of the more difficult trails in the Sullivan Lake area. After crossing its namesake, Slate Creek Trail climbs steeply through the forest to a small depression within a small ridge. From there, lace your boots tightly for a quick descent into Uncas Gulch, only to climb right out of it again. It's a significant up and down of about 500 feet and is likely to leave you a bit spent for the extra effort. Plenty of good things will more than make up for your effort. Hikers who wallk quietly are likely to encounter wildlife, whether it be as small as a rabbit or grouse, or as large as an elk, caribou, or grizzly bear. The trail is mostly used only during the fall hunting seasons, so the animals are unlikely to be expecting you. A campsite and the trail's only water are at Uncas Gulch Creek. The trail ends after 4.3 miles at a junction with North Fork Sullivan Trail, where the forest finally opens to reveal the surrounding mountains.

User Groups: Hikers, leashed dogs, and horses. No mountain bikes are allowed. No wheelchair access.

Open Seasons: This trail is accessible June–October.

Permits: Permits are not required. Parking and access are free.

Maps: For a map of Colville National Forest, contact the Outdoor Recreation Information Center at the downtown Seattle REI. For a topographic map, ask the USGS for Gypsy Peak.

Directions: From Metaline Falls, drive north on Highway 31 for 9 miles to Forest Service Road 3155. Turn right and drive 5.5 miles to the trailhead on the right side of the road.

Contact: Colville National Forest, Sullivan Lake Ranger Station, 12641 Sullivan Lake Road, Metaline Falls, WA 99153, 509/446-7500.

36 SALMO LOOP

17.8 mi/2–3 days

east of Metaline Falls in the Salmo-Priest Wilderness of Colville National Forest

Map 4.3, page 203

Backcountry trekkers, this is the hike for you. Salmo Loop explores the old-growth forests of Salmo River while also climbing to the peak of Snowy Top, a 7,500-foot peak that's actually in Idaho. The route feels as if it's some of the deepest wilderness in the country for a reason: It is. The symbol of wilderness in North America, the grizzly bear, still lives here. Not to mention herds of deer, elk, caribou, and moose. The trail encounters old-growth western hemlock and western red cedar within the Salmo Basin but passes through sublime alpine meadows near the peak of Little Snowy Top. This is one trail that certainly makes the long drive out to this little-known corner of the state worthwhile.

Salmo Basin Trail drops from Salmo Divide Trailhead steeply to South Salmo River (3.1 miles). The bridge may or may not be passable when you get there, so be sure to consider carefully before fording this river during times of high snow runoff. The trail then follows the South Salmo River up to the ridgeline between Snowy Top and Little Snowy Top (8.8 miles). It may be out of the way to hike the side trail up to Snowy Top, but it's the perfect spot for a long break. Possession of a camera is recommended here. The route then follows Shedroof Divide Trail back down to Salmo Divide Trail (14.8 miles), three miles from the car.

Campsites are scattered liberally throughout the trip, most notably along the South Salmo River. A pair are also up on the Shedroof Divide. Water is plentiful in the Salmo Basin, but may be tricky if not impossible to secure once you're on the ridge. Be sure to top off your water before leaving the river. Other than that, be prepared for an amazing trip.

User Groups: Hikers, leashed dogs, and horses. No mountain bikes are allowed. No wheelchair access.

Open Seasons: This trail is accessible mid-June–October.

Permits: Permits are not required. Parking and access are free.

Maps: For a map of Colville National Forest, contact the Outdoor Recreation Information Center at the downtown Seattle REI. For topographic maps, ask the USGS for Salmo Mountain and Continental Mountain (Idaho).

Directions: From Metaline Falls, drive north 2 miles on Highway 31. Turn right onto County Road 9345 and drive 5 miles to Forest Service Road 22. Turn left and drive 20 miles (the road becomes Forest Service Road 2220 at 6.5 miles) to the road's end and the trailhead.

Contact: Colville National Forest, Sullivan Lake Ranger Station, 12641 Sullivan Lake Road, Metaline Falls, WA 99153, 509/446-7500.

37 SHEDROOF DIVIDE

18.7 mi one-way/2 days 3 10

east of Metaline Falls in the Salmo-Priest Wilderness of Colville National Forest

Map 4.3, page 203

Cutting through the heart of Salmo-Priest Wilderness, Shedroof Divide Trail revels in open meadows and expansive views of the surrounding Selkirk Mountains. This high route along the crest of a long ridge is hard to equal in its beauty, making for a backpacker's dream. Big game abounds in this high country, with scores of deer, elk, and even caribou roaming the hillsides. Hikers may encounter a bear (both black bears and grizzly bears live here) or a more elusive cougar. Don't worry, these big predators prefer to mind their own business; just remember to look big if you come across one.

Shedroof Divide Trail is accessible via several trails and trailheads, including Shedroof Mountain (the northern trailhead), Pass Creek Pass (southern trailhead), Thunder Creek Trail, and Shedroof Cutoff Trail. A through-hike is recommended to take in all of the route, but bringing two cars to this remote part of Washington can prove problematic. Single-car hikers are best advised to start at the northern trailhead and hike in from there as time allows. Shedroof Divide Trail follows the crest, passing below a number of peaks, including Shedroof, Thunder, and Round Top Mountains. Side trails to their peaks are a must-do diversion. Much of the route is awash in open meadows and grand views deep into Idaho and Canada. Water may be difficult to find along the trail, but there are a couple of seasonal cold-water springs for help. Camps are

dispersed along the route, with good, established sites just north of Round Top and just south of Thunder Mountain. Shedroof Divide Trail is the way best way to experience the vastness of the Selkirk Mountains.

User Groups: Hikers, leashed dogs, and horses. No mountain bikes are allowed. No wheelchair access.

Open Seasons: This trail is accessible mid-June–October.

Permits: Permits are not required. Parking and access are free.

Maps: For a map of Colville National Forest, contact the Outdoor Recreation Information Center at the downtown Seattle REI. For topographic maps, ask the USGS for Salmo Mountain, Helmer Mountain, and Pass Creek.

Directions: North access: From Metaline Falls, drive north 2 miles on Highway 31. Turn right onto County Road 9345 and drive 5 miles to Forest Service Road 22. Turn left and drive 20.5 miles to the end of the road and the signed trailhead.

South access: From Metaline Falls, drive north 2 miles on Highway 31. Turn right onto County Road 9345 and drive 5 miles to Forest Service Road 22. Turn left and drive 6.5 miles to a signed junction. Stay to the right on Forest Service Road 22 and drive 7.5 miles to Pass Creek Pass and the signed trailhead.

Contact: Colville National Forest, Sullivan Lake Ranger Station, 12641 Sullivan Lake Road, Metaline Falls, WA 99153, 509/446-7500.

38 CROWELL RIDGE

12.0 mi/8.0 hrs

east of Metaline Falls in the Salmo-Priest Wilderness of Colville National Forest

Map 4.3, page 203

Visitors to Crowell Ridge will think they have accidentally hiked into the North Cascades. Glacial basins and snowy peaks greet hikers as they traverse this high ridge in the northern arm of Salmo-Priest Wilderness. Undisturbed forests of subalpine fir and Englemann spruce give way to big meadows and bigger vistas. Expect to see a large assortment of wildlife, from bald eagles patrolling the skies for a meal to deer, elk, and bighorn sheep grazing along the steep hillsides.

Crowell Ridge Trail leaves Bear Pasture Trailhead and immediately climbs to Crowell Ridge. The trees quickly disappear from the rocky ridge and open meadows. At more than 7,300 feet, Gypsy Peak stands as a beacon from the north with a large glacial basin and lakes at the bottom of steep slopes. If you're interested in seeing wildflowers, try late June and early July, when the winter's snowpack has finally melted out. The trail heads south and makes a junction with North Fork Sullivan Trail at 3.7 miles. Here is the trail's only campsite, a grand place to set up camp. Crowell Ridge Trail continues 4.1 miles through open meadow over to Sullivan Mountain Trailhead, the trail's end. If you had only one day to spend in the Sullivan Lake area, this would be the trail to hike.

User Groups: Hikers, leashed dogs, and horses. No mountain bikes are allowed. No wheelchair access.

Open Seasons: This trail is accessible mid-June–October.

Permits: Permits are not required. Parking and access are free.

Maps: For a map of Colville National Forest, contact the Outdoor Recreation Information Center at the downtown Seattle REI. For a topographic map, ask the USGS for Gypsy Peak.

Directions: From Metaline Falls, drive north 2 miles on Highway 31. Turn right onto County Road 9345 and drive 5 miles to Forest Service Road 22. Turn left and drive 8 miles (the road becomes Forest Service Road 2220 at 6.5 miles) to Forest Service Road 2212. Turn left and drive 3 miles to Forest Service Road 200. Turn right and drive 6 miles to the road's end and Bear Pasture Trailhead.

Contact: Colville National Forest, Sullivan Lake Ranger Station, 12641 Sullivan Lake Road, Metaline Falls, WA 99153, 509/446-7500.

39 THUNDER CREEK

10.2 mi/5.0 hrs

east of Metaline Falls in the Salmo-Priest Wilderness of Colville National Forest

Map 4.3, page 203

Less traveled than many other trails in the region, Thunder Creek Trail serves as an excellent way to step into the heart of Shedroof Divide. The first half of the trail follows an old road through the forest, passing many small streams and wet spots. After 2.2 miles, the road ends and the trail becomes a true footpath as it crosses into Salmo-Priest Wilderness. Old-growth western hemlock and western red cedar fill the forests, making prime habitat for a variety of big game animals. Deer, elk, bear, and even caribou are found in these forests. Thunder Creek Trail finds Shedroof Divide Trail after 5.1 miles, complete with open meadows and encouraging views. From here, hikers can head north or south along the backbone of Salmo-Priest Wilderness. Although the trail can often be wet, suitable drinking water may be difficult to find. Folks looking to make a night out of it will want to pitch their tents up on the divide in previously used spots.

User Groups: Hikers, leashed dogs, and horses. No mountain bikes are allowed. No wheelchair access.

Open Seasons: This trail is accessible mid-June–October.

Permits: Permits are not required. Parking and access are free.

Maps: For a map of Colville National Forest, contact the Outdoor Recreation Information Center at the downtown Seattle REI. For topographic maps, ask the USGS for Salmo Mountain and Helmer Mountain.

Directions: From Metaline Falls, drive north 2 miles on Highway 31. Turn right onto County Road 9345 and drive 5 miles to Forest Service Road 22. Turn left and drive 13 miles (the road becomes Forest Service Road 2220 at 6.5 miles) to Gypsy Meadows. The signed trailhead is on the right side of Forest Service Road 2220.

Contact: Colville National Forest, Sullivan Lake Ranger Station, 12641 Sullivan Lake Road, Metaline Falls, WA 99153, 509/446-7500.

40 SULLIVAN LAKESHORE

8.4 mi/4.0 hrs

east of Metaline Falls in Colville National Forest

Map 4.3, page 203

Situated between two national forest campgrounds, Sullivan Lakeshore Trail is a great hike for families. Four miles of level hiking along Sullivan Lake is highlighted by a great self-guided nature trail at one end. The trail runs between East Sullivan and Noisy Creek Campgrounds along the eastern shore of Sullivan Lake, making for two easily accessible trailheads. The better bet is to start from East Sullivan, where a short .5-mile nature loop cuts off the main trail into the heart of the forest. Hikers can pick up a brochure to follow as they hike, learning about different processes of the forest ecosystem. This short trail is ideal for little ones.

Sullivan Lakeshore Trail runs along the edge of Sullivan Lake, passing in and out of a mixed forest of hardwoods and conifers. The trail frequently breaks out to views of the lake and Sand Creek Mountain to the west. Often, hikers will turn around and peer up from the foot of Hall Mountain to see mountain goats scaling the rocky cliffs. Hikers young and old will appreciate this lakeside trail.

User Groups: Hikers and leashed dogs. No horses or mountain bikes are allowed. The nature trail is wheelchair accessible.

Open Seasons: This trail is accessible year-round.

Permits: Permits are not required. Parking and access are free.

Maps: For a map of Colville National Forest, contact the Outdoor Recreation Information Center at the downtown Seattle REI. For a topographic map, ask the USGS for Metaline Falls.

Directions: From Metaline Falls, drive north

2 miles on Highway 31. Turn right onto County Road 9345 and drive 5 miles to Forest Service Road 22. Turn left and drive .5 mile to East Sullivan Campground. Turn right and drive .3 mile to the well-signed trailhead on the left.

Contact: Colville National Forest, Sullivan Lake Ranger Station, 12641 Sullivan Lake Road, Metaline Falls, WA 99153, 509/446-7500.

41 HALL MOUNTAIN

5.0 mi/2.5 hrs

east of Metaline Falls in Colville National Forest

Map 4.3, page 203

Hall Mountain Trail is one of the best day hikes in the Sullivan Lake area. The trail up Hall Mountain is relatively short, never too steep for even younger hikers, and ends at an old lookout site, an obvious spot for views of the surrounding mountains. Hall Mountain Trail starts along an old road before arriving at a junction with Noisy Creek Trail (.7 mile). Take a right and keep climbing through the forest of subalpine fir and Englemann spruce. Big-game encounters are possible, with scores of deer, elk, and even caribou filling the woods during different seasons. More likely, you'll be startled by the sudden noise of a grouse taking off from under your feet. Hall Mountain Trail breaks out of the forest to find old remains of the Hall Mountain fire lookout. Sand Creek Mountain stands opposite the deep, blue water of Sullivan Lake, a tempting refresher for the end the day. Lucky hikers will peer down the steep slopes of Hall Mountain to find bighorn sheep scaling the hillside.

User Groups: Hikers, leashed dogs, horses, and mountain bikes. No wheelchair access.

Open Seasons: This trail is accessible June–October.

Permits: Permits are not required. Parking and access are free.

Maps: For a map of Colville National Forest, contact the Outdoor Recreation Information Center at the downtown Seattle REI. For topographic maps, ask the USGS for Metaline Falls and Pass Creek.

Directions: From Metaline Falls, drive north 2 miles on Highway 31. Turn right onto County Road 9345 and drive 5 miles to Forest Service Road 22. Turn left and drive 3.5 miles to Forest Service Road 500. Turn right and drive 7 miles to the road's end and the trailhead. This road is open only July 1–August 14, to minimize disturbances to wildlife habitat. Hall Mountain is accessible via Grassy Top or Noisy Creek during other times of the year.

Contact: Colville National Forest, Sullivan Lake Ranger Station, 12641 Sullivan Lake Road, Metaline Falls, WA 99153, 509/446-7500.

42 NOISY CREEK

10.6 mi/4.0 hrs

east of Metaline Falls in Colville National Forest

Map 4.3, page 203

In a region of high mountains, Noisy Creek Trail offers an easier hike perfectly suited for more laid-back hikers. The trail follows Noisy Creek, an appropriate name for the gushing stream during the spring snowmelt, for five miles through forests new and old. The first 1.3 miles climbs gently through the valley up to a vista of Sullivan Lake. This is a great turnaround for those seeking a shorter day hike, as it's about the only view you're going to find. More serious hikers will want to follow the trail farther up the creek valley as it makes its way through a forest of western hemlock, western red cedar, grand fir, and western larch, a hard-to-find species in Washington. Watch for camp robbers (not bandits, just gray jays) following you from the trailhead, hoping for a trail-mix handout. Woodpeckers pound away on dead snags while deer and elk frequently cross hikers' paths. Noisy Creek Trail crosses its namesake once (1.8 miles), a wet and even troublesome ford when the stream is running strongly. The trail makes a steep, mile-long climb out of the valley before ending at a junction with Hall Mountain Trail, at 5.3 miles.

User Groups: Hikers, leashed dogs, horses, and mountain bikes. No wheelchair access.
Open Seasons: This trail is accessible year-round.
Permits: Permits are not required. Parking and access are free.
Maps: For a map of Colville National Forest, contact the Outdoor Recreation Information Center at the downtown Seattle REI. For topographic maps, ask the USGS for Metaline Falls and Pass Creek.
Directions: From Metaline Falls, drive north 2 miles on Highway 31. Turn right onto County Road 9345 and drive 9.8 miles to Noisy Creek Campground. The well-signed trailhead is between the group and individual camp sections.
Contact: Colville National Forest, Sullivan Lake Ranger Station, 12641 Sullivan Lake Road, Metaline Falls, WA 99153, 509/446-7500.

43 PASS CREEK/GRASSY TOP

7.6 mi/4.0 hrs

east of Metaline Falls in Colville National Forest

Map 4.3, page 203

A mountain summit covered in grass means few trees. Few trees means expansive views of the surrounding mountains. One of the easier and more beautiful peaks to bag in the Sullivan Lake area is Grassy Top, a challenging but not overwhelming trail to the mountain's summit. All of this lies just outside of Salmo-Priest Wilderness but that is no harm to the appeal of this hike.

Grassy Top Trail begins at lofty Pass Creek Pass, a low point in the Shedroof Divide. The trail heads south along the ridge and steadily climbs toward Grassy Top. The forest of subalpine fir, Englemann spruce, and whitebark pine breaks open into expansive meadows of wildflowers (during the early summer) and waves of grass. These meadows are great places to catch deer grazing or bears scavenging. The trail passes just below Grassy Top, but a side trail leads to the summit. The surrounding Selkirk Range is in full splendor from this vantage, a delight on clear days. Remember to pack enough water, as it's nonexistent along the trail. Overnight hikers will need to find a place to camp off trail as there are no developed sites. We recommend atop Grassy Top.
User Groups: Hikers, leashed dogs, horses, and mountain bikes. No wheelchair access.
Open Seasons: This trail is accessible mid-June–October.
Permits: Permits are not required. Parking and access are free.
Maps: For a map of Colville National Forest, contact the Outdoor Recreation Information Center at the downtown Seattle REI. For a topographic map, ask the USGS for Pass Creek.
Directions: From Metaline Falls, drive north 2 miles on Highway 31. Turn right onto County Road 9345 and drive 5 miles to Forest Service Road 22. Turn left and drive 6.5 miles to a signed junction. Stay to the right on Forest Service Road 22 and drive 7.5 miles to Pass Creek Pass and the signed trailhead.
Contact: Colville National Forest, Sullivan Lake Ranger Station, 12641 Sullivan Lake Road, Metaline Falls, WA 99153, 509/446-7500.

44 LITTLE SPOKANE RIVER NATURAL AREA

7.5 mi/4.0 hrs

east of Spokane in Little Spokane River Natural Area

Map 4.4, page 204

Little Spokane River Natural Area provides a great escape from the city into an undisturbed wilderness. Contrasting greatly with the dry pine forests common to the Spokane area, the lowland bordering the river is rich in life. It's a prime spot to see animals normally viewed only on wildlife shows. The river ecosystem is fertile habitat for wildlife, including beaver, muskrat, porcupines, raccoons, coyotes, white-tailed deer, and even the occasional moose. The river also serves as important habitat for birds, including woodpeckers, bald eagles, red-tailed hawks, mergansers, and wood ducks. During the spring,

this area serves as a rookery (nesting site) for great blue herons. The Little Spokane River is also a great place to cast a fishing line, and the trail offers access to many secluded fishing holes where rainbow and cutthroat trout lurk below the surface.

From the central Painted Rocks Trailhead, the main trail runs to the east and west along the river. An informative brochure is available at the trailhead, providing a natural-history lesson as one wanders the trails. There is no true destination along the trail; a hike of any length is certain to be great trip. Be sure to investigate rock outcroppings for ancient Indian pictographs; these paintings are found all along the trail. Hikers who lead a double life as river rats will be happy to know that the Little Spokane River is a favorite haunt for canoeists and kayakers.

User Groups: Hikers only. No dogs, horses, or mountain bikes are allowed. No wheelchair access.

Open Seasons: This trail is accessible year-round.

Permits: Permits are not required. Parking and access are free.

Maps: For topographic maps, ask the USGS for Dartford and Ninemile Falls.

Directions: From Spokane, drive north on Highway 291 to Rutter Parkway. Turn right (east) and drive to the trailhead, on the left just after you cross the river.

Contact: Riverside State Park, 9711 West Charles Street, Nine Mile Falls, WA 99026, 509/465-5537.

Chapter 5

© SCOTT LEONARD

Mount Rainier and the Southern Cascades

Mount Rainier and the Southern Cascades

Easily the Northwest's tallest point (by more than 2,000 feet), Mount Rainier never seems to be far from view. At 14,411 feet, the towering mass of The Mountain looms over life in Puget Sound, southern Washington, and a good chunk of the east side as well. Perhaps because Mount Rainier is such familiar sight, many of the forests and mountains to her south go unnoticed. That's a shame, for the South Cascades of Washington are home to some excellent adventures in waiting. This area not only contains the living outdoor laboratory that is Mount St. Helens, it also has the glaciers and meadows of Mount Adams and Goat Rocks.

First and foremost on the agendas of most visitors to the region is Mount Rainier, since it is, to say the least, the embodiment of hiking in the Evergreen State. From old-growth forest to alpine meadows, from icy glaciers to milky white rivers, Mount Rainier has it all. A total of 26 glaciers grace the slopes of Takhoma (which, in Puyallup, means "breast of the milk-white waters"). These glistening masses of ice give birth to opalescent rivers flowing in every direction.

There are several points of access to one of the nation's most famous and heavily visited national parks: Route 410 and 123 transect the eastern side of the park, accessing Sunrise (6,400 feet), where great day hikes and longer trips exploring the north and east sides of Mount Rainier begin. Along the south side of the park, Nisqually and Stevens Canyon Roads meet at the high country of glory of Paradise. Again, numerous trails branch out from the visitor center and historic Park Lodge, exploring the meadows and glaciers of the area. Skyline Trail is a mecca for wildflowers. Although the west side of the park is inaccessible by car, Mowich Lake and Carbon River in the northwest corner can still be reached by road, the easiest park access from Seattle.

To the south is the Cascades' most restless sister, Mount St. Helens. Once one of the nation's most majestic mountains, it erupted in a mighty explosion in 1980, drastically altering its figure. Cubic miles of rock and mud slid off the mountain, and many square miles of forest were completely leveled. Today, life around the mountain is making a comeback. Shrubs and wildflowers are taking hold, and trees are even popping up here and there. But the devastation of the eruption is still readily evident. Coldwater Ridge and Johnston Ridge Visitor Centers are great stops, with trails leading from each into the blast zone. Folks can actually drive right into the blast zone at Windy Ridge Viewpoint, on the east side. A hike along Plains of Abraham or Meta Lake are great day trips.

Not to be outdone, the Gifford Pinchot National Forest boasts two beautiful wildernesses. Near White Pass are the snowcapped and rocky peaks of Goat Rocks. Numerous trails access this complex of obsolete volcanoes. Snowgrass Flats and Goat Ridge are the most scenic—and popular—routes into the area. And yes, there are goats here: A bet that you'll see a few is definitely worth a wager. Farther south in Indian Heaven, another group of high peaks and ridges were left over from old volcanoes. Thomas Lake and Indian Heaven Trails are great routes to explore the meadows and get good views of Mounts Hood, Adams, St. Helens, and even Rainier.

The rest of the Gifford Pinchot National Forest is crisscrossed by a large network of paved and unpaved roads. Numerous campgrounds and trails are easy to access, and even Sunday drivers will enjoy a trip into the Gipo. Mount Adams stands as Washington's second tallest peak and enjoys a wealth of trails and campgrounds. Although Round-the-Mountain doesn't actually make it all the way around, it's a great through-hike amongst meadows and waterfalls. Mount Adams is also one of Washington's easiest summits. Well, easy as in no ropes or climbing, but there is still the small matter of 8,000 feet elevation gain via South Climb. Much of the Gifford Pinchot remains unprotected as federal wilderness. Before hikers rise up in protest, mountain bikers should remind them that there are other users out there. In fact, many ridge trails are perfect for those on wheels (check out Langille Ridge, Boundary Trail, or Badger Ridge). Thanks to all the volcanic soil of the South Cascades, huckleberries are a plentiful backcountry harvest, and Juniper Ridge, Dark Meadows, and Hidden Lakes are great berry-picking trails. Rounding out the hiking selection is every kid's favorite school field trip: Ape Cave, a long underground lava tube. For water lovers, there's the White Salmon River, a very popular white-water rafting river, and while driving along the Columbia River Gorge, perhaps on your way to hike Beacon Rock, you're sure to notice hundreds of windsurfers on the river near Hood River.

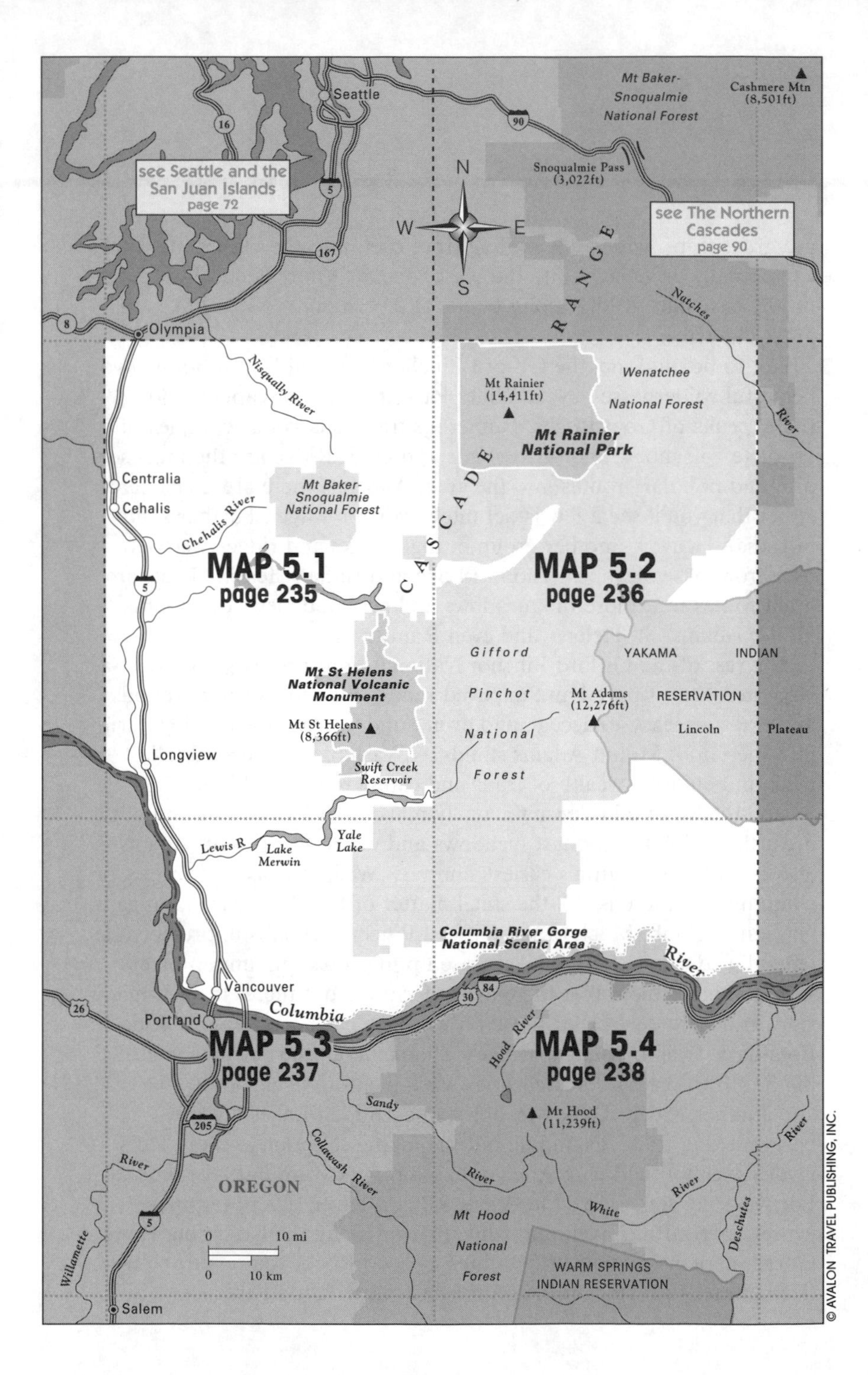

Seattle
16
5
167
see Seattle and the San Juan Islands page 72
Olympia
8
90
Mt Baker-
Snoqualmie
National Forest
Cashmere Mtn (8,501ft)
Snoqualmie Pass (3,022ft)
N
W
E
S
see The Northern Cascades page 90
Natches
CASCADE RANGE
Nisqually River
Mt Rainier (14,411ft)
Wenatchee
National Forest
Mt Rainier National Park
River
Centralia
Cehalis
Chehalis River
Mt Baker-
Snoqualmie
National Forest
MAP 5.1
page 235
MAP 5.2
page 236
5
Gifford
Pinchot
National
Forest
YAKAMA
INDIAN
RESERVATION
Mt St Helens National Volcanic Monument
Mt St Helens (8,366ft)
Mt Adams (12,276ft)
Lincoln
Plateau
Longview
Swift Creek Reservoir
Lewis R
Lake Merwin
Yale Lake
Columbia River Gorge National Scenic Area
River
Vancouver
84
30
26
Portland
Columbia
MAP 5.3
page 237
MAP 5.4
page 238
Hood River
Sandy
Mt Hood (11,239ft)
205
River
Collawash River
River
White
River
River
Deschutes
OREGON
5
Willamette
0
10 mi
0
10 km
Mt Hood
National
Forest
WARM SPRINGS
INDIAN RESERVATION
Salem

Map 5.1

Hikes 1–17
Pages 239–248

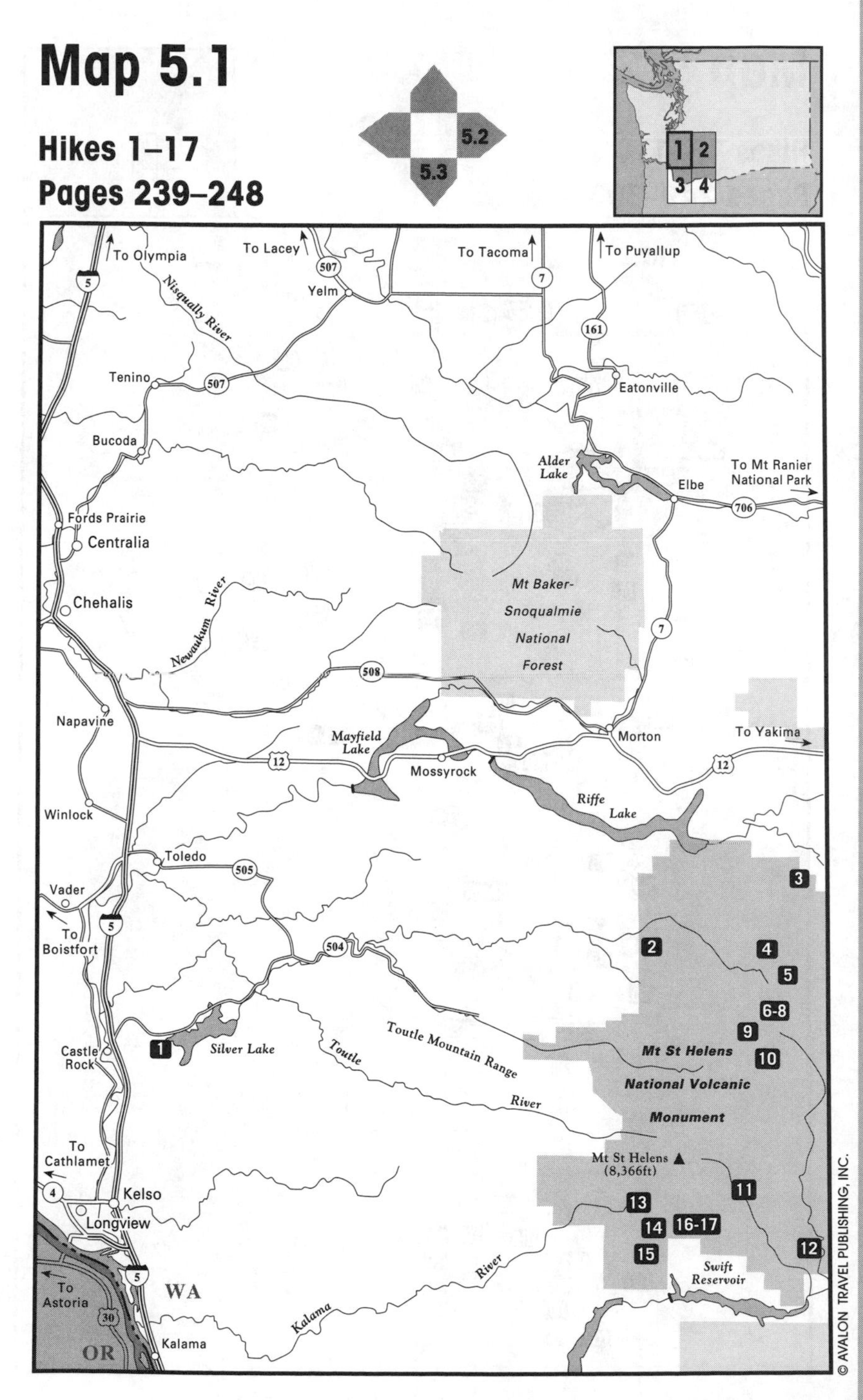

Map 5.2

Hikes 18–110
Pages 249–305

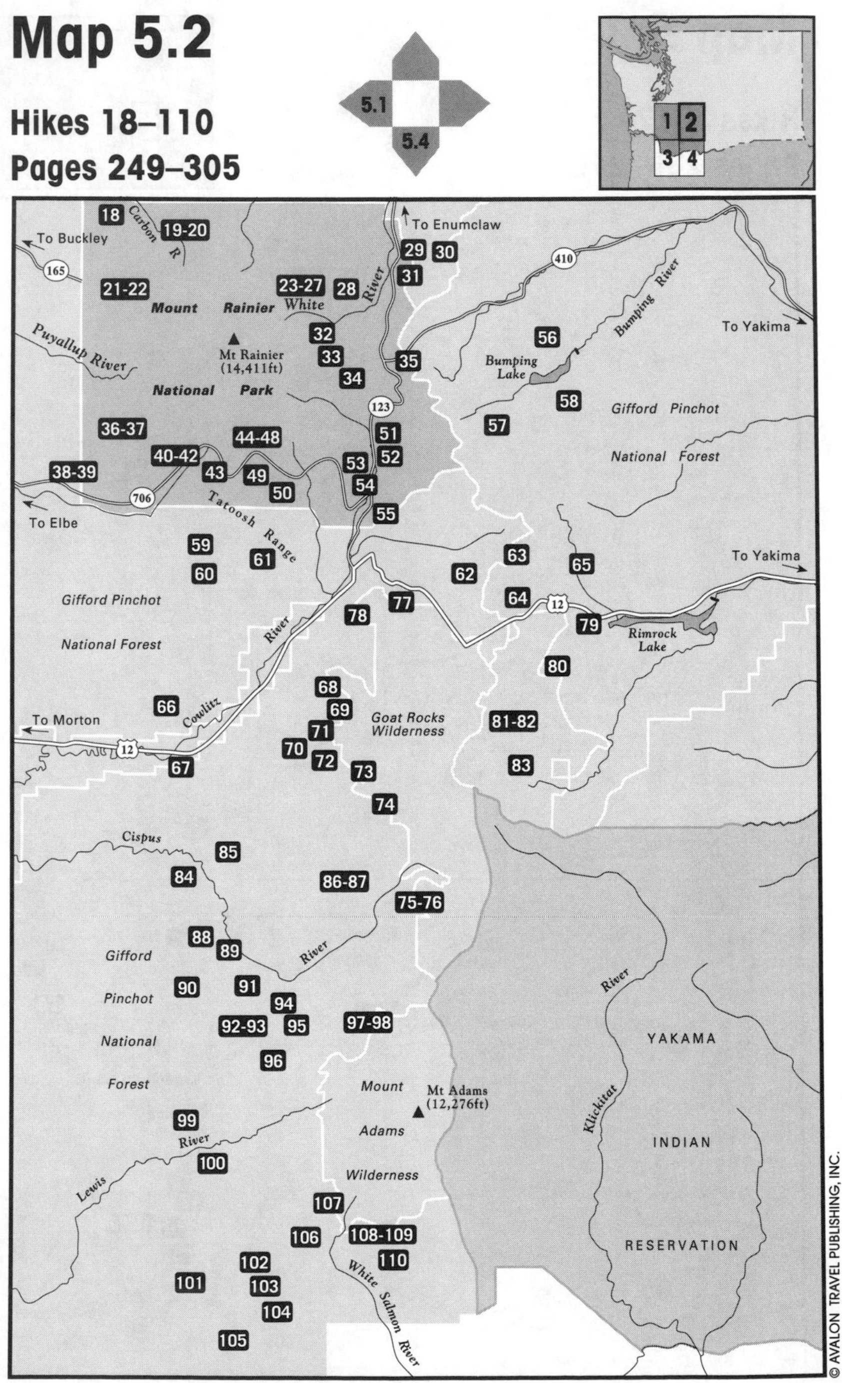

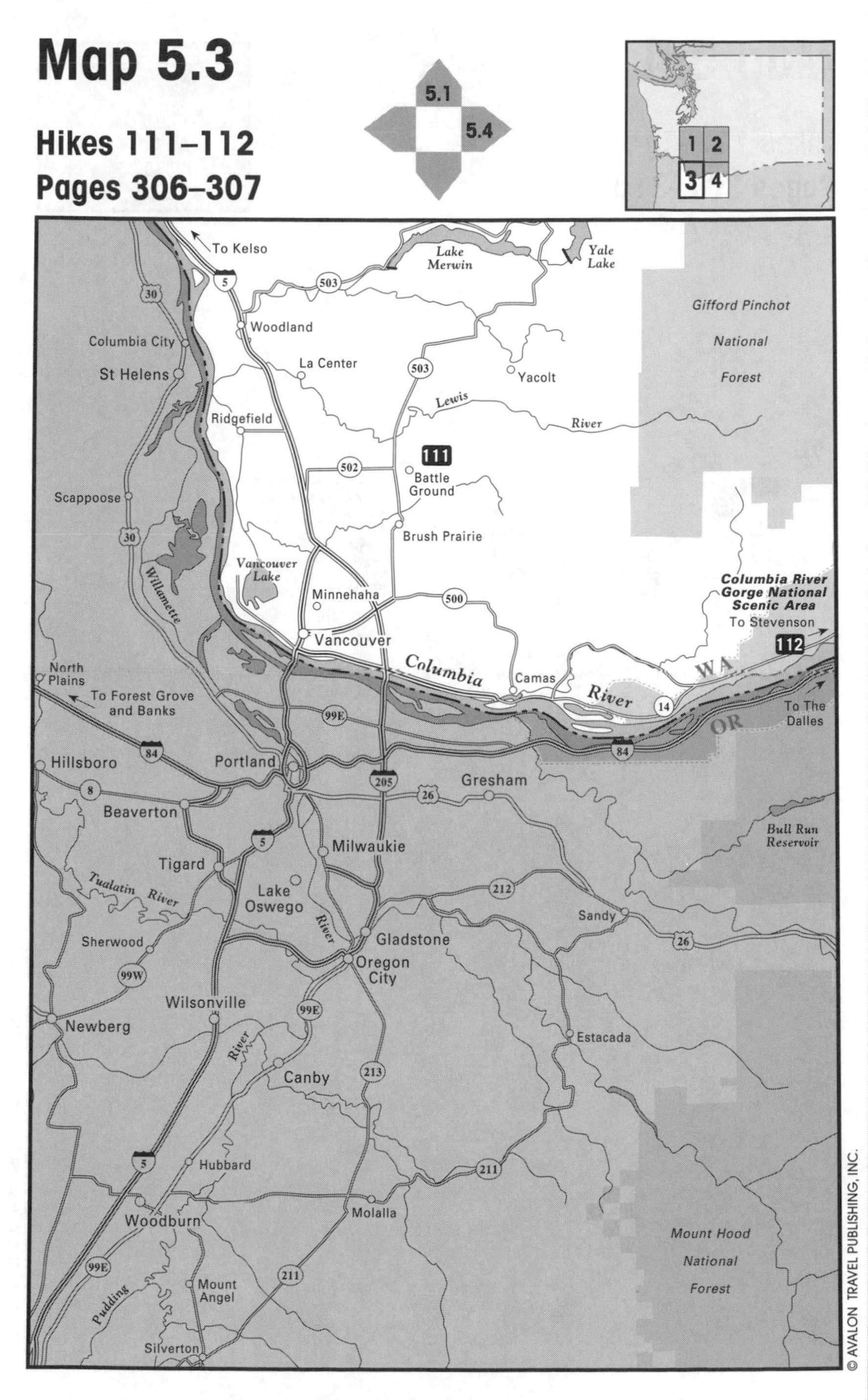
Map 5.3
Hikes 111–112
Pages 306–307
5.1
5.4
1
2
3
4
To Kelso
Lake Merwin
Yale Lake
5
503
30
Woodland
Columbia City
St Helens
La Center
503
Yacolt
Gifford Pinchot
National
Forest
Lewis
River
Ridgefield
111
502
Battle Ground
Scappoose
30
Brush Prairie
Vancouver Lake
Willamette
Columbia River Gorge National Scenic Area
Minnehaha
500
To Stevenson
Vancouver
112
Columbia
WA
North Plains
Camas
River
To Forest Grove and Banks
14
To The Dalles
99E
OR
84
84
Hillsboro
Portland
205
Gresham
8
26
Beaverton
Bull Run Reservoir
5
Milwaukie
Tigard
Tualatin River
Lake Oswego
212
River
Sandy
Sherwood
Gladstone
26
Oregon City
99W
Wilsonville
99E
Newberg
Estacada
River
Canby
213
5
Hubbard
211
Woodburn
Molalla
Mount Hood
National
Forest
99E
211
Mount Angel
Pudding
Silverton
© AVALON TRAVEL PUBLISHING, INC.

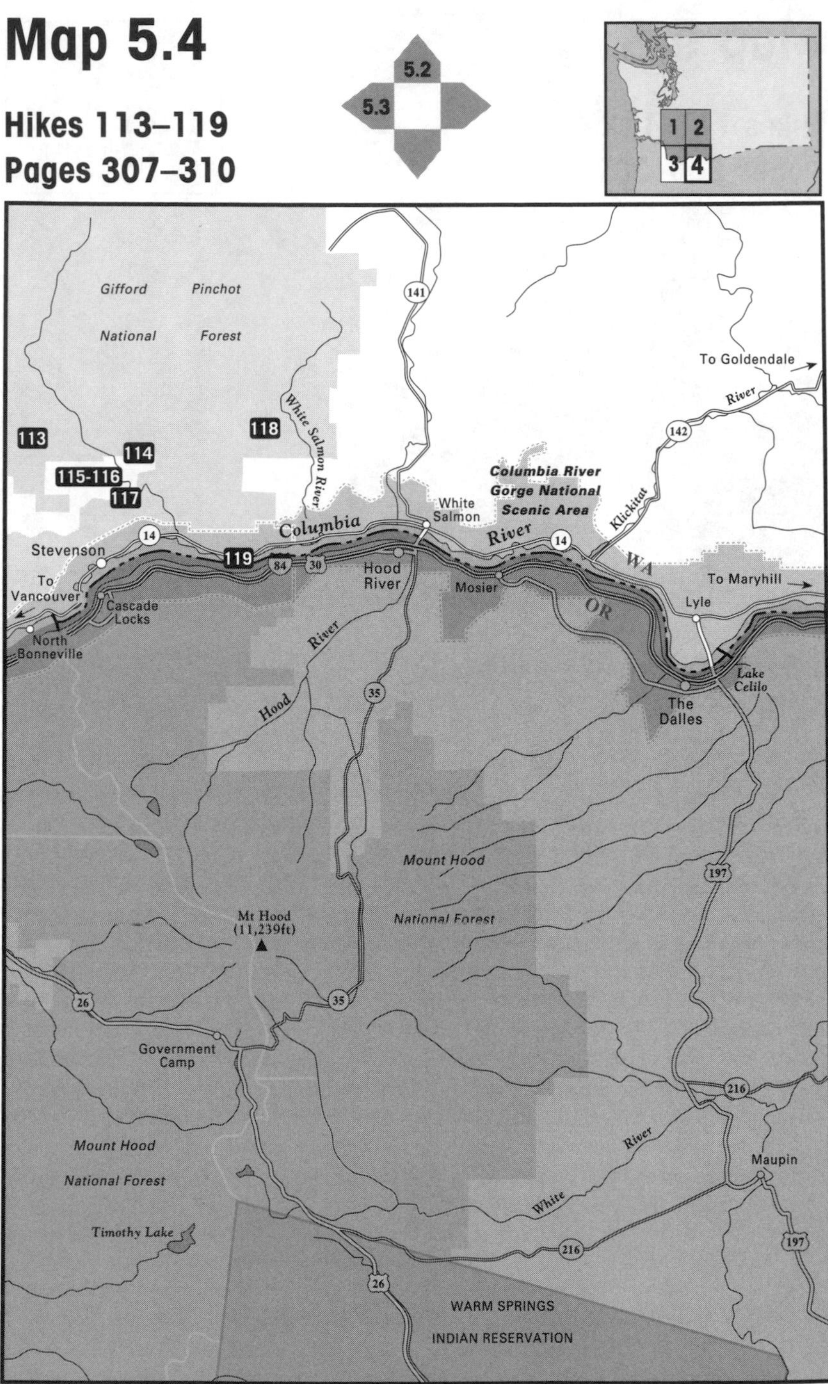
Map 5.4
Hikes 113–119
Pages 307–310
5.2
5.3
1 2
3 4
Gifford Pinchot
National Forest
White Salmon River
113
114
115-116
117
118
119
141
142
14
84
30
35
26
197
216
To Goldendale
River
Klickitat
Columbia River
Gorge National
Scenic Area
White
Salmon
Columbia
River
WA
OR
Stevenson
To
Vancouver
Cascade
Locks
North
Bonneville
Hood
River
Mosier
To Maryhill
Lyle
Lake
Celilo
The
Dalles
Hood
River
Mount Hood
National Forest
Mt Hood
(11,239ft)
Government
Camp
Mount Hood
National Forest
Timothy Lake
White
River
Maupin
WARM SPRINGS
INDIAN RESERVATION
© AVALON TRAVEL PUBLISHING, INC.

1 SILVER LAKE

1.0 mi/0.5 hr

east of Castle Rock in Silver Lake State Park

Map 5.1, page 235

The quick, one-mile loop of Silver Lake Trail is a great leg stretcher for folks hitting up the Silver Lake Visitor Center. The trail delves into the growing wetlands that in turn are slowly shrinking Silver Lake. The lake itself was formed by lava flows more than 2,000 years ago and is now on its last legs. Although the outlook may not be good for the lake, wildlife still finds it a happy home and is abundant around the lake. This is a favorite winter haunt for deer and elk, while spring and fall bring loads of migrating waterfowl. On clear days, Mount St. Helens is visible across Silver Lake. The trail is barrier free and accessible to wheelchairs.

User Groups: Hikers and leashed dogs. No horses or mountain bikes are allowed. The trail is wheelchair accessible.

Open Seasons: This trail is accessible year-round.

Permits: A federal Northwest Forest Pass is required to park here.

Maps: For a topographic map, ask the USGS for Silver Lake.

Directions: From Castle Rock, drive east 5 miles on Highway 504 to Silver Lake Mount St. Helens Visitor Center. The trailhead is on the south side of the visitors center.

Contact: Gifford Pinchot National Forest, Mount St. Helens National Volcanic Monument, 42218 Northeast Yale Bridge Road, Amboy, WA 98601, 360/449-7871.

2 COLDWATER LAKE

5.5 mi/3.0 hr

east of Castle Rock in Mount St. Helens National Volcanic Monument of Gifford Pinchot National Forest

Map 5.1, page 235

Hikers along the shores of Coldwater Lake can thank the 1980 eruption of Mount St. Helens for the trail they're enjoying. That's because before the blast, there was no Coldwater Lake. Massive amounts of mud and debris rushed down from the erupting volcano and created a large natural dam on Coldwater Creek, slowly filling up to become Coldwater Lake.

Coldwater Lake Trail follows the shores of this lake before climbing abruptly to the ridge above. The trail is easy to reach, beginning at the Coldwater Ridge Visitor Center. The trail follows the shores, now regenerating with small shrubs and plants. Although the gray, ashen hillsides look unfit for survival, many species of wildlife are spotted here, including deer, elk, squirrels, and frogs, and trout have been stocked in the lake. The trail hugs the shoreline for nearly three miles before climbing steeply. It's best to turn around and enjoy the walk back before the steep ascent.

User Groups: Hikers only. No dogs, horses, or mountain bikes are allowed. No wheelchair access.

Open Seasons: This trail is accessible April–November.

Permits: A federal Northwest Forest Pass is required to park here.

Maps: For a map of Gifford Pinchot National Forest, contact the Outdoor Recreation Information Center at the downtown Seattle REI. For a topographic map, ask Green Trails for No. 364, Mount St. Helens, or ask the USGS for Elk Rock and Spirit Lake West.

Directions: From Castle Rock, drive east 35 miles to the Coldwater Visitor Center in Mount St. Helens National Monument. The signed trailhead is immediately following the visitors center on the left.

Contact: Gifford Pinchot National Forest, Mount St. Helens National Volcanic Monument, 42218 Northeast Yale Bridge Road, Amboy, WA 98601, 360/449-7871.

3 STRAWBERRY MOUNTAIN

12.0 mi/6.0 hr 2 9

south of Randle in Mount St. Helens National Volcanic Monument of Gifford Pinchot National Forest

Map 5.1, page 235

Running south to north along the edge of Mount St. Helens' blast zone, Strawberry Mountain tells a great story of the effects of the 1980 eruption. Strawberry Mountain Trail rides the crest of the long mountain (which is more a ridge than a mountain). Along the western side, entire forests were leveled by a wave of searing gas and ash. The blast leveled the trees like blades of grass, leaving them arranged in neat rows. On the eastern side, it's business as usual. Subalpine meadows filled with wildflowers now dominate the southern part of the route, which climbs to a pair of open peaks.

Strawberry Mountain Trail runs the length of the ridge, 11 miles in all. The southern trailhead saves a lot of elevation gain and is more open and scenic. Thus it's the preferred route. Start at Bear Meadows and hike Boundary Trail to Strawberry Mountain Trail (.4 mile). Turn left and follow Strawberry Mountain Trail north. Old-growth forest is mixed with open meadows. A short side trail (2.7 miles) cuts off to the west and quickly finds an expansive viewpoint. Views of the alpine Mount Margaret backcountry and the crater within Mount St. Helens are terrific. The trail continues into open meadows of heather and lupine (5 miles). It's a good time to turn around and retrace your steps to the car when you've had your fill of views. Don't expect to find any water along this high route.

User Groups: Hikers, leashed dogs, horses, and mountain bikes. No wheelchair access.

Open Seasons: This trail is accessible June–October.

Permits: A federal Northwest Forest Pass is required to park here.

Maps: For a map of Gifford Pinchot National Forest, contact the Outdoor Recreation Information Center at the downtown Seattle REI. For a topographic map, ask Green Trails for No. 332, Spirit Lake, or ask the USGS for Cowlitz Falls and Vanson Peak.

Directions: From Randle, drive south 1 mile on Highway 131 to Forest Service Road 25. Stay to the right and drive 19 miles to Forest Service Road 99. Turn right and drive 6 miles to Bear Meadow Trailhead. The trail starts on the north side of Road 99.

Contact: Gifford Pinchot National Forest, Mount St. Helens National Volcanic Monument, 42218 Northeast Yale Bridge Road, Amboy, WA 98601, 360/449-7871.

4 QUARTZ CREEK BIG TREES

0.5 mi/0.5 hr 1 9

southwest of Randle in Gifford Pinchot National Forest

Map 5.1, page 235

So close to such devastated landscape, it's amazing to see what much of the forest near Mount St. Helens previously looked like. Not far from the blast zone, Quartz Creek Big Trees Trail is a short loop into an ancient forest of Douglas fir, western hemlock, and western red cedar. Mosses and ferns blanket every branch and inch of ground, a moist contrast to the barren landscapes just a few miles away over the ridge. Quartz Creek Big Trees Trail is flat, level, and barrier free, perfect for hikers of all ages and abilities. The trail makes a short .5-mile loop within this old-growth forest.

User Groups: Hikers and leashed dogs. No horses or mountain bikes are allowed. The trail is wheelchair accessible.

Open Seasons: This trail is accessible year-round.

Permits: A federal Northwest Forest Pass is required to park here.

Maps: For a map of Gifford Pinchot National Forest, contact the Outdoor Recreation Information Center at the downtown Seattle REI. For a topographic map, ask Green Trails for No. 332, Spirit Lake, or ask the USGS for Cowlitz Falls.

Directions: From Randle, drive south 1 mile on

Highway 131 to Forest Service Road 25. Stay to the right and drive 8 miles to Forest Service Road 26. Turn right and drive 8 miles to Forest Service Road 2608. Turn left and drive 1.5 miles to the signed trailhead on the right.

Contact: Gifford Pinchot National Forest, Cowlitz Valley Ranger Station, 10024 U.S. 12, Randle, WA 98377, 360/497-1100.

5 GOAT MOUNTAIN

8.0 mi/5.0 hr

north of Mount St. Helens in Gifford Pinchot National Forest

Map 5.1, page 235

Situated 12 miles north of Mount St. Helens (as the crow flies), Goat Mountain managed to escape much of the eruption's devastating impact. Thank goodness, for Goat Mountain is a subalpine wonderland. Covered in open meadows, this rocky ridge provides great views of the eruption's impact to the south. Goat Mountain is an excellent way to see the altered landscape yet still enjoy a hike among lush meadows.

Goat Mountain Trail climbs from Ryan Lake, zigzaging in and out of affected forest, now a graveyard of standing dead trees. The trail reaches the ridge (1.5 miles) and navigates a mix of meadows and rocky bluffs, each awash in wildflowers (bear grass, lupine, siprea, and stonecrop, to name a few). The towering slopes of Mount Margaret loom from the south.

Goat Mountain Trail traverses the ridge for three spectacular miles, eventually dropping to Deadman Lake (4.8 miles) and on to Vanson Lake (8.1 miles). Unless you're looking for a long hike or tough climb back, the best turnaround is before the trail drops to Deadman Lake. You'll see that Goat Mountain is an appropriate name. Fluffy white goats are a common sight, scrambling along the rocky cliffs.

User Groups: Hikers, leashed dogs, horses, and mountain bikes. No wheelchair access.

Open Seasons: This trail is accessible June–September.

Permits: A federal Northwest Forest Pass is required to park here.

Maps: For a map of Gifford Pinchot National Forest, contact the Outdoor Recreation Information Center at the downtown Seattle REI. For a topographic map, ask Green Trails for No. 332, Spirit Lake, or ask the USGS for Cowlitz Falls and Vanson Peak.

Directions: From Randle, drive south 1 mile on Highway 131 to Forest Service Road 25. Stay to the right and drive 8 miles to Forest Service Road 26. Turn right and drive 14 miles to Forest Service Road 2612. Turn right and drive .5 mile to the trailhead on the right.

Contact: Gifford Pinchot National Forest, Mount St. Helens National Volcanic Monument, 42218 Northeast Yale Bridge Road, Amboy, WA 98601, 360/449-7871.

6 BOUNDARY, WEST END

12.0 mi/5.0–6.0 hr

in Mount St. Helens National Monument

Map 5.1, page 235

This western end of Boundary Trail is the most glorious stretch of trail in Mount St. Helens National Monument. Every step is better than the one before it, as you experience beautiful meadows of wildflowers with expansive views of the eruption's impact. This section of Boundary Trail runs 13.8 miles (one-way) between Johnston Ridge Observatory and Norway Pass, near Winder Ridge Viewpoint. A car-drop between these two points involves hundreds of miles of driving and is hardly worthwhile. No worries, because each trailhead offers access to a great peak in about 12 miles.

Visitors to Johnston Ridge Observatory can hike to Coldwater Peak (12.2 miles round-trip), an up-close look at the crater. From the observatory, hike east on Boundary Trail above sprawling plains of ash and mud. The trail heads north and climbs above St. Helens Lake, a site of total devastation. A side trail leads to the summit (elevation 5,727 feet).

From Forest Service Road 99, a hike to Mount Margaret (11.6 miles round-trip) makes for an incredible trip through alpine meadows

and views of sparkling lakes. From Norway Pass Trailhead, hike west on Boundary Trail to Norway Pass (2.2 miles). The trail travels through the heart of the blast zone, but lush meadows survived to the north. A side trail leads to Margaret's summit.

Both hikes are exposed and dry, with no water to be found. They also have rocky sections along steep slopes; care is necessary at times.

User Groups: Hikers only. No dogs, horses, or mountain bikes are allowed. No wheelchair access.

Open Seasons: This trail is accessible June–mid-October.

Permits: A federal Northwest Forest Pass is required to park here.

Maps: For a map of Gifford Pinchot National Forest, contact the Outdoor Recreation Information Center at the downtown Seattle REI. For a topographic map, ask Green Trails for No. 332, Spirit Lake, or ask the USGS for Spirit Lake West and Spirit Lake East.

Directions: From Randle, drive south 1 mile on Highway 131 to Forest Service Road 25. Stay to the right and drive 19 miles to Forest Service Road 99. Turn right and drive 11 miles to Forest Service Road 26. Turn right and drive 1.5 miles to Norway Pass Trailhead.

Contact: Gifford Pinchot National Forest, Mount St. Helens National Volcanic Monument, 42218 Northeast Yale Bridge Road, Amboy, WA 98601, 360/449-7871.

7 BOUNDARY TRAIL

27.8 mi one-way/3.0 days

across Gifford Pinchot National Forest

Map 5.1, page 235

Boundary Trail is a long through-hike traversing Gifford Pinchot National Forest west to east. The trail previously began near the Mount Margaret backcountry, but the 1980 eruption destroyed the western trailhead and made the western six miles an adventuresome and entirely new out-and-back hike (see previous listing). The eastern contiguous section of Boundary Trail gets in miles of meadow rambling and even some old-growth shade. Views of surrounding valleys and peaks are nonstop in the middle segment.

The best place to start is Elk Pass, an easy access on Forest Service Road 25. From here, Boundary Trail travels alternating patches of old-growth and clear-cuts for about seven miles. The trail gets interesting as it skirts Badger and Craggy Peaks, where meadows and views reign supreme. The trail leads to the southern ends of Langille and Juniper Ridges, an exposed and beautiful 11-mile segment. The remainder of the trail (9 miles) sticks mostly to forest, ending at Council Lake.

Many so-called feeder trails offer access to Boundary Trail, making numerous segments of the route accessible for day hikes. Water is often scarce along the route, so plan well and bring plenty of capacity. Campsites are rarely designated; low-impact cross-country camping is necessary. Although few hikers complete the whole trip in one go, occasional crowds are likely because of the many access points. Also, be ready for noisy motorcycles on summer weekends.

User Groups: Hikers, leashed dogs, horses, mountain bikes, and motorcycles. No wheelchair access.

Open Seasons: This trail is accessible July–mid-October.

Permits: A federal Northwest Forest Pass is required to park at the trailheads.

Maps: For a map of Gifford Pinchot National Forest, contact the Outdoor Recreation Information Center at the downtown Seattle REI. For a topographic map, ask Green Trails for No. 332, Spirit Lake, No. 333, McCoy Peak, and No. 334, Blue Lake, or ask the USGS for French Butte, McCoy, Spirit Lake East, and Spirit Lake West.

Directions: From Randle, drive south 1 mile on Highway 131 to Forest Service Road 25. Stay to the right and drive 23 miles to the well-signed trailhead.

Contact: Gifford Pinchot National Forest, Cowlitz Valley Ranger Station, 10024 U.S. 12, Randle, WA 98377, 360/497-1100.

8 META LAKE

0.5 mi/0.5 hr

northeast of Mount St. Helens in Mount St. Helens National Volcanic Monument in Gifford Pinchot National Forest

Map 5.1, page 235

Lying behind a small ridge, Meta Lake received less than a death blow from Mount St. Helens' eruption despite being squarely in the blast zone. It helped that a snowpack lingered around the still-frozen lake, providing plants and trees a modest insulation from the searing heat and gas. With such protection in place, Meta Lake survived the blast and today provides a great example of the regeneration of life after the 1980 eruption.

Meta Lake Trail makes a quick trip to the lake (just .25 mile one-way). Several interpretive signs line the route, filling visitors in on the ability of life to survive and thrive here. Firs and hemlocks are once again creating a forest among blown-down logs, with lots of huckleberry bushes filling in the holes. Brook trout are still found in the lake, as are salamanders and frogs. The path is paved and is one of the best in the area with access for wheelchairs.

User Groups: Hikers only. No dogs, horses, or mountain bikes are allowed. The trail is wheelchair accessible.

Open Seasons: This trail is accessible June–September.

Permits: A federal Northwest Forest Pass is required to park here.

Maps: For a map of Gifford Pinchot National Forest, contact the Outdoor Recreation Information Center at the downtown Seattle REI. For a topographic map, ask Green Trails for No. 332, Spirit Lake, or ask the USGS for Spirit Lake East.

Directions: From Randle, drive south 1 mile on Highway 131 to Forest Service Road 25. Stay to the right and drive 19 miles to Forest Service Road 99. Turn right and drive 11.5 miles to the signed trailhead on the right.

Contact: Gifford Pinchot National Forest, Mount St. Helens National Volcanic Monument, 42218 Northeast Yale Bridge Road, Amboy, WA 98601, 360/449-7871.

9 HARMONY FALLS

2.0 mi/1.5 hr

northeast of Mount St. Helens in Mount St. Helens National Volcanic Monument in Gifford Pinchot National Forest

Map 5.1, page 235

Before the 1980 eruption of Mount St. Helens, Spirit Lake was home to houses and lodges, campgrounds, and an old, lush forest. All of that was quickly destroyed by the eruption, which left behind a surreal landscape. Harmony Trail passes right through this devastated area down to Spirit Lake, surveying the enormously changed scene.

Harmony Trail provides the only access to Spirit Lake, reaching the lakeshore where Harmony Falls drops in. The trail drops 600 feet to the lake, a considerable climb out. Bare trees lie scattered on the hillsides in neat rows, leveled by the searing gases of the eruption. Part of Spirit Lake is covered by dead trees, neatly arranged in the northern arm. On the hillsides, now covered in fine ash, small plants and shrubs work hard to revegetate the land. With a significant chunk of the mountain now lying at the bottom of the lake, the shores of Spirit Lake were raised 200 feet. This significantly enlarged the lake and cut off much of the height of Harmony Falls. Harmony Trail is a great way to experience one of the most affected areas of the blast zone.

User Groups: Hikers only. No dogs, horses, or mountain bikes are allowed. No wheelchair access.

Open Seasons: This trail is accessible June–September.

Permits: A federal Northwest Forest Pass is required to park here.

Maps: For a map of Gifford Pinchot National Forest, contact the Outdoor Recreation Information Center at the downtown Seattle REI. For a topographic map, ask Green Trails for

No. 332, Spirit Lake, or ask the USGS for Spirit Lake West and Spirit Lake East.

Directions: From Randle, drive south 1 mile on Highway 131 to Forest Service Road 25. Stay to the right and drive 19 miles to Forest Service Road 99. Turn right and drive 16 miles to the signed trailhead on the right.

Contact: Gifford Pinchot National Forest, Mount St. Helens National Volcanic Monument, 42218 Northeast Yale Bridge Road, Amboy, WA 98601, 360/449-7871.

10 PLAINS OF ABRAHAM

9.0 mi/5.0 hr

south of Randle in Mount St. Helens National Volcanic Monument in Gifford Pinchot National Forest

Map 5.1, page 235

Other than Loowit Trail, a round-the-mountain trek, no route gets closer to Mount St. Helens than Abraham Trail. Even better, Plains of Abraham makes a loop, with only two miles of trail hiked twice. The route, shaped like a lasso, spends its entirety within the blast zone, a barren landscape leveled by the 1980 eruption. During summer, when wildflowers speckle the slopes with color, this is undoubtedly the best option for a longer day hike near Mount St. Helens.

The route begins at popular Windy Ridge Viewpoint and follows the ridge on Truman Trail. Turn left on Abraham Trail (1.7 miles) as the path rounds five narrow draws (3 miles) to Loowit Trail (4 miles), within the Plains of Abraham. The plains are a wide, barren landscape repeatedly pounded by mud and landslides. Other than the smallest of plants and mosses, life is absent. It's an eerie but impressive scene.

Turn right on Loowit Trail to climb to Windy Pass (5 miles), an appropriate name on most days. The loop returns to the car via Truman Trail (6 miles) and Windy Ridge. July and August are great months to hike Abraham Trail, when wildflowers are at their peak. Water and shade are not found at any time along the trail, so consider extra water and sunscreen.

User Groups: Hikers only. No dogs, horses, or mountain bikes are allowed. No wheelchair access.

Open Seasons: This trail is accessible June–October.

Permits: A federal Northwest Forest Pass is required to park here.

Maps: For a map of Gifford Pinchot National Forest, contact the Outdoor Recreation Information Center at the downtown Seattle REI. For a topographic map, ask Green Trails for No. 364S, Mount St. Helens NW, or ask the USGS for Spirit Lake East.

Directions: From Randle, drive south 1 mile on Highway 131 to Forest Service Road 25. Stay to the right and drive 19 miles to Forest Service Road 99. Turn right and drive to Windy Ridge Trailhead at road's end.

Contact: Gifford Pinchot National Forest, Mount St. Helens National Volcanic Monument, 42218 Northeast Yale Bridge Road, Amboy, WA 98601, 360/449-7871.

11 LAVA CANYON

2.0 mi/1.5 hr

northeast of Cougar in Mount St. Helens National Volcanic Monument in Gifford Pinchot National Forest

Map 5.1, page 235

Removed from the blast zone of the 1980 eruption, Sheep Canyon nonetheless felt a few effects. The eruption created a raging torrent of mud and debris that gushed through the narrow gorge. The violent flow scoured the canyon bottom clean, leaving only barren bedrock for the Muddy River. That was a good thing, as it created a colorful river canyon with numerous pools and cascades. The trail through the gorge is one of the coolest places in Mount St. Helens National Volcanic Monument.

The first section of Lava Canyon Trail descends a steep series of switchbacks to several views of the canyon (.5 mile). Platforms are in place with interpretive signs. This section is paved and accessible to wheelchairs, although it's very steep and assistance is usually needed.

From here, a signed loop crosses the river via a bridge and follows the river down. This section of river has many pools and channels carved into the bedrock. The loop crosses back over the river via a high suspension bridge (1 mile). Although Lava Canyon Trail continues to a lower trailhead (2.5 miles), the lower suspension bridge marks a good time to head back.

User Groups: Hikers and leashed dogs. No horses or mountain bikes are allowed. Part of the trail is wheelchair accessible (for the first half mile, down to a viewpoint of the canyon, although very steep).

Open Seasons: This trail is accessible May–November.

Permits: A federal Northwest Forest Pass is required to park here.

Maps: For a map of Gifford Pinchot National Forest, contact the Outdoor Recreation Information Center at the downtown Seattle REI. For a topographic map, ask Green Trails for No. 364, Mount St. Helens, or ask the USGS for Smith Creek Butte.

Directions: From Vancouver, drive north on I-5 to Highway 503 (Woodland, exit 21). Drive east 35 miles to Forest Service Road 83. Turn left and drive 10 miles to the signed trailhead at road's end.

Contact: Gifford Pinchot National Forest, Mount St. Helens National Volcanic Monument, 42218 Northeast Yale Bridge Road, Amboy, WA 98601, 360/449-7871.

12 CEDAR FLATS

1.0 mi/0.5 hr

north of Cougar in Gifford Pinchot National Forest

Map 5.1, page 235

Quick and easy, Cedar Flats Trail ventures through Southern Washington's most impressive old-growth forest. It's easy to imagine you've been transported to the Olympic Peninsula when wandering among these giants. Douglas fir, western hemlock, and western red cedar create a forest of immense proportions. The area is preserved as part of Cedar Flats Natural Area, which was set aside in the 1940s. This area serves as important, undisturbed habitat for a variety of animals. Herds of elk winter in this area and deer are year-round inhabitants. Cedar Flats Trail makes a short and flat loop, arranged like a lasso, making this a great walk for families and hikers who prefer to avoid difficult hikes. Part of the trail nears the steep cliffs overlooking the Muddy River (inaccessible from the trail). The trail can be easily walked in a half hour, but it's well worth spending an afternoon in this peaceful setting.

User Groups: Hikers and leashed dogs. No horses or mountain bikes are allowed. No wheelchair access.

Open Seasons: This trail is accessible year-round.

Permits: A federal Northwest Forest Pass is required to park here.

Maps: For a map of Gifford Pinchot National Forest, contact the Outdoor Recreation Information Center at the downtown Seattle REI. For a topographic map, ask Green Trails for No. 364, Mount St. Helens, or ask the USGS for Cedar Flat.

Directions: From Cougar, drive east on Highway 503 (Forest Service Road 90) to Forest Service Road 25, at Pine Creek Information Station. Turn left and drive 6 miles to the trailhead on the right.

Contact: Gifford Pinchot National Forest, Mount St. Helens National Volcanic Monument, 42218 Northeast Yale Bridge Road, Amboy, WA 98601, 360/449-7871.

13 SHEEP CANYON

4.4 mi/3.0 hr

3 8

north of Cougar in Mount St. Helens National Volcanic Monument of Gifford Pinchot National Forest

Map 5.1, page 235

Not all of Mount St. Helens' destruction in May 1980 was the result of searing gas and ash. Areas not directly in the line of fire were instead affected by torrents of mud, water, and

debris. That's what happened along Sheep Creek, a muddy, ashen stream running through a steep canyon. The trail provides access to Loowit Trail, the route running around the mountain, home to impressive views of the flattened volcano.

Sheep Canyon Trail quickly leaves a patch of clear-cut land to enter an old-growth forest of noble fir. The route climbs much of its length, gaining more than 1,400 feet, rendering the shady, old forest a welcome friend. The highlight of the trail is Sheep Canyon, where Sheep Creek flows between vertical rock walls. Raging mudflows scoured the bottom of the canyon, leaving debris scattered over bare bedrock. Finally, the trail climbs harshly to Loowit Trail, where hikers can add extra miles by exploring to the north or south.

User Groups: Hikers and leashed dogs. No horses or mountain bikes are allowed. No wheelchair access.

Open Seasons: This trail is accessible June–October.

Permits: A federal Northwest Forest Pass is required to park here.

Maps: For a map of Gifford Pinchot National Forest, contact the Outdoor Recreation Information Center at the downtown Seattle REI. For a topographic map, ask the USGS for Mount St. Helens and Goat Mountain.

Directions: From Vancouver, drive north on I-5 to Highway 503 (Woodland, exit 21). Drive east 35 miles to Forest Service Road 83. Turn left and drive 3.5 miles to Forest Service Road 81. Turn left and drive to Forest Service Road 8123. Turn right and drive to the signed trailhead at road's end.

Contact: Gifford Pinchot National Forest, Mount St. Helens National Volcanic Monument, 42218 Northeast Yale Bridge Road, Amboy, WA 98601, 360/449-7871.

14 APE CAVE

2.5 mi/3.0 hr

north of Cougar in Mount St. Helens National Volcanic Monument in Gifford Pinchot National Forest

Map 5.1, page 235

The name Ape Cave conjures images of Sasquatch huddled in a narrow underground passage, hiding from people and their cameras. Sorry to disappoint. The caves were first explored by members of a local outdoors club, "The Apes," hence the name. Ape Cave is a long, large cave (known as a lava tube) naturally carved into the basalt by lava and water through thousands of years. Explored by thousands of visitors each year (including busloads of schoolchildren), these deep, pitch-black tunnels are an eerie and memorable experience.

From the main entrance, the cave heads in two directions. The Lower Passage is easier and shorter. It delves about .7 mile past a number of formations, including a Lava Ball and mudflow floor. The Upper Passage is 1.3 miles long underground with a 1.3-mile trail aboveground that returns to the trailhead. Upper Passage is more challenging, with segments that climb over rock piles and a small lava ledge. Near the upper exit, a large hole in the ceiling of the cave creates a natural skylight.

Be prepared for a chilly hike. Year-round temperature is a steady 42°F. Imagine that, 85 outside but 42 inside! Two sources of light are recommended, and headlamps don't count. The deep darkness of the caves requires very strong flashlights or, preferably, large gas lanterns. Parts of the upper passage are rocky, so sturdy shoes and pants are also recommended.

User Groups: Hikers only. No dogs, horses, or mountain bikes are allowed. No wheelchair access.

Open Seasons: This trail is accessible year-round.

Permits: A federal Northwest Forest Pass is required to park here.

Maps: For a map of Gifford Pinchot National Forest, contact the Outdoor Recreation Information Center at the downtown Seattle REI. For a topographic map, ask Green Trails for No. 364, Mount St. Helens, or ask the USGS for Mount Mitchell.

Directions: From Vancouver, drive north on I-5 to Highway 503 (Woodland, exit 21). Drive east 35 miles to Forest Service Road 83. Turn left and drive 2 miles to Forest Service Road 8303. Turn left and drive 1.5 miles to the signed trailhead on the right.

Contact: Gifford Pinchot National Forest, Mount St. Helens National Volcanic Monument, 42218 Northeast Yale Bridge Road, Amboy, WA 98601, 360/449-7871.

15 TRAIL OF TWO FORESTS

0.3 mi/0.5 hr

northeast of Cougar in Mount St. Helens National Volcanic Monument in Gifford Pinchot National Forest

Map 5.1, page 235

Trail of Two Forests is a quick nature loop into one of the most unlikely natural phenomena in the Northwest. Nearly two millennia ago, Mount St. Helens sent a wave of molten lava down her south flank. This wave of lava consumed everything in its path before eventually cooling and stopping. Trail of Two Forests is perfectly situated near the bottom of the flow, where the lava still moved but was not hot enough to immediately destroy trees. Here, lava cooled around the trees, which eventually decomposed and left small tunnels, caves, and pits as a testament to the old forest. The second of the two forests is the one that stands today. Interpretive signs do a great job of explaining the story in depth. Conveniently, boardwalk lines the entire route, making Trail of Two Forests accessible to wheelchairs. The boardwalk also protects the fragile forest ground, so please stay on the trail. The one chance visitors have to get off-trail is a chance to crawl through a tunnel, or lava tube, nearly 30 feet long. It's a trip!

User Groups: Hikers and leashed dogs. No horses or mountain bikes are allowed. No wheelchair access.

Open Seasons: This trail is accessible March–November.

Permits: A federal Northwest Forest Pass is required to park here.

Maps: For a map of Gifford Pinchot National Forest, contact the Outdoor Recreation Information Center at the downtown Seattle REI. For a topographic map, ask Green Trails for No. 364, Mount St. Helens, or ask the USGS for Mount Mitchell.

Directions: From Vancouver, drive north on I-5 to Highway 503 (Woodland, exit 21). Drive east 35 miles to Forest Service Road 83. Turn left and drive 2 miles to Forest Service Road 8303. Turn left and drive .1 mile to the signed trailhead on the left.

Contact: Gifford Pinchot National Forest, Mount St. Helens National Volcanic Monument, 42218 Northeast Yale Bridge Road, Amboy, WA 98601, 360/449-7871.

16 JUNE LAKE

2.8 mi/2.0 hr

northeast of Cougar in Mount St. Helens National Volcanic Monument in Gifford Pinchot National Forest

Map 5.1, page 235

June Lake achieves recognition by being the only subalpine lake on the slopes of Mount St. Helens. As the volcano forms a nice, neat cone, few basins are created to host a beautiful lake. Well, that's what Mount St. Helens has done here, nestling a great lake below a cliff of basalt, complete with waterfall. Subalpine forest and meadow ring the lake, which has a sandy beach perfect for summer afternoon lounging.

June Lake Trail gains just 500 feet in 1.4 miles and is ideal for families. It courses its way through young forest with views of a gorge before emerging upon a large field of basalt boulders (1 mile). The trail sticks to the forest and soon finds June Lake. For a view of Mount St. Helens, hike past the lake a few hundred yards on Loowit Trail. Several campsites are scattered around the lake, and campers are expected to follow strict Leave-No-Trace principles.

User Groups: Hikers and leashed dogs. No horses or mountain bikes are allowed. No wheelchair access.
Open Seasons: This trail is accessible May–November.
Permits: A federal Northwest Forest Pass is required to park here.
Maps: For a map of Gifford Pinchot National Forest, contact the Outdoor Recreation Information Center at the downtown Seattle REI. For a topographic map, ask Green Trails for No. 364S, Mount St. Helens NW, or ask the USGS for Mount St. Helens.
Directions: From Vancouver, drive north on I-5 to Highway 503 (Woodland, exit 21). Drive east 35 miles to Forest Service Road 83. Turn left and drive 6 miles to the signed trailhead on the left.
Contact: Gifford Pinchot National Forest, Mount St. Helens National Volcanic Monument, 42218 Northeast Yale Bridge Road, Amboy, WA 98601, 360/449-7871.

17 LOOWIT TRAIL

30.5 mi/3–4 days

around the mountain in Mount St. Helens National Volcanic Monument in Gifford Pinchot National Forest

Map 5.1, page 235

Loowit Trail is the grand loop encircling Mount St. Helens. It was an interesting trip before 1980, and the eruption of the mountain turned this trek into an unforgettable outing. Loowit experiences everything imaginable–old-growth forest, alpine meadows, and barren, ravaged landscapes. Compared to Wonderland Trail, elevation changes along the route are modest. Still, many sections of the trail are difficult and rocky.

Loowit Trail has no definite trailhead. Instead, several feeder trails lead to the 27.7-mile loop. Among these trails are June Lake in the south (1.7 miles one-way), Truman Trail at Windy Ridge (3 miles), and Sheep Canyon on the west side (2.2 miles). Diligent planning is a must before setting out on Loowit Trail. Water sources and campsites are limited throughout the route and often change year to year. The Forest Service suggests that you call ahead to get the current scoop. Finally, be ready for ash, lots and lots of ash. The fine, gray particles will invade everything you own. Bring a coffee filter to tie around your water filter and protect it. Also, take special care with cameras, binoculars, or eyeglasses, all easily damaged by ash.

Loowit Trail is often hiked counterclockwise. From June Lake, the trail climbs beneath the rocky toe of the Worm Flows to Shoestring Glacier, from the barren Plains of Abraham to Loowit Falls and impressive views of the crater. Loowit Trail traverses the blast zone, a real lesson in the magnitude of the destructive blast, before crossing the mud-ravaged Toutle River. Meadow and old-growth forest line the route as it returns to June Lake.
User Groups: Hikers only. No dogs, horses, or mountain bikes are allowed. No wheelchair access.
Open Seasons: This trail is accessible June–October.
Permits: A federal Northwest Forest Pass is required to park here.
Maps: For a map of Gifford Pinchot National Forest, contact the Outdoor Recreation Information Center at the downtown Seattle REI. For a topographic map, ask Green Trails for No. 364S, Mount St. Helens NW, or ask the USGS for Mount St. Helens, Smith Creek Butte, and Goat Mountain.
Directions: From Vancouver, drive north on I-5 to Highway 503 (Woodland, exit 21). Drive east 35 miles to Forest Service Road 83. Turn left and drive 6 miles to the signed trailhead on the left for June Lake (the shortest access on the south side).
Contact: Gifford Pinchot National Forest, Mount St. Helens National Volcanic Monument, 42218 Northeast Yale Bridge Road, Amboy, WA 98601, 360/449-7871.

18 GREEN LAKE

3.6 mi/2.0 hr

in northwest Mount Rainier National Park

Map 5.2, page 236

You don't need amnesia to forget about Mount Rainier when hiking the trail to Green Lake. Grabbing your attention from the start are granddaddy Douglas firs and western hemlocks. These giants tower over the trail in the Carbon River Valley and are estimated to be more than 800 years of age. The trail then climbs alongside Ranger Creek, within earshot but mostly out of sight. A must-see stop is a small side trail to Ranger Falls (1 mile). During the spring snowmelt, this large series of cascades creates a thunderous roar heard throughout the forest. The trail switchbacks .5 mile before leveling and crossing the creek. Green Lake sits among pristine forest and a little meadow. Anglers can try their luck here for trout. South of the lake and peeking through a large valley stands Tolmie Peak. Green Lake is a great day hike during the summer but also makes a good snowshoe trek during the winter. Old-growth forest, big waterfalls, and a serene mountain lake—now what was the name of that mountain everyone keeps talking about?

User Groups: Hikers only. No dogs, horses, or mountain bikes are allowed. No wheelchair access.

Open Seasons: This area is usually accessible April–November.

Permits: A National Parks Pass is required to enter the park.

Maps: For a map of Mount Rainier National Park, contact the Outdoor Recreation Information Center at the downtown Seattle REI. For a topographic map, ask Green Trails for No. 269, Mount Rainier West, or ask the USGS for Mowich Lake.

Directions: From Tacoma, drive east on Highway 410 to Buckley. Turn south on Highway 165 and drive 14 miles to Carbon River Road. Turn left and drive 8 miles to Carbon River Entrance Station. Continue 3 miles to the trailhead on the right.

Contact: Mount Rainier National Park, Wilkeson Wilderness Information Center, P.O. Box 423, Wilkeson, WA 98396, 360/569-6020.

19 WINDY GAP

13.0–17.0 mi/8.0 hr–2 days

4 10

in northern Mount Rainier National Park

Map 5.2, page 236

Mount Rainier grabs the most attention (it stands more than 14,000 feet tall, after all). But the park holds miles of amazing terrain, tucked away from the mountain's view. Windy Gap is a perfect example. The enjoyable trail climbs into a high-country playground of meadows and rocky peaks, with plenty to see and do. Hikes to Lake James and the Natural Bridge (a large rock arch) start here. A full day of hiking, Windy Gap features two backcountry camps for overnight visits.

The route starts from Ipsut Creek Campground and joins Wonderland Trail (.5 mile), eventually leaving to cross the Carbon River (2.4 miles). Turn left and do the switchback shuffle up Northern Loop Trail to Windy Gap. The sighting of colorful Yellowstone Cliffs (5.1 miles) signals the arrival of parkland meadows, reflective tarns, and craggy horizons. Boulder-strewn Windy Gap (6.4 miles), a good place to turn around, is truly a blustery experience, and mountain goats roam the surrounding ridges.

Beyond Windy Gap, Northern Loop Trail drops 1.5 miles to lightly visited Lake James, clad in subalpine meadows. Beyond Windy Gap .25 mile, a signed trail leads to Natural Bridge. Rising out of the forest, the large rock formation seems lost from the sea. After crossing the Carbon, the trail is dry; bring plenty of water. Beautiful backcountry camps are situated at Yellowstone Cliffs and Lake James and require camping permits.

User Groups: Hikers only. No dogs, horses, or mountain bikes are allowed. No wheelchair access.

Open Seasons: This area is usually accessible mid-July–September.

Permits: A National Parks Pass is required to enter the park. Overnight stays within the national park require backcountry camping permits, which are available at Wilkeson Wilderness Information Center.
Maps: For a map of Mount Rainier National Park, contact the Outdoor Recreation Information Center at the downtown Seattle REI. For a topographic map, ask Green Trails for No. 269, Mount Rainier West, and No. 270, Mount Rainier East, or ask the USGS for Mowich Lake and Sunrise.
Directions: From Tacoma, drive east on Highway 410 to Buckley. Turn south on Highway 165 and drive 14 miles to Carbon River Road. Turn left and drive 8 miles to Carbon River Entrance Station. Continue 5 miles to Ipsut Creek Campground at road's end. The trailhead is well marked.
Contact: Mount Rainier National Park, Wilkeson Wilderness Information Center, P.O. Box 423, Wilkeson, WA 98396, 360/569-6020.

20 CARBON GLACIER/ MYSTIC LAKE

15.5 mi/8.0 hr–2 days 4 10

north of The Mountain in Mount Rainier National Park

Map 5.2, page 236

Situated on the famed Wonderland Trail, there isn't a lake closer to Mount Rainier than Mystic Lake. This seven-mile stretch of Washington's most esteemed trail is incredibly diverse. It travels through old-growth forest on the Carbon River, past Rainier's lowest and longest glacier, and upward to rocky alpine meadows and a majestic lake. This is one of the park's premier hikes.

The length of the route follows Wonderland Trail. The trail starts mildly, cruising through ancient forests. After crossing Carbon River (3 miles), however, the trail climbs unrelentingly to Mystic Lake. Somehow, the trail finds a path between Carbon Glacier and the valley wall. Those cracking noises you hear are the glacier giving way to the hot summer sun; walking on the glacier is ill advised without an ice ax and proper training.

Wonderland Trail parts ways with the glacier as it enters Moraine Park (5.5 miles), acres of wildflower meadows. A welcome sight on hot days, Mystic Lake lies just below Mineral Mountain. Although it stands 800 feet above the lake, Mineral Mountain can do little to block Mount Rainier and its ragged Willis Wall. Backcountry camps are situated at Dick Creek (4 miles) and Mystic Lake (7.7 miles); they require permits and are usually occupied by Wonderland trekkers.
User Groups: Hikers only. No dogs, horses, or mountain bikes are allowed. No wheelchair access.
Open Seasons: This area is usually accessible mid-July–September.
Permits: A National Parks Pass is required to enter the park. Overnight stays within the national park require backcountry camping permits, which are available at Wilkeson Wilderness Information Center.
Maps: For a map of Mount Rainier National Park, contact the Outdoor Recreation Information Center at the downtown Seattle REI. For a topographic map, ask Green Trails for No. 269, Mount Rainier West, or ask the USGS for Mowich Lake.
Directions: From Tacoma, drive east on Highway 410 to Buckley. Turn south on Highway 165 and drive 14 miles to Carbon River Road. Turn left and drive 8 miles to Carbon River Entrance Station. Continue 5 miles to Ipsut Creek Campground at road's end. The trailhead is well marked.
Contact: Mount Rainier National Park, Wilkeson Wilderness Information Center, P.O. Box 423, Wilkeson, WA 98396, 360/569-6020.

21 TOLMIE PEAK LOOKOUT

6.5 mi/3.5 hr 2 10

northwest of Tahoma in Mount Rainier National Park

Map 5.2, page 236

The best job in the United States is a summer spent staffing the Tolmie Peak Lookout. The job description includes: a three-mile commute through pristine subalpine forest, picturesque Eunice Lake surrounded in parkland meadows, and panoramic views from the office, encompassing The Mountain and miles of national forest. Ready to sign up?

Tolmie Peak Trail begins at Mowich Lake, a spectacular setting itself. The trail leaves the large, forested lake and rises gently to Ipsut Pass (1.5 miles), a junction with Carbon River Trail. Stay to the left and continue climbing to Eunice Lake (2.3 miles), where meadows reach to the lake's edges. The trail then climbs steeply one more mile to Tolmie Lookout (elevation 5,939 feet) atop the windswept peak. Mount Rainier is the obvious attraction, but Mount St. Helens and the North Cascades make appearances as well. Talk about your prime picnic spots. If the final steep climb to the lookout sounds unappealing, stopping short at Eunice Lake is a good hike as well. In late July, wildflowers fill the meadows bordering Eunice, and views of Mount Rainier are still to be had.

User Groups: Hikers only. No dogs, horses, or mountain bikes are allowed. No wheelchair access.

Open Seasons: This area is accessible June–October.

Permits: A National Parks Pass is required to enter the park.

Maps: For a map of Mount Rainier National Park, contact the Outdoor Recreation Information Center at the downtown Seattle REI. For a topographic map, ask Green Trails for No. 269, Mount Rainier West, or ask the USGS for Mowich Lake and Golden Lakes.

Directions: From Tacoma, drive east on Highway 410 to Buckley. Turn south on Highway 165 and drive 14 miles to Carbon River Road junction. Stay to the right on Mowich Lake Road and drive 17 miles to Mowich Lake Campground at road's end. The trailhead is well marked.

Contact: Mount Rainier National Park, Wilkeson Wilderness Information Center, P.O. Box 423, Wilkeson, WA 98396, 360/569-6020.

22 SPRAY PARK

8.8 mi/4.5 hr

northwest of The Mountain in Mount Rainier National Park

Map 5.2, page 236

Spray Park is without a doubt one of the most beautiful places on Mount Rainier. Meadows measured by the square mile cover the upper reaches of this trail, dominated by the imposing stature of The Mountain. Wildflowers erupt and blanket the high country in late July, while black bears in search of huckleberries roam in late August. The trail is one of the greats in the national park and receives heavy use.

Spray Park Trail leaves from Mowich Lake, an inviting dip after a hot summer day on the trail. The trail meanders through the forest to Eagle Cliff (1.5 miles), where the trail follows the precipitous slope. A side trail wanders over to Spray Falls (1.9 miles) before making a steep ascent on switchbacks. The reward for the effort is a breakout from forest into open meadow. Spray Park Trail wanders through this open country, past tarns and rock fields to a saddle (elevation 6,400 feet) with views of even more meadows. The saddle is a good turnaround point, as the trail drops beyond it to Carbon River. Be sure to bring ample water, a rarity beyond Spray Falls. And remember, the meadows here are very fragile; please stay on established trails.

User Groups: Hikers only. No dogs, horses, or mountain bikes are allowed. No wheelchair access.

Open Seasons: This area is usually accessible July–September.

Permits: A National Parks Pass is required to enter the park.

Maps: For a map of Mount Rainier National Park, contact the Outdoor Recreation Information Center at the downtown Seattle REI. For a topographic map, ask Green Trails for No. 269, Mount Rainier West, or ask the USGS for Mowich Lake.

Directions: From Tacoma, drive east on Highway 410 to Buckley. Turn south on Highway

165 and drive 14 miles to Carbon River Road junction. Stay to the right on Mowich Lake Road and drive 17 miles to Mowich Lake Campground at road's end. The trailhead is well marked.

Contact: Mount Rainier National Park, Wilkeson Wilderness Information Center, P.O. Box 423, Wilkeson, WA 98396, 360/569-6020.

23 SUNRISE NATURE TRAILS

1.5–3.2 mi/0.5–1.5 hr

near Sunrise in Mount Rainier National Park

Map 5.2, page 236

The beauty of Sunrise's high placement means that hikers don't have to venture far for an incredible hike. Although the views start at the parking lot, pavement is usually something we're trying to avoid. Several great options are well suited to hikers of all abilities. Options vary from trips to Shadow Lake or Frozen Lake to a nature trail and a walk through a silver forest. These are perfect trails for families with little ones or for folks conducting an auto tour around the park.

Although the network of trails surrounding Sunrise seems like a jumbled cobweb, every junction is well signed and easy to navigate. Trails to the two lakes are easy walks. Shadow Lake is a level three-mile round-trip, with meadows and views of Rainier all the way. Frozen Lake gains a little more elevation and peers out over the colorful meadows of Berkeley Park (3.2 miles round-trip).

The west end of Sourdough Ridge Trail features a self-guided nature trail, a 1.5-mile loop with some elevation gain. Lupine and bistort are on full display in July. On the south side of the visitors center is Silver Forest Trail (2.4 miles), a unique path through a forest of bare snags, long ago killed but not toppled by fire.

User Groups: Hikers only. No dogs, horses, or mountain bikes are allowed. No wheelchair access.

Open Seasons: This area is usually accessible July–September.

Permits: A National Parks Pass is required to enter the park.

Maps: For a map of Mount Rainier National Park, contact the Outdoor Recreation Information Center at the downtown Seattle REI. For a topographic map, ask Green Trails for No. 270, Mount Rainier East, or ask the USGS for Sunrise.

Directions: From Puyallup, drive east 52 miles on Highway 410 to Sunrise Road in Mount Rainier National Park. Turn right and drive 15 miles to the trailhead at Sunrise Visitor Center.

Contact: Mount Rainier National Park, White River Wilderness Information Center, 70004 Highway 410 East, Enumclaw, WA 98022, 360/569-6030.

24 BERKELEY AND GRAND PARKS

7.6–15.2 mi/4.0–8.0 hr

out of Sunrise in Mount Rainier National Park

Map 5.2, page 236

A grand destination indeed, wide, flat Grand Park stretches for more than a mile with incredible views of Mount Rainier. On the way, Berkeley Park dazzles with its own wildflower displays and beautiful stream. In a land of many high-country meadows, this is a dandy of a choice.

The route leaves the high country of Sunrise and gently wanders through meadows to Frozen Lake (1.5 miles), tucked beneath Mount Fremont and Burroughs Mountain. Follow the Wonderland Trail for one mile to Northern Loop Trail and drop into Berkeley Park (2.5 miles), where streams crisscross the lush meadows. This is a good turnaround for hikers uninterested in making the longer trip to Grand Park.

Northern Loop Trail leaves Berkeley Park and travels through open subalpine forest to Grand Park (7.6 miles). Grand Park and its meadows stretch more than a mile to the north. Deer and elk are frequent visitors to the meadows, where they find an abundance

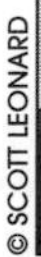

Mount Rainier from Grand Park

of summer grazing. Although Grand Park is preferably accomplished in a day, hikers hoping to spend the night can pitch camp at Berkeley Camp (3.8 miles) or hike 3.3 miles beyond Grand Park to Lake Eleanor (11.4 miles one-way). Access to Lake Eleanor via an unofficial trail from national forest land is frowned upon by the Park Service; besides, it misses out on the best sections of the route.

User Groups: Hikers only. No dogs, horses, or mountain bikes are allowed. No wheelchair access.

Open Seasons: This area is usually accessible mid-July–September.

Permits: A National Parks Pass is required to enter the park.

Maps: For a map of Mount Rainier National Park, contact the Outdoor Recreation Information Center at the downtown Seattle REI. For a topographic map, ask Green Trails for No. 270, Mount Rainier East, or ask the USGS for Sunrise.

Directions: From Puyallup, drive east 52 miles on Highway 410 to Sunrise Road in Mount Rainier National Park. Turn right and drive 15 miles to the trailhead at Sunrise Visitor Center.

Contact: Mount Rainier National Park, White River Wilderness Information Center, 70004 Highway 410 East, Enumclaw, WA 98022, 360/569-6030.

25 MOUNT FREMONT LOOKOUT

6.0 mi/3.0 hr

out of Sunrise in Mount Rainier National Park

Map 5.2, page 236

Where there's a lookout, there are views. And there's no lookout closer to Mount Rainier than the one atop Mount Fremont. Never mind that the lookout doesn't sit on Fremont's summit. There are still plenty of views along this great trail. Hiking in Rainier high country is all about meadows, and this trail is no different. It travels exclusively through open meadows, and as long as the weather is clear (never a guarantee around The Mountain), you can expect knock-your-boots-off views. Best of all, Mount Fremont is an easy trail to navigate for hikers, gaining just 1,200 feet in about three miles.

Mount Fremont Trail leaves the popular Sunrise Visitor Center and quickly climbs to Sourdough Ridge. Mount Rainier is almost too close, crowding much of the southern horizon. Pass picturesque Frozen Lake at 1.5 miles as the trail encounters a large but well-signed junction. Mount Fremont Trail heads north along the rocky ridge, tops out in elevation, and drops to the lookout, built in the 1930s. Although it's hard to take your eyes off Tahoma and its glaciers, the Cascades and Olympics will call from distant

horizons. The vast meadows of Grand Park below the lookout are a painter's palette of color in July. Be sure to carry enough water for the trip; there's none to be found along the way.

User Groups: Hikers only. No dogs, horses, or mountain bikes are allowed. No wheelchair access.

Open Seasons: This trail is accessible mid-July–September.

Permits: A National Parks Pass is required to enter the park.

Maps: For a map of Mount Rainier National Park, contact the Outdoor Recreation Information Center at the downtown Seattle REI. For a topographic map, ask Green Trails for No. 270, Mount Rainier East, or ask the USGS for Sunrise.

Directions: From Puyallup, drive east 52 miles on Highway 410 to Sunrise Road in Mount Rainier National Park. Turn right and drive 15 miles to the trailhead at Sunrise Visitor Center.

Contact: Mount Rainier National Park, White River Wilderness Information Center, 70004 Highway 410 East, Enumclaw, WA 98022, 360/569-6030.

26 SOURDOUGH RIDGE/ DEGE PEAK

2.5 mi/1.5 hr

2 9

near Sunrise in Mount Rainier National Park

Map 5.2, page 236

Sourdough Ridge Trail covers more than four miles of immaculate subalpine meadows immersed in grand views of Mount Rainier and much more. The trail follows Sourdough Ridge from Sunrise Visitor Center out to Dege Peak and Sunrise Point on the east end. A visit here in July will yield acre upon acre of blooming wildflowers, with swaths of paintbrush, lupine, and daisies on the mountainside. This is a popular and heavily used trail near the Sunrise Visitor Center, and rightfully so. There may be no easier or quicker way to get a view of Tahoma.

Sourdough Ridge Trail quickly climbs away from Sunrise Visitor Center into meadows. Every step leads to a better view. Of course The Mountain is impressively big, but the Cowlitz Chimneys and Sarvent Glaciers are seen best from this route. Those who survive the ascent of the first mile have seen the worst. The trail follows the ridge beneath Antler Peak and Dege Peak, the trail's highlight (a side trail leads to its summit). Look north over meadowy ridges to the Palisades and all the way up to Glacier Peak. This is a great hike for families visiting Sunrise; the trail gains less than 600 feet.

User Groups: Hikers only. No dogs, horses, or mountain bikes are allowed. No wheelchair access.

Open Seasons: This area is usually accessible mid-June–September.

Permits: A National Parks Pass is required to enter the park.

Maps: For a map of Mount Rainier National Park, contact the Outdoor Recreation Information Center at the downtown Seattle REI. For a topographic map, ask Green Trails for No. 270, Mount Rainier East, or ask the USGS for Sunrise.

Directions: From Puyallup, drive east 52 miles on Highway 410 to Sunrise Road in Mount Rainier National Park. Turn right and drive 15 miles to the trailhead at Sunrise Visitor Center.

Contact: Mount Rainier National Park, White River Wilderness Information Center, 70004 Highway 410 East, Enumclaw, WA 98022, 360/569-6030.

27 BURROUGHS MOUNTAIN LOOP

5.5 mi/3.0 hr

near Sunrise in Mount Rainier National Park

Map 5.2, page 236

One of Mount Rainier's best day hikes, Burroughs Mountain is also one of its most challenging. Many hikers set out on this hike only to be turned back by snowfields that linger well into August. It's best to check in with the ranger at Sunrise and get a trail report. Snow or not, there's definitely lots to see along the way. Along the way you'll find meadows of flowers and marmots before reaching the tundralike expanses atop Burroughs Mountain. Add to it a lake for lunch and views of glaciers, and Burroughs Loop seems to have it all.

Burroughs Mountain Trail makes a five-mile loop up to the high, rocky plateau of Burroughs Mountain. A clockwise direction is best, especially if the north side is still snowy. From the visitors center, the trail crosses over crystal streams and colorful meadows to Shadow Lake and an overlook of Emmons Glacier and the White River (1.4 miles). Hikers start dropping off as the trail climbs 900 feet to First Burroughs Mountain (2.8 miles). Guaranteed: Mount Rainier has never looked so big in your life.

Burroughs Mountain Trail wanders the wide, flat plateau and drops to Frozen Lake (3.6 miles). Snowfields like to linger along this northern half of the loop. These steep slopes can be crossed when snowy, but an ice ax is highly, highly recommended. The well-signed trail heads back to the visitors center.

User Groups: Hikers only. No dogs, horses, or mountain bikes are allowed. No wheelchair access.

Open Seasons: This area is usually accessible July–September.

Permits: A National Parks Pass is required to enter the park.

Maps: For a map of Mount Rainier National Park, contact the Outdoor Recreation Information Center at the downtown Seattle REI. For a topographic map, ask Green Trails for No. 270, Mount Rainier East, or ask the USGS for Sunrise.

Directions: From Puyallup, drive east 52 miles on Highway 410 to Sunrise Road in Mount Rainier National Park. Turn right and drive 15 miles to the trailhead at Sunrise Visitor Center.

Contact: Mount Rainier National Park, White River Wilderness Information Center, 70004 Highway 410 East, Enumclaw, WA 98022, 360/569-6030.

28 PALISADES LAKES

6.6 mi/3.5 hr–2 days

near Sunrise in Mount Rainier National Park

Map 5.2, page 236

There is no easier lake hike in Mount Rainier National Park than Palisades Lakes Trail. It has no big views of Tahoma; those are blocked by the rugged Sourdough Mountains. But Palisades Lakes Trail offers seven subalpine lakes and many smaller tarns, each among acres of meadows and rocky ridges. The trail is up and down but never significantly, making this a perfect hike for younger hikers. The short length of the trail means it's easily hiked in an afternoon, but a pair of backcountry camps are enticing enough to warrant an overnight visit.

Palisades Lakes Trail leaves Sunrise Road and quickly climbs to Sunrise Lake (.4 mile), where a short side trail leads to the small, forested lake. Palisades Trail continues past Clover Lake (1.4 miles) and Hidden Lake (2.5 miles), each surrounded by subalpine groves and meadows. Another mile of trail through acres of meadows, brimming with wildflowers in early August, arrives at Upper Palisades Lake. The lake gets its name from the rocky ridge, known as the Palisades, framing the basin. Marmots and picas are sure to be heard whistling from the talus slopes, and mountain goats are residents of the area too. For an overnight stay, you must make camp at either Dicks Lake or Upper Palisades.

User Groups: Hikers only. No dogs, horses, or mountain bikes are allowed. No wheelchair access.

Open Seasons: This area is usually accessible mid-June–September.

Permits: A National Parks Pass is required to enter the park. Overnight stays within the national park require backcountry camping permits, which are available at Sunrise Visitor Center.

Maps: For a map of Mount Rainier National Park, contact the Outdoor Recreation Information Center at the downtown Seattle REI.

For a topographic map, ask Green Trails for No. 270, Mount Rainier East, or ask the USGS for White River Park.

Directions: From Puyallup, drive east 52 miles on Highway 410 to Sunrise Road in Mount Rainier National Park. Turn right and drive 13 miles to Sunrise Point and the trailhead.

Contact: Mount Rainier National Park, White River Wilderness Information Center, 70004 Highway 410 East, Enumclaw, WA 98022, 360/569-6030.

29 CRYSTAL MOUNTAIN

9.0 mi/4.5 hr

3 9

near Crystal Mountain Ski Resort in Mount Baker–Snoqualmie National Forest

Map 5.2, page 236

Better known for ski runs, Crystal Mountain features a good hiking trail. Getting there isn't quite as easy as using a ski lift, however, unless you actually ride the resort's chair lift, which is possible. Crystal Mountain Trail spends a fair amount of time in unimpressive woods before breaking out into miles of more-than-wonderful ridge hiking. This is a great place to view Mount Rainier and munch on huckleberries.

Crystal Mountain Trail begins with little flair, enduring clear-cuts and second-growth forest for three miles as it ascends 1,600 feet. That's the requirement to achieve Crystal Ridge and any notable rewards. At the ridge, Mount Rainier appears above the White River Valley. The trail climbs another three miles along the ridge through wide, rounded meadows mixed with steep, rocky slopes. Wildflowers are in full gear during early June while huckleberries make the trip twice as sweet in early August. Anywhere along the ridge is a good turnaround. Water is nonexistent, so carry plenty of extra water.

Crystal Mountain Trail can be completed several other ways, but they aren't as enjoyable. The trail forms a loop back to the ski resort, passing several small mountain lakes (a total of 13.8 miles, 2.5 on the road). An all-downhill version can be had by riding a ski lift up to the ridge and hiking back down.

User Groups: Hikers, leashed dogs, horses, and mountain bikes. No wheelchair access.

Open Seasons: This trail is accessible June–September.

Permits: A federal Northwest Forest Pass is required to park here.

Maps: For a map of Mount Baker–Snoqualmie National Forest, contact the Outdoor Recreation Information Center at the downtown Seattle REI. For topographic maps, ask Green Trails for No. 270, Mount Rainier East, and No. 271, Bumping Lake, or ask the USGS for Bumping Lake and White River.

Directions: From Puyallup, drive east 47 miles on State Highway 410 to Crystal Mountain Road (Forest Service Road 7190). Turn left (east) and drive 4.4 miles to Forest Service Road 7190-510. Turn right and drive .4 mile to Sand Flats camping area and the trailhead.

Contact: Mount Baker–Snoqualmie National Forest, Enumclaw Ranger Station, 450 Roosevelt Avenue East, Enumclaw, WA 98022, 360/825-6585.

30 NORSE PEAK

11.2–13.8 mi/6.0–7.5 hr

4 10

near Crystal Mountain Ski Resort in Mount Baker–Snoqualmie National Forest

Map 5.2, page 236

Ignored by the masses at Mount Rainier, Norse Peak and Cascade Crest are equally deserving of attention. Although steep, Norse Peak Trail travels miles of meadows to a former lookout site west of Rainier. Conveniently, the trail offers a detour of even more meadowy hiking on the way. When in this region, it's often hard to justify not visiting the national park. Not here. Norse Peak is worth it.

Norse Peak Trail spends all of its time climbing, gaining 2,900 feet to the lookout. It's well laid out and never too steep, but it's certainly tiring under a hot summer sun. Most of the trail is exposed in high-country meadows, so bringing plenty of water and sunscreen are good ideas. Norse Peak Trail spends less than two miles in the forest before emerging into the open. As the trail climbs, Tahoma rises from behind Crystal Mountain. At 3.6 miles lies Goat Lake junction and at 4.9 miles is Norse Peak Lookout junction; stay to the right both times for the lookout, 6,856 feet of views. Tahoma is its usual magnificent self, but numerous other peaks are noteworthy too.

You can make a loop to visit beautiful Big Crow Basin. Descend from the lookout to the upper junction. Turn right and pass through the large basin of meadows to Pacific Crest Trail and back again via Goat Lake Trail. Even with a trip to the lookout, the loop is less than 14 miles.

User Groups: Hikers, leashed dogs, horses, and mountain bikes (no mountain bikes in Big Crow Basin). No wheelchair access.

Open Seasons: This trail is accessible mid-June–September.

Permits: A federal Northwest Forest Pass is required to park here.

Maps: For a map of Mount Baker–Snoqualmie National Forest, contact the Outdoor Recreation Information Center at the downtown Seattle REI. For a topographic map, ask Green Trails for No. 271, Bumping Lake, or ask the USGS for Norse Peak.

Directions: From Puyallup, drive east 47 miles on State Highway 410 to Crystal Mountain Road (Forest Service Road 7190). Turn left (east) and drive 4 miles to Forest Service Road 7190-410. Parking is on the right side of Crystal Mountain Road (Forest Service Road 7190); the signed trailhead is several hundred yards up Forest Service Road 7190-410.

Contact: Mount Baker–Snoqualmie National Forest, Enumclaw Ranger Station, 450 Roosevelt Avenue East, Enumclaw, WA 98022, 360/825-6585.

31 CRYSTAL LAKES

6.0 mi/3.5 hr

near Sunrise in Mount Rainier National Park

Map 5.2, page 236

Crystal Lakes Trail presents hikers a choice between two inspiring destinations. One route heads to Crystal Lakes, a pair of sublime subalpine lakes cloaked in wildflower meadows. As the lakes are in a large basin beneath Sourdough Gap and Crystal Peak, the distant views are limited (but hardly missed). The second option bypasses the two lakes and climbs to Crystal Peak Lookout. Naturally, the views of The Mountain are great. Either way, a great trip is assured.

Crystal Lakes Trail leaves Highway 410 and hastily climbs the valley wall within forest. At 1.3 miles lies the decisive junction. Left for the lakes, right for the lookout. Crystal Lakes Trail keeps climbing, soon entering the open subalpine and Lower Crystal Lake (2.3 miles). Upper Crystal Lake is just a short climb away (3 miles). Acres of wildflowers light up the basins in early August. Backcountry camps are at each lake and require a camping permit. For those itching to get to a high viewpoint, the Crystal Peak Trail climbs 2.5 miles from the junction along a dry, open slope to the lookout (elevation 6,615 feet). On a clear day, five Cascades volcanoes are within view, not to mention much of the national park and surrounding national forest.

User Groups: Hikers only. No dogs, horses, or mountain bikes are allowed. No wheelchair access.

Open Seasons: This trail is usually accessible mid-July–September.

Permits: A National Parks Pass is required to enter the park. Overnight stays within the national park require backcountry camping permits, which are available at Sunrise Visitor Center.

Maps: For a map of Mount Rainier National Park, contact the Outdoor Recreation Information Center at the downtown Seattle REI. For a topographic map, ask Green Trails for No. 270, Mount Rainier East, or ask the USGS for White River Park.

Directions: From Puyallup, drive east 51 miles on Highway 410 to Crystal Lakes Trailhead, just before the White River Wilderness Information Center.

Contact: Mount Rainier National Park, White River Wilderness Information Center, 70004 Highway 410 East, Enumclaw, WA 98022, 360/569-6030.

32 GLACIER BASIN

3.8–7.0 mi/2.0–3.5 hr

near Sunrise in Mount Rainier National Park

Map 5.2, page 236

Mount Rainier may be known best for the immense glaciers covering its slopes. More than two dozen massive ice sheets radiate from the mountain's summit, sculpting entire valleys and ridges. Glacier Basin Trail provides a close look at two of Mount Rainier's glaciers, Emmons Glacier and Inter Glacier, hard at work. If you find glaciers boring, then shift your attention to the hillsides and look for mountain goats among the meadows.

Here's a little geology lesson first. Glaciers are massive sheets of ice produced through thousands of years. Snowfall slowly accumulates through the years and becomes compacted into a sheet of ice. Enter gravity, which slowly pulls the glacier down the valley, scraping and sculpting the terrain as it moves. It may take a while (millennia), but glaciers are heavy-duty landscapers. When glaciers retreat (melt faster than they form, as they are now), they leave a denuded valley filled with moraine (piles of rock and dirt), which you'll see here. Got it? You're ready for Glacier Basin Trail.

The trail has two forks: Glacier Basin Trail (7 miles round-trip) and Emmons Glacier Trail (3.8 miles). The trail departs White River Campground and gently climbs to the junction (.9 mile): Head left for Emmons Glacier (the largest in the lower 48 states), right for Inter Glacier. Both trails provide great views of the glaciers. Being a glacier is dirty work, apparent from the enormous piles of rock and mud covering the ice. Glacier Basin is most popular with mountaineers seeking a summit of The Mountain.

User Groups: Hikers only. No dogs, horses, or mountain bikes are allowed. No wheelchair access.

Open Seasons: This trail is usually accessible mid-July–September.

Permits: A National Parks Pass is required to enter the park.

Maps: For a map of Mount Rainier National Park, contact the Outdoor Recreation Information Center at the downtown Seattle REI. For a topographic map, ask Green Trails for No. 270, Mount Rainier East, or ask the USGS for White River Park.

Directions: From Puyallup, drive east 52 miles on Highway 410 to Sunrise Road in Mount Rainier National Park. Turn right and drive 5.5 miles to White River Road. Turn left and drive 2 miles to White River Campground and signed trailhead.

Contact: Mount Rainier National Park, White River Wilderness Information Center, 70004 Highway 410 East, Enumclaw, WA 98022, 360/569-6030.

33 SUMMERLAND/ PANHANDLE GAP

8.6–11.4 mi/4.5–6.0 hr

near Sunrise in Mount Rainier National Park

Map 5.2, page 236

Many hikers who have completed Wonderland Trail, a 93-mile trek around The Mountain, claim the country surrounding Panhandle Gap as their favorite. The meadows of Summerland and Ohanapecosh Park lie on either side of Panhandle Gap. Above, the ancient volcano of Little Tahoma stands before its big sister, Mount Rainier. Traveling this high country via Wonderland Trail at White River is a diverse and scenic trip.

The route leaves White River Campground and follows Wonderland through old-growth forest of large western hemlock, western red cedar, and Douglas fir. Little Tahoma, with Fryingpan Glacier hanging off its side, signals your arrival in the meadows and wildflowers of Summerland (4.3 miles). Large herds of mountain goats are frequently seen on the rocky slopes surrounding Summerland.

The curious and energetic can follow Wonderland Trail another 1.4 miles as it ascends steeply to the wind-swept terrain of Panhandle Gap. From this high point, the meadows of Ohanapecosh Park unfold beneath several high waterfalls. A word of caution: This high country is rocky and fairly barren. In many places, the trail is designated by rock cairns. No matter the season, be prepared for adverse weather. Tahoma has a system of its own, one that changes rapidly and unexpectedly, so bring warm clothes and know how to use your compass.

User Groups: Hikers only. No dogs, horses, or mountain bikes are allowed. No wheelchair access.

Open Seasons: This area is usually accessible August–September.

Permits: A National Parks Pass is required to enter the park.

Maps: For a map of Mount Rainier National Park, contact the Outdoor Recreation Information Center at the downtown Seattle REI. For a topographic map, ask Green Trails for No. 270, Mount Rainier East, or ask the USGS for Sunrise and White River Park.

Directions: From Puyallup, drive east 52 miles on Highway 410 to Sunrise Road in Mount Rainier National Park. Turn right and drive 4.5 miles to Fryingpan Trailhead on the left.

Contact: Mount Rainier National Park, White River Wilderness Information Center, 70004 Highway 410 East, Enumclaw, WA 98022, 360/569-6030.

34 OWYHIGH LAKES

7.6 mi/4.0 hr

east of Tahoma in Mount Rainier National Park

Map 5.2, page 236

With such a dominating presence, Mount Rainier makes it easy to miss some of the other outstanding scenery in the park. Plenty of great hiking is to be had that doesn't include bulky views of the massive volcano. Owyhigh Lakes Trail is one such hike, traveling up through old but dense forest to parkland lakes. Meadows of wildflowers surround the several lakes and light up the scenery during early August. If you're worried about missing out on seeing rocky peaks and ridges, don't fret. The lakes are situated between craggy Governors Ridge and stately Tamanos Mountain, home of four prominent pinnacles known as the Cowlitz Chimneys.

Adding to Owyhigh Trail's allure is its lack of people. When the crowds at the park visitors centers make you begin to think it's holiday shopping season at the mall, Owyhigh Lakes is likely to be vacant. Folks hoping to spend the night can pitch their shelters at Tamanos Creek Camp, .5 mile before the lakes; just remember to pick up your permit. The trail continues beyond the lakes, crests a pass, and drops five miles to Deer Creek Trailhead, requiring a car-drop. Day hikers should turn around at Owyhigh Lakes.

User Groups: Hikers only. No dogs, horses, or mountain bikes are allowed. No wheelchair access.

Open Seasons: This trail is accessible mid-July–September.

Permits: A National Parks Pass is required to enter the park.

Maps: For a map of Mount Rainier National Park, contact the Outdoor Recreation Information Center at the downtown Seattle REI. For a topographic map, ask Green Trails for No. 270, Mount Rainier East, or ask the USGS for White River Park and Chinook Pass.

Directions: From Puyallup, drive east 52 miles on Highway 410 to Sunrise Road in Mount Rainier National Park. Turn right and drive 3 miles to the signed trailhead on the left.

Contact: Mount Rainier National Park, White River Wilderness Information Center, 70004 Highway 410 East, Enumclaw, WA 98022, 360/569-6030.

35 CHINOOK PASS HIKES

1.0–13.0 mi/0.5–6.0 hr

at Chinook Pass in Mount Baker–Snoqualmie National Forest

Map 5.2, page 236

Chinook Pass is one of the most beautiful of Washington's Cascade passes. So it comes as no surprise that it is a starting point for some amazing hiking. Three great hikes originate here, two of them routes along famed Pacific Crest Trail. Tipsoo Lake Trail is extremely easy, perfect for families with little ones. Naches Loop is longer but also easy, full of big-time views. Sourdough Gap and Pickhandle Point offer views and meadows along PCT.

Tipsoo Lake is a short one-mile walk around the high mountain lake. Wildflowers light up the meadows in July, with views of Mount Rainier. The trail around Tipsoo Lake is flat with many picnic sites.

Making a four-mile loop around Naches Peak, PCT connects to Naches Trail among acres of wildflower-filled meadows. The preferred route is clockwise, so as to keep Mount Rainier in front of you. The trail gains just 400 feet but is exposed and dry, becoming hot on summer afternoons.

A longer trip from Chinook Pass heads along PCT to Sourdough Gap and Pickhandle Point. This is one of PCT's most beautiful segments, traveling through open meadows to Sourdough Gap (3 miles one-way) and Pickhandle Point (6.5 miles). Pickhandle Point lies south and above the lifts of the local ski resort; skiers accustomed to a snowy landscape will be just as pleased with the summertime look.

User Groups: Hikers, leashed dogs, and horses. No mountain bikes are allowed. Tipsoo Lake Trail is wheelchair accessible.

Open Seasons: This area is accessible June–mid-October.

Permits: A federal Northwest Forest Pass is required to park here.

Maps: For a map of Mount Baker–Snoqualmie National Forest, contact the Outdoor Recreation Information Center at the downtown Seattle REI. For a topographic map, ask Green Trails for No. 270, Mount Rainier East, and No. 271, Bumping Lake, or ask the USGS for Chinook Pass.

Directions: From Puyallup, drive east 60 miles on Highway 410 to Tipsoo Lake Trailhead, on the west side of Chinook Pass.

Contact: Wenatchee National Forest, Naches Ranger Station, 10237 Highway 12, Naches, WA 98937, 509/653-2205.

36 KLAPATCHE PARK

21.0 mi/2 days

near Longmire in Mount Rainier National Park

Map 5.2, page 236

The one sure way to instantly turn a popular backcountry destination into a remote and lonely journey is to close the access road. That's exactly what happened to Klapatche Park, now mostly enjoyed by trekkers on Wonderland Trail. A washout on Westside Road extended a trip into Klapatche from five miles round-trip into 21 miles. That's 16 miles of road—but don't miss out on the miles of meadows and high country lakes of Klapatche Park. Instead, hop on a mountain bike and turn this into Washington's best ride and hike.

The best access to Klapatche Park is via Klapatche Ridge Trail, eight miles up Westside Road. The trail climbs through old-growth forest to the high meadows of Klapatche Park and Aurora Lake (2.5 miles). Mount Rainier towers above fields of lupine, aster, and penstemon. The giant meadows of St. Andrew's Park are a must side trip, just a mile south on Wonderland Trail. This certainly qualifies as some of the park's best high country. Return back via Klapatche Ridge Trail or make a loop of it via South Puyallup Trail. Camping is allowed only at Klapatche Park Camp or South Puyallup Camp and requires reservations. Road or not, this is a gorgeous hike.

User Groups: Hikers and mountain bikes (mountain bikes on Westside Road). No dogs or horses are allowed. No wheelchair access.

Open Seasons: This trail is accessible July–mid-October.

Permits: A National Parks Pass is required to enter the park.
Maps: For a map of Mount Rainier National Park, contact the Outdoor Recreation Information Center at the downtown Seattle REI. For a topographic map, ask Green Trails for No. 269, Mount Rainier West, or ask the USGS for Mount Wow and Mount Rainier West.
Directions: From Tacoma, drive south 40 miles on Highway 7 to Elbe. Turn east on Highway 706 and drive 10 miles to the Nisqually Entrance Station. Continue 1 mile to Westside Road. Turn left and drive to the trailhead at the washout. Hike or bike 8 miles on the closed road to the trailhead on the right.
Contact: Mount Rainier National Park, Longmire Wilderness Information Center, Tahoma Woods, Star Route, Ashford, WA 98304, 360/569-4453.

37 EMERALD RIDGE LOOP

16.2 mi/1–2 days 3 10

near Longmire in Mount Rainier National Park

Map 5.2, page 236

More remote and less accessible than other faces, Mount Rainier's western side features few trails outside of Mowich. And the trails that do explore The Mountain's western slopes are fading into obscurity thanks to the closure of Westside Road. That's a shame, as Emerald Ridge is a beauty of a trail. With old-growth forest, alpine meadows, and an almost-close-enough-to-touch encounter with Tahoma Glacier, there's little left to desire.

Westside Road once provided easy access to the trailheads. But after a washout, the Park Service decided not to reopen it. That has kept the crowds out and the animals wild. It also means some road walking, about 8.3 miles of road out of a 16.2-mile total loop. The park does allow mountain bikes on the road; the smart hiker bikes to the upper trailhead, hikes the loop, and coasts back to the car.

On the trail, the loop follows Round Pass Trail and South Emerald Ridge Trail up to Wonderland Trail (2.1 miles). An interesting outcrop of columnar basalt (hexagonal columns formed as erupted lava cooled) is found just before the junction. Wonderland Trail climbs to emerald meadows and Tahoma Glacier (4.3 miles). Glacier Island, encircled by glaciers as recently as the 1930s, stands before the towering bulk of Mount Rainier. The loop drops to Tahoma Creek Trail (5.8 miles) and to the lower trailhead (7.9 miles). Backpackers need to plan on setting up for the night at South Puyallup Camp (the only site along the trail), located at the junction of South Emerald Ridge and Wonderland Trails.
User Groups: Hikers and mountain bikes (mountain bikes on Westside Road). No dogs or horses are allowed. No wheelchair access.
Open Seasons: This trail is accessible July–mid-October.
Permits: A National Parks Pass is required to enter the park.
Maps: For a map of Mount Rainier National Park, contact the Outdoor Recreation Information Center at the downtown Seattle REI. For a topographic map, ask Green Trails for No. 269, Mount Rainier West, or ask the USGS for Mount Wow and Mount Rainier West.
Directions: From Tacoma, drive south 40 miles on Highway 7 to Elbe. Turn east on Highway 706 and drive 10 miles to the Nisqually Entrance Station. Continue 1 mile to Westside Road. Turn left and drive to the trailhead at the washout. Hike or bike 5 miles on the closed road to the trailhead on the right.
Contact: Mount Rainier National Park, Longmire Wilderness Information Center, Tahoma Woods, Star Route, Ashford, WA 98304, 360/569-4453.

38 GLACIER VIEW WILDERNESS

1.5–7.0 mi/1.0–3.5 hr 1 9

west of Mount Rainier in Glacier View Wilderness of Gifford Pinchot National Forest

Map 5.2, page 236

Excluded from the national park but protected by wilderness designation, Glacier View

Wilderness is a gem hidden from the masses. This small enclave on the west side of Mount Rainier National Park features several pristine mountain lakes and a pair of gorgeous viewpoints. When you want to see The Mountain in all its glory but don't want to bump elbows with the crowds at Sunrise or Paradise, head to Glacier View Wilderness.

The wilderness is bisected by Glacier View Trail, which runs north to south and has two trailheads. The southern trailhead provides easy access to Lake Christine. The trail climbs gently to the mountain lake (.75 mile), cloaked by mountain hemlock and subalpine fir. There are several great campsites, and the fishing is supposedly not half bad either. From the lake, a side trail leads one mile to the summit of Mount Beljica, awash in big views of Rainier.

The northern trailhead provides access to Glacier View Lookout. Glacier View Trail runs north along a forested ridge to Glacier View Lookout (2 miles; elevation 5,450). This high forest is chock-full of ancient trees and bear grass with its huge blooms. The lookout provides great views of Rainier and surrounding countryside. Beyond the lookout are Lake West (2.3 miles) and Lake Helen (3.5 miles). Both lakes have several campsites. You'll likely be able to count on one hand the people you run across.

User Groups: Hikers and leashed dogs. No horses or mountain bikes are allowed. No wheelchair access.

Open Seasons: This area is accessible mid-June–October.

Permits: A federal Northwest Forest Pass is required to park here.

Maps: For a map of Gifford Pinchot National Forest, contact the Outdoor Recreation Information Center at the downtown Seattle REI. For a topographic map, ask Green Trails for No. 269, Mount Rainier West, or ask the USGS for Mount Wow.

Directions: From Tacoma, drive south 40 miles on Highway 7 to Elbe. Turn east on Highway 706 and drive to Copper Creek Road (Forest Service Road 59). Turn left and drive 4.5 miles to Forest Service Road 5920. Turn right and drive to the unsigned trailhead at road's end.

Contact: Gifford Pinchot National Forest, Cowlitz Valley Ranger Station, 10024 U.S. 12, Randle, WA 98377, 360/497-1100.

39 GOBBLER'S KNOB/ LAKE GEORGE

6.4–8.8 mi/3.5–4.5 hr

west of Mount Rainier in Glacier View Wilderness and Mount Rainier National Park

Map 5.2, page 236

Gobbler's Knob is the best deal in the Mount Rainier area. Pristine old-growth forest blankets this grand route as it passes a beautiful mountain lake on its way to the national park, a viewpoint, and another impressive lake. From atop Gobbler's Knob, Mount Rainier looms large with its impressive stature. Lake George lies beneath Mount Wow. Wow means "goat" in the Salish, the language of local American Indians in the Puget Sound region, and it's likely what you'll be mouthing as you watch mountain goats rambling along the steep slopes.

The preferred route to Gobbler's Knob and Lake George crosses Glacier View Wilderness. A washout on Westside Road increased access via the national park by three miles (all on old road). Avoid park fees and an unsightly road walk by hiking through the wilderness. Puyallup Trail meanders through Beljica Meadows to the junction with Lake Christine Trail (.9 mile). Head left as the trail drops through old-growth mountain hemlock and subalpine fir to Goat Lake (2.3 miles). Campsites are scattered around the lake and require no backcountry permits.

Puyallup Trail then climbs to a saddle between Gobbler's Knob and rocky Mount Wow (3.2 miles). A side trail leads to Gobbler's Knob Lookout and its drop-dead views of Mount Rainier and its glaciers. What a place to watch a sunset! Lake George lies 1,200 feet below, surrounded by forest and rocky slopes. Lake George Camp requires backcountry permits

from the National Park Service. The trail continues .8 mile to the abandoned Westside Road.
User Groups: Hikers only. No dogs, horses, or mountain bikes are allowed. No wheelchair access.
Open Seasons: This area is accessible mid-June–October.
Permits: A federal Northwest Forest Pass is required to park here.
Maps: For a map of Mount Rainier National Park and Gifford Pinchot National Forest, contact the Outdoor Recreation Information Center at the downtown Seattle REI. For a topographic map, ask Green Trails for No. 269, Mount Rainier West, or ask the USGS for Mount Wow.
Directions: From Tacoma, drive south 40 miles on Highway 7 to Elbe. Turn east on Highway 706 and drive to Copper Creek Road (Forest Service Road 59). Turn left and drive 4.5 miles to Forest Service Road 5920. Turn right and drive to the unsigned trailhead at road's end. (For access via the national park, follow directions for the Emerald Ridge listing in this chapter.)
Contact: Mount Rainier National Park, Longmire Wilderness Information Center, Tahoma Woods, Star Route, Ashford, WA 98304, 360/569-4453.

40 INDIAN HENRY'S HUNTING GROUND

11.4 mi/7.0 hr

near Longmire in Mount Rainier National Park

Map 5.2, page 236

Home to some of Mount Rainier's most beautiful scenery, Kautz Creek Trail to Indian Henry's Hunting Ground has it all. The trail passes through old-growth forest, where Douglas firs, western hemlocks, and western red cedars have been standing together for centuries. Upper sections of the route are enveloped in subalpine meadows, where bear, deer, and marmots roam the parkland. And of course, The Mountain makes a grand appearance, towering above the high country with rocky arms and glistening glaciers. It's a full day of hiking, but enjoyable every step of the way.

There are three ways into Indian Henry's Hunting Ground, the best being via Kautz Creek, described below. Other options include Wonderland Trail out of Longmire (an up and down 13.8 miles) and Tahoma Creek Trail (a steeper, less scenic 10 miles). Kautz Creek Trail quickly crosses its namesake on an old floodplain. The trail then climbs through stands of old-growth forest on its way to high-country meadows (3.5 miles). The grade becomes more gentle in its final two miles, providing plenty of time to snack on huckleberries in the fall. A great side trip is Mirror Lakes (an extra 1.2 miles round-trip), where Tahoma reflects in the small subalpine tarns. At Indian Henry's Hunting Ground stands a historic patrol cabin still staffed by the Park Service. The only campground within the area is Devils Dream Camp (reservations required), usually full with Wonderland Trail trekkers.
User Groups: Hikers only. No dogs, horses, or mountain bikes are allowed. No wheelchair access.
Open Seasons: This area is usually accessible year-round.
Permits: A National Parks Pass is required to enter the park. Overnight stays within the national park require backcountry camping permits, which are available at Longmire Wilderness Information Center in Ashford.
Maps: For a map of Mount Rainier National Park, contact the Outdoor Recreation Information Center at the downtown Seattle REI. For a topographic map, ask Green Trails for No. 269, Mount Rainier West, and No. 301, Randle, or ask the USGS for Mount Rainier West.
Directions: From Tacoma, drive south 40 miles on Highway 7 to Elbe. Turn east on Highway 706 and drive 10 miles to the Nisqually Entrance Station. Continue 7 miles to Longmire Wilderness Information Center. The trailhead is across the street in Kautz Creek Picnic Area.

Contact: Mount Rainier National Park, Longmire Wilderness Information Center, Tahoma Woods, Star Route, Ashford, WA 98304, 360/569-4453.

41 RAMPART RIDGE LOOP

4.5 mi/2.5 hr

near Longmire in Mount Rainier National Park

Map 5.2, page 236

Climbing atop one of Rainier's ancient lava flows, Rampart Ridge Trail delivers the requisite views and meadows needed in any hike. The trail offers some of the best views of Tahoma (Mount Rainier) from the Longmire Visitor Center. Included in the deal are old-growth forests and some likely encounters with wildlife. Deer, grouse, squirrels, and woodpeckers are regular residents of the area. Gaining little more than 1,100 feet, it's a great trail for all hikers.

The loop is best done clockwise, hiking along the ridge toward the mountain. Rampart Ridge Trail begins on Trail of the Shadows, just 300 yards from the parking lot. From there, it switchbacks at a moderate but steady grade around the steep cliffs of Rampart Ridge. The forest here is great old-growth mountain hemlocks and subalpine firs, decked out in gowns of moss and lichens. The trail finds the top of the ridge (1.5 miles) and follows the level plateau for more than a mile. Forest is regularly broken up by meadows of wildflowers (try the month of July) and huckleberries (usually ripe in August). Although The Mountain dominates the skyline, Rampart Ridge offers a great view of the large, U-shaped Nisqually River Valley (thank you, glaciers). The trail circles back to Longmire via Wonderland Trail.

User Groups: Hikers only. No dogs, horses, or mountain bikes are allowed. No wheelchair access.

Open Seasons: This trail is usually accessible July–mid-October.

Permits: A National Parks Pass is required to enter the park.

Maps: For a map of Mount Rainier National Park, contact the Outdoor Recreation Information Center at the downtown Seattle REI. For a topographic map, ask Green Trails for No. 269, Mount Rainier West, or ask the USGS for Mount Rainier West.

Directions: From Tacoma, drive south 40 miles on Highway 7 to Elbe. Turn east on Highway 706 and drive 10 miles to the Nisqually Entrance Station. Continue 18 miles to the National Park Inn at Paradise. The trailhead is behind the inn.

Contact: Mount Rainier National Park, Longmire Wilderness Information Center, Tahoma Woods, Star Route, Ashford, WA 98304, 360/569-4453.

42 COMET FALLS/ VAN TRUMP PARK

6.2 mi/3.5 hr

near Longmire in Mount Rainier National Park

Map 5.2, page 236

Two of the most scenic spots in Mount Rainier National Park are conveniently on the same trail. One of Rainier's highest waterfalls, Comet Falls, plunges off a rocky cliff more than 320 feet. It's the largest of several cascades along the route. As great as Comet Falls may be, Van Trump Park is arguably even better. Acre upon acre of meadow unfolds beneath behemoth Tahoma, with wildflowers coloring the entire scene during the summer. That rumbling is just Kautz and Van Trump Glaciers doing their thing, cracking and breaking in the summer heat.

You can bet that with so much to see, the trail will be busy. In fact, this is one of the park's most popular hikes. Unfortunately, it has a small trailhead with no alternate parking; be ready to choose another hike if the parking lot is full. Van Trump Park Trail leaves the trailhead and briskly climbs alongside the constantly cascading Van Trump Creek. Christine Falls is a short 10-minute walk from the trailhead. Old-growth forest provides shade all the way to Comet Falls. Shutterbugs rejoice, but save some film for later. From the falls, Van Trump Park Trail switchbacks up to open meadows and prime views. Clear days reveal the Tatoosh Range, Mount Adams, and Mount St. Helens to the south. Be sure to stick to established trails; in such a heavily used area, meadows are quickly destroyed by wayward feet.

User Groups: Hikers only. No dogs, horses, or mountain bikes are allowed. No wheelchair access.

Open Seasons: This trail is usually accessible July–mid-October.

Permits: A National Parks Pass is required to enter the park.

Maps: For a map of Mount Rainier National Park, contact the Outdoor Recreation Information Center at the downtown Seattle REI. For a topographic map, ask Green Trails for No. 269, Mount Rainier West, or ask the USGS for Mount Rainier West.

Directions: From Tacoma, drive south 40 miles on Highway 7 to Elbe. Turn east on Highway 706 and drive 10 miles to the Nisqually Entrance Station. Continue 12 miles to the signed trailhead on the left.

Contact: Mount Rainier National Park, Longmire Wilderness Information Center, Tahoma Woods, Star Route, Ashford, WA 98304, 360/569-4453.

43 EAGLE PEAK

7.2 mi/4.0 hr

near Longmire in Mount Rainier National Park

Map 5.2, page 236

Directly out of Longmire, Eagle Peak Trail climbs skyward through old-growth forest and meadows to Eagle Peak Saddle on the north side of Tatoosh Range. At an elevation of 5,700 feet, Mount Rainier looms large while several other Cascade volcanoes are well within sight. The trail is fairly steep, gaining 2,700 feet in just 3.6 miles. Despite its close proximity to Longmire, the ascent keeps the trail less traveled than those near Sunrise or Paradise Visitor Centers.

Eagle Peak Trail climbs quickly and steeply through the mature forest. Douglas fir and mountain hemlock quickly give way to their relatives, mountain hemlock and subalpine fir. The forest covers the trail for three miles, keeping it relatively cool; the only water is found when the trail crosses a small stream (2 miles). The final .5 mile is a steep ascent in flower-clad meadows, with Eagle Peak towering above. The trail ends in a large saddle between Eagle and Chutla Peaks. Scrambles to either peak are recommended only for experienced and outfitted climbers. From this outpost of the Tatoosh Range, miles and miles of surrounding countryside (some forested, some denuded) are revealed. Hikers who neglect to bring a camera never fail to regret it.

User Groups: Hikers only. No dogs, horses, or mountain bikes are allowed. No wheelchair access.

Open Seasons: This area is usually accessible mid-July–September.

Permits: A National Parks Pass is required to enter the park.

Maps: For a map of Mount Rainier National Park, contact the Outdoor Recreation Information Center at the downtown Seattle REI. For a topographic map, ask Green Trails for No. 269, Mount Rainier West, and No. 301, Randle, or ask the USGS for Mount Rainier West and Wahpenayo.

Directions: From Tacoma, drive south 40 miles on Highway 7 to Elbe. Turn east on Highway 706 and drive 10 miles to the Nisqually Entrance Station. Continue 7 miles to Longmire Museum for parking. The signed trailhead is on the opposite side of the suspension bridge crossing the Nisqually River, on the left.

Contact: Mount Rainier National Park, Longmire Wilderness Information Center, Tahoma Woods, Star Route, Ashford, WA 98304, 360/569-4453.

44 PARADISE NATURE TRAILS

1.5–2.8 mi/0.7–1.5 hr

near Paradise in Mount Rainier National Park

Map 5.2, page 236

World-famous and Mount Rainier's most visited setting, Paradise fails to disappoint even the highest expectations. Directly below The Mountain among acres of subalpine meadows, Paradise sports a striking visitors center as well as the historic Paradise Inn. Folks have been coming here to experience Mount Rainier for well over 100 years. And Paradise is a great place to become acquainted with Washington's tallest peak on a number of easy and highly scenic trails. From glacier viewpoints to wildflower rambles, the trails of Paradise easily put visitors into seventh heaven.

The large network of trails near Paradise may appear confusing on a map, but all junctions are well signed. The meadows of this high country are extremely fragile and wither away quickly under the stomp of a boot. Be sure to stick to designated trails at all times. For a view of enormous Nisqually Glacier and its expansive moraine, hike from the visitors center to Nisqually Vista (1.6 miles). This level and wide trail makes a loop (shaped like a lasso) and is perfect for hikers of any ability. Also accessible from the visitors center is Alta Vista Trail (1.5 miles), a gentle climb to a viewpoint. From this small knob, Rainier's bulk astounds even the most veteran of hikers. Look south to take in views of southern Washington's other volcanic peaks, Mount St. Helens and Mount Adams.

Paradise Inn also offers an array of trails, easily customized to any length desired. A good hike is to Golden Gate (2.8 miles) and the vast meadows of Edith Creek Basin. Also beginning in Paradise but long enough to warrant their own listings in this chapter are Skyline Loop, Mazama Ridge, and Paradise Glacier Trails (see next listings).

User Groups: Hikers only. No dogs, horses, or mountain bikes are allowed. No wheelchair access.

Open Seasons: This area is accessible mid-June–October.

Permits: A National Parks Pass is required to enter the park.

Maps: For a map of Mount Rainier National Park, contact the Outdoor Recreation Information Center at the downtown Seattle REI. For a topographic map, ask Green Trails for No. 270S, Paradise, or ask the USGS for Mount Rainier East.

Directions: From Tacoma, drive south 40 miles on Highway 7 to Elbe. Turn east on Highway 706 and drive 10 miles to the Nisqually Entrance Station. Continue 17.5 miles to the Henry M. Jackson Visitor Center or 18 miles to the Paradise National Park Inn. The trails emanate from the visitors center and the lodge. Consult a map to see which trailhead to access.

Contact: Mount Rainier National Park, Longmire Wilderness Information Center, Tahoma Woods, Star Route, Ashford, WA 98304, 360/569-4453.

45 PARADISE GLACIER

6.0 mi/3.0 hr

near Paradise in Mount Rainier National Park

Map 5.2, page 236

To discover what millions of tons of ice look and sound like, take scenic Paradise Glacier Trail, which gently climbs through wide open meadows, rock fields, and snowfields to the living Paradise Glacier. Centuries of snowfall built up this massive block of ice slowly sliding down Mount Rainier. The upper reaches of the trail reveal the barren landscapes that are trademarks of retreating glaciers. Paradise Glacier Trail is the park's best chance to view up close the mountain's most famous features.

The route to Paradise Glacier follows Skyline Trail (counterclockwise from Paradise Inn) 1.9 miles to Paradise Glacier Trail junction, just above Sluiskin Falls. Also here is Stevens–Van Trump Historical Memorial, commemorating their 1870 ascent of Mount

Rainier, one of the first by white men. Paradise Glacier Trail begins here and heads directly for the glacier (3 miles), cracking, creaking, and breaking apart before your very eyes and ears. Although the terrain appears barren, it is very fragile; be sure to stick to designated trails. The high country here is pretty close to true tundra, with tiny plants doing their best to survive on the barren slopes. Streams cascade all around. Paradise Glacier used to sport several large ice caves that could be explored, but warm weather through the last few decades has left them destroyed or unsafe. Walking on the glacier is also unsafe and prohibited.

User Groups: Hikers only. No dogs, horses, or mountain bikes are allowed. No wheelchair access.

Open Seasons: This trail is accessible mid-June–October.

Permits: A National Parks Pass is required to enter the park.

Maps: For a map of Mount Rainier National Park, contact the Outdoor Recreation Information Center at the downtown Seattle REI. For a topographic map, ask Green Trails for No. 270S, Paradise, or ask the USGS for Mount Rainier East.

Directions: From Tacoma, drive south 40 miles on Highway 7 to Elbe. Turn east on Highway 706 and drive 10 miles to the Nisqually Entrance Station. Continue 18 miles to the National Park Inn at Paradise. The trailhead is behind the inn.

Contact: Mount Rainier National Park, Longmire Wilderness Information Center, Tahoma Woods, Star Route, Ashford, WA 98304, 360/569-4453.

46 MAZAMA RIDGE

5.4 mi/2.5 hr

near Paradise in Mount Rainier National Park

Map 5.2, page 236

Walking away from The Mountain, Mazama Ridge avoids the mall-like crush of visitors along other Paradise trails. Such a beautiful hike still gets plenty of use, however, and for good reason. The easy trail spends its entirety wandering amid subalpine meadows with big views of the big mountain. To the south stands the jagged Tatoosh Range. And to cap it all off is a series of small tarns, idyllic spots for lunch.

The theme of Mazama Ridge Trail is meadows, meadows, meadows. The route leaves Paradise Inn and follows Skyline Trail 1.5 miles to a signed junction; to the right is Mazama Ridge Trail. The trail follows the wide, flat ridgeline south. During July, lupine, daisies, and countless other wildflowers add shrouds of color to green meadows.

The trail reaches a number of small lakes and tarns (2.5 miles) along the flat top of Faraway Rock. Below its steep slopes lie Louise and Reflection Lakes and Wonderland Trail. With little elevation change, this is a great trail for families with little ones.

User Groups: Hikers only. No dogs, horses, or mountain bikes are allowed. No wheelchair access.

Open Seasons: This trail is accessible mid-June–October.

Permits: A National Parks Pass is required to enter the park.

Maps: For a map of Mount Rainier National Park, contact the Outdoor Recreation Information Center at the downtown Seattle REI. For a topographic map, ask Green Trails for No. 270S, Paradise, or ask the USGS for Mount Rainier East.

Directions: From Tacoma, drive south 40 miles on Highway 7 to Elbe. Turn east on Highway 706 and drive 10 miles to the Nisqually Entrance Station. Continue 18 miles to the National Park Inn at Paradise. The trailhead is behind the inn.

Contact: Mount Rainier National Park, Longmire Wilderness Information Center, Tahoma Woods, Star Route, Ashford, WA 98304, 360/569-4453.

47 SKYLINE LOOP

5.0 mi/3.0 hr

out of Paradise in Mount Rainier National Park

Map 5.2, page 236

Skyline Trail may well be the premier hike in Mount Rainier National Park. The trail delivers miles of alpine meadows, peers over the enormous Nisqually Glacier, and summits Panorama Point. This high vista is as close to The Mountain as you can get without ropes and a harness. Acres of blooming wildflowers line the trail in late July, and if big-time views bore you, several streams and waterfalls are thrown in for good measure. This is a popular trip for folks visiting the Paradise Visitor Center. The overall elevation gain is 1,400 feet, a respectable but not strenuous workout.

The best route is a clockwise one. Although numerous trails crisscross this area, Skyline Trail is well signed at every junction. Starting at Paradise, the trail skirts Alta Vista Peak and climbs through meadows to the ridge above Nisqually Glacier (1.3 miles). On hot summer days, the silence of the high country is broken only by whistling marmots and the cracking glacier.

Panorama Point (2.5 miles; elevation 6,800 feet) is an appropriate name for this high vista. Mount Rainier towers above the viewpoint, and the rocky and jagged Tatoosh Range stands to the south. On clear days, Mount Adams, Goat Rocks, Mount St. Helens, and even Mount Hood in Oregon make appearances. Panorama indeed! Because you definitely packed your camera, save some film for the last half of the trail. Descending to Paradise, Skyline Trail passes Stevens–Van Trump Memorial (commemorating an ascent of Mount Rainier), Sluiskin Falls, and Myrtle Falls. Camping is not permitted in the Paradise area.

User Groups: Hikers only. No dogs, horses, or mountain bikes are allowed. Part of the trail is wheelchair accessible (but somewhat steep).

Open Seasons: This trail is accessible mid-July–September.

Permits: A National Parks Pass is required to enter the park.

Maps: For a map of Mount Rainier National Park, contact the Outdoor Recreation Information Center at the downtown Seattle REI. For a topographic map, ask Green Trails for No. 270S, Paradise, or ask the USGS for Mount Rainier East.

Directions: From Tacoma, drive south 40 miles on Highway 7 to Elbe. Turn east on Highway 706 and drive 10 miles to the Nisqually Entrance Station. Continue 18 miles to the National Park Inn at Paradise. The trailhead is behind the inn.

Contact: Mount Rainier National Park, Longmire Wilderness Information Center, Tahoma Woods, Star Route, Ashford, WA 98304, 360/569-4453.

48 WONDERLAND TRAIL

93.0 mi/10 days

around Tahoma in Mount Rainier National Park

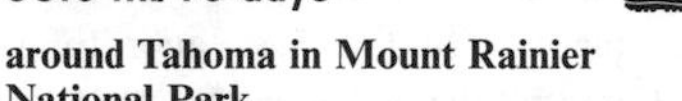

Map 5.2, page 236

Wonderland Trail is considered by many to be the be-all and end-all of Washington hiking. The long, demanding trek makes a full circle around the behemoth mountain, exploring old-growth forest, high alpine meadows, and everything in between. Tahoma (Mount Rainier's Native American name) is the center of attention at almost every turn, towering above the trail with massive glaciers and windswept snowfields. The Wonderland passes through the park's most beautiful terrain. Acres and acres of wildflower meadows dominate Spray Park, Indian Henry's Hunting Ground, and Summerland. Outstanding lakes and streams are repeat encounters, with Mowich Lake, Carbon River, and Martha Falls a sampling of many highlights.

Wonderland Trail is certainly one of the most demanding hikes in the state. The route repeatedly climbs out of low river valleys to high ridges radiating from Tahoma. Although some folks complete the hike in as few as seven or eight days, plan for at least 10 full days. This makes for a leisurely pace of about 10 miles per day. Besides, there's far too much to see to rush through it. The best starting points include Longmire, Sunrise, or Paradise Visitor Centers. Smart hikers plan carefully and leave a food cache at a visitors center halfway through the route. Because of the trail's popularity, the Park Service requires reservations for all backcountry camps (cross-country camping–that is, selecting a temporary site somewhere off-trail, is not allowed). Spots are limited and regularly fill up in April (reservations can be made after April 1). And finally, be prepared for adverse weather in any season. Tahoma creates its own weather systems, sometimes in just minutes. Set out upon this epic trail and you will not be disappointed, guaranteed!

User Groups: Hikers only. No dogs, horses, or mountain bikes are allowed. No wheelchair access.

Open Seasons: This trail is accessible mid-July–September.

Permits: A National Parks Pass is required to enter the park.

Maps: For a map of Mount Rainier National Park, contact the Outdoor Recreation Information Center at the downtown Seattle REI. For a topographic map, ask Green Trails for No. 269, Mount Rainier West, and No. 270, Mount Rainier East, or ask the USGS for Mount Rainier West, Mount Rainier East, Mowich Lake, Sunrise, Golden Lakes, Mount Wow, White River Park, and Chinook Pass.

Directions: From Tacoma, drive south 40 miles on Highway 7 to Elbe. Turn east on Highway 706 and drive 10 miles to the Nisqually Entrance Station. Continue 18 miles to the National Park Inn at Paradise. The well-signed trailhead is beside the inn. Other access points include Sunrise Visitor Center or Mowich Lake.

Contact: Mount Rainier National Park, Longmire Wilderness Information Center, Tahoma Woods, Star Route, Ashford, WA 98304, 360/569-4453.

49 PINNACLE SADDLE

2.6 mi/2.5 hr

near Paradise in Mount Rainier National Park

Map 5.2, page 236

Pinnacle Peak Trail is one of the park's steepest trails. An elevation gain of 1,050 feet passes underfoot in a short 1.3 miles, delivering hikers to a wonderful viewpoint. The steep, rocky path keeps the crowds at bay, leaving the route for only the most determined hikers and view junkies. Although it starts gently, much of the trail does little but climb skyward. Mount Rainier remains visible the entire way. Because the trail is situated on the north-facing slopes of the Tatoosh Range, snow lingers here late, sometimes into August. Marmots and picas whistle and scurry about the rocky meadows while mountain goats frequently patrol the jagged ridge. The trail eventually reaches Pinnacle Saddle, between Pinnacle and Denham Peaks, in the heart of the Tatoosh Range. To the north stands The Mountain, above Paradise meadows; to the south, snowy Goat Rocks and Mount Adams are visible. The truly adventurous can undertake a rocky scramble to the summit of Pinnacle Peak. It's a gain of 600 feet, but few views are to be gained for the extra effort. Other than snowmelt, little water is to be found along the way; be sure to pack your own.

User Groups: Hikers only. No dogs, horses, or mountain bikes are allowed. No wheelchair access.

Open Seasons: This area is accessible August–September.

Permits: A National Parks Pass is required to enter the park.

Maps: For a map of Mount Rainier National Park, contact the Outdoor Recreation Information Center at the downtown Seattle REI. For a topographic map, ask Green Trails for No. 270, Mount Rainier East, or ask the USGS for Mount Rainier East.

Directions: From Tacoma, drive south 40 miles on Highway 7 to Elbe. Turn east on Highway

706 and drive 10 miles to the Nisqually Entrance Station. Continue 16 miles to Stevens Canyon Road. Turn right and drive 2.5 miles to the signed trailhead on the right.

Contact: Mount Rainier National Park, Longmire Wilderness Information Center, Tahoma Woods, Star Route, Ashford, WA 98304, 360/569-4453.

50 SNOW AND BENCH LAKES

2.6 mi/1.5 hr 1 9

near Paradise in Mount Rainier National Park

Map 5.2, page 236

Short, flat, and beautiful best describe Snow Lake Trail. The perfect hike for folks young and old, Snow Lake Trail features a pair of subalpine lakes enclosed by meadows and rocky peaks. The total elevation gain is about 200 feet, practically unnoticeable. Away from the bustle of the Paradise area, Snow Lake offers visitors prime hiking without the crowds.

Snow Lake Trail leaves Stevens Canyon Road and quickly reaches The Bench, a wide, flat meadow with perfect views of Mount Rainier. Bear grass occupies the large meadows, sending its large blooms skyward during August. Bench Lake occupies part of the large meadow. The trail continues another .5 mile to Snow Lake, tucked away within a large basin. The lake got its name from the heavy snowpack that lingers around the lake (and on the trail) until late July. Craggy Unicorn Peak rises above the lake and talus slopes from the south. Visitors interested in spending the night will appreciate Snow Lake Camp, the park's most accessible backcountry campground (permits required).

User Groups: Hikers only. No dogs, horses, or mountain bikes are allowed. No wheelchair access.

Open Seasons: This trail is usually accessible August–September.

Permits: A National Parks Pass is required to enter the park. Overnight stays within the national park require backcountry camping permits, which are available at Sunrise Visitor Center.

Maps: For a map of Mount Rainier National Park, contact the Outdoor Recreation Information Center at the downtown Seattle REI. For a topographic map, ask Green Trails for No. 270, Mount Rainier East, or ask the USGS for Mount Rainier East.

Directions: From Tacoma, drive south 40 miles on Highway 7 to Elbe. Turn east on Highway 706 and drive 10 miles to the Nisqually Entrance Station. Continue 16 miles to Stevens Canyon Road. Turn right and drive 4 miles to the signed trailhead on the right.

Contact: Mount Rainier National Park, Longmire Wilderness Information Center, Tahoma Woods, Star Route, Ashford, WA 98304, 360/569-4453.

51 SHRINER PEAK LOOKOUT

8.4 mi/5.0 hr–2 days 5 9

near Stevens Canyon entrance in Mount Rainier National Park

Map 5.2, page 236

Probably nothing is more beautiful than waking to Mount Rainier basking in the glow of the rising sun. And probably there is no better place to behold such a sight than Shriner Peak. But this extraordinary place requires extraordinary effort. Shriner Peak Trail gains extensive elevation in open terrain, made hot by the afternoon sun. Easily done in a day, Shriner Camp invites hikers to spend the night and enjoy the daybreak view.

Shriner Peak Trail is not for the faint of heart. The trail gains more than 3,400 feet in just 4.2 miles, a steep ascent by any standard. Plus, much of the route lies on an exposed, south-facing slope (the hottest of them all). As you sweat and trudge uphill, keep in mind that nature rewards those who work the hardest. The trail winds its way through shady forest before entering an old burn area and eventually open meadows (2.5 miles). The upper half of the route is awash in views of Mount Rainier and surrounding valleys. Shriner Camp is just below the summit off a short side trail; unfortunately it's a dry camp. Shriner Peak is best undertaken early in the day, before the sun is high. Finally, be sure to carry extra water; even if it's cloudy and cool, you'll need it.

User Groups: Hikers only. No dogs, horses, or mountain bikes are allowed. No wheelchair access.

Open Seasons: This area is accessible August–September.

Permits: A National Parks Pass is required to enter the park. Overnight stays within the national park require backcountry camping permits, which are available at the Longmire and White River Wilderness Information Centers.

Maps: For a map of Mount Rainier National Park, contact the Outdoor Recreation Information Center at the downtown Seattle REI. For a topographic map, ask Green Trails for No. 270, Mount Rainier East, or ask the USGS for Chinook Pass.

Directions: From Puyallup, drive east 56 miles on Highway 410 to Highway 123. Turn right (south) and drive 7.5 miles to the trailhead on the left side of the road.

Contact: Mount Rainier National Park, White River Wilderness Information Center, 70004 Highway 410 East, Enumclaw, WA 98022, 360/569-6030.

52 LAUGHINGWATER CREEK

11.4 mi/6.0 hr–2 days 2 8

near Stevens Canyon entrance in Mount Rainier National Park

Map 5.2, page 236

A rarity in this national park, Laughingwater Creek Trail forsakes mountain meadows and views of Mount Rainier. Instead, this lightly used trail makes a grand trip through old-growth forest to Three Lakes, set among open subalpine forest. The trail provides a quiet reintroduction to the Cascade Mountains after the crowds of Mount Rainier's visitors centers. The only sounds around these parts are the noisy rumbling of Laughingwater Creek and the bellows of elk.

Laughingwater Creek Trail gains more than 2,500 feet between the trailhead and Three Lakes. Most of the climb is spread moderately along the route, easy enough for hikers young and old. The trail sticks close to the creek and passes within view of a waterfall at 2.5 miles. Western hemlocks gives way to mountain hemlocks and subalpine fir replaces Douglas fir as the trail nears the crest of the hike.

Three Lakes lie in a small basin atop the ridge. A wonderful backcountry camp is situated here with an aged shelter. This is an out-of-the-way section of the national park (if any remain these days), with few visitors spending the night at Three Lakes Camp. If you have an itch to see The Mountain, continue on the trail past Three Lakes toward Pacific Crest Trail and meadow vistas.

User Groups: Hikers and horses. No dogs or mountain bikes are allowed. No wheelchair access.

Open Seasons: This area is usually accessible July–September.

Permits: A National Parks Pass is required to enter the park.

Maps: For a map of Mount Rainier National Park, contact the Outdoor Recreation Information Center at the downtown Seattle REI. For a topographic map, ask Green Trails for No. 270, Mount Rainier East, and No. 271, Bumping Lake, or ask the USGS for Chinook Pass.

Directions: From Puyallup, drive east 56 miles on Highway 410 to Highway 123. Turn right (south) and drive 10.5 miles to the trailhead on the left side of the road, just south of Stevens Canyon entrance.

Contact: Mount Rainier National Park, White River Wilderness Information Center, 70004 Highway 410 East, Enumclaw, WA 98022, 360/569-6030.

53 SILVER FALLS LOOP

3.0 mi/1.5 hr 1 8

out of Ohanapecosh in Mount Rainier National Park

Map 5.2, page 236

Silver Falls Loop is one of Mount Rainier's

best river trails, perfect for families and hikers of all abilities. The route is a gentle grade along the bustling river to one of the park's most impressive cascades. Silver Falls Trail follows Ohanapecosh River a gentle 1.5 miles to Silver Falls. Old-growth trees dominate the forest found along the route, making the trail a cool and shady respite from hot and sunny meadows. Squirrels and woodpeckers are often found scurrying among the timber while deer and elk browse the forest floor. Anglers are frequent visitors to the trail, thanks to its easy access to the trout-laden river.

Silver Falls is a thunderous waterfall, where the glacial-fed Ohanapecosh makes a series of cascades. The climax is a 70-foot drop into a large punch bowl. The trail crosses a deep gorge via a bridge immediately below the falls, showering hikers in mist when the river is roaring. Although beautiful, the falls are dangerous if explored off-trail. Keep a short leash on little ones and stick to the established trail. The loop heads directly back to Ohanapecosh Campground along the opposite bank of the river, a quick and easy outing.

User Groups: Hikers only. No dogs, horses, or mountain bikes are allowed. No wheelchair access.

Open Seasons: This trail is accessible year-round.

Permits: A National Parks Pass is required to enter the park.

Maps: For a map of Mount Rainier National Park, contact the Outdoor Recreation Information Center at the downtown Seattle REI. For a topographic map, ask Green Trails for No. 270, Mount Rainier East, or ask the USGS for Ohanapecosh Hot Springs and Chinook Pass.

Directions: From Puyallup, drive east 56 miles on Highway 410 to Highway 123. Turn right (south) and drive 13 miles to Ohanapecosh Campground. Turn left into the campground; the trailhead is near the visitor center.

Contact: Mount Rainier National Park, White River Wilderness Information Center, 70004 Highway 410 East, Enumclaw, WA 98022, 360/569-6030.

54 GROVE OF THE PATRIARCHS

1.5 mi/1.0 hr 1 9

near Stevens Canyon entrance in Mount Rainier National Park

Map 5.2, page 236

Competing with Olympic rainforests, here, in the low valley of the Ohanapecosh River, is one of Washington's most impressive stands of old-growth timber. On a small island in the middle of the river, this grove of Douglas fir, western hemlock, and western red cedar has been growing undisturbed for nearly 1,000 years. That's right, a full millennium. Isolated by the river from the surrounding forest, Grove of the Patriarchs has been able to avoid fire and other natural disturbances, living up to its full potential. This is a true climax forest. The trail to Grove of the Patriarchs is flat and easily navigated. The trail heads upstream for .5 mile through an impressive (yet comparatively small) forest. The trail crosses the river via bridge and loops around the island. Many of the trees measure more than 25 feet around the trunk, with one granddaddy fir rounding out at 35 feet in circumference. In this ancient place, the only hazard is a strained neck.

User Groups: Hikers only. No dogs, horses, or mountain bikes are allowed. No wheelchair access.

Open Seasons: This area is accessible mid-May–October.

Permits: A National Parks Pass is required to enter the park.

Maps: For a map of Mount Rainier National Park, contact the Outdoor Recreation Information Center at the downtown Seattle REI. For a topographic map, ask Green Trails for No. 270, Mount Rainier East, or ask the USGS for Ohanapecosh Hot Springs.

Directions: From Puyallup, drive east 56 miles on Highway 410 to Highway 123. Turn right (south) and drive 11 miles to Stevens Canyon

Road/entrance. Turn right and the trailhead is just beyond the guard station on the right.
Contact: Mount Rainier National Park, White River Wilderness Information Center, 70004 Highway 410 East, Enumclaw, WA 98022, 360/569-6030.

55 EAST SIDE TRAIL

3.0–5.0 mi/1.5–3.5 hr

near Stevens Canyon entrance in Mount Rainier National Park

Map 5.2, page 236

East Side Trail follows Chinook Creek and Ohanopecosh River as they wind their ways through exceptional old-growth forests. The trail has three trailheads, including near Cayuse Pass and Ohanapecosh Campgrounds. The distance between these two endpoints is 12 miles. The best access, however, is via Deer Creek in the middle of the route. This .5-mile access trail joins East Side Trail within a mile of spectacular waterfalls to the north and south. Deer Creek Trail drops to East Side Trail at the backcountry camp of Deer Creek. The best option is to turn left (south) and follow the level trail one mile to where it crosses Chinook Creek. Here, the stream cascades through a narrow gorge directly below the footbridge. Bigger Stafford Falls is another mile down the trail. From Deer Creek Camp, the trail climbs kindly toward Cayuse Pass, passing more falls and cascades. This is a great trail for families with little ones; just keep a short leash on them near all stream crossings.
User Groups: Hikers only. No dogs, horses, or mountain bikes are allowed. No wheelchair access.
Open Seasons: This area is usually accessible April–October.
Permits: Permits are not required. Parking and access are free.
Maps: For a map of Mount Rainier National Park, contact the Outdoor Recreation Information Center at the downtown Seattle REI. For a topographic map, ask Green Trails for No. 270, Mount Rainier East, or ask the USGS for Ohanapecosh Hot Springs and Chinook Pass.
Directions: From Puyallup, drive east 56 miles on Highway 410 to Highway 123. Turn right (south) and drive 4 miles to the signed trailhead on the right side of the road.
Contact: Mount Rainier National Park, White River Wilderness Information Center, 70004 Highway 410 East, Enumclaw, WA 98022, 360/569-6030.

56 AMERICAN RIDGE

10.2–26.2 mi/5.0 hr–3 days

in William O. Douglas Wilderness of Wenatchee National Forest

Map 5.2, page 236

A major route bisecting the northern William O. Douglas Wilderness, American Ridge Trail offers hikers many options to customize a hike. From the Bumping River all the way up to Pacific Crest Trail, American Ridge stretches more than 26 miles. Eight different access trails, including PCT, create a whole slew of opportunities. The eastern end is primarily high forests; the middle third reaches into high, ridgeline meadows with lots of views; the western end offers access to a number of high-country lakes and meadows (see next listing).

Four trails reach American Ridge from Highway 410, with Mesatchee Creek Trail a favorite. Mesatchee Trail climbs 5.3 miles and 2,200 feet through forest and intermittent meadows to the ridge. East of this junction delivers more than five miles of meadows. Also from Highway 410, Goat Peak Trail climbs 3,000 feet in four miles to a lookout.

Three trails reach the ridge from Bumping River, Goose Prairie Trail being the preferred route. This is a 5.1-mile ascent to the ridge. Hike west for tiny Kettle Lake and miles of meadows. All of these trails are very hot in the late summer and always lack any water, an important consideration. They're also lonely routes into a beautiful backcountry.
User Groups: Hikers, leashed dogs, and horses.

No mountain bikes are allowed. No wheelchair access.

Open Seasons: This trail is accessible April–October.

Permits: A federal Northwest Forest Pass is required to park here.

Maps: For a map of Wenatchee National Forest, contact the Outdoor Recreation Information Center at the downtown Seattle REI. For a topographic map, ask Green Trails for No. 271, Bumping Lake, and No. 272, Old Scab Mountain, or ask the USGS for Norse Peak, Cougar Peak, Bumping Lake, Goose Prairie, and Old Scab Mountain.

Directions: From Yakima, drive west on Highway 410 to Forest Service Road 460, just west of Lodgepole Campground. Turn left and drive .3 mile to the trailhead at road's end.

Contact: Wenatchee National Forest, Naches Ranger Station, 10237 Highway 12, Naches, WA 98937, 509/653-2205.

57 COUGAR LAKES

12.0–20.0 mi/6.0 hr –2 days 2 9

in William O. Douglas Wilderness of Wenatchee National Forest

Map 5.2, page 236

Cougar Lakes lie at the western end of American Ridge, directly below the Cascade Crest. They make a great day hike or easy overnighter. Also in the area is Pacific Crest Trail, which lends itself to an excellent loop hike connecting to Cougar Lakes. This is a great weekend hike, encompassing one of the best sections of PCT in southern Washington. Meadows and mountain lakes are prominent themes on both routes. Each route is great for hikers of all abilities, gaining moderate elevation gently.

To reach Cougar Lakes, the route begins with Swamp Lake Trail, a gradual, forested ascent to Swamp Lake (4 miles) and American Ridge Trail (4.6 miles). Hike west toward PCT; Cougar Lakes junction (5.2 miles) cuts south to the two lakes (6 miles). Around the lakes, subalpine meadows unfold beneath tall, rocky cliffs. Numerous campsites are around the basin. Whether on a day hike or overnighter, be sure to scramble the crest for a view of Mount Rainier.

To hike the longer loop on PCT, continue west on American Ridge Trail toward PCT (6.7 miles). The loop route goes south on PCT, passing Two Lakes, Crag Lake, and Buck Lake. This is meadow country with prime viewing of Mount Rainier and many other mountains. The route intersects Bumping River Trail (13.1 miles) and turns east to return to the trailhead (20 miles). All lakes along the way offer camping and are the sole sources of water.

User Groups: Hikers, leashed dogs, and horses. No mountain bikes are allowed. No wheelchair access.

Open Seasons: This trail is accessible June–mid-October.

Permits: A federal Northwest Forest Pass is required to park here.

Maps: For a map of Wenatchee National Forest, contact the Outdoor Recreation Information Center at the downtown Seattle REI. For a topographic map, ask Green Trails for No. 271, Bumping Lake, or ask the USGS for Cougar Lake.

Directions: From Yakima, drive west on Highway 410 to Bumping Lake Road (Forest Service Road 1800). Turn left and drive 17 miles to the trailhead at road's end.

Contact: Wenatchee National Forest, Naches Ranger Station, 10237 Highway 12, Naches, WA 98937, 509/653-2205.

58 MOUNT AIX

11.0 mi/6.0 hr 5 10

in William O. Douglas Wilderness of Wenatchee National Forest

Map 5.2, page 236

Steep, rocky, and downright treacherous at times, Mount Aix does its best to discourage visitors. It stands at 7,766 feet, and hikers must scale 4,000 feet in just 5.5 miles to reach the summit. And the mountain offers no water to aid the trek, a harsh slight on the hot, exposed slopes. Demanding as it may be, Mount Aix rewards with much more than it asks. Miles of meadows chock-full of wildflowers highlight the upper half as do exceptional views of Mount Rainier and surrounding mountains. Mount Aix is definitely best for seasoned hikers who are looking for a good workout.

Mount Aix Trail rests on the east side of the Cascade Crest, meaning the route receives less snow than trails just a few miles west. This is one of the earliest high-country routes to open in the state. Switchbacks are the name of the game, rising out of the forest into the open meadows. At 3.7 miles is a junction with Nelson Ridge Trail. This is a nice option, offering several miles of ridgeline meadows before dozens of miles in the William O. Douglas Wilderness. Head right and climb another two miles to the summit. This last effort to the trail's climax is rocky and sometimes a scramble.

User Groups: Hikers, leashed dogs, and horses. No mountain bikes are allowed. No wheelchair access.

Open Seasons: This trail is accessible mid-May–mid-October.

Permits: A federal Northwest Forest Pass is required to park here.

Maps: For a map of Wenatchee National Forest, contact the Outdoor Recreation Information Center at the downtown Seattle REI. For a topographic map, ask Green Trails for No. 271, Bumping Lake, or ask the USGS for Timberwolf Mountain and Bumping Lake.

Directions: From Yakima, drive west on Highway 410 to Bumping Lake Road (Forest Service Road 1800). Turn left and drive 14 miles to Forest Service Road 1808. Turn left and drive 1.5 miles to the signed trailhead on the left side.

Contact: Wenatchee National Forest, Naches Ranger Station, 10237 Highway 12, Naches, WA 98937, 509/653-2205.

59 SAWTOOTH LAKES

7.0 mi/4.0 hr

south of Mount Rainier in Gifford Pinchot National Forest

Map 5.2, page 236

Along the north side of Sawtooth Ridge lie four high lakes among forest and meadows. Just outside the national park boundary, these lakes are highly ignored by the masses headed for Mount Rainier. That's good news for peace and quiet, at least until July 1. After that date motorcycles are allowed on the trail. Visit here in late May or June, and you'll have these great swimming holes all to yourself. Old forest and peek-a-boo views of The Mountain vie for attention along the way. And to cap off the hike is a neck-straining view of High Rock's 600-foot vertical cliff.

The best route to Sawtooth Lakes is via Teeley Creek Trail. After a quick climb past Pothole Lake, the trail levels out completely. At Osborne Mountain Trail junction (.7 mile), stay left on Teeley Creek Trail and soon reach the two largest and best lakes, Bertha May (1.2 miles) and Granite (1.8 miles). The trail continues along the north side of Sawtooth Ridge to meadows directly beneath the cliffs of High Rock (3.1 miles). Although the trail continues two miles to Cora Lake and additional trailheads, the meadows below High Rock are a great turnaround. On hot summer days, a dip in the lakes will be calling your name.

User Groups: Hikers, leashed dogs, horses, mountain bikes, and motorcycles (motorcycles allowed after June 30). No wheelchair access.

Open Seasons: This trail is accessible mid-June–October.

Permits: A federal Northwest Forest Pass is required to park here.

Maps: For a map of Gifford Pinchot National Forest, contact the Outdoor Recreation Information Center at the downtown Seattle REI. For a topographic map, ask Green Trails for No. 301, Randle, or ask the USGS for Sawtooth Ridge.

Directions: From Tacoma, drive south 40 miles

on Highway 7 to Elbe. Turn east on Highway 706 and drive 7 miles to Forest Service Road 52. Turn right and drive 4.5 miles to Forest Service Road 84. Turn right and drive 1.5 miles to Forest Service Road 8410. Turn right and drive 4.5 miles to the trailhead on the left.

Contact: Gifford Pinchot National Forest, Cowlitz Valley Ranger Station, 10024 U.S. 12, Randle, WA 98377, 360/497-1100.

60 HIGH ROCK LOOKOUT

3.2 mi/2.0 hr

south of Mount Rainier in Gifford Pinchot National Forest

Map 5.2, page 236

Towering over the adjacent Sawtooth Ridge at 5,685 feet, this peak is certainly high. And with a sheer 600-foot drop on its north face, it definitely qualifies as a rock. And yet the name is an understatement. High Rock might be an imposing sight from below, but the Forest Service Lookout stationed on the summit boasts some of the best views in the Gifford Pinchot. The mountain is separated from Mount Rainier National Park only by Nisqually Valley. Thus, broad views but sparse crowds.

Atop the tallest peak in Sawtooth Range, High Rock Lookout Trail endures a short but sharp climb: 1,600 feet in just 1.5 miles. It wastes little time reaching high meadows and glorious views along High Rock's southern arm. Southern-oriented meadows means sunny, exposed, and dry. Bring water. The lookout stands at 5,685 feet and revels in views of Goat Rocks, Mount Adams, and Mount St. Helens. That enormous mountain just a stone's throw away is Mount Rainier. The northern edge is a sharp drop, so watch your step. Over the edge lie three high lakes along Sawtooth Ridge (see previous listing).

User Groups: Hikers and leashed dogs. No horses or mountain bikes are allowed. No wheelchair access.

Open Seasons: This trail is accessible mid-June–October.

Permits: A federal Northwest Forest Pass is required to park here.

Maps: For a map of Gifford Pinchot National Forest, contact the Outdoor Recreation Information Center at the downtown Seattle REI. For a topographic map, ask Green Trails for No. 301, Randle, or ask the USGS for Sawtooth Ridge.

Directions: From Tacoma, drive south 40 miles on Highway 7 to Elbe. Turn east on Highway 706 and drive 7 miles to Forest Service Road 52. Turn right and drive 1 mile to Forest Service Road 85. Continue straight and drive 5 miles to Forest Service Road 8440. Stay to the left and drive 4.5 miles to the trailhead on the left at Towhead Gap.

Contact: Gifford Pinchot National Forest, Cowlitz Valley Ranger Station, 10024 U.S. 12, Randle, WA 98377, 360/497-1100.

61 TATOOSH RIDGE

5.0 mi/3.5 hr

south of Mount Rainier in Tatoosh Wilderness of Gifford Pinchot National Forest

Map 5.2, page 236

Tatoosh Range stands less than 10 miles from Mount Rainier (as the crow flies), practically a smaller sister to the dominating mountain. And Tatoosh Ridge Trail boasts incredible views of The Mountain, yet it seems so far away—far away from the crowds in the national park, that is. Just south of the park boundary but protected by its own wilderness, Tatoosh Range receives just a fraction of the visitors that trails inside the park do. It's good habitat for lonely views, high lakes, and mountain meadows.

Tatoosh Ridge Trail runs along the southern spine of Tatoosh Ridge, with trailheads at either end. Both ends are steep switchback shuffles, but the northern trailhead offers access to much more scenic terrain. Tackle 2,600 feet of elevation in just two miles before reaching Tatoosh Lakes junction. This side trail (1 mile round-trip) leads up to a saddle of epic views and down to Tatoosh Lakes, lying among rocky slopes and meadows. Several great camps are found along the lakeshore.

From the first junction, Tatoosh Ridge Trail

continues over rocky and exposed terrain to another junction (3.9 miles), this time leading up to Tatoosh Lookout. At 6,310 feet, here are your epic views. The trail drops from the second junction, below Butter Peak and to the southern trailhead (9 miles one-way). Pack sunscreen and extra water, as the trail is hot, often exposed, and without water, save for the lakes.

User Groups: Hikers, leashed dogs, and horses. No mountain bikes are allowed. No wheelchair access.

Open Seasons: This trail is accessible July–September.

Permits: A federal Northwest Forest Pass is required to park here.

Maps: For a map of Gifford Pinchot National Forest, contact the Outdoor Recreation Information Center at the downtown Seattle REI. For a topographic map, ask Green Trails for No. 302, Packwood, or ask the USGS for Tatoosh Lakes.

Directions: To the northern trailhead: From Packwood, drive north 4 miles on Skate Creek Road (Forest Service Road 52) to Forest Service Road 5270. Turn right and drive 6 miles to the signed trailhead on the right.

To the southern trailhead: From Packwood, drive north on Skate Creek Road and turn right on Forest Service Road 5290. Drive 5 miles, staying on the main gravel road, then veer left, remaining on Forest Service Road 5290 for 3.5 miles to the trailhead at road's end.

Contact: Gifford Pinchot National Forest, Cowlitz Valley Ranger Station, 10024 U.S. 12, Randle, WA 98377, 360/497-1100.

62 DUMBBELL LAKE LOOP

15.8 mi/2 days — 2 8

southeast of Mount Rainier in William O. Douglas Wilderness of Gifford Pinchot National Forest

Map 5.2, page 236

Dumbbell Lake knows how to treat a hiker well. It offers not only beautiful scenery but the opportunity for lots of exploring. It's situated on a high plateau, where the firs are plentiful and form a nice surrounding forest. On the north side, a connected chain of small islands extends into the lake and encourages lots of investigation.

The hike to Dumbbell begins along Pacific Crest Trail out of White Pass. Follow PCT for 6.5 miles as it climbs gently onto the plateau. The trail passes small Sand Lake before dropping to Buesch Lake, where good camping is to be had. Abandon PCT and join Trail 56, where Dumbbell lies just .5 mile away. The best camping is found near the middle of the lake on the north side, beyond the burned section at the west end. The trail continues past Cramer Lake while gradually dropping elevation back to the trailhead.

On these high flatlands, dense groves of subalpine firs and mountain hemlocks frequently give way to open meadows. The many small lakes and large open meadows on this high plateau make for great day excursions. If you try this hike in the summer, expect people and bugs. Both can be pesky, but don't miss this hike.

User Groups: Hikers, leashed dogs, and horses. No mountain bikes are allowed. No wheelchair access.

Open Seasons: This trail is usually accessible July–mid-October.

Permits: A federal Northwest Forest Pass is required to park here.

Maps: For a map of Gifford Pinchot National Forest, contact the Outdoor Recreation Information Center at the downtown Seattle REI. For topographic maps, ask Green Trails for No. 303, White Pass, or ask the USGS for White Pass and Spiral Lake.

Directions: From Randle, drive east on Highway 12 to White Pass Campground, on the north side of the highway just east of the pass. The trailhead is located just before the campground entrance and is signed as the Pacific Crest Trail.

Contact: Gifford Pinchot National Forest, Cowlitz Valley Ranger Station, 10024 U.S. 12, Randle, WA 98377, 360/497-1100.

63 TWIN SISTERS

2.4 mi/1.5 hr

southeast of Mount Rainier in William O. Douglas Wilderness of Gifford Pinchot National Forest

Map 5.2, page 236

It's almost too easy to get to Twin Sisters. A place so beautiful usually loses out when access is so easy, and that's nearly the case here. A pair of large, stunning high lakes are the Twin Sisters, surrounded by a wilderness of firs and hemlocks. The lakes are popular destinations for folks of all types because of their easy accessibility, great camping, and extensive opportunities for side trips, including the great Tumac Mountain.

This hike serves well both as a day hike or as an extended backpacking trip. The grade up Deep Creek is short and never taxing. The lakes are surrounded by forests of subalpine fir and mountain hemlock. To the north, almost between the lakes, lies a small butte. Most of the terrain in this area is gentle, rolling hills. At the lakes, excessive use through the years created numerous campsites. Camping must now be at least 200 feet from the lakeshore to keep damage to a minimum. If the crowds feel too thick at Twin Sisters, many other small lakes are worth seeking out.

A necessary side trip is Tumac Mountain, a relatively small and young High Cascades volcano. Just two miles from the east lake, the 6,340-foot summit of Tumac includes a crater and stunning views of Mount Rainier. Other easy expeditions are to Fryingpan Lake, Snow Lake, or Blakenship Lakes, and Pacific Crest Trail is not far.

User Groups: Hikers, leashed dogs, and horses. No mountain bikes are allowed. No wheelchair access.

Open Seasons: This area is usually accessible July–early October.

Permits: A federal Northwest Forest Pass is required to park here.

Maps: For a map of Gifford Pinchot National Forest, contact the Outdoor Recreation Information Center at the downtown Seattle REI. For a topographic map, ask Green Trails for No. 303, White Pass, or ask the USGS for Spiral Lake, Bumping Lake, and White Pass.

Directions: From Yakima, drive west on Highway 410 to Bumping Lake Road (Forest Service Road 1800). Turn left and drive 13 miles to Forest Service Road 1808. Turn left and drive 6.5 miles to Deer Creek Campground and the trailhead at road's end.

Contact: Gifford Pinchot National Forest, Cowlitz Valley Ranger Station, 10024 U.S. 12, Randle, WA 98377, 360/497-1100.

64 SPIRAL BUTTE

12.0 mi/6.0 hr

southeast of Mount Rainier in William O. Douglas Wilderness of Gifford Pinchot National Forest

Map 5.2, page 236

Forget all the gear, time, and trouble it takes to summit Mount Rainier or Mount Adams. Getting atop a High Cascades volcano can be done in a day with nothing more than a sturdy pair of hiking boots. That's the allure of Spiral Butte, a small peak just north of Highway 12 near White Pass. The scene from the top is panoramic, offering views of Mount Rainier, Goat Rocks, and other surrounding peaks and ridges.

The trail is a steady climb nearly all the way, gaining 2,500 feet. Sand Ridge Trail climbs through a typical east-side forest. Take a left onto Shellrock Lake Trail (3 miles) and another left on Spiral Butte Trail (4 miles). Here, western larches begin to appear and add some needed color on autumn days. Spiral Butte is so named because of a long, twisting arm of the mountain that swings out from the north. It is on this arm that the trail climbs, providing a great alternative to switchbacks but nevertheless gaining 1,100 feet in the final two miles.

Spiral Butte is relatively young, about one million years old, and consists of andesite, a volcanic rock that breaks into large and beautiful gray chunks. Large slopes of talus are visible, revealing the difficulty vegetation can encounter when trying to pioneer such tough terrain.

User Groups: Hikers, leashed dogs, mountain bikes, and horses. No wheelchair access.

Open Seasons: This trail is usually accessible mid-June–early October.

Permits: A federal Northwest Forest Pass is required to park here.

Maps: For a map of Gifford Pinchot National Forest, contact the Outdoor Recreation Information Center at the downtown Seattle REI. For topographic maps, ask Green Trails for No. 303, White Pass, or ask the USGS for Spiral Butte.

Directions: From Randle, drive east on Highway 12 to White Pass. Continue east on Highway 12 for 6 miles to the trailhead (signed "Sand Ridge") on the north side of the highway.

Contact: Gifford Pinchot National Forest, Cowlitz Valley Ranger Station, 10024 U.S. 12, Randle, WA 98377, 360/497-1100.

65 IRONSTONE MOUNTAIN

11.0 mi/6.0 hr

north of White Pass in William O. Douglas Wilderness of Wenatchee National Forest

Map 5.2, page 236

Aided by a high trailhead (elevation 6,300 feet), Ironstone Mountain presents the easiest ridge hike in the area. Sparse, open forest regularly gives way to open meadows and great views. Ironstone Mountain Trail leaves Forest Service Road 199 and follows the ups and downs of the ridge to Ironstone Mountain. Along the way are several trail junctions, including Burnt Mountain Trail (2.5 miles) and Shellrock Peak (4.5 miles). These two side trails can be combined to form a loop option down (way down) to Rattlesnake Creek and back. A full trip out to Ironstone Mountain is nearly 20 miles roundtrip. The best option is to hike the ridge to Shellrock Peak Trail and head north on this trail. Within a mile is easy access to Shellrock Peak, a panoramic vista at 6,835 feet. This is a great viewpoint to see Mount Rainier, the Cascade Crest, and Goat Rocks. Remember to carry plenty of water. This trail is on the east side of the Cascades and can be extremely hot and dry.

User Groups: Hikers, leashed dogs, and horses. No mountain bikes are allowed. No wheelchair access.

Open Seasons: This trail is accessible June–October.

Permits: A federal Northwest Forest Pass is required to park here.

Maps: For a map of Wenatchee National Forest, contact the Outdoor Recreation Information Center at the downtown Seattle REI. For a topographic map, ask Green Trails for No. 304, Rimrock, or ask the USGS for Spiral Butte and Rimrock Lake.

Directions: From White Pass, drive east 18 miles to Bethel Ridge Road (Forest Service Road 1500) at Bethel Ridge Sno-Park. Turn left and drive 9.5 miles to Forest Service Road 199. Turn left and drive 2.5 miles to the trailhead at road's end.

Contact: Wenatchee National Forest, Naches Ranger Station, 10237 Highway 12, Naches, WA 98937, 509/653-2205.

66 PURCELL MOUNTAIN

7.4–15.4 mi/4.0–8.0 hr

north of Randle in Gifford Pinchot National Forest

Map 5.2, page 236

Conveniently situated along Highway 12 near Randle, Purcell Mountain reaches into the high country and snags meadows and views. It's not an easy trip, however, despite two separate access trails. Expect some significant climbing along either end, with switchbacks the name of the game. The reward for such efforts? Expansive meadows of flowers spread before vast mountain vistas.

Purcell Mountain Trail runs the ridge of the long mountain, almost eight miles from end to end with a total elevation gain of 4,500 feet. From Highway 12, the trail wastes no time and quickly climbs among old timber. The forest provides welcome shade but breaks occasionally for valley views. Meadows appear before Prairie

Mountain (5 miles) and dominate the eastern slopes at Little Paradise (6 miles). The trail ends atop Purcell Mountain (7.7 miles).

A shorter but more strenuous option is Purcell Lookout Trail to the upper ridge. The trail climbs from a logging road to the top of Purcell Mountain (elevation 5,442 feet), gaining 2,400 feet in 3.7 miles. The lookout is long gone, but the views stuck around. Across miles of logged national forest land, Mount Rainier, Mount St. Helens, and Goat Rocks make inspiring neighbors.

On either route, water is a scarce commodity; be sure to carry adequate supplies. Campsites are also scarce, but a couple may be found below Little Paradise Meadows and at the two trails' junction.

User Groups: Hikers, leashed dogs, horses, and mountain bikes. No wheelchair access.

Open Seasons: This trail is accessible mid-June–October.

Permits: A federal Northwest Forest Pass is required to park here.

Maps: For a map of Gifford Pinchot National Forest, contact the Outdoor Recreation Information Center at the downtown Seattle REI. For a topographic map, ask Green Trails for No. 301, Randle, or ask the USGS for Randle.

Directions: Lower trailhead: From Randle, drive east 6 miles on Highway 12 to the signed trailhead, on the left (north) side.

Upper trailhead: From Randle, drive east 6 miles to Davis Creek Road. Turn left and drive 1 mile to Forest Service Road 63. Turn left and drive 4.5 miles to Forest Service Road 6310. Turn left and drive 1 mile to the trailhead on the right.

Contact: Gifford Pinchot National Forest, Cowlitz Valley Ranger Station, 10024 U.S. 12, Randle, WA 98377, 360/497-1100.

67 POMPEY PEAK

3.2 mi/2.0 hr

southwest of Packwood in Gifford Pinchot National Forest

Map 5.2, page 236

Pompey Peak Trail offers a quick, beautiful, but steep trip to a high viewpoint overlooking the Cowlitz River Valley. The trailhead actually bisects the trail, eliminating 2,500 feet of knee-knocking elevation gain along Kilborn Creek. That sounds good. From Kilborn Springs at the trailhead, Pompey Peak Trail climbs quickly and steadily through shady old-growth forest. Douglas fir and western hemlock give way to silver fir as the trail climbs. A social trail breaks off from the main trail (1.5 miles) and makes a short scramble to the summit (elevation 5,180 feet). Mount Rainier towers above the Tatoosh Range, while the peaks of Goat Rocks peek out from the east. Those with a hankering to put more trail underfoot can wander along Pompey Peak Trail another 2.8 miles along the ridge to Klickitat Trail, near Twin Sisters Mountain. And for a bit of history: Pompey Peak was named for a pack mule belonging to an old settler. The mule fell to its death on the upper part of the trail in the 1890s.

User Groups: Hikers, leashed dogs, horses, and mountain bikes. No wheelchair access.

Open Seasons: This trail is accessible June–October.

Permits: A federal Northwest Forest Pass is required to park here.

Maps: For a map of Gifford Pinchot National Forest, contact the Outdoor Recreation Information Center at the downtown Seattle REI. For a topographic map, ask Green Trails for No. 301, Randle, or ask the USGS for Purcell Mountain.

Directions: From Randle, drive south 1. mile on Highway 131 to Forest Service Road 23. Turn left and drive 3.5 miles to Forest Service Road 2404. Turn left and drive to the trailhead at road's end.

Contact: Gifford Pinchot National Forest, Cowlitz Valley Ranger Station, 10024 U.S. 12, Randle, WA 98377, 360/497-1100.

68 PACKWOOD LAKE

9.2 mi/5.0 hr

east of Packwood in Goat Rocks Wilderness of Gifford Pinchot National Forest

Map 5.2, page 236

Here's a hike the whole family can enjoy. Packwood Lake Trail skirts the base of Snyder Mountain through a forest of big trees to the large, scenic lake. Peaks of the Goat Rocks are visible to the south and Mount Rainier's summit to the north. The lake's crystal-blue water is inviting to swimmers and anglers alike; it holds a healthy population of trout. Elk are a frequent visitor during the winter. The idyllic setting is punctuated by a small forested island in the middle.

Although Packwood Lake Trail is forested and shady, little water is to be found along the way. The elevation gain of 900 feet is barely noticeable, well spread over the 4.6 miles of trail. Clear-cuts and second-growth forests are quickly passed by before you enter stands of old timber. The lake is a favorite overnight destination for families, with campsites found around the shores of the lake. A trail winds around the east shore, with trails leading to Mosquito (6.8 miles) and Lost Lakes (8.8 miles).

User Groups: Hikers, leashed dogs, and horses. No mountain bikes are allowed. No wheelchair access.

Open Seasons: This trail is accessible year-round.

Permits: A federal Northwest Forest Pass is required to park here.

Maps: For a map of Gifford Pinchot National Forest, contact the Outdoor Recreation Information Center at the downtown Seattle REI. For a topographic map, ask Green Trails for No. 302, Packwood, or ask the USGS for Packwood.

Directions: From Randle, drive east 16 miles to Packwood. Turn right on Forest Service Road 1260 (near the ranger station) and drive south 5 miles to the trailhead at road's end.

Contact: Gifford Pinchot National Forest, Cowlitz Valley Ranger Station, 10024 U.S. 12, Randle, WA 98377, 360/497-1100.

69 LILY BASIN

12.0 mi/6.0 hr

south of Mount Rainier in Goat Rocks Wilderness of Gifford Pinchot National Forest

Map 5.2, page 236

Lily Basin Trail is full of great views of the South Cascade volcanoes and blooming wildflowers. Contouring around the head of Glacier Creek, the trail gives a bird's-eye view of Lily Basin, where bugling elk and howling coyotes are frequently heard. Johnson Peak towers above the trail before Heart Lake, set within subalpine meadows, comes into view below the trail. Many hikers leave with a camera full of great pictures.

The trail begins quite high, at 4,200 feet, and quickly enters Goat Rocks Wilderness. The trees along the ridge fight the heavy winter snowpack to attain large girths. The trail follows the ridge for four miles before arriving high above Lily Basin. Large populations of elk often graze in Lily Basin. The trail becomes tricky as it contours around the basin through avalanche chutes and talus. The slope falls away quickly, and hikers should take care when tackling this section. Wildflowers are abundant in these high open slopes.

At six miles is the junction with Angry Mountain Trail. From here, one can gaze down onto either side of the ridge, and no fewer than three of the major volcanoes are within view. A couple of possible camps lie along the trail, with the best camping a quick descent to Heart Lake.

User Groups: Hikers, leashed dogs, and horses (horses may have difficulty navigating the last couple of miles around the basin). No mountain bikes are allowed. No wheelchair access.

Open Seasons: This area is accessible July–October.

Permits: A federal Northwest Forest Pass is required to park here.

Maps: For a map of Gifford Pinchot National Forest, contact the Outdoor Recreation Information Center at the downtown Seattle REI. For a topographic map, ask Green Trails for No. 302, Packwood, or ask the USGS for Packwood.

Directions: From Randle, drive east 14 miles on Highway 12 to Forest Service Road 48. Turn right (south) and drive 9.5 miles to the trailhead on the right. This is shortly after a sharp left-hand turn in a creek bottom.

Contact: Gifford Pinchot National Forest, Cowlitz Valley Ranger Station, 10024 U.S. 12, Randle, WA 98377, 360/497-1100.

70 SOUTH POINT LOOKOUT

7.0 mi/4.0 hr

south of Randle in Gifford Pinchot National Forest

Map 5.2, page 236

The lookout may be long gone, but the far-reaching views remain. South Point Lookout Trail makes a rugged assault on South Point Mountain, gaining 3,200 feet in just 3.5 miles. That's steep by anyone's standards. The payoff is grand, though, with views of Mount Rainier, Mount St. Helens, and Goat Rocks, not to mention many surrounding ridges and peaks. Much of the trail climbs within an open forest burned long ago. The resulting forest of snags provides increasingly better vistas along the ascent but also makes the hike a hot one (and dry, so bring extra water). The trail ends at the summit, where the lookout once stood. Adventurous folk will enjoy scrambling south along the rocky, meadowy ridge.

User Groups: Hikers, leashed dogs, horses, and mountain bikes. No wheelchair access.

Open Seasons: This trail is accessible June–October.

Permits: A federal Northwest Forest Pass is required to park here.

Maps: For a map of Gifford Pinchot National Forest, contact the Outdoor Recreation Information Center at the downtown Seattle REI. For a topographic map, ask Green Trails for No. 302, Packwood, or ask the USGS for Packwood.

Directions: From Randle, drive east 11 miles on Highway 12 to Forest Service Road 20. Turn right (south) and drive 4 miles (crossing Smith Creek) to the signed trailhead on the left.

Contact: Gifford Pinchot National Forest, Cowlitz Valley Ranger Station, 10024 U.S. 12, Randle, WA 98377, 360/497-1100.

71 GLACIER LAKE

4.0 mi/2.0 hr

south of Mount Rainier in Goat Rocks Wilderness of Gifford Pinchot National Forest

Map 5.2, page 236

The trail to Glacier Lake is short, has just 800 feet of gain, and leads to a great lake full of trout. The name is misleading, as there are no glaciers near the lake. Instead, beautiful forests of old-growth fir and hemlock encase the lake with a small meadow at the west end making for a great picnicking spot. Elk roam Lily Basin farther up the creek and often make it down to the lake.

Glacier Lake Trail starts off from the trailhead in a young forest logged several decades ago. Within a mile the trail enters the wilderness and virgin forests. The trail is well maintained and never very steep, making easy access for all. A footpath skirts the large lake for exploration by anglers and families alike.

User Groups: Hikers, leashed dogs, and horses. No mountain bikes are allowed. No wheelchair access.

Open Seasons: This trail is accessible May–November.

Permits: A federal Northwest Forest Pass is required to park here.

Maps: For a map of Gifford Pinchot National Forest, contact the Outdoor Recreation Information Center at the downtown Seattle REI. For a topographic map, ask Green Trails for No. 302, Packwood, or ask the USGS for Packwood.

Directions: From Randle, drive east 12 miles on Highway 12 to Forest Service Road 21. Turn right (south) and drive 5 miles to Forest Service Road 2110. Turn left and drive .5 mile to the trailhead on the right.

Contact: Gifford Pinchot National Forest, Cowlitz Valley Ranger Station, 10024 U.S. 12, Randle, WA 98377, 360/497-1100.

72 ANGRY MOUNTAIN

16.8 mi/8.0 hr

south of Mount Rainier in Goat Rocks Wilderness of Gifford Pinchot National Forest

Map 5.2, page 236

Despite the name of the mountain, few people leave Angry Mountain in a foul mood. Out of breath and quite tired, but angry, not likely. The trail climbs 3,400 feet along the long ridge of the mountain with the help of plenty of switchbacks. Mount Rainier seems never to be far off, constantly in view to the north. The route ventures deep into the Goat Rocks Wilderness, ending at Heart Lake, a beautiful high lake sure to calm flared tempers and sore feet.

Angry Mountain Trail is difficult from the get-go. It quickly switchbacks up the west end of the mountain through nice forests of Douglas fir and hemlock. The forest soon opens, with large trees spaced farther apart because of heavy winter snowpacks. The trail follows the ridge, which drops steeply to the south. The severe cliffs along the south side of the mountain are a likely source of the name Angry Mountain. Or maybe it's the steep ascent.

Angry Mountain Trail continues by making another series of steep switchbacks, nearing the high point of the mountain and a viewpoint. The trail enters its prime from here, meandering along the ridge. Wildflowers go crazy during June and July. The trail eventually connects to Lily Basin Trail, near the head of Jordan Basin. A great overnight stay is found at Heart Lake (9 miles).

User Groups: Hikers, leashed dogs, and horses. No mountain bikes are allowed. No wheelchair access.

Open Seasons: This area is usually accessible mid-June–October.

Permits: A federal Northwest Forest Pass is required to park here.

Maps: For a map of Gifford Pinchot National Forest, contact the Outdoor Recreation Information Center at the downtown Seattle REI. For topographic maps, ask Green Trails for No. 302, Packwood, or ask the USGS for Packwood Lake.

Directions: From Randle, drive east 12 miles on Highway 12 to Forest Service Road 21. Turn right (south) and drive 7.5 miles to Forest Service Road 2120. Turn left and drive .5 mile to the trailhead on the right.

Contact: Gifford Pinchot National Forest, Cowlitz Valley Ranger Station, 10024 U.S. 12, Randle, WA 98377, 360/497-1100.

73 GOAT RIDGE

11.0 mi/6.0 hr

south of Mount Rainier in Goat Rocks Wilderness of Gifford Pinchot National Forest

Map 5.2, page 236

This is one of the most popular trails in Goat Rocks and for good reason. After climbing into the subalpine with miles of views, the trail finds beautiful but cold Goat Lake. Guarantees are rare, but it's likely that you'll see mountain goats on the high ridges surrounding the lake in the evening. So if you're after goats, wildflowers, or views, Goat Ridge is your hike.

The trail begins from Berry Patch Trailhead and climbs quickly through the forest. A loop option is available (1.2 miles) and is highly recommended. It climbs to the site of a former lookout, where three Cascade volcanoes sit close by. The loop returns to the main Goat Ridge Trail and adds little distance to the hike.

Scaling the slopes of Jordan Basin, the trail passes through wide open meadows that ignite with wildflower blooms in the summer. The trail intercepts Jordan Basin Trail (5.1 miles), a great side trip. Goat Lake lies another .5 mile on Goat Ridge Trail, set deep among high alpine ridges, home to white fuzzy goats.

Goat Ridge makes a great loop. Beyond Goat Lake, hike to Snowgrass Flats (7.8 miles), where hikers can drop back to the trailhead (13.3 miles) via Snowgrass Trail. This is an outstanding overnight trip.

User Groups: Hikers, leashed dogs, and horses.

No mountain bikes are allowed. No wheelchair access.

Open Seasons: This trail is usually accessible July–September.

Permits: A federal Northwest Forest Pass is required to park here.

Maps: For a map of Gifford Pinchot National Forest, contact the Outdoor Recreation Information Center at the downtown Seattle REI. For topographic maps, ask Green Trails for No. 334, Blue Lake, and No. 303, White Pass, or ask the USGS for Hamilton Butte and Old Snowy Mountain.

Directions: From Randle, drive east 12 miles on Highway 12 to Forest Service Road 21. Turn right (south) and drive 14 miles to Forest Service Road 2150. Turn left and drive 3.5 miles. Stay right at the Chambers Lake turnoff and then left to the north Berry Patch Trailhead. (There are two trailheads named Berry Patch—check signboards to verify you're at the one you want.)

Contact: Gifford Pinchot National Forest, Cowlitz Valley Ranger Station, 10024 U.S. 12, Randle, WA 98377, 360/497-1100.

74 SNOWGRASS FLATS

8.4 mi/5.0 hr

south of Mount Rainier in Goat Rocks Wilderness of Gifford Pinchot National Forest

Map 5.2, page 236

Some trails feature smile-inducing views or open vistas. Others showcase beautiful vegetation or wildlife. When a trail delivers both, it enters a realm reserved for few hikes. Snowgrass Flats is one of those hikes. The trail starts with a diverse forest featuring trees of inspiring size. Next are a pair of beautiful streams. And at the top lies Snowgrass Flats, a wide open parkland featuring more than acres of meadow. And last, the towering peaks of the Goat Rocks.

Snowgrass Trail leaves Berry Patch Trailhead and climbs over the end of Goat Ridge. It crosses Goat Creek on a nice bridge, where the stream cascades and courses over bedrock. Giant yellow cedars, Douglas firs, silver firs, and mountain hemlocks grow here. The trail passes another cascading stream, and the scenery only gets better. Numerous trees cost hikers time on the trail to ponder their ages.

After fairly steady climbing, the trail reaches Snowgrass Flats. This is open parkland for the most part, with meadows spreading far and wide. Here the trail runs into Pacific Crest Trail. Hiking about two miles south on PCT is well worth the effort, as the trail climbs to the base of Old Snowy and the views north become wide open. Old Snowy, at almost 8,000 feet, beckons you to climb farther with a very steep but trouble-free way trail to the summit. This is a hike to remember. Unfortunately, camping is prohibited within Snowgrass Flats.

User Groups: Hikers, leashed dogs, and horses. No mountain bikes are allowed. No wheelchair access.

Open Seasons: This trail is usually accessible July–September.

Permits: A federal Northwest Forest Pass is required to park here.

Maps: For a map of Gifford Pinchot National Forest, contact the Outdoor Recreation Information Center at the downtown Seattle REI. For topographic maps, ask Green Trails for No. 334, Blue Lake, No. 335, Walupt Lake, and No. 303, White Pass, or ask the USGS for Hamilton Butte and Walupt Lake.

Directions: From Randle, drive east 12 miles on Highway 12 to Forest Service Road 21. Turn right (south) and drive 14 miles to Forest Service Road 2150. Turn left and drive 3.5 miles. Stay right at Chambers Lake turnoff and then right on Forest Service Road 2150-405, toward the south Berry Patch Trailhead. (There are two trailheads named Berry Patch—check signboards to verify you're at the one you want.)

Contact: Gifford Pinchot National Forest, Cowlitz Valley Ranger Station, 10024 U.S. 12, Randle, WA 98377, 360/497-1100.

© ANDREA PENGLASE

Goat Lake, seen here from the PCT near Snowgrass Flats, is a popular destination.

75 NANNIE RIDGE

9.0 mi/5.5 hr

south of White Pass in Goat Rocks Wilderness of Gifford Pinchot National Forest

Map 5.2, page 236

Nannie Ridge Trail, in the southern Goat Rocks Wilderness, makes a scenic trip along the high crest. Nannie Ridge is between the craggy peaks of Goat Rocks and the commanding presence of Mount Adams. The trail passes an old lookout site on its way to the meadows of Sheep Lake and Pacific Crest Trail. Understandably, Nannie Ridge is a popular trail in the Gifford Pinchot.

Beginning from the shores of Walupt Lake, Nannie Ridge Trail climbs steadily and steeply to the crest of the ridge. A social trail leads to Nannie Peak (2.5 miles, elevation 6,106), the first but not last opportunity for expansive views. The trail traverses the ridge beneath tall, rocky cliffs and over open meadows of heather. This is hot and dry country, demanding that hikers pack extra water and sunscreen. Nannie Ridge Trail ends at Sheep Lake, a favorite campsite and swimming hole for hikers passing through on PCT. If Sheep Lake doesn't tempt you into the water, Walupt Lake will.

User Groups: Hikers, leashed dogs, and horses. No mountain bikes are allowed. No wheelchair access.

Open Seasons: This trail is accessible June–October.

Permits: A federal Northwest Forest Pass is required to park here.

Maps: For a map of Gifford Pinchot National Forest, contact the Outdoor Recreation Information Center at the downtown Seattle REI. For a topographic map, ask Green Trails for No. 335, Walupt Lake, or ask the USGS for Walupt Lake.

Directions: From Randle, drive east 12 miles on Highway 12 to Forest Service Road 21. Turn right (south) and drive 18.5 miles to Forest Service Road 2160. Turn left and drive 5.5 miles to Walupt Lake Trailhead.

Contact: Gifford Pinchot National Forest, Cowlitz Valley Ranger Station, 10024 U.S. 12, Randle, WA 98377, 360/497-1100.

76 WALUPT CREEK

8.6–13.5 mi/4.5 hr–2 days

south of White Pass in Goat Rocks Wilderness of Gifford Pinchot National Forest

Map 5.2, page 236

Short, easy, and not exceptionally scenic, Walupt Creek Trail is about more than just the creek.

The up-and-back along the trail is a great hike, with pleasant forest and meadows, and even a few high tarns thrown in at the end. But more importantly, Walupt Creek Trail provides two great loops along Pacific Crest Trail.

Walupt Creek Trail provides great access to PCT, gaining just 1,000 feet in more than four miles. The trail spends its first 1.5 miles along the shores of Walupt Lake. Good luck getting past here on a hot summer day without a quick dip to cool off. The trail briefly follows the creek before leaving it to climb out of the glacially shaped valley (notice the U shape) to a large, flat basin. Here are your open subalpine meadows and small tarns. Campsites are found along Walupt Creek and here, near the tarns and PCT.

Walupt Creek is the starting leg to a pair of great loops. From the end of Walupt Creek Trail, head north on PCT to Sheep Lake and along Nannie Ridge (see previous listing) to Walupt Lake (12.3 miles). This route has the most views, especially along Nannie Ridge. Or head south on PCT (13.5 miles), through a large basin and the meadows of Coleman Weedpatch. Both loops turn Walupt Creek from mundane into terrific.

User Groups: Hikers, leashed dogs, and horses. No mountain bikes are allowed. No wheelchair access.

Open Seasons: This trail is accessible June–October.

Permits: A federal Northwest Forest Pass is required to park here.

Maps: For a map of Gifford Pinchot National Forest, contact the Outdoor Recreation Information Center at the downtown Seattle REI. For a topographic map, ask Green Trails for No. 335, Walupt Lake, or ask the USGS for Walupt Lake.

Directions: From Randle, drive east 12 miles on Highway 12 to Forest Service Road 21. Turn right (south) and drive 18.5 miles to Forest Service Road 2160. Turn left and drive 5.5 miles to Walupt Lake Trailhead.

Contact: Gifford Pinchot National Forest, Cowlitz Valley Ranger Station, 10024 U.S. 12, Randle, WA 98377, 360/497-1100.

77 CLEAR FORK

19.2 mi/8.0 hr

east of Packwood in Goat Rocks Wilderness of Gifford Pinchot National Forest

Map 5.2, page 236

Clear Fork Trail offers something rarely found south of the North Cascades: a long, undisturbed river valley hike up to Pacific Crest Trail. Although many river valleys in the area were logged long ago, the upper Clear Fork of Cowlitz River survived the ax and saw. That's a good thing, for the bubbling water of this stream makes for a serene scene. This is an ideal hike for families, with lots to see and very little elevation change in the first seven miles.

Clear Fork Trail begins on a level, timbered plateau above the river. Situated in an open meadow, Lily Lake (1.5 miles) makes a great swimming hole and turnaround for hikers seeking a shorter hike. Beyond, Clear Fork rambles through old-growth forest and meets the river (5.5 miles). Anglers will note that trout inhabit this wild, rarely fished water. The forests are full of deer and elk, and maybe even a black bear or two. The trail eventually fords the river (7 miles) and climbs to PCT (9.6 miles).

User Groups: Hikers, leashed dogs, and horses. No mountain bikes are allowed. No wheelchair access.

Open Seasons: This trail is accessible year-round.

Permits: A federal Northwest Forest Pass is required to park here.

Maps: For a map of Gifford Pinchot National Forest, contact the Outdoor Recreation Information Center at the downtown Seattle REI. For a topographic map, ask Green Trails for No. 303, White Pass, or ask the USGS for White Pass and Packwood.

Directions: From Randle, drive east 21 miles on Highway 12 to Forest Service Road 46. Turn right (south) and drive 9 miles to the trailhead at road's end.

Contact: Gifford Pinchot National Forest, Cowlitz Valley Ranger Station, 10024 U.S. 12, Randle, WA 98377, 360/497-1100.

78 BLUFF LAKE

3.0–13.2 mi/2.0–8.0 hr

east of Packwood in Goat Rocks Wilderness of Gifford Pinchot National Forest

Map 5.2, page 236

On the map, Bluff Lake fails to muster much excitement, appearing as nothing more than a small body of water atop a low ridge. Once boots hit trail, however, it's apparent that a great trip is in store. Bluff Lake Trail climbs to its namesake and beyond, running 6.6 miles along the crest of Coal Creek Mountain. Old-growth forest gives way to subalpine meadows. No map mentions that your most likely traveling companions will be deer, elk, and mountain goats. And the map's biggest secret is huckleberries, acres of them.

Bluff Lake Trail gets under way in a mean way, quickly rising 1,000 feet to Bluff Lake (1.5 miles) in the forest atop the ridge. The lake is a good place to turn around for a short hike, but the best is yet to come. The trail maintains its ascent to the crest of Coal Creek Mountain and mellows out along the ridge. The forest grows increasingly sparse, giving way to meadows full of views and huckleberries. This is a good place to see the Goat Rocks, several miles to the southeast. At 6.6 miles, Bluff Lake Trail ends atop a high butte, at a junction with Clear Lost Trail (dropping to Lost Hat Lake, 1 mile) and Packwood Lake Trail (dropping to Lost Lake, 1.4 miles). Trips to these lakes can make your hike slightly longer. Other than Bluff Lake, there's no water to be found along the route.

User Groups: Hikers, leashed dogs, and horses. No mountain bikes are allowed. No wheelchair access.

Open Seasons: This trail is accessible mid-May–October.

Permits: A federal Northwest Forest Pass is required to park here.

Maps: For a map of Gifford Pinchot National Forest, contact the Outdoor Recreation Information Center at the downtown Seattle REI. For a topographic map, ask Green Trails for No. 302, Packwood, or ask the USGS for Ohanapecosh.

Directions: From Randle, drive east 21 miles on Highway 12 to Forest Service Road 46. Turn right (south) and drive 2 miles to Forest Service Road 4610. Turn right and drive 2 miles to Forest Service Road 4612. Turn left and drive 3 miles to the trailhead at a sharp left turn in the road.

Contact: Gifford Pinchot National Forest, Cowlitz Valley Ranger Station, 10024 U.S. 12, Randle, WA 98377, 360/497-1100.

79 ROUND MOUNTAIN

5.0 mi/3.0 hr

south of White Pass in Goat Rocks Wilderness of Gifford Pinchot National Forest

Map 5.2, page 236

Short but steep, Round Mountain Trail climbs to an abandoned lookout and onward over Twin Peaks to Pacific Crest Trail. This rugged trail shows few qualms about reaching its destination, gaining 1,600 feet in just 2.5 miles. Round Mountain Trail begins in open forest, but the timber gives way to rocky meadows near the top of Round Mountain. This is a good place to see elk and deer foraging in the forest. At the summit, 5,970 feet, stands an old, shuttered lookout no longer in use by the Forest Service. The views, looking out over miles of the Cascade Crest, are grand—north to Spiral Butte and Mount Rainier and south to Goat Rocks. Beyond the summit, Round Mountain Trail continues over Twin Peaks (4.5 miles) to PCT (6.5 miles). Be sure to carry plenty of water and sunscreen, as this is a hot and dry trail.

User Groups: Hikers, leashed dogs, and horses. No mountain bikes are allowed. No wheelchair access.

Open Seasons: This trail is accessible June–October.

Permits: A federal Northwest Forest Pass is required to park here.

Maps: For a map of Gifford Pinchot National Forest, contact the Outdoor Recreation Information Center at the downtown Seattle REI.

For a topographic map, ask Green Trails for No. 303, White Pass, or ask the USGS for Spiral Butte.
Directions: From White Pass, drive east 7.5 miles on Highway 12 to Tieton Road (Forest Service Road 1200). Turn right (south) and drive 3 miles to Forest Service Road 830. Turn right and drive 4.5 miles to the trailhead on the left side.
Contact: Wenatchee National Forest, Naches Ranger Station, 10237 Highway 12, Naches, WA 98937, 509/653-2205.

80 SHOE LAKE

13.5 mi/8.0 hr

south of White Pass in Goat Rocks Wilderness of Gifford Pinchot National Forest

Map 5.2, page 236

Some of the best stretches of Pacific Crest Trail are here in Goat Rocks Wilderness. Though not as celebrated as the rocky crags of the Goat Rocks peaks, Shoe Lake is a scenic hike and certainly carries its own weight. Starting directly from Highway 12, PCT traverses seven miles of open forest and wide open meadows to reach refreshing Shoe Lake.

Pacific Crest Trail leaves White Pass and progressively climbs through open forest, passing small Ginette Lake (2.2 miles). PCT eventually finds itself swamped in meadows (5 miles) and awash in wildflower color in late June. For those who have made it this far, the best is still to come. Mount Rainier comes into view as PCT skirts Hogback Mountain and ascends to a high saddle (6.3 miles) overlooking the basin of Shoe Lake with Pinegrass Ridge in the distance. Reaching Shoe Lake requires a steep, short drop into the basin.

The hike to Shoe Lake is very hot and dry, especially during late summer. Until you reach the lake, water is nonexistent, an important consideration when packing before your trip. Camping is highly discouraged in Shoe Lake Basin because of heavy use in the past. Overnight hikers must continue to Hidden Spring (8.5 miles) or cross-country camp more than 200 yards from the trail.

User Groups: Hikers, leashed dogs, and horses. No mountain bikes are allowed. No wheelchair access.
Open Seasons: This trail is accessible June–October.
Permits: A federal Northwest Forest Pass is required to park here.
Maps: For a map of Gifford Pinchot National Forest, contact the Outdoor Recreation Information Center at the downtown Seattle REI. For a topographic map, ask Green Trails for No. 303, White Pass, or ask the USGS for White Pass.
Directions: From White Pass, drive east .7 mile on Highway 12 to the Pacific Crest Trailhead at White Pass Campground. Park here, on the north side of the highway. The trailhead is on the south side.
Contact: Wenatchee National Forest, Naches Ranger Station, 10237 Highway 12, Naches, WA 98937, 509/653-2205.

81 NORTH FORK TIETON

14.0 mi/1–2 days

south of White Pass in Goat Rocks Wilderness of Wenatchee National Forest

Map 5.2, page 236

North Fork Tieton Trail makes a terrific run up to Pacific Crest Trail and an amazing basin below the glaciers of Goat Rocks. This is one of the best ways to reach PCT, just before it climbs into the Goat Rocks. Although this isn't Mount Rainier, Goat Rocks still gets fairly crowded on a summer weekend. This northern side of Goat Rocks, however, sees a fraction of the use compared to the western side.

North Fork Tieton Trail climbs at a steady grade before making a steep rise to Tieton Pass (4.9 miles). Old-growth forests line the trail, with large timber despite being east of the Cascade Crest. Along the way are views of enormous Tieton Valley, ringed by tall, snowy peaks. Gilbert Peak and Old Snowy tower from the heart of the Goat Rocks, at the head of the basin. To the east stand the rugged, rocky slopes of Tieton Peak and Devils Horns.

Pacific Crest Trail runs north-south from Tieton Pass. Head south to reach a junction for McCall Basin (6.5 miles). Break south along McCall Basin Trail and wander into a subalpine wonderland. Acres of meadows run into rocky slopes. Large herds of mountain goats are regular visitors in the area. Since McCall Basin makes a long day hike, campsites are scattered about, ideal for Leave-No-Trace camping.

User Groups: Hikers, leashed dogs, and horses. No mountain bikes are allowed. No wheelchair access.

Open Seasons: This trail is accessible mid-June–mid-October.

Permits: A federal Northwest Forest Pass is required to park here.

Maps: For a map of Wenatchee National Forest, contact the Outdoor Recreation Information Center at the downtown Seattle REI. For a topographic map, ask Green Trails for No. 303, White Pass, or ask the USGS for Pinegrass Ridge and Old Snowy Mountain.

Directions: From White Pass, drive east 7.5 miles on Highway 12 to Tieton Road (Forest Service Road 1200). Turn right (south) and drive 3 miles to Forest Service Road 1207. Continue straight onto Road 1207 and drive 4.5 miles to the trailhead at road's end.

Contact: Wenatchee National Forest, Naches Ranger Station, 10237 Highway 12, Naches, WA 98937, 509/653-2205.

82 BEAR CREEK MOUNTAIN

12.8 mi/8.0 hr 4 10

southeast of White Pass in Goat Rocks Wilderness of Wenatchee National Forest

Map 5.2, page 236

As far as forgotten and ignored trails in the Goat Rocks go, this is it. Bear Creek Mountain Trail makes a steep trip to the summit along the ridge dividing the North and South Fork Tieton Rivers. Because of an elevation gain of more than 3,000 feet, most hikers select other trails in the area. That's a shame, because high-country meadows full of wildflowers, maybe even mountain goats, reward those who make the trip.

Bear Creek Mountain Trail wastes little time before starting a steep ascent out of the South Fork Tieton Valley. The trees are big, but this being the east side of the Cascade Crest, the forest is open. Meadows begin to appear as the trail reaches a junction with Tieton Meadows Trail (5.4 miles). The views are grand from this north-facing vista, including Mount Rainier, which outshines any other peak.

To gain panoramic views, one must turn south and scramble nearly 1,000 feet in one mile to the summit of Bear Creek Mountain. To say the least, this is an impressive location from which to study Goat Rocks. Hikers who pack a pair of binoculars this far will be glad they did. Bear Creek Mountain Trail passes no water along the way, so plan to carry plenty.

User Groups: Hikers, leashed dogs, and horses. No mountain bikes are allowed. No wheelchair access.

Open Seasons: This trail is accessible July–October.

Permits: A federal Northwest Forest Pass is required to park here.

Maps: For a map of Wenatchee National Forest, contact the Outdoor Recreation Information Center at the downtown Seattle REI. For a topographic map, ask Green Trails for No. 303, White Pass, or ask the USGS for Pinegrass Ridge.

Directions: From White Pass, drive east 7.5 miles on Highway 12 to Tieton Road (Forest Service Road 1200). Turn right (south) and drive 12 miles to Forest Service Road 1000. Turn right and drive 12 miles to the trailhead at road's end.

Contact: Wenatchee National Forest, Naches Ranger Station, 10237 Highway 12, Naches, WA 98937, 509/653-2205.

83 SOUTH FORK TIETON RIVER

13.9 mi/1–2 days 2 10

southeast of White Pass in Goat Rocks Wilderness of Wenatchee National Forest

Map 5.2, page 236

Free from the crowds that pack much of the Goat Rocks Wilderness in summer, South Fork

Tieton River Trail offers access to one of the mountains' most beautiful basins. The trail follows the river upstream before splitting to make a loop around the top of the expansive basin. The beauty of this trail layout (it's shaped like a lasso) is that very little of the trail is walked twice. Rocky peaks of Gilbert Peak and Klickitat Divide loom over the loop, home to fields of wildflowers and herds of mountain goats.

South Fork Tieton Trail remains exceptionally level and easy for the first several miles. Open Conrad Meadows features some very large timber. Elk and deer are common. The trail comes to a junction (4.3 miles), where the loop begins. This is also where the climbing starts. Either side of the loop climbs quickly to the upper slopes of the basin before leveling out. Long, narrow Surprise Lake is truly a surprise along the forested slopes, and it makes a great place to pitch camp. Mountain goats are frequent along the rocky rim bordering the basin. Hikers can make great excursions among the rocky meadows to the crest of Klickitat Divide for views of the surrounding Goat Rocks.

User Groups: Hikers, leashed dogs, and horses. No mountain bikes are allowed. No wheelchair access.

Open Seasons: This trail is accessible July–October.

Permits: A federal Northwest Forest Pass is required to park here.

Maps: For a map of Wenatchee National Forest, contact the Outdoor Recreation Information Center at the downtown Seattle REI. For a topographic map, ask Green Trails for No. 303, White Pass, or No. 335, Walupt Lake, or ask the USGS for Jennies Butte and Pinegrass Ridge.

Directions: From White Pass, drive east 7.5 miles on Highway 12 to Tieton Road (Forest Service Road 1200). Turn right (south) and drive 12 miles to Forest Service Road 1000. Turn right and drive 12 miles to the trailhead at road's end.

Contact: Wenatchee National Forest, Naches Ranger Station, 10237 Highway 12, Naches, WA 98937, 509/653-2205.

84 CISPUS BRAILLE

0.5 mi/0.5 hr

south of Randle in Gifford Pinchot National Forest

Map 5.2, page 236

This nature trail at the Cispus Environmental Learning Center investigates a forest recovering from fire. The trail is level and easy to negotiate, an ideal outing for families or those using a wheelchair. Interpretive signs lead the way and describe the flora and fauna helping to recreate a forest. The folks at the Learning Center have also designed this trail to be accessible to the visually impaired, with Braille markings and roping to guide hikers around the loop. This is a wonderful place to find elk or deer grazing the understory, especially in the winter when the high country lies under several feet of wet snow.

User Groups: Hikers and leashed dogs. No horses or mountain bikes are allowed. The trail is wheelchair accessible.

Open Seasons: This trail is accessible year-round.

Permits: A federal Northwest Forest Pass is required to park here.

Maps: For a map of Gifford Pinchot National Forest, contact the Outdoor Recreation Information Center at the downtown Seattle REI. For a topographic map, ask Green Trails for No. 333, McCoy Peak, or ask the USGS for Tower Rock.

Directions: From Randle, drive south 1 mile on Highway 131 to Forest Service Road 23. Veer left and drive 8 miles to Forest Service Road 28. Turn right and drive 1.5 miles to Forest Service Road 76. Stay to the right and drive 1 mile to the Cispus Environmental Learning Center. The trailhead is on the opposite side of Road 76.

Contact: Gifford Pinchot National Forest, Cowlitz Valley Ranger Station, 10024 U.S. 12, Randle, WA 98377, 360/497-1100.

85 KLICKITAT TRAIL

17.1 mi one-way/9.0 hr

4 9

south of Packwood in Gifford Pinchot National Forest

Map 5.2, page 236

Following an ancient Native American trail through the high country, Klickitat Trail makes an excellent ridge run. Bathed in summer sun, with miles of huckleberry bushes and mountain views, Klickitat Trail is an ideal day (or two) in the Gifford Pinchot. The length and orientation of the trail make an out-and-back hike very unappealing; a car-drop is best if it can be arranged. If not, the two trailheads are supplemented with several additional access points. Although the trail starts and ends high, the route encounters numerous ups and downs, making for some challenging elevation changes. Because much of the trail rides the crest of a ridge, snowfields are common on north slopes well into August.

From west to east, the trail skirts the rocky masses of Twin Sisters and Castle Butte. A side trail leads to the summit of Cispus Lookout (3.2 miles). Huckleberries and views of Mount Rainier dominate the scenery on the way to Horseshoe Point (7.5 miles), Cold Spring Butte (9 miles), and Mission Mountain (12.4 miles). The ridge (and trail) head south to the eastern trailhead, below Elk Peak (17.1 miles). The trail is dry except for Jackpot Lake (4.4 miles) and St. Michael Lake (off-trail below Cold Springs Butte).

User Groups: Hikers, leashed dogs, horses, and mountain bikes. No wheelchair access.

Open Seasons: This trail is accessible mid-July–October.

Permits: A federal Northwest Forest Pass is required to park here.

Maps: For a map of Gifford Pinchot National Forest, contact the Outdoor Recreation Information Center at the downtown Seattle REI. For a topographic map, ask Green Trails for No. 334, Blue Lake, or ask the USGS for Tower Rock, Hamilton Butte, and Blue Lake.

Directions: From Randle, drive south 1 mile on Highway 131 to Forest Service Road 25. Stay to the right and drive 21 miles to Forest Service Road 28. Turn left and drive 2.5 miles to the signed trailhead.

Contact: Gifford Pinchot National Forest, Cowlitz Valley Ranger Station, 10024 U.S. 12, Randle, WA 98377, 360/497-1100.

86 HAMILTON BUTTES

5.6 mi/3.0 hr

south of Randle in Gifford Pinchot National Forest

Map 5.2, page 236

Hamilton Buttes Trail features a pair of trailheads, one low and one high. Pick the starting location that's right for you, but the upper trailhead is 1.5 miles shorter and saves 1,000 feet of elevation gain. Hamilton Buttes Trail leads to the twin peaks on a route primarily cloaked in carpets of wildflower meadows and huckleberries.

From the upper trailhead, Hamilton Buttes Trail scales the side of a forested basin to reach a small ridgeline and junction (2.2 miles). Turning right drops to the lower trailhead, so don't do that. Head left, uphill, and climb to the top of the two peaks. This is divine country, with outstanding views of Goat Rocks and Mount Adams. August is the prime month to find ripe huckleberries. Carry plenty of water, as none is to be found once you leave the car.

User Groups: Hikers, leashed dogs, horses, mountain bikes, and motorcycles. No wheelchair access.

Open Seasons: This trail is accessible June–October.

Permits: A federal Northwest Forest Pass is required to park here.

Maps: For a map of Gifford Pinchot National Forest, contact the Outdoor Recreation Information Center at the downtown Seattle REI. For a topographic map, ask Green Trails for No. 334, Blue Lake, or ask the USGS for Hamilton Butte.

Directions: From Randle, drive south 1 mile on Highway 131 to Forest Service Road 23. Veer left and drive 12 miles to Forest Service

Road 22. Turn left and drive 6 miles to Forest Service Road 78. Turn right and drive 8.5 miles to the trailhead at the pass.

Contact: Gifford Pinchot National Forest, Cowlitz Valley Ranger Station, 10024 U.S. 12, Randle, WA 98377, 360/497-1100.

87 YOZOO

8.0 mi/4.0 hr

south of Randle in Gifford Pinchot National Forest

Map 5.2, page 236

Don't ask where the name came from, just enjoy the huckleberries and views of Mount Rainier. That's easy enough, because Yozoo Trail spends a big chunk of its length in open meadows along the high ridge. Through large, old forest, the trail skirts a ridge and climbs through the small valley of Grouse Creek (1.5 miles). This is the last chance for water before Yozoo Trail enters the high country with open meadows of small trees and huckleberry bushes. The trail runs just below the rim of Yozoo Basin, where views of Mount Rainier are constant. Several peaks frame the basin and make great scrambles to even bigger views. Mountain goats, elk, and black bear are all regular visitors to this area during the summer and early fall. Just be mindful of the most annoying of beasts, roaring motorbikes. Yozoo Trail ends at Bishop Ridge Trail (4 miles), overlooking the sparkling and tempting water of Blue Lake.

User Groups: Hikers, leashed dogs, horses, mountain bikes, and motorcycles. No wheelchair access.

Open Seasons: This trail is accessible April–October.

Permits: A federal Northwest Forest Pass is required to park here.

Maps: For a map of Gifford Pinchot National Forest, contact the Outdoor Recreation Information Center at the downtown Seattle REI. For a topographic map, ask Green Trails for No. 334, Blue Lake, or ask the USGS for Hamilton Butte.

Directions: From Randle, drive south 1 mile on Highway 131 to Forest Service Road 23. Veer left on Forest Service Road 23 and drive 12 miles to Forest Service Road 22. Turn left and drive 6 miles to Forest Service Road 78. Turn right and drive 5 miles to the signed trailhead.

Contact: Gifford Pinchot National Forest, Cowlitz Valley Ranger Station, 10024 U.S. 12, Randle, WA 98377, 360/497-1100.

88 LANGILLE RIDGE

8.4 mi/5.0 hr

south of Randle in Gifford Pinchot National Forest

Map 5.2, page 236

In the heart of Gifford Pinchot National Forest, Langille Ridge stands as a lonely place. Because of a road washout at one end and a steep, rocky access trail, few hikers have the pleasure of hiking this high ridge. Thus the spoils of Langille Ridge are left to the few, a tantalizing prospect for hikers looking for solitude. The jagged ridge runs more than 10 miles from end to end, but the best spots are close to the car.

With the washout of the northern trailhead, Langille Ridge Trail is best reached via Rough Trail. Appropriately named, Rough Trail climbs 2,000 feet over a rocky path to Langille Ridge Trail (1.7 miles). This is the worst of it, however. From the junction, Langille Ridge Trail runs north and south, making some ups and downs along the jagged ridge. A hike south travels through rocky meadows, complete with huckleberries, to Boundary Trail (5.6 miles one-way).

The preferred option is to head north from the Rough Trail junction along Langille Ridge to McCoy Peak (4.2 miles) and Langille Peak (5.9 miles). Both peaks offer panoramic views of the surrounding countryside and forests. The northern half of Langille Ridge features uninterrupted views of Juniper Ridge and Mount Adams. This is a great place to see mountain goats along the rocky slopes and to hear elk bellowing from the basins below. Plan on packing plenty of water, as much of the ridge is exposed and dry.

User Groups: Hikers, leashed dogs, horses,

mountain bikes, and motorcycles. No wheelchair access.

Open Seasons: This trail is accessible May–October.

Permits: A federal Northwest Forest Pass is required to park here.

Maps: For a map of Gifford Pinchot National Forest, contact the Outdoor Recreation Information Center at the downtown Seattle REI. For a topographic map, ask Green Trails for No. 333, McCoy Peak, or ask the USGS for Tower Rock and McCoy Peak.

Directions: From Randle, drive south 1 mile on Highway 131 to Forest Service Road 23. Veer left on Forest Service Road 23 and drive 8 miles to Forest Service Road 28. Turn right and drive 1.5 miles to Forest Service Road 29. Turn left and drive 12 miles to Forest Service Road 29-116. Turn right and drive .5 mile to the signed trailhead.

Contact: Gifford Pinchot National Forest, Cowlitz Valley Ranger Station, 10024 U.S. 12, Randle, WA 98377, 360/497-1100.

89 TONGUE MOUNTAIN

3.4 mi/2.0 hr

south of Randle in Gifford Pinchot National Forest

Map 5.2, page 236

Standing slightly apart from Juniper Ridge, Tongue Mountain towers over lush Cispus River Valley. Although the peak looks as if it belongs to the neighboring ridge, Tongue Mountain is actually the remains of an old volcano. Tongue Mountain Trail makes a gentle climb through old-growth forest to an open saddle (1 mile). Folks interested in views but not a workout can enjoy looking out over the valley to Mount Adams and Mount Rainier from here. More determined hikers can make the sharp and steep ascent to the peak's summit (1.7 miles, elevation 4,838 feet). This section of trail is a tough climb, but it's over quickly and is certainly rewarding. Cascades volcanoes tower over the Gifford Pinchot, and the noisy Cispus River roars from below. Lucky hikers will spot fluffy white mountain goats along the peaks' sheer cliffs.

User Groups: Hikers, leashed dogs, horses, and mountain bikes. No wheelchair access.

Open Seasons: This trail is accessible April–October.

Permits: A federal Northwest Forest Pass is required to park here.

Maps: For a map of Gifford Pinchot National Forest, contact the Outdoor Recreation Information Center at the downtown Seattle REI. For a topographic map, ask Green Trails for No. 333, McCoy Peak, or ask the USGS for Tower Rock.

Directions: From Randle, drive south 1 mile on Highway 131 to Forest Service Road 23. Veer left on Forest Service Road 23 and drive 8 miles to Forest Service Road 28. Turn right and drive 1.5 miles to Forest Service Road 29. Turn left and drive 4 miles to Forest Service Road 2904. Turn left and drive 4 miles to the signed trailhead.

Contact: Gifford Pinchot National Forest, Cowlitz Valley Ranger Station, 10024 U.S. 12, Randle, WA 98377, 360/497-1100.

90 BADGER PEAK

2.0 mi/1.5 hr

south of Randle in Gifford Pinchot National Forest

Map 5.2, page 236

Such easy access to a former lookout point is hard to come by, but Badger Ridge Trail delivers. It's just one short mile to the summit of Badger Peak (elevation 5,664 feet), where a lookout stood until the 1960s. Even harder to find is a refreshing lake nearby to enjoy after the climb to the summit, but that is found here also. Badger Ridge Trail starts high and climbs to the crest of Badger Ridge (.6 mile). Already, the views of Mount St. Helens are grand. They have competition, however, from fields of huckleberries. The trail now splits, dropping slightly to Badger Lake or climbing to Badger Peak. From the summit, volcanoes new and old dominate the landscape. Mount St. Helens, Mount

Rainier, and Mount Adams represent the new school, still busy at building themselves up. Older, extinct volcanoes include craggy Pinto Rock, jagged Langille Ridge, and other surrounding peaks. Your best bet is to climb the summit before dipping into Badger Lake.

User Groups: Hikers, leashed dogs, horses, mountain bikes, and motorcycles. No wheelchair access.

Open Seasons: This trail is accessible May–October.

Permits: A federal Northwest Forest Pass is required to park here.

Maps: For a map of Gifford Pinchot National Forest, contact the Outdoor Recreation Information Center at the downtown Seattle REI. For a topographic map, ask Green Trails for No. 333, McCoy Peak, or ask the USGS for French Butte.

Directions: From Randle, drive south 1 mile on Highway 131 to Forest Service Road 25. Stay to the right and drive 21 miles to Forest Service Road 28. Turn left (east) and drive 2.5 miles to Forest Service Road 2816 (a bit rocky). Turn right and drive 5 miles to the trailhead at road's end.

Contact: Gifford Pinchot National Forest, Cowlitz Valley Ranger Station, 10024 U.S. 12, Randle, WA 98377, 360/497-1100.

91 JUNIPER RIDGE

6.4–8.8 mi/5.0 hr 2 10

south of Randle in Gifford Pinchot National Forest

Map 5.2, page 236

High, open, and awash in huckleberries and views, Juniper Ridge Trail is a southern Washington favorite. The long ridge run follows the crest of Juniper Ridge over Juniper, Sunrise, and Jumbo Peaks. The hiker's reward is miles of huckleberries and views of Mount Adams, Mount Rainier, Mount St. Helens, and even Mount Hood. Between gazing and grazing, be sure not to bump into the numerous elk, mountain goats, deer, or bear that live here. Juniper Ridge is tremendously scenic and wild (except for the occasional dirt bike roaring through).

Juniper Ridge Trail runs 11.4 miles along the crest of the high ridge. Fortunately, the trail is bisected by Sunrise Trail, a short access trail (1.4 miles) conveniently starting at 4,500 feet. From Sunrise, hikers have options to head north to two separate peaks or south to miles of huckleberry meadows. Backpackers thinking of spending the night here will need to pack extra water; the ridge is dry.

The southern half of Juniper Ridge is certainly the best. The route is one big meadow ramble. Huckleberries are ripest in August. Juniper Ridge Trail skirts Jumbo Peak (3.2 miles), a good turnaround, before dropping to Dark Meadows and Boundary Trail.

The northern half of Juniper Ridge Trail leaves Sunrise Trailhead and climbs Sunrise Peak (1.4 miles), a steep but manageable endeavor. This is Juniper Ridge's highest point. The trail follows the rocky ridge north to Juniper Peak (4.4 miles), a good turnaround, before dropping into clear-cuts.

User Groups: Hikers, leashed dogs, horses, mountain bikes, and motorcycles. No wheelchair access.

Open Seasons: This trail is accessible May–October.

Permits: A federal Northwest Forest Pass is required to park here.

Maps: For a map of Gifford Pinchot National Forest, contact the Outdoor Recreation Information Center at the downtown Seattle REI. For a topographic map, ask Green Trails for No. 333, McCoy Peak, and No. 334, Blue Lake, or ask the USGS for McCoy Peak and Tower Rock.

Directions: From Randle, drive south 1 mile on Highway 131 to Forest Service Road 23. Veer left on Forest Service Road 23 and drive 24 miles to Forest Service Road 2324. Turn right and drive 5 miles to Forest Service Road 2324-063. Turn left and drive .3 mile to the trailhead at road's end.

Contact: Gifford Pinchot National Forest,

Cowlitz Valley Ranger Station, 10024 U.S. 12, Randle, WA 98377, 360/497-1100.

92 YELLOWJACKET PASS/ HAT ROCK

5.4 mi/3.0 hr

south of Randle in Gifford Pinchot National Forest

Map 5.2, page 236

Hat Rock is but one of many things to see or travel to from this trailhead. Yellowjacket Trail is merely a shortcut to other trails, heading in every direction through the high country. This is also known as a cheater trail; that is, quick and easy access to terrain normally approached by longer, more traditional routes. In this instance, Yellowjacket Trail provides a quick route to Boundary Trail's scenic eastern segment and Langille Ridge.

Yellowjacket Trail climbs sharply to Boundary Trail, gaining 800 feet in just one mile. Head left for Langille Ridge junction (1.2 miles from the trailhead) or to follow Boundary Trail to the huckleberry riches of Dark Meadow. Turning right from Yellowjacket Trail leads through open meadows with stunning views of Mount Adams to Hat Rock (2.4 miles from the trailhead) and Yellowjacket Pass (2.7 miles). A boot-beaten path leads to the top of Hat Rock (elevation 5,599 feet) and a remarkable view of Badger Peak, Craggy Peak, Langille Ridge, and Juniper Ridge. The flattened top of Mount St. Helens rises to the west. Although short, this is an exposed and dry hike; remember plenty of water.

User Groups: Hikers, leashed dogs, horses, mountain bikes, and motorcycles. No wheelchair access.

Open Seasons: This trail is accessible June–October.

Permits: A federal Northwest Forest Pass is required to park here.

Maps: For a map of Gifford Pinchot National Forest, contact the Outdoor Recreation Information Center at the downtown Seattle REI. For a topographic map, ask Green Trails for No. 333, McCoy, or ask the USGS for McCoy Peak.

Directions: From Randle, drive south 1 mile on Highway 131 to Forest Service Road 23. Veer left on Forest Service Road 23 and drive 8 miles to Forest Service Road 28. Turn right and drive 11 miles to Forest Service Road 2810. Stay to the left and drive 9 miles to trailhead at road's end.

Contact: Gifford Pinchot National Forest, Mount St. Helens National Volcanic Monument, 42218 Northeast Yale Bridge Road, Amboy, WA 98601, 360/449-7871.

93 CRAGGY PEAK

8.8 mi/5.0 hr

northeast of Cougar in Gifford Pinchot National Forest

Map 5.2, page 236

Craggy Peak Trail makes a great ridge run in the heart of the Gifford Pinchot, with meadow views to craggy peaks (including Craggy Peak!) and distant volcanoes. Enjoy the virgin forest shading the trail before it breaks out into spectacular meadows. Craggy Peak Trail also offers great access to Boundary Trail. With lots of campsites, this is a great day hike or an easy overnighter. Elk, deer, and mountain goats are frequent visitors to the area, and black bears appear in late summer to browse the huckleberries.

Craggy Peak Trail gets most of the climbing done early, ascending through an old forest of fir trees, dominated on the ground by bear grass. Quick glimpses of Mount Adams can be had through the trees, but the real views are reserved until the meadows (3 miles). The trail continues through prime huckleberry habitat to Boundary Trail, at the base of Craggy Peak (4.4 miles). Exploration along Boundary Trail is a meadow delight, north to Shark Rock or east to Yellowjacket Pass. The peaks tower over the deep, glaciated valleys, lush with old forests. Great campsites are situated along the trail, often down faint boot-worn paths to big views. Basin Camp is .5 mile east

on Boundary Trail. Just be prepared for a dry trip with extra packed water.

User Groups: Hikers, leashed dogs, horses, mountain bikes, and motorcycles. No wheelchair access.

Open Seasons: This trail is accessible June–October.

Permits: A federal Northwest Forest Pass is required to park here.

Maps: For a map of Gifford Pinchot National Forest, contact the Outdoor Recreation Information Center at the downtown Seattle REI. For a topographic map, ask Green Trails for No. 333, McCoy Peak, and No. 365, Lone Butte, or ask the USGS for Spencer Butte, Quartz Creek, and McCoy Peak.

Directions: From Vancouver, drive north on I-5 to Highway 503 (Woodland, exit 21). Drive east 45 miles to Forest Service Road 25. Continue straight on Forest Service Road 25 and drive 6 miles to Forest Service Road 93, just beyond the Muddy River. Turn right and drive 13 miles to Forest Service Road 93-040. Turn left and drive .5 mile to the signed trailhead on the right.

Contact: Gifford Pinchot National Forest, Mount St. Helens National Volcanic Monument, 42218 Northeast Yale Bridge Road, Amboy, WA 98601, 360/449-7871.

94 SUMMIT PRAIRIE

17.8 mi/1–2 days

northeast of Cougar in Gifford Pinchot National Forest

Map 5.2, page 236

Miles from the nearest trailhead, Summit Prairie is isolated, to say the least. Access to the open meadows, chock-full of huckleberry bushes, requires a long climb of nearly 3,000 feet. That keeps the crowds out of Summit Prairie and the wildlife wild, despite the occasional motorbike (they're still allowed in this "roadless" area). Herds of elk and mountain goats live in Quartz Creek Ridge and Summit Prairie, one of the Gifford Pinchot's most remote places.

In honor of full disclosure, a cheater trail does offer access to Summit Prairie (Boundary Trail, via Table Mountain). It's a little shorter, but nowhere near as scenic. Better access is via Summit Prairie Trail, which climbs Quartz Creek Ridge and runs the long, open ridgeline to Summit Prairie. Leaving from Forest Service Road 90, Summit Prairie Trail climbs harshly to the ridgeline (4 miles). The only water on the route is found in this first segment. Open subalpine forest and frequent meadows cover the ridge to Summit Prairie (8.9 miles) and Boundary Trail.

This is a tough trip to complete in one day, but campsites are few and far between. Overnight campers should plan on cross-country camping without a water source. If you've made it this far, the best option is to turn the trip into a 20.7-mile loop on Boundary Trail, Quartz Creek Trail (see listing in this chapter), and Quartz Creek Butte Trail (a 1.5-mile trail that serves as connector between Summit Prairie and Quartz Creek Big Trees).

User Groups: Hikers, leashed dogs, horses, mountain bikes, and motorcycles. No wheelchair access.

Open Seasons: This trail is accessible mid-June–October.

Permits: A federal Northwest Forest Pass is required to park here.

Maps: For a map of Gifford Pinchot National Forest, contact the Outdoor Recreation Information Center at the downtown Seattle REI. For a topographic map, ask Green Trails for No. 334, Blue Lake, No. 365, Lone Butte, and No. 366, Mount Adams West, or ask the USGS for Steamboat Mountain and East Canyon Ridge.

Directions: From Vancouver, drive north on I-5 to Highway 503 (Woodland, exit 21). Drive east 45 miles to Pine Creek Information Center. Turn right and continue on Forest Service Road 90 for 25 miles to the signed trailhead on the left (1.5 miles before Forest Service Road 88).

Contact: Gifford Pinchot National Forest, Mount St. Helens National Volcanic Monument, 42218 Northeast Yale Bridge Road, Amboy, WA 98601, 360/449-7871.

95 DARK MEADOW

8.4 mi/4.5 hr

south of Randle in Gifford Pinchot National Forest

Map 5.2, page 236

Yet another locale with an ill-fitting name, the only thing dark in Dark Meadows are black huckleberries, juicy and ripe in August. In fact, these open meadows are lit up with summer sun, revealing great views of Jumbo Peak, Langille Ridge, and Mount Adams. Dark Meadow Trail endures several miles of shady forest before emerging into the dueling glories of huckleberry fields and vistas.

Dark Meadow Trail begins by gently wandering up the level valley of Dark Creek. The forest here is old Douglas fir and western hemlock, a perfect home for elk. After one mile, the trail climbs steeply to a junction with Juniper Ridge Trail (3.2 miles). The forest opens occasionally to reveal views of the valleys below. A short mile south on Juniper Ridge Trail finds Dark Meadow. Black huckleberry bushes fill the open meadows, attracting hikers and black bears alike. A short footpath leads through the meadow to the summit of Dark Mountain for a panoramic viewpoint (Mount Adams, wow!).

User Groups: Hikers, leashed dogs, horses, mountain bikes, and motorcycles. No wheelchair access.

Open Seasons: This trail is accessible May–October.

Permits: A federal Northwest Forest Pass is required to park here.

Maps: For a map of Gifford Pinchot National Forest, contact the Outdoor Recreation Information Center at the downtown Seattle REI. For a topographic map, ask Green Trails for No. 333, McCoy Peak, and No. 334, Blue Lake, or ask the USGS for McCoy Peak and East Canyon Ridge.

Directions: From Randle, drive south 1 mile on Highway 131 to Forest Service Road 23. Veer left on Forest Service Road 23 and drive 25 miles to the signed trailhead on the right.

Contact: Gifford Pinchot National Forest, Cowlitz Valley Ranger Station, 10024 U.S. 12, Randle, WA 98377, 360/497-1100.

96 QUARTZ CREEK

21.2 mi/1–2 days

northeast of Cougar in Gifford Pinchot National Forest

Map 5.2, page 236

Lesser known for old-growth forests than other forests of Washington, Gifford Pinchot features forests as magnificent as any other. Quartz Creek Trail is a wonderful example of these ancient timberlands, where towering Douglas fir, western hemlock, and western red cedar grow to immense proportions. Quartz Creek Trail spends more than 10 miles wandering up the valley. Numerous streams enter Quartz Creek, including Straight Creek and its waterfalls. Regardless of how far one ventures up Quartz Creek Trail, the trip is sure to be grand.

Although Quartz Creek Trail gains 2,500 feet net elevation, numerous ups and downs make total elevation change more than twice that amount. The trail encounters Straight Creek (2 miles), home to a beautiful series of waterfalls. The occasional sections of logged forest are worth tolerating, balanced by the many miles of ancient old-growth forest. Campsites dot the trail as it wanders up the valley, passing Quartz Creek Butte Trail (a 1.5-mile connector between Summit Prairie and Quartz Creek Big Trees) junction at 4.5 miles. The upper section of the trail passes through forest burned long ago and now replaced by a subalpine setting. The trail connects to Boundary Trail (10.6 miles).

Folks who decide to hike the length of the trail are well advised to turn the trip into a loop. Summit Prairie Trail (see listing in this chapter) traverses Quartz Creek Ridge, awash in distant views and berry bushes. At the junction with Boundary Trail, hike east 2.3 miles to Summit Prairie Trail and turn south toward Quartz Creek Butte Trail, descending to Quartz Creek. Total mileage is 22 miles.

User Groups: Hikers, leashed dogs, horses, and mountain bikes. No wheelchair access.

Open Seasons: This trail is accessible mid-June–October.
Permits: A federal Northwest Forest Pass is required to park here.
Maps: For a map of Gifford Pinchot National Forest, contact the Outdoor Recreation Information Center at the downtown Seattle REI. For a topographic map, ask Green Trails for No. 333, McCoy Peak, No. 334, Blue Lake, No. 365, Lone Butte, and No. 366, Mount Adams West, or ask the USGS for Quartz Creek Butte, East Canyon Ridge, and Steamboat Mountain.
Directions: From Vancouver, drive north on I-5 to Highway 503 (Woodland, exit 21). Drive east 45 miles to Pine Creek Information Center. Turn right and continue on Forest Service Road 90 for 20 miles to the signed trailhead on the left (just beyond Forest Service Road 93).
Contact: Gifford Pinchot National Forest, Mount St. Helens National Volcanic Monument, 42218 Northeast Yale Bridge Road, Amboy, WA 98601, 360/449-7871.

97 HIGH LAKES

8.0 mi/3.5 hr

south of Packwood in Gifford Pinchot National Forest

Map 5.2, page 236

Take much of what is great about the Gifford Pinchot, combine it into one trail, and High Lakes Trail is the result. The trail does indeed visit several high, meadow-rimmed lakes along the way. Views of Mount Adams make regular appearances along the route. And during the later summer, delicious, ripe huckleberries make this trip an appetizing day hike.

High Lakes Trail connects Olallie and Horseshoe Lakes. Save for a small segment in the middle, much of the route is easy to negotiate with little elevation gain. From the western end, the trail travels the dense forest around Olallie Lake to the open forest and meadows of Chain Lakes (1.3 miles). The trail crosses a large lava flow punctuating the valley of Adams Creek (2.8 miles) and climbs to Horseshoe Lake and campground. August is usually the best month to harvest mouthfuls of huckleberries along the way. These juicy berries constitute a large part of the summer diets for local black bears.

User Groups: Hikers, leashed dogs, horses, mountain bikes, and motorcycles. No wheelchair access.
Open Seasons: This trail is accessible May–November.
Permits: A federal Northwest Forest Pass is required to park here.
Maps: For a map of Gifford Pinchot National Forest, contact the Outdoor Recreation Information Center at the downtown Seattle REI. For a topographic map, ask Green Trails for No. 334, Blue Lake, or ask the USGS for Green Mountain.
Directions: From Randle, drive south 1 mile on Highway 131 to Forest Service Road 23. Veer left on Forest Service Road 23 and drive 33 miles to Forest Service Road 2329. Turn left and drive 1 mile to the signed trailhead on the left.
Contact: Gifford Pinchot National Forest, Cowlitz Valley Ranger Station, 10024 U.S. 12, Randle, WA 98377, 360/497-1100.

98 TAKHLAKH LAKE AND MEADOWS

2.6 mi/1.5 hr

north of Trout Lake in Gifford Pinchot National Forest

Map 5.2, page 236

Families on the lookout for an easy but scenic hike will want to pay attention here. Two trails combine to enjoy Takhlakh Lake, a 1.1-mile loop, and Takhlakh Meadows, a 1.5-mile loop situated off the first trail (imagine a figure eight). Both trails are flat and extremely level, perfect for hikers of any age. The trails are even barrier free, making them accessible for folks in wheelchairs, although in a few sections assistance will be appreciated. Both trails enjoy views of Mount Adams to the southeast. Takhlakh Lake Trail loops around the lake.

From the southeast part of this loop, Takhlakh Meadows Trail makes a separate loop. In August, these open meadows are full of delicious, ripe huckleberries.

User Groups: Hikers and leashed dogs. No horses or mountain bikes are allowed. These trails are wheelchair accessible.

Open Seasons: This trail is accessible May–November.

Permits: A federal Northwest Forest Pass is required to park here.

Maps: For a map of Gifford Pinchot National Forest, contact the Outdoor Recreation Information Center at the downtown Seattle REI. For a topographic map, ask Green Trails for No. 334, Blue Lake, or ask the USGS for Green Mountain.

Directions: From Randle, drive south 1 mile on Highway 131 to Forest Service Road 23. Veer left on Forest Service Road 23 and drive 33 miles to Forest Service Road 2329. Turn left and drive 2 miles to the signed trailhead at road's end.

Contact: Gifford Pinchot National Forest, Mount Adams Ranger District, 2455 Highway 141, Trout Lake, WA 98650, 509/395-3400.

99 SPENCER BUTTE

3.8 mi/2.0 hr

north of Cougar in Gifford Pinchot National Forest

Map 5.2, page 236

Spencer Butte Trail leads to one of the most beautiful views of a volcano you're likely to find anywhere. From atop Spencer Butte, a natural rock arch frames Mount St. Helens, a memorable and picturesque view. Short and accessible, with trailheads at either end of the three-mile route, Spencer Butte is a great trip for folks looking for views on a quick day hike.

The best access is from the upper (north) trailhead in Spencer Meadows. It's not unlikely that you'll spot a herd of elk before you've even hit the trail. Spencer Butte Trail climbs steadily from the open meadows along a wide ridge. White pines give way to noble fir as the trail ascends through an open forest with regular views of the surrounding valleys. The trail crests atop Spencer Butte (elevation 4,247 feet). On the south side, a side trail drops slightly to a cold-water spring and the natural archway. Bring a camera, and you'll have a picture to display for years.

User Groups: Hikers, leashed dogs, horses, mountain bikes, and motorcycles. No wheelchair access.

Open Seasons: This trail is accessible May–November.

Permits: A federal Northwest Forest Pass is required to park here.

Maps: For a map of Gifford Pinchot National Forest, contact the Outdoor Recreation Information Center at the downtown Seattle REI. For a topographic map, ask Green Trails for No. 365, Lone Butte, or ask the USGS for Spencer Butte.

Directions: From Vancouver, drive north on I-5 to Highway 503 (Woodland, exit 21). Drive east 45 miles to Forest Service Road 25. Continue straight on Forest Service Road 25 and drive 6 miles to Forest Service Road 93, just beyond the Muddy River. Turn right and drive 9 miles to the signed trailhead on the left. This road is accessible for a passenger car but a high-clearance vehicle is recommended.

Contact: Gifford Pinchot National Forest, Mount St. Helens National Volcanic Monument, 42218 Northeast Yale Bridge Road, Amboy, WA 98601, 360/449-7871.

100 BIG CREEK FALLS

1.4 mi/0.5 hr

north of Cougar in Gifford Pinchot National Forest

Map 5.2, page 236

This is one of the best and easiest trails in the Gifford Pinchot National Forest. Big Creek Falls Trail follows the steep cliffs alongside Big Creek to an overlook with an excellent view of the 110-foot cascade. Big Creek is exactly that, a thunderous gusher of a stream. The sound alone of Big Creek dropping into a pool beside the Lewis

River is impressive, not to say anything of the enormous cloud of mist the fall generates. The trail has some interpretive signs discussing the old-growth forest through which the trail travels. Granddaddy Douglas firs and western hemlocks dominate the forest, draped in shrouds of ferns and mosses. The trail ends at a viewpoint over the falls, overlooking the Lewis River and Hemlock Falls on the opposite side. This is an ideal trail for young hikers-in-training.

User Groups: Hikers and leashed dogs. No horses or mountain bikes are allowed. Part of this trail (a loop to a viewpoint) is wheelchair accessible.

Open Seasons: This trail is accessible year-round.

Permits: A federal Northwest Forest Pass is required to park here.

Maps: For a map of Gifford Pinchot National Forest, contact the Outdoor Recreation Information Center at the downtown Seattle REI. For a topographic map, ask Green Trails for No. 365, Lone Butte, or ask the USGS for Burnt Peak.

Directions: From Vancouver, drive north on I-5 to Highway 503 (Woodland, exit 21). Drive east 45 miles to Pine Creek Information Center. Turn right and continue on Forest Service Road 90 for 11 miles to the signed trailhead on the left.

Contact: Gifford Pinchot National Forest, Mount St. Helens National Volcanic Monument, 42218 Northeast Yale Bridge Road, Amboy, WA 98601, 360/449-7871.

101 THOMAS LAKE

6.6 mi/3.0 hr

north of Carson in Indian Heaven Wilderness of Gifford Pinchot National Forest

Map 5.2, page 236

The high country of Indian Heaven is covered by small lakes in beautiful subalpine settings. Thomas Lake Trail encounters more of these lakes than any other trail in Indian Heaven Wilderness. It's also one of the easiest trails here, gaining just 600 feet in three miles. That makes Thomas Lake Trail a popular route into the huckleberry fields and wildflower meadows that characterize this high, volcanic plateau.

Thomas Lake Trail gets much of the work out of the way early, quickly climbing through dense forest to Thomas, Dee, and Heather Lakes (.6 mile). The forest begins to break frequently, revealing meadows full of lupine and huckleberries in August. Elk and deer are frequently seen in this area, grazing in the meadows or wallowing in the small lakes and tarns. The trail ascends gently through meadows, passing yet more lakes. It crests at Rock Lake before dropping slightly to Blue Lake and Pacific Crest Trail. Although the trail is easily accomplished in a morning, it's advisable to plan on spending a full day exploring the many meadows and lakes. Just remember a fly rod or swimsuit.

User Groups: Hikers, leashed dogs, and horses. No mountain bikes are allowed. No wheelchair access.

Open Seasons: This trail is accessible May–October.

Permits: A federal Northwest Forest Pass is required to park here.

Maps: For a map of Gifford Pinchot National Forest, contact the Outdoor Recreation Information Center at the downtown Seattle REI. For a topographic map, ask Green Trails for No. 365S, Indian Heaven, or ask the USGS for Gifford Peak and Lone Butte.

Directions: From Vancouver, drive east 55 miles on Highway 14 to the town of Carson. Turn north on Wind River Road and drive 5 miles to Forest Service Road 65. Turn right and drive 17 miles to the signed trailhead on the right.

Contact: Gifford Pinchot National Forest, Mount Adams Ranger District, 2455 Highway 141, Trout Lake, WA 98650, 509/395-3400.

102 HIDDEN LAKES

0.4 mi/0.5 hr

west of Trout Lake in Indian Heaven Wilderness of Gifford Pinchot National Forest

Map 5.2, page 236

Hidden Lakes is a short and easy hike for everyone. Traveling around several small subalpine lakes, Hidden Lakes Trail provides a great sampler of this scenic area. On the northeast side of Indian Heaven Wilderness, the lakes are home to a primitive car campground. Small forest and open meadows dominate this area of the Gifford Pinchot National Forest, famous for its berry fields. Hidden Lakes is no different, basking in large fields of huckleberries, with peak season typically arriving in early August. Enjoy the berries, but leave some for others. A view of Mount Adams completes the scene.

User Groups: Hikers, leashed dogs, mountain bikes, and horses. No wheelchair access.

Open Seasons: This trail is accessible June–October.

Permits: A federal Northwest Forest Pass is required to park here.

Maps: For a map of Gifford Pinchot National Forest, contact the Outdoor Recreation Information Center at the downtown Seattle REI. For a topographic map, ask Green Trails for No. 365S, Indian Heaven, or ask the USGS for Sleeping Lady.

Directions: From Vancouver, drive east 70 miles on Highway 14 to Highway 141. Turn north and drive 22 miles to Trout Lake. Continue north on Highway 141 as it becomes Forest Service Road 24 for 16 miles (past Little Goose Campground) to the trailhead on the right.

Contact: Gifford Pinchot National Forest, Mount Adams Ranger District, 2455 Highway 141, Trout Lake, WA 98650, 509/395-3400.

103 INDIAN HEAVEN

6.6 mi/3.5 hr

west of Trout Lake in Indian Heaven Wilderness of Gifford Pinchot National Forest

Map 5.2, page 236

Strewn with high country lakes and subalpine meadows, Indian Heaven is heavenly indeed. A visit to this volcanic highland in August is divine, when ripe black huckleberries are ubiquitous. Indian Heaven Trail is the best way to the meadows and lakes of this subalpine playground. The short and accessible trail delivers every step of the way, whether it be old-growth forest, wildflower meadows, or scenic vistas.

Indian Heaven Trail wastes no time in reaching the high plateau of Indian Heaven. The trail climbs steadily through superb old-growth forest of subalpine fir, mountain hemlock, Englemann spruce, and white pine. Peek-a-boo views of Mount Adams whet the appetite for the meadows to come. The arrival into the high country is signaled when the trail reaches Cultus Lake, directly next to the trail (2.3 miles). A signed side trail leads a few hundred yards to Deep Lake. The trail junctions with Lemei Trail (2.5 miles) and bypasses Clear Lake before continuing to Pacific Crest Trail (3.3 miles). Rambling along any of these trails is well recommended.

Hikers looking for a little variety can turn Indian Heaven Trail into part of a great loop. The 6.7-mile loop uses PCT to encircle Bird Mountain, passing numerous lakes along the way. Hike east on Indian Heaven Trail to PCT (3.3 miles). Turn north and hike to Cultus Creek Trail (5.2 miles), which quickly descends back to Cultus Creek Campground and trailhead.

User Groups: Hikers, leashed dogs, and horses. No mountain bikes are allowed. No wheelchair access.

Open Seasons: This trail is accessible June–October.

Permits: A federal Northwest Forest Pass is required to park here.

Maps: For a map of Gifford Pinchot National Forest, contact the Outdoor Recreation Information Center at the downtown Seattle REI. For a topographic map, ask Green Trails for No. 365S, Indian Heaven, or ask the USGS for Lone Butte.

Directions: From Vancouver, drive east 70 miles on Highway 14 to Highway 141. Turn north and drive 22 miles to Trout Lake. Continue north on Highway 141 as it becomes Forest Service Road 24 for 18 miles to the signed trailhead within Cultus Creek Campground.

Contact: Gifford Pinchot National Forest, Mount Adams Ranger District, 2455 Highway 141, Trout Lake, WA 98650, 509/395-3400.

104 LEMEI

10.6 mi/5.0 hr

west of Trout Lake in Indian Heaven Wilderness of Gifford Pinchot National Forest

Map 5.2, page 236

Lemei Trail provides a scenic route to the volcanic plateau of Indian Heaven Wilderness. The trail is a decent workout, ascending through much of its length. Views, huckleberries, and lakes are ample reward for the effort. After enjoying the meadows teeming with wildflower displays and feasting on August-ripe huckleberries, hikers will find that the waters of Lake Wapiki make a refreshing dip. One of the prettiest lakes in the high country of Indian Heaven, Lake Wapiki is enclosed by the area's tallest peak, jagged Lemei Rock.

Lemei Trail spends its first mile in dense second-growth forest. As the trail enters the wilderness (1 mile), the timber becomes old and large, in a more open forest. An understory of huckleberry bushes helps to ease the sting of the continuous climb. A side trail (3 miles) leads .5 mile to Lake Wapiki in the basin of Lemei Rock. Small forest and meadow fill the basin under craggy Lemei Rock. Lemei Trail continues beyond the junction to Indian Heaven Trail (5.3 miles) and miles of meadow exploration.

User Groups: Hikers, leashed dogs, and horses. No mountain bikes are allowed. No wheelchair access.

Open Seasons: This trail is accessible June–October.

Permits: A federal Northwest Forest Pass is required to park here.

Maps: For a map of Gifford Pinchot National Forest, contact the Outdoor Recreation Information Center at the downtown Seattle REI. For a topographic map, ask Green Trails for No. 365S, Indian Heaven, or ask the USGS for Sleeping Beauty and Lone Butte.

Directions: From Vancouver, drive east 70 miles on Highway 14 to Highway 141. Turn north and drive 22 miles to Trout Lake. Continue north on Highway 141 as it becomes Forest Service Road 24 for 13 miles to the trailhead on the left (before Little Goose Campground).

Contact: Gifford Pinchot National Forest, Mount Adams Ranger District, 2455 Highway 141, Trout Lake, WA 98650, 509/395-3400.

105 RACE TRACK

6.2 mi/3.5 hr

west of Trout Lake in Indian Heaven Wilderness of Gifford Pinchot National Forest

Map 5.2, page 236

Huckleberries and history are the story of this trail. Race Track Trail delves into the southern section of Indian Heaven Wilderness, a former meeting place for Native Americans. Each year, thousands of people from Yakama, Klickitat, and Columbia River nations gathered here during the height of the berry-harvesting season (August). The huckleberry bushes that flourish in this volcanic soil were a major source of food for Native Americans. And as it's situated along an important cross-Cascades trade route, it's easy to see how this area came to be known as an "Indian Heaven." During their time here, Native Americans entertained themselves by staging pony races, hence the name Race Track. The dirt track used is still visible today within an open meadow.

A popular trail into the wilderness, Race Track Trail climbs steadily but gently, emerging from large timber to open subalpine meadows. During August, huckleberries will be sure to be the main attraction. But don't let them keep you from spotting the abundant wildlife, including deer, elk, hawk, and even black bear. Race Track Trail reaches Race Track Lake (2.3 miles), where the dirt track can be seen, and then ascends to the peak of Red Mountain. This lofty peak with big views is home to one of Gifford Pinchot's three remaining fire lookouts.

User Groups: Hikers, leashed dogs, and horses. No mountain bikes are allowed. No wheelchair access.

Open Seasons: This trail is accessible June–October.

Permits: A federal Northwest Forest Pass is required to park here.
Maps: For a map of Gifford Pinchot National Forest, contact the Outdoor Recreation Information Center at the downtown Seattle REI. For a topographic map, ask Green Trails for No. 365S, Indian Heaven, or ask the USGS for Gifford Peak.
Directions: From Vancouver, drive east 55 miles on Highway 14 to the town of Carson. Turn north on Wind River Road and drive 5 miles to Forest Service Road 65. Turn right and drive 13 miles to the signed trailhead at Falls Creek Horse Camp.
Contact: Gifford Pinchot National Forest, Mount Adams Ranger District, 2455 Highway 141, Trout Lake, WA 98650, 509/395-3400.

106 SLEEPING BEAUTY

2.8 mi/2.0 hr

north of Trout Lake in Gifford Pinchot National Forest

Map 5.2, page 236

As close to Mount Adams as one can be without actually scaling its slopes, Sleeping Beauty offers a grand view of the mountain. A tall outcrop of craggy rock sticking out above the surrounding forest, Sleeping Beauty gazes at the mass of Mount Adams from just eight miles distant. Access to the rocky peak is a steep but quick trip through dense second-growth forest. The trail finds the edge of logging and enjoys old timber for a short time. Any views are reserved until the very end.

Sleeping Beauty is so named because it apparently resembles the profile of a sleeping woman; we'll let you decide. All personifications aside, the view from the top is spectacular. Rainier, St. Helens, and Hood dot the distant horizons. The peaks of Indian Heaven rise on the western skyline. The peak was formerly home to a Forest Service lookout.

User Groups: Hikers and leashed dogs. No horses or mountain bikes are allowed. No wheelchair access.
Open Seasons: This trail is accessible May–November.
Permits: A federal Northwest Forest Pass is required to park here.
Maps: For a map of Gifford Pinchot National Forest, contact the Outdoor Recreation Information Center at the downtown Seattle REI. For a topographic map, ask Green Trails for No. 366, Mount Adams West, or ask the USGS for Sleeping Beauty.
Directions: From Vancouver, drive east 70 miles on Highway 14 to Highway 141. Turn north and drive 22 miles to Forest Service Road 88, just beyond the town of Trout Lake. Turn right on Forest Service Road 88 and drive 5 miles to Forest Service Road 8810. Turn right and drive 5 miles to Forest Service Road 8810-040. Turn right and drive .5 mile to the trailhead on the left.
Contact: Gifford Pinchot National Forest, Mount Adams Ranger District, 2455 Highway 141, Trout Lake, WA 98650, 509/395-3400.

107 STAGMAN RIDGE

8.0–12.8 mi/4.0–7.0 hr

north of Trout Lake in Mount Adams Wilderness of Gifford Pinchot National Forest

Map 5.2, page 236

Stagman Ridge Trail provides great access to the high-country meadows flanking the western slopes of Mount Adams. The trail steadily but gently climbs to Horseshoe Meadows, home of juicy huckleberries, roaming mountain goats, and some pretty spectacular views. A trip to Horseshoe Meadows is indeed a great day, but hikers looking to throw in a subalpine lake (think refreshing swim) can continue an extra 2.4 miles to Lookingglass Lake.

Stagman Ridge Trail begins at a lofty elevation of 4,200 feet and gains about 1,600 feet over four miles. The forested trail quickly opens to reveal tremendous views of the mountain. It crosses several small streams, and Stagman Ridge Trail intersects PCT (4 miles) on the lower slopes of Horseshoe Meadows. Although

you could turn around here, hikers are well advised to continue on PCT in either direction for at least a mile; the meadows are full of huckleberries in late summer and offer outstanding views year-round.

If the cold and refreshing water of Lookingglass Lake entices you to continue (it's well worth it), turn right on PCT, turn right again on Round the Mountain Trail (4.4 miles), and one more right turn onto Lookingglass Trail (5.5 miles). The lake (6.4 miles) is situated within high meadows, underneath the mountain.

User Groups: Hikers, leashed dogs, and horses. No mountain bikes are allowed. No wheelchair access.

Open Seasons: This trail is accessible June–October.

Permits: A federal Northwest Forest Pass is required to park here.

Maps: For a map of Gifford Pinchot National Forest, contact the Outdoor Recreation Information Center at the downtown Seattle REI. For a topographic map, ask Green Trails for No. 367S, Mount Adams, or ask the USGS for Mount Adams West.

Directions: From Vancouver, drive east 70 miles on Highway 14 to Highway 141. Turn north and drive 22 miles to Forest Service Road 23 (Buck Creek Road), near the town of Trout Lake. Turn right and drive 8 miles to Forest Service Road 8031. Turn right and drive .5 mile to Forest Service Road 070. Turn left and drive 3.5 miles to Forest Service Road 120. Turn right and drive .5 mile to the trailhead at road's end.

Contact: Gifford Pinchot National Forest, Mount Adams Ranger District, 2455 Highway 141, Trout Lake, WA 98650, 509/395-3400.

108 ROUND-THE-MOUNTAIN

22.2 mi one-way/2 days 4 10

north of Trout Lake in Mount Adams Wilderness of Gifford Pinchot National Forest

Map 5.2, page 236

Like Washington's other big volcanoes, Mount Adams is circumnavigated by a long, demanding trail. Set high in the subalpine meadows gracing the slopes of Mount Adams, Round-the-Mountain Trail is the best way to fully experience Washington's second-tallest peak. Here's the catch. The east side of Mount Adams is managed by the Yakima Indian Nation, and special permits are required to hike within the reservation (a vexing process). Additionally, this section of trail is extremely difficult. East-side streams turn into dangerous glacial torrents during the summer, and no maintained trail exists over enormous lava fields. Thus, Round-the-Mountain is best completed as a through-hike, along the western side of Mount Adams.

Round-the-Mountain Trail is best begun from Cold Springs on the south side of Mount Adams. Hike South Climb Trail to Round-the-Mountain Trail (1.3 miles) and turn north. The scenery is supreme every step of the way, with alpine meadows and distant mountain views the norm. Expect to see an abundance of wildflowers in midsummer and huckleberries in early fall. The trail encounters Pacific Crest Trail (7 miles) and follows it to Muddy Meadows Trail (19.8 miles). Turn north to reach the northern trailhead at Keenee Campground (22.2 miles).

Highlights along the way include Lookingglass Lake (5.9 miles), Horseshoe Meadows (7 miles), Sheep Lake (11 miles), and Adams Meadows (14.5 miles, below Adams Glacier). Campsites are frequent along the route; stick to already established sites to minimize damage to fragile meadows. The views of Mount Adams improve with progress around the peak, with great looks at the glaciers. If a true circumnavigation of the mountain is an unshakable goal, please contact the Mount Adams Ranger Station for full details on trail conditions.

User Groups: Hikers, leashed dogs, and horses. No mountain bikes are allowed. No wheelchair access.

Open Seasons: This trail is accessible July–mid-October.

Permits: A federal Northwest Forest Pass is required to park here.

Maps: For a map of Gifford Pinchot National Forest, contact the Outdoor Recreation Information Center at the downtown Seattle REI. For a topographic map, ask Green Trails for No. 367S, Mount Adams, or ask the USGS for Mount Adams West, Mount Adams East, and Green Mountain.

Directions: From Vancouver, drive east 70 miles on Highway 14 to Highway 141. Turn north and drive 22 miles to Forest Service Road 23 (Buck Creek Road), near the town of Trout Lake. Turn right and drive 3 miles to Forest Service Road 82. Turn right and drive .5 mile to Forest Service Road 80. Turn left and drive 4 miles to Forest Service Road 8040. Continue 5 miles on Road 8040 to Morrison Creek Campground and Forest Service Road 500. Turn right and drive 2 miles to the trailhead at road's end.

Contact: Gifford Pinchot National Forest, Mount Adams Ranger District, 2455 Highway 141, Trout Lake, WA 98650, 509/395-3400.

109 KILLEN CREEK

6.2 mi/4.0 hr

north of Trout Lake in Mount Adams Wilderness of Gifford Pinchot National Forest

Map 5.2, page 236

By the time the first views of Mount Adams emerge (which is quickly), hikers on Killen Creek Trail know they've selected a beauty of a hike. This popular route on the north side of Mount Adams climbs steadily through open forest to wide open meadows beneath towering glaciers. This is undoubtedly great rambling country, where the hike gets better every step of the way. Day hikes this grand are hard to come by in Southern Washington, and this is one of the best in the state.

Killen Creek Trail starts high (4,600 feet) and climbs slowly but steadily to Pacific Crest Trail (3.1 miles). Much of the trail traverses open forest with repeated views of Mount Adams, but the last mile or so revels in meadows. Wildflowers take turns blooming throughout the summer. Rambling in either direction along PCT is highly recommended to soak up the scenery. Hikers hoping to approach even closer to the mountain are welcome to do so along High Camp Trail, a continuation of Killen Creek Trail on the uphill side of PCT. This is a one-mile trail to High Camp, one of Adams' best, among rocky meadows and glacier moraine.

User Groups: Hikers, leashed dogs, and horses. No mountain bikes are allowed. No wheelchair access.

Open Seasons: This trail is accessible mid-June–October.

Permits: A federal Northwest Forest Pass is required to park here.

Maps: For a map of Gifford Pinchot National Forest, contact the Outdoor Recreation Information Center at the downtown Seattle REI. For a topographic map, ask Green Trails for No. 367S, Mount Adams, or ask the USGS for Green Mountain and Mount Adams West.

Directions: From Vancouver, drive east 70 miles on Highway 14 to Highway 141. Turn north and drive 22 miles to Forest Service Road 23 (Buck Creek Road), near the town of Trout Lake. Turn right and drive about 30 miles to Forest Service Road 2329. Turn right and drive 5 miles (around Takhlakh Lake) to the trailhead on the right.

Contact: Gifford Pinchot National Forest, Mount Adams Ranger District, 2455 Highway 141, Trout Lake, WA 98650, 509/395-3400.

110 SOUTH CLIMB

6.8 mi/4.5 hr

north of Trout Lake in Mount Adams Wilderness of Gifford Pinchot National Forest

Map 5.2, page 236

Not for the faint of heart, South Climb is exactly what the name implies: an ascent of Mount Adams from the south side. The summit needn't be one's goal to embark on this beautiful trail, but well-conditioned legs certainly are always helpful. South Climb Trail assaults the mountain straight on and reaches 8,500 feet of elevation before petering out beside Crescent Glacier. From here, it's a mad scramble to the top. Stopping at Crescent Glacier reveals spectacular views of the surrounding valleys, forests,

and distant mountain ridges. If the wildflower meadows alongside the trail and beautiful views don't take your breath away, the steep pitch of South Climb will.

Should a summit of Mount Adams be on your wish list, keep several things in mind. One, it's steep as hell and strenuous. Experienced climbers take at least 6–8 hours to reach the summit from Cold Springs, an elevation gain of 6,700 feet. Visibility decreases after early morning, so smart mountaineers camp at Cold Springs Car Campground and hit the trail by 3 A.M. That's 3 o'clock in the morning. And the climb requires permits from the ranger station in Trout Lake. The summit is certainly achievable and is relatively easy compared to Mount Hood or Mount Rainier. Novices frequently reach the peak. At the top are views conceivable only if you've been there.

User Groups: Hikers, leashed dogs, and horses. No mountain bikes are allowed. No wheelchair access.

Open Seasons: This trail is accessible July–September.

Permits: A federal Northwest Forest Pass is required to park here. Climbing permits are required for summits of Mount Adams. The $15 permits are available at Trout Lake Ranger Station.

Maps: For a map of Gifford Pinchot National Forest, contact the Outdoor Recreation Information Center at the downtown Seattle REI. For a topographic map, ask Green Trails for No. 367S, Mount Adams, or ask the USGS for Mount Adams West.

Directions: From Vancouver, drive east 70 miles on Highway 14 to Highway 141. Turn north and drive 22 miles to Forest Service Road 23 (Buck Creek Road), near the town of Trout Lake. Turn right and drive 3 miles to Forest Service Road 82. Turn right and drive .5 mile to Forest Service Road 80. Turn left and drive 4 miles to Forest Service Road 8040. Continue 5 miles on Road 8040 to Morrison Creek Campground and Forest Service Road 500. Turn right and drive 2 miles to the trailhead at road's end.

Contact: Gifford Pinchot National Forest, Mount Adams Ranger District, 2455 Highway 141, Trout Lake, WA 98650, 509/395-3400.

111 BATTLE GROUND LAKE LOOP

7.0 mi/3.5 hr

north of Vancouver in Battle Ground Lake State Park

Map 5.3, page 237

There's no need to drive all the way to southern Oregon to see Crater Lake. Washington has its own miniature version here in Battle Ground Lake. Like Crater Lake, Battle Ground Lake was created by a massive volcanic explosion. The resulting crater filled with spring water and created Battle Ground Lake. Today, conifer forests of Douglas fir and western hemlock surround the lake, creating peaceful and quiet surroundings. The trail circles the lake within the shady forest, never venturing far from the lakeshore. Anglers will appreciate the access to solitary fishing holes, where monster trout hide out. The state park has a large car campground, but it fills quickly on summer weekends.

User Groups: Hikers, leashed dogs, and horses. No mountain bikes are allowed. No wheelchair access.

Open Seasons: This trail is accessible year-round.

Permits: A $5 day-use fee is required to park here and is payable at the trailhead, or you can get an annual State Parks Pass for $30; contact Washington State Parks and Recreation, 360/902-8500.

Maps: For a topographic map, ask the USGS for Battleground and Wacolt.

Directions: From Vancouver, drive north on I-5 to Exit 14. Turn right on Northeast 179th Street and drive to the city of Battle Ground. Drive to the east end of town and turn left on Grace Avenue. Drive three miles to Battle Ground Lake State Park. The signed trailhead is near the day-use area within the park.

Contact: Battle Ground Lake State Park, 18002

Northeast 249th Street, Battle Ground WA, 98604, 360/687-4621.

112 BEACON ROCK

2.0 mi/2.0 hr

east of Vancouver in Beacon Rock State Park

Map 5.3, page 237

Visible from miles away and towering over the Columbia River, Beacon Rock offers an unbeatable view of the Columbia River Gorge. Geologically speaking, Beacon Rock is a true rock. That is, it's one solid piece of rock, not a conglomeration of different types of rock like many mountains are. That makes Beacon Rock the second tallest "rock" in the world! Beacon Rock is actually the core of an old volcano, exposed when the Missoula Floods eroded softer rock encasing it. The resulting hulk towers 848 feet over the mighty Columbia. It's quite a perch from the top.

Beacon Rock State Park offers nearly 20 miles of trail and road to explore, but the most popular and scenic is the trail to the summit. It's a little under one mile to the top, but don't let the short distance fool you. It's a steep climb every step of the way. Old forest shades the trail where trees can find a small ledge to grow, but many areas are on steep, exposed cliffs. Boardwalks, stairways, and handrails have been installed to present a safer experience. The summit is an ideal picnic spot, with great views of the gorge and Mount Hood.

User Groups: Hikers and leashed dogs. No horses or mountain bikes are allowed. No wheelchair access.

Open Seasons: This trail is accessible March–November.

Permits: A $5 day-use fee is required to park here and is payable at the trailhead, or you can get an annual State Parks Pass for $30; contact Washington State Parks and Recreation, 360/902-8500.

Maps: For a topographic map, ask the USGS for Bonneville Dam and Tanner Butte.

Directions: From Vancouver, drive east on Highway 14 to Beacon Rock State Park (near Mile Marker 35). The trailhead is on the right side of the highway.

Contact: Beacon Rock State Park, Highway 14, Skamania, WA, 509/427-8265.

113 SIOUXON

8.0 mi/4.0 hr

east of Cougar in Gifford Pinchot National Forest

Map 5.4, page 238

Deep within old forest, Siouxon Trail journeys alongside the noisy creek. Waterfalls and deep pools are regular highlights, making this a great winter hike when higher routes are closed by snow. Siouxon Trail quickly descends from the trailhead to the creek. Large and gushing West Creek is crossed by a large wooden bridge (.5 mile). Peer downstream to see the first of many waterfalls. The trail encounters another cascade on Siouxon Creek (4 miles), where the creek empties into a large emerald pool. During the summer, good luck avoiding the urge for a quick dip in the cold water. This is a common turnaround for many day hikers, but Siouxon Trail travels along the creek for a total of 5.5 miles through grand forest the entire length. This is a great place to spend a night with little ones or first-time backpackers. Numerous campsites are on the stream banks, where the noisy stream lulls one to sleep.

User Groups: Hikers, leashed dogs, horses, and mountain bikes. No wheelchair access.

Open Seasons: This trail is accessible year-round.

Permits: A federal Northwest Forest Pass is required to park here.

Maps: For a map of Gifford Pinchot National Forest, contact the Outdoor Recreation Information Center at the downtown Seattle REI. For a topographic map, ask Green Trails for No. 396, Lookout Mountain, or ask the USGS for Siouxon Peak and Bear Mountain.

Directions: From Vancouver, drive north on I-5 to Highway 503 (Woodland, exit 21). Drive east 45 miles to Pine Creek Information Center. Turn right and continue on Forest Service

Road 90 to Northeast Healy Road, in the town of Clehatchie. Turn right and drive 10 miles to Forest Service Road 57. Turn left and drive 1.5 miles to Forest Service Road 5701. Turn left and drive 4 miles to the trailhead at road's end.
Contact: Gifford Pinchot National Forest, Mount Adams Ranger District, 2455 Highway 141, Trout Lake, WA 98650, 509/395-3400.

114 LOWER FALLS CREEK

3.4 mi/2.0 hr

north of Carson in Gifford Pinchot National Forest

Map 5.4, page 238

About the only thing keeping the masses from Lower Falls Creek is the short length of the trail. It's not a destination in itself. But anyone visiting the town of Carson should certainly spend the time to visit Lower Falls Creek. The trail follows this beautiful stream as it passes through a narrow gorge and ends at the base of a large waterfall. On hot summer days, the forest is cool and shady, and the water of Falls Creek is especially appealing.

Lower Falls Creek Trail climbs gently throughout its short length. Deer and elk are frequently seen browsing in the forest, filled with the sounds of woodpeckers and wrens. The trail crosses Falls Creek as it gushes through a rock gorge; fortunately, a suspension bridge spans the gap. Falls Creek Trail ends at the base of a large waterfall, where Falls Creek cascades down a steep wall.

User Groups: Hikers, leashed dogs, and mountain bikes. No horses are allowed. No wheelchair access.

Open Seasons: This trail is accessible year-round.

Permits: A federal Northwest Forest Pass is required to park here.

Maps: For a map of Gifford Pinchot National Forest, contact the Outdoor Recreation Information Center at the downtown Seattle REI. For a topographic map, ask Green Trails for No. 397, Wind River, or ask the USGS for Termination Point.

Directions: From Vancouver, drive east 55 miles on Highway 14 to the town of Carson. Turn north on Wind River Road and drive 9 miles to Forest Service Road 30. Turn right and drive 3 miles to the signed trailhead on the right.
Contact: Gifford Pinchot National Forest, Mount Adams Ranger District, 2455 Highway 141, Trout Lake, WA 98650, 509/395-3400.

115 TRAPPER CREEK

9.5 mi/4.5 hr

north of Carson in Trapper Creek Wilderness of Gifford Pinchot National Forest

Map 5.4, page 238

Any opportunity to hike in old-growth forest should be seized, sooner rather than later. Trapper Creek, one of the least-known wildernesses in the state of Washington, preserves a small chunk of ancient timberland just north of the Columbia River Gorge. Trapper Creek Trail makes a full immersion into the wilderness, following the beautiful, restless creek to its headwaters as it flows over waterfalls and through narrow gorges. Trapper Creek Trail connects to Observation Trail (see next listing), so if you're itching for views, you can have them by making a large loop.

Trapper Creek Trail spends much of its length alongside the noisy creek. The forest is a diverse mix of giants, with Douglas fir, western hemlock, and western red cedar, all draped with mosses and lichens, growing to immense proportions. Trapper Creek Trail junctions with Observation Peak Trail (1 mile) but continues alongside the creek. The creek is a long sequence of cascades and pools, but Trapper Creek Falls (4.5 miles) are the highlight of the trip and a good turnaround point. The trail ends at another junction with Observation Trail, the option for a loop trip (about 12 miles).

User Groups: Hikers, leashed dogs, and horses. No mountain bikes are allowed. No wheelchair access.

Open Seasons: This trail is accessible year-round.

Permits: A federal Northwest Forest Pass is required to park here.
Maps: For a map of Gifford Pinchot National Forest, contact the Outdoor Recreation Information Center at the downtown Seattle REI. For a topographic map, ask the USGS for Bare Mountain.
Directions: From Vancouver, drive east 55 miles on Highway 14 to the town of Carson. Turn north on Wind River Road and drive 10 miles to Forest Service Road 3065. Turn left and drive 1.5 miles to the signed trailhead at Government Mineral Springs.
Contact: Gifford Pinchot National Forest, Mount Adams Ranger District, 2455 Highway 141, Trout Lake, WA 98650, 509/395-3400.

116 OBSERVATION PEAK

6.0–13.0 mi/3.0–7.0 hr 2 10

north of Carson in Trapper Creek Wilderness of Gifford Pinchot National Forest

Map 5.4, page 238

Options, options, options. Observation Peak provides great views from the heart of Trapper Creek Wilderness, over lush, green valleys out to several snowcapped volcanic peaks. Best of all, there are several ways to enjoy this pristine and unlogged section of the Gifford Pinchot. A trip to Observation Peak can be a short hike (5.6 miles), a long up and down (13 miles), or one of two loop trips (12 miles). These loops are by far the best way to experience the wilderness, where misty forests are full of ancient timber.

Observation Trail runs from the valley bottom up along a high ridge to Observation Peak and out to Forest Service Road 58. For a short hike, park on Forest Service Road 58 and hike south through Sister Rocks Natural Area (big trees!) to the peak (2.8 miles). Reaching Observation Peak from the south is certainly longer and more strenuous, but remember that rule: no pain, no gain.

From Government Mineral Springs, Observation Trail climbs steadily from old-growth lowland forest into a mix of subalpine trees. Views are frequent along the lightly forested ridge, as are huckleberries and deer. Hearty hikers can pass the peak and descend back to the trailhead via Trapper Creek Trail (see previous listing) or Dry Creek (Big Hollow Trail, another big tree and beautiful creek route).
User Groups: Hikers, leashed dogs, and horses. No mountain bikes are allowed. No wheelchair access.
Open Seasons: This trail is accessible April–November.
Permits: A federal Northwest Forest Pass is required to park here.
Maps: For a map of Gifford Pinchot National Forest, contact the Outdoor Recreation Information Center at the downtown Seattle REI. For a topographic map, ask Green Trails for No. 396, Lookout Mountain, and No. 397, Wind River, or ask the USGS for Bare Mountain.
Directions: From Vancouver, drive east 55 miles on Highway 14 to the town of Carson. Turn north on Wind River Road and drive 10 miles to Forest Service Road 3065. Turn left and drive 1.5 miles to the signed trailhead at Government Mineral Springs.
Contact: Gifford Pinchot National Forest, Mount Adams Ranger District, 2455 Highway 141, Trout Lake, WA 98650, 509/395-3400.

117 BUNKER HILL

3.6 mi/1.5 hr

north of Carson in Gifford Pinchot National Forest

Map 5.4, page 238

Great for folks in Carson with a couple of hours to kill, Bunker Hill Trail is a quick but strenuous climb to the summit. The first .5 mile of the route follows Pacific Crest Trail north. Most folks on PCT are through-hikers coming from Oregon and on their way to big, grand country in the coming months. Turn left onto Bunker Hill Trail and do the switchback shuffle up to the summit. Views are reserved until the very top, where a fire lookout once stood. Views of the Wind River Valley are revealed, as are numerous surrounding ridges.
User Groups: Hikers and leashed dogs. No

horses or mountain bikes are allowed. No wheelchair access.
Open Seasons: This trail is accessible April–December.
Permits: A federal Northwest Forest Pass is required to park here.
Maps: For a map of Gifford Pinchot National Forest, contact the Outdoor Recreation Information Center at the downtown Seattle REI. For a topographic map, ask Green Trails for No. 397, Wind River, or ask the USGS for Stabler.
Directions: From Vancouver, drive east 55 miles on Highway 14 to the town of Carson. Drive north 5.5 miles on Wind River Road to Hemlock Road. Turn left and drive 1.5 miles to Forest Service Road 43. Turn right and drive .5 mile to Forest Service Road 43-417. Turn right and drive .2 mile to the Pacific Crest Trailhead. Head to the right (north) on the PCT.
Contact: Gifford Pinchot National Forest, Mount Adams Ranger District, 2455 Highway 141, Trout Lake, WA 98650, 509/395-3400.

118 LITTLE HUCKLEBERRY

5.0 mi/3.0 hr

west of Trout Lake in Gifford Pinchot National Forest

Map 5.4, page 238

One of the more accessible viewpoints from Highway 14, Little Huckleberry Trail makes a quick and at times steep trip to an old lookout site. Views of Mount Adams and Mount Hood, across the Colombia River, are quite nice. And a feast of huckleberries along the way sweetens the deal on August trips to the mountain. This is a nice trail for a weekend morning, if you're coming from Vancouver or Portland.

Little Huckleberry Trail gains 1,800 feet in just 2.5 miles, a steady and soon tiring ascent within a small draw. Enjoy the old forest and take your time. Early in the summer, a coldwater spring runs (2 miles), offering a great place to break. The final .5 mile climbs through open berry fields and rock slopes to the summit. A lookout once stood atop this rounded top, perched over a wide expanse of the Gifford Pinchot. With room for a tent, this is a fun overnighter for beginning backpackers (think of the stars).
User Groups: Hikers, leashed dogs, horses, and mountain bikes. No wheelchair access.
Open Seasons: This trail is accessible April–November.
Permits: A federal Northwest Forest Pass is required to park here.
Maps: For a map of Gifford Pinchot National Forest, contact the Outdoor Recreation Information Center at the downtown Seattle REI. For a topographic map, ask Green Trails for No. 398, Willard, or ask the USGS for Sleeping Beauty.
Directions: From Vancouver, drive east 70 miles on Highway 14 to Highway 141. Turn north and drive 22 miles to Trout Lake. Continue north on Highway 141 as it becomes Forest Service Road 24 for 10 miles to Forest Service Road 66. Turn left (south) and drive 5 miles to the trailhead on the left.
Contact: Gifford Pinchot National Forest, Mount Adams Ranger District, 2455 Highway 141, Trout Lake, WA 98650, 509/395-3400.

119 DOG MOUNTAIN

6.0 mi/3.5 hr

east of Carson in Gifford Pinchot National Forest

Map 5.4, page 238

Getting to Dog Mountain, with a trailhead directly on Highway 14, is no problem. Getting up Dog Mountain is a bit more of a workout, however. Dense forest mixes with open wildflower meadows along the trail, cresting at the open summit of Dog Mountain. The views of the Columbia River Gorge are outstanding, with snowcapped Mount Hood standing across the way. This is a very popular hike with folks coming from Vancouver or Portland, especially on the weekends. Expect to see a neighbor or two.

Dog Mountain Trail makes the best of what it has been given, forming a loop instead of a straight up and down. The loop is arranged like a lasso. Climb steeply to the loop junction (.5 mile). Head to the right for a more gradual and scenic route to the top. Regular breaks in the forest provide room for open meadows of wildflowers (May is a great month here). This is dry country, meaning water is nonexistent; pack plenty, because overall elevation gain is 2,700 feet. Do be on the lookout for poison oak and rattlesnakes, things that most hikers don't care to mess with. The summit is the former home to a Forest Service lookout. The loop returns to the junction via a steep, densely forested route.

User Groups: Hikers and leashed dogs. No horses or mountain bikes are allowed. No wheelchair access.

Open Seasons: This trail is accessible March–December.

Permits: A federal Northwest Forest Pass is required to park here.

Maps: For a map of Gifford Pinchot National Forest, contact the Outdoor Recreation Information Center at the downtown Seattle REI. For a topographic map, ask the USGS for Mount Defiance.

Directions: From Vancouver, drive east on Highway 14 to Mile Marker 53 and the signed trailhead.

Contact: Gifford Pinchot National Forest, Mount Adams Ranger District, 2455 Highway 141, Trout Lake, WA 98650, 509/395-3400.

Chapter 6

© SCOTT LEONARD

Southeast Washington

Southeast Washington

What's that? You didn't know that there was any hiking in the southeast portion of our state? There surely is, and most of it is unlike anything else found in a state famous for cloudy and rainy days. Better known for its agricultural base, this region offers up some beautiful and wild places for hiking, although not much. This is the sparsest region for trails, and most of them are concentrated in the very southeastern corner of the state in the Blue Mountains. That's a long drive for most Washington residents, especially those living on the west side of the Cascades. Still, thanks to the warm weather that makes wheat, hops, and wine grapes major crops in the region, some great trails exist for spring hiking, when snow still blankets the high country of the Cascades.

Near Yakima, the Cascades devolve into a mass of rolling foothills. Just a few dozen miles from the rain forests on the west side of the Cascades, this is dry country for sure. Much of this region receives just 20 inches or less of rain each year, so you can almost always count on sunny skies. Yakima Rim Trail is a hike for the first outing of the year. While snow measured by the foot still lingers in the Cascades, wildflowers are beginning to blossom in this desert-steppe environment. Yakima Rim runs along Umtanum Ridge, delivering views of the snow-capped Stuart Range on the horizon, colorful blossoms, and dry, moderate temperatures in April and May. Umtanum Creek Trail wanders up a low valley, one of the few places to find water year-round. Each of these hikes is located on the Yakima River, a world-class trout river and a pretty good river raft, too.

Spread amidst miles of agricultural land are several unlikely environments for Washington. Potholes Sand Dunes are an expansive landscape in the middle of our state. Countless small lakes and the larger Potholes reservoir break up large dunes of sand. Near the Tri-Cities are Juniper Dunes Wilderness, another desertlike landscape seemingly out of place in Washington. In fact, it's so unusual that it is affectionately known as "Washington's Sahara," and vast dunes spread out over the high desert, dotted by small shrubs and the occasional tree. You may even find the grove of ancient juniper trees, many of them centuries old and subsisting on just inches of rain each year. Coyotes, deer, and owls far outnumber bipeds in this area. This is one of the region's best places to set out and explore cross-country. Folks who don't want to venture far from the car will love the easy access to Palouse Falls, Washington's version of Niagara Falls. Smack dab in the middle of nowhere (ever heard of Washtucna?), the Palouse River makes a mighty and vociferous drop into a large bowl. The falls are just one of the many land features left by the Missoula Glacial Floods, when billions of gallons of water rushed from Montana to the Pacific, scouring eastern Washington along the way.

The jackpot of hiking in southeast Washington is the Wenaha-Tucannon Wilderness. This federally protected wilderness envelops more than 177,000 acres of the Blue Mountains, stretching across the border of Washington and Oregon. The Blue Mountains are an untamed, rarely visited place, where bighorn sheep, deer, and elk are plentiful and draw hundreds of hunters in the fall. The Wenaha-Tucannon Wilderness is unique in that access points start from on high, usually around 5,000 feet, and require hikers to drop down into the vast canyons and gorges to explore. The lookout atop Oregon Butte is a popular (and easy) place to visit here, where you can get a panoramic view of the arid mountains and valleys. Longer trips can be made along Crooked Creek or Smooth Ridge down to the Wenaha River, an excellent trout and salmon river. Despite its remote location, the Wenaha-Tucannon Wilderness is a beautiful Washington landscape and should be visited at least once by all devout hikers.

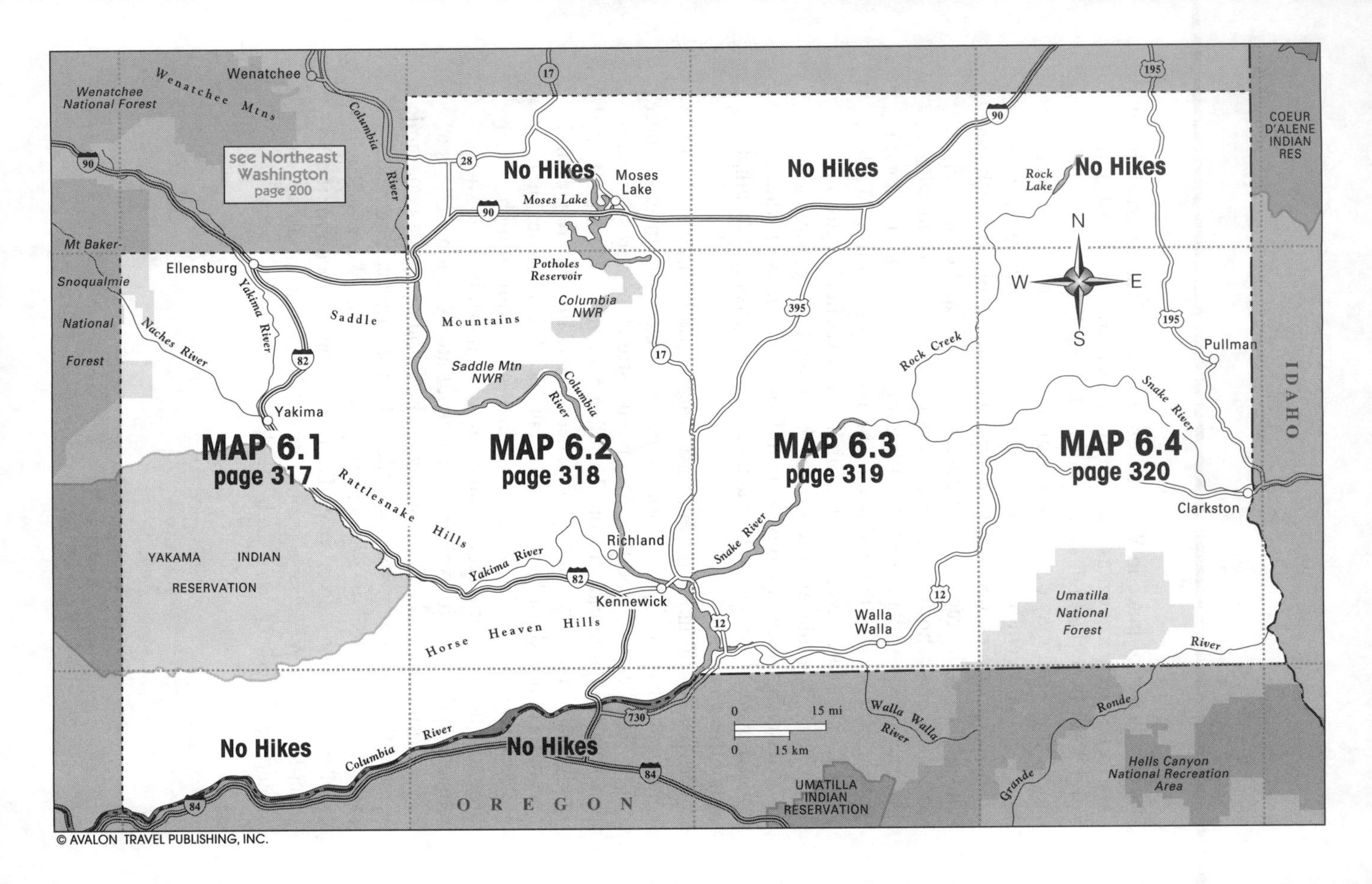

Wenatchee
Wenatchee National Forest
Wenatchee Mtns
Columbia River
see Northeast Washington page 200
No Hikes
Moses Lake
Moses Lake
No Hikes
Rock Lake
No Hikes
COEUR D'ALENE INDIAN RES
N
W
E
S
Mt Baker-Snoqualmie National Forest
Ellensburg
Yakima River
Saddle Mountains
Potholes Reservoir
Columbia NWR
Saddle Mtn NWR
Columbia River
Naches River
Yakima
Rock Creek
Pullman
Snake River
IDAHO
MAP 6.1
page 317
MAP 6.2
page 318
MAP 6.3
page 319
MAP 6.4
page 320
Clarkston
Rattlesnake Hills
Richland
Snake River
YAKAMA INDIAN RESERVATION
Yakima River
Kennewick
Walla Walla
Umatilla National Forest
Horse Heaven Hills
River
Ronde
0
15 mi
15 km
Walla Walla River
No Hikes
Columbia River
No Hikes
Grande
Hells Canyon National Recreation Area
UMATILLA INDIAN RESERVATION
OREGON

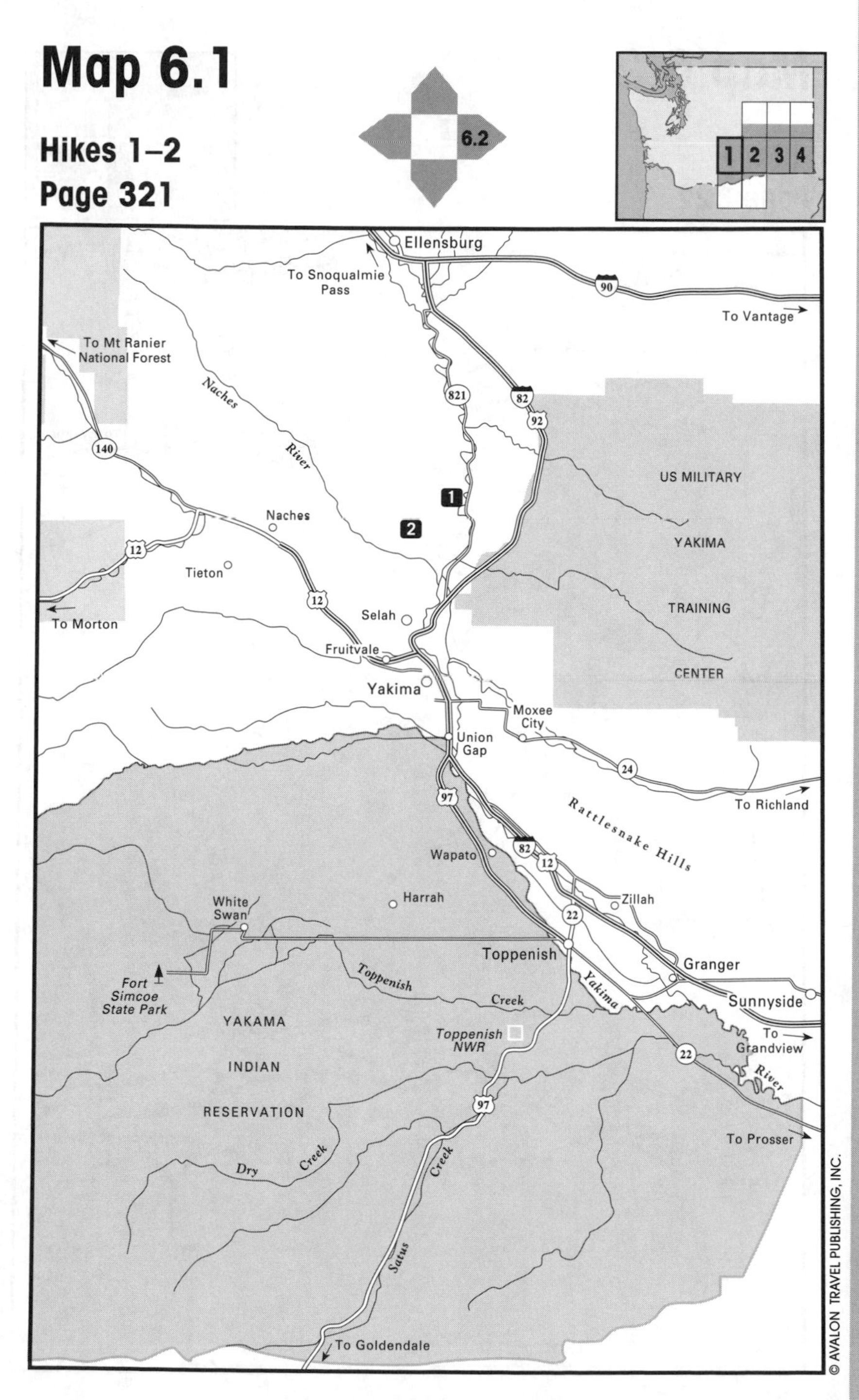
Map 6.1
Hikes 1–2
Page 321
6.2
1
2
3
4
Ellensburg
To Snoqualmie Pass
90
To Vantage
To Mt Ranier National Forest
Naches
River
821
82
92
140
US MILITARY
YAKIMA
TRAINING
CENTER
Naches
Tieton
12
To Morton
Selah
Fruitvale
Yakima
Moxee City
Union Gap
24
To Richland
97
Rattlesnake Hills
Wapato
Harrah
Zillah
White Swan
Toppenish
Fort Simcoe State Park
Toppenish
Creek
Yakima
Granger
Sunnyside
To Grandview
River
YAKAMA
INDIAN
RESERVATION
Toppenish NWR
22
To Prosser
Dry
Creek
Creek
Satus
To Goldendale
© AVALON TRAVEL PUBLISHING, INC.

Map 6.2

Hike 3
Page 322

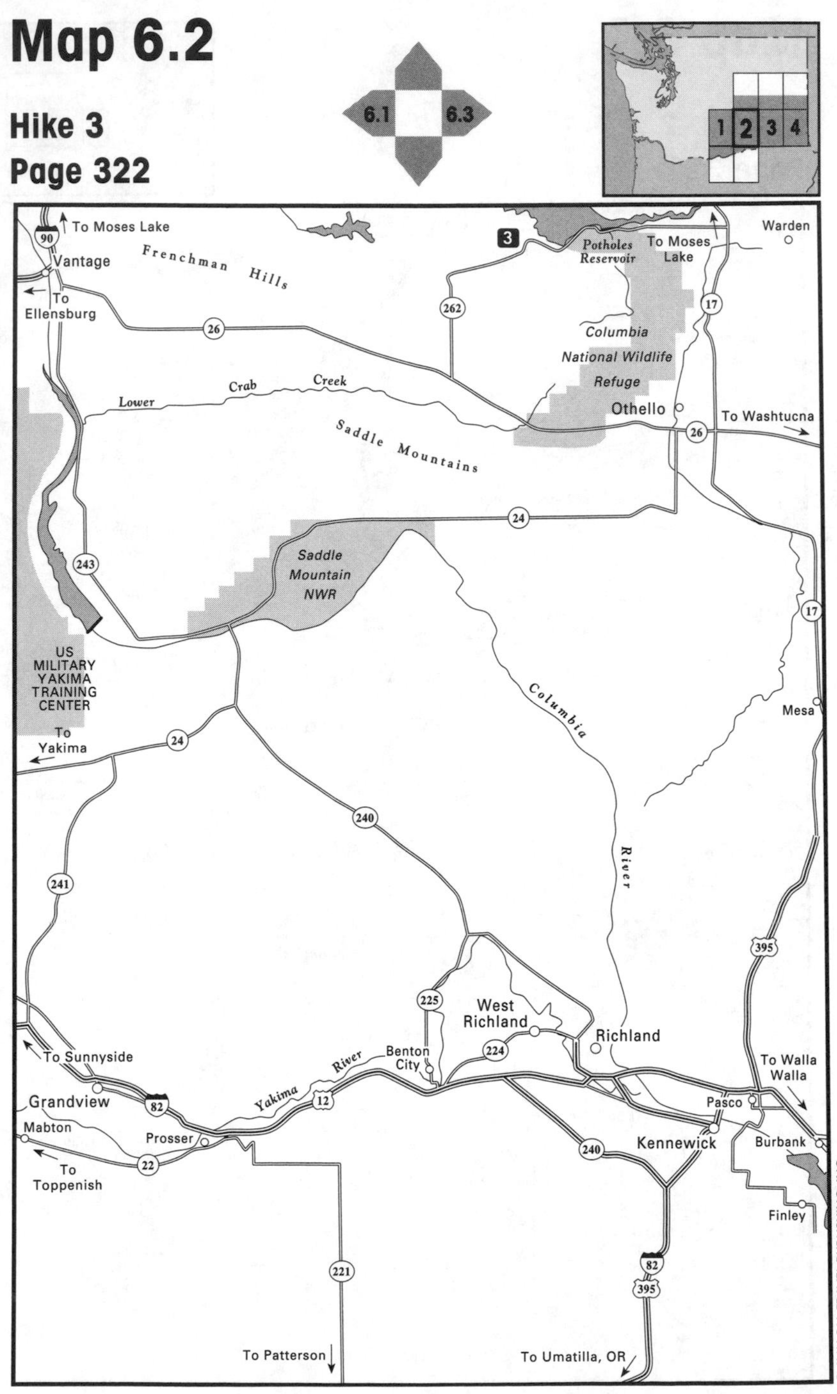

Map 6.3

Hikes 4–5
Pages 323–324

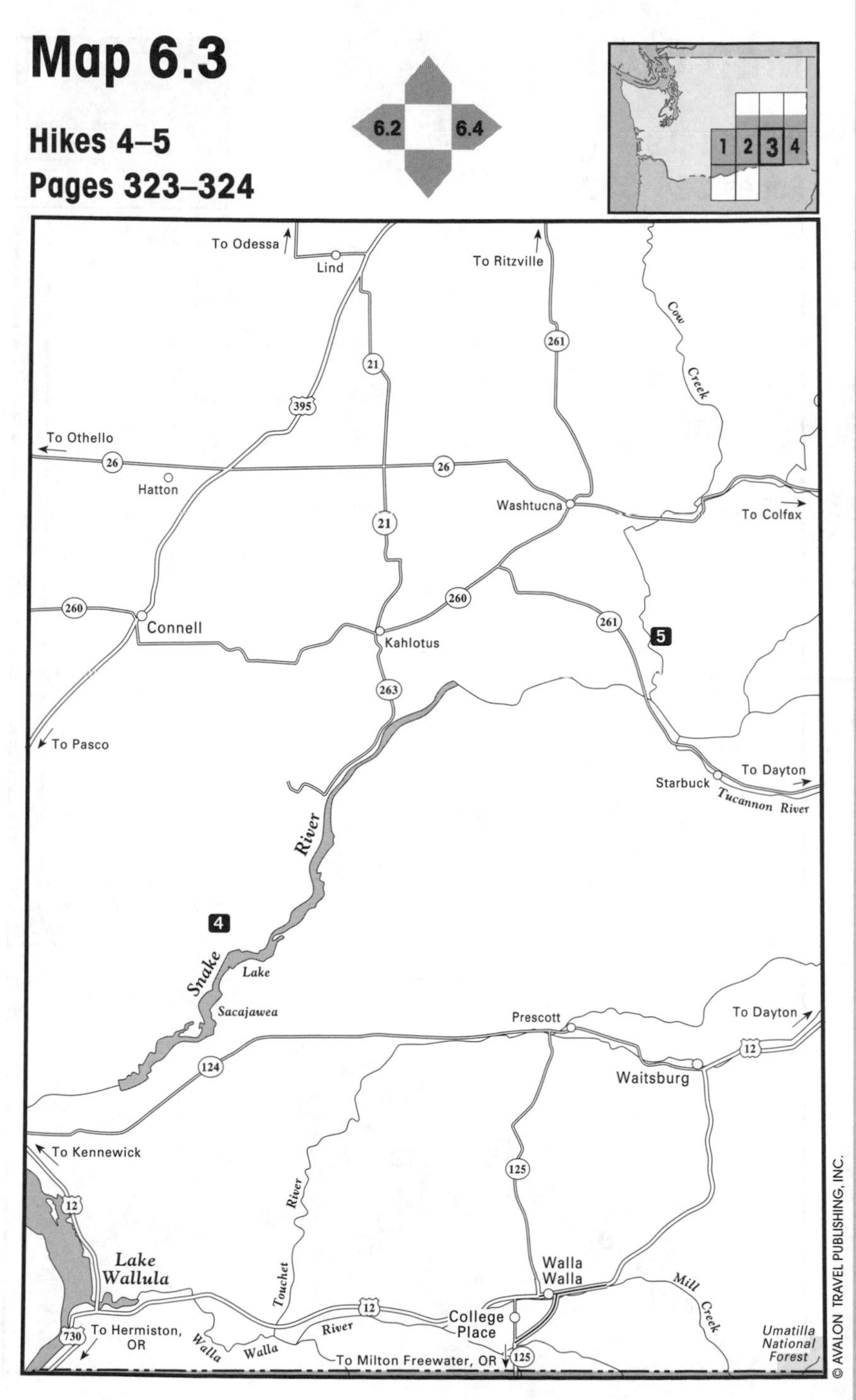

Map 6.4

Hikes 6–19
Pages 324–332

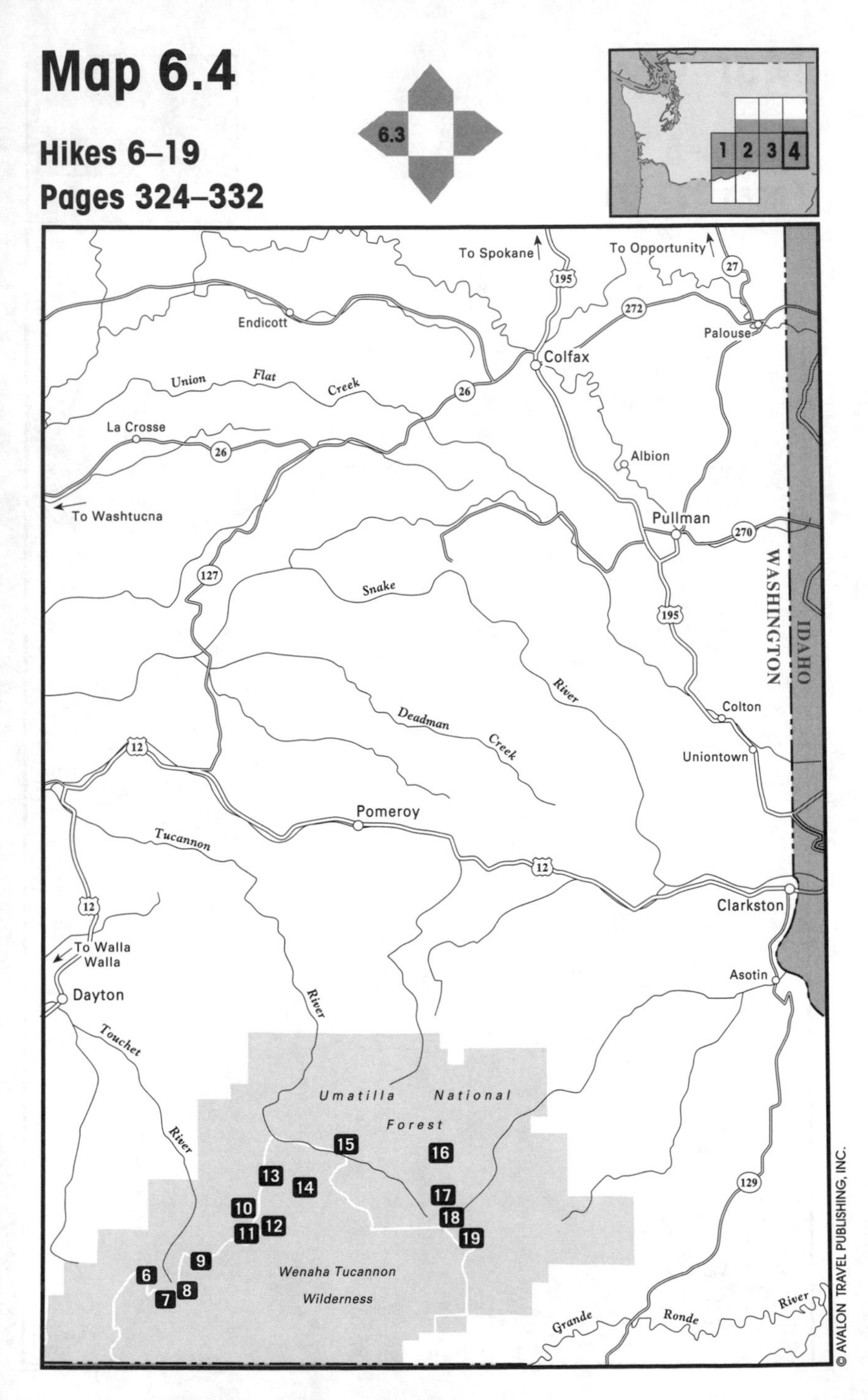

1 UMTANUM CREEK

4.0 mi/2.0 hrs

north of Yakima in L. T. Murray Wildlife Refuge

Map 6.1, page 317

Umtanum Creek offers the ideal early season hike. You know that time of year, when Cle Elum and Yakima are hitting 75°F but Seattle is still mired in May showers, and snow blankets the Cascades. This is the trail to hit. Umtanum Creek Trail begins within one of Washington's most beautiful canyons, home to the Yakima River. Basalt cliffs and large rounded mountains dominate the valley, with small creek drainages running in between. Umtanum Creek Trail follows the creek through rarely experienced east-side meadows, a rich habitat for wildlife. Spring is the best season to hike here, especially in May, when wildflowers smother the hillsides in color.

The trail begins by crossing the Yakima River on a suspension bridge and quickly crosses railroad tracks, entering the L. T. Murray Wildlife Refuge. Although it gets extremely dry in summer, this area is home to an array of wildlife, including deer, eagles, hawks, coyotes, amphibians, snakes, and, some say, bighorn sheep. Umtanum Creek Trail follows the gently flowing creek up the valley. Willows and cottonwoods mark the creek, a sharp contrast to the meadows on the hillsides. The maintained trail ends about two miles upstream. If a longer hike is your intention, it's only a short scramble to the top of the bordering ridges. From on top, views stretch from the valley below to the Stuart Range.

User Groups: Hikers, leashed dogs, horses, and mountain bikes. No wheelchair access.

Open Seasons: This trail is accessible March–November.

Permits: The Washington Department of Fish and Wildlife requires an annual Vehicle Use Permit to park here. Permits are issued free with the purchase of a hunting or fishing license; additional permits are $10 each. Permits are available anywhere hunting or fishing licenses are sold, by telephone at 866/246-9453, or online at website: fishhunt.dfw.wa.gov.

Maps: For topographic maps, ask the USGS for Wymer and The Cottonwoods.

Directions: From Ellensburg, drive south 16.5 miles on Highway 821 to the signed trailhead and parking area on the right (west) side of the road.

Contact: Washington Department of Fish and Wildlife, 201 North Pearl Street, Ellensburg, WA 98926, 509/925-6746.

2 YAKIMA RIM

4.0–18.0 mi/2.0 hrs–2 days

north of Yakima in L. T. Murray Wildlife Refuge

Map 6.1, page 317

When snow still blankets the high country and the rains are still drenching the west side (that is, much of the spring), there is no better trail than Yakima Rim. It's an east-side gem, especially considering that you can tally on one hand the number of trees you encounter. The route traverses a high, rolling ridge with views of the surrounding countryside and far-off mountains. Wildflowers are everywhere, bringing much-needed life to a normally brown and dry terrain. It's a completely different world from the forests of the Cascades and every bit as beautiful.

Yakima Rim Trail is more of a route than a trail. Often following an old road through the L. T. Murray Wildlife Refuge, the trail makes a long loop, with half along a high ridge and the other half through a narrow valley. From the lower trailhead, head to the left and climb along the old, abandoned, but signed Jacob Durr Road to the crest of the ridge, about 4.5 miles, and an upper trailhead. Mount Rainier pokes up from the southwest while the Stuart Range is visible in all its glory to the north. A closed dirt road heads east along the ridge, dropping to the Yakima River in about 10 miles. The way back to the trailhead is 4 miles through the lush Rosa Creek Valley, full of grasses, willows, snakes, and deer.

Yakima Rim Trail, the chapter's most accessible hike from Seattle

Spring is by far the best time to visit, when the daytime air is still cool. Be sure to carry water, especially on the ridge, as water is found only in Rosa Creek. The best campsite is on Rosa Creek 1.5 miles from the Yakima River at Birdsong Tree, an old locust tree planted nearly 150 years ago by homesteaders. For a shorter and less demanding trip, head to the left from the trailhead to find Birdsong Tree (2.0 miles). Deer are a frequent companion within the willow groves alongside Rosa Creek.

User Groups: Hikers, leashed dogs, horses, and mountain bikes. No wheelchair access.

Open Seasons: This trail is accessible March–November.

Permits: The Washington Department of Fish and Wildlife requires an annual Vehicle Use Permit to park here. Permits are issued free with the purchase of a hunting or fishing license; additional permits are $10 each. Permits are available anywhere hunting or fishing licenses are sold, by telephone at 866/246-9453, or online at website: fishhunt.dfw.wa.gov.

Maps: For topographic maps, ask the USGS for Wymer and The Cottonwoods.

Directions: From Selah, drive 5 miles on Wenas Road to Sheep Company Road. Turn right and drive 5 miles (enter the wildlife refuge at Mile 2.6) to the unsigned trailhead. The key to finding the start of the trail is a small sign at a junction naming the Jacob Durr Road. Head left on the road to reach the ridge. Head right to find Rosa Creek Valley.

Contact: Washington Department of Fish and Wildlife, 201 North Pearl Street, Ellensburg, WA 98926, 509/925-6746.

3 POTHOLES SAND DUNES

3.0–6.0 mi/1.5–3.0 hrs 1 9

south of Moses Lake in South Columbia Basin Wildlife Area

Map 6.2, page 318

Don't show up expecting to find any trails at Potholes Sand Dunes, because you're unlikely to find any. Instead, this is true cross-country hiking, setting out over miles of sand dunes spread out among a number of small lakes, or potholes. They seem oddly out of place here in the middle of eastern Washington, a sort of desert oasis. The small lakes and larger Potholes Reservoir were created when the lengthy O'Sullivan Dam was built in the 1940s; the low, flat land was flooded, creating a sort of wetland among sand dunes. Grasses and juniper grow thickly, supporting a rich population of wildlife—mule deer, coyotes, and a vast abundance of birds. As there are no trails, an excursion of any size is possible. The best bet is to head out north from the parking area (crossing Winchester Wasteway via bridge) and hike roughly 1.5 miles to the edge of Potholes Reservoir. Since there aren't any trails to follow, other than faint game trails, it's ideal to bring a map and compass to help you find your way back to the car. If you can't, civilization and help are never far away. Bring water, as the area is quite hot during summer, and the potholes aren't recommended for drinking. Wide open horizons make this a great place for a night hike. Set out under a full moon and witness the night shift of wildlife do business.

User Groups: Hikers, leashed dogs, horses, and mountain bikes. No wheelchair access.

Open Seasons: This area is accessible year-round.

Permits: The Washington Department of Fish and Wildlife requires an annual Vehicle Use Permit to park here. Permits are issued free with the purchase of a hunting or fishing license; additional permits are $10 each. Permits are available anywhere hunting or fishing licenses are sold, by telephone at 866/246-9453, or online at website: fishhunt.dfw.wa.gov.

Maps: For topographic maps, ask the USGS for Royal Camp and Mae.

Directions: From Royal City, drive east 9 miles on Highway 26 to Highway 262. Turn left (north) and drive 8.5 miles to C Street Southeast. Turn left (north) and drive 1.5 miles to road's end and signed parking area.

Contact: Washington Department of Fish and Wildlife, 6653 Road K Northeast, Moses Lake, WA 98837, 509/765-6641.

4 JUNIPER DUNES

5.5 mi/4.0 hrs

northeast of Pasco in Juniper Dunes Wilderness

Map 6.3, page 319

One of Washington's smallest and certainly most isolated wildernesses, Juniper Dunes promises to be unique. Covering more than 7,100 acres of pristine high desert, the Juniper Dunes preserve what once was and still is a small gem in the middle of eastern Washington. Sagebrush and desert grasses do their best to hold together the large mounds of sand, some more than 100 feet high. This layer of vegetation keeps the dunes in place and provides habitat for wildlife. Mule deer, coyotes, porcupines, and mice do their business on the ground while red-tailed hawks and owls work from the skies. The highlight of a trip to Juniper Dunes is surely the six small groves of juniper trees found near the center of the wilderness. From the trailhead, walk the road roughly 1.5 miles before turning due north for one mile. These groves of juniper trees have existed here in relative isolation for thousands of years, with many individual trees having grown for two or three centuries. The trees are surprisingly big and seem fairly out of place, in light of the fact that the region receives on average only 12 inches of rain a year. Special considerations include water (there is none to be found here) and a map and compass (other than the jeep trail bisecting the wilderness, there are no discernable trails). A field guide and binoculars will also prove helpful, for wildlife is sure to be a part of your trip to Juniper Dunes.

User Groups: Hikers, leashed dogs, and horses. No mountain bikes are allowed. No wheelchair access.

Open Seasons: This trail is accessible year-round.

Permits: No permits are needed. Parking and access are free.

Maps: For topographic maps, ask the USGS for Levey, Levey SW, and Levey NE.

Directions: From Pasco, drive east 2 miles on Highway 12 to Pasco/Kahlotus Highway. Turn left and drive 5.5 miles to Peterson Road. Turn left and drive 4.5 miles to a large sandy parking area, where the jeep trail starts.

Contact: Bureau of Land Management, Spokane District Office, 1103 North Fancher Street, Spokane, WA 99212-1275, 509/536-1200.

5 PALOUSE FALLS

0.2 mi/0.5 hrs

north of Walla Walla on the Palouse River

Map 6.3, page 319

The trail may be short, but the falls are big. From a high viewpoint, watch the Palouse River make a thunderous plummet nearly 200 feet into a large bowl before rolling downstream to the Snake River. Adding to the scenic beauty are enormous cliffs and columns of basalt stationed around the falls. The enormous falls were created by the Missoula Floods more than 15,000 years ago. Mile-thick sheets of ice in Montana blocked glacial meltwater, creating an enormous lake. When the dams eventually broke (dozens of times through thousands of years), the released torrents raced from Montana down through the Columbia Basin of Washington. Much of eastern Washington was scoured and altered, as were eastern Oregon and the Willamette Valley. Palouse Falls is just one of the more interesting and noisy changes the floods left behind. The heavy flows of water quickly eroded the basalt, producing the falls. The official trail is short, but there are several nonofficial side trails leading (safely) to viewpoints upriver from the parking lot. A trail is visible down around the falls, but it is dangerous and should not be attempted. It's not a destination hike (don't drive from Seattle just to see it), but Palouse Falls is a good stopover when passing through the area. A number of trees provide welcome shade for picnics and lounging. The only safety consideration is an important one: This is rattlesnake country, so be cautious at all times. Rattlers enjoy basking on side trails, in the grass, or even in the parking lot.

User Groups: Hikers and leashed dogs. No horses or mountain bikes are allowed. This trail is wheelchair accessible.

Open Seasons: This trail is accessible year-round.

Permits: A $5 day-use fee is required to park here and is payable at the trailhead, or you can get an annual State Parks Pass for $30; contact Washington State Parks and Recreation, 360/902-8500.

Maps: For a topographic map, ask the USGS for Palouse Falls.

Directions: From Kennewick, drive north on U.S. 395 to Highway 260. Head east for 25 miles to Highway 261. Turn north and drive 14.5 miles to Palouse Falls Road. Turn left and drive 2 miles to the parking area where the trail starts.

Contact: Palouse Falls State Park, Highway 261, Washtucna, WA, 509/549-3551.

6 SAWTOOTH RIDGE

28.0 mi/3–4 days

east of Walla Walla in the Wenaha-Tucannon Wilderness of Umatilla National Forest

Map 6.4, page 320

The trail along Sawtooth Ridge is the epitome of the Wenaha-Tucannon Wilderness—long and high, dry and secluded, but chock-full of gorgeous views of the surrounding country. The trail makes a long traverse of Sawtooth Ridge, passing in and out of forests and meadows on its way into Oregon and down to the Wenaha River. The trail's placement along the ridge means that you shouldn't expect to find any water until the Wenaha. On such a long trail, it's necessary to plan carefully and carry plenty of extra fluids. Much of the path is rocky and difficult, not surprising for a ridge named Sawtooth. As far as camping is concerned, set up camp in the scenic meadow of your choice, as long as it's low impact. Wildlife in the forms of deer, bighorn sheep, and elk abound, while other hikers certainly do not (save for hunting seasons). In May and early June, Sawtooth Ridge will pleasantly surprise hikers with a grand display of wildflowers.

User Groups: Hikers, leashed dogs, and horses. No mountain bikes are allowed. No wheelchair access.

Open Seasons: This trail is accessible mid-June–October.

Permits: A federal Northwest Forest Pass is required to park here.

Maps: For a map of Umatilla National Forest, contact the Outdoor Recreation Information Center at the downtown Seattle REI. For topographic maps, ask the USGS for Godman Spring and Wenaha Forks.
Directions: From Dayton, drive south on North Fork Touchet River Road (following signs toward Bluewood Ski Area). This road becomes Forest Service Road 64 and eventually intersects Forest Service Road 46. Turn left on Forest Service Road 46 and drive .5 mile to the signed trailhead on the right side of the road.
Contact: Umatilla National Forest, Pomeroy Ranger District, 71 West Main Street, Pomeroy, WA 99347, 509/843-1891.

7 SLICK EAR

12.0 mi/7.0 hrs

east of Walla Walla in the Wenaha-Tucannon Wilderness of Umatilla National Forest

Map 6.4, page 320

More than half of this trail actually lies within Oregon, but it would be a shame to omit such a beautiful route to the Wenaha River. Heavily used by hunters in the fall but rarely during other times of the year, Slick Ear offers hikers outstanding views of the surrounding landscape before dramatically dropping into a beautiful forested canyon ending at the Wenaha. Don't expect to find much water along the first two miles, where the trail rides the ridge top. At that point (a good turnaround for less serious excursions), the trail drops steeply into the canyon containing Slick Ear Creek. Down here is where you'll find water, campsites, and, unfortunately, rattlesnakes too. The trail ends at the Wenaha River, a prime spot for both trout and salmon fishing (Wenaha salmon are endangered and federally protected, so be sure to check Oregon fishing regulations). The trail works especially well as a loop if hikers travel east on the Wenaha River Trail to Grizzly Bear Trail, a total of 18.2 miles.
User Groups: Hikers, leashed dogs, and horses. No mountain bikes are allowed. No wheelchair access.
Open Seasons: This trail is accessible June October.
Permits: A federal Northwest Forest Pass is required to park here.
Maps: For a map of Umatilla National Forest, contact the Outdoor Recreation Information Center at the downtown Seattle REI. For topographic maps, ask the USGS for Godman Spring and Wenaha Forks.
Directions: From Dayton, drive south on North Fork Touchet River Road (following signs toward Bluewood Ski Area). This road becomes Forest Service Road 64 and eventually intersects Forest Service Road 46. Turn left on Forest Service Road 46 and drive 3 miles to Forest Service Road 46-300. Turn right and drive 5 miles to Twin Buttes Trailhead at road's end.
Contact: Umatilla National Forest, Pomeroy Ranger District, 71 West Main Street, Pomeroy, WA 99347, 509/843-1891.

8 GRIZZLY BEAR RIDGE

15.0 mi/2 days

east of Walla Walla in the Wenaha-Tucannon Wilderness of Umatilla National Forest

Map 6.4, page 320

This is one more of the many great ridge hikes in the wilderness. Putting it near the top of the list is a pair of cold-water springs supplying much-needed refreshment on hot summer days and panoramic views leading to the Wenaha River. The Wenaha is an outstanding river for trout fishing with Grizzly Bear offering access to one of the most remote sections. The trail follows an old road for about two miles, at which point Coyote Spring can be found on the south side. The trail then follows the ridge into Oregon, slowly losing elevation for four miles to Meadow Spring (on the north side of the trail). Meadow Spring is a good turnaround point for folks out for just a day hike. The descent continues as the trail makes its way to the Wenaha River. Camps are best made near Meadow Spring or preferably at the Wenaha. Hikers can make a great loop by combining Grizzly Bear Ridge with

Slick Ear, a total of 18.2 miles. Grizzly bears may be gone in this area, but a lot of other wildlife still lives in this place. Black bears roam the meadows, as do mule deer, elk, and bighorn sheep. Hawks and ravens soar in the skies, while trout and salmon ply the the Wenaha.

User Groups: Hikers, leashed dogs, and horses. No mountain bikes are allowed. No wheelchair access.

Open Seasons: This trail is accessible June–October.

Permits: A federal Northwest Forest Pass is required to park here.

Maps: For a map of Umatilla National Forest, contact the Outdoor Recreation Information Center at the downtown Seattle REI. For topographic maps, ask the USGS for Godman Spring, Oregon Butte, and Elbow Creek.

Directions: From Dayton, drive south on North Fork Touchet River Road (following signs toward Bluewood Ski Area). This road becomes Forest Service Road 64 and eventually intersects Forest Service Road 46. Turn left on Forest Service Road 46 and drive 3 miles to Forest Service Road 46-300. Turn right and drive 5 miles to Twin Buttes Trailhead at road's end.

Contact: Umatilla National Forest, Pomeroy Ranger District, 71 West Main Street, Pomeroy, WA 99347, 509/843-1891.

9 WEST BUTTE CREEK

16.0 mi/2 days

east of Walla Walla in the Wenaha-Tucannon Wilderness of Umatilla National Forest

Map 6.4, page 320

West Butte Creek has a bit of everything. After spending several miles along a high open ridge with panoramic views of the wilderness, the trail drops through the Rainbow Creek Natural Research Area. Wildlife is extremely abundant along this route. Mule deer, elk, bighorn sheep, and black bear are frequent sightings in this wild area.

The trail begins from Godman, a Forest Service station on the edge of Wenaha-Tucannon Wilderness. Soak in the views as you slowly traverse the ridge for two miles. The trail then steeply drops to Rainbow Creek and campsites (4 miles). This is in the heart of the Rainbow Creek Natural Research Area, a large section of wilderness devoted to the study of this unique and natural ecosystem. Large Douglas and grand firs provide welcome shade and lower the temperature significantly during the summer. The route ends at a junction with East Butte and Twin Buttes Trails, two primitive and rarely maintained routes back up to high ridge trailheads that would require car-drops. The trail is hot and dry along the ridge but water is available year-round from Rainbow Creek.

User Groups: Hikers, leashed dogs, and horses. No mountain bikes are allowed. No wheelchair access.

Open Seasons: This trail is accessible June–October.

Permits: A federal Northwest Forest Pass is required to park here.

Maps: For a map of Umatilla National Forest, contact the Outdoor Recreation Information Center at the downtown Seattle REI. For topographic maps, ask the USGS for Godman Spring and Oregon Butte.

Directions: From Dayton, drive 1 mile south on 4th Street to Mustard Hollow Road. Turn left and drive 28 miles (as the road turns to Eckler Mountain Road, Skyline Drive, and Forest Service Road 46) to the Godman Guard Station. The trailhead is on the left immediately after the guard station.

Contact: Umatilla National Forest, Pomeroy Ranger District, 71 West Main Street, Pomeroy, WA 99347, 509/843-1891.

10 SMOOTH RIDGE

28.0 mi one-way/3 days

east of Walla Walla in the Wenaha-Tucannon Wilderness of Umatilla National Forest

Map 6.4, page 320

Smooth Ridge is the chief high route through the Wenaha-Tucannon Wilderness, offering constant views of mountains near and far. No route through the wilderness is as scenic or as likely to provide wildlife sightings as Smooth Ridge. Numerous cold-water springs along the route provide water well into summer, and campsites are found regularly along the way, making the long journey easy. Smooth Ridge is a trekker's dream, either as an excellent through-hike or an outstanding (but extremely long) loop hike.

The best access to Smooth Ridge is via Mount Misery Trail out of Teepee Trailhead. After 2.5 miles, the trail intersects Smooth Ridge below the north slope of Oregon Butte, a quick, must-see side trip. Smooth Ridge Trail heads south over Danger Point and encounters the first set of springs at about five miles. From here, the trail follows the ridge through forest and meadow up to Weller Butte at 10 miles and slowly drops to the Wenaha River and the state of Oregon (18 miles). On clear days (which is nearly every day during summer), the Wallowa Range in Oregon and the Seven Devils Range in Idaho are plainly visible.

It's highly recommended to carry a map on this trip to help find the many springs (usually just off the main trail). Most springs provide water well into August, unless it's been a very dry spring. Campsites are situated throughout the route, with the best ones found next to the springs. From the Wenaha River, hike nine miles east to Troy, Oregon, and the logical drop-off for your return ride. Another option is to hike Crooked Creek north and return via Indian Corral, a long, tiring, and beautiful loop of more than 50 miles.

User Groups: Hikers, leashed dogs, and horses. No mountain bikes are allowed. No wheelchair access.

Open Seasons: This trail is accessible June–October.

Permits: A federal Northwest Forest Pass is required to park here.

Maps: For a map of Umatilla National Forest, contact the Outdoor Recreation Information Center at the downtown Seattle REI. For topographic maps, ask the USGS for Oregon Butte, Eden, and Diamond Peak.

Directions: From Dayton, drive 1 mile south on 4th Street to Mustard Hollow Road. Turn left and drive 28 miles (as the road turns to Eckler Mountain Road, Skyline Drive, and Forest Service Road 46) to the Godman Guard Station. Turn left onto Forest Service Road 4608 and drive 5 miles to Teepee Trailhead at road's end.

Contact: Umatilla National Forest, Pomeroy Ranger District, 71 West Main Street, Pomeroy, WA 99347, 509/843-1891.

11 TURKEY CREEK

8.0 mi/4.5 hrs 4 8

east of Walla Walla in the Wenaha-Tucannon Wilderness of Umatilla National Forest

Map 6.4, page 320

While much of Southeastern Washington receives little rain or snow, Turkey Creek is an exception. Turkey Creek drains to the north, meaning much of the valley gets less sunshine than other valleys. That results in Turkey Creek's holding on to a hefty snowpack well into May. With a source of water lasting so long, the creek supports a more lush forest. And that makes for great hiking scenery: many large trees with a thick, green understory. Water also means an abundance of wildlife, with deer and elk finding Turkey Creek a cool refuge from the area's dry, hot ridges.

Turkey Creek Trail drops from Teepee Trailhead, the one and only vista along the route (in the opposite direction, no less). The trail descends sharply into a valley of enormous Douglas firs and western larches. The strongly flowing creek is never out of ear's reach as the trail travels four miles to the confluence with Panjab Creek. Several camps lie along the route (mainly used by hunters in the fall), including a pair near the midpoint and the best site at the junction with Panjab Trail. Turkey Creek flows year-round, meaning water is readily available, even on hot summer days. Good on its own, the trail works especially well as part of a 16-mile loop with Panjab and Oregon Butte Trails.

User Groups: Hikers, leashed dogs, and horses. No mountain bikes are allowed. No wheelchair access.
Open Seasons: This trail is accessible June–November.
Permits: A federal Northwest Forest Pass is required to park here.
Maps: For a map of Umatilla National Forest, contact the Outdoor Recreation Information Center at the downtown Seattle REI. For topographic maps, ask the USGS for Panjab Creek and Oregon Butte.
Directions: From Dayton, drive 1 mile south on 4th Street to Mustard Hollow Road. Turn left and drive 28 miles (as the road turns to Eckler Mountain Road, Skyline Drive, and Forest Service Road 46) to the Godman Guard Station. Turn left onto Forest Service Road 4608 and drive 5 miles to Teepee Trailhead at road's end.
Contact: Umatilla National Forest, Pomeroy Ranger District, 71 West Main Street, Pomeroy, WA 99347, 509/843-1891.

12 OREGON BUTTE

5.5 mi/3.0 hrs

east of Walla Walla in the Wenaha-Tucannon Wilderness of Umatilla National Forest

Map 6.4, page 320

Where there are fire lookouts, there are views. Oregon Butte is no exception to this high-country rule. With easy access and knockout vistas, Oregon Butte is undoubtedly the most beautiful day hike in the Wenaha-Tucannon Wilderness. The high, open mountaintop reveals all of the surrounding wilderness, and on clear days, the jagged, snowy peaks of the Wallowa Range in Oregon and Seven Devils Range in Idaho are readily visible. And to top it off, mule deer and bighorn sheep are frequently seen along the route.

The trip to Oregon Butte follows Mount Misery Trail east out of Teepee Trailhead. At 2.5 miles, the trail passes Oregon Butte Spring, the route's only source of water. Just beyond is the junction for Smooth Ridge, along with several campsites. An easily found side trail heads straight up to the summit of Oregon Butte and the fire lookout, still staffed by the Forest Service during the summer. The views extend in every direction, with most of the wilderness's drainages easily traced back to their sources. The trail is easy to follow at all times and fairly gentle and easy. It's important to know that Mount Misery Trail lies on the north side of a ridge, meaning snow can linger along the trail well into June.
User Groups: Hikers, leashed dogs, and horses. No mountain bikes are allowed. No wheelchair access.
Open Seasons: This trail is accessible June–October.
Permits: A federal Northwest Forest Pass is required to park here.
Maps: For a map of Umatilla National Forest, contact the Outdoor Recreation Information Center at the downtown Seattle REI. For a topographic map, ask the USGS for Oregon Butte.
Directions: From Dayton, drive 1 mile south on 4th Street to Mustard Hollow Road. Turn left and drive 28 miles (as the road turns to Eckler Mountain Road, Skyline Drive, and Forest Service Road 46) to the Godman Guard Station. Turn left onto Forest Service Road 4608 and drive 5 miles to Teepee Trailhead at road's end.
Contact: Umatilla National Forest, Pomeroy Ranger District, 71 West Main Street, Pomeroy, WA 99347, 509/843-1891.

13 PANJAB

11.2 mi/6.0 hrs

east of Walla Walla in the Wenaha-Tucannon Wilderness of Umatilla National Forest

Map 6.4, page 320

Panjab provides the best access to Indian Corral, the Wenaha-Tucannon Wilderness's largest and most popular high-country camp. Indian Corral is an intersection for several long, highly scenic trails spreading into the far reaches of the wilderness. Having such a crossroads as a end makes Panjab useful as a starting point for long treks. With wide expansive meadows, Panjab is also a great day hike.

The trail starts from large Panjab Trailhead and gently climbs alongside Panjab Creek through cool forests for 1.5 miles to an intersection with Turkey Creek Trail and the route's only camp. Notice the diverse forests, full of Douglas fir, yews, grand fir, ponderosa pine, and western larch. This a good turnaround for casual hikers, as the trail only gets steeper. The next 2.5 miles climb steadily through the forest to Indian Corral and wide meadows of wildflowers. Water is common along the route, important on those hot summer days. Numerous camps are available at Indian Corral, and for water Dunlap Springs is just a few hundred yards down Crooked Creek Trail. Except in the fall, during hunting season, don't expect to see many people; the Wenaha-Tucannon is desolate country.

User Groups: Hikers, leashed dogs, and horses. No mountain bikes are allowed. No wheelchair access.

Open Seasons: This trail is accessible June–October.

Permits: A federal Northwest Forest Pass is required to park here.

Maps: For a map of Umatilla National Forest, contact the Outdoor Recreation Information Center at the downtown Seattle REI. For topographic maps, ask the USGS for Panjab Creek.

Directions: From Dayton, drive east 12 miles on Highway 12 to Tucannon River Road. Turn right and drive 35 miles to a fork. Stay to the right as the road turns into Forest Service Road 4713 and drive 3 miles to the well-signed trailhead.

Contact: Umatilla National Forest, Pomeroy Ranger District, 71 West Main Street, Pomeroy, WA 99347, 509/843-1891.

14 CROOKED CREEK

29.2 mi one-way/2–3 days

east of Walla Walla in the Wenaha-Tucannon Wilderness of Umatilla National Forest

Map 6.4, page 320

This is the trail for those seeking a long trek through the heart of the Wenaha-Tucannon Wilderness. Starting high at Indian Corral, overlooking the surrounding Blue Mountains, Crooked Creek Trail drops into cool, shady forests and travels 18 miles to the Wenaha River. By the time you're done, you'll be in Oregon. And you'll likely be tired. Crooked Creek Valley is full of life, passing through prime wildlife country where deer, elk, bighorn sheep, and black bears are common residents.

The route begs for a car-drop, with one vehicle stationed at Panjab Trailhead and another in Troy, Oregon. Otherwise, it's a long trip back to your car, either via the same route or via Smooth Ridge (a 52-mile loop). Start at Panjab Trailhead and hike to Indian Corral (5.6 miles). Crooked Creek Trail drops beside Trout Creek, which runs into Third Creek (12 miles), which runs into Crooked Creek (18 miles). Another five miles brings hikers to the Wenaha River; Troy is six miles to the east.

Much of the route is well forested, a big plus in this hot, dry region. Frequent breaks in the trees, however, reveal the high open ridges that define this wilderness. Water is never a problem since the creeks run year-round. Camps are situated regularly along the trail as well. A fishing pole is a nice luxury, as Crooked Creek and the Wenaha are prime fishing streams. Solitude seekers will be in heaven here; except during the fall hunting seasons, you likely won't encounter another soul.

User Groups: Hikers, leashed dogs, and horses. No mountain bikes are allowed. No wheelchair access.

Open Seasons: This trail is accessible June–October.

Permits: A federal Northwest Forest Pass is required to park here.

Maps: For a map of Umatilla National Forest, contact the Outdoor Recreation Information Center at the downtown Seattle REI. For topographic maps, ask the USGS for Diamond Peak, Eden, Oregon Butte, and Panjab Creek.

Directions: From Dayton, drive east 12 miles on Highway 12 to Tucannon River Road. Turn right and drive 35 miles to a fork in the road. Veer to the left onto Forest Service Road 4712 and drive 5 miles to the well-signed trailhead at road's end.

Contact: Umatilla National Forest, Pomeroy Ranger District, 71 West Main Street, Pomeroy, WA 99347, 509/843-1891.

15 TUCANNON RIVER

8.2 mi/4.5 hrs

east of Walla Walla in Umatilla National Forest

Map 6.4, page 320

The Tucannon River provides the setting for the area's most laid-back hike, a gentle walk through a striking canyon among surprisingly large trees. The route gains little elevation over its five-mile length, making it great for families and casual hikers. Though after 4.1 miles in, the trail begins a steep climb out of the valley. For a more relaxed hike, turn back after 4.1 miles. The Tucannon is well stocked with trout, making it an angler's dream. Although the trail isn't within the wilderness boundaries, there's little trace of people other than the easy-to-follow footpath. The narrow valley of the Tucannon is made of steep cliffs giving way to rounded ridges, with thick forests in the valley bottom. Ponderosa pine, yew, Douglas fir, and grand fir grow quite large here, creating a forest as impressive as those of the West Cascades, at least in light of what little precipitation the area receives. The trail ends at a junction with Jelly Springs Trail (a steep ascent to Diamond Peak) and Bear Creek (a steep ascent to Hunter's Spring). The Tucannon is a protected stream, so anglers will want to check state fishing regulations on the way in. Also keep in mind that this is rattlesnake country. They're most often found in sunny, rocky sections of the trail and are likely to warn you of their presence with a few shakes of their tails. Nevertheless, keep your eyes and ears peeled.

User Groups: Hikers, leashed dogs, and horses. No mountain bikes are allowed. No wheelchair access.

Open Seasons: This trail is accessible April–November.

Permits: A federal Northwest Forest Pass is required to park here.

Maps: For a map of Umatilla National Forest, contact the Outdoor Recreation Information Center at the downtown Seattle REI. For a topographic map, ask the USGS for Stentz Spring.

Directions: From Dayton, drive east 12 miles on Highway 12 to Tucannon River Road. Turn right and drive 35 miles to a fork in the road. Veer to the left onto Forest Service Road 4712 and drive 5 miles to the well-signed trailhead at road's end.

Contact: Umatilla National Forest, Pomeroy Ranger District, 71 West Main Street, Pomeroy, WA 99347, 509/843-1891.

16 BEAR CREEK

6.0 mi/4.0 hrs

east of Walla Walla in Umatilla National Forest

Map 6.4, page 320

Bear Creek serves as a route to the wildest parts of the Tucannon River. The trail drops from Hunter's Spring atop a high ridge into a rough canyon encasing the Tucannon River. This section of the river is at least three miles from any road, making visitors scarce. Few visitors means even fewer anglers. Which in turn means these parts are mostly unfished water, otherwise known as a trout angler's dream. The hike down is not easy, though, losing more than 1,600 feet along a steep and rocky descent. Although the trail is rough, the view is great. Pine, spruce, and larch create an open parkland forest with plenty of views of the rocky canyon below. The rustling in the bushes is probably mule deer or elk, both of which are plentiful in this wild area. Also present in the area are rattlesnakes, so be sure to keep eyes and ears alert. The trail empties on the valley floor at the shores of the Tucannon River. A couple of campsites can be found here at this junction, where trails lead down the river or up the other side of the canyon to Jelly Springs.

User Groups: Hikers, leashed dogs, and horses. No mountain bikes are allowed. No wheelchair access.

Open Seasons: This trail is accessible June–November.

Permits: A federal Northwest Forest Pass is required to park here.

Maps: For a map of Umatilla National Forest, contact the Outdoor Recreation Information Center at the downtown Seattle REI. For a topographic map, ask the USGS for Stentz Spring.

Directions: From Pomeroy, drive south 10 miles on County Road 128 to Mountain Road 40. Stay to the right and drive about 16 miles to Blue Mountain Trail sign. Turn right and drive .25 mile to the signed trailhead.

Contact: Umatilla National Forest, Pomeroy Ranger District, 71 West Main Street, Pomeroy, WA 99347, 509/843-1891.

17 JELLY SPRINGS

9.0 mi/5.0 hrs

east of Walla Walla in Umatilla National Forest

Map 6.4, page 320

Within the Blue Mountains just north of the Wenaha-Tucannon Wilderness, Jelly Springs Trail offers a unique perspective on the area. The trail is one of the few to bear due north from the wilderness, offering views not seen from the region's other trails. From Diamond Peak Trailhead, the route makes an easy traverse of a high ridge (over 6,000 feet in elevation) for three miles. Hawks frequently patrol the skies in search of a meal while Rocky Mountain elk and mule deer graze within the high meadows. Jelly Springs, a cold-water spring that runs well into August, serves as a good turnaround point for those not interested in making the sharp, steep descent to the Tucannon River. The trail encounters the Tucannon River Trail at 4.5 miles, a potential route for a through-hike. While most of the trail lies outside the wilderness boundary, the uppermost section is protected, keeping out noisy motorbikes.

User Groups: Hikers, leashed dogs, and horses. Motorcycles are allowed on the lower section of the trail and must turn around at the wilderness boundary. No mountain bikes are allowed. No wheelchair access.

Open Seasons: This trail is accessible June–October.

Permits: A federal Northwest Forest Pass is required to park here.

Maps: For a map of Umatilla National Forest, contact the Outdoor Recreation Information Center at the downtown Seattle REI. For topographic maps, ask the USGS for Stentz Spring and Diamond Peak.

Directions: From Pomeroy, drive south 10 miles on County Road 128 to Mountain Road (Forest Service Road 40). Continue straight (on Forest Service Road 40) for 24 miles to Forest Service Road 4030. Turn right and drive 5 miles to Diamond Trailhead at road's end. Jelly Springs Trail begins 1.5 miles west on Mount Misery Trail.

Contact: Umatilla National Forest, Pomeroy Ranger District, 71 West Main Street, Pomeroy, WA 99347, 509/843-1891.

18 MOUNT MISERY

14.7 mi one-way/2 days

east of Walla Walla in the Wenaha-Tucannon Wilderness of Umatilla National Forest

Map 6.4, page 320

It may be known as Mount Misery Trail, but in fact, it has little to do with its namesake. Mount Misery is quickly skirted in the first few miles and soon forgotten. Instead, the trail continues to Diamond Peak, the Wenaha-Tucannon Wilderness's highest point, and onward for 12 miles through exceptional meadows packed full of far-flung vistas. This is some of the area's best hiking along a trail that starts high and stays there. Throw in a number of cold-water springs and scenic camps, and you have yourself a wonderful trip.

The trail is best completed as a through-hike, with a start at Diamond Peak Trailhead and ending at Teepee Trailhead. Pass on the side trip to Mount Misery (although it isn't a miserable view) and make a short side trip up

Diamond Peak (at 2.5 miles) and big-time views. From there the trail travels seven miles to Indian Corral, wandering in and out of meadows along Horse Ridge. Views extend over the whole of the Wenaha-Tucannon Wilderness, all the way to the Wallowa Range in Oregon and Seven Devils Range in Idaho. The route passes five springs along the way and campsites are plentiful, with the best spots usually near the springs. From Indian Corral, the trail heads south three miles to Oregon Butte (another great, short side trip) then east two miles to Teepee Trailhead. Expect to encounter a fair amount of wildlife, including mule deer, Rocky Mountain elk, and bighorn sheep. Don't expect to run into many other hikers, save for during the fall hunting seasons.

User Groups: Hikers, leashed dogs, and horses. No mountain bikes are allowed. No wheelchair access.

Open Seasons: This trail is accessible June–October.

Permits: A federal Northwest Forest Pass is required to park here.

Maps: For a map of Umatilla National Forest, contact the Outdoor Recreation Information Center at the downtown Seattle REI. For topographic maps, ask the USGS for Panjab Creek, Diamond Peak, and Stentz Spring.

Directions: From Pomeroy, drive south 10 miles on County Road 128 to Mountain Road (Forest Service Road 40). Continue straight (on Forest Service Road 40) for 24 miles to Forest Service Road 4030. Turn right and drive 5 miles to Diamond Trailhead at road's end.

Contact: Umatilla National Forest, Pomeroy Ranger District, 71 West Main Street, Pomeroy, WA 99347, 509/843-1891.

19 MELTON CREEK

19.4 mi/2 days

east of Walla Walla in the Wenaha-Tucannon Wilderness of Umatilla National Forest

Map 6.4, page 320

It's a shame that so few people travel Melton Creek Trail, for it's packed full of exceptional views and awe-inspiring terrain. The first five miles traverse a high ridge immersed in panoramic views of the surrounding wilderness. There are loads of opportunities to see bighorn sheep and Rocky Mountain elk in this country. As if that weren't good enough, the trail then drops to the shady forest of Melton Creek, which flows through a stunning canyon. This is one of the more secluded spots within the Wenaha-Tucannon Wilderness, an attractive consideration for those seeking a little solitude. Water is nonexistent along the ridge but Melton Creek flows year-round. The trail intersects Crooked Creek Trail at the 10-mile mark, a decent day's travel (day hikers will want to turn around before the trail drops to Melton Creek). A few camps are spread out along the route, with the best ones in the valley. The few who set out on this trail will surely not be disappointed.

User Groups: Hikers, leashed dogs, and horses. No mountain bikes are allowed. No wheelchair access.

Open Seasons: This trail is accessible June–October.

Permits: A federal Northwest Forest Pass is required to park here.

Maps: For a map of Umatilla National Forest, contact the Outdoor Recreation Information Center at the downtown Seattle REI. For a topographic map, ask the USGS for Diamond Peak.

Directions: From Pomeroy, drive south 10 miles on County Road 128 to Mountain Road (Forest Service Road 40). Continue straight (on Forest Service Road 40) for 24 miles to Forest Service Road 4030. Turn right and drive 5 miles to Diamond Trailhead at road's end. Melton Creek Trail begins 1.5 miles west on Mount Misery Trail.

Contact: Umatilla National Forest, Pomeroy Ranger District, 71 West Main Street, Pomeroy, WA 99347, 509/843-1891.

Resources

Resources

National Parks

Mount Rainier National Park

Longmire Wilderness Information Center
Tahoma Woods, Star Route
Ashford, WA 98304
360/569-4453

White River Wilderness Information Center
70004 Highway 410 East
Enumclaw, WA 98022
360/569-6030

Wilkeson Wilderness Information Center
P.O. Box 423
Wilkeson, WA 98396
360/569-6020

North Cascades National Park

Golden West Visitor Center
Stehekin, WA
360/856-5700, ext. 340

Marblemount Wilderness Information Center
7280 Ranger Station Road
Marblemount, WA 98267
360/873-4500

Olympic National Park

Olympic Wilderness Information Center
600 East Park Avenue
Port Angeles, WA 98362
360/565-3130

National Forests

Colville National Forest

www.fs.fed.us/r6/colville

Newport Ranger District
315 North Warren
Newport, WA 99156
509/447-7300

Republic Ranger District
180 North Jefferson
Republic, WA 99166
509/775-7400

Sullivan Lake Ranger District
12641 Sullivan Lake Road
Metaline Falls, WA 99153
509/446-7500

Three Rivers Ranger District,
Colville Ranger Station
755 South Main
Colville, WA 99114
509/684-7000

Three Rivers Ranger District,
Kettle Falls Ranger Station
255 West 11th Avenue
Kettle Falls, WA 99141
509/738-7700

Gifford Pinchot National Forest

www.fs.fed.us/r6/gpnf

Cowlitz Valley Ranger District
10024 U.S. 12
Randle, WA 98377
360/497-1100

Mount Adams Ranger District
2455 Highway 141
Trout Lake, WA 98650
509/395-3400

Mount Baker–Snoqualmie National Forest

www.fs.fed.us/r6/mbs

Glacier Public Service Center
Glacier, WA 98244
360/599-2714

Verlot Public Service Center
33515 Mountain Loop Highway
Granite Falls, WA 98252
360/691-7791

Darrington Ranger District
1405 Emmens Street
Darrington, WA 98241
360/436-1155

Mount Baker Ranger District Office
810 Highway 20
Sedro-Woolley, WA 98284
360/856-5700

Skykomish Ranger District
74920 Northeast Stevens Pass Highway
P.O. Box 305
Skykomish, WA 98288
360/677-2414

Snoqualmie Ranger District,
Enumclaw Ranger Station
450 Roosevelt Avenue East
Enumclaw, WA 98022
360/825-6585

Snoqualmie Ranger District,
North Bend Ranger Station
42404 Southeast North Bend Way
North Bend, WA 98045
425/888-1421

Okanogan National Forest

www.fs.fed.us/r6/oka

Methow Valley Ranger District
24 West Chewuch Road
Winthrop, WA 98862
509/996-4003

Tonasket Ranger District
1 West Winesap
Tonasket, WA 98855
509-486-2186

Olympic National Forest

www.fs.fed.us/r6/olympic

Forks Ranger District
437 Tillicum Lane
Forks, WA 98331
360/374-6522

Hoodsport Ranger District
150 North Lake Cushman Road
P.O. Box 68
Hoodsport, WA 98548
360/877-5254

Quilcene Ranger District
295142 U.S. 101 South
P.O. Box 280
Quilcene, WA 98376
360/765-2200

Quinault Ranger District
353 South Shore Road
P. O. Box 9
Quinault, WA 98575
360/288-2525

Umatilla National Forest

www.fs.fed.us/r6/uma

Pomeroy Ranger District
Route 1, Box 53-F
Pomeroy, WA 99347
509/843-1891

Wenatchee National Forest

www.fs.fed.us/r6/wenatchee

Chelan Ranger District
428 West Woodin Avenue
Chelan, WA 98816-9724
509/682-2576

Cle Elum Ranger District
803 West 2nd Street
Cle Elum, WA 98922
509/852-1100

Entiat Ranger District
2108 Entiat Way
P.O. Box 476
Entiat, WA 98822
509/784-1511

Lake Wenatchee Ranger District
22976 Highway 207
Leavenworth, WA 98826
509/763-3103

Leavenworth Ranger District
600 Sherbourne
Leavenworth, WA 98826
509/548-6977

Naches Ranger District
10237 Highway 12
Naches, WA 98937
509/653-2205

Parks, Recreation Areas, and Other Resources

Bureau of Land Management
Spokane District Office
1103 North Fancher Street
Spokane, WA 99212-1275
509/536-1200

Mount St. Helens National Volcanic Monument
www.fs.fed.us/gpnf/mshnvm

Monument Headquarters
(Gifford Pinchot National Forest)
42218 Northeast Yale Bridge Road
Amboy, WA 98601
360/449-7800
Mount Margaret Backcountry: 360/449-7871
Climbing Info-Line: 360/449-7861

Mount St. Helens–Coldwater Ridge Visitor Center
3029 Spirit Lake Highway
Castle Rock, WA 98611
360/274-2114

Mount St. Helens–Johnston Ridge Observatory
3029 Spirit Lake Highway
Castle Rock, WA 98611
360/274-2140

Seattle City Parks and Recreation
100 Dexter Avnue North
Seattle, WA 98109
206/684-4075
www.cityofseattle.net/parks

Washington Department of Fish and Wildlife
201 North Pearl Street
Ellensburg, WA 98926
509/925-6746
6653 Road K Northeast
Moses Lake, WA 98837
509/765-6641

Washington Department of Natural Resources
P.O. Box 47001
Olympia, WA 98504-7001
360/902-1375

Washington State Parks and Recreation Commission
P.O. Box 42650
Olympia, WA 98504-2669
360/902-8844 (information) or
360/902-8500 (State Parks Pass)
www.parks.wa.gov

Map Resources

Green Trails
P.O. Box 77734
Seattle, WA 98177
206/546-MAPS (206/546-6277)
www.greentrails.com

USGS Information Services
Box 25286
Denver, CO 80225
www.store.usgs.gov

Outdoor Recreation Information Center
In the Seattle REI Building
222 Yale Avenue North
Seattle, WA 98109-5429
206/470-4060

Hiking Clubs and Groups

Cascade Chapter of Sierra Club
180 Nickerson Street
Suite 202
Seattle, WA 98109-1631
206/523-2147
www.cascade.sierraclub.org

Cascadians of Yakima, WA
www.cascadians.org

Mazamas
909 Northwest 19th Avenue
Portland, OR 97209
503/227-2345
www.mazamas.org

Mountaineers
300 3rd Avenue West
Seattle, WA 98119
206/284-8484
www.mountaineers.org

Mountains-to-Sound Greenway
1011 Western Avenue
Suite 606
Seattle, WA 98104
206/812-0122
www.mtsgreenway.org

Pacific Northwest Trail Association
P.O. Box 1817
Mount Vernon, WA 98273
877/854-9415
www.pnt.org

Washington Trails Association
1305 4th Avenue
Suite 512
Seattle, WA 98101-2401
206/625-1367
www.wta.org

Acknowledgments

Writing a hiking guide that covers the entire state of Washington turned out to be quite an endeavor. Such a monumental task could not have been completed without the assistance of many great people.

Thank you to Robin Clark for imparting her knowledge of the Alpine Lakes. Similar gratitude is due to Professor Doug McKeever for sharing his expertise of the North Cascades, Ray and Sam Warner for recommendations for the South Cascades, and friendly Park Ranger Lizza Demsetz for helping with Mount Rainier National Park.

Many thanks to my friends David Dow, Ben Cate, Andrea Penglase, Erica Capuana, Al Her, Pete Lenaker, Pete Kingham, Andy Kingham, and my step dad Justus Mills for their time on the trail and for taking part in many stories.

Appreciation goes to Liz Westbrook, James Herndon, and Andy Leung for providing a place to stay for a summer. Thanks Victrola Coffee & Art for the office.

The editors at Avalon have been great to work with. Thank you Grace Fujimoto and Marisa Solís. A big thank you to Rebecca Browning for this opportunity.

Washingtonians benefit from a rich history of hiking guides. I would like to thank Harvey Manning and Ira Spring for spreading a passion for wilderness in each of their books while setting a high standard for outdoor writing. Robert L. Wood has written extensively on the Olympics, and his work is indispensable.

I can't say thank you enough to Louise Alexander, who was there for me too many times to count. You are a beautiful woman, without whom I couldn't have written this book. Thank you.

And last, but not least, thanks to Venus the dog, the best trail buddy ever.

Index

Page numbers in **bold** *are references to maps.*

A

Abercrombie Mountain: **203,** 222
Adams Mountain: **202**
Agnes Gorge Trail: 143
Alder Lake: **235**
Alexander Island: 37
Alpine Lakes Wilderness: **94,** 160–164, 169–182, 187–191, 194
Alpine Lookout: 165
American Ridge: 273–274
Amphitheater Mountain: 138
Anacortes: 77
Anderson and Watson Lakes: 108
Anderson Island: **27**
Andrews Creek: 138
Angry Mountain: 283
Annette Lake: 175
Anti-Aircraft Peak: 83
Antler Peak: 254
Ape Cave: 246–247
Appleton Pass: 39–40
Ashland Lakes/Bald Mountain: 122–123

B

Badger Peak: 293–294
Bainbridge Island: **27**
Baker Lake and Baker River: **91,** 107–108
Bandera Mountain: 171–172
Barnaby Butte: 220–221
Battle Ground Lake Loop: 306–307
Battle Ground Lake State Park: 306
Beacon Rock State Park: 307
Beacon Rock: 307
Bear Creek Mountain: 289
Bear Creek: **320,** 330–331
bears: 6–8, 7
Beaver Loop: 113–114
Bell Pass/Cathedral Pass/Mazama Park: 106
Bellevue: 82
Bellingham Bay: **73**
Bellingham: 75–76
Berkeley and Grand Parks: 252–253
Bernhardt Mine: 209
berry picking: 16
Beverly Turnpike: 193–194
Big Creek Falls: 299–300
Big Tree Botanical Loop: 208
Birch Point: **73**
Bird Mountain: 301
Birdsong Tree: 322
Blake Island: **27**
Blanca Lake: 157–158
Blue Lake: 130–131
Bluff Lake: 287
bobcats: 8
Bogachiel River: 37–38
Bolton Peninsula: **27**
Boulder Lake: 40
Boulder River Wilderness: 116, 120
Boulder River: 116–117
Boundary Trail (Gifford Pinochet National Forest): 242
Boundary Trail (Okanogan National Forest): 205
Boundary, West End: 241–242
Bridle Trails: 82
Brothers, The: 59–60
Brothers Wilderness: 59–50
Brown Point: **74**
Buck Creek Pass: 154
Buckhorn Wilderness: 51, 52–55, 66
Buckskin Ridge: 132
Bullion Loop: 143
Bumping Lake: **236**
Bumping River: **236**
Bunker Hill: 309–310
Burch Mountain: 135–136
Burroughs Mountain Loop: 254–255

C

Cady Creek/Little Wenatchee Loop: 159
Calispell Peak: **203**
Camano Island: **73**
Cameron Creek: 43–44
camping and campfires: 9–10
Canyon Creek: 39, 127
Cape Alava: **23,** 31
Cape Disappointment: **28**
Cape Disappointment State Park: 68
Cape Elizabeth: **25**
Cape Flattery: **23,** 29
Capitol State Forest: **28**
Carbon Glacier/Mystic Lake: 250
Carbon River: **74, 236**
Carkeek Park: 81
Carr Inlet: **27**
Cascade Falls Trail: 76
Cascade Pass: 111–112
Case Inlet: **27**
Cashmere Mountain: **94**
Cathedral Basin: 137–138
Cathedral Peak: 138
Cathedral Rock: 180–181
Cedar Flats: 245
Cedar River: **74, 93**
Cedar River Municipal Watershed: 168
Central Wilderness Beach: 37
Chain Lakes: 164–165

Chatter Creek/Lake Edna: 188
Chehalis River: **28**
Chelan Lakeshore: 143–144
Chelan Mountains: **92**
Chelan Summit Trail: 149
Chester Morse Lake: **93**
Chewuch Falls: 136
Chewuch River: **92,** 136
Chilean Memorial: 31
Chilliwack River: 103
Chinook Creek: 273
Chinook Pass Hikes: 260
Chiwaukum Creek: 187–188
Chiwaukum Mountains: **94**
Christine Falls: 264
Chromatic Moraine: 97
Chuckanut Mountain: 76–77
Church Mountain: 95–96
Cispus Braille: 290
Cispus River: **236**
Clayton Beach: 76
Cle Elum Lake: **93**
Clear Fork: 286
Clearwater River: **25**
Clearwater Wilderness: 184
clothing: 3
Colchuck and Stuart Lakes: 190–191
Coldwater Lake: 239
Coleman Glaciers: 97
Coleman Pinnacle: 105
Coleman Ridge: 136–137
Colonel Bob Mountain: 48–49
Columbia Mountain: 218
Columbia River: **28, 94, 201, 203, 237, 238, 318**
Colville Indian Reservation: **201, 202**
Colville National Forest: **202, 203,** 211–229
Colville River: **203**
Columbia River Gorge National Scenic Area: **237, 238**
Columbia National Wildlife Refuge: **318**
Comet Falls/Van Trump Park: 264–265
Commonwealth Basin/Red Pass: 177
Company/Devore Creeks Loop: 142–143
compasses: 4–5
Copper Butte: **202,** 216
Copper Ridge Loop: 101–102
Cougar Lakes: 274
Cougar Mountain: 83
Cougar Mountain Regional Park: 83
cougars: 8
Cowap Peak: 95
Cow Creek: **319**
Cowlitz Chimneys: 254, 259
Cowlitz River: **236**
Craggy Peak: 295–296
Crater Lake: 153
Crater Mountain: 127
Crooked Creek: **320,** 329–330
Crowell Ridge: 226
Crystal Lakes: 257–258
Crystal Mountain: 256
Cultus Mountains: **73**
Curlew Lake: **202**
Cutthroat Lakes: 122–123
Cutthroat Pass: 131

D

Damfino Lakes: 95
Dark Meadow: 297
Deadman Creek: **320**
Deception Creek: 163
Deception Pass Loop: 180–181
Deception Pass State Park: 78
Deer Lake: 39
Denham Peak: 269
Denny Creek and Lake Melakwa: 175–176
Desolation Peak: 115
Devil's Dome Loop: 127
Diablo Lake: 113
Dingford Creek: 169–170
Dirty Face: 187
Discovery Park: 81–82
Dog Mountain: 310–311
dogs, hiking with: 10
Domke Lake: 145
Driveway Butte: 133
Dry Creek: **317**
Duckabush River: 57–58
Dumbbell Lake Loop: 277
Dungeness National Wildlife Refuge: **24,** 35
Dungeness Spit: 35
Dunn Mountain: **203**
Dutch Miller Gap: 170–171

E

Eagle Lakes: 153–154
Eagle Peak: 265
East Creek: 127–128
East Fork Buttermilk Creek: 151–152
Easton Glacier: 107
East Side Trail: 273
easy hikes, author's top ten: 13
Easy Pass/Fisher Creek: 128–129
ecology and environment: 9–10
Edds Mountain: 220
Eightmile and Trout Lake Loop: 190
Elk Mountain: 42
Elwha River: **24, 26,** 41
Emerald Park: 145–146
Emerald Ridge Loop: 261
emergency kits: 6
Emmons Glacier: 255
Enchanted Valley: 47
Enchantments, The: 191–192
Entiat Meadows: 155–156
Entiat Mountains: **92, 94**

Esmerelda Basin: 192
Excelsior Ridge: 96

F

Falls Creek: 33
Fidalgo Head: 77
Fidalgo Island: **73,** 78
Fir Mountain: 211
fire starters: 4
first aid kits: 5
Fisher Creek Valley: 128
Flapjack Lakes: 63–64
flashlights: 6
Flattery Rocks National Wildlife Refuge: **23**
food: 4
Fort Ebey: 78–79
Fort Simcoe State Park: **317**
Fortune Ponds: 159–160
Foss Lakes: 161
Four Point Lake: 136
Fourth of July Pass: 126–127
Fourth of July Ridge: 210
Fox Island: **27**
Fragrance Lake: 76–77
Franklin Roosevelt Lake: **202**
Frenchman Hills: **318**

G

Galena Chain Lakes: 104–105
Gardner Meadows: 150–151
Gedney Island: **73**
Giants Graveyard: 37
Gifford Pinchot National Forest: **236–238** 239–248, 261, 275–288, 290–305, 307–311
Gilbert Mountain: 146–147
Gillette Ridge: 221–222
glacial exploration: 97
Glacier Basin (Mount Baker-Snoqualmie National Forest): 125–126
Glacier Basin (Mount Rainier National Park): 258
Glacier Lake: 282
Glacier Meadows: 44
Glacier Peak: **91,** 254
Glacier Peak Wilderness: **92,** 117–119, 142, 144, 145, 154–156, 185–186
Glacier View Wilderness: 261–262, 262
Goat Flats: 120
Goat Mountain (Gifford Pinochet National Forest): 241
Goat Mountain (Mount Baker-Snoqualmie National Forest): 99–100
Goat Peak Trail: 273
Goat Ridge: 283–284
Goat Rocks: 269
Goat Rocks Wilderness: **236,** 280–289
goats, trails allowing: Granite Mountain 173–174
Gobbler's Knob/Lake George: 262–263
Goblin's Gate: 41
Gold Creek Valley: 178
Goldmeyer Hot Springs: 169
Goode Ridge: 140–141
Goose Prairie Trail: 273
Gothic Basin: 124–125
Grand Pass: 43
Grand Ridge: 42
Grande Ronde River: **320**
Granite Falls: 121
Granite Mountain: 173–174, 209–210
Graves Creek: 47–48
Gray Wolf River: 50
Grays Harbor: **25, 28**
Green Lake: 249
Green Mountain: 117–118
Green River: **74**
Greenwater River: 184–185
Grenville Bay: **25**
Grizzly Bear Ridge: **320,** 325–326
Grove of the Patriarchs: 272–273
Guemes Island: **73**

H

Hall Mountain: 228
Halliday/North Fork: 223–224
Hamilton Buttes: 291–292
Hangman Creek: **204**
Hannegan Pass: 101
Happy Lake Ridge Trail: 40
Harmony Falls: 243–244
Hartstene Island: **27**
Hayes Lake: 105
headlamps: 6
Heart Lake: 39, 281, 283
Heather Lake: 121–122
Heather Park/Mount Angeles: **24,** 34
Heliotrope Ridge: 96–97
Henry M. Jackson Wilderness: 124–125, 157–159
Hester Lake: 169–170
Hidden Lake Peaks: 110–111
Hidden Lakes: 300–301
High Divide Trail: 96
High Lakes: 298
High Rock Lookout: 276
hiking tips: 3–12
Hoh River: **25, 26,** 37, 44–45
Hole in the Wall: 31
Hood Canal: **26, 27**
Hoodoo Canyon: 221
Hoodoo Pass: 151
Horseshoe Basin (Pasayten): 205–206
Horseshoe Basin (Stehekin): 139
hot springs: 40
Hovander Park Trail: 75
Howard Hanson Reservoir: **93**
Huckleberry Mountain: 117
Huckleberry Range: **202**
Humptulips River: **25, 26**
Hurricane Hill: 41–42

IJK

Iceberg Lake: 105
Ice Lakes: 156
Icicle Ridge: 189–190
Image Lake: 118–119
Indian Heaven: 301
Indian Heaven Wilderness: 300–302
Indian Henry's Hunting Ground: 263–264
Ingalls Creek: 194–195
Iron Goat: 165–166
Ironstone Mountain: 279
Jack Creek: 188–189
Jelly Springs: **320,** 331
Johnson Peak: 281
Jolly Mountain: 183
June Lake: 247–248
Juniper Dunes: 323
Juniper Dunes Wilderness: 323
Juniper Ridge: 294–295
Kachess Lake: **93**
Kachess Ridge: 180
Kalama River: **235**
Kaniksu National Forest: **203**
Kautz Creek: 263
Keekwulee Falls: 175
Kendall Katwalk: 177–178
Kettle Crest North: 218–219
Kettle Crest South: 219–220
Kettle Crest Trail: 216, 217
Killen Creek: 305
Kitsap Lake: **27**
Klahhane Ridge: **24,** 34–35
Klapatche Park: 260–261
Klickitat Trail: **236, 238,** 291
knives, multipurpose: 6

L

L. T. Murray Wildlife Refuge: 321
Lake 22: 122
Lake Angeles: 34–35
Lake Ann/Maple Pass: 129–130
Lake Ann: 103–104
Lake Chelan: **92, 94,** 111
Lake Chelan National Recreation Area: **92,** 141
Lake Chelan-Sawtooth Wilderness: 143–145, 146–153
Lake Constance: 57
Lake Crescent: **24,** 33
Lake Cushman: **26**
lake hikes: author's top ten 14
Lake Juanita 149
Lake Merwin: **237**
Lake Meten 119
Lake of the Angels: 60
Lake Ozette: 31
Lake Quinault: **26**
Lake Quinault Loop: 49
Lake Roosevelt National Recreation Area: **202**
Lake Sacajawea: **319**
Lake Sammamish: **74**
Lake Shannon: **91**
Lake Tapps: **74**
Lake Wallula: **319**
Lake Washington: **74,** 82–83
Lake Wenatchee: **94**
Lake Whatcom: **73**
Lane Mountain: **203**
Langille Ridge: 292–293
Larch Lake: 187
Larrabee State Park: 76–77
Laughingwater Creek: 271
Lava Canyon: 244–245
Leadbetter Point: **28,** 67
Leadbetter Point State Park: **28**
Leave-No-Trace principles: 9–10
Lemei: 302
Lena Lakes: 58–59
Leona: 215
Lewis River: **236**
Libby Creek: 152
light sources: 6
Lily Basin: 281–282
Little Giant Pass: 186
Little Huckleberry: 310
Little Pend Oreille National Wildlife Refuge: **203**
Little Si: 167–168
Little Spokane River Natural Area: 229–230
Little White Salmon River: **238**
llamas, trails allowing: Damfino Lakes 95; Excelsior Ridge 96; Granite Mountain 173–174; Pratt Lake 174–175
Long Beach: 67
Long Island: 67–68
Long Lake: **204**
Longs Pass and Lake Ingalls: 192–193
Lookingglass Lake: 304
Loon Lake: **203**
Loowit Trail: 248
Lopez Island: **73**
Lost Lake: 76–77
Lost River: **92,** 135
Louis Lake: 147
Louise Lake: 267
Lower Crab Creek: **318**
Lower Falls Creek: 308
Lummi Island: **73**
Lyall Glacier: 129
Lyman Lakes: 144–145
lynx: 8

M

Maiden Peak: 42
Main Fork Dosewallips River: 26, 56–57
Makah Indian Reservation: **23,** 29
maps: 4–5, *See also specific place*
Marcus: 216–217
Margaret and Lillian Lakes: 178–179

Martin Lakes: 152–153
Marymere Falls: **24,** 33–34
Maury Island: **74**
Mayfield Lake: **235**
Mazama Lake: 104
Mazama Ridge: 267
McClellan Butte: 172–173
McCoy Peak: 292
McGee Creek: 133
McGregor Mountain: 141–142
McNeil Island: **27**
Meadow Mountain: 119–120
Melton Creek: **320,** 332
memorials: 31
Mercer Island: **74**
Merritt Lake: 165
Mesatchee Creek Trail: 273
Meta Lake: 243
Metcalf Moraine: 107
Methow River: **92**
Middle Fork Snoqualmie River: 169
Mildred Lakes: 61
Miller River: 160
Monogram Lake/Lookout Mountain: 110
Moran State Park: 76
Mount Adams: **236,** 269, 304
Mount Adams Wilderness: **236,** 303–305
Mount Aix: 274–275
Mount Appleton: 39
Mount Baker: **91**
Mount Baker-Snoqualmie National Forest: **91–94,** 95–101, 103–110, 117–125, 157–163, 160–163, 169–178, 184–185, **235,** 256, 260
Mount Baker Wilderness: **91,** 96–101, 103–106
Mount Beljica: 262
Mount Challenger: 102
Mount Constitution: 76
Mount David: 185–186
Mount Deception: **26,** 50, 52, 54
Mount Defiance/Mason Lakes: 171
Mount Dickerman: 124
Mount Ellinor: 64–65
Mount Forgotten Meadows: 123
Mount Fremont Lookout: 253–254
Mount Higgins: 115–116
Mount Logan: 128
Mount Misery: **320,** 331–332
Mount Mystery: 54
Mount Olympus: **26,** 44, 46
Mount Pilchuck: 121
Mount Pilchuck State Park: 121
Mount Pugh (Stujack Pass): 119
Mount Rainier: **236**
Mount Rainier National Park: **236,** 249–255, 257–273; passes and permits 12
Mount Rose: 65
Mount Shuksan: 96
Mount Si: 166–167
Mount Si Natural Resources Conservation Area: 166–167
Mount Skokomish Wilderness: 60–61, 64–65
Mount Spokane State Park: **204**
Mount St Helens: **235**
Mount St. Helens National Monument: 241
Mount St. Helens National Volcanic Monument: **235,** 239–230, 243–248
Mount Townsend: 53–54
Mount Triumph: 109
Mount Zion: 50–51
Mountain Lake: 76
Mountain, The: 254, 257
Mud Mountain Lake: **93**
Myrtle Lake: 169–170

N

Naches Loop: 260
Naches River: **317**
Nannie Ridge: 285
Naselle River: **28**
Nason Ridge: 165
National Parks passes and permits: 11–12
National Wildlife Refuge: 67
Nature Loop Trail: 81
Necklace Valley: 161–162
Needles: 50, 52
Newaukum River: **235**
Nisqually Glacier: 266
Nisqually National Wildlife Refuge: 84–85
Nisqually River: **235**
Noble Knob: 185
Noisy Creek: 228–229
Noisy-Diobsud Wilderness: 108
Nooksack Cirque: 100–101
Nooksack River: 75
Norse Peak: 256–257
Norse Peak Wilderness: 184–185
North Beach Peninsula: **28**
North Cascades National Park: **91, 92,** 101–103, 109–115, 126–127, 128, 139–141; passes and permits 11
North Cascades Scenic Highway: 127
North Creek: 146–147
North Fork Bridge Creek: 139–140
North Fork Quinault: 46–47
North Fork Skokomish: 62
North Fork Tieton: 288–289
North River: **28**
North War Creek: 149–150
North Wilderness Beach: 31–32
Northwest Forest Pass: 11
Norwegian Memorial: 31

O

Observation Peak: 309
Obstruction Point: 43
Okanogan National Forest: **92,** 127, 129–138, 143, 146–153, **201, 202,** 205–211
Okanogan River: **201**
Old Stage Road: 216
Olympic Coast: 36–37
Olympic Coast National Marine Sanctuary: 29
Olympic Hot Springs: 40
Olympic National Forest: **23–27,** 48–49, 50–55, 60–61, 64–66
Olympic National Park: **23–26,** 29–34, 37–50, 52, 55–58, 60–65; passes and permits 11–12
Olympic Peninsula: 35
Omak Lake: **201**
Orcas Island: **73,** 76
Oregon Butte: **320,** 328
Osoyoos Lake: **201**
O'Toole Mountain: **203**
Oval Lakes: 150
overnight hikes, author's top ten: 13
Owyhigh Lakes: 259
Ozette Lake: **23**
Ozette Triangle: 30–31

P

Pacific Crest Trail: 131, 133, 141, 143, 288
Packwood Lake: 280–281
Paddy-Go-Easy Pass: 182
Padilla Bay: **73,** 80
Palisades Lakes: 255–256
Palmer Lake: **201**
Palouse Falls: 324
Panjab: **320,** 328–329
Panorama Point: 268
Panther Creek: 126
Paradise Glacier: 266–267
Paradise Nature Trails: 266
Park Butte/Railroad Grade/Scott Paul Trail: 106–107
Pasayten Wilderness: 127, 132–138, 205–206
Pass Creek/Grassy Top: 229
Peepsight: 138–139
Pend Oreille River: **203**
permits and passes: 10–12
Perry Creek Falls: 123
petroglyphs: 30–31
Phelps Creek (Spider Meadow): 154–155
Picket Range: **91**
Pickhandle Point: 260
Picnic Point: **74**
Pilchuck River: **74**
Pine and Cedar Lakes: 77
Pinnacle Peak: 269
Pinnacle Saddle: 269–270
Pipeline Trail: 75
Piper Creek: 81
Plains of Abraham: 244
Point Defiance: 83–84
Point of Arches: 29–30
Pompey Peak: 280
Poodle Dog Pass/Twin Lakes: 125
Port Susan: **73**
Possession Point: **74**
Possession Sound: **73**
Potholes Reservoir: **318**
Potholes Sand Dunes: 322–323
Pratt Lake: 174–175
Profanity: 214
Ptarmigan Ridge: 105–106
Puget Sound: **74,** 77, 80, 81, 83–85
Purcell Mountain: 279–280
Putvin: 60
Puyallup River: **74, 236**
Pyramid Lake: 112
Pyramid Mountain: **24,** 32, 156–157

QR

Quartz Creek: 297–298
Quartz Creek Big Trees: 240–241
Queets River: **25, 26,** 45
Quillayute Needles National Wildlife Refuge: **25**
Quinault Indian Reservation: **25, 26**
Quinault River: **25, 26**
Race Track: 302–303
Rachel Lake: 179–180
Rainbow Canyon: 66
Rainbow Creek Natural Research Area: 326
Rainbow Lake: 141
Rainbow Loop Trail: 143
Rainy Lake Nature Trail: 129
Rampart Ridge Loop: 264
Rattlesnake Hills: **317**
Rattlesnake Mountain: 168
rattlesnakes: 8
Reflection Lake: 267
Remmel Lake: 136
Riffe River: **235**
Rimrock Lake: **236**
Robinson Pass: 134
Rock Mountain and Lake: 165
Ross Lake: **91,** 127
Ross Lake National Recreation Area: **91, 92,** 112–113, 126
Round Mountain: 287–288
Round-The-Mountain: 304–305
Royal Basin: 52
Ruth Creek: 100
Ruth Mountain: 101

S

Saddle Mountains: **318**
Saddle Mountain National Wildlife Refuge: **318**
Salmo Loop: 224–225
Salmo-Priest Wilderness: 223–227

Samish Bay: **73**
Sand Point Trail: 31
Sanpoil River: **202**
Sarvent Glaciers: 254
Satus Creek: **317**
Sauk Mountain: 108–109
Sauk River: **91**
Sawtooth Lakes: 275–276
Sawtooth Ridge: **320,** 324–325
Sawtooth Wilderness: 143
Scatter Creek: 147–148
Seattle: 81, 82
Second Beach: 36
Seven Lakes Basin Loop: 39
Seward Park: 82–83
Shadow Lake: 255
Shaw Island: **73**
Shedroof Divide: 225–226
Sheep Canyon: 245–246
Sherlock Peak: 222–223
Sherman: 217
Sherman Creek: **202**
Shi Shi Beach: 29–30
Shoe Lake: 288
Shore Trail: 80
Shriner Peak Lookout: 270–271
signal mirror: 6
Silver Falls Loop: 271–272
Silver Lake: **235,** 239
Silver Lakes: 54
Silver Lake State Park: 239
Similkameen River: **201**
Siouxon: 307–308
Six Ridge: 64
Skagit Bay: **73**
Skagit River: **73**
Skykomish River: **93**
Skyline Divide: 97–98
Skyline Loop: 268
Skyline Ridge: 45–46
Slate Creek: 148, 224
Slate Pass: 132
Slate Peak: 133
Sleeping Beauty: 303
Slick Ear: **320,** 325
Small Oyster Lake: 39
Smooth Ridge: **320,** 326–327
Snake River: **319, 320**
snakes: 8
Snohomish Centennial Trail: 80–81
Snohomish County: 80–81
Snohomish River: **74**
Snoqualmie Falls: **93**
Snoqualmie River: **93**
Snoqualmie and Dorothy Lakes: 160–161
Snow and Bench Lakes: 270
Snow Lake: 176
Snowgrass Flats: 284
Snowshoe Falls: 175
Sol Duc Falls/Lover's Lane: 38
Sourdough Gap: 260
Sourdough Mountain: 112–113
Sourdough Ridge/Dege Peak: 254
South Climb: 305–306
South Columbia Basin Wildlife Area: 322
South Fork Tieton River: 289–290
South Point Lookout: 282
South Side Bonaparte: 207
South Whidbey State Park: 79
Southern Travelway: 37
space blankets: 6
Spada Lake: **93**
Spencer Butte: 299
Spiral Butte: 278–279
Spokane Indian Reservation: **204**
Spray Park: 251–252
Spruce Railroad: **24,** 33
Stagman Ridge: 303–304
Staircase Rapids: 61–62
Stehekin: 139–143
Stehekin River: **92,** 111
Stehekin Trails: 143
Stevens Pass: 165
Stevens-Van Trump Historical Memorial: 266–267
Stick Pin: 214–216
Strawberry Mountain (Gifford Pinochet National Forest): 240
Strawberry Mountain (Okanogan National Forest): 207–208
Strawberry Point: 37
Stujack Pass: 119
Suiattle River: **91**
Sullivan Lakeshore: 227–228
Sultan River: **93**
Summerland/Panhandle Gap: 258–259
summit hikes, author's top ten: 16
Summit Lake/Bearhead Mountain: 184
Summit Prairie: 296
sun protection: 5
Sunrise Nature Trails: 252
Sunrise Trail: 34
Surprise Lake: 163–164
Swan and Long Lake Loops: 211–212
Swift Reservoir: **235**
Swiss army knife: 6

TUV

13 Mile: **202,** 212–213
Table Mountain: 105
Tacoma: 83–84
Takhlakh Lake and Meadows: 298–299
Talapus and Olallie Lakes: 173
Tatoosh Range: **236**
Tatoosh Ridge: 276–277
Tatoosh Wilderness: 276
Taylor Ridge: 213–214
Taylor River: 160
Teahwhit Head: **25**

Teddy Bear Cove: 76
Tenmile: 212
Tennant Lake: 75
Tennant Lake County Park: 75
Tennant Lake Wildlife Area: 75
Third Beach: 36
Thomas Lake: 300
Thornton Lakes: 109–110
Three Fingers Trail: 120
Three Lakes: 271
Thunder Creek: 114–115, 128, 227
Tiffany Mountain: 208–209
Tiger Mountain: 166
Tiger Mountain State Forest: 166
Tiger/Coyote Rock Loops: 223
Tipsoo Lake Trail: 260
Toandos Peninsula: **27**
Toleak Point: 37
Tolmie Peak Lookout: 250–251
Tomyhoi Lake Trail: 98
Tonga Ridge: 162–163
Tongue Mountain: 293
Toppenish Creek: **317**
Toppenish National Wildlife Refuge: **317**
Touchet River: **319, 320**
Toutle Lake: **235**
Toutle Mountain Range: **235**
Trail of Two Forests: 247
Trapper Creek: 308–309
Trapper Creek Wilderness: 308–309
Tubal Cain: 51–52
Tucannon River: **319, 320,** 330
Tuck and Robin Lakes: 181–182
Tulalip Indian Reservation: **73**
Tunnel Creek: 55
Turkey Creek: **320,** 327–328
Turnbull National Wildlife Refuge: **204**
Twin Falls: 123, 168–169
Twin Falls State Park: 168–169
Twin Lakes: **202**
Twin Lakes Trail: 76
Twin Sisters: 278
Twisp Pass: 146
Twisp River: **92**
Umatilla National Forest: **319, 320,** 324–332
Umtanum Creek: 321
Unicorn Peak: 270
Union Flat Creek: **320**
Upland Trail: 80
Upper Big Quilcene: 54–55
Upper Dungeness: 52–53
Upper South Fork Skokomish: 65–66
US Military Yakima Training Center: **317, 318**
US Mountain: 215
utility knife: 6
Valley of Heaven: 60
Vancouver Lake: **237**
Vashon Island: **74**

W

Wagonwheel Lake: 62–63
Waitts Lake: **203**
Walla Walla River: **319**
Wallace Falls: 157
Wallace Falls State Park: 157
Walupt Creek: 285–286
Wapaloosie: 217
Waptus River Valley: 182–183
War Creek Pass: 149
Washington Department of Natural Resources Land: 122–123, 168
Washington Park: 77–78
water supply: 3–4
Wedding Rocks: 30–31
weekend hikes, author's top ten: 13
Welcome Pass Trail: 96
Wenaha-Tucannon Wilderness: **320,** 324–329, 331–332
Wenatchee Mountains: **94**
Wenatchee National Forest: **94,** 142, 144–145, 154–156, 165, 178–183, 185–195, 273–274, 279, 288–289
West Butte Creek: **320,** 326
West Cady Ridge: 158–159
West Fork Dosewallips: 55–56
West Fork Methow River: 131–132
West Fork Pasayten: 133–134
Whatcom Falls: 75–76
Whatcom Pass: 102–103
wheelchair accessible trails: Big Creek Falls 299–300; Big Tree Botanical Loop 208; Chinook Pass Hikes 260; Cispus Braille 290; Deception Pass State Park 78; Dungeness Spit 35; Iron Goat 165–166; Lava Canyon 244–245; Meta Lake 243; Nisqually National Wildlife Refuge 84–85; Padilla Bay 80; Palouse Falls 324; Point Defiance 83–84; Seward Park 82–83; Silver Lake 239; Snohomish Centennial Trail 80–81; Sullivan Lakeshore 227–228; Takhlakh Lake and Meadows 298–299; Trail of Two Forests 247
Whidbey Island: **73,** 78–79
whistles: 6
White River: **74, 236,** 255
White Salmon River: **236, 238**

wildlife: 6–8, 10
Willapa Bay: **28,** 67
Willapa River: **28**
William O. Douglas Wilderness: 273–274, 277–279
Williams Creek: **92,** 149
Wilson Creek: 123
Winchester Mountain: 99
Windy Gap: 249–250
Windy Peak: 206–207
Wolf Creek: 150–151
Wonder Mountain Wilderness: 65–66
Wonderland Trail: 250, 258–259, 260, 268–269
Wynoochee Pass: 49–50

XYZ

Yakama Indian Reservation: **236, 317**
Yakima Rim: 321–322
Yakima River: **93, 317, 318**
Yale Lake: **237**
Yellow Aster Butte: 98–99
Yellow Bank: 31
Yellow Hill and Elbow Peak: 195
Yellow Jacket Pass/Hat Rock: 295
Yozoo: 292

Notes

Notes

Notes

Notes